2014

Social Panorama of Latin America

UNITED NATIONS

ECLAC

The *Social Panorama of Latin America* is prepared each year by the Social Development Division and the Statistics Division of the Economic Commission for Latin America and the Caribbean (ECLAC), under the supervision of María Nieves Rico and Pascual Gerstenfeld, respectively, and with participation by the Latin American and Caribbean Demographic Centre (CELADE)-Population Division of ECLAC, directed by Dirk Jaspers_Faijer. The Division for Gender Affairs, under Sonia Montaño, and the ECLAC subregional headquarters for the Caribbean, under Diane Quarless, were also involved in the preparation of this year's edition.

The 2014 edition was coordinated by María Nieves Rico, Daniela Trucco and Xavier Mancero, who also worked on the preparation of the text together with Verónica Amarante, Ernesto Espíndola, Álvaro Fuentes, Jorge Rodríguez, María Emma Santos and Pablo Villatoro. Mario Acuña, Martín Brun, David Candia, Maira Colacce, Fabiana del Popolo, Andrés Espejo, Fabiola Fernández, Marco Galván, Marcela Gómez, Daniela González, Carlos Howes, Amanda Loptspike, Jorge Martínez, Vivian Milosavljevic, Claudio Moris, Miguel Ojeda, Amalia Palma, Lucía Scuro, Conrado Soto, Humberto Soto, Sheila Stuart and Heidi Ullmann prepared substantive inputs and processed statistical data. Input and comments on different sections of the document were received from Martín Hopenhayn, Ricardo Jordán, Rodrigo Martínez, Andrea Murden, Alejandro Parraguez, Carlos Perea and Matías Salces.

Explanatory notes:

- In this publication, the term "country" is used to refer to territorial entities, whether these are States as understood by international law and practice or simply territories for which statistical data are maintained on a separate and independent basis.
- Three dots (...) indicate that data are not available or are not separately reported.
- Two dashes and a full stop (-.-) indicate that the sample size is too small to be used as a basis for estimating the corresponding values with acceptable reliability and precision.
- A dash (-) indicates that the amount is nil or negligible.
- A blank space in a table indicates that the concept under consideration is not applicable or not comparable.
- A minus sign (-) indicates a deficit or decrease, unless otherwise indicated.
- The use of a hyphen (-) between years (e.g. 2000-2008) indicates reference to the complete number of calendar years involved, including the beginning and end years.
- A slash (/) between years (e.g. 2003/2005) indicates that the information given corresponds to one of these two years.
- The world "dollars" refers to United States dollars, unless otherwise specified.
- Individual figures and percentages in tables may not always add up to the corresponding total because of rounding.
- The boundaries and names shown on the maps of this publication do not imply official endorsement or acceptance by the United Nations.

United Nations publication
ISBN 978-92-1-121876-3 (print and pdf)
ISBN: 978-92-1-057210-1 (ePub)
LC/G.2635-P
Sales No.: E.15.II.G.6

Printed at United Nations, Santiago, Chile

This publication should be cited as: Economic Commission for Latin America and the Caribbean (ECLAC), *Social Panorama of Latin America, 2014*, (LC/G.2635-P), Santiago, Chile, 2014.

Contents

Tables

Figures

Boxes

Maps

Introduction

The 2014 edition of *Social Panorama of Latin America* presents ECLAC measurements for the analysis of income poverty, taking, as well, a multidimensional approach to poverty. Applying these two approaches to data for the countries of the region provides confirmation that despite the progress made over the past decade, structural poverty is still a feature of Latin American society. In order to contribute to a more comprehensive design of public policies aimed at overcoming poverty and socioeconomic inequality, this edition examines recent trends in social spending and sets out a deeper gap analysis focused on three areas: youth and development, gender inequality in the labour market and urban residential segregation.

Since 2010 the United Nations Economic Commission for Latin America and the Caribbean (ECLAC) has been laying out and condensing its proposed agenda for the development of Latin America and the Caribbean in the documents that make up the trilogy of equality, which were presented at its past three sessions: *Time for equality: Closing Gaps, Opening Trails*; *Structural Change for Equality: An Integrated Approach to Development*; and *Compacts for Equality: Towards a Sustainable Future*. According to this vision of development and public policy, equality must be the core guiding ethical principle and the ultimate goal of development. Every year, *Social Panorama of Latin America* takes up the challenge of a more in-depth examination of social gaps, the mechanisms that reproduce them and options for closing them.

As in previous editions, chapter I of the 2014 edition sets out updated figures on poverty and indigence in Latin America. With the region's economy slowing since 2010, the data for 2013 show that, regionwide, the income poverty rate has not changed since 2011 and there are no significant differences in the poverty and indigence rates compared with the figures for 2012.

This edition also sets forth the results of applying a multidimensional poverty index built on the measurement approaches proposed in the 2013 edition of *Social Panorama of Latin America*. This new index combines monetary and non-monetary indicators of well-being, taking into account deprivations in employment and social protection, and an indicator of low educational achievement, and applies new deprivation thresholds to some of the indicators commonly used in poverty measurement, in order to provide more up-to-date standards that reflect the reality in the region.

The results show that the incidence of multidimensional poverty declined between 2005 and 2012, mainly in urban areas. Poverty intensity according to the percentage of deprivations experienced by households identified as poor also declined during the period. Although the situation varies widely from country to country, in all of them monetary poverty is the deprivation that contributes the most to multidimensional poverty.

Chapter II examines income distribution. Despite dissimilar scenarios, the downtrend in the degree of concentration is confirmed, meaning that inequality continues to decline in most of the countries of the region.

Polarization indices are used to describe income distribution in Latin America and how it is related to conflict and social identity. Here, the results show a lessening of polarization and a growing weight of the groups in the middle of the distribution. At the same time, in 2011 the proportion of the population that reported feeling part of the middle class tended to be higher in countries with a less bipolar distribution of income. And those who felt they were middle class had more confidence in their children's future economic well-being than those who considered themselves in the lower class, which is indicative of higher expectations of intergenerational mobility.

Chapter III looks at three key issues on the current agenda for youth and development in Latin America. First, the link between education and paid work (which is a pillar of social inclusion) is taken not only as the bridge between a dependent life and an independent one but is also viewed as a key area for youth participation in production development and access to conditions for greater well-being and personal development.

Second, in many of the countries of the region, the violent settings in which young people live, amid growing insecurity in which they sometimes are key players, directly affect them as victims and stigmatize them, too, to the extent that violence is considered a condition of youth. This exacerbates the sense of social exclusion and contributes to a vicious circle where the formation of urban gangs poses a threat to society, and public policies generally have yet to generate an appropriate response.

For young people in Latin America, political participation is the best way to bring about social change. But at present their social participation tends to fall into two main areas: youth demonstrations in city streets and organization via virtual social networks.

Chapter IV focuses on gender, linking inequalities in labour market insertion between men and women (along with conditioning factors such as care work and unpaid domestic work) to household income inequality in the economies of the region. While most of the countries of Latin America have seen participation gaps narrow over the past decade, in all of them there is still much room for increasing the participation of women in the paid labour market. In the English-speaking countries of the Caribbean the gaps are smaller, but there is still a long way to go to achieve greater equality. The pattern is similar for the number of hours worked, occupational segregation and the higher proportion of women in the low-productivity sector.

There are significant gender differentials in labour income as well. All of these gaps go beyond economic cycles and production heterogeneity across countries, revealing entrenched gender discrimination that must be addressed effectively.

Against this backdrop, chapter IV also examines what would happen to the levels of income inequality and poverty in the region if the participation gap between men and women were closed and if there were equal pay for workers with equal qualifications. The study shows that incorporating women into the labour market would bring about significant progress in reducing poverty and achieving equality. This would call for active and forceful policies to foster and encourage participation and improve its quality.

One of the markers of urbanization in Latin America has been the concentration of the poorest and most excluded population segments in the outskirts of cities while more affluent groups are concentrated in other areas with better infrastructure and living conditions. Chapter V looks at residential segregation and how it reflects socioeconomic, ethnic and national-origin inequalities, providing data on some 20 major cities in 10 countries of the region. This pattern also operates as an intermediate variable for internal migration, including intrametropolitan migration. Its impact on residential segregation and the social landscape of cities is therefore calculated on the basis of its effects on age and education-level composition and what is referred to as the "neighbourhood effect".

Previous editions of *Social Panorama* have examined social spending. Chapter VI of this edition does too, analysing its priority within total spending in the framework of the economic cycle. This cycle is marked at present by a global and regional slowdown following slight upticks after the global financial crisis of 2008-2009. This provides a context for discussing the degree of procyclicality of social spending and its most recent trends, as well as the sectoral distribution of and medium- and long-term trends in public social spending.

The second part of chapter VI, which is an adaptation of a number of ECLAC contributions to the Third Ibero-American Youth Report submitted at the XVII Ibero-American Conference of Ministers of Youth (Burgos, Spain, 18-20 September 2014), is devoted to public social investment in young people. Social spending is broken down by sector (education, health, housing and social care) and by how young people receive its benefits (direct, extended, indirect or general). This overall approach highlights the imbalance between spending aimed at this age group and the total population, and the need to expand and redirect spending to achieve greater equality in State budgets from the point of view of youth needs and interests, as well as their demographic weight relative to the total population.

Summary

Chapter I
Poverty in Latin America: achievements so far and challenges ahead

As set out in *Compacts for Equality: Towards a Sustainable Future* (ECLAC, 2014), Latin America and the Caribbean is standing at a crossroads: how to maintain the significant progress made in reducing poverty and unemployment as well as incipient gains in income distribution, which have taken place alongside democratic consolidation, macroeconomic stability and social policies. Efforts to sustain and expand these achievements seem to be hitting limits as the pace of poverty and indigence reduction and improvement in income distribution slows, especially in the wake of the 2008 international crisis. This will be discussed in this chapter and the following one.

This edition of Social Panorama takes a multidimensional approach for a fresh look at poverty from an income perspective. Doing so confirms that despite the progress made over the past decade, structural poverty is still a feature of Latin American society. The estimates provided quantify the magnitude and intensity of poverty in different population groups, setting out stylized facts that can be useful for targeting policies to overcome poverty, to make these achievements sustainable over time and to work towards higher levels of well-being and development.

A. Analysis of income poverty

The global economy started growing again in 2013, with developed-country economies showing improvement and China growing by some 7%. The economy of Latin America expanded by 2.5% in 2013, outperforming the global average of 2.2% but coming in under the 2.9% recorded in 2012. Per capita GDP rose by only 1.5%, continuing the slowdown that began in 2010.

Even as GDP expansion slackened, the urban unemployment rate fell slightly as a declining labour force participation rate more than offset the drop in the employment rate. Average wage purchasing power either showed no substantial changes or posted moderate increases in most countries, albeit at a slower pace than in previous years. The inflation rate in the region rose, as a simple average, from 5.3% to 6.8% as prices climbed in the Bolivarian Republic of Venezuela.

In this setting, the poverty rate in Latin America in 2013 was around 28.1% of the population; indigence (extreme poverty) stood at 11.7%. These percentages are equivalent to 165 million persons in poverty, of which 69 million are extremely poor (see figure 1). These figures show no significant differences compared with the poverty rate for 2012 (28.1%). There were no statistically significant changes in extreme poverty, either: the figure for 2013 is only 0.4 percentage points higher than in 2012 (11.3%). This means that there were no substantial changes in the number of poor in 2013, but the number in extreme poverty rose by about 3 million while the number of non-indigent poor decreased by a similar figure.

Despite the minimal changes in terms of rates, the new estimates show that extreme poverty has returned to the levels estimated for 2011 and thus lost some of the ground gained in previous years. This is nothing new —the data set out in previous editions of Social Panorama have shown similar trends. According to regional estimates, the downtrend in the rate of poverty and extreme poverty slowed and even reversed in the early years of this decade. This, combined with population growth, pushed the number of extreme poor up for 2013.

Compared with the figures reported in 2002 (when they were the highest in the past 15 years), poverty has decreased by almost 16 percentage points, of which 10.4 percentage points are for until 2008 (at an annual rate of 1.7%). The decline was slower between 2008 and 2013: a cumulative decrease of 5.4 percentage points, equivalent to an annual rate of 1.0%. The regional poverty rate has held steady at around 28% from 2011 on.

The trend was similar for extreme poverty, with a drop of 6.4 percentage points between 2002 and 2008 and 1.2 percentage points between 2008 and 2013. In a pattern similar to the poverty rate, the percentage in extreme poverty has remained between 11% and 12% over the past three years.

Figure 1
Latin America: poverty and indigence, 1980-2014 [a]
(Percentages and millions of people)

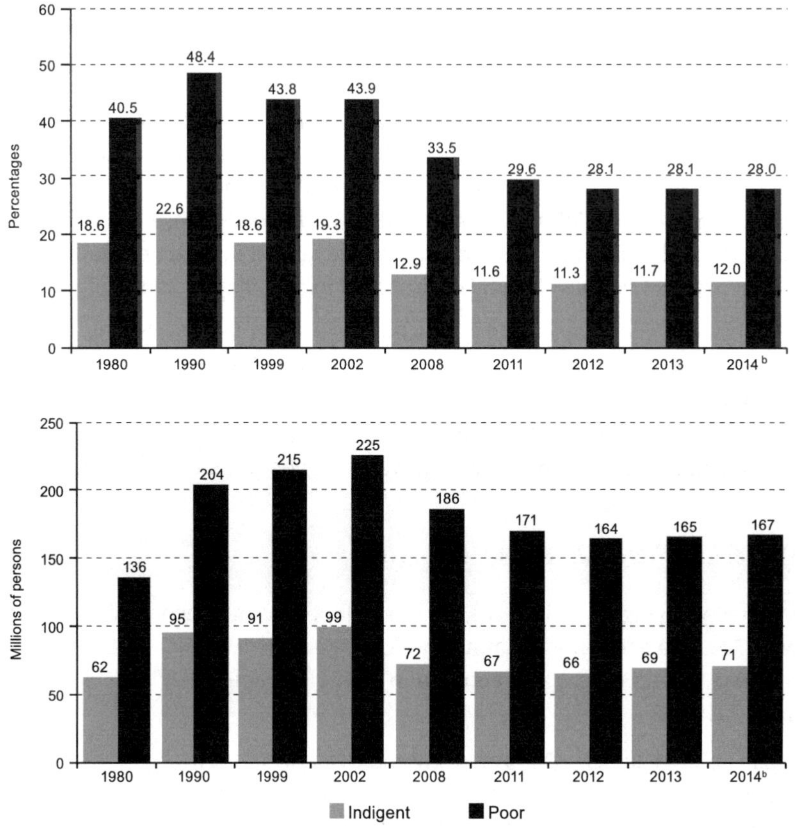

Source: Economic Commission for Latin America and the Caribbean (ECLAC), on the basis of special tabulations of data from household surveys conducted in the respective countries.
[a] Estimate for 18 countries of the region plus Haiti. The figures above the bars are the percentages and total numbers of poor (indigent plus non-indigent poor). The figures for 2014 are projections.
[b] Projection.

A look at recent trends by country shows that 6 of the 12 countries with data available for 2013 posted statistically significant reductions in poverty and indigence. Paraguay showed the sharpest decline, at 4.5 percentage points per year, from 49.6% to 40.7% between 2011 and 2013; indigence fell at the same annual pace, from 28.0% down to 19.2%. In El Salvador, poverty decreased by 4.4 percentage points between 2012 and 2013 (from 45.3% to 40.9%) and indigence dropped by 1.0 percentage point (from 13.5% to 12.5%) during the same period. Colombia recorded a 2.2 percentage-point drop in poverty levels between 2012 and 2013 (from 32.9% to 30.7%) and a 1.3 percentage-point decrease in extreme poverty (from 10.4% to 9.1%).

In Peru poverty decreased by 1.9 percentage points (from 25.8% to 23.9%) and the extreme poverty rate dropped 1.3 percentage points (from 6.0% to 4.7%) between 2012 an 2013. Chile posted a 1.6 percentage point drop per year, from 10.9% in 2011 to 7.8% in 2013, and a yearly fall of 0.3 percentage point from 3.1% in 2011 to 2.5% in 2013. Poverty came down in Ecuador as well between 2011 and 2013, at a rate of 0.9 percentage point per year (from 35.4% in 2011 to 33.6% in 2013), and extreme poverty by 1.0 percentage point per year (from 13.9% in 2011 to 12.0% in 2013). In the remaining countries (Costa Rica and Uruguay), the poverty and indigence rate decreases were smaller, around 0.3 percentage points or even less (see table 1).

Brazil, meanwhile, recorded a 0.6 percentage-point drop in the poverty rate but a similar increase (0.5 percentage points) in indigence between 2012 and 2013. A similar picture —falling poverty but rising indigence— was seen in the Dominican Republic in the same period, and in Panama between 2011 and 2013, although the changes are not statistically significant. In the Bolivarian Republic of Venezuela, the poverty rate climbed by 6.7 percentage points (from 25.4% to 32.1%) and the indigence rate increased by 2.7 percentage points, from 7.1% to 9.8%, both between 2012 and 2013.

Table 1

Latin America (18 countries): persons living in poverty and indigence, around 2005, 2012 and 2013

(Percentages)

Country	Around 2005			Around 2012			2013		
	Year	Poverty	Indigence	Year	Poverty	Indigence	Year	Poverty	Indigence
Argentina [a]	2006	24.8	9.6	2012	4.3	1.7	...	...	...
Bolivia (Plurinational State of)	2004	63.9	34.7	2011	36.3	18.7	...	...	...
Brazil	2005	36.4	10.7	2012	18.6	5.4	2013	18.0	5.9
Chile	2006	13.7	3.2	2011	10.9	3.1	2013	7.8	2.5
Colombia [b]	2005	45.2	13.9	2012	32.9	10.4	2013	30.7	9.1
Costa Rica [c]	2005	21.1	7.0	2012	17.8	7.3	2013	17.7	7.2
Dominican Republic	2005	47.5	24.6	2012	41.2	20.0	2013	40.7	20.2
Ecuador	2005	48.3	21.2	2011	35.3	13.8	2013	33.6	12.0
El Salvador	2004	47.5	19.0	2012	45.3	13.5	2013	40.9	12.5
Guatemala	2002	60.2	30.9	2006	54.8	29.1	...	...	...
Honduras	2007	68.9	45.6	2010	69.2	45.6	...	...	...
Mexico	2006	31.7	8.7	2012	37.1	14.2	...	...	...
Nicaragua	2005	61.9	31.9	2009	58.3	29.5	...	...	...
Panama	2005	31.0	14.1	2011	24.0	11.3	2013	23.2	12.2
Paraguay	2005	56.9	27.6	2011	49.6	28.0	2013	40.7	19.2
Peru [d]	2003	52.5	21.4	2012	25.8	6.0	2013	23.9	4.7
Uruguay [a]	2005	18.8	4.1	2012	6.1	1.2	2013	5.7	0.9
Venezuela (Bolivarian Republic of)	2005	37.1	15.9	2012 [e]	25.4	7.1	2013 [e]	32.1	9.8

Source: Economic Commission for Latin America and the Caribbean (ECLAC), on the basis of special tabulations of data from household surveys conducted in the respective countries.

[a] Urban areas.

[b] Figures from the National Administrative Department of Statistics (DANE) of Colombia.

[c] Figures for 2012 and 2013 are not strictly comparable with data from previous years.

[d] Figures from the National Institute of Statistics and Informatics (INEI) of Peru.

[e] Figures from the National Institute of Statistics (INE) of the Bolivarian Republic of Venezuela. Figures for 2012 and 2013 are not comparable with those for earlier years.

No statistically significant changes in the levels of poverty and indigence for the region as a whole are expected for 2014 because growth in per capita GDP will be similar or somewhat lower than in 2013 and no significant changes are expected in employment or inflation in most of the countries. However, projections show a slight increase in the indigence rate, to around 12%, which would mean not only sliding back to the rates seen at the beginning of the decade but also a marked rise in the number of indigent people.

B. A multidimensional measure of poverty in Latin America

This section sets out the findings from applying a multidimensional index of poverty in 17 countries of Latin America. The index builds on the exploration of different dimensions and thresholds of poverty in the previous edition of *Social Panorama* (ECLAC, 2013) and is the product of a joint effort by ECLAC and Oxford Poverty & Human Development Initiative (OPHI).

The index presented here has the following main innovations in that it: (i) aggregates non-monetary and monetary dimensions in order to minimize errors of inclusion and exclusion in identifying the poor; (ii) considers deprivation in employment and social protection, expanding the dimensions commonly used in the measurement of poverty and adding an indicator for low educational achievement; (iii) uses new deprivation cut-offs for some dimensions usually employed in poverty measurement, in order to have standards that are more in line with the situation in Latin America.[1]

This index follows the methodology described in Alkire and Foster (2007 and 2011), which consists of: (i) choosing the dimensions and measures and weighting them; (ii) setting the multidimensional cut-off (k) or the proportion of deprivations (weighted) that a subject must show in order to be considered poor; and (iii) calculating the deprivation score for each subject and determining, by comparing the score and the value of k, whether the subject is multidimensionally poor.

Table 2 shows the dimensions, indicators and weighting structure for the index. All of the deprivations are weighted the same (7.4%), except for social protection (3.7%) and income (14.8%). Deprivations in social protection

[1] For more details on construction of the index, see Santos and others (2015).

were weighted less because they indicate a situation of insufficient well-being that goes a step beyond the traditional concept of poverty.[2] Income, in turn, is weighted more because it is a synthetic indicator built by validating and aggregating data from a wide variety of questions and income streams.[3]

Table 2

Multidimensional poverty index: dimensions, deprivation indicators and weightings

Dimensions	Deprivation indicators: persons living in...	Weighting *(percentages)*
Dwelling		22.2
Makeshift building materials [a]	Dwellings with a dirt floor or walls or roof of makeshift materials (waste material, cardboard, cans, thatch, palm fronds, straw or other materials).	7.4
Overcrowding [b]	Households with three or more people per room, rural and urban areas.	7.4
Insecure housing tenure [c]	Households: (i) living as squatters; or (ii) living in ceded or borrowed housing.	7.4
Basic services		22.2
Lack of access to improved water sources [d]	Urban areas: Households obtaining water from: -Mains network off the premises -Unprotected wells or lacking a motor pump -Mobile sources (village tank, tank cart, tanker truck, etc.) - Bottled water - River, stream, rainwater, other Rural areas: households obtaining water from: -Unprotected wells or with a hand pump -Mobile sources (village tank, tank cart, tanker truck, etc.) -Bottled water -River, stream, rainwater, other	7.4
Lack of improved sanitation [d]	Urban areas: -Waste not connected to a sewer system or septic tank -Shared toilet -No sanitation Rural areas: -No sanitation -Shared toilet -Waste going untreated to ground surface, river or sea.	7.4
Lack of source of energy [e]	Households without electricity or using firewood, coal or waste for cooking.	7.4
Living standard		22.2
Insufficient resources	Households with insufficient per capita income to meet food and non-food needs.	14.8
Lack of durable goods [f]	Households that have none of the following goods: (i) vehicle; (ii) refrigerator; (iii) washing machine.	7.4
Education		22.2
Non-attendance at school	Household has at least one child of school age (6 to 17 years old) who does not attend school.	7.4
Schooling gap	Household has at least one child or adolescent aged 6 to 17 who is more than two years behind schooling grade for age.	7.4
Low educational attainment	Household has nobody aged 20 or above with a minimum level of schooling. - Persons aged 20 to 59: have not completed lower secondary education. - Persons aged 60 and above: have not completed primary education.	7.4
Employment and social protection		11.1
Unemployment	Household has at least one person aged 15 to 65 in one of the following situations: - Unemployed - Employed without pay - Discouraged worker	7.4
Lack of social protection [g]	Household meets all the following conditions: - Nobody has any kind of contributory or co-payment health insurance - Nobody is affiliated with a contributory social security system - Nobody has income from a pension or contribution-based retirement scheme	3.7

Source: Economic Commission for Latin America and the Caribbean (ECLAC) on the basis of Santos and others (2014).

[a] No information was available on walls for Argentina (2005 and 2012), on floors for Brazil (2005 and 2012), on roofs for Colombia (2008 and 2012) and Ecuador (2005), or on dwelling materials for Uruguay (2005).

[b] The correction proposed by Katzman was used for non-exclusion of kitchen and/or toilet regarded as rooms for Brazil, Costa Rica, Honduras and Mexico (see Katzman, 2011).

[c] Living in housing given in usufruct is not considered housing deprivation.

[d] For the Dominican Republic (2006 and 2012), urban criterion applies to rural areas because the question does not allow for other criteria.

[e] No information was available on electricity for Argentina (2005 and 2012), Dominican Republic (2006) and Uruguay (2005); no information on fuel for Bolivarian Republic of Venezuela (2005 and 2012), Chile (2003 and 2011), and Honduras (2006).

[f] No information was available on goods for Argentina (2005 and 2012) and Plurinational State of Bolivia (2003); no information on vehicle for Brazil (2005), replaced with cooking stove; no information on vehicle for Chile (2003), replaced by water heater; no information on washing machine for Costa Rica (2012) no information on washing machine, replaced by plasma or liquid crystal display (LCD) television set; no information on washing machine for Honduras (2010 and 2006), replaced with cook stove.

[g] No information on health insurance for Brazil (2005 and 2012) and the Bolivarian Republic of Venezuela (2005 and 2012); the indicator for social protection is not included for Nicaragua (2009) because of lack of information on pension and health insurance affiliation.

---

2 There is also a technical reason for affording less weight to social protection indicators. The effective weighting of each indicator is determined by two factors: the relative weight it is assigned in the index and the threshold selected. So indicators with high thresholds, which translate into high deprivation rates, will account for a larger part in the composition of poverty, even if their relative weight is the same as that assigned to other indicators. This is precisely the case of social protection.

3 The overall poverty threshold is used here because the indicator of extreme poverty encompasses a very small percentage of the population of Latin America and therefore is not enough to capture income insecurity.

For the multidimensional cut-off k, an option between the union and intersection approaches is used. The union approach, which requires only one deprivation for a household to be identified as poor, increases the probability of errors of inclusion because all of the indicators have measurement errors. And the intersection method, which requires that a household be deprived in all dimensions, markedly increases the probability of errors of exclusion. The cut-off used corresponds to k=25%. With this value, persons identified as poor must be deprived in the equivalent of an entire dimension plus some other indicator, or must be deprived in income and show at least two additional deprivations. Consequently, no individual deprived in just one dimension is identified as multidimensionally poor.[4]

In 2012, approximately 28% of the region's population was living in multidimensional poverty. The highest levels were in Nicaragua (74.1%), Honduras (70.5%), Guatemala (70.3%), and the Plurinational State of Bolivia (58%). The lowest levels were in Chile (6.8%), Argentina (8.1%), Uruguay (9%), Brazil (14.5%) and Costa Rica (14.9%) (see figure 2).

Figure 2

Latin America (17 countries): multidimensional poverty, around 2005 and 2012

(Percentages of the population)

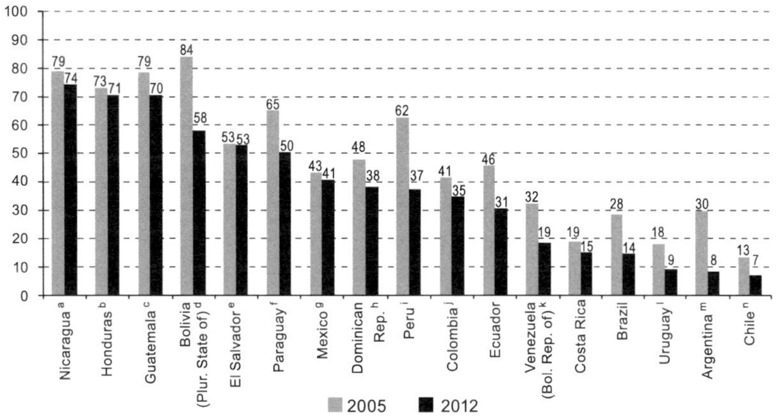

Source: Economic Commission for Latin America and the Caribbean (ECLAC), on the basis of special tabulations of data from household surveys conducted in the respective countries.

[a] Data for Nicaragua refer to 2005 and 2009.
[b] Data for Honduras refer to 2006 and 2010.
[c] Data for Guatemala refer to 2000 and 2006.
[d] Data for the Plurinational State of Bolivia refer to 2003 and 2011.
[e] Data for El Salvador refer to 2004 and 2012.
[f] Data for Paraguay refer to 2005 and 2011.
[g] Data for Mexico refer to 2004 and 2012.
[h] Data for the Dominican Republic refer to 2006 and 2012.
[i] Data for Peru refer to 2003 and 2012.
[j] Data for Colombia refer to 2008 and 2012
[k] Data for the Bolivarian Republic of Venezuela for 2005 and 2012 refer to urban areas.
[l] Data for Uruguay for 2005 refer to urban areas.
[m] Data for Argentina for 2005 and 2012 refer to urban areas.
[n] Data for Chile refer to 2003 and 2011.

All the countries saw a decline in multidimensional poverty between 2005 and 2012. The sharpest decreases were in Argentina, Uruguay, Brazil, Peru, Chile and the Bolivarian Republic of Venezuela, equivalent to a decrease in the headcount ratio of 7% or more per year. El Salvador, Mexico, Honduras and Nicaragua posted decreases of 1% or less (see figure 2).

The poverty reduction trend was more pronounced in countries with lower baseline incidence (around 2005). However, countries like the Dominican Republic, Ecuador, Paraguay and the Plurinational State of Bolivia, where the baseline incidence was in excess of 45%, posted very significant reductions in poverty (decreases between 3% and 6% per year).

Poverty intensity indicates the percentage of deprivation experienced by households classified as poor. In both 2005 and 2012, this indicator was higher in countries with the highest incidence of poverty. In these countries, then, not only are there more poor people, but the poor are deprived in more dimensions.

[4] The maximum score for an individual deprived in all of the indicators for a single dimension is 22.2%.

The findings show that between 2005 and 2012 poverty intensity declined in all the countries, especially in Peru, the Plurinational State of Bolivia, Argentina and Uruguay, with percentage decreases between 1.7% and 2.8% per year.

As for poverty incidence by area of residence, a higher percentage of the population was poor in rural than in urban areas around 2012. The highest rural poverty levels were in Nicaragua, Guatemala, Honduras and the Plurinational State of Bolivia, and the lowest in Chile, Uruguay and Costa Rica (see figure 3). The pattern is similar for poverty intensity, which was also higher in rural areas than in urban areas.

Figure 3

Latin America (15 countries): poverty rate by area of residence, around 2012

(Percentages of the population)

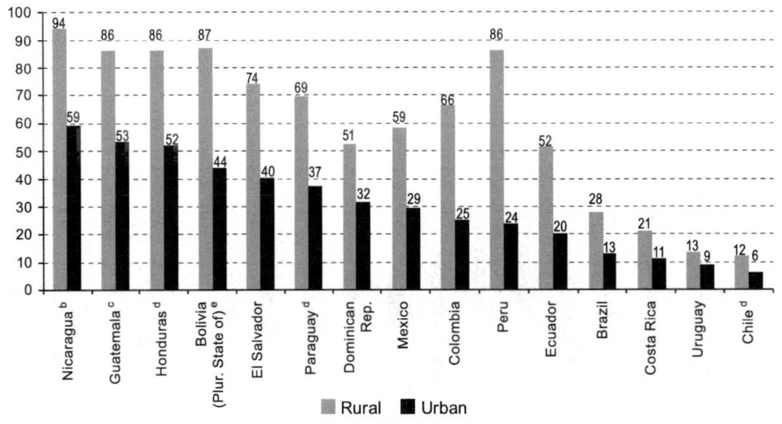

Source: Economic Commission for Latin America and the Caribbean (ECLAC), on the basis of special tabulations of data from household surveys conducted in the respective countries.

[a] Countries shown in order of poverty incidence around 2012.

[b] Data for Nicaragua refer to 2009.

[c] Data for Guatemala refer to 2006.

[d] Data for Honduras refer to 2010.

[e] Data for Chile, Paraguay and the Plurinational State of Bolivia refer to 2011.

Regarding changes in poverty levels by area of residence between 2005 and 2012, only in Costa Rica and Chile did poverty decline more in rural than in urban areas. In the remaining countries, urban poverty decreased more than rural poverty.

Figure 4 shows the contributions of the different deprivations to overall poverty[5] around 2012. Considering the simple average for the region, in 2012 monetary poverty was the deprivation that contributed the most to overall multidimensional poverty (28%). Next were the educational attainment of adults in the household (12%), employment deprivation (8%), social protection and sanitation (7% each) and deficiencies in relation to overcrowding, energy and ownership of durable goods (6% each).

The contribution of income to overall poverty tends to be larger in countries with the lowest adjusted incidence of poverty (or total poverty). The largest contribution of monetary poverty was in Chile (41%), Brazil (37%) and the Bolivarian Republic of Venezuela (35%). The contribution of income to overall poverty did not reach 25% in the five countries with the highest adjusted poverty rates (Nicaragua, Guatemala, Honduras, the Plurinational State of Bolivia and El Salvador).

Makeshift housing, insufficient electricity and lack of durable goods contributed most to overall poverty in countries with higher levels of poverty (adjusted headcount ratio). By contrast, the contribution of unsecure housing tenure tended to be higher in countries with lower levels of poverty. For the rest of the deprivations, no substantial differences linked to the level of multidimensional poverty were found.

5 Overall poverty is measured by the adjusted headcount ratio (M0), which is headcount ratio (H) times poverty intensity (A).

Figure 4
Latin America (17 countries): contribution of each of the deprivations a to overall poverty by country, 2012
(Percentages)

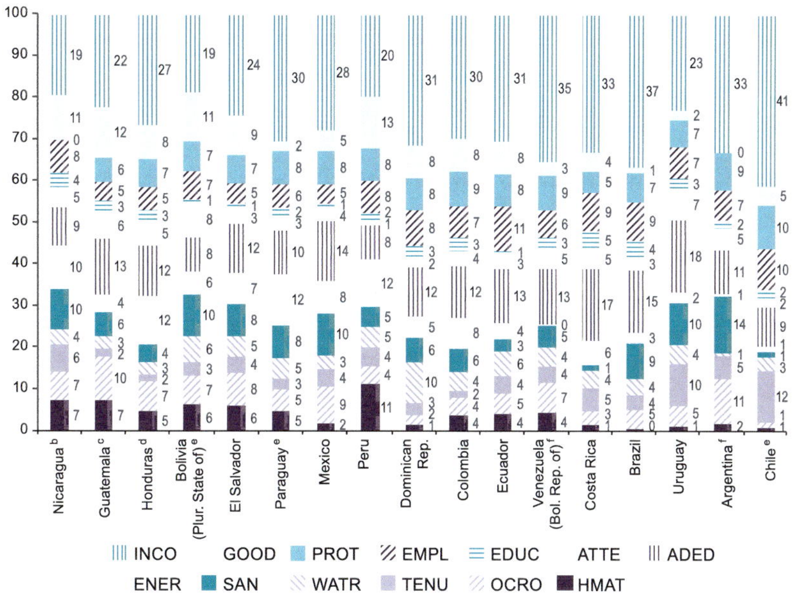

Source: Economic Commission for Latin America and the Caribbean (ECLAC), on the basis of special tabulations of data from household surveys conducted in the respective countries.

[a] Countries shown in order of adjusted headcount ratio (M0). The following abbreviations are used for deprivations: INCO=monetary income; GOOD=durable goods in the household; PROT=social protection; EMPL=Employment: EDUC=low education achievement; ATTE=attendance; LOED=Educational attainment of adults; ENER=Energy; SANI=sanitation; WATR=water: TENU=secure housing tenure; OCRO=overcrowding; HMAT=housing materials.
[b] Data for Nicaragua refer to 2009.
[c] Data for Guatemala refer to 2006.
[d] Data for Honduras refer to 2010.
[e] Data for Chile, Paraguay and the Plurinational State of Bolivia refer to 2011.
[f] Data for Argentina and the Bolivarian Republic of Venezuela refer to urban areas.

The results obtained from applying this measurement of multidimensional poverty show that the form and intensity of poverty varies between countries. This heterogeneity must necessarily be taken into account for effective policymaking to combat poverty. Any one policy solution is unlikely to produce the same results across all countries.

The fact that poverty manifests in multiple dimensions also shows how important it is that poverty reduction policies be designed and implemented in a coordinated manner across different sectors. In particular, income shortages, however significant among the array of lacks suffered by poor households, are far from being the only ones. Given that marginal increases in household income are insufficient to resolve several non-monetary deprivations, poverty reduction needs not only monetary transfers, but also substantial efforts in the areas of housing policy (especially in terms of housing materials and overcrowding) and basic services (water, sanitation and energy), particularly in the poorer countries.

Chapter II
Income distribution, polarization and perceptions

One of the region's distinguishing features has been its inequality in resource distribution and the exercise of rights. While Latin America is not the poorest region of the world, it stands out as the most unequal. This is strangling current well-being and the future development of its societies and economies. In a series of publications referred to as the trilogy of equality (ECLAC, 2010, 2012 and 2014), ECLAC has outlined this challenge and argued that overcoming it is a prerequisite for protecting recent gains and opening a new path towards a virtuous circle of growth and inclusion. This chapter of *Social Panorama* tracks trends in income inequality, focusing on the slowing of progress in this area in recent years. It examines the degree of distributive polarization in Latin American societies, in search of an approach to understanding the lack of social cohesion and recent manifestations of collective unrest in some of the countries in the region.

A. Income distribution: a status report

In the early 2000s inequality began to decrease in most of the countries of the region and this trend is still holding. Between 2002 and 2013 the average Gini coefficient for the region fell approximately 10%, from 0.542 to 0.486.

The dynamics of inequality reduction during the subperiod 2008-2013 did not follow the same patterns as in 2002-2008. In some countries reduction in inequality began to pick up speed in 2008, especially in the Plurinational State of Bolivia, Uruguay, Argentina, Brazil, Mexico and Colombia. Of these countries, three (the Plurinational State of Bolivia, Argentina and Brazil) also saw striking improvements in inequality reduction in 2002-2008 (see figure 5).

Figure 5

Latin America (15 countries): annual variation of Gini coefficient, 2002-2008 and 2008-2013 [a]

(Percentages)

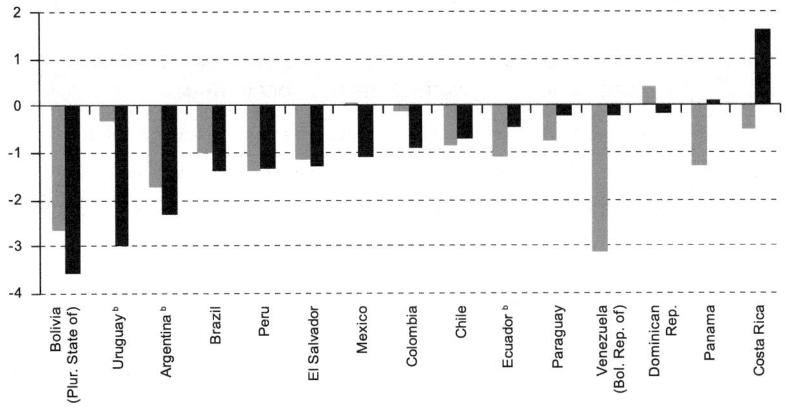

Source: Economic Commission for Latin America and the Caribbean (ECLAC), on the basis of special tabulations of data from household surveys in the respective countries.

[a] Includes only countries with data available for 2011-2013. Countries are ordered by variation in the second subperiod (2008-2013).

[b] Urban areas.

Other countries saw similar improvements (on the order of 1% per year) in both subperiods; among them were Peru, El Salvador, Brazil and Chile. In the Bolivarian Republic of Venezuela, Ecuador, Paraguay and Panama, inequality fell much faster between 2002 and 2008 than in the subsequent period. In particular, Panama saw a slight trend towards concentration between 2008 and 2013. Lastly, in the Dominican Republic, worsening distribution in the first period was followed by a partial reversal of this trend in the second. Costa Rica registered a slight improvement between 2002 and 2008 and marked concentration between 2008 and 2013, at rates in excess of 1% a year (see figure 5).

With regard to income distribution across population groups, the share of the poorest 20% of households increased between 2008 and 2013, from an average of 5.2% to 5.6% of the total.[6] By contrast, the same period saw the average share of the richest quintile decrease from 48.4% in 2008 to 46.7% in 2013.

The share of the poorest quintile rose in 11 of the 15 countries during the period, with increases of one percentage point or more in Argentina and Uruguay. The share of the richest quintile shrank in 11 of the 15 countries reviewed, dropping by more than 4% in Argentina, Brazil and Uruguay. Between 2008 and 2013, Costa Rica, Panama and Paraguay posted simultaneous drops in the income share of the poorest quintile and rises in the share of the richest population quintile (see table 3).

6 Calculated on the basis of the 15 countries for which the most recent data are available. Does not include Guatemala, Honduras or Nicaragua.

Table 3
Latin America (17 countries): distribution of household income by extreme quintiles, around 2008 and 2013
(Percentages)

Country	Around 2008				Around 2013			
	Year	Share in total income *(percentages)*		Ratio of average per capita income	Year	Share in total income *(percentages)*		Ratio of average per capita income
		Poorest quintile (QI)	Richest quintile (QV)	QV/QI		Poorest quintile (QI)	Richest quintile (QV)	QV/QI
Argentina [a]	2009	5.7	47.8	16.6	2012	6.9	43.6	13.2
Bolivia (Plurinational State of)	2009	3.9	46.0	19.8	2011	4.4	42.6	15.9
Brazil	2008	4.1	58.0	26.2	2013	4.6	53.6	21.3
Chile	2009	5.3	53.5	15.9	2013	5.7	52.1	14.5
Colombia	2008	4.1	52.1	24.5	2013	4.7	50.1	20.0
Costa Rica	2008	5.2	47.3	13.5	2013	4.5	50.9	16.9
Dominican Republic	2008	3.5	53.0	25.4	2013	3.8	53.5	21.2
Ecuador	2008	5.2	48.5	15.6	2013	6.2	46.2	12.2
El Salvador	2009	5.8	46.4	13.0	2013	6.6	44.2	11.0
Mexico	2008	5.8	49.0	16.0	2012	6.6	46.2	14.0
Panama	2008	4.5	47.7	18.8	2013	4.2	48.0	20.2
Paraguay	2008	4.8	49.3	18.6	2013	4.3	50.6	19.1
Peru	2008	5.2	45.2	14.4	2013	5.3	42.9	12.3
Uruguay	2008	8.7	42.0	9.6	2013	10.0	36.4	7.2
Venezuela (Bolivarian Republic of)	2008	6.6	40.3	9.7	2013	6.5	39.0	10.1

Source: Economic Commission for Latin America and the Caribbean (ECLAC), on the basis of special tabulations of data from household surveys conducted in the respective countries.
[a] Urban total.

B. Distributive polarization

Recent years have brought conceptual and methodological developments that provide a different take on types of income distribution and their relationship to social conflict. These new developments include polarization indices, which until now have been little used to yield a comparative description of income distribution in the countries of Latin America. This section therefore describes and analyses trends in income distribution polarization indicators in the countries of Latin America between 2004 and 2012.

Interest in polarization stems from concern about social cohesion and equality. Polarization indices add new elements that complement the analysis of income distribution performed on the basis of traditional indicators. This is because conventional indicators of inequality are not suitable for differentiating between concentration around the mean of an income distribution or concentration around the poles of the distribution. The usual measures of inequality would therefore not necessarily pick up on the level of social tension associated with a distribution.

Polarization indices are used to estimate the extent to which the population is clustered around a small number of poles of income. The main idea is that individuals feel identified with the members of their income group and feel alienated from those outside their group. Alienation is captured by the distance between groups' income and identification by group size.

One of the most widely used indices for analysing the bipolarization of income distribution is the Wolfson index. This index was constructed to indirectly determine the weight of the middle class. It analyses bipolarization by dividing the income distribution into two groups of the same size; the median is the cut-off point. A higher value means a higher degree of bipolarization, and, consequently, a lower weight for the middle class.

There are also several indices for analysing distributive polarization in an arbitrary number of groups. In these cases, polarization is the sum of all effective antagonisms (alienation and identification). These indexes typically use a polarization aversion parameter known as alpha (the higher the value of this parameter, the greater the weight of the identification component), and they use different methods to determine the number of groups and find distribution cut-offs. One of these indices is the EGR. A higher EGR index value means greater polarization.

The data show a downtrend in income bipolarization, with the Wolfson index[7] declining in 15 of the 18 countries between 2004 and 2012. The only countries where it increased were Costa Rica, Paraguay and Guatemala.[8] In terms of relative changes,[9] the sharpest declines were seen in Nicaragua (-2.8%), Argentina (-2.6%), El Salvador (-2.4%), Uruguay (-2.3%) and Brazil (-2.3%) (see figure 6). A similar trend is obtained when using the EGR index[10] to measure bipolarization for two groups.

Figure 6

Latin America (18 countries): Wolfson index [a] of income distribution bipolarization, 2004 [b] and 2012 [c d]

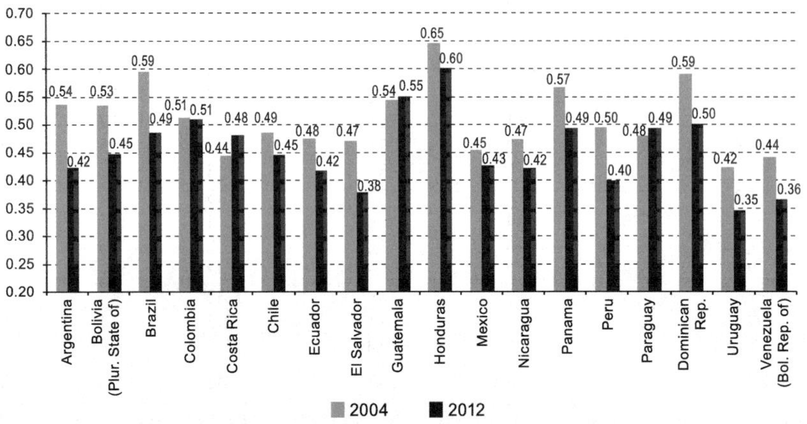

Source: Economic Commission for Latin America and the Caribbean (ECLAC), on the basis of special tabulations of data from household surveys conducted in the respective countries.

[a] Countries ordered by percentage change in the index between 2004 and 2012.

[b] Data refer to 2005 in Nicaragua; 2003 in Chile, Honduras, Peru and the Plurinational State of Bolivia; and 2002 in Guatemala.

[c] Data refer to 2011 in Chile, Paraguay and the Plurinational State of Bolivia; 2010 in Honduras; 2009 in Nicaragua; and 2006 in Guatemala.

[d] Data refer to urban areas for Argentina and the Bolivarian Republic of Venezuela in 2004 and 2012, and in Uruguay in 2004.

As for income polarization, in 16 of 18 countries the EGR[11] index values fell by 0.5 between 2004 and 2012. The most significant declines, measured as annualized relative variations, were in Nicaragua, Argentina, the Plurinational State of Bolivia and Uruguay, in that order. Bipolarization of income increased in Guatemala and Costa Rica.

Falling polarization was mainly due to the patterns in urban areas. As for bipolarization, the average Wolfson index value for urban areas in 15 countries (excluding Uruguay[12]) fell from 0.473 to 0.425 between 2004 and 2012, while in rural areas it increased slightly, from 0.435 in 2004 to 0.445 in 2012. A similar trend is seen when examining polarization in three or more groups.

C. Social classes: perceptions and expectations

Between 2004 and 2012, income distribution polarization decreased in most of the countries of Latin America. Correlatively, poverty also showed a sustained downtrend. Both factors point to an increasing weight for the groups in the middle of the distribution.

In conventional theories, declining polarization should lessen social conflict. But Chile and Brazil, which have brought polarization and poverty down, have recently been hit by expressions of social unrest. One possibility is that

7 See Foster and Wolfson (2002).

8 For Guatemala, the data are for 2002 and 2006.

9 There are differences between countries in the number of years between baseline measurements (2004) and follow-up measurements (2012). Therefore it was decided to divide the relative differences in the polarization index values between the initial and final year by the number of years between the two periods. Thus, the annualized relative change (ARC) for each country based on the formula ARC = ((IPas-IPab/Ipab) * 100) / AT, where Ipas = polarization value in the follow-up year; IPab = polarization value in the baseline year; AT = years elapsed between initial and final measurement.

10 Esteban, Gradín and Ray polarization index (1999).

11 See Duclos, Esteban and Ray (2005).

12 In the baseline measurement there are no data for rural areas of Uruguay.

declining polarization and poverty have boosted the sense of identification with the middle class[13] and fed higher expectations, which could lead to conflicts if not met.[14]

This study does not provide a direct test of these hypotheses, because of data limitations. Instead, two more limited propositions are compared. First, in countries with less polarization and less poverty there should be a stronger sense of identification with the middle class. Second, expectations of mobility should be higher in the groups that identify with the middle class than among those who identify with the lower class.

In 2011 the proportion of the population with a sense of belonging to the middle class tended to be higher in countries with a less bipolar distribution of income, but the association was not statistically significant. By contrast, the percentage of the population identifying with the middle class was significantly higher in countries where the incidence of poverty was lower (see figure 7).

Figure 7

Latin America (18 countries): population with a sense of belonging to the middle class, and incidence of monetary poverty, [a b c d e] **2011**

(Percentages)

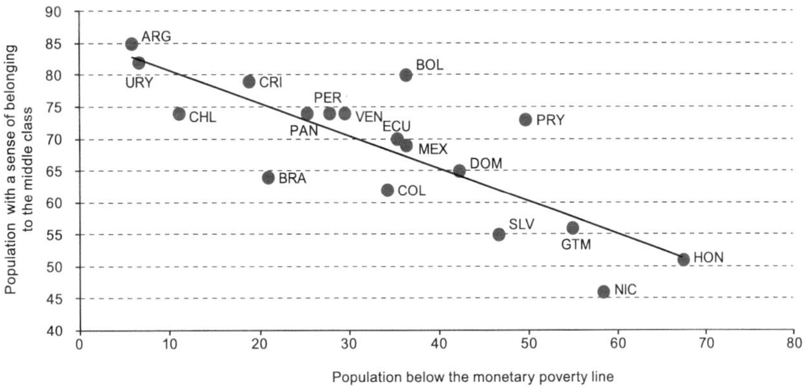

Source: Economic Commission for Latin America and the Caribbean (ECLAC), on the basis of tabulations of data from the 2011 Latinobarómetro database and from household surveys conducted in Argentina, Bolivarian Republic of Venezuela, Brazil, Chile, Colombia, Costa Rica, Dominican Republic, Ecuador, El Salvador (2010), Guatemala (2006), Honduras (2010), Nicaragua (2009), Panama, Paraguay, Peru, Plurinational State of Bolivia, Uruguay.

a The middle class population includes individuals who reported belonging to the middle or lower-middle class.

b The incidence of monetary poverty corresponds to ECLAC estimates for 2011, except for El Salvador, Honduras and Mexico (2010), Nicaragua (2009) and Guatemala (2006).

c Spearman's rho non-parametric correlation=-0.767, p=0.000***. OLS regression, standardized Beta coefficient Poverty=-0.804, p=0.000***. Highest residuals: Brazil =-1.6, Nicaragua=-1.5, Paraguay=1.8, Plurinational State of Bolivia=1.9.

d OLS regression model controlling for polarization: poverty, p=0.000***, polarization=0.841, adjusted R-squared=60%. Durbin Watson=2.219 (independent residuals between 1.5 and 2.5), VIF (variance inflation, lowest possible value 1, values greater than 10 indicate collinearity)=1.321. Excluding Honduras and Nicaragua, poverty, p=0.013* and Wolfson, p=0.384, adjusted R-squared=44%.

e OLS regression model, controlling for GDP per capita: poverty, p=0.001**, GDP=0.296, adjusted R-squared=62.8%. Durbin Watson=2.255 (independent residuals between 1.5 and 2.5), VIF (variance inflation, lowest possible value 1, values greater than 10 indicate collinearity)=2.640. Excluding Mexico and Plurinational State of Bolivia, poverty, p=0.010* and GDP, p=0.565, adjusted R-squared=68%.

On average for the region, expectations for offspring's economic well-being are higher among those who identify with the middle class than for those who reported being in the lower class. Just 23% of the population that reported being in the middle class feels that the economic well-being attained by their offspring will not go above the fourth step of a poverty-wealth ladder.[15] Among those who reported being in the lower-middle class, the figure was 37%; among those who reported being in the lower class, the figure was 53%.

Figure 8 charts evaluations of present economic well-being and expectations for offspring's well-being, disaggregated by countries. In 8 of 18 countries, expectations for the future of offspring are higher than evaluations of present well-being, and therefore express expectations of intergenerational mobility. In the rest of the countries there is no difference. This is mainly the case in countries with higher poverty rates, although there are exceptions such as Uruguay.

13 The link between decreasing absolute poverty and a growing middle class will not necessarily show in measurements of social classes based strictly on relative criteria.

14 The goal is not to analyse the relationship between polarization and conflict, which would be hard to do because of the lack of data on conflict in the region.

15 The question used was: Imagine a ladder with 10 steps, where the poorest people are on the first step and the richest people are on the tenth step. Where do you think your children will be?

Figure 8

Latin America (18 countries): present economic well-being and expectations for offspring's future 2011 [a b]

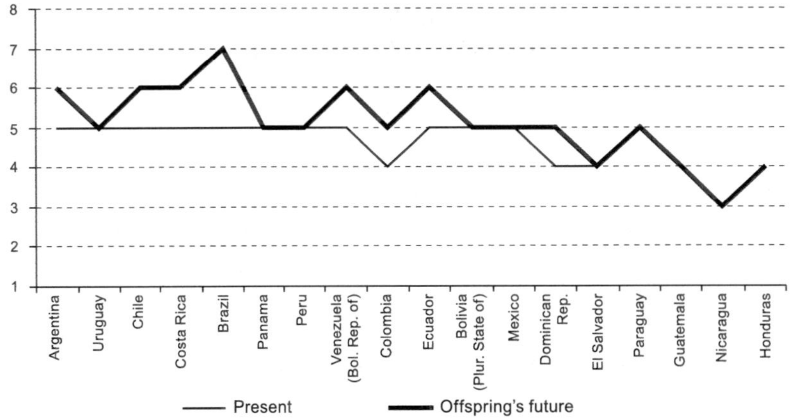

Source: Economic Commission for Latin America and the Caribbean (ECLAC), on the basis of tabulations of data from the 2011 Latinobarómetro database.
[a] Results are the median for each country. A value of 1 indicates worst level of poverty.
[b] Countries are ordered by rates of monetary poverty rate, from lowest to highest.

Brazil is the country where expectations of offspring's future well-being are highest. Next are Chile, Argentina, Costa Rica, the Bolivarian Republic of Venezuela and Ecuador. Nicaragua simultaneously shows the lowest level of expectations for future well-being and the worst evaluation of present economic well-being. Then come Honduras, Guatemala and El Salvador. In these latter four countries, with monetary poverty rates close to or above 50%, there are no differences between the median values for expectations and for present evaluation.

In short, in countries with less poverty and greater relative development there is a greater sense of identification with the middle class. And expectations of economic progress are higher among individuals who identify with the middle class than among individuals who feel they are in the lower class. All of these factors should be considered when designing policies for equality and social cohesion, especially in the economic slowdown scenario that the countries of the region are currently facing.

Chapter III
Youth: critical areas of the agenda for development with equality

Integrating the youth population into development processes is crucial for progress towards a more egalitarian society. The link between education and employment is one of the keys to social inclusion at this stage of life. It is important to understand the diversity of young people's current situations and life paths, which can coexist rather uneasily with inclusion difficulties specific to this age group, rather than stigmatizing them when they become separated, even if only temporarily, from both these institutions. The stereotype of violent youth also needs to be done away with, as it is a hindrance to development with equality. Understanding how social participation develops in contexts of growing violence in the region is vital for creating escape routes from these situations.

The position taken in the current debate on the post-2015 development agenda is that the sustainable development targets which this will have to include should be people-centred and aim for a just and inclusive world. It is also proposed that the greatest attention should be paid to the new generations, with particular emphasis on avoiding discrimination. Youth must also participate in the discussion of development strategies to achieve significant progress and more egalitarian societies.

A. Opportunities and capabilities: education and work for the young

It is in youth that the link between education and paid work, which are among the keys to social inclusion, becomes most firmly established. More years of education mean greater job opportunities, while creating the conditions for fuller participation in democratic societies. In the past 20 years, the region has made great progress with the proportion of young people completing some cycle of education (see figure 9).

Figure 9

Latin America (18 countries):[a] proportion of people aged 15 to 29 with complete primary, secondary and tertiary education, by age group, 1990, 2002 and 2012

(Percentages)

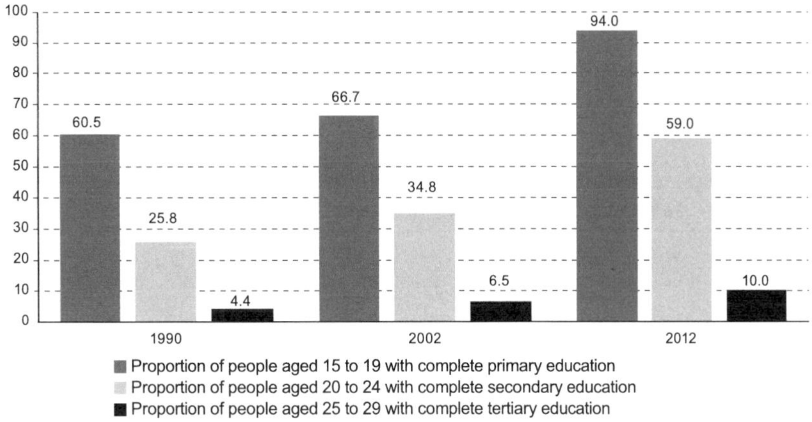

Source: Economic Commission for Latin America and the Caribbean (ECLAC), on the basis of special tabulations of data from household surveys conducted in the respective countries.

[a] Argentina (urban areas), Bolivarian Republic of Venezuela, Brazil, Chile, Colombia, Costa Rica, Dominican Republic, Ecuador, El Salvador, Guatemala, Honduras, Mexico, Nicaragua, Panama, Paraguay, Peru, Plurinational State of Bolivia and Uruguay.

Despite these major attainments in terms of education coverage and lower inequality, there are still large structural divides in capacity-building opportunities between the region's young people. There is a need to design flexible strategies to give all groups of young people the opportunity to pursue educational processes that are not necessarily linear or confined exclusively to the formal system, but provide tools and develop lifelong learning capabilities while easing entry into the labour market.

The move from education to employment in youth largely represents the transition from dependent to independent living (Rico and Trucco, 2014). Although youth employment has improved in recent decades, it still typically involves poor quality jobs, lower wages and a low level of affiliation to social security. As figure 10 shows, unemployment rates are considerably higher for the population aged 15 to 24 than for the total population in all countries of Latin America and the Caribbean. The situation in most of the English-speaking Caribbean is particularly worrying, as some countries have youth unemployment rates in excess of 30%. These barriers may result in discontent and frustration among many who are not included in the region's collective development process. Young people aspire to high-quality employment opportunities enabling them to participate fully in productive and civic development processes and achieve the conditions for personal development and well-being.

In 2012, around 30 million young people aged 15-29 in 18 Latin American countries (that is, 22% of the total population of that age group in the region) were not in formal education or employment. A better understanding is needed of the complexity and diversity of situations experienced by this large group of young people, so that key determinants of young lives are not overlooked. When the specific activity status of this group is looked into further, it can be concluded that being outside education and employment is not synonymous with apathy or a lack of interest in participating in society (see figure 11).

Figure 10

Latin America and the Caribbean (26 countries): unemployment rates among those aged 15 to 24 and those aged 15 and over, around 2012

(Percentages)

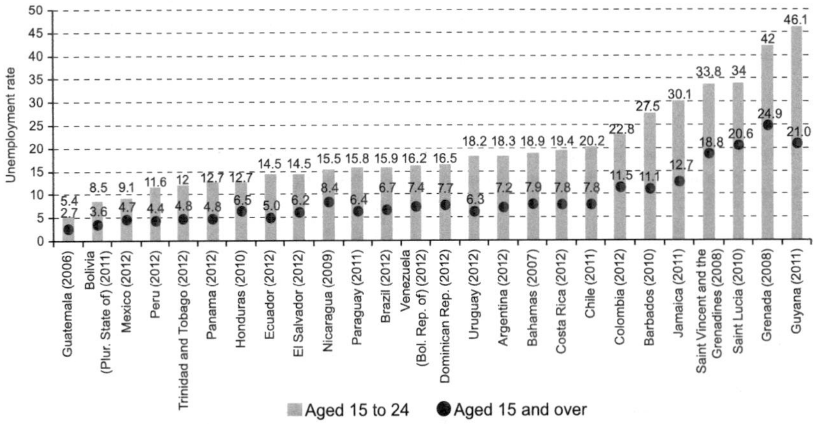

Source: Economic Commission for Latin America and the Caribbean (ECLAC), on the basis of special tabulations of data from household surveys conducted in Latin American countries. For Caribbean countries: Mónica Parra-Torrado, "Youth unemployment in the Caribbean", *Caribbean Knowledge Series*, Washington, D.C., World Bank, 2014.

Figure 11

Latin America (18 countries):[a] activity status of people aged 15 to 29 who are neither studying nor in paid employment, around 2012

(Percentages)

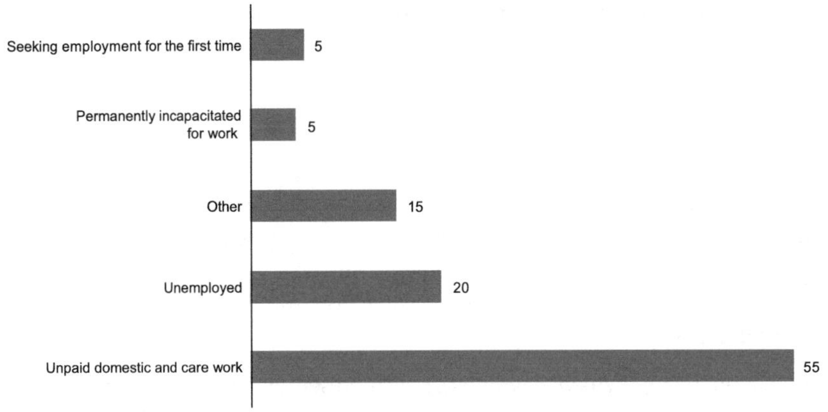

Source: Economic Commission for Latin America and the Caribbean (ECLAC), on the basis of special tabulations of data from household surveys conducted in the respective countries.

[a] Argentina (urban areas), Bolivarian Republic of Venezuela, Brazil, Chile, Colombia, Costa Rica, Dominican Republic, Ecuador, El Salvador, Guatemala, Honduras, Mexico, Nicaragua, Panama, Paraguay, Peru, Plurinational State of Bolivia and Uruguay.

The segment of young people not in education or paid employment is diverse, with some falling out of the system temporarily and a substantial proportion of young women devoting themselves to unpaid care and domestic work (70% of those who report performing these activities are women). The analysis makes clear the imperative need for policies to address the demands of care and domestic work from a gender and poverty reduction perspective, and for broader first job opportunities.

B. Young people and environments of violent social inclusion

Paradoxically, the major advances in development that the Latin American countries have achieved in recent years and the positive effects these have had on the young now coexist with increases in indices of violence in the region, exposing the population at large, but most particularly the youth of Latin America and the Caribbean, to a context of growing violence and insecurity. Seven of the 14 most violent countries in the world are in Latin America and the Caribbean: Bolivarian Republic of Venezuela, Belize, Colombia, El Salvador, Guatemala, Honduras and Jamaica.

The concept of violence is a complex one to address owing to its multidimensional character, deriving from the diverse areas of people's lives in which it can manifest itself and the different causes and consequences it can have. Given today's situations of violence, there is a need to look into the existence of a close relationship with social exclusion processes, where violence and context feed upon and into each other, so that social, territorial and family settings can end up encouraging the young to seek violent solutions. The stigmatization of the young for their supposedly violent way of life represents a breakdown in solidarity and worsens exclusion.

Several perception surveys conducted in the last few years show high crime figures, indicating that young people are living in societies where violence is strongly present and which are fractured by a sense of insecurity and lack of solidarity and cohesion. According to the Latinobarómetro Study (2013), on average a majority of young people stating that they or a family member had been the victim of some crime during the past year said that the crime involved violence (see figure 12).

Figure 12
Latin America (18 countries): people aged 16 to 29 stating they have been victims of violent and non-violent crime in the past 12 months, 2013
(Percentages)

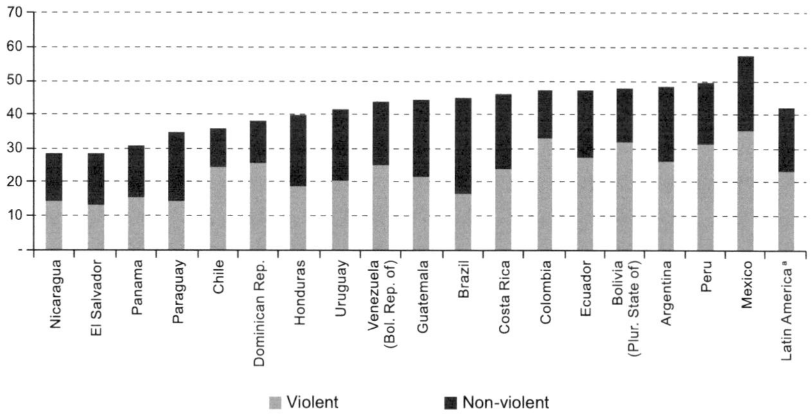

Source: Economic Commission for Latin America and the Caribbean (ECLAC), on the basis of special tabulations of the 2013 Latinobarómetro Survey.
[a] Simple average of the results for the 18 countries included in the measurement.

Little is known about the perpetrators of violence and their age distribution. A general approach to gauging participation in acts of violence are the figures for victims of extreme violence, such as homicide. The average figures for Latin America and the Caribbean between 1990 and 2010 do not suggest that violent deaths among young people are significantly different in nature to those among people aged 30 to 44 (see figure 13). A look at the statistics of involvement in violent behaviour based on victim figures indicates that the stigma attached to violent youth derives not so much from the scale of their participation in acts of violence as in the way they participate. What the mass media most highlight are organized forms of urban violence among the young (usually males) in gangs going by the name of *pandillas, maras, clicas* or *combos*, depending on the country.

Youth involvement in different forms of organized urban violence in the region is undeniable. The territorial role of gangs within cities is one of the things that do most to create a feeling of insecurity among the population at large, as it directly affects community life. It represents a threat to civic order and the city as a cultural project because its sovereignty is based on the local district or *barrio* (Perea, 2008). Gangs have emerged as a direct effect of people's exclusion and marginalization from the development of society. Gangs give them power, cash incomes, a space and a feeling of belonging that no other social institution provides. In this context, there is one thing that it is important to highlight, as it is common to a number of the region's countries (particularly those that have suffered from alarming cycles of violence) and is also particularly characteristic of the region: cocaine trafficking. In some countries, such as those of Central America and Mexico, the cartels are increasingly tending to use gangs to "outsource" abduction and contract killing activities, particularly when they come into conflict with one another and have to find more recruits quickly and at lower cost. Cocaine trafficking in the region has played a key role as a driver of conflict and a multiplier of violence.

Figure 13

Latin America and the Caribbean (33 countries): rate of mortality from interpersonal violence, by age group, 1990-2010

(Deaths per 100,000 inhabitants)

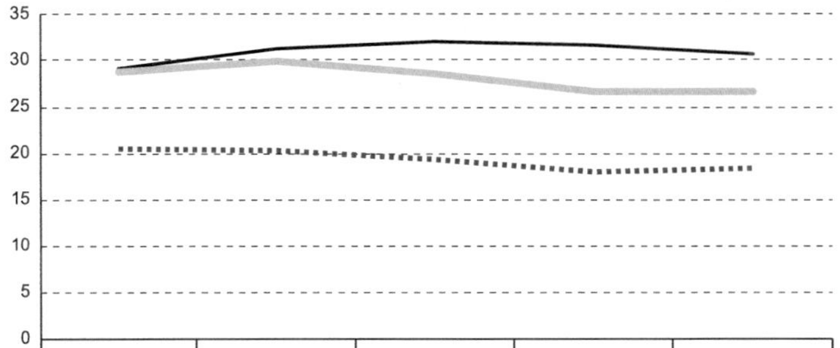

	1990	1995	2000	2005	2010
Aged 15-29	29	31	32	32	31
Aged 30-44	29	30	29	27	27
Aged 45-59	20	20	19	18	18

Source: Institute for Health Metrics and Evaluation [online] http://vizhub.healthdata.org/gbd-compare/.

Describing young people from the perspective of the stigma of violence distorts appreciations of the roots of the problem and opens the way to alarmist and exaggerated proposals for preventing and solving it. It is important to grasp the sociocultural factors that have come into play in each of the territories where violence has broken out most strongly and where young people are involved. Territorial inequality in a city makes criminal organizations very attractive for the part of the population that is being excluded from established mechanisms of social participation. To be able to solve this problem, it is important to understand the corrupt ties that criminal organizations have developed with the various State political, police and judicial authorities, but also the links they establish with local communities themselves and the degree of support and protection they receive from the population where they hold sway.

C. Youth and the development agenda

Support for political participation by the young, with consideration of their diversity, is essential to strengthen their commitment to the development of public policies that can overcome the persistent inequalities of Latin America and the Caribbean. As part of the global debate on new development goals, a number of youth forums have been held in the past few years to identify the main challenges this age group faces in the region. The priority development areas for the young on the development agenda are education, employment, enterprise, health, peace, personal security, good governance and participation.

On the whole, young people consider that the best way of bringing about social change is through political participation. But the ways in which the new generations participate have been transformed: they perceive that the best way to do this is through social movements and youth organizations. The Internet, and particularly social networks, have played a key role in the youth-led social movements that have sprung up in different parts of the world in the past few years. This has translated into mobilizations that have mainly catalysed social discontent, organized through these new platforms and capturing the attention of both the mass media and their governments.

The underrepresentation of the young in all their plurality affects the democratic quality of institutions, facilitated the emergence of movements like those described. Policies that are inappropriate for the young have significant costs for all, both because they worsen the problems described in the earlier sections and because of the consequences of failing to include this population group properly in economic development efforts and thereby sacrificing their creativity and energy. In other words, a virtuous circle is foregone and a vicious circle is entrenched.

Chapter IV Gender inequality in the labour market and its impact on socioeconomic inequality: what gains could be made?

In recent years, ECLAC has placed the issue of equality front and centre on the region's agenda, setting forth a broad concept of equality whose scope extends beyond distributive justice to include subjects' demands for recognition, dignity and autonomy (ECLAC, 2014). The autonomy of individuals is dependent on the range of options and resources that society makes available to them (Lechner, 2002). ECLAC has also highlighted the issue of equality between men and women, with an emphasis on the unpaid work performed by women within households, its economic value and how these activities prevent women from achieving economic autonomy and full integration into the labour market (ECLAC, 2013). In this context, a gender perspective is indispensable to analysing prevailing societal inequalities and their interlinkages. Several studies have argued that the absence of a gender perspective impedes an understanding of the different positions of men and women as economic agents and subjects of economic policies (Giosa and Rodríguez, 2010), while also masking the role of unpaid domestic work as a factor that both conditions and sustains the labour market.

Inequalities are generated in various dimensions of the market, in connection with variables such as income, participation and access to different occupations. Not only does the labour market offer an unparalleled space for social relations, mutual recognition and building autonomy and identity, it is also one of the arenas in which the struggle to overcome poverty and extend citizenship plays out, making it a crucial sphere for advancing towards the goal of equality.

The gaps in economic participation, employment and income must be reduced, as doing so will have positive effects at different levels. For one, there will be productivity gains, higher household income and, as shown in this chapter, lower levels of socioeconomic inequality and household poverty. But it will also give impetus to equality in other spheres, such as the full exercise of autonomy, the development of individual capacities and potential, access to contributory social protection and broader participation in society beyond the household. Against this backdrop, this chapter links the gender inequalities in labour market integration and the household income inequalities prevalent in the region's economies.

A. Interlinkages between paid and unpaid work

Work can be defined as the physical or mental effort that people make with the aim of generating wealth. When this work is carried out in the market in exchange for pay, it is referred to as employment. Employment is valued socially and economically, measured in statistics and included in national accounts.

One special case is unpaid employment, that is, work carried out within the scope of the market without pay. The individuals in this group are considered to be employed for the purposes of labour statistics. This type of employment is more prevalent among women, and is particularly common in some countries of the region. This category should not be confused with unpaid work in a wider sense, which extends to domestic and care work in households and communities.

Unpaid domestic work, done mostly by women, is not included in countries' labour statistics and accounts of economic activity. However, paid and unpaid work are strongly interlinked and both are productive, the only difference is that in one case the production is market-oriented and in the other it is destined for the home and community.

Distinguishing between work and employment is important for at least three reasons. First, because the interaction between the two types of activity conditions the lives of men and women in different ways. Second, because the distinction helps to identify individuals', and in particular women's, overall economic contribution, beyond whether the task performed is paid or not. And third, because in order to analyse female employment, its contribution to countries' development and the benefits and rights derived therefrom, it is essential to relate the two concepts. A full examination of the issues surrounding women's labour market participation and gender inequalities requires an acknowledgement that people's contribution to the economy consists of market and non-market work.

Spotlighting and analysing the sexual division of labour and the links between the spheres of production and reproduction provides insight into the origin of gender inequalities in various areas. The large amount of time that women devote to unpaid work and the almost complete lack of male involvement in domestic and care work prevent women from entering the labour market on equal terms.

B. Female labour force participation

1. Participation, employment and unemployment

The overall participation rate in Latin America has held relatively steady over the past decade. The female participation rate, despite losing some momentum in relation to previous decades, continued to show moderate growth in some countries; while the growth in labour force participation rates for men has been less pronounced. On the back of these developments, the gender-based economic participation gap has narrowed in most countries. Yet despite the considerable differences between countries, there remains broad scope for increasing women's labour market participation in all cases.

Figure 14
Latin America (18 countries): ratio of female to male participation rates, around 2002 and 2012

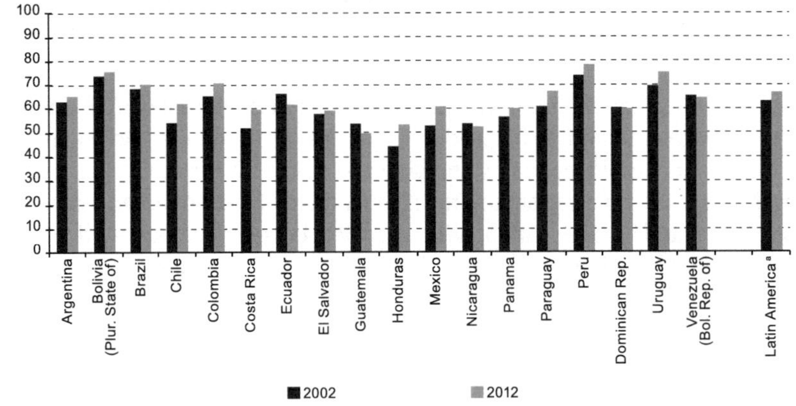

Source: Economic Commission for Latin America and the Caribbean (ECLAC), on the basis of special tabulations of data from household surveys conducted in the respective countries.
ª Weighted average.

The English-speaking Caribbean countries are no exception to the rule and their participation rates are also lower for women than for men. However, the gap is smaller in most of the Caribbean countries for which information is available than in many of the countries of Latin America.

The moderate economic growth in the last decade has led to declines in the unemployment rate for both men and women. In aggregate terms for the region, the female-to-male unemployment ratio has held relatively steady, although there are significant variations between countries. However, in all countries of the region unemployment rates are significantly higher for women than for men.

Most countries in the region saw a rise in the employment rate over the decade. While the employment rate for women expanded in all countries except Ecuador and Guatemala, the male employment rate fell in several countries. As a result, the gender gap in employment between men and women has narrowed significantly, although some large gaps remain, as is the case for participation. On average for the region, the female employment rate stood at 65% of the male employment rate in 2012, compared with 61% in 2002. The largest gender gaps in employment were found in Guatemala, Honduras and Nicaragua.

2. The labour market outlook in the current climate

Today, a new economic scenario is taking shape in the region. The most recent projections forecast modest growth and an economic slowdown, with a corresponding loss of momentum in the labour market indicators (ECLAC/ILO, 2014). First, for Latin America as a whole, the participation rate has declined for men and has remained constant for women in the last year, bringing to a halt the recent expansion in the number of women in the workforce. Second, the unemployment rate for the entire region has continued to fall, although much more slowly. Third, although the total number of employed persons has increased in all countries, job creation is beginning to slow. In fact, in some countries that increase is attributable to own-account employment rather than wage employment, contrary to the trend in previous years. Lastly, with regard to income, in 2013 average wages continued to grow in real terms in a context of low unemployment and moderate inflation.

3. Economic cycles and differential gender impacts

Workers suffer when economic activity contracts, as it leads to diminished earnings and loss of jobs. Given the differential inclusion of men and women in the labour market and the unequal amount of time they spend on unpaid work, it is logical to expect different outcomes by sex during downturns. Economic theory posits that labour supply reacts in one of two ways in a period of economic crisis. The first is a countercyclical approach, which seeks to increase labour participation in response to a decline in economic activity, often referred to as the added worker effect. The alternative is a procyclical perspective whereby the slump in economic activity is matched by a fall in labour participation, which is known as the discouraged worker effect. Several studies have suggested that the first of these effects tends to predominate among women and the second among men (Espino, 2012; Antonopoulos, 2009; Arroyo and others, 2010).

In order to analyse the impact of crises on key labour market indicators, five countries that have reported major declines in economic activity at some point in recent decades were selected: Brazil (1989-1990), Argentina (2001), Uruguay (2002), Paraguay (2008) and the Bolivarian Republic of Venezuela (2009). All these countries recorded an increase in the female participation rate and a decrease in the male rate during the downturn. This evidence appears to support the hypothesis that female labour supply expands in crisis situations owing to the added worker effect and that male labour supply diminishes owing to the discouraged worker effect. The fact that the female participation rates did not subsequently fall as the economy picked up suggests that women who enter the labour market in times of crisis tend to stay there even after the crisis is over (Montaño and Milosavljevic, 2010).

4. Traits associated with male and female labour market participation

The gender differences in the key labour market indicators that are revealed by comparing the aggregate averages for each country mask other, more specific patterns that are clearly repeated in all of the economies. For example, the gender gap in participation rates is narrower for men and women with higher education levels: more educated men and women display more similar labour market behaviour. Thus, in the region the female-to-male ratio for the participation rate among workers with incomplete primary education is 54%, compared with 87% for workers with secondary or higher education.

Gender differences in labour force participation also vary with workers' household composition. When there are children aged 6 years or under in the household, that is, when care demands are very high, women's participation rates are equivalent to 60% of those of men. When the youngest child in the household is between 6 and 14 years, the ratio rises to 75%, and if there are no young children in the household the ratio goes up to 80%. The differences are much more pronounced in the poorest households in the first quintile than in households in the wealthiest quintile. The greatest scope for increasing female labour participation is therefore among women with lower educational levels who have household responsibilities, which will require specific public policy efforts. The efforts targeting this segment should focus on education and training, care services and active employment.

A comparison of employed men and women reveals differences in several areas. Women work considerably fewer hours per week in the labour market, for example, than men (37 hours for women compared with 45 hours for men) in all countries. This very significant gap is linked to women's unpaid work responsibilities, especially care within households. As has been widely documented, when total work hours, including paid and unpaid work, are taken into account, women shoulder a heavier overall burden than men in most countries (see, for example, ECLAC, 2014). Another recognized feature of female labour force participation is the high concentration of women in certain occupations and sectors, otherwise known as occupational segregation. In terms of the quality of employment, the rates of social security affiliation for men and women increased between 2002 and 2012, and the prevailing rates of formal employment are similar for men and women.

5. Heterogeneity in the production structure and gender inequality

One of the hallmarks of the region's economies is the striking heterogeneity of their production structures, manifested in sharp differences in worker productivity. One way of analysing this structural heterogeneity is to take a sectoral approach and to focus on the productivity differentials between sectors or branches of economic activity. In this context, it is also interesting to compare the employment of men and women in sectors with different productivity levels. To this end, the sectors were divided into three groups on the basis of their average labour productivity (at purchasing power parity 2005 dollars): the low-productivity sector, which includes agriculture, commerce and services; the medium-productivity sector, which covers construction, manufacturing and transport; and the high-productivity sector, encompassing finance, electricity and mining. As shown below, women make up a larger proportion of workers in the low-productivity sector than in other sectors and, furthermore, this sector employs the bulk of women in the region.

Figure 15
Latin America (18 countries):[a] sectoral distribution of workers by sex, around 2012
(Percentages)

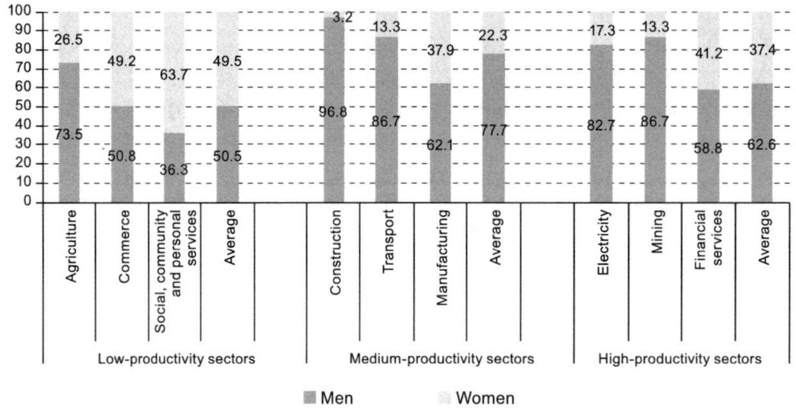

Source: Economic Commission for Latin America and the Caribbean (ECLAC), on the basis of special tabulations of data from household surveys conducted in the respective countries.
[a] Weighted average.

In terms of contribution to GDP, in 2012 the low-productivity sector generated 39% of GDP in Latin America, compared with 28% of GDP for the high-productivity sector.

C. Labour income of women and men

A persistent feature of the region's labour markets is that the average monthly earnings of women are lower than those of men. The gaps vary significantly between countries: in the Plurinational State of Bolivia and Peru men earn on average over 50% more per month than women, but in El Salvador, Honduras and Panama this difference is less than 10%. This gap may in part be attributable to the fact that women spend fewer hours on paid work per month than men. Indeed, in 2012 men spent an average of 8 hours per week more than women on paid work. But even when this factor is taken into account, there remains a considerable gender gap in average earnings in most countries, although it does narrow somewhat. In some countries, such as Argentina, Costa Rica, El Salvador, Honduras and Nicaragua, wage differentials tend to disappear when controlling for hours worked.

Figure 16

Latin America (18 countries): difference between average wages for men and women, around 2012

(Percentages of female income)

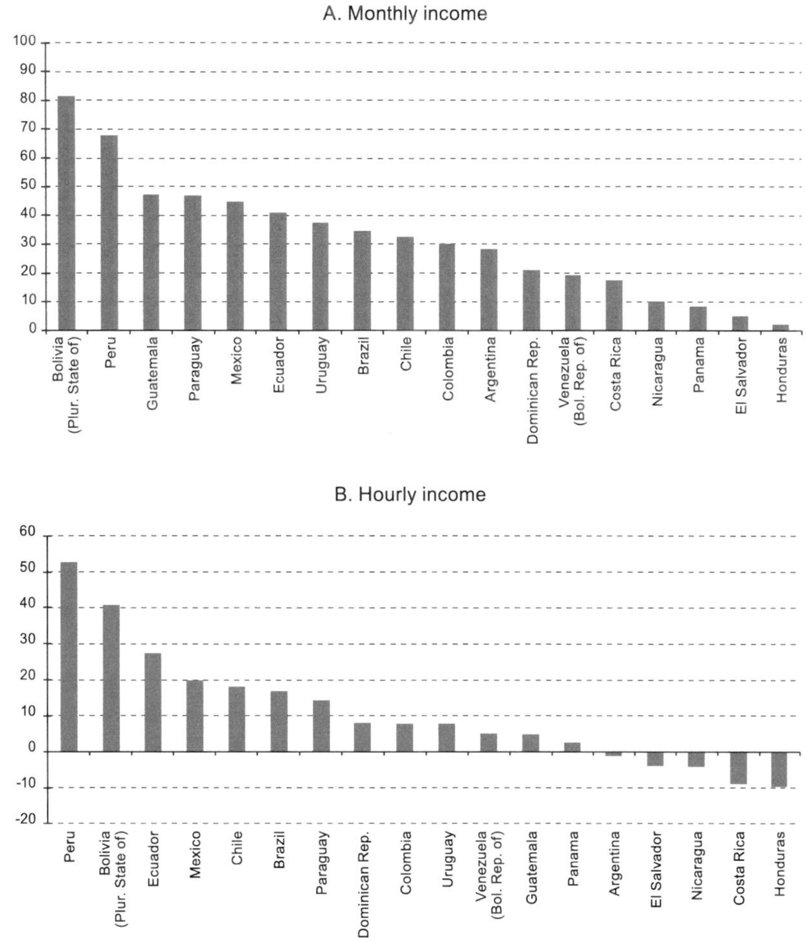

Source: Economic Commission for Latin America and the Caribbean (ECLAC), on the basis of special tabulations of data from household surveys conducted in the respective countries.

As discussed in ECLAC (2014), there is a negative association between female participation and employment rates and the average gender wage gap for the countries. For example, the countries of Central America, which have wider participation and employment gaps between women and men, show fewer gender differences in earnings on average. The explanation for this finding lies in the selection process that women undergo to gain entry to the labour market. It is the women with better education levels who are more likely to participate actively in the labour market and get jobs, while employment among men is more widespread.

The differences in participation rates, employment and wages between men and women combine to set a scenario in which female earnings contribute significantly less to household income than male earnings. Indeed, women consistently contribute less than half of total household labour income. In fact, that proportion fell short of 40% in all of the countries in the region in 2012. They make the largest proportional contribution in Uruguay, furnishing 39% on average of total household earnings, and the smallest in Dominican Republic, where their share is 26%.

Even greater heterogeneity is detected in the region regarding women's contribution to total household labour income in the lowest income quintile in each country. The significantly smaller share contributed by women in the lower quintiles may reflect the reduced labour market participation of women in these economic strata.

Figure 17
America Latina (18 countries): women's contribution to total household labour income in the first and fifth income quintiles, around 2012
(Percentages)

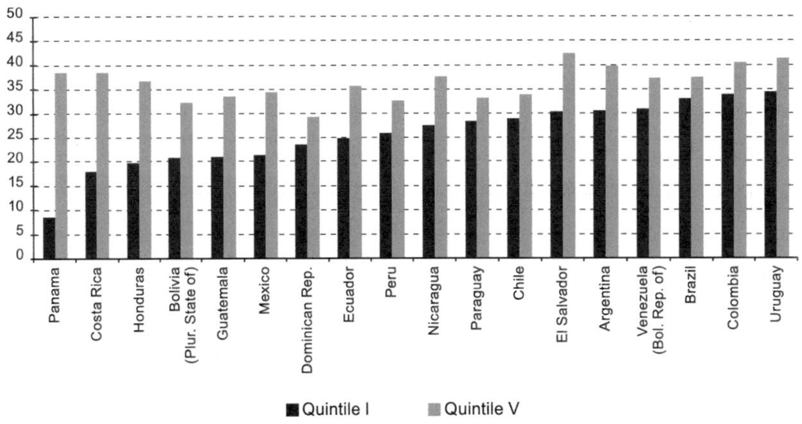

Source: Economic Commission for Latin America and the Caribbean (ECLAC), on the basis of special tabulations of data from household surveys conducted in the respective countries.

There is therefore scope for increasing women's contribution to household income, either by expanding their labour market participation or eliminating wage discrimination. Depending on the starting position of each country, the greatest gains can be achieved by advancing on one of these two fronts, although they are obviously not mutually exclusive.

D. Women's labour income and its effects on inequality and poverty

This section attempts to quantify what the levels of income inequality and poverty would be in the region in two scenarios: (i) if the participation gap between men and women were closed; and (ii) if women earned the same as men (with the same qualifications). The simulations are based on the latest information available from household surveys conducted in the respective countries, which in most cases corresponds to 2012.

Setting out to close these gaps is not a utopian exercise. The fact that these disparities are ingrained in multiple mechanisms of cultural reproduction may make them difficult to reverse, but international experience has shown that public policies on labour and care have much to contribute in these areas.

1. Closing the participation gap

The first analysis looked at what would happen if the participation rate for women in the intermediate age group (14-65 years) was similar to that for men. Such a rise in female participation would lead to an increase in average household income ranging from 3% to 4% in Argentina, Brazil, Colombia, Mexico and Uruguay, and reaching over 10% in El Salvador, Honduras, Nicaragua and Peru. The countries with the largest gender gaps in participation would gain the most in terms of average household income if those participation gaps disappeared. Evening up the rates of female and male participation would reduce poverty and inequality in the countries.

If more women were to enter the labour market, great strides would be made in reducing poverty and inequality. These findings give an idea of the magnitude of the improvements that could be expected as a result of increased female labour market participation. Nevertheless, it is clear that even the massive incorporation of women into the labour market would not eliminate poverty in Latin America owing to the structural characteristics of the region's labour markets. The income that these women would earn would help to improve their situation, but only to some extent. However, some countries would record very significant progress, especially with regard to inequality. Even more importantly, the entry of women into the labour market would have a profound impact in terms of the full exercise of autonomy, the development of capacities and personal potential, access to contributory social protection and broader participation in society beyond the household.

Figure 18

Latin America (18 countries): changes in poverty and inequality in a scenario of closing the labour participation gap compared with a baseline scenario

(Percentages)

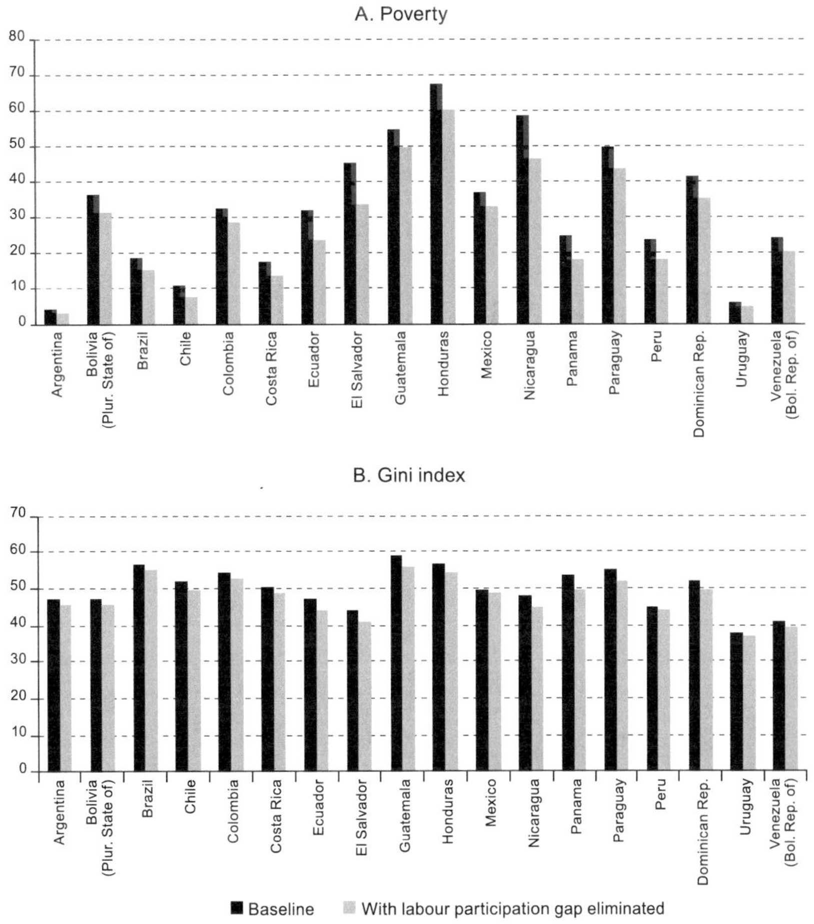

Source: Economic Commission for Latin America and the Caribbean (ECLAC), on the basis of special tabulations of data from household surveys conducted in the respective countries.

Changes cannot be hastened in the proposed direction without active, resolute policies that promote and encourage such transformations, including policies on care. The region has much ground to cover in this respect because although progress has been made in legal and regulatory terms, scant substantial changes have been seen. Care services generally have low coverage and operate in a weak institutional framework, thus failing to meet the growing needs of societies. Nevertheless, several countries have incorporated the issue into their policy agendas and have made different degrees of progress (ECLAC, 2012). Active labour market policies can encourage greater participation by women in the labour market by helping to ensure that they are properly qualified and facilitating their labour market integration. Of course, there are other policies that can influence the female participation rate, such as the provision of preschool education and extended schooldays at the primary stage. Lastly, as ECLAC has highlighted in several studies, what is needed is a new gender compact that involves a more equitable distribution of roles within the household and is thus conducive to female labour force participation.

2. Closing the income gap

Closing the gender income gap would lead to milestone achievements in poverty reduction in countries such as the Plurinational State of Bolivia and Peru. A significant percentage of women in these countries are employed but not paid, which explains the dramatic changes that would take place if these women were to receive a similar income to men with the same level of education and work experience.

Figure 19

Latin America (18 countries): changes in poverty and inequality in a scenario of closing the gender income gap compared with a baseline scenario

(Percentages)

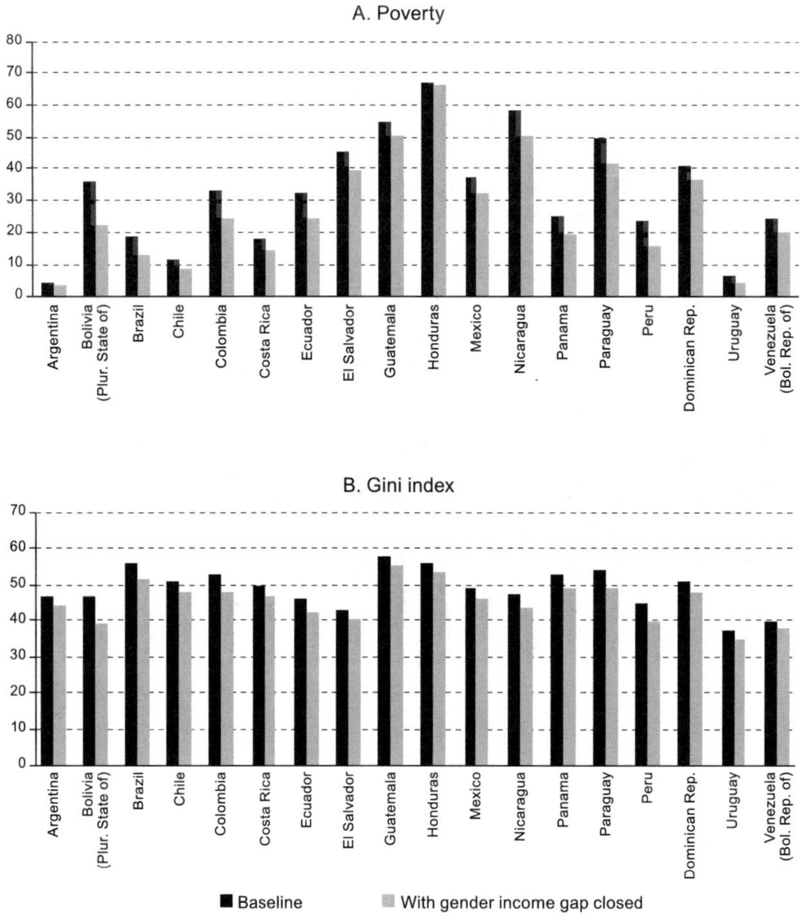

Source: Economic Commission for Latin America and the Caribbean (ECLAC), on the basis of special tabulations of data from household surveys conducted in the respective countries.

Again, progress will not be made on this front without public policy. Governments in the region have ratified international agreements and passed domestic legislation to endorse the principles of equal opportunity and non-discrimination between women and men. However, the figures indicate that these actions alone are insufficient to eradicate gender discrimination in the labour market. In addition to enacting specific legislation on equal pay, labour market institutions can play a role in helping to close gaps. Expanding the coverage of collective bargaining to include workers in traditionally excluded sectors, such as domestic workers, rural workers and homeworkers, can help to narrow the gender income gap. Another approach is to address issues relating to the protection of maternal and paternal labour rights (Maurizio, 2010). Improving labour inspections can also help to eliminate discriminatory practices. Furthermore, as several studies have indicated that occupational segregation is responsible for a significant part of the gender wage gap (for example, Macpherson and Hirsch, 1995; Miller, 2009), policies to address occupational segregation, for example, by training women for occupations that are not typically female, would narrow the wage gap.

E. Concluding remarks

This chapter details the various spheres in which gender inequalities occur and shows how they are reflected and reproduced in the labour market, despite originating in forms of discrimination that predate the labour market and are related to sociocultural conditioning. The simulation exercises conducted show that eliminating the participation gap between men and women or closing the gender pay gap can result in significant improvements in household well-being, in terms of both increased household income and lower poverty and socioeconomic inequality levels. The potential for progress varies between countries and is greater in the countries where the gaps are more pronounced. In all cases, the changes would be significant and entirely attainable for the region. Specific labour market policies and care policies can directly influence both women's labour market participation and income discrimination.

Chapter V
Residential segregation and the reproduction of inequalities

In Latin America, socioeconomic groups generally exhibit distinctive location patterns within cities. If these patterns involve physical distances that hinder or prevent interaction, recognition and cooperation between these groups, social cohesion and city governance are likely to be weakened. Where the location pattern of socioeconomic groups helps perpetuate social inequalities in the city (either by blocking the upward social mobility of disadvantaged groups, by creating privileges and rents for affluent groups, or by segmenting and excluding the poor from the circuits through which the different kinds of capital flow), socioeconomic residential segregation ensues, posing a fundamental challenge for the development of inclusive and sustainable cities.

One of the hallmarks of urbanization in the region is the concentration of populations of low socioeconomic level in peripheral areas, especially in large cities (those with a population of more than 1 million inhabitants). This pattern is typically disadvantageous, since these groups are subject to more precarious conditions in terms of access to housing, basic services and community infrastructure, and suffer greater exposure to security risks and natural disasters, more expensive transport costs and longer journey times, greater physical and social distance from the spheres and channels through which economic resources flow, a lack of awareness and interest on the part of the State and predominant groups in respect of their problems and needs, and stigmatization and even fear among other socioeconomic groups.

The other side of the coin is that groups with high socioeconomic status have consolidated their presence in a few areas of the city which, as well as having abundant private resources owing to residents' income levels, are usually relatively close (or have easier access) to city centres and hubs of good quality employment. Residents of these areas benefit from a higher quality of life and more efficient urban services than in the rest of the city. Of course, this clustering of the affluent population tends to create an identity conducive to mutual exchange and familiarity within the group, but which simultaneously isolates it and even disconnects it from other social groups.

In Latin American cities, this highly differentiated geographical location pattern leads to socioeconomic residential segregation, which causes concern for authorities and experts alike. There is fierce debate over future trends in segregation, the magnitude of its effects, and the relevance and effectiveness of policies designed to reduce it. This chapter of *Social Panorama 2014* provides an input to that debate, by contributing updated indicators obtained from the processing of census microdata from a score of cities and 10 of the region's countries.

A. Socioeconomic residential segregation: arguments and measures

Until the 1990s, the broadly prevailing view was that socioeconomic residential segregation was increasing and would continue to do so. This view was founded on the increase in poverty and social inequality caused by the debt crisis and neoliberal structural adjustments, the weakening of social cohesion and the public institutions that underpin social integration, and the segregation-intensifying effects of State interventions, particularly under authoritarian regimes.

Theories that directly linked globalization with the configuration of dual cities, divided along social and territorial lines, also contributed to this point of view.

By contrast, the first decade of the twenty-first century was marked by opposing arguments. In some quarters it is maintained that socioeconomic residential segregation continued to increase, since the periphery has consolidated its status as the habitat of low-income groups, poor families have withdrawn from affluent and middle-class neighbourhoods, and some central areas have regained their appeal to migrants, driving up land prices and forcing out poor families. Other studies anticipate a fall in socioeconomic residential segregation, driven mainly by the relocation of middle- and high-income households to certain parts of the periphery, in some cases forming middle and upper-class suburbs that could be termed the "gentrified periphery". Such movements fragment the territorial distribution of this group and diversify the socioeconomic composition of destination areas, which in turn helps reduce overall segregation. Moreover, residential developments at the city edge —some of which are social housing, others private and aimed at middle-income groups— along with rising incomes among the poorest population segments and urban renewal and investment programmes, have consolidated formal housing across swathes of the periphery, and may therefore also reduce rates of socioeconomic residential segregation.

Thanks to census microdata, estimates of socioeconomic residential segregation are possible for different geographical scales. Nevertheless, comparability between cities is somewhat limited, so indicators are calculated for "broad urban areas", which distinguish between central and peripheral areas and usually identify pericentral areas and two or more types of periphery.

B. The sociodemographic dynamics of large cities and trends in socioeconomic residential segregation during the 2000s

All the cities studied have expanding populations, though growth rates are slowing and have dipped below 1% in some cases. There remains a clear contrast between city centres and peripheries, since central areas are growing much more slowly (and are even losing population in some cases), while peripheral areas continue to have a lower socioeconomic status. The cities reported widespread improvements in education levels, albeit with variations from one country to the next, with the fastest progress in educational and socioeconomic status occurring at the periphery. This helped narrow social inequality between broad urban areas.

Most cities are still seeing positive net migration, albeit rates are slowing and net emigration is a reality in several cases. A clear and persistent pattern has emerged, in that all cities are a magnet for young people (aged 15 to 29). The territorial impact of migration, and particularly intrametropolitan migration, remains highly centrifugal, with most migrants settling in the periphery (see map 1).

Map 1

Mexico City, São Paulo (Brazil), San José and Santo Domingo: minor administrative divisions (MIADs) by average annual net migration rate, five-year period prior to the 2010 census round [a]

(Per 1,000 inhabitants)

A. Mexico City: net internal migration rate, by municipality, 2005-2010

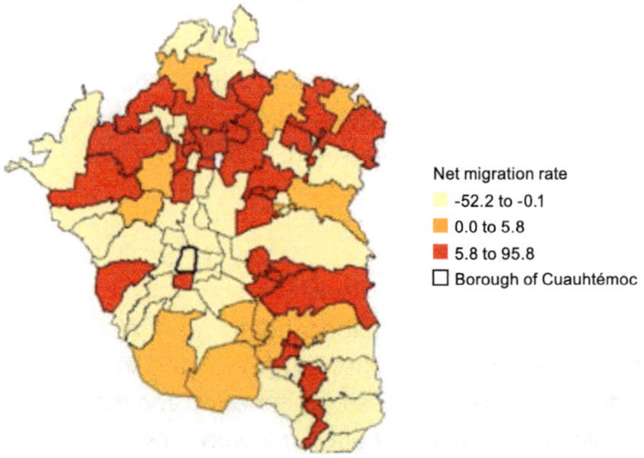

Map 1 (concluded)

B. São Paulo: net internal migration rate, by municipality, 2005-2010

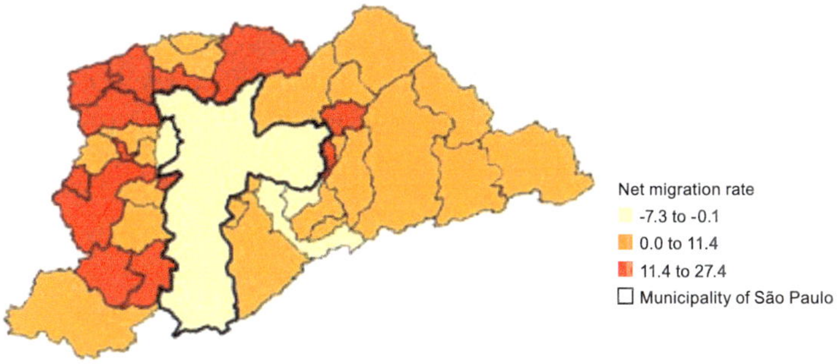

C. San José: net internal migration rate, by canton, 2006-2011

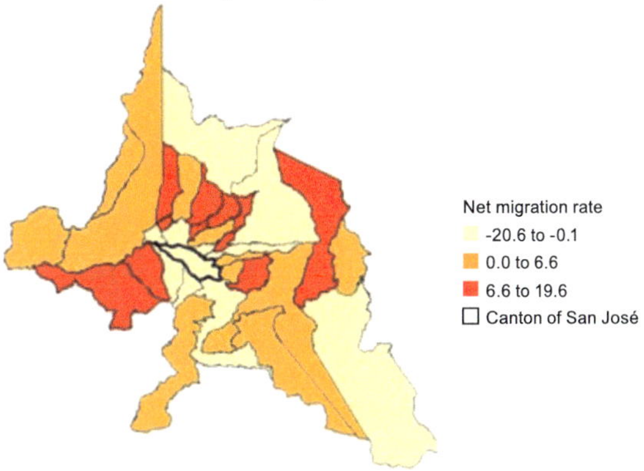

D. Santo Domingo: net internal migration rate, by municipality, 2005-2010

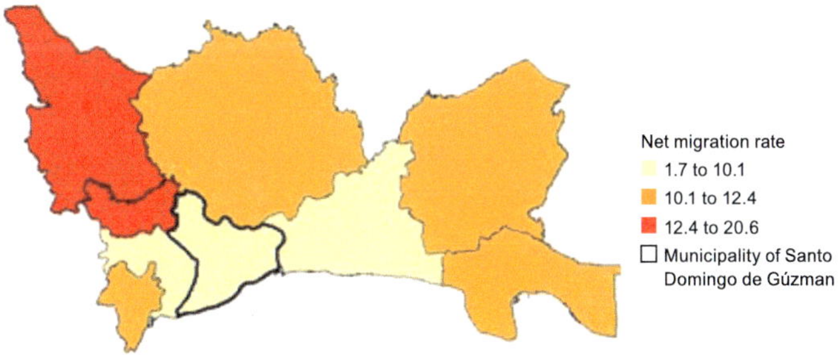

Source: Economic Commission for Latin America and the Caribbean (ECLAC), on the basis of special processing of census microdata.
[a] The three categories used in each map refer to terciles of the distribution of municipalities or boroughs, according to population growth rate. Borders outlined in bold denote the central MIAD, to give an indication of where the centre and periphery of each city is located. Note that in some cities the central MIAD corresponds to the "broad urban area," but in other it does not.

Socioeconomic residential segregation, measured as the average of the index of dissimilarity for the cities studied, diminished during the study period, though this outcome was almost entirely dependent on the decreases in Brazilian cities (see figures 20A, 20B and 20C). In fact, if the average of the sample is calculated for all countries excluding Brazil, not only is the overall downtrend much less pronounced, but is actually reversed in the cases of the least educated group and the group with the lowest socioeconomic status. Segregation is invariably greater among groups with higher socioecomic status, which reflects how strongly they are influenced by mechanisms that perpetuate residential exclusion and the desire for territorial distinctiveness and exclusivity (see figures 20A, 20B and 20C). The simple average of the index of dissimilarity at the minor administrative division (MIAD) level is greater than 0.2 for the most educated group and for the top socioeconomic decile. This means that a fifth of the population is thought to be residing in areas in which it is underrepresented in comparison with the spatial distribution of the rest of the population. By contrast, the simple average of the index of dissimilarity is in the region of 0.15 for the group with the lowest education and the decile with the lowest socioeconomic status.

Figure 20

Latin America (selected cities): index of dissimilarity by education group, highest and lowest socioeconomic deciles, and wealthiest and poorest deciles of the household income distribution, including and excluding Brazilian cities, 2000 and 2010 censuses

(Simple averages)

A. Latin America (22 selected cities):[a] index of dissimilarity (at the level of minor administrative divisions) of three education groups, including and excluding Brazilian cities, 2000 and 2010 censuses

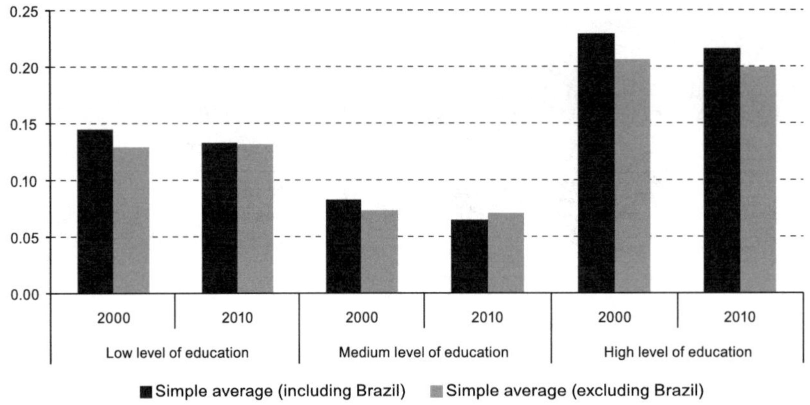

B. Latin America (17 selected cities):[b] simple average of the index of dissimilarity (at the level of minor administrative divisions) of the top and bottom socioeconomic deciles, including and excluding Brazilian cities, 2000 and 2010 censuses

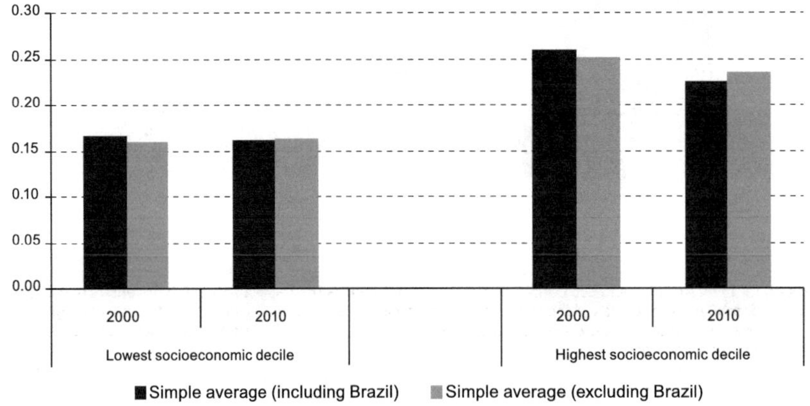

Figure 20 (concluded)

C. Latin America (8 selected cities):[c] simple average of the index of dissimilarity (at the level of minor administrative divisions) of the top and bottom deciles of the per capita household income distribution, 2000 and 2010 censuses

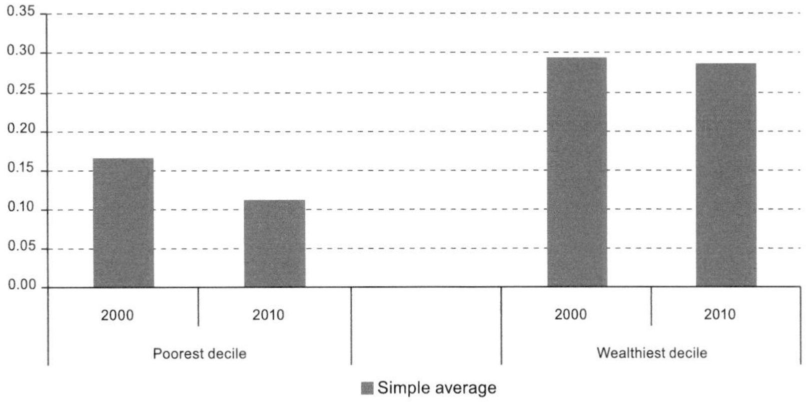

Source: Economic Commission for Latin America and the Caribbean (ECLAC), on the basis of special processing of census microdata.
[a] Buenos Aires (Argentina), Caracas, Maracaibo (Bolivarian Republic of Venezuela), Belo Horizonte, Brasilia, Curitiba, Recife, Rio de Janeiro, Salvador, São Paulo (Brazil), San José (Costa Rica), Santo Domingo (Dominican Republic), Cuenca, Guayaquil, Quito (Ecuador), Guadalajara, Mexico City, Monterrey, Toluca (Mexico), Panama City (Panama), Lima (Peru), Montevideo (Uruguay).
[b] Caracas, Maracaibo (Bolivarian Republic of Venezuela), Belo Horizonte, Brasilia, Curitiba, Recife, Rio de Janeiro, Salvador, São Paulo (Brazil), San José (Costa Rica), Santo Domingo (Dominican Republic), Guadalajara, Mexico City, Monterrey, Toluca (Mexico), Panama City (Panama), Montevideo (Uruguay).
[c] Belo Horizonte, Brasilia, Curitiba, Recife, Rio de Janeiro, Salvador, São Paulo (Brazil) and Panama City (Panama).

C. Impact of internal migration on socioeconomic residential segregation in large cities in the region

An analysis of how migration affects the social composition of "broad urban areas" (see table 4) revealed that migration is pushing down the proportion of children (aged 15 and under) in the central areas of the selected cities. In peripheral areas, the main effect of migration is to reduce the percentage of older adults (aged 60 and over). Migration tends to improve education indicators in the periphery, mostly by reducing the proportion of heads of household with low levels of education, in some cases combined with an increase in the proportion of heads of household with higher education. In most cities, the centre is trending towards an education-based dualization because of migration, which increases the proportion of heads of household in the lowest and highest educational categories (owing to the emigration of those with medium education levels and the immigration of those with high levels of education). Migration also reinforces the characteristics of gentrified peripheries by significantly boosting their education indicators owing to the arrival of highly educated (and the departure of the least educated) heads of household.

On applying the procedure devised by the Latin American and Caribbean Demographic Centre (CELADE)-Population Division of ECLAC to estimate the effect of migration on socioeconomic residential segregation, the selected cities exhibited no common pattern. However, where the analysis focused on the five-year period prior to the latest census, it was observed that internal migration did not play a decisive role in reducing segregation. In fact, migration exerted a positive influence on the index of dissimilarity in several Brazilian cities. Accordingly, the reduction in segregation in these cities is the result of the other proximate determinants of segregation, especially the increase in the education levels of the population as a whole and in the municipalities or neighbourhoods with lower education levels, which was the prevailing trend in the region and especially in Brazil during a decade of well-documented social and educational improvements (ECLAC, 2014).

Table 4

Latin America (18 selected cities): effect of total internal migration on the age and educational composition of populations living in central and peripheral urban areas, 2000 and 2010 censuses [a]

(Percentages)

Metropolitan area	Broad urban area	2000 census round				2010 census round			
		Children	Older adults	Heads of household with low education level	Heads of household with high education level	Children	Older adults	Heads of household with low education level	Heads of household with high education level
Belo Horizonte	Centre	-3.03	2.29	-1.78	4.91	-3.61	1.45	-1.12	1.70
	Periphery	0.28	-5.11	-0.19	-2.40	-0.24	-2.66	-0.37	-0.19
	Gentrified periphery	-0.26	-3.84	-2.88	29.81	-0.94	-2.38	-5.11	18.24
Brasilia	Centre	-2.99	-2.76	-3.13	8.44	-3.63	-1.56	-1.72	3.78
	Periphery	-2.43	-11.09	-0.13	-5.64	-1.48	-3.31	-0.78	2.35
Curitiba	Centre	-3.11	0.08	-1.78	3.63	-3.57	0.65	-1.18	2.41
	Periphery	-0.09	-6.25	-1.69	11.00	-1.48	-2.61	-1.56	8.41
Recife	Centre	-0.69	2.62	0.60	1.37	-0.69	2.03	0.24	1.30
	Periphery	-0.26	-0.35	-1.23	5.74	-0.36	-0.25	-0.28	-1.53
Rio de Janeiro	Centre	-1.01	-0.52	0.43	0.26	-1.17	-0.65	0.30	-0.20
	Periphery	-0.17	-0.91	-0.11	-0.37	-0.13	-0.17	0.26	-1.20
	Gentrified periphery	-2.25	-3.35	-7.11	21.44	1.86	-3.71	-6.05	12.65
Salvador	Centre	-1.32	0.48	-0.01	0.46	-0.85	0.59	0.29	-1.12
	Periphery	-1.08	1.34	-0.78	11.64	-0.19	-0.91	-0.87	0.75
	Gentrified periphery	-4.54	-4.01	-7.71	33.94	-4.00	-1.53	-5.77	16.73
São Paulo	Centre	-2.13	-0.17	-0.21	1.62	-2.38	-0.27	-0.00	0.87
	Periphery	-0.82	-2.99	-1.37	2.15	-1.11	-1.80	-0.35	1.25
	Periphery elitizada	-0.58	-3.36	-0.24	5.85	-0.68	-1.11	-0.51	3.75
San José	Centre	-1.9	1.2	0.83	-0.60	-1.99	1.12	-0.31	0.02
	Near periphery	-0.8	-0.8	-0.62	1.25	-1.34	-0.31	-0.87	2.00
	Far periphery	-0.3	-2.3	-1.84	8.16	-0.09	-0.82	-2.04	5.09
Santo Domingo	Centre	-2.2	0.6	0.14	0.17	-1.66	-0.06	0.05	0.31
	Near periphery	-1.7	0.1	0.17	0.15	-1.19	1.99	-0.25	0.32
	Far periphery	-1.2	-0.2	-0.01	0.22	-1.45	-0.52	-0.43	1.63
Cuenca	Centre	-2.4	-3.2	1.6	-2.20	-2.20	-1.39	1.09	-1.57
	Periphery	-0.9	-2.7	-0.7	4.75	-0.07	-1.27	-0.27	2.23
Guayaquil	Centre	-1.0	1.0	2.47	-2.35	0.04	-1.87	1.19	-3.33
	Periphery	-2.9	-2.8	-0.62	11.52	-0.03	0.32	-0.99	-6.23
Quito	Centre	-2.7	-1.6	2.03	-2.61	-1.88	-0.71	0.74	-0.66
	Periphery	-2.3	-5.7	-4.71	7.93	-0.95	-2.62	-0.41	0.07
Guadalajara	Centre	-2.1	5.6	2.86	-2.83	-5.10	9.52	7.67	-5.11
	Periphery	-0.7	-4.3	-4.82	9.09	-0.71	-4.58	-8.20	15.73
Mexico City	Centre	-4.5	3.1	-0.2	3.1	-3.53	0.23	-1.54	3.75
	Periphery	-0.3	-0.6	-0.7	-0.4	-0.20	-0.57	-0.75	-1.04
Monterrey	Centre	-2.0	3.1	2.37	1.28	-4.99	10.03	8.31	3.80
	Periphery	-1.4	-11.6	-4.57	16.03	0.90	-20.07	-11.78	16.26
Toluca	Centre	0.3	1.5	-1.07	3.19	-0.61	0.52	-2.45	7.62
	Periphery	-0.0	0.9	-0.48	4.69	-0.29	-5.48	-4.15	9.80
Montevideo	Centre	-2.3	-0.5	0.43	-0.24	-2.65	-0.53	0.20	0.16
	Periphery elitizada	0.4	-8.9	-4.56	2.89	-1.54	-3.12	-5.77	7.23
	Poor periphery	0.7	-3.1	-0.42	-0.02	0.98	-0.91	0.22	-4.97
Caracas	Centre	-1.2	3.0	1.91	-3.90	-1.19	2.99	1.91	-3.90
	First ring	-1.1	-1.6	-1.90	2.41	-1.15	-0.57	-1.90	2.41
	Inner periphery	-0.9	-1.4	-1.27	1.65	-0.94	-0.77	-1.27	1.65
	Outer periphery	-0.1	-4.2	-1.11	1.66	-0.05	-0.55	-1.11	1.66

Source: Economic Commission for Latin America and the Caribbean (ECLAC), on the basis of special processing of census microdata.

[a] The "periphery" category in the above table refers to one of the types of periphery that make up the "broad urban areas"; unless otherwise indicated it refers to the "traditional periphery".

D. Effects of segregation on households and communities

Another area of analysis is the "neighbourhood effect" on the behaviours of children and adolescents, especially, in the case of women, with regard to the likelihood of adolescent motherhood. The neighbourhood effect is illustrated by the case of Brazil's favelas, in that the probability of a Brazilian woman becoming a mother by the age of 19 is, according to the 2000 census, invariably higher for favela residents, even after controlling for household income (see figure 21). In the 2010 census, these results were corroborated for well-known favelas (Rocinha, Complexo do Alemão and Maré) and affluent areas (Tijuca); the likelihood of teenage motherhood in the three favelas was higher than the city average and much higher than in wealthy neighbourhoods.

Figure 21
Brazil: women aged 19 who are mothers and who have always resided in the same municipality, by per capita household income and favela residence or non-residence, 2000
(Percentages and multiples of the minimum wage)

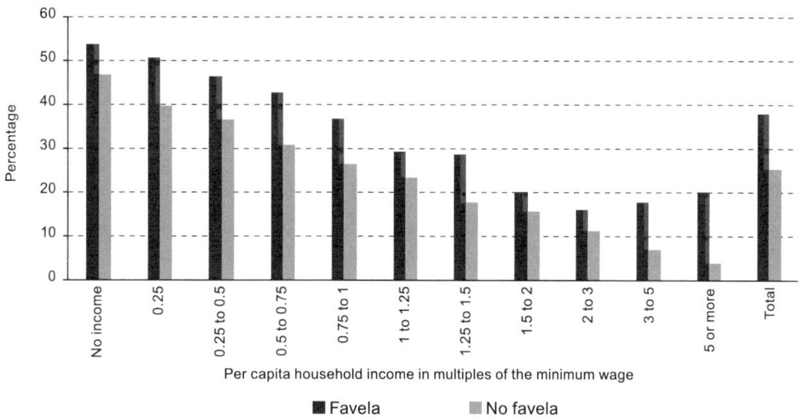

Source: Economic Commission for Latin America and the Caribbean (ECLAC), on the basis of special processing of 2000 census microdata.

E. Special cases: ethnic segregation and international migration

Two phenomena have been observed in Latin America's large cities: (i) the presence of indigenous peoples has increased in recent decades, and (ii) cities have become magnets for international migrants. In both cases, the reasons for settling in specific neighbourhoods may be functional to the process of integrating into a new society or habitat. However, if concentrations of migrants occur in deprived areas, which are also subject to stigmatization, discrimination and neglect, it may be deemed that residential segregation is present.

Both indigenous and international migrants record high indices of dissimilarity. This is especially true of indigenous groups, some of whom tend to settle on city edges, while others establish themselves near commercial districts where they can sell agricultural and handcrafted products. In the selected cities, the data indicated that indigenous and Afro-descendant residents were often more concentrated in places with housing and education deficits, and that Afro-descendant populations tended to be even more segregated in these precarious parts of the city.

International immigrants typically cluster in central areas, which allow them to take advantage of support networks and other benefits such as better access to jobs, services and public transport. However, the living conditions that immigrants face in these central areas are usually rather insecure, which somewhat diminishes the benefits of this location.

F. Public policies: experiences and general guidelines for the region

In Latin America, few policies and programmes are intended to directly reduce socioeconomic residential segregation. In addition, some of the policy instruments deployed by developed countries to curb or reduce segregation are either unavailable or are, in practical terms, ineffective in the region. The very notion of social housing —in the sense of publicly owned real estate set aside to meet the housing requirements of vulnerable or special-needs households— is non-existent in the region. In Latin America, social housing is that which is provided to the poor, either free or at subsidized prices. The focus is therefore on reducing housing costs, which incentivizes the construction of massive social housing projects at the urban edge, creating new neighbourhoods whose inhabitants remain poor and who suffer from a lack of public facilities and accessibility. Moreover, once the housing has been handed over, the State is no longer able to use it as part of schemes to reduce socioeconomic residential segregation.

The absence of instruments to ensure that low-income housing is built in middle- or upper-class neighbourhoods makes it impossible to break the pattern of market selection determined by land prices. Moreover, serious public budget constraints and a lack of mechanisms for the territorial redistribution of local revenues, as well as coordination issues between municipal governments in the absence of a city-wide authority and institutional structure, make it difficult for local governments to balance inequalities between rich and poor neighbourhoods.

Public policies to promote and facilitate non-segregated residential patterns should include, first, means of resolving the accumulated deficits in poor and segregated neighbourhoods. They should also include mechanisms for social integration and exchange, as well as measures to minimize or offset market-driven impacts on housing prices as a result of social and residential diversity. Initiatives in favour of social empowerment, price regulation and barriers to the purchase and sale of real estate may be essential to counteract the various forces that displace poor populations from wealthy neighbourhoods. Conversely, high quality public services, citizen security and safety, and easy accessibility are crucial to ensuring that the flow of people from intermediate and upper socioeconomic backgrounds to traditionally poor neighbourhoods is not reversed.

Lastly, a number of methodological challenges must be addressed if more in-depth studies are to be conducted on socioeconomic residential segregation in the region. In Latin America, the availability of census microdata, digital mapping and new demographic and statistical techniques are opening up promising avenues for future research. But there is also a need to tackle segregation, given the consensus regarding its negative repercussions for equality in cities and countries.

Chapter VI
Recent trends in social spending and social investment in young people

In spite of ups and downs in the economic cycle over the past five years, including the global financial crisis of 2008-2009, the slight rally in the economy in the following years and the global slowdown since 2012, the trend in the region until 2013 was towards a real increase in the resources available for financing social services and cash transfers to households.

A. Social spending in Latin America

This rise in disposable public resources was also reflected in the priority accorded to social spending at the macroeconomic level: in the early 1990s, social spending as a share of gross domestic product (GDP) stood at 13.8%, rising steadily, albeit slowly, in the bienniums under review to reach 16.7% in 2006-2007. It then soared to 19.1% of the region's GDP in 2012-2013 (see figure 22). In the last year under consideration, social spending in the region (21 countries) amounted to nearly US$ 685 billion (at constant 2005 prices). In 2012 the overall growth trend in social spending in both absolute and relative terms began to weaken somewhat. This trend reversal has led to ever-slower growth in public social spending owing to the persistent fiscal deficits incurred by a number of governments to tackle the global financial crisis and to the expected falls in revenue owing to the slowdown in growth in most countries, with a few exceptions that include several countries in Central America and the Caribbean.

Until the mid-2000s, social public spending had been markedly procyclical, but, even by 2005, several countries had embarked on systematic efforts to strengthen their social programmes, in particular those designed to combat poverty, which reversed this procyclicality. The change in the pattern of social spending in the region is due to gradual measures to cope with external shocks: the escalation in food and fuel prices in 2008, the sustained rise in commodity exports which began in 2003; the worst of the world financial crisis towards the end of 2008 and in 2009; and, more recently, the climate of uncertainty across the world as the global economy slows.

Figure 22
Latin America and the Caribbean (21 countries):[a] public social spending and total public spending as shares of GDP, and social public spending as a share of total spending, 1990-1991 to 2012-2013[b]
(Percentages of GDP and of total public spending)

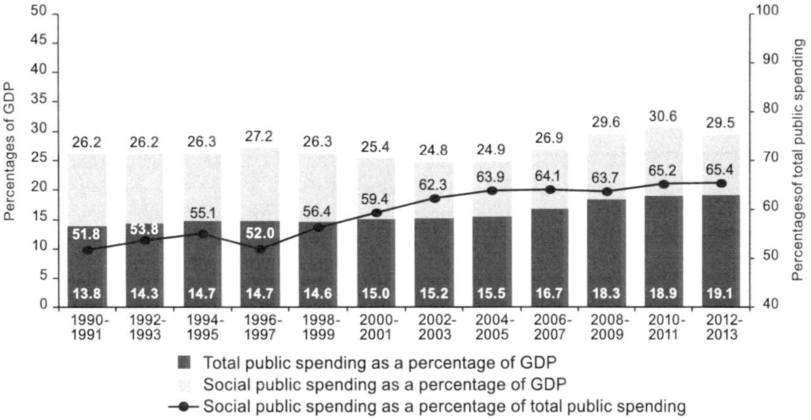

Source: Economic Commission for Latin America and the Caribbean (ECLAC), on the basis of social spending data.
[a] Argentina, Bolivarian Republic of Venezuela, , Brazil, Chile, Colombia, Costa Rica, Cuba, Dominican Republic, Ecuador, El Salvador, Guatemala, Honduras, Jamaica, Mexico, Nicaragua, Panama, Paraguay, Peru, Plurinational State of Bolivia, Trinidad and Tobago, and Uruguay.
[b] Weighted average for the countries. The figures on total public spending correspond to official data, mostly from the functional classification of public spending, and may not correspond to those based on an economic classification of spending .The regional figures are affected by the Brazilian official report's inclusion within total public spending of domestic and external debt refinancing, which was equivalent to 14.8% of total public spending on average over the last 4 years. For this reason, the data used for Brazil correspond to primary public spending.

Since 2010, several countries have embarked on fiscal reforms on both the revenue and the spending side in order to consolidate their public finances. This is because after some five years (from 2003 to 2008) of primary surpluses and falling public debt, the spike in public expenditure to finance measures to address the short- and medium-term effects of the global financial crisis led to a public accounts deficit as GDP stagnated or began to fall. Although the figures for 2010 show a continued countercyclical expansion in spending, this was accompanied by faster growth in social public spending and, in some cases, a decline in public spending in the economic and administrative spheres. At the regional level in 2010, social public spending grew by 7.9% compared with the financial crisis years of 2008-2009, and non-social spending by 7.2%. In 2011 expenditure in both categories was up, but public non-social spending rose at a faster rate.

Partial data for 2012 and 2013 point to a slowdown in social spending growth (3.5%) and a contraction in spending in non-social sectors, because, particularly in 2012, non-public social spending appears to have fallen (-5.2%).

1. Social spending by country

The region's countries differ greatly both in the amount of resources they can effectively channel towards the social sectors and in the macroeconomic effort represented by their public social budgets. Of course, the capacity to assign greater macroeconomic priority to social spending depends on a host of economic, political and social variables. One of the determining factors is fiscal revenue, which sets a certain limit for the overall budget. Notwithstanding the rise in social expenditure as a percentage of GDP in the region (from 13.8% in 1990-1991 to 19.1% in 2012-2013), the initial and current levels of this indicator vary considerably between the countries. In 1990-1991 (or the most recent period for which data are available), countries such as Ecuador, Honduras, Mexico, Nicaragua and Trinidad and Tobago allocated less than 7% of GDP to social sectors, whereas Argentina, the Bolivarian Republic of Venezuela, Costa Rica, Cuba and Uruguay earmarked 15% or more.

Except in specific periods, almost all the countries have made efforts to increase both the proportion of social public spending within total public spending (the fiscal priority of social spending) and its macroeconomic priority, and many of them have boosted social spending in relation to GDP. By the end of the period under consideration, the macroeconomic priority of social spending has risen significantly in almost all the countries. In 2012-2013 (or the nearest period with data available), no country in the region was devoting less than 7% of GDP to social sectors and only the Dominican Republic, Ecuador, Guatemala, Jamaica and Peru were spending less than 10% of GDP on these sectors. In addition, by that point, Paraguay had joined the group of countries that were spending over 15% of GDP on social sectors at the beginning of the 1990s (see figure 24).

Figure 23

Latin America and the Caribbean (21 countries): public social spending, 1990-1991 to 2012-2013

(Percentages of GDP)

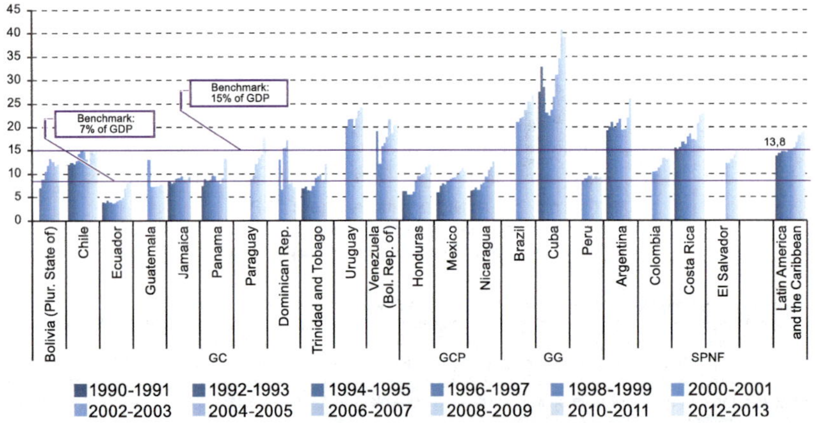

Source: Economic Commission for Latin America and the Caribbean (ECLAC), social expenditure database.
Note: CG: Central government; BCG: Budgetary central government; GG: General government; NFPS: Non-financial public sector (for Costa Rica: total public sector).

Figure 24

Latin America and the Caribbean (21 countries): per capita social public spending, 1990-1991 to 2012-2013

(Dollars at constant 2005 prices)

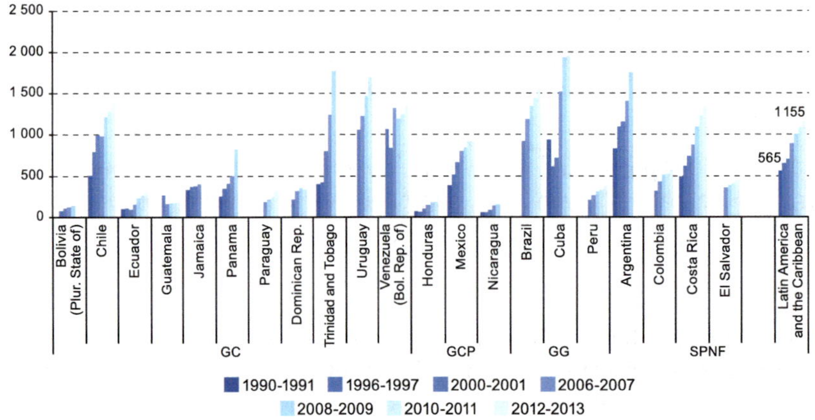

Source: Economic Commission for Latin America and the Caribbean (ECLAC), social expenditure database.
Note: CG: Central government; BCG: Budgetary central government; GG: General government; NFPS: Non-financial public sector (for Costa Rica: total public sector).

Despite persistent differences in the level of macroeconomic priority of social spending, some countries have made a proportionally larger effort to increase the percentage allocated to such spending. As a share of GDP, the macroeconomic priority of public social spending rose by 9.2% in Argentina between 1990 and 2009, by 8.7 percentage points in the Bolivarian Republic of Venezuela between 1997 and 2012, by 10 percentage points in Cuba between 1990 and 2011, by 10.4 percentage points in Panama until 2012, and by 8.9 percentage points in Paraguay between 2003 and 2012. In contrast, a comparison between the most recent data available (in most cases 2012-2013) and the initial series (1990-1991 or the most recent period for which data are available) shows no significant increase in the share of resources allocated to such spending by Chile, El Salvador, Guatemala, Jamaica or Peru.

2. Social spending by sector

Growth in social spending has not been uniform across all sectors. This is partly because the importance attached to investment in different sectors varies, but also because growth in any given sector also depends on how developed the institutional framework and social services coverage were at the start of the period under review (1990-1991), as well as on the pressures that various social groups can bring to bear on the State to obtain a more rapid increase in certain types of expenditure, on contractions in the economy requiring mobilization of welfare resources, and on the level of population ageing.

Figure 25

Latin America and the Caribbean (21 countries): [a] **social public spending by sector, 1990-1991 to 2012-2013** [b]

(Percentages of GDP)

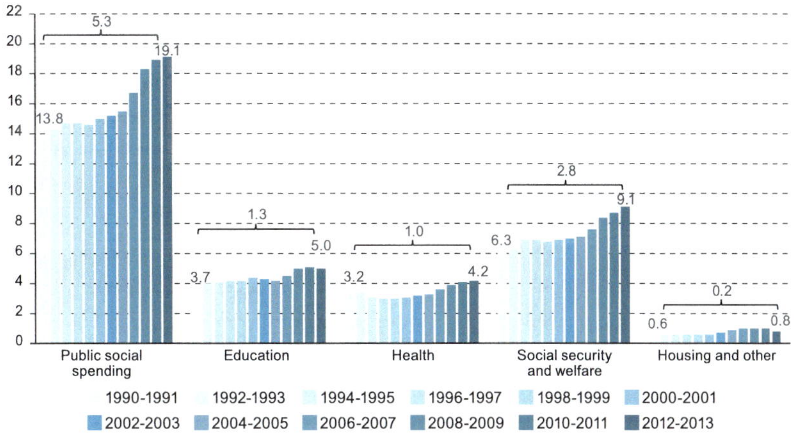

Source: Economic Commission for Latin America and the Caribbean (ECLAC), social expenditure database.

[a] Argentina, Bolivarian Republic of Venezuela, Brazil, Chile, Colombia, Costa Rica, Cuba, Dominican Republic, Ecuador, El Salvador, Guatemala, Jamaica, Mexico, Nicaragua, Panama, Paraguay, Peru, Plurinational State of Bolivia, Trinidad and Tobago, and Uruguay.

[b] Weighted average of the countries.

Generally speaking, the increase in social expenditure equal to 5.3 percentage points of GDP is largely attributable to greater spending on social security and welfare (2.8 GDP points over the period). The progressive ageing of the population in many countries in the region has meant that resources used to pay social security benefits have gradually increased. Although a significant proportion of these resources comes from revenues based on contributory social security schemes (in this case, public or mixed), more countries have gradually introduced solidarity mechanisms for financing social-security payments in addition to the normal solidarity-based redistribution mechanisms that already existed within these systems.

Although there is no disaggregated information that distinguishes between social security and non-contributory social protection systems, the data indicate that a number of welfare programmes were expanded (mostly during the 2000s) —especially anti-poverty programmes consisting of mechanisms for direct conditional or non-conditional transfers to households. In Argentina, from 2000 to 2007, spending on social assistance rose by almost 85% (even considering the fall of almost 20% in 2002); in Brazil (federal government), it tripled over the same period. In Chile, it went up by just 5.5% (with sharp falls in 2003, 2004 and 2006); in Colombia it almost doubled between 2004 and 2007, and in Costa Rica it has increased by more than 75% since 2002. Notwithstanding this expansion, it should be borne in mind that in 2007 public spending on social assistance in these and other countries for which this type of information is available represented as little as between 10% and 35% of the aggregate total for social security and assistance.

In the wake of the global financial crisis, various emergency programmes and other measures were implemented to avoid a contraction in the real economy. This accounts for much of the rise in social spending (equal to 0.8 percentage points of GDP) over the past five years. Most of this increase (three quarters of the total) was in social security and welfare. Since social security commitments usually show less elasticity to the business cycle, the increase was likely associated with strengthening or implementing social welfare programmes (including stepping up efforts to combat poverty through conditional and non-conditional transfers) targeting those persons and households most vulnerable to economic contraction, and with boosting the solidarity-based pillars of social security systems (or, more generally, of social protection systems).

The other sector in which there has been a noteworthy increase in spending (of 1.3 percentage points of GDP) over the past 22 years was education. This increase is related to the expansion in coverage of and access to primary education in the poorest countries, and secondary education in the others (in terms of infrastructure, and, above all, of current expenditure, associated mainly with the increase in teacher staffing) as well as, to a lesser extent, an expanded supply of public post-secondary education.

This has come at the expense of health sector expansion, which saw its level of macroeconomic priority expand only very slightly (by 1 percentage point of GDP). Declining budgets for this sector usually mean that investments or reinvestments in infrastructure, renewal of equipment and replacement of medical supplies are sacrificed, which causes problems in the public health sector that have a negative impact on coverage and, above all, on the quality of services. It takes a long time to return to normal after such situations.

Lastly, the sector receiving the least attention —0.2% of GDP over the period— is housing (which includes drinking water, sanitation, community infrastructure and, lately, the environment) despite the fact that practically all countries and major cities still have large pockets of substandard housing and segregation. There has even been a contraction over in the past biennium, owing in part to an expansion in the preceding period when housing was used as a tool to boost job creation and revitalize the region's domestic economies, particularly the construction industry.

Scanty investment in this area has also hampered or slowed environmental conservation initiatives involving the establishment of biodiversity conservation areas and implementation of measures needed for regulating human activity, in particular productive ventures, so as to prevent environmental degradation and pollution.

B. Social investment in youth

One of the most widely used definitions of social expenditure is that of the Organization for Economic Cooperation and Development (OECD), which considers it to be the provision by public and private institutions of benefits to, and financial contributions targeted at, households and individuals in order to provide support during circumstances which adversely affect their welfare. Public-sector social investment —unlike compensatory policies, which address the effects of an incident or a hazard that has already occurred— aims to help prevent or prepare for adverse events, and to support and equip people for coping with them, rather than compensate those affected by, for example, market deregulation.

From this perspective, public spending is not a cost for the economy but rather a series of investments that are necessary to ensure strong, lasting and shared growth, meet new social needs and safeguard economic, social and cultural rights (DESC). Social investment strategies set priorities with a view to supporting people throughout their life cycle, focusing on groups that are subject to social exclusion (including women, young people and children) in fundamental areas of human development (such as education, health, employment and housing).

Social investment can encompass spending in both the public and the private sectors. However, public spending, particularly public social expenditure, makes up the bulk of it. Therefore, although these two categories are not strictly speaking the same, for the purposes of estimating the magnitude of social investment in youth, this analysis considers public social expenditure on this population group.

In their annual public budgets, governments set out their priorities and objectives as expressed by their estimated income and expenditure. Young people can thus be the target population of certain public policies, and can benefit either directly from resources allocated exclusively to them or indirectly from policies targeting not them but their environment. Four types of social spending can be identified, which differ in the way in which young people benefit from it:

i) Direct
This kind of social investment works through policies and programmes whose target population are young people, as direct beneficiaries. The basic eligibility criterion for these initiatives is simply to be young.

ii) Expanded
This kind of social investment is made through programmes that are not specifically aimed at young people but at a wider population of which they form part. Young people are therefore beneficiaries alongside other age groups.

iii) Indirect
Another part of public spending that can be considered to be social investment benefits young people indirectly and only to the extent that they are part of households receiving resources allocated by the programmes. This category chiefly consists of initiatives targeting households, such as programmes to combat poverty, and for housing and other subsidies.

iv) General
Spending not specifically aimed at young people or their households but affecting the areas in which they live or spend time (such as investment in communities or neighbourhood unions) should also be considered investment in young people.

Owing to the absence of comprehensive, sector-disaggregated studies on social investment in youth, there are variations in the methodology and sources employed to obtain the information used in this chapter to estimate the magnitude of social spending in the different areas considered, namely education, health, welfare and housing.

The data used on spending on education came from the functional distributions of public expenditure provided by countries which is compiled in the ECLAC social expenditure database. [16] To estimate total spending on education targeting young people, data was used on gross enrolment rates at selected levels of education (upper secondary and postsecondary) and the share of pupils enrolled in public or private establishments. The information used comes from the database of the United Nations Educational, Scientific and Cultural Organization (UNESCO-UIS).

Social investment in young people's health was estimated using information from the database of the World Health Organization (WHO)/Pan American Health Organization (PAHO).[17] Unlike investment in education, the data available on health are insufficient for estimating the breakdown of spending between age groups each year. For that reason, the calculations also draw on studies carried out for OECD countries and on the national transfer accounts (NTA) initiative, which contains estimates of the distribution of public spending on health by age group and sex. The resulting profile of health spending by age group and sex was used to estimate public resources devoted to youth in each country.

Social assistance spending on young people, by its very nature, varies greatly between countries and over time, and is chiefly made up of programmes (often to combat poverty) benefiting young people directly or indirectly. The amount of investment in social assistance for young people was therefore estimated by analysing conditional cash transfer programmes, the most common form of such assistance in the countries of Latin America, on which ECLAC has collected and systematized the information necessary to analyse, on a comparable basis, the resources the region's countries allocate to social assistance.

The other component of social investment is public expenditure on housing, which, in addition to housing construction programmes, includes investment in basic water and sanitation services and other spending on improving community infrastructure (such as electricity, sports centres and social centres). The Inter-American Development Bank (IDB) has conducted studies on certain countries showing how public spending on social housing programmes breaks down according to beneficiary-household income. In order to estimate the amount of social investment in housing and infrastructure allocated to young people it was assumed that this spending benefits young people in households in the three lowest-income population quintiles (per the information obtained in the IDB studies).

1. Overview of social investment in young people in Latin America

Given that the way in which social investment in Latin America is measured differs from country to country, and that the figures presented below understate the actual amount of such investment made at all levels of the State, total social investment around 2012 can, for purposes of illustration, can be put at 19.1% of GDP, or around US$ 660 billion.

[16] See [online] http://dds.cepal.org/gasto/indicadores/.

[17] World Health Organization (WHO)/Pan American Health Organization (PAHO), Global Health Observatory Data Repository [online] http://apps.who.int/gho/data/?theme=main.

According to estimates, out of total public expenditure on social investment, the region allocates around US$ 102 billion to social programmes which directly or indirectly benefit young people (US$ 183 billion at 2005 prices at PPP). Share of social public spending allocated to young people is 13.8%, which is equivalent to 2.65% of GDP for the Latin American countries under review (see table 5).

Table 5

Latin America (19 countries): social investment in young people, around 2012

(Percentages)

Country	Investment in young people as a percentage of social spending	Investment in young people as a percentage of GDP	Percentage of young people in the total population
Argentina	11.9	3.3	24.3
Bolivia (Plurinational State of)	24.2	2.8	28.2
Brazil	10.6	2.8	25.7
Chile	15.5	2.3	24.9
Colombia	12.5	1.6	26.3
Costa Rica	14.4	3.3	27.4
Cuba	26.0	9.7	20.4
Dominican Republic	17.8	1.4	26.8
Ecuador	31.4	2.6	26.7
El Salvador	12.1	1.6	30.2
Guatemala	19.1	1.8	28.4
Honduras	...	0.5	29.9
Mexico	18.0	2.1	26.4
Nicaragua	...	1.4	30.2
Panama	21.5	3.7	25.1
Paraguay	25.8	2.8	28.9
Peru	17.9	1.9	27.3
Uruguay	13.0	3.3	22.1
Venezuela (Bolivarian Republic of)	19.2	4.0	26.7
Latin America	**13.8**	**2.65**	**26.3**

Source: Economic Commission for Latin America and the Caribbean (ECLAC), social expenditure database and calculations on the basis of conditional cash transfer programmes and data provided by the UNESCO Institute of Statistics, World Health Organization and Inter-American Development Bank (IDB).

The data available for the different sectors show social investment in youth in Latin America breaking down as set forth below.

(a) Education

Social investment in youth is focused on education. Almost 60% of the resources allocated directly or indirectly to young people are used to fund education systems. At least since the 2000s, spending on education has been rising steadily. This trend was enhanced by a steady increase in enrolment rates, especially at the secondary level. So, while total spending on education (as a simple average) was 3.7% of GDP at the start of the decade, by 2012 it had reached 5.2% of GDP. Public spending on youth education, while of course lower than overall expenditure on education, has followed the same sustained increase. In 2012, public investment in youth education stood at nearly 2.1% of GDP (as a simple average), which is 0.7 percentage points more than in 2000.

(b) Health

Young people are, comparatively, the healthiest age group or population segment. For young people, the major health events requiring specialized care are, for young women, pregnancy and motherhood, especially at early ages (adolescence). Young men face issues associated with alcohol and drug abuse, accidents, violence and the prevention and treatment of HIV.

Thus, when compared with spending on the rest of the population, the amount of resources allocated by States to youth health would appear rather low, but demand is markedly lower too. While total public spending on health around 2000 averaged 3.1% of GDP, spending on youth health was only 0.65% of GDP. But while spending on health services for young people rose between 2000 and 2012, it grew more slowly than total spending on health. This meant that its relative share of overall health spending fell to 17.3% of total public expenditure on health in 2012 (see table 6).

Table 6

Latin America (17 countries): public spending on young people as a percentage of GDP and of sectoral public spending, around 2000 and 2012

(Percentages)

Country	Education spending on youth: As a percentage of GDP		Education spending on youth: As a percentage of public spending on education		Health spending on youth: As a percentage of GDP		Health spending on youth: As a percentage of public spending on health		Spending on conditional cash transfer schemes as a percentage of GDP	Youth beneficiaries of schemes as a percentage of total youth	Spending on housing and basic services for youth as a percentage of GDP
	2000	2012	2000	2012	2000	2012	2000	2012	Around 2012	Around 2012	2012
Argentina	1.63	2.36	32.6	35.3	0.74	0.80	14.9	13.6	0.06	11.8	0.55
Bolivia (Plurinational State of)	1.96	2.43	37.8	46.2	0.73	0.83	20.1	20.1	0.05	11.7	0.07
Brazil	1.74	1.81	35.5	31.3	0.56	0.71	19.4	16.4	0.09	21.7	0.56
Chile	1.38	1.81	35.4	42.9	0.53	0.51	15.7	14.5	0.02	6.3	0.13
Colombia	0.93	0.95	28.6	31.4	0.92	0.91	19.6	17.5	0.08	22.4	0.19
Costa Rica	1.29	1.95	26.5	26.3	1.02	1.33	18.4	17.6	0.06	2.3	0.64
Cuba	3.27	7.92	37.8	49.7	0.74	0.84	13.4	10.4	...	...	0.89
Ecuador	0.68	2.10	39.1	44.3	0.22	0.51	19.5	17.6	0.23	38.9	0.09
El Salvador	1.59	1.90	14.8	24.1	0.70	0.82	18.6	19.5	0.01	7.8	0.26
Guatemala	0.46	0.51	16.9	16.0	0.45	0.49	20.2	20.3	0.07	19.6	0.93
Honduras	...	...	...	...	0.75	0.93	20.9	21.4	0.05	7.7	0.05
Mexico	1.14	1.22	33.2	32.4	0.48	0.56	20.5	17.5	0.10	19.9	0.42
Nicaragua	...	...	...	...	0.64	0.96	22.2	21.5	...	...	0.98
Panama	1.84	2.18	37.8	51.4	1.00	0.83	19.0	16.0	0.04	9.7	1.02
Paraguay	0.93	0.97	28.6	52.1	0.64	0.86	19.7	19.9	0.07	7.0	0.06
Peru	2.06	2.37	32.2	34.1	0.56	0.54	20.4	18.2	0.03	7.7	0.65
Dominican Republic	0.58	0.52	24.6	21.0	0.43	0.49	19.5	17.7	0.10	18.6	0.54
Uruguay	1.03	1.86	39.4	41.9	0.76	0.65	12.4	10.9	0.08	11.7	0.96
Venezuela (Bolivarian Republic of)	2.71	3.50	27.8	32.4	0.47	0.28	19.7	17.9	...	...	0.37
Latin America *(simple average)*	**1.48**	**2.14**	**31.1**	**36.1**	**0.65**	**0.73**	**18.6**	**17.3**	**0.07**	**14.0**	**0.49**

Source: Economic Commission for Latin America and the Caribbean (ECLAC), on the basis of social spending and conditional cash transfer databases; official figures from the UNESCO Institute of Statistics, Pan American Health Organization (PAHO)/World Health Organization (WHO) and Inter-American Development Bank (IDB).

(c) Social assistance and poverty reduction schemes

Social assistance programmes have taken many different forms in Latin America, but for the most part they have all sought ways to increase or at least safeguard the human capital of households. In the past decade a new generation of such initiatives, known as conditional cash transfer (CCT) programmes have become the most widely used mechanism for combating the intergenerational transmission of poverty in the countries of the region.

The target population of such programmes varies from country to country, but generally the beneficiaries are families, especially those with children under 18 years old, living in poverty or extreme poverty. Young people indirectly benefit from these programmes as members of beneficiary households and in some cases may also receive benefits directly —sometimes up until the age of 29— as in the case with *Oportunidades* (opportunities) in Mexico, *Bolsa familia* (family grant) in Brazil and *Jóvenes en Acción* (young people in action) in Colombia.

Despite this, the regional picture with regard to CCT schemes remains mixed. The average budget allocated to conditional transfer programmes in the countries of Latin America amounts to around 0.3% of GDP. On average, about 13% of the population belongs to beneficiary households, although the percentage varies depending on the scope of programmes and the proportion of poor or vulnerable people meeting the relevant eligibility criteria. Certain programmes are notable for their extremely broad coverage, but this makes it more likely that there will be errors of inclusion (households that are not in the target population).

Taking the universe of analysis as the total number of young people aged 15 to 29, conditional transfer programmes cover 14% of all young people and the amount spent directly or indirectly on this population group comes to little more than an estimated US$ 170 million regionwide, mainly through access to different types of services (as a simple average, around 0.07% of the GDP of the countries reviewed).

(d) Housing

Public social spending on housing and basic services such as clean water, sanitation, slum improvement and community facilities is the item of social expenditure that receives the smallest proportion of resources. In 2012, total expenditure on housing and basic services stood at 1.8% of GDP as a simple average for 19 countries in the region. Spending devoted directly or indirectly to young people through access to programmes targeting housing, water, sanitation and other services comes to around 0.5% of GDP (see table 6).

It may be concluded that, given the currently small margins for expanding spending on youth, efforts need to be redoubled to improve planning of expenditure and to develop and strengthen assessment mechanisms with a view to making more efficient and effective use of resources. Part of this increased effectiveness and efficiency can be achieved by bringing spending more in line with the needs of various population groups, such as young men and women. By allocating resources to the general programmes and specific initiatives most likely to benefit the well-being of the population and to provide the necessary opportunities and capacities, a new development model can be built to reduce inequalities and help break the chains that transmit poverty from generation to generation.

Bibliography

Alkire, Sabina and James Foster (2011), "Counting and multidimensional poverty measurement", *Journal of Public Economics*, vol. 95, No. 7–8.

___(2007), "Counting and multidimensional poverty measurement", *OPHI Working Paper,* No. 7 [online] http://www.ophi.org.uk/wp-content/uploads/ophi-wp7.pdf.

Antonopoulos, R. (2009), "The current economic and financial crisis: a gender perspective", *The Levy Economics Institute of Bard College*, No. 562, May.

Arroyo, L. and others (2010), "Los efectos de la crisis sobre las mujeres: Empleo, segregación ocupacional y modelo productivo", *Informes de la Fundación*, Madrid, March.

Duclos, Jean Yves, Joan Esteban and Debraj Ray (2004), "Polarization: Concepts, measurement, estimation", *Econometrica,* No. 72.

ECLAC (Economic Commission for Latin America and the Caribbean) (2014), *Compacts for Equality: Towards a sustainable future* (LC/G.2586(SES.35/3)), Santiago, Chile.

___(2013), *Social Panorama of Latin America, 2013* (LC/G.2580), Santiago, Chile.

___(2012), *Structural Change for Equality: an integrated approach to development* (LC/G.2524(SES.34/3)), Santiago, Chile.

___(2010), *Time for Equality: clsoing gaps, opening trails* (LC/G.2432(SES.33/3)), Santiago, Chile.

ECLAC/ILO (Economic Commission for Latin America and the Caribbean/International Labour Organization) (2014), "Conditional transfer programmes and the labour market", *The Employment Situation in Latin America and the Caribbean*, No. 10 (LC/L.3815), Santiago, Chile, Economic Commission for Latin America and the Caribbean (ECLAC).

Espino, Alma (2012), "La dimensión de género de la crisis. ¿Existe una agenda feminista?", *Nueva Sociedad,* No. 237, January-February.

Esteban, Joan, Carlos Gradín and Debraj Ray (1999), "Extensions of a measure of polarization with and application to the income distribution of five OECD countries", *Luxembourg Income Study Working Paper Series,* No. 218, New York, Maxwell School of Citizenship and Public Affairs, Syracuse University.

Foster, James E. and Michael C. Wolfson (2002), "Polarization and the decline of the middle class: Canada and the US", *OPHI Working Paper,* No. 31 [online] http://www.ophi.org.uk/wp-content/uploads/OPHI-wp31.pdf?92fa97.

Giosa, Z. and C. Rodríguez (2010), "Estrategias de desarrollo y equidad de género: Una propuesta de abordaje y su aplicación al caso de las industrias manufactureras de exportación en México y Centroamérica", *Mujer y Desarrollo series,* No. 97 (LC/L.3154-P), Santiago, Chile, Economic Commission for Latin America and the Caribbean (ECLAC). United Nations publication, Sales No. S.09.II.G.127.

Kaztman, Rubén (2011), "Infancia en América Latina: privaciones habitacionales y desarrollo de capital humano", *Project Document* (LC/W.431), Santiago, Chile, Economic Commission for Latin America and the Caribbean (ECLAC)/United Nations Children's Fund (UNICEF).

Lechner, N. (2002), *Las sombras del mañana. La dimensión subjetiva de la política*, Santiago, Chile, Editorial Lom.

Macpherson, D.A. and B.T. Hirsch (1995), "Wages and gender composition: why do women's jobs pay less?", *Journal of Labor Economics*, vol. 13, No. 3, Chicago, University of Chicago Press.

Maurizio, R. (2010), "Enfoque de género en las instituciones laborales y las políticas del mercado de trabajo en Argentina", *Macroeconomía del Desarrollo series*, No. 104 (LC/L.3230-P), Santiago, Chile, Economic Commission for Latin America and the Caribbean (ECLAC). United Nations publication, Sales No. S.10.II.G.34.

Miller, P. (2009), "The gender pay gap in the US: does sector make a difference?", *Journal of Labor Research*, vol. 30, No. 1, Springer.

Montaño, S. and V. Milosavljevic (2010), "La crisis económica y financiera. Su impacto sobre la pobreza, el trabajo y el tiempo de las mujeres", *Mujer y Desarrollo series*, No. 98 (LC/L.3168-P), Santiago, Chile, Economic Commission for Latin America and the Caribbean (ECLAC). United Nations publication, Sales No. S.09.II.G.141.

Perea Restrepo, Carlos (2008), *¿Qué nos une? Jóvenes, cultura y ciudadanía*, Medellín, La Carreta.

Rico, María Nieves and Daniela Trucco (2014), "Adolescentes. Derecho a la educación y al bienestar futuro", *Políticas Sociales series*, No. 190 (LC/L.3791), Santiago, Chile, Economic Commission for Latin America and the Caribbean (ECLAC).

Santos, María Emma and others (2014), "Un índice multidimensional de pobreza para América Latina", Santiago, Chile, Santiago, Chile, Economic Commission for Latin America and the Caribbean (ECLAC), unpublished.

Chapter I

Poverty in Latin America: achievements so far and challenges ahead

Introduction

As noted in *Compacts for Equality: Towards a sustainable future* (ECLAC, 2014c), the countries of Latin America and the Caribbean are currently faced with the challenge of maintaining the significant progress made in reducing poverty and unemployment and consolidating the initial steps taken to improve income distribution by strengthening democracy, achieving macroeconomic stability and implementing social policies. Attempts to shore up and go beyond this progress would appear to be constrained by certain limitations which have halted or slowed the reduction of poverty and indigence and the improvement of income distribution, especially following the global financial crisis of 2008, as will be shown in the first and the second chapters of this document.

This edition of *Social Panorama* again explores poverty from an income-based perspective and with a multidimensional approach, both of which bear out the theory that, despite the progress made in the last decade, poverty remains a characteristic structural phenomenon in Latin America. The various estimates presented gauge the magnitude and intensity of poverty in different population groups, and provide stylized facts which can be used to guide poverty eradication policies aimed at achieving sustainable improvements in well-being and development.

A. Analysis of income poverty

In line with the trend seen in recent years, poverty rates in 2013 remained similar to those of 2011 and 2012, which may be a sign that the process of poverty reduction seen in the region over the past ten years has stalled. Rates of extreme poverty show a similar pattern, having returned to levels similar to those seen two years ago. The number of indigent people has begun to trend upwards, although significant variations are yet to be seen.

1. Economic context

The global economy returned to growth in 2013, spurred by consolidation in the economies of the United States and Japan and the end of the recession in the eurozone. Growth in China remained at around 7%, but is expected to slow in 2014 as a result of financial tensions and the weaker performance of the country's manufacturing industry.

Against this backdrop, the growth rate in Latin America in 2013 (2.5%) outperformed the global average (2.2%) but was lower than in 2012 (2.9%). As in previous years, household consumption was the driving force for growth, expanding by 3.1% and thus offsetting the slowdown in gross fixed capital formation and slack export growth in the wake of lower export prices (ECLAC, 2014a).

Per capita GDP rose by 1.5% in Latin America, continuing the slowdown seen since 2010.

Thirteen countries posted GDP growth rates above the regional average, including Paraguay (11.8%), Panama (6.6%), Peru (4.5%), the Plurinational State of Bolivia (5.2%) and Uruguay (4.0%). Outside this group of countries, per capita output increased by around 3% in Chile, Colombia, the Dominican Republic, Ecuador and Nicaragua, and by around 2% in Argentina, Brazil and Costa Rica. Per capita GDP grew by rates of around 1% in El Salvador, Honduras and Guatemala, and contract slightly (by 0.1%) in the economies of the Bolivarian Republic of Venezuela and Mexico.

Labour markets in Latin America and the Caribbean lost momentum in 2013, after the steady advances that marked the last 10 years. The employment rate edged up from 55.3% in 2012 to 55.7% in 2013, while the urban unemployment rate was down again, slipping from 6.4% in 2012 to 6.3% in 2013, a historic low. This was the result of the aforementioned increase in the employment rate and a fall in labour market participation, which declined from 59.8% in 2012 to 59.6% in 2013. The rate of unemployment showed a similar variation in the individual countries and in the region as a whole. Rates in eight countries either remained the same or slipped back by up to 0.2 points on the previous year (Argentina, Brazil, Ecuador, Guatemala, Mexico, Panama, Paraguay and Uruguay), whereas seven others saw contractions of more than 0.2 percentage points (Barbados, Belize, the Bolivarian Republic of Venezuela, Chile, Colombia, Peru and Trinidad and Tobago) and five more posted falls of 0.4 percentage points or more (Bahamas, Costa Rica, Dominican Republic, Honduras and Jamaica) (ECLAC/ILO, 2014).

The purchasing power of average wages held steady or rose —albeit at lower rates than in previous years— in most countries with available information. The largest increase was seen in Chile (around 4%), followed by Uruguay (3%), Colombia (2.6%), Paraguay (2.2%), and Brazil (1.1%). The only fall in average real wages (of 4.1%) was in the Bolivarian Republic of Venezuela, mainly owing to an upswing in inflation (ECLAC/ILO, 2014).

The simple average rate of inflation in the region increased from 5.3% to 6.8%. The bulk of this was attributable to inflation in the Bolivarian Republic of Venezuela, which surged from 20.1% in 2012 to 56.2% in 2013. Inflation that year was also slightly up on 2012 in Chile (1.6 percentage points), the Plurinational State of Bolivia (2 percentage points), and Guatemala and and Uruguay (1 percentage point) and down sharply in Haiti (-4.2 percentage points), Cuba (-2.0 percentage points) and Nicaragua (-1.7 percentage points).

Output is expected to grow by some 2.2% in 2014, or around 1% in per capita terms. The behaviour of indicators over the first half-year suggests no major changes in employment. Meanwhile, the expected slowdown in nominal wage rises, coupled with a slight uptick in inflation, will temper real wage growth (ECLAC, 2014b).

Table I.1
Latin America (20 countries): selected socioeconomic indicators, 2000-2013
(Percentages)

Country and year	Per capita GDP	Unemployment	Average real wage [c]	Consumer price index [d]
	(average annual rate of variation) [a]	*(simple average over the period)* [b]	*(average annual rate of variation)*	
Argentina				
2000-2010	2.4	12.5	5.2	9.1
2011	7.6	7.2	...	9.5
2012	0.1	7.2	...	10.8
2013	2.1	7.1	...	10.9
Bolivia (Plurinational State of)				
2000-2010	1.9	7.6	-0.5	5.0
2011	3.6	...	-1.3	6.9
2012	3.6	...	0.9	4.5
2013	5.2	...	...	6.5
Brazil				
2000-2010	2.5	9.1	-0.6	6.6
2011	1.9	6.0	2.4	6.5
2012	0.2	5.5	3.7	5.8
2013	1.7	5.4	1.1	5.9
Chile				
2000-2010	2.8	9.0	1.9	3.3
2011	4.9	7.1	2.5	4.4
2012	4.5	6.4	3.2	1.5
2013	3.2	5.9	3.9	3.1
Colombia				
2000-2010	2.4	14.6	1.4	5.7
2011	5.1	11.5	9.2	3.7
2012	2.6	11.2	-7.2	2.4
2013	3.3	10.6	2.6	1.9
Costa Rica				
2000-2010	2.3	6.2	1.1	10.1
2011	3.1	7.7	5.7	4.7
2012	3.7	7.8	1.4	4.5
2013	2.2	8.2	1.3	3.7

Table I.1 (continued)

Country and year	Per capita GDP	Unemployment	Average real wage [c]	Consumer price index [d]
	(average annual rate of variation) [a]	*(simple average over the period)* [b]	*(average annual rate of variation)*	
Cuba				
2000-2010	5.1	2.6	4.8	2.6
2011	2.8	3.2	0.3	1.3
2012	3.0	3.5	0.3	2.0
2013	2.7	...	...	0.04
Dominicana Republic				
2000-2010	3.8	6.6	...	11.6
2011	3.1	5.8	...	7.8
2012	2.6	6.5	...	3.9
2013	2.8	7.0	...	3.9
Ecuador				
2000-2010	2.0	8.8	...	12.2
2011	6.0	6.0	...	5.4
2012	3.4	4.9	...	4.2
2013	2.8	4.7	...	2.7
El Salvador				
2000-2010	1.5	6.4	-1.3	3.4
2011	1.7	6.6	-2.9	5.1
2012	1.3	6.2	0.2	0.8
2013	1.1	...	0.5	0.8
Guatemala				
2000-2010	0.9	4.9	-0.5	6.6
2011	1.7	3.1	0.4	6.2
2012	0.5	4.0	4.0	3.4
2013	1.2	3.8	-0.2	4.4
Haiti				
2000-2010	-1.3	...	...	13.6
2011	4.2	...	...	8.3
2012	1.6	...	...	7.6
2013	3.0	...	...	3.4
Honduras				
2000-2010	2.2	5.7	...	7.7
2011	1.8	6.8	...	5.6
2012	1.9	5.6	...	5.4
2013	0.6	6.0	...	4.9
Mexico				
2000-2010	1.0	4.2	2.0	4.9
2011	2.7	5.9	0.9	3.8
2012	2.8	5.8	0.2	3.6
2013	-0.1	5.7	-0.1	4.0
Nicaragua				
2000-2010	1.6	9.0	0.7	9.3
2011	4.2	...	0.1	8.6
2012	3.5	...	0.4	7.1
2013	3.1	...	0.3	5.4
Panama				
2000-2010	3.8	11.9	-0.3	2.6
2011	8.9	5.4	0.1	6.3
2012	8.4	4.8	3.4	4.6
2013	6.6	4.7	1.8	3.7
Paraguay				
2000-2010	1.0	9.4	0.6	8.0
2011	2.6	7.1	2.7	4.9
2012	-2.8	8.1	0.7	4.0
2013	11.8	8.1	2.2	3.7
Peru				
2000-2010	4.0	8.8	1.1	2.4
2011	5.3	7.7	...	4.7
2012	4.7	6.8	...	2.6
2013	4.5	5.9	...	2.9

Table I.1 (concluded)

Country and year	Per capita GDP (average annual rate of variation)[a]	Unemployment (simple average over the period)[b]	Average real wage[c] (average annual rate of variation)	Consumer price index[d] (average annual rate of variation)
Uruguay				
2000-2010	2.7	12.1	0.1	8.4
2011	7.0	6.6	4.0	8.6
2012	3.3	6.7	4.2	7.5
2013	4.0	6.7	3.0	8.5
Venezuela (Bolivarian Republic of)				
2000-2010	1.4	11.9	-2.5	21.6
2011	2.6	8.3	3.0	27.6
2012	4.0	8.1	5.8	20.1
2013	-0.1	7.8	-4.4	56.2
Latin America[e]				
2000-2010	2.0	9.2	...	7.7
2011	3.3	6.7	...	7.0
2012	1.9	6.4	...	5.3
2013	1.5	6.3	...	6.8

Source: Economic Commission for Latin America and the Caribbean (ECLAC), on the basis of official figures.
[a] Calculated on the basis of per capita GDP in dollars, at constant 2005 prices. The average for Latin America is the weighted average of GDP variations in the countries in the subregion.
[b] The information for the countries comes from official national sources. For 2000-2010, data for Guatemala refers to 2002-2004 and 2010 onwards, and data for Honduras refers to 2001 onwards. The unemployment figures given for Peru are for the city of Lima.
[c] The coverage of this indicator is generally very patchy. In most of the countries, it refers to industrial workers in the formal sector only.
[d] Year-on-year variations, with December as the reference month. The regional aggregate is the simple average of the different rates of variation.
[e] The (weighted) regional average unemployment rate for Latin America and the Caribbean, calculated using data from 25 countries, including all those referred to in the table, with the exception of the Bahamas, Barbados, Belize, Haiti, Jamaica, Suriname and Trinidad and Tobago, and weighted using projections of the working-age population provided by CELADE-Population Division of ECLAC.

2. Recent trends in poverty in Latin America

Against the backdrop described, the poverty rate in Latin America stood at 28.1% in 2013, while the indigence or extreme poverty rate was 11.7%. These percentages represent 165 million poor, including 69 million living in extreme poverty (see figure I.1).

Figure I.1
Latin America: poverty and indigence, 1980-2014[a]
(Percentages and millions of persons)

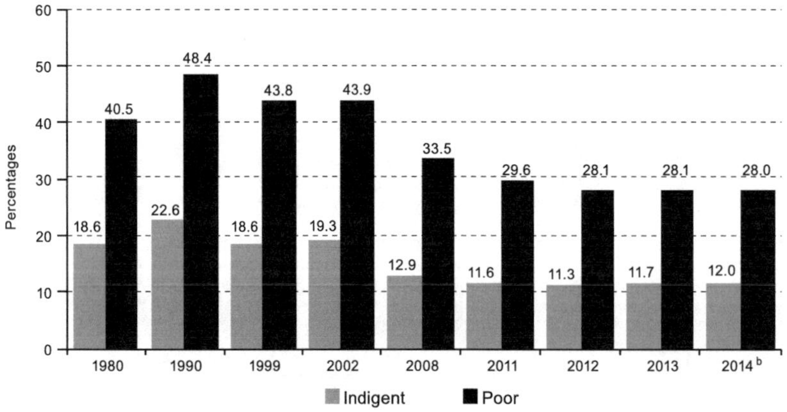

Figure I.1 (concluded)

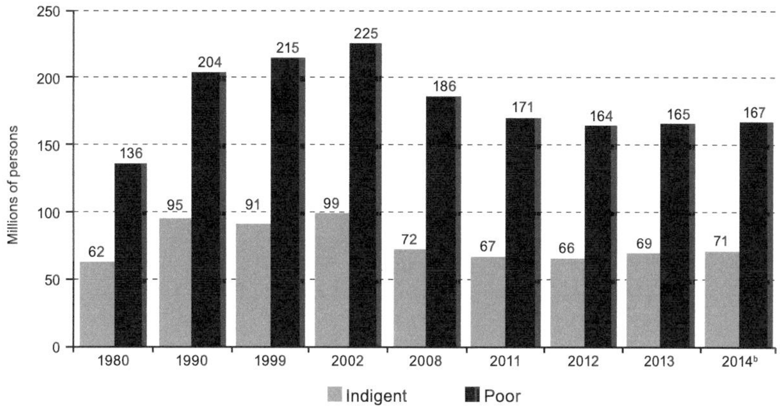

Source: Economic Commission for Latin America and the Caribbean (ECLAC), on the basis of special tabulations of data from household surveys conducted in the respective countries.
[a] Estimate for 19 countries, including Haiti. Cuba not included.
[b] Projection.

These values show that the poverty rate was largely unchanged in respect of levels seen in 2012 (28.1%). There was, however, a slight uptick in extreme poverty, which rose by 0.4 percentage points on 2012 levels (11.3%). No significant change was thus seen in numbers of poor in 2013, while the number of indigents increased by around 3 million.

Although the percentage variations are very small, extreme poverty has reached levels close to those last seen in 2011, according to the new projections. Ground has therefore been lost following the progress made in the intervening years. This is not a new development; similar trends were also evident in the data presented in previous editions of the *Social Panorama*. Indeed, estimates for the region show that the downward trend in poverty and extreme poverty has slowed and even gone into reverse since 2010, a situation which, coupled with population growth, has increased the number of people living in extreme poverty in 2013.

By way of example, a comparison can be made between the periods 2002-2008 and 2008-2013. The period 2002-2008 was initially marked by very high rates of poverty, which decreased rapidly, at a rate of 1.7% per year to accumulate a fall of 10.4 percentage points. In this period the indigence rate fell by 1.0% annually, giving a decrease of 6.4 percentage points overall. Between 2008 and 2013, however, both rates fell more slowly, with poverty contracting by 5.4 percentage points —a rate of 1.0% per year— and indigence by a mere 1.2 percentage points, around 0.2% per year.

No statistically significant changes are expected in the levels of poverty and indigence in the region as a whole in 2014, since growth in per capita output will similar to, or slightly lower than, that of 2013, and employment and inflation are unlikely to vary greatly in most countries. However, projections point to a slight increase in the indigence rate to around 12%, which would mean not only a return to around the rate seen early this decade, but also a sharp rise in the number of extremely poor owing to population growth.

3. Recent trends in poverty by country

In respect of developments in poverty by country, of the 12 countries with available data for 2013, six saw statistically significant falls in levels of poverty and indigence. Paraguay was most successful in reducing poverty, by 4.5 percentage points per year from 49.6% to 40.7% between 2011 and 2013, while indigence also fell at almost the same annual rate over the period, from 28.0% to 19.2%. In El Salvador poverty fell by 4.4 percentage points between 2012 and 2013 (from 45.3% to 40.9%) and indigence contracted by 1.0 percentage point (from 13.5% to 12.5%) over the same period. Colombia reported a drop of 2.2 percentage points in poverty levels (from 32.9% to

30.7%) and a 1.3-percentage-point reduction in extreme poverty (from 10.4% to 9.1 %). Poverty in Peru decreased by 1.9 percentage points (from 25.8% to 23.9%), and extreme poverty fell by 1.3 points (6.0% to 4.7%). In Chile, meanwhile, poverty decreased by 1.6 percentage points per year, from 10.9% in 2011 to 7.8% in 2013, while extreme poverty fell at an annual rate of 0.3 percentage points per year, from 3.1% in 2011 to 2.5% in 2013. Ecuador also saw poverty contract at a rate of 0.9 percentage points per year between 2011 and 2013 (from 35.4% in 2011 to 33.6% in 2013), while extreme poverty fell by 1.0 percentage points per year (from 13.9% in 2011 to 12.0% in 2013). The remaining countries (Costa Rica and Uruguay) saw less significant reductions, of around 0.3 percentage points or less, in both poverty and indigence (see figure I.2).

Figure I.2
Latin America (12 countries): variation in poverty and indigence rates, 2012-2013 [a]
(Percentage points)

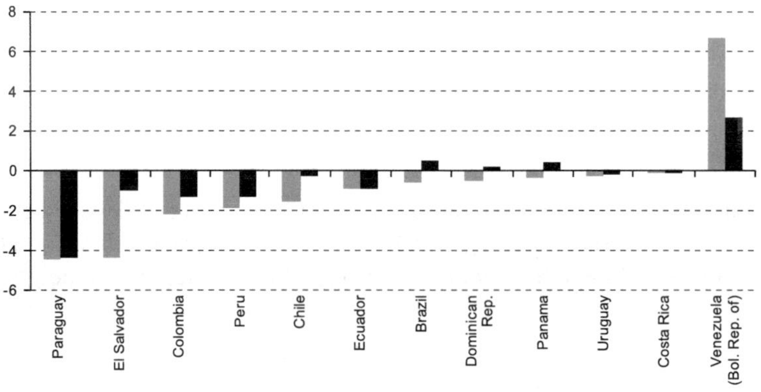

Source: Economic Commission for Latin America and the Caribbean (ECLAC), on the basis of special tabulations of data from household surveys conducted in the respective countries.
[a] Average annual variations between 2011 and 2013 are used for Chile, Ecuador, Panama and Paraguay.

Between 2012 and 2013, Brazil recorded a drop of 0.6 percentage points in the poverty rate, but an increase of 0.5 percentage points in the rate of indigence. A similar picture of falls in poverty but rises in indigence was seen in the Dominican Republic over the same period and Panama between 2011 and 2013, but these variations were not statistically significant. Between 2012 and 2013, the Bolivarian Republic of Venezuela saw rises of 6.7 percentage points in the poverty rate (from 25.4% to 32.1%) and 2.7 percentage points in the indigence rate (from 7.1% to 9.8%).[1]

An overview of trends in poverty in the countries can be supplemented by using indicators of the poverty gap and the severity of poverty (or poverty gap squared). The former provides a weighting of the percentage of poor people by the average difference between their income and the poverty line. The latter is similar but also captures income distribution among the poor (see box I.2 and table I.A1 in the annex to this chapter).

Between 2012 and 2013 the percentage variation in these three poverty indicators in countries with significant rates of change were broadly similar to the two countries with the largest falls in percentage terms (Chile and El Salvador). In four other countries (Colombia, Ecuador, Paraguay, and Peru) the poverty gap and poverty severity indicators fell more steeply than the headcount ratio (i.e. the poverty rate) as a result of a significant rise in the income of the very poorest households. In Brazil, the poverty gap remained constant and the severity of poverty rose although the headcount ratio fell during the period under review. In the Bolivarian Republic of Venezuela, meanwhile, the poverty gap and poverty severity indicators both increased (see figure I.3).

An examination of trends over a longer period (2008-2013) reveals that by and large the poverty gap and poverty severity indicators came down more than the headcount ratio. This was the case in Uruguay, Peru, Chile, the Plurinational State of Bolivia, Paraguay, Colombia, Ecuador, El Salvador and the Dominican Republic. In these countries, therefore, poverty reduction has been accompanied by an improvement in the relative conditions of all those living below the poverty line, rather than just an increase in income for those closer to this threshold. Argentina,

1 These figures may vary from those presented in annex table I.A.1, owing to differences in the coverage of the estimated.

Brazil and Panama showed a different pattern in this period, in which poverty fell faster in absolute terms than both the poverty gap and severity, indicating that conditions improved for the least poor among the poor. In Mexico, these three indicators performed in a similar manner over the period, while in Costa Rica an increased the headcount ratio was accompanied by a worsening of both the poverty gap and the severity of poverty.

Figure I.3

Latin America (14 countries): annual variations in poverty indicators, 2008-2013 and 2012-2013

(Percentages)

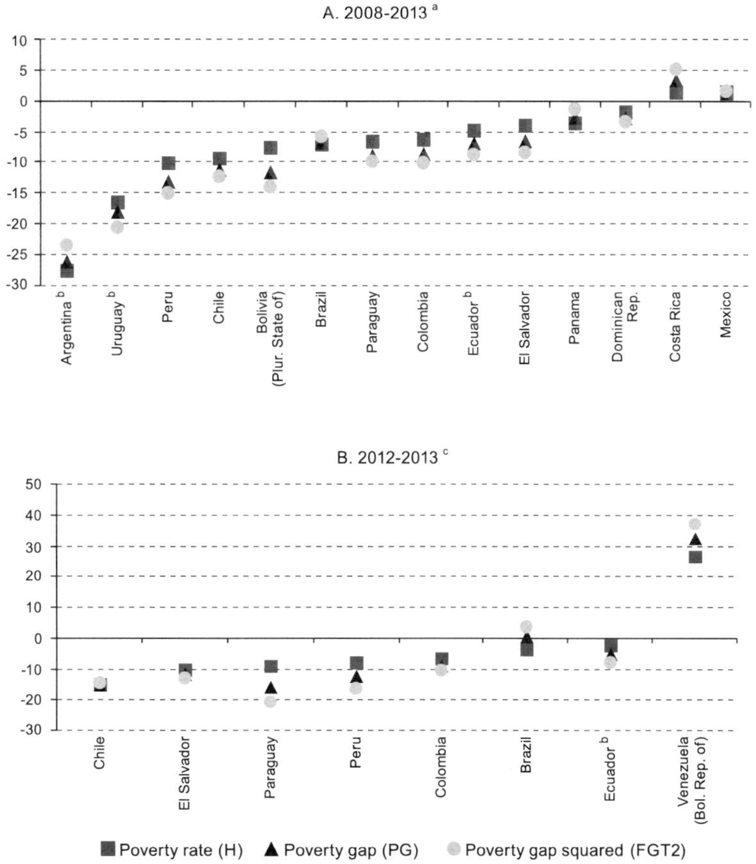

Source: Economic Commission for Latin America and the Caribbean (ECLAC), on the basis of special tabulations of data from household surveys conducted in the respective countries.

[a] Data refer to 2008-2013, except in the cases of the Plurinational State of Bolivia (2009-2011), Chile (2009-2011), El Salvador (2009-2013), Honduras (2007-2010), Mexico (2008-2012) and Nicaragua (2005-2009).

[b] Data refer to urban areas.

[c] Includes eight countries with significant variations in poverty. Data refer to the period between 2012 and 2013, except those for Chile, Ecuador and Paraguay, which refer to the 2011-2013 period.

Box I.1

Method used to measure poverty

The approach used in this report to estimate poverty classifies a person as poor when the per capita income of his or her household is below the poverty line, which is the minimum level of income needed to meet their basic needs. Poverty lines, expressed in each country's currency, are calculated from the cost of a basket of goods and services using the cost of basic needs method.

The basic food basket used to measure poverty contains the goods required to cover people's nutritional needs, taking into account consumption habits, the actual availability of foodstuffs and their prices for each country and geographical area. In most cases, data on the make-up of household consumption patterns for both foodstuffs and other goods and services are derived from national household budget surveys carried out in the 1980s.

The total value of the poverty line is calculated by taking the indigence line and then adding the amount that households require in order to meet their basic non-food needs. In order to carry out this calculation, the indigence line is multiplied by a factor that varies between urban and rural areas. For poverty estimates for up to 2006, a factor of 2 was used for urban areas and a factor of 1.75 for rural areas.[a] The factors applied since 2007 vary depending on the difference between price trends for foodstuffs and for other goods and services.

Box I.1 (concluded)

Indigence lines and poverty lines are updated each year to reflect cumulative changes in the consumer price index (CPI). For estimates calculated up to December 2006, the same rate of variation was applied to both lines. Since 2007, the indigence line has been adjusted to reflect changes in CPI for foodstuffs, while the part of the poverty line corresponding to expenditure on non-food goods has been adjusted to reflect changes in the non-food CPI. The values used as indigence and poverty lines in this publication can be found in table 4 of the statistical annex.[b]

Household income data are taken from household surveys conducted in each country in the years corresponding to the poverty estimates presented in this edition. In line with standard procedure at ECLAC, the data have been corrected to account for non-response to some income-related questions by wage earners, the self-employed and retirees and to mitigate probable underreporting biases. This was done by comparing the responses to income-related questions in the survey with figures from an estimate of the household income and spending account taken from each country's system of national accounts prepared for this purpose using official information.

The income figures used refer to total current income, i.e. income from wage labour (in both money and kind), self-employment (including self-supply and the consumption value of home-made or home-grown products), property income, retirement and other pensions and other transfers received by households. In most countries, household income also includes the imputed rental value of owner-occupied dwellings.

Source: Economic Commission for Latin America and the Caribbean (ECLAC).

[a] The sole exceptions to this general rule were the estimates for Brazil, Colombia and Peru. For Brazil, this study used the indigence lines estimated jointly by the Brazilian Geographical and Statistical Institute (IBGE), the Brazilian Institute of Applied Economic Research (IPEA) and ECLAC in the late 1990s. For Colombia, the cut-offs proposed by the Colombian Mission for the Linkage of Employment, Poverty and Inequality Series (MESEP) were used. For Peru, indigence and poverty lines were estimated by the National Institute of Statistics and Informatics (INEI).

[b] Available online.

Box I.2

Indicators for measuring poverty

The poverty indicators used in this study belong to the family of parametric indices proposed by Foster, Greer and Thorbecke (1984) and have been obtained from the following formula:

$$(1)\quad FGT_{\alpha} = \frac{1}{n}\sum_{i=1}^{q}\left(\frac{z-y_i}{z}\right)^{\alpha}$$

where n represents population size, q denotes the number of people with incomes below the poverty or indigence line (z) and the parameter $\alpha > 0$ assigns differing levels of shortfall between the income (y) of each poor or indigent individual and the poverty or indigence line.

When α takes a value of 0, then formula (1) corresponds to the headcount ratio (H), which indicates the percentage of people with incomes below the poverty or indigence line:

$$(2)\quad H = q/n$$

When α equals 1, the expression yields the poverty gap (PG) (or indigence gap), which weights the percentage of poor (or indigent) people by how far their incomes fall short of the poverty (or indigence) line:

$$(3)\quad PG = \frac{1}{n}\sum_{i=1}^{q}\left[\frac{z-y_i}{z}\right]$$

Lastly, when α has a value of two, a greater relative weight is assigned in the final result to those who fall furthest below the poverty (or indigence) line by squaring the relative income deficit:

$$(4)\quad FGT_{2} = \frac{1}{n}\sum_{i=1}^{q}\left(\frac{z-y_i}{z}\right)^{2}$$

Source: Economic Commission for Latin America and the Caribbean (ECLAC), on the basis of James Foster, Joel Greer and Erik Thorbecke, "A class of decomposable poverty measures", Econometrica, vol. 52, No. 3, 1984.

4. Factors contributing to trends in poverty

Variations in poverty and indigence rates may be broken down into two components: growth in average individual income (the growth effect) and changes in the way in which that income is distributed (the distribution effect).[2]

The growth effect was predominant in changes in poverty levels between 2012 and 2013, since the distribution effect was adjudged to have had a minimal or even negative impact. Only in Chile, Paraguay and Peru was there a positive distribution effect, which reinforced the contribution made by the growth effect in reducing poverty. In Ecuador and El Salvador worsening income distribution curtailed the positive effects of the fall in the poverty rate caused by the growth effect. In the Bolivarian Republic of Venezuela and Colombia, meanwhile, the distribution effect was nil (see figure I.4).

2 This breakdown is based on a method proposed by Datt and Ravallion (1992).

Figure I.4
Latin America (14 countries): [a] **cumulative changes in poverty rates and the impact of growth and distribution effects, 2008-2013 and 2012-2013**
(Percentages)

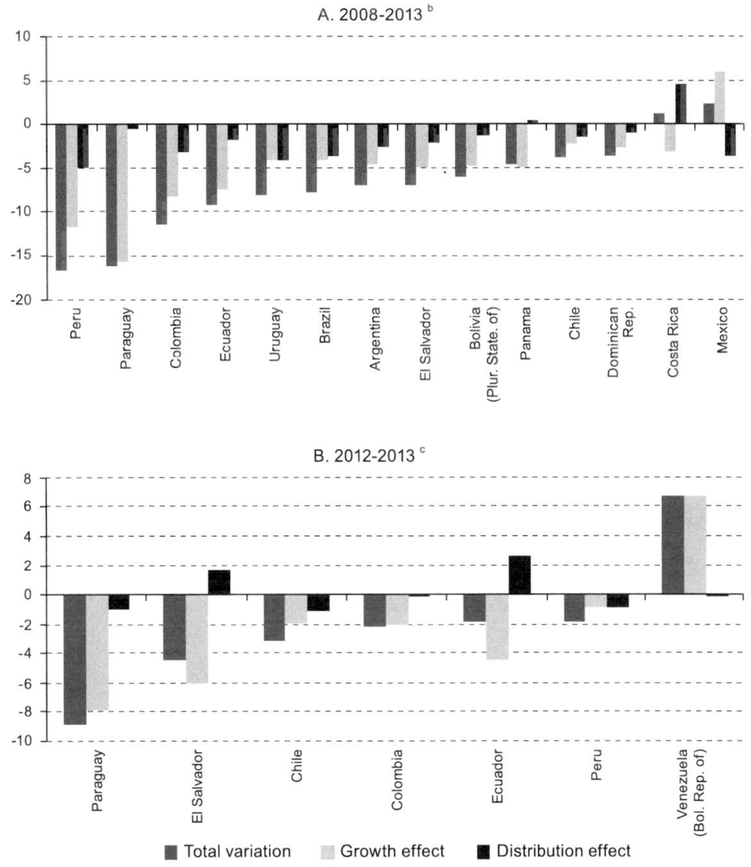

Source: Economic Commission for Latin America and the Caribbean (ECLAC), on the basis of special tabulations of data from household surveys conducted in the respective countries.
[a] Includes countries whose rates of poverty increased or decreased by more than 1% in the periods under review.
[b] Data refer to 2008-2013, except for Argentina (2008-2012), Bolivia (Plurinational State of) (2009-2011), Chile (2009-2013), El Salvador (2009-2013) and Mexico (2008-2012).
[c] Data for Chile, Ecuador and Paraguay refer to 2011-2013.

The relative contributions of the growth and distribution effects are different when the period 2008-2013 is considered in its entirety. While the growth effect accounted for more than half of the reduction in poverty over this period, the distribution effect was responsible for a third or more thereof in most countries where poverty fell significantly. Uruguay and Brazil were among the countries in which the contributions of two effects were most evenly balanced. In Mexico, meanwhile, improved distribution helped prevent falling income from pushing up poverty rates. In Costa Rica, however, the opposite happened: a worsening in distribution curtailed the ability of household income growth to reduce poverty over the period.

Quantifying the contribution made by the various revenue streams to overall variations in the income of the poorest households[3] provides a different perspective with which to analyse trends in poverty. Changes in the overall income of poor households are usually driven mainly by employment income —wages, salaries, and pay of own-account workers— as is shown in countries reporting positive or negative variations in such income between 2008 and 2013. Indeed, in 10 of the countries under review this category of income grew, and it accounted for at least 60% of total income variation in eight of them.

[3] Since the data used come from cross-sectional surveys, the reference groups in both years have been identified approximately. Comparisons between rates are made using the income of all households below the income distribution percentile corresponding to the estimated poverty line in the initial period.

Retirement benefits, pensions and other transfers made a positive contribution to variations in income in 12 countries, having the greatest impact on the incomes of the poorest households in Panama, Chile, Colombia and the Plurinational State of Bolivia. In Panama growth in this category mitigated the decline in labour earnings over the period, while in the remaining countries it provided a boost to household income from employment. In Uruguay, Brazil and Mexico, the other sources of income recorded in surveys also made a significant contribution (see figure I.5).

Figure I.5

Latin America (14 countries): annual rate of change in total per capita labour income of poor households, by source of income, around 2008-2013 [a]

(Percentages)

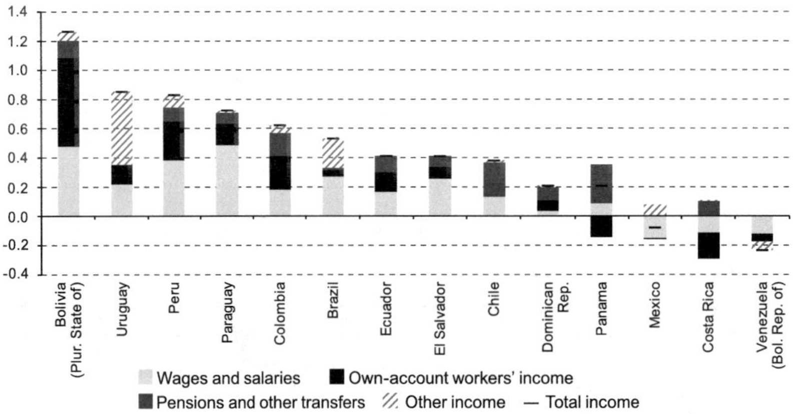

Source: Economic Commission for Latin America and the Caribbean (ECLAC), on the basis of special tabulations of data from household surveys conducted in the respective countries.

[a] Data refer to the period from 2008 to 2013, except for Bolivia (Plurinational State of) (2007-2011), Chile (2006-2013), El Salvador (2009-2013) and Mexico (2008-2012).

Earnings from work can be examined to ascertain whether variations are due to changes in employment or average income, or a combination of both. The dominant trend over the period 2008-2013 was for rises in both employment and labour income per employed person, as seen in six of the 13 countries under review (Colombia, the Dominican Republic, El Salvador, Paraguay, Peru, and Uruguay). In four countries (Brazil, Chile, Ecuador and the Plurinational State of Bolivia) labour income per employed person increased and employment fell, although in all cases the net effect was a rise in earnings over the period. In Costa Rica, Mexico and Panama, meanwhile, an increase in employment caused earnings to fall at a slower rate than average labour income (see table I.2).

Table I.2

Latin America (13 countries): variation in labour earnings of poor households, by changes in employment and labour income per employed person, around 2008-2013 [a]

	Rise in employment	Fall in employment
Labour income per employed person increased	Colombia (+) El Salvador (+) Paraguay (+) Peru (+) Dominican Republic (+) Uruguay (+)	Bolivia (Plurinational State of) (+) Brazil (+) Chile (+) Ecuador (+)
Labour income per employed person fell	Costa Rica (-) Mexico (-) Panama (-)	

Source: Economic Commission for Latin America and the Caribbean (ECLAC), on the basis of special tabulations of data from household surveys conducted in the respective countries.

[a] A "+" or "–" sign indicating a rise or fall in total labour income is included in brackets. In Peru, the variation in employment was close to zero over the period, but slightly positive.

By and large, labour income per worker had a greater impact on variations in earnings than overall employment, except in Colombia and El Salvador, where the increase in employment was the main driver of rising incomes among poor households (see figure I.6).

Figure I.6
Latin America (13 countries): annual rate of change in labour income per employed person and in employed persons in poor households, around 2008-2013 [a]
(Percentages)

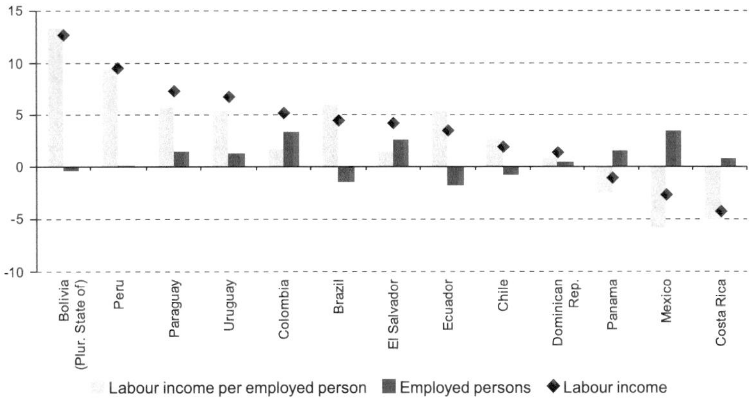

Source: Economic Commission for Latin America and the Caribbean (ECLAC), on the basis of special tabulations of data from household surveys conducted in the respective countries.

[a] The data refer to 2008-2013, except for Bolivia (Plurinational State of) (2007-2011), Chile (2006-2013), El Salvador (2009-2013) and Mexico (2008-2012).

5. Poverty in different population groups

One of hallmarks of poverty in Latin America is its higher incidence among younger rather than older segments of the population. This is illustrated by comparing the ratio between the poverty rates for young people and for those aged over 55 years (on average the population group least likely to suffer poverty in the region as a whole). Poverty rates among children under age 15 are 2.8 times higher than those aged 55 or over, while rates among young people aged 15-24 are 1.9 times greater than in the aforementioned age group.

The highest ratios are found in the four countries of the Southern Cone: in Uruguay the poverty rate is eight times higher among children under 15 years than among people over 55, in Brazil it is 5.5 times greater, in Argentina 5.1 times greater and in Chile 2.9 times greater. The ratio in the remaining countries of Latin America is below the regional average, although in the Bolivian Republic of Venezuela, Colombia, Mexico and Panama the incidence of poverty among children under 15 is more than twice as high as in the aforementioned older age group. A similar picture, albeit of a slightly lower order of magnitude, is seen in the 15-to-24 age category in comparison with the older group (see figure I.7).

Figure I.7
Latin America (14 countries): ratio between poverty rates among people aged 0-14 years and those aged 15-24 years, in respect of those aged 55 years and over, around 2013

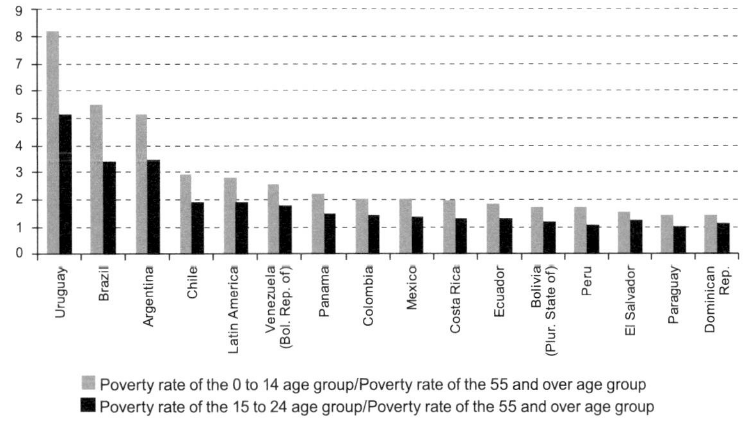

Source: Economic Commission for Latin America and the Caribbean (ECLAC), on the basis of special tabulations of data from household surveys conducted in the respective countries.

Poverty also varies by gender, particularly in the age group comprising adults most likely to participate in the labour market. In Latin America on average the poverty rate among women aged 25-49 years is 1.2 times that of men in the same age group. This ratio, which is higher than one in all countries of the region, is highest in the countries with the lowest incidence of poverty, particularly Argentina, Chile and Uruguay, where poverty rates among women are 1.5 times those for men. These differences are most likely attributable chiefly to the characteristics of labour markets and gender gaps in wages and workforce participation in these countries. In urban areas of the region in 2012, 50.5% of women were employed in low-productivity jobs —as opposed to 43.7% of men— and women's total earnings were on average 73.5% of men's.

These disparities in poverty rates are also associated with education level and employment type. Regarding education, poverty rates among those who have completed upper-secondary or tertiary education are, respectively, 26% and 74% lower than among the population at large. Poverty among those with three years or fewer of education is 66% higher than the average for the general population, while it is 34% and 15% higher among those with four to six years and seven to nine years of education, respectively. As for employment type, poverty rates are 90% higher among the unemployed, 23% higher among inactive persons and 18% higher among self-employed workers than in the total population. Poverty rates among wage workers are on average 41% below those of the general population, further evidence of the crucial role of employment in staving off poverty and indigence.

B. The multiple dimensions of poverty in Latin America[4]

Using a multidimensional poverty index to quantify poverty provides a complementary view of the phenomenon in the region. Although poverty fell between 2005 and 2012, some 28% of the population continue to suffer from simultaneous deprivations in different dimensions of well-being. To assess these dimensions for Latin America, it is necessary to broaden the analysis beyond basic lacks and look at shortfalls in areas such as employment and social protection.

This section presents the findings of an analysis of 17 countries in Latin America using a multidimensional poverty index. This index builds further on the exploration of different dimensions and thresholds of poverty made in the previous edition of *Social Panorama* (ECLAC, 2013), and is the product of a joint effort between ECLAC and the Oxford Poverty and Human Development Initiative (OPHI).

This multidimensional index has three main innovations with respect to previous poverty measures in the region: (i) the addition of monetary and non-monetary dimensions, so as to minimize errors of inclusion and exclusion in identifying the poor; (ii) the consideration of deprivations in terms of employment, social protection and schooling gap, thus widening the set of dimensions commonly used to measure poverty in the region; and (iii) the inclusion of new deprivation cut-offs for the commonly used dimensions with a view to defining standards that better reflect the current regional reality (for more details on the index, see Santos and others, 2015).

This new index represents an attempt to provide the region with a useful instrument to monitor public policies and reflect situations in which deprivations in various aspects of well-being occur simultaneously. However, although the index seeks to make the best possible use of information available in household surveys in the countries, data limitations remain a major drawback. Making progress in the multidimensional measurement of poverty in the region entails not only stepping up efforts to increase the availability and quality of information, but also ensuring that these efforts give rise to greater harmonization of the concepts and tools used for data collection.

4 The index presented in this section and its findings are based on Santos and others (2015).

This section is structured as follows: first, the conceptual framework on which the index was built is presented, then the basic rationale for the selection of dimensions, indicators and cut-offs included in the index is explained; third, the structure of the index is described, including the weighting of the various dimensions and the value used for the multidimensional poverty cut-off, as well as the justifications for those decisions. Lastly, the main empirical findings obtained by applying the index are presented and discussed.

1. Background and basic concepts

There are currently a great many reasons for working towards building a multidimensional measure of poverty. These include: (i) the spread and prevalence of new conceptual frameworks for development and well-being, as well as the rights- and capabilities-based approaches, in which income shortfall is only an incomplete proxy for standard of living, and (ii) the availability of new methodologies that have overcome some of the obstacles to the inclusion of various dimensions of poverty in an index (Alkire and Foster, 2007, 2011).

This new context has been reflected in the increasing number of multidimensional poverty indices involving several countries of the region,[5] as part of initiatives supported by the national governments and international agencies. ECLAC, continuing in its pioneering tradition in multidimensional poverty measurement in Latin America, has developed a multidimensional child poverty index grounded in the rights-based approach (ECLAC/UNICEF, 2010) and exploring the various dimensions of poverty and poverty thresholds for the entire population of the region (ECLAC, 2013).

Continuing in this vein, this section provides the findings of an examination of 17 countries in the region using the multidimensional poverty index. This index comprises non-monetary and monetary dimensions, including indicators of deprivations in respect of employment, social protection and schooling gap, and proposes new thresholds for the dimensions traditionally considered in measurements of poverty. The index was developed to make best possible use of information from surveys in the countries of the region, with a view to providing the region with an instrument to monitor public policies that is comparable between countries and can be applied to its entire population and used continually over the long term, as noted above.

The index used here incorporates elements from the capabilities-based, rights-based and unmet-basic-needs (UBN) approaches because they can be used in a complementary manner as they capture different aspects of deprivation. The rights-based approach describes the institutional means necessary for achieving well-being, while needs and capabilities —or functionings— are a way of describing and expressing the various constituent parts of well-being. The guaranteed exercise of rights enables people to satisfy their basic needs and function at a basic level. If their basic needs are not met or if they are prevented from performing essential functions, however, people will be less able to exercise their rights, which entrenches poverty reproduction (ECLAC, 2013).[6]

There are also practical reasons for combining complementary approaches. Although the capabilities- and rights-based approaches are clearly valid from a conceptual perspective, in practice household surveys capture lacks or deprivations, of which some may be interpreted simultaneously as constraints on meeting needs, as proxies for infringements of rights or as obstacles to the performance of functions (ECLAC, 2013). A direct measurement of these functions may require information which cannot be obtained through surveys or, even where such measurement is possible, information is generally not available for enough countries (as is the case, for example, with the nutritional status of the population) (Santos and others, 2010).

For Latin America, the best starting point for multidimensional poverty measurement is the set of core indicators of critical deficiencies in living conditions, which are the classic method of measuring UBN. This is because they are relatively well-established measures of poverty (constituting part of the prevailing notions of poverty in academic and policymaking circles) and are widely available in surveys. This starting point provides dimensions and indicators that

---

5 For a review of the regional experience in multidimensional poverty measurement in the region, see Santos (2013).

6 In Latin America, poverty is measured on the basis of determining the amount of resources needed to meet basic needs (poverty line method), or by attempting to determine directly whether such needs are fulfilled (UBN method). From the perspective of capabilities, poverty measurement based solely on resources is inadequate, since it does not provide information on the things that people can do or actually do with these resources (or means). From a rights-based perspective, meanwhile, the poor are not persons who are deprived or needy but rather citizens and rights-holders. However, even if capabilities or functionings have intrinsic value, not all of them are rights that States are legally obliged to uphold.

provide a fairly good picture of whether people have access to goods that can often not be bought from current income (such as public goods).[7] However, in the region today, where progress has been made in reducing the most extreme deprivations in living conditions, an index measuring classic UBN would not appear the most comprehensive way of identifying poverty.

Common practice in Latin America has been to calculate separate poverty indicators for income insufficiencies and UBN. Two, not necessarily consistent, reasons have been put forward to justify this: (i) poverty in terms of UBN and insufficient income are two distinct types of poverty that can be measured using complementary methods, but which nonetheless remain different, and (ii) there is a high correlation between the two indicators, which implies risks of redundancy and suggests that the best option would to be to employ only one of them. However, from a very early stage some authors advocated combining the two methods, with a view to identifying poor individuals and households as accurately as possible (Beccaria and Minujín 1985: Kaztman and Gerstenfeld, 1988; Boltvinik, 1990 and 1992).

In recent years the view that classic UBN indicators should be combined with monetary measures in a multidimensional index has been gaining ground. This is because both measures are imperfect, which means that errors of inclusion and exclusion can arise when only one is used to identify the poor (Santos and others, 2010; ECLAC, 2013). Indeed, there is ample empirical evidence from different countries of discrepancies arising between the numbers of poor as identified by income and by non-monetary dimensions.[8] Since the ultimate purpose of a poverty index is to identify who is poor with as much accuracy as possible, and since insufficient income is one of the clearest expressions of poverty, it would appear unwise to ignore the information contained in this variable.

ECLAC (2013) has observed that the combined use of a set of classic UBN indicators with a monetary measurement of extreme deprivation (indigence) yields incidences of poverty that are low and decrease over time, especially in countries where the living conditions of the population have improved the most. Thus, with a view to providing a measurement of poverty that is more in line with the reality of the region, two complementary paths can be followed: (i) amending certain cut-offs used for the deprivations normally included in measures of poverty (more on this later), and (ii) incorporating information on insufficiencies in other spheres.

Regarding the latter, the index presented here includes deprivations that reflect the weakness of links with institutions. Although this field has been little considered in measurements of poverty in the region, there are good reasons to include it. ECLAC has stated that poverty entails both lacking the income to met basic needs, and suffering social exclusion, which prevents full participation in society (Bárcena, 2010). This approach is a way of incorporating the social structure and the functioning of labour market institutions and social protection as an explicit element in poverty measurement (Kaztman, 2001).[9]

In short, the index set out here represents an attempt to quantify hardships, deprivations and infringements of rights that prevent or hinder people or households from meeting their basic needs and performing essential functions for their well-being. Nonetheless, this conceptualization of poverty remains incomplete. It is an ad hoc construct, built by combining the prevailing approaches to well-being and the possibilities offered by surveys conducted by the countries and tailored to the need for a measurement of poverty in line with the regional reality that can provide data suitable for informing policymakers in the public and social spheres.

2. Dimensions and thresholds

Measuring poverty on a multidimensional basis necessitates evaluating whether people succeed in achieving minimum thresholds of well-being in a narrow set of dimensions and indicators. In this case, the dimensions and indicators were selected with reference to the notion of poverty mentioned earlier. The aim was to provide the most comprehensive representation possible of the various areas that make up well-being, although data limitations sometimes prevented this (a proposal on aspects of the data sources in need of improvement is presented in box I.3).

---

7 This is not always the case, however, especially in the most market-orientated societies.

8 See for example Ruggeri Laderchi (1997) who considers data from Chile, Peru and India; Stewart and others (2007) who consider data from India; Bradshaw and Finch (2003) for the United Kingdom; and Whelan, Layte and Maitre (2004) for nine European countries.

9 It is also a way to include elements of the definition of poverty put forward by Townsend (1979).

Box I.3

Towards improved data sources

The index used here was developed to make best possible use of information available from household surveys conducted in the region. It should, however, be noted that the difficulties inherent in building it means it still leaves a great deal to be desired.

Although great strides have been made in surveys in the region over the past two decades, there are still many aspects in need of improvement. Many of the proposals made with a view to improving both surveys in general[a] and multidimensional measurements of poverty[b] would not necessarily incur greater costs and could bring significant benefits for poverty measurement and for public policymaking.

In respect of multidimensional poverty measurement, it is necessary to expand and improve the coverage of the dimensions and move towards greater international harmonization of questions. The dimension of health, which is conspicuous by its absence from this index, is a salient example. The only indicator which is widely available in surveys is access to health insurance, and that fails to take account of effective use of services or health outcomes. With some exceptions, the surveys contain no health-care performance indicators such as anthropometric data and measurements of infant mortality, incidence of chronic diseases, disabilities and/or the inability to perform daily activities independently.

Since health is such an important dimension of well-being, expanding and improving indicators in this area should be a priority objective. This would not entail including an exhaustive module on health; choosing a few key indicators would suffice. With this in mind, and in line with the post-2015 development agenda, the Multidimensional Poverty Peer Network (MPPN) and the Oxford Poverty and Human Development Initiative (OPHI) have proposed a set of short modules for data collection, including some that have been referred to above.[c]

The available indicators on other dimensions are also far from perfect. In the field of education for example, there is great scope for improvement in the measurement of aspects relating to the quality of education. The inclusion of a concise instrument to measure certain fundamental age-appropriate cognitive skills would be a source of valuable information (Grosh and Glewwe, 2000). The modules proposed by MPPN include dedicated questions to that end. This is not only applicable to the school population; it is valid for adults too, since there is no information on whether they have the cognitive skills to participate adequately in modern societies.

Data sources on employment are also in need of improvement, especially those on the quality and formality of work. There are conceptual frameworks that can act as guidelines for this purpose, such as the concept of decent work promoted by ILO and the technical recommendations of the Nineteenth International Conference of Labour Statisticians.[d]

Although income is one of the most widely used indicators in surveys, the way in which information on it is gathered varies greatly within the region, which acts as an obstacle to data comparability. Aspects such as income from second jobs, payment in kind, the distinction between gross and net income or how to measure public transfers, to name but a few, are issues that need to be properly addressed before the monetary resources of households can begin to be measured more adequately.

With regard to housing and basic services, the categories used need to be further harmonized and adapted, as far as possible, in line with the standards of the Millennium Development Goals, and an indicator of quality should be added where applicable.[e] Greater harmonization of categories is particularly important in respect of the water sources and sanitation available to the household, as well as the durable goods they possess. There is a particular need for the inclusion of a question on the continuity of services in terms of access to mains water, electricity and natural gas, so as to reflect any deprivations that would not be revealed by merely asking whether households are connected to these networks.

Importantly, the incorporation of the aforementioned indicators on health, employment and access to services would represent genuine progress in the measurement of the effective functionings of members of households and would be a way of overcoming the restrictions imposed by measurements that merely quantify the means at their disposal. The collection of information on multiple dimensions in the same survey would also enable analysis of the interplay of different dimensions, their combined distribution and causal interrelationships, which would facilitate the formulation and monitoring of policies.

But beyond improving questions, many challenges remain in respect of the drawing-up, carrying out and distribution of household surveys. It is to be hoped that the various efforts being made in the region, under the banner of the Statistical Conference of the Americas of ECLAC, or globally through initiatives such as the International Household Survey Network, will give rise to the greater availability of more useful and reliable sources of information that can adequately meet the growing demand for information.

Source: Economic Commission for Latin America and the Caribbean (ECLAC).

[a] See, for example, documentation on the workshops held between 1998 and 2004 under the programme for the improvement of surveys and the measurement of living conditions in Latin America and the Caribbean (MECOVI).

[b] See Alkire (2014), Alkire and others (2014) and Santos (2013).

[c] See [online] http://www.ophi.org.uk/wp-content/uploads/MPPN_SDG-Pov_QuoxPoct2015_Sopt 14a.pdf?0a8fd7.

[d] See [online] http://ilo.org/global/statistics-and-databases/meetings-and-events/international-conference-of-labour-statisticians/19/WCMS_234036/lang--en/index.htm.

[e] Not all of the countries' surveys ask whether toilets are shared with other households, for example.

The indicators that measure severe deprivations in the habitability of housing, such as overcrowding and precarious building materials, have commonly been included in measurements of UBN poverty in Latin America. Deprivation in housing habitability is understood to exist when it fails to provide its occupants with a minimum level of protection from the natural and social environment. This means that the dwelling fails to provide protection against various environmental factors (such as rain or humidity), as well as privacy and comfort for basic biological and social activities (Feres and Mancero, 2001).

A dwelling's ability to insulate individuals against the natural elements is usually assessed by looking at the construction materials used in the roof, walls and floor. This indicator considers people living in houses with dirt floors or with ceilings or walls made of unsound materials to be deprived.[10]

A dwelling's adequacy to provide social insulation is established through the indicator of overcrowding, the commonly used standard being more than three persons per room. This bar would appear to be rather undemanding for some countries in the region; Chile and Mexico, for example, apply thresholds of around 2.5 persons per room.[11] Nonetheless, given that other countries in the region continue to use the old standard, the value of three or more persons per room has been taken in this work as representing an intermediate benchmark.[12]

With regard to housing, the index includes an indicator to measure insecurity of tenure of homes. According to the United Nations (2013) all persons should possess a degree of security of tenure which guarantees legal protection against forced eviction and other threats, and enables them to live in peace and dignity. Unlike the United Nations (2013), which considers security of tenure to be safeguarded by common law, here it is deemed to be protected by civil (written) law only. People occupying dwellings illegally (squats) or living in loaned housing are thus deemed not to have secure tenure.

Deprivation in access to water and sanitation has also been a regular part of measurements of UBN poverty in Latin America, and its importance is internationally recognized. In 2010, the United Nations affirmed the human right to water and sanitation, since both are essential for preventing undernutrition, infectious diseases and maternal and child mortality.

The standard set by the World Health Organization (WHO) defines as appropriate access to improved water sources that each individual should have access to at least 20 litres of clean water per day from a source situated less than one kilometre from the home.[13] Unimproved water sources, meanwhile, are vendors, water trucks, unprotected wells or watersheds, and bottled water, whereas rainwater is classified as an improved source (UNICEF/WHO, 2012).

However, the information provided by the surveys of the Latin American countries does not allow for direct measurement of access to improved water sources, and presents gaps and discrepancies which hinder comparison between countries. What is more, not all countries in the region have adopted the international standard so notions of what constitutes improved water sources differ from country to country (Taccari and Stockins, 2013), thus giving rise to —often large— discrepancies in empirical estimates of access to water sources (and improved sanitation services) (see Cecchini and Azócar, 2007, for further details).

The WHO definition also provides criteria for determining whether a water source can be considered to be improved, namely the quality and quantity of water available and the effort necessary to obtain it. ECLAC (2013) attempted to implement the aforementioned international standard, based on survey data, with water from vendors, water trucks and unprotected wells considered to be unimproved, as was rainwater since its availability could not be guaranteed on a year-round basis.[14]

In designing this index it was decided to continue efforts to improve the measurement of access to water sources. Thus, in urban areas, households are not considered to be deprived if they have access either to mains water from a tap on the premises, whether inside or outside the dwelling itself, or to a well with a pump.[15] Other situations are deemed to constitute deprivation. In rural areas, households with a protected well, well with a pump (if surveys allow this distinction to be ascertained) or access to a communal tap are not considered to constitute water-related deprivation.

---

10 Information on the materials used in the construction of dwellings is usually obtained differently in national surveys from country to country, partly because of the features peculiar to those contexts (Feres and Mancero, 2001).

11 For Chile, see Ministry of Social Development [online] http://www.ministeriodesarrollosocial.gob.cl/casen/definiciones/vivienda.html; for Mexico, see State System of Information and Indicators on Land and Housing [online] https://www.coveg.gob.mx/seiisv/modulos/secciones/indicadores/indicadores/Indicador%2014.pdf.

12 This is the cut-off used in the indicator on overcrowding for gauging progress in the Millennium Development Goals (see [online] http://mdgs.un.org/unsd/mdg/Host.aspx?Content=Indicators/OfficialList.htm).

13 See the WHO website [online] http://www.who.int/water_sanitation_health/mdg1/en/.

14 A situation liable to get worse as the effects of climate change manifest themselves.

15 Surveys in most countries provide no information on whether or not the well is protected. Some, however, state whether the wells have pumps, which enables application of the criterion of the necessary effort to obtain water (per the international standard).

An improved sanitation installation, meanwhile, is one which allows for the hygienic separation of faeces from human contact (Taccari and Stockins, 2013). As in the case of water sources, a usual practice in the evaluation of improved sanitation is consideration of the features of the surroundings. For example, in some rural settings, households, irrespective of their poverty status, would not have access to a sewerage system or to mains water.

As with water sources, some changes were made to the definitions of improved sanitation in ECLAC (2013), most notably to the effect that in both urban and rural areas households sharing toilets are considered to be deprived. Households in urban areas are deemed not to suffer deprivation if they have sanitation systems for removal of waste into a sewerage system or a well with a septic tank. Households in rural areas are deemed not deprived if they have some form of sanitation (including latrines) with removal and disposal of waste neither aboveground nor in rivers or seas.

One aspect overlooked by commonly used UBN indicators is energy poverty. Households are said to be energy poor when they do not consume enough energy to meet their daily requirements and use fuel that is hazardous to the health of their members (Nussbaumer and others, 2011). The resources of households have been linked to the level of toxicity and the efficiency of the fuel that they use, with the worst fuels being waste matter, wood and charcoal, in that order[16] (Duflo and others, 2008). In this index, as in ECLAC (2013), households without electricity and those using toxic fuels for cooking are considered to be deprived in respect of energy.

The overall multidimensional poverty index of Alkire and Santos (2010) includes a measurement of the amount of durable goods that households possess as an indicator of standard of living. Although information on durable goods is usually available in national surveys in the region, it has not been particularly widely used in multidimensional measurements of poverty. It was therefore decided to include a durable goods deprivation indicator in the index, as a more lasting proxy for the standard of living of households. The goods considered are vehicles, washing machines and refrigerators.

Again in respect of the dimension of living standards, the exercise carried out by ECLAC (2013) included a monetary indicator of deprivation, which deemed households below the indigence line to be deprived. The indigence indicator was preferred as a cut-off partly because the indicator of total monetary poverty could increase the possibility of double counting, given that part of the income poverty measurement that does not correspond to indigence is a proxy for the ability of households to satisfy non-food needs, including some which are already covered by the set of UBN indicators. Moreover, although the fungible nature of income means that revenue cannot be equated with food consumption, the indigence line represents a minimum amount of resources necessary for people to satisfy their basic requirements for daily sustenance, an aspect not captured by the other indicators considered by ECLAC (2013).

On this occasion the criteria used previously have been modified, however, and the overall poverty line has been employed as a cut-off to determine monetary deprivation. The reason for this is twofold: first, the indicator of extreme poverty covers a very small percentage of the population in Latin America, and is thus unable to capture income insecurity. Second, although there is greater co-occurrence between some critical gaps and income insufficiencies when the poverty line is used rather than the indigence line, not all of this co-occurrence is redundancy (when the same deprivation is determined more than once), since another part of the covariance corresponds to the systematic association of different deprivations, which is essential for the identification of multidimensional poverty (see further details on redundancy in box I.6).

Education, moreover, is essential in order to build the skills that people need in order to participate adequately in productive and social life. Lack of education is therefore a very real obstacle to escaping from poverty and can contribute to its reproduction. The indicator of school attendance has been traditionally used in multidimensional poverty measurements in the region. It is usually calculated for the population aged from 6 to 14 years but, given the legislative reforms undertaken in some countries in the region to make full secondary education mandatory, here households with at least one child or adolescent (aged from 6 to 17 years) not attending an educational institution are considered to be deprived.

[16] No differentiated cut-offs have been set for urban and rural areas in relation to the use of cooking fuel, since the very harmful effects of the use of toxic fuels are believed to take precedence over cultural differences or differences in resources.

At any rate, the increase of school coverage has led to a substantial increase in enrolment in primary and secondary education in the region. This index therefore includes a schooling gap indicator, following the example of the national poverty measurements in Mexico (National Council for the Evaluation of Social Development Policy (CONEVAL), 2010) and Colombia (Angulo, Díaz and Pardo Pinzón, 2013). Although imperfect, the schooling gap indicator provides a proxy for the quality of education children receive (and reflects the education system's inability to help children progress through the levels of schooling at an adequate pace), which can be used to supplement the indicator of school attendance. A household is understood to be deprived when at least one child between 6 and 17 years is lagging behind their school year group. A cut-off of two years or more was used, since a cut-off of one year could give rise to confusion as a result of the particularities of school years, effective school starting ages and the date on which the countries take measurements.[17]

Given that the school attendance and schooling gap indicators are insufficient to determine the educational status of the adults in the household, an indicator on completion of education is also included for the members of the household aged 20 years or over. Usually the deprivation cut-off is completion of primary education, but people in Latin America now require a level of education far beyond primary school to have a good chance of escaping income poverty (Villatoro, 2007). The cut-off used here for persons aged between 20 and 59 years is completion of lower-secondary education, while that for those of 60 years or over remains completion of primary school.

In turn, attending school, progressing through the school system or completing a given level of schooling does not ensure the acquisition of knowledge and cognitive tools needed to overcome poverty and participate adequately in the knowledge society and networks (which requires skills such as the ability to analyse written texts, process information, build relationships and come up with new ideas). However, household surveys in the region do not currently include indicators of cognitive skills for either children of school age or adults.

So far, only indicators frequently used in multidimensional measurements of poverty have been selected. Naturally, any comprehensive measurement of poverty requires data on other aspects. It would be particularly relevant to include indicators of people's health and nutritional status (Santos, 2013), but this information is not available for a sufficient number of countries in the region. Indeed, the health dimension is notably absent from household surveys in Latin America. Very little information is generally collected on this dimension, and the indicators used vary greatly from country to country in those that do compile more comprehensive information. It is therefore essential to increase the amount of information collected on this dimension in household surveys in the near future (see box I.3).

One of the innovations of this index is the inclusion of deprivations stemming from precarious links with institutions, a hardship affecting people in their relations with other members of society. Thus, alongside the more extreme deprivations, which have typically been part of the absolute measures of poverty, the index also includes deprivations that reflect relative disadvantage. In the Latin American region, these include living in socially segregated urban areas,[18] access to only poor quality services (education, health, transport, housing, among others), and lack of connection to social networks and institutional frameworks that would facilitate dealing with shocks and accessing opportunities of upward mobility (Kaztman, 2001).

One of the most important mechanisms for ensuring social inclusion is employment. The International Labour Organization (ILO) has stated that work is a source of personal dignity, family stability and peace in the community. The concept of decent work expresses the principle that people should have safe, worthwhile jobs that they may carry out in conditions of freedom and equity.[19] Decent work is characterized by the safeguarding of labour rights and the presence of social protection and social dialogue.

There is, however, no internationally accepted method for measuring decent work, and a cut-off to determine it may be set too high for the purposes of measuring poverty in Latin America. As a first step, an unemployment indicator

17 For example, it could be assumed that in a given country the school year begins in March and that the official age for entering the first year of primary education is 6 years. If a child turning six in June is not admitted in the first year for being younger than the official age, he or she will begin school at age seven; with a cut-off of one year he or she would be considered to be lagging behind.

18 This dimension was not included in the measurements made here owing to data limitations.

19 See the ILO website for further details [online] http://www.ilo.org/global/about-the-ilo/decent-work-agenda/lang--en/index.htm.

has been included in the multidimensional poverty index, both because of the importance of the issue and the fact that it is one of the most commonly covered aspects in surveys of the countries of the region.

Although unemployment is considered to be one of the causes of monetary poverty, comparative evidence at international level suggests that there is no linear correlation between these two phenomena (Atkinson and others, 2002). Unemployment is included in this index because of the risk it implies of social exclusion and detachment from the lifestyle and the prevailing culture of society (Atkinson and others, 2002). People deemed to be deprived in this regard are those living in households where at least one person of working age is in any of the following situations: (i) unemployed; (ii) employed without pay; or (iii) discouraged (able to work but having ceased to look for employment).[20]

Access to adequate social protection is a fundamental right enshrined in international labour standards and recognized by the United Nations and, as such, a principle of the ILO decent work agenda.[21] There are in fact very serious shortcomings in terms of social protection in Latin America: the segmented nature of the structure of production means that the poorest individuals work in informal jobs with either precarious social protection arrangements or no social protection whatsoever (Katzman, 2010).

The question of whether people have access to adequate social protection cannot be directly determined from household surveys. Recent practice in the multidimensional measurement of poverty in the region has been to consider lack of access to social protection —in terms of health insurance coverage, affiliation to social protection schemes and receipt of pensions— as deprivation (see CONEVAL, 2010; Angulo Pardo Diaz and Finch, 2013; ECLAC, 2013).

This index uses the approach taken by ECLAC (2013) to social protection, with some modifications. Households in which no member has any form of contributory insurance (based on mandatory or voluntary contributions from individuals) are considered to be deprived in respect of social protection. This cut-off is used for both social security and health, and has the advantage of using a constant delimiting criterion across the different indicators of social protection.

As for social security, people living in households where no member is either affiliated to a social security system (or contributes to one) or receives any contribution-based pension or retirement benefits are considered to be deprived. Receipt of a non-contribution-based pension (such as a solidarity-based or basic pension) is thus insufficient to prevent an individual being considered deprived in respect of social security.

With regard to health insurance, households in which no member is covered by a contribution-based health insurance scheme are considered to be deprived. This definition was adopted on the basis that, to a greater or lesser degree, fees in the health systems of all of the countries covered by this indicator are adjusted for purchasing power.

The cut-off employed for health insurance differs from that of ECLAC (2013), which deemed households not to be deprived in this respect if they had health insurance of any kind. This criterion presented problems of comparability, since it judged differently two households in different countries but in similar situations in respect of access to health care.[22]

---

20 The indicator used here follows the guidelines proposed by Atkinson and others (2002) (the "jobless households" indicator), as a social indicator for the European Union (pp. 144-147). The possibility of counting as deprivations certain situations where people do not participate in the labour market for other reasons (as a result of employment discrimination, responsibilities associated with the care economy or cultural bias, for instance) was considered but, since this would have led to very high incidences of employment derivation, it was decided to leave them out.

21 See ILO [online] http://ilo.org/global/about-the-ilo/decent-work-agenda/social-protection/lang--en/index.htm.

22 For example, in Chile almost the entire population has some form of health insurance; in Argentina, meanwhile, a portion of the population has no insurance but the public health system is required to treat them free of charge. In respect of the hierarchical stratification of users of the systems, the proportion of Chileans holding a free card (i.e. those living in indigence) are in a position similar in relative terms to those without insurance in Argentina. The difference is that in Chile means testing is carried out to ascertain and categorize the most vulnerable in society, while in the Argentine system relies on a self-selection that does not explicitly classify the most vulnerable. In terms of figures, under the definition of deprivation of ECLAC (2013), there is practically no deprivation in Chile (what is more, the proportion of uninsured people is spread more or less evenly across the different socioeconomic groups). When a cut-off based on contribution-based insurance is used, the levels of deprivation are similar in the two countries.

The definition of deprivation in respect of health insurance used here can be taken as a proxy for the quality of the health-care services people receive, provided that individuals or households able to pay more rationally prefer health protection schemes that provide the best quality of care. However, owing to the opacity of health insurance markets, this is not necessarily the case.

In respect of social linkages, one dimension that was considered but ultimately rejected was deprivations in access to information and communications technology (ICT). While there is extensive literature on the existence of a digital divide that reproduces socioeconomic gaps, the emergence of mobile telephony in the region compromises the effectiveness of this dimension. At present, access to Internet-enabled mobile telephones tends to cut across different socioeconomic groups, so assessing deprivations in access to information and networks via technological devices does not seem appropriate.

What is more, including deprivations in terms of links with other people or institutions would most likely mean exceeding the scope of the conventional notion of poverty, which could lead to a greater likelihood of inclusion error. However, this risk is reduced by using a method of aggregation under which the presence of just one deprivation is insufficient to identify a household as poor. Some of these indicators serve, albeit imperfectly, as a proxy for the dimensions of health and employment, which are important aspects of well-being.

3. Building the index

The index was developed on the basis of the methodology described in Alkire and Foster (2007 and 2011) (see box I.4 for further details). This entailed: (i) choosing the dimensions and indicators and weighting them; (ii) setting the multidimensional cut-off (k) or the proportion of deprivations that a subject must suffer in order to be considered poor; and (iii) calculating the deprivation score for each person and determining, by comparing the score and the value of k, whether he or she is multidimensionally poor.

Table I.3 shows the dimensions, indicators and weighting structure of the index. All the deprivations are weighted the same (7.4%), except for social protection (3.7%) and income (14.8%). Deprivations in social protection were weighted less for two reasons: (i) because they are hardships that account for a lack of well-being that goes a step beyond the traditional concept of poverty, and (ii) because otherwise the effective weight of this dimension, which is created by combining the weighting and the selected cut-off, would have been very high, thus leading to something of an imbalance between dimensions in the index.[23] Income, in turn, is weighted more because it is itself a synthetic indicator that reflects insufficiencies in various dimensions of well-being. The other indicators used do not have this characteristic.

The union approach was not used to calculate the multidimensional cut-off k, as it requires only one deprivation for a household to be identified as poor, thus greatly increasing the likelihood of errors of inclusion because all of the indicators have measurement errors.[24] The intersection method, which requires that a household be deprived in all dimensions, was not used either since it markedly increases the probability of errors of exclusion.

For the purposes of this index an intermediate criterion was preferred, k=25%. With this value, persons identified as poor must be deprived in the equivalent of an entire dimension plus one other indicator, or must be deprived in income and have at least two additional deprivations. Setting this k value also ensured that no individual deprived in just one dimension could be identified as multidimensionally poor,[25] thus reducing the chances of inclusion error.

Because there is an element of discretion in selecting weightings and cut-offs, it is very important to establish whether the estimates provided by the index are sufficiently robust. In particular, checks need to be made to ascertain whether the ranking of countries tends to be similar when different values are used for the multidimensional cut-off and changes are made to the weightings of the dimensions or indicators. As box I.5 shows, the index remains robust for changes to weightings, indicators, deprivation cut-offs and k values.

23 The effective weighting of each indicator is determined by two factors: the relative weighting accorded in the aggregation of the index and the cut-off selected. Thus, indicators with high cut-offs, which yield high rates of deprivation, have a greater influence in ascertaining poverty, although the relative weight assigned is equal to that of other indicators. This is the case with the social protection indicator.

24 This risk is greater when insufficiencies going beyond those traditionally associated with poverty are included.

25 The maximum score that can be obtained by a person deprived in respect of all indicators in a single dimension is 22.2%.

Table I.3

Multidimensional poverty index: dimensions, deprivation indicators and weightings

Dimensions	Deprivation indicators: persons living in...	Weighting (percentages)
Dwelling		22.2%
Makeshift building materials[a]	Dwellings with a dirt floor or walls or roof of makeshift materials (waste material, cardboard, cans, thatch, palm fronds, straw or other materials).	7.4%
Overcrowding[b]	Households with three or more people per room, rural and urban areas.	7.4%
Insecure housing tenure[c]	Households: (i) living as squatters; or (ii) living in ceded or borrowed housing.	7.4%
Basic services		22.2%
Lack of access to improved water sources[d]	Urban areas: Households obtaining water from: -Mains network off the premises -Unprotected wells or lacking a motor pump -Mobile sources (village tank, tank cart, tanker truck, etc.) - Bottled water - River, stream, rainwater, other Rural areas: households obtaining water from: -Unprotected wells or with a hand pump -Mobile sources (village tank, tank cart, tanker truck, etc.) - Bottled water - River, stream, rainwater, other	7.4%
Lack of improved sanitation[d]	Urban areas: -Waste not connected to a sewer system or septic tank -Shared toilet -No sanitation Rural areas: -No sanitation -Shared toilet -Waste going untreated to ground surface, river or sea.	7.4%
Lack of source of energy[e]	Households without electricity or using firewood, coal or waste for cooking.	7.4%
Living standard		22.2%
Insufficient resources	Households with insufficient per capita income to meet food and non-food needs.	14.8%
Lack of durable goods[f]	Households that have none of the following goods: (i) vehicle; (ii) refrigerator; (iii) washing machine.	7.4%
Education		22.2%
Non-attendance at school	Household has at least one child of school age (6 to 17 years old) who does not attend school.	7.4%
Schooling gap	Household has at least one child or adolescent aged 6 to 17 who is more than two years behind schooling grade for age.	7.4%
Low educational attainment	Household has nobody aged 20 or above with a minimum level of schooling. - Persons aged 20 to 59: have not completed lower secondary education. - Persons aged 60 and above: have not completed primary education.	7.4%
Employment and social protection		11.1%
Unemployment	Household has at least one person aged 15 to 65 in one of the following situations: - Unemployed - Employed without pay - Discouraged worker	7.4%
Lack of social protection[g]	Household meets all the following conditions: - Nobody has any kind of contributory or co-payment health insurance - Nobody is affiliated with a contributory social security system - Nobody has income from a pension or contribution-based retirement scheme	3.7%

Source: Economic Commission for Latin America and the Caribbean (ECLAC) on the basis of Santos and others (2014).

[a] No information was available on walls for Argentina (2005 and 2012), on floors for Brazil (2005 and 2012), on roofs for Colombia (2008 and 2012) and Ecuador (2005), or on dwelling materials for Uruguay (2005).

[b] The correction proposed by Katzman was used for non-exclusion of kitchen and/or toilet regarded as rooms for Brazil, Costa Rica, Honduras and Mexico (see Katzman, 2011).

[c] Living in housing given in usufruct is not considered housing deprivation.

[d] For the Dominican Republic (2006 and 2012), urban criterion applies to rural areas because the question does not allow for other criteria.

[e] No information was available on electricity for Argentina (2005 and 2012), Dominican Republic (2006) and Uruguay (2005); no information on fuel for Bolivarian Republic of Venezuela (2005 and 2012), Chile (2003 and 2011), and Honduras (2006).

[f] No information was available on goods for Argentina (2005 and 2012) and Plurinational State of Bolivia (2003); no information on vehicle for Brazil (2005), replaced with cooking stove; no information on vehicle for Chile (2003), replaced by water heater; no information on washing machine for Costa Rica (2012) no information on washing machine, replaced by plasma or liquid crystal display (LCD) television set; no information on washing machine for Honduras (2010 and 2006), replaced with cook stove.

[g] No information on health insurance for Brazil (2005 and 2012) and the Bolivarian Republic of Venezuela (2005 and 2012), the indicator for social protection is not included for Nicaragua (2009) because of lack of information on pension and health insurance affiliation.

Lastly, all the deprivations included in the index are operationalized at the household level. This is not only because of issues related to data characteristics, but also because many of the deprivations experienced in principle individually have important externalities for all members of the household. For example, income is obtained individually but is used to meet the needs of all members of the household. The same is true for health insurance and social security, which are usually contracted individually, but their benefits are extended to most or all household members (especially dependents). Even individual educational attainment and underperformance have positive or negative effects, respectively, on other household members (Basu and Foster, 1998). Furthermore, a considerable proportion of public policies target households.

Box I.4
The Alkire-Foster method

The Alkire-Foster method links the counting tradition, which identifies the poor by the number of deprivations that affect them, with the axiomatic tradition, which sets out a group of desirable properties that poverty measures must satisfy at the identification and aggregation stages.

The Alkire-Foster approach proposes: (i) an identification method ρk, which links and extends traditional intersection and union approaches, and (ii) a class of poverty measures $M\alpha$, which are extensions of the traditional measures proposed by Foster, Greer and Thorbecke (the FGT index), but adjusted for multidimensionality and satisfying a variety of axioms.

For the process of identification, the authors suggest a cut-off level k for ci (the number of weighted deprivations suffered by an individual) lying somewhere between $k=1$ and $k=d$. Thus, ρk (the identification method) identifies person i as poor when the number of weighted deprivations is at least k. Since ρk is dependent on both the within- dimension cut-off line zj and the across-dimension cut-off line k, ρk is a dual cut-off method of identification.

The basic input for the Alkire-Foster methodology is a deprivations matrix g0 = $[gij0]$, where each individual is assigned the value of zero when there is no deprivation, and the value of one when there is ($yij < zj$). Then the people's deprivation scores (ci) are calculated using the (weighted) sum of their score in the different dimensions, thus identifying who is poor ($ci \geq k$). The matrix is then censored ($g0k$), which means that the deprivations of the non-poor are excluded (they are assigned a value of zero).

The Alkire and Foster measurement used to construct the multidimensional poverty index presented in this chapter is the adjusted headcount ratio (M0). This is made up of two basic indicators: the poverty headcount ratio (H) and the poverty intensity rate (A), as defined below:

- The headcount ratio (H) is the proportion of individuals identified as poor. $H=q/n$, where q is the number of poor people and n is the total population.
- The poverty intensity rate (A): is the (weighted) average of the deprivations suffered by people identified as poor: $A=\sum ci(k)/dq$.

To estimate A, it is necessary to calculate the proportion of deprivations experienced by individuals, taking ci(k)/d the censored vector of deprivation counts as a benchmark (discounting deprivations among the non-poor). This value is then divided by the total number of poor individuals (q).

The adjusted headcount ratio (M0) is the result of multiplying H by A.

Source: Economic Commission for Latin America and the Caribbean (ECLAC), on the basis of S. Alkire and J. Foster, "Counting and multidimensional poverty measurement", *Journal of Public Economics*, vol. 95, No. 7–8, 2011; and "Counting and multidimensional poverty measurement", *OPHI Working Paper*, No. 7, 2007.

4. Findings

The methodology described was used to estimate the percentage of poor in 17 countries in Latin America, around 2005 and 2012. In 2012, approximately 28% of the region's population was living in multidimensional poverty. The highest levels were in Nicaragua (74.1%), Honduras (70.5%), Guatemala (70.3%), and the Plurinational State of Bolivia (58%). The lowest levels were in Chile (6.8%), Argentina (8.1%), Uruguay (9%), Brazil (14.5%) and Costa Rica (14.9%) (see figure I.8).

Multidimensional poverty incidence declined in all the countries between 2005 and 2012. The sharpest decreases were in Argentina, Uruguay, Brazil, Peru, Chile and the Bolivarian Republic of Venezuela, equivalent to a decrease in the headcount ratio of 7% or more per year, while El Salvador, Mexico, Honduras and Nicaragua posted decreases of 1% or less per year.

Poverty reduction was steeper in countries with lower baseline incidence (around 2005). However, the Plurinational State of Bolivia, Ecuador, Paraguay and the Dominican Republic, where the baseline incidence was in excess of 45%, posted very significant reductions in poverty (of between 3% and 6% per year).

A complementary method of quantifying poverty is determining its intensity. This indicator is obtained by dividing the weighted deprivation values of poor individuals in all dimensions (indicators) by the total number of poor (see box I.4).

Figure I.9 shows that the intensity of poverty declined in all of the countries under review between the two years considered, especially in Peru, the Plurinational State of Bolivia Argentina and Uruguay, which saw decreases of between around 1.7% and 2.8% per year.

In both around 2005 and 2012, poverty was most intense in countries with the highest incidence of poverty. In these countries, then, are not only are there more poor individuals, but the poor are deprived in more dimensions.

Figure I.8
Latin America (17 countries): incidence of multidimensional poverty around 2005 and 2012
(Percentages of the population)

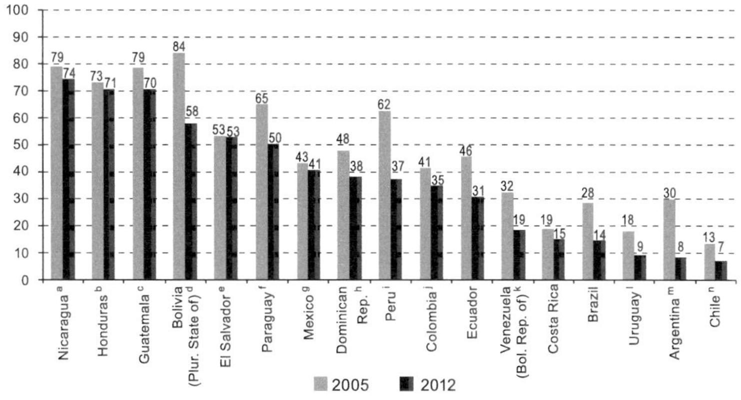

Source: Economic Commission for Latin America and the Caribbean (ECLAC), on the basis of special tabulations of data from household surveys conducted in the respective countries.

[a] Data for Nicaragua refer to 2005 and 2009.
[b] Data for Honduras refer to 2006 and 2010.
[c] Data for Guatemala refer to 2000 and 2006.
[d] Data for the Plurinational State of Bolivia refer to 2003 and 2011.
[e] Data for El Salvador refer to 2004 and 2012.
[f] ata for Paraguay refer to 2005 and 2011.
[g] Data for Mexico refer to 2004 and 2012.
[h] Data for the Dominican Republic refer to 2006 and 2012.
[i] ata for Peru refer to 2003 and 2012.
[j] Data for Colombia refer to 2008 and 2012
[k] Data for the Bolivarian Republic of Venezuela for 2005 and 2012 refer to urban areas.
[l] Data for Uruguay for 2005 refer to urban areas.
[m] Data for Argentina for 2005 and 2012 refer to urban areas.
[n] Data for Chile refer to 2003 and 2011.

Figure I.9
Latin America (17 countries): intensity of multidimensional poverty, around 2005 and 2012 [a]
(Percentages of deprivation suffered by poor households)

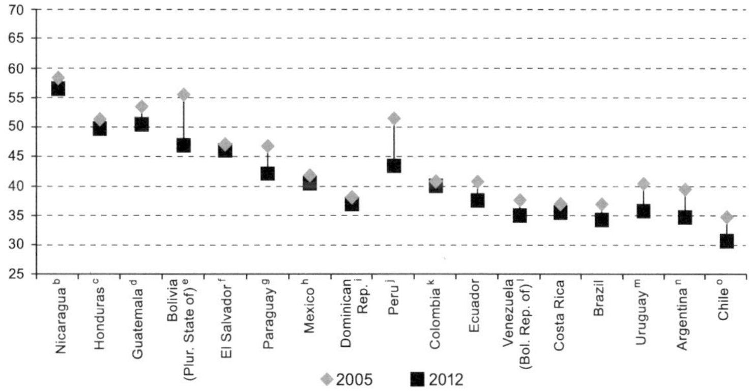

Source: Economic Commission for Latin America and the Caribbean (ECLAC), on the basis of special tabulations of data from household surveys conducted in the respective countries.

[a] Countries shown in order of poverty incidence around 2012.
[b] Data for Nicaragua refer to 2005 and 2009.
[c] Data for Honduras refer to 2006 and 2010.
[d] Data for Guatemala refer to 2000 and 2006.
[e] Data for the Plurinational State of Bolivia refer to 2003 and 2011.
[f] Data for El Salvador refer to 2004 and 2012.
[g] Data for Paraguay refer to 2005 and 2011.
[h] Data for Mexico refer to 2004 and 2012.
[i] Data for the Dominican Republic refer to 2006 and 2012.
[j] Data for Peru refer to 2003 and 2012.
[k] Data for Colombia refer to 2008 and 2012.
[l] Data for the Bolivarian Republic of Venezuela for 2005 and 2012 refer to urban areas.
[m] Data for Uruguay for 2005 refer to urban areas.
[n] Data for Argentina for 2005 and 2012 refer to urban areas.
[o] Data for Chile refer to 2003 and 2011.

Figure I.10 presents the incidence of multidimensional poverty by area of residence around 2012. In all the countries, a higher percentage of the population was poor in rural than in urban areas. The highest rural poverty levels were in Nicaragua, Guatemala, Honduras and the Plurinational State of Bolivia. The pattern was very similar for urban poverty, which also had the highest incidence in these four countries.

Figure I.10

Latin America (15 countries): rate of multidimensional poverty by area of residence, around 2012 [a]

(Percentages)

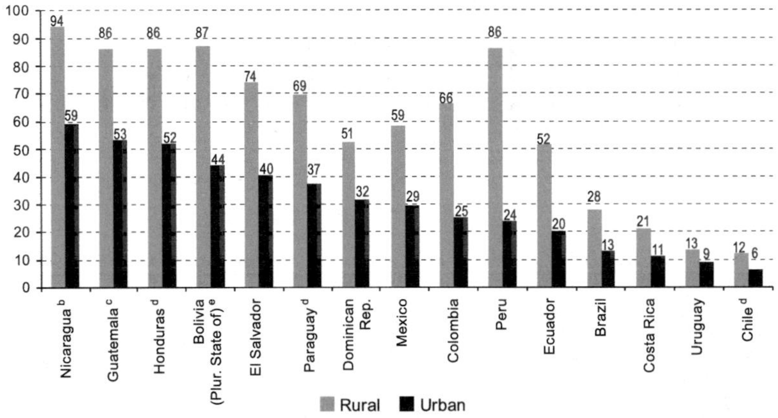

Source: Economic Commission for Latin America and the Caribbean (ECLAC), on the basis of special tabulations of data from household surveys conducted in the respective countries.

[a] Countries shown in order of poverty incidence around 2012.

[b] Data for Nicaragua refer to 2009.

[c] Data for Guatemala refer to 2006.

[d] Data for Honduras refer to 2010.

[e] Data for Chile, Paraguay and the Plurinational State of Bolivia refer to 2011.

Regarding changes in poverty incidence by area of residence between 2005 and 2012, in all countries poverty fell more in rural areas than in urban areas. The greatest differences between the declines in rural and urban poverty were in Peru, the Plurinational State of Bolivia, Ecuador, Brazil and Paraguay.

It is therefore not surprising that the largest increases in imbalances between rural and urban headcount rates occurred in some of these countries. In Peru, for example, rural poverty was 3.6 times urban poverty in 2012, compared to twice in 2003; in the Plurinational State of Bolivia, the ratio rose from 1.8 times in 2003 to 2.6 times in 2011; and in Ecuador, this ratio was twice in 2012, compared to 1.3 times in 2005 (see figure I.11).

Around 2012, rural poverty was more intense than urban poverty in practically all countries, with the sole exception of Uruguay. The most intense rural poverty around 2012 was seen in Nicaragua, the Plurinational State of Bolivia, Honduras and Guatemala. In urban areas, meanwhile, poverty was most intense in Nicaragua, Guatemala, El Salvador and Honduras (see figure I.12).

The largest reductions in rural poverty intensity between 2005 and 2012 took place in Peru, the Plurinational State of Bolivia, Ecuador, Paraguay and Chile. Trends in rural poverty in the first four countries merit special attention. In these countries, poverty rates fell much less in rural areas than in urban areas, but the intensity of rural poverty declined considerably. In other words, although a large proportion of the rural population in these countries remained in poverty in 2012, they were deprived in fewer dimensions than around 2005. Rural poverty intensity increased slightly in El Salvador, meanwhile, and remained constant in Costa Rica.

In respect of urban poverty intensity, the greatest reductions between 2005 and 2012 were seen in the Plurinational State of Bolivia, Peru, Chile and Paraguay, while levels in Nicaragua and Honduras remained practically unchanged.

Figure I.11
Latin America (14 countries): ratio of rural and urban multidimensional poverty rates, around 2005 and 2012 [a]
(Number of times)

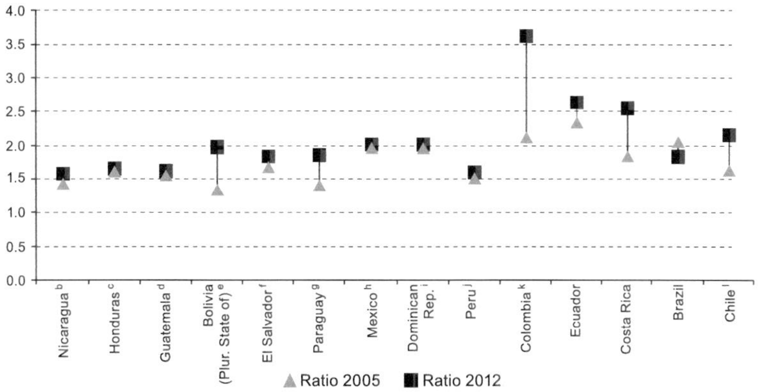

Source: Economic Commission for Latin America and the Caribbean (ECLAC), on the basis of special tabulations of data from household surveys conducted in the respective countries.
[a] Countries shown in order of the incidence of poverty at national level around 2012.
[b] Data for Nicaragua refer to 2005 and 2009.
[c] Data for Honduras refer to 2006 and 2010.
[d] Data for Guatemala refer to 2000 and 2006.
[e] Data for the Plurinational State of Bolivia refer to 2003 and 2011.
[f] Data for El Salvador refer to 2004 and 2012.
[g] Data for Paraguay refer to 2005 and 2011.
[h] Data for Mexico refer to 2004 and 2012.
[i] Data for the Dominican Republic refer to 2006 and 2012.
[j] Data for Peru refer to 2003 and 2012.
[k] Data for Colombia refer to 2008 and 2012.
[l] Data for Chile refer to 2003 and 2011.

Figure I.12
Latin America (15 countries): intensity of multidimensional poverty by area of residence, around 2012 [a]
(Percentages of deprivation suffered by poor households)

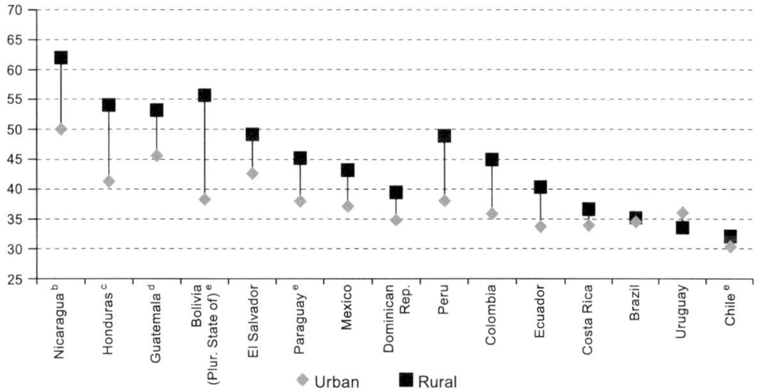

Source: Economic Commission for Latin America and the Caribbean (ECLAC), on the basis of special tabulations of data from household surveys conducted in the respective countries.
[a] Countries shown in order of poverty incidence at national level around 2012.
[b] Data for Nicaragua refer to 2009.
[c] Data for Honduras refer to 2010.
[d] Data for Guatemala refer to 2006.
[e] Data for Chile, Paraguay and the Plurinational State of Bolivia refer to 2011.

As noted above, a headcount ratio such as the indicator of poverty intensity can provide useful information for quantifying poverty from a multidimensional perspective. A way of synthesizing the information obtained in both indices is to calculate a measurement of overall poverty (M0), or adjusted headcount ratio by multiplying the unadjusted headcount ratio (or incidence of poverty) by the intensity of poverty (see box I.4).

Figure I.13 shows that the countries with the highest adjusted poverty headcount ratios (M0) around 2012 were Nicaragua, Guatemala and Honduras, while Chile, Argentina and Uruguay had the lowest. These ratios were generally higher in rural than in urban areas, with the widest disparities between areas of residence in the poorest countries.

Figure I.13

Latin America (17 countries): adjusted poverty headcount ratio (M0), total and by area of residence, around 2012

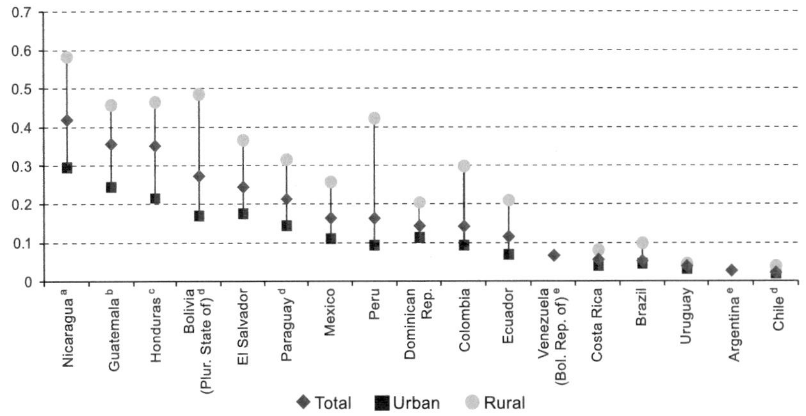

Source: Economic Commission for Latin America and the Caribbean (ECLAC), on the basis of special tabulations of data from household surveys conducted in the respective countries.

[a] Data for Nicaragua refer to 2009.

[b] Data for Guatemala refer to 2006.

[c] Data for Honduras refer to 2010.

[d] Data for Chile, Paraguay and the Plurinational State of Bolivia refer to 2011.

[e] Data for Argentina and the Bolivarian Republic of Venezuela refer to urban areas.

The adjusted poverty headcount ratio (M0) can be broken down to show the contribution made by each deprivation (and dimension) to overall poverty. Considering the simple average for the region, in 2012 income deprivations contributed the most to overall multidimensional poverty (28%). Next were deprivations in the educational attainment of adults in the household (12%), employment, social protection and sanitation (7% each), then deprivations in relation to overcrowding, energy and ownership of durable goods (6% each).

Figure I.14 shows the relative contributions of the various derivations to overall poverty in each country around 2012. The contribution of income to overall poverty tends to be larger in countries with the lowest adjusted incidence of poverty (M0). The largest contributions by monetary poverty were seen in Chile (41%), Brazil (37%) and the Bolivarian Republic of Venezuela (35%). The contribution of income to total poverty was below 25% in the five countries with the highest adjusted poverty rates (Nicaragua, Guatemala, Honduras, Plurinational State of Bolivia and El Salvador).

Precarious housing, insufficient energy and lack of durable goods contributed most to overall poverty in countries with higher levels of poverty (adjusted headcount ratios). By contrast, the contribution of unsecure housing tenure tended to be higher in countries with lower levels of poverty. For the rest of the deprivations, no substantial differences linked to the level of multidimensional poverty were found.

Table I.4 presents variations in the contribution of the various deprivations to overall poverty between around 2005 and 2012. As can be seen, the contributions of the different deprivations to the adjusted headcount ratio remained fairly stable in both periods under review. The most marked change was the drop of 20 percentage points in the contribution of income-based deprivation to total poverty in Argentina between 2005 and 2012. Another notable change was the fall in the contribution of the same deprivation (income) to total poverty in the Plurinational State of Bolivia (down by 15.8 percentage points between 2003 and 2011).

Tables I.5 and I.6 show the contributions of the various deprivations to total poverty around 2012, broken down by area of residence. In urban areas, considering the simple average of all countries, the largest contribution to the adjusted poverty index was made by income deprivation (31.8%), followed by the educational attainment of adults (11.6%), sanitation (8.2%), employment (7.4%), social protection (7.2%) and ownership of durable goods (6.3%). In rural areas, income deprivation was once more the largest contributor to total poverty (22.7%), ahead of educational attainment (13.2%), energy (10.1%) and ownership of durable goods (7.8%).

The most marked differences in contributions by area of residence are in deprivations relating to energy, housing materials and water, which contributed more to rural than urban poverty. Deprivations in sanitation and income, meanwhile, contribute more to poverty in urban areas than in rural areas.

Figure I.14

Latin America (17 countries): contribution of the various deprivations to overall poverty, around 2012 [a]

(Percentages)

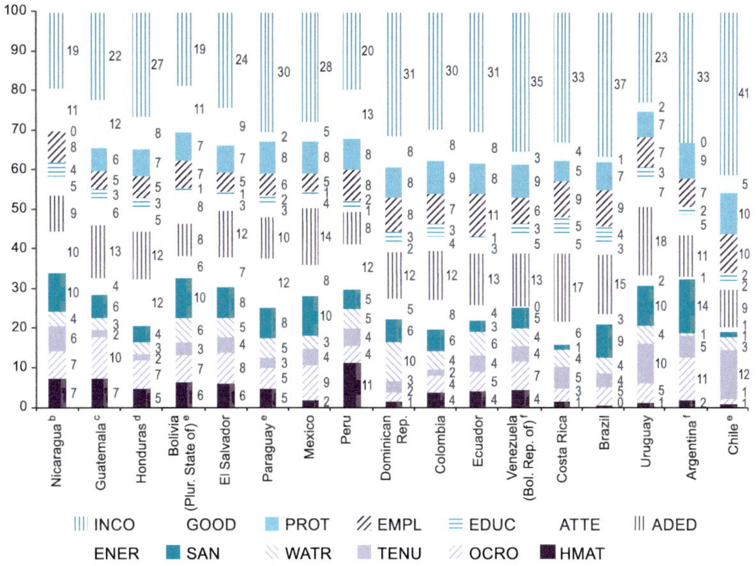

Source: Economic Commission for Latin America and the Caribbean (ECLAC), on the basis of special tabulations of data from household surveys conducted in the respective countries.

[a] Countries shown in order of adjusted headcount ratio (M0). Deprivations are abbreviated as follows: INCO=monetary income; GOOD=durable goods in the household; PROT=social protection; EMPL=employment; EDUC=low education achievement; ATTE=school attendance; ADED=educational attainment of adults; ENER=energy; SANI=sanitation; WATR=water; TENE=secure housing tenure; OCRO=overcrowding; HMAT=housing materials.

[b] Data for Nicaragua refer to 2009.

[c] Data for Guatemala refer to 2006.

[d] Data for Honduras refer to 2010.

[e] Data for Chile, Paraguay and the Plurinational State of Bolivia refer to 2011.

[f] Data for Argentina and the Bolivarian Republic of Venezuela refer to urban areas.

Table I.4

Latin America (17 countries): variations in the contribution of the various deprivations to overall poverty, around 2005 and 2012 [a]

(Percentage points)

Country	Years	HMAT	OCRO	TENU	WATR	SANI	ENER	ADED	ATTE	EDUC	EMPL	PROT	INCO	GOOD
Argentina [b]	2005 and 2012	0.7	4.5	2.6	-0.2	3.7	-0.2	3.2	2.7	0.3	0.5	2.2	-20.0	...
Bolivia (Plurinational State of) [c]	2003 and 2011	-0.6	-0.5	1.6	1.0	-2.0	-1.7	0.2	4.5	-0.7	1.6	1.0	-15.8	...
Brazil	2005 and 2012	0.2	-0.1	-0.1	-0.5	-0.7	-0.8	-0.3	-0.2	0.8	-0.3	1.4	-0.1	0.8
Chile	2003 and 2011	-0.6	-3.3	2.8	0.1	-3.4	-0.3	-1.1	-0.7	0.0	1.6	2.5	7.0	-4.6
Colombia	2008 and 2012	0.5	-0.1	0.8	0.6	0.7	0.2	-0.4	0.0	0.1	0.5	0.1	-1.7	-1.3
Costa Rica	2005 and 2012	-1.1	-0.3	0.6	1.4	0.4	-0.6	-0.8	-1.0	-0.8	1.2	-0.6	0.8	0.9
Dominican Republic	2006 and 2012	0.0	0.3	0.8	0.4	-0.5	0.3	-0.4	0.1	-1.4	-0.4	-0.8	0.1	1.6
Ecuador	2005 and 2012	-1.1	-1.6	1.2	-1.1	-4.0	-0.4	0.5	-1.6	-0.4	3.6	0.0	0.1	5.0
El Salvador	2004 and 2012	0.9	-1.4	0.3	0.3	1.2	0.1	-0.7	-0.5	-0.9	0.8	0.2	0.5	-0.9
Guatemala	2000 and 2006	-0.6	-0.2	-0.5	0.0	0.2	-1.4	0.3	-0.9	0.2	0.5	0.0	2.5	-0.1
Honduras	2006 and 2010	-0.8	-1.2	-0.1	-0.6	-0.9	5.4	-0.6	-0.4	-1.1	1.7	0.2	0.0	-1.5
Mexico	2004 and 2012	-2.7	-1.1	0.9	1.4	-2.0	4.2	-0.7	-0.9	-0.7	0.9	0.4	1.2	-0.6
Nicaragua [d]	2005 and 2009	0.6	0.7	-0.2	0.4	1.0	0.3	-0.1	0.7	-0.7	2.9	...	-0.2	-0.2
Paraguay	2005 and 2011	0.5	-0.2	0.4	-1.7	0.2	0.3	-0.7	0.0	-0.6	0.0	0.8	4.0	-3.1
Peru	2003 and 2012	0.8	-0.8	1.7	-1.3	-1.7	0.2	0.5	1.0	-1.0	-0.3	1.0	-3.3	3.1
Uruguay [e]	2005 and 2012	...	-1.7	-5.7	0.9	4.3	2.4	3.7	2.9	0.3	-1.7	1.7	-6.8	-1.5
Venezuela (Bolivarian Republic of) [f]	2005 and 2012	-0.1	-0.4	1.0	0.7	0.4	-0.2	-1.2	0.2	-0.6	-0.7	0.7	2.7	-2.6
Simple average		**-0.2**	**-0.4**	**0.5**	**0.1**	**-0.2**	**0.5**	**0.1**	**0.3**	**-0.4**	**0.7**	**0.7**	**-1.7**	**-0.3**

Source: Economic Commission for Latin America and the Caribbean (ECLAC), on the basis of special tabulations of data from household surveys conducted in the respective countries.

[a] Deprivations are abbreviated as follows: HMAT=housing materials; OCRO=overcrowding; TENU=secure housing tenure; WATR=water; SANI=sanitation; ENER=energy; ADED=educational attainment of adults; ATTE=school attendance; EDUC=low education achievement; EMPL=employment; PROT=social protection; INCO=monetary income; GOOD=durable goods in the household.

[b] Data refer to urban areas; information on goods in the household is not available.

[c] Information not available on goods in the household.

[d] No estimate was made for deprivations in social protection for 2009 owing to a lack of information on social security affiliation and health insurance.

[e] Data for Uruguay from 2005 refer to urban areas and include no information on housing materials.

[f] Data refer to urban areas.

Table I.5
Latin America (15 countries): contribution of the various deprivations to overall poverty in urban areas, around 2012 [a]
(Percentages)

Country	Year	HMAT	OCRO	TENU	WATR	SANI	ENER	ADED	ATTE	EDUC	EMPL	PROT	INCO	GOOD
Nicaragua [b]	2009	6	6	7	2	11	9	9	4	3	8	....	24	10
Guatemala	2006	5	10	2	3	10	3	14	5	2	4	6	24	12
Honduras	2010	2	8	3	1	7	8	12	4	3	7	7	33	5
Bolivia (Plurinational State of)	2011	3	9	5	3	13	1	7	11	1	5	9	22	12
El Salvador	2012	4	7	4	5	11	4	11	2	1	5	7	28	9
Paraguay	2011	2	4	3	5	13	9	10	2	2	5	8	35	1
Mexico	2012	1	10	6	2	12	3	14	4	1	4	8	33	3
Peru	2012	10	5	8	5	6	8	7	2	1	7	8	22	13
Dominican Republic	2012	1	2	2	8	8	2	10	3	3	10	8	35	7
Colombia	2012	2	5	2	3	6	2	12	4	3	9	9	37	7
Ecuador	2012	2	5	5	5	2	1	12	3	1	11	9	39	5
Costa Rica	2012	1	3	5	4	1	1	17	4	5	10	5	39	3
Brazil	2012	0	5	3	5	10	1	15	3	4	8	7	38	1
Uruguay	2012	1	5	10	4	11	1	17	7	3	7	7	24	2
Chile	2011	0	1	12	1	2	1	8	2	2	10	10	45	4
Simple average		**3**	**6**	**5**	**4**	**8**	**4**	**12**	**4**	**2**	**7**	**7**	**32**	**6**

Source: Economic Commission for Latin America and the Caribbean (ECLAC), on the basis of special tabulations of data from household surveys conducted in the respective countries.

[a] Countries shown in order of poverty incidence around 2012. Deprivations are abbreviated as follows: HMAT=housing materials; OCRO=overcrowding; TENU=secure housing tenure; WATR=water; SANI=sanitation; ENER=energy; ADED=educational attainment of adults; ATTE=school attendance; EDUC=low education achievement; EMPL=employment; PROT=social protection; INCO=monetary income; GOOD=durable goods in the household.

[b] No estimate was made of the social protection indicator owing to a lack of information on health insurance and social security affiliation.

Table I.6
Latin America (15 countries): contribution of the various deprivations to overall poverty in rural areas, around 2012 [a]
(Percentages)

Country	Year	HMAT	OCRO	TENU	WATR	SANI	ENER	ADED	ATTE	EDUC	EMPL	PROT	INCO	GOOD
Nicaragua [b]	2009	8	7	6	5	9	12	9	5	4	8	.....	17	11
Guatemala	2006	9	11	2	3	4	5	13	6	3	5	6	21	12
Honduras	2010	6	7	1	3	3	13	13	6	3	5	7	24	9
Bolivia (Plurinational State of)	2011	9	6	2	9	8	8	9	6	1	8	6	17	11
El Salvador	2012	8	8	4	5	5	10	12	4	2	5	7	21	10
Paraguay	2011	7	6	2	5	4	15	11	4	2	6	8	27	3
Mexico	2012	2	8	3	4	9	12	14	4	1	5	8	24	6
Peru	2012	13	4	2	6	4	14	9	1	2	9	7	18	12
Dominican Republic	2012	2	2	4	12	3	9	13	2	3	7	8	28	8
Colombia	2012	5	4	2	6	6	13	13	4	3	6	8	23	9
Ecuador	2012	5	5	3	6	3	6	14	4	1	11	7	25	9
Costa Rica	2012	2	3	6	4	1	10	17	5	4	8	6	29	5
Brazil	2012	1	2	6	1	4	8	17	2	4	12	8	33	2
Uruguay	2012	5	2	10	10	6	14	19	8	1	8	6	8	2
Chile	2011	2	2	14	10	1	3	15	2	2	7	10	27	7
Simple average		**6**	**5**	**4**	**6**	**5**	**10**	**13**	**4**	**2**	**7**	**7**	**23**	**8**

Source: Economic Commission for Latin America and the Caribbean (ECLAC), on the basis of special tabulations of data from household surveys conducted in the respective countries.

[a] Countries shown in order of poverty incidence around 2012. Deprivations are abbreviated as follows: HMAT=housing materials; OCRO=overcrowding; TENU=secure housing tenure; WATR=water; SANI=sanitation; ENER=energy; ADED=educational attainment of adults; ATTE=school attendance; EDUC=low education achievement; EMPL=employment; PROT=social protection; INCO=monetary income; GOOD=durable goods in the household.

[b] No estimate was made of the social protection indicator owing to a lack of information on health insurance and social security affiliation.

5. Final remarks

In conclusion, the results of applying this index for multidimensional poverty measurement show that the deprivations suffered by the poor vary from country to country in respect of intensity and the forms they take. This heterogeneity must therefore be taken into account in drawing up effective policies to overcome poverty, as the same policy solutions are unlikely to yield similar results in all countries.

Furthermore, the evidence that poverty manifests itself in many areas shows just how urgent it is to devise and implement poverty reduction-related policies in a coordinated manner across multiple sectors. More specifically, although income insufficiencies are an important component of the set of deprivations affecting poor households, they are not the only hardships that they suffer. Since several of the non-monetary deprivations cannot be adequately resolved by marginal increases in household income, the reduction of poverty necessitates, in addition to cash transfers, substantial efforts to be made in the field of housing policy (especially concerning housing materials and overcrowding) and the provision of basic utilities (water, sanitation and energy), particularly in the poorest countries.

Box I.5

Robustness of the multidimensional poverty index

In the development of any measurement of poverty a series of decisions need to be taken that affect the estimates obtained. The indicators and deprivation cut-offs and their weightings must be selected, and the multidimensional poverty threshold "k" —the proportion of deprivations that are required to identify a person as poor— has to be set. If changing these parameters substantially alters the order in which countries are ranked, the index is unlikely to be sufficiently robust to provide effective guidance in public policymaking. In this case, the evidence shows that the proposed index is extremely robust to changes in these parameters.

One way of analysing degree of robustness is to modify k values without changing the structure of the index (indicators and weightings). For a ranking to be robust, a country that is poorer than another with a given k value must remain so when other k values are set. When all k values between 10% and 70% were considered, 93% of all possible comparisons between pairs of observations were robust.[a] When k values were restricted to a range of between 20% and 40%, the percentage of robust comparisons rose to 98%.

The Spearman and Kendall rank correlation coefficients are also high between the rankings of countries with the different k values used. The Kendall coefficient for k values between 10% and 70% varies between 0.89 and 0.99, while the Spearman coefficient ranges between 0.98 and 0.99. The robustness of the index to changes in the k value is shown in the figure below, which presents the adjusted headcount ratios (M0) with the various k values for the 34 observations.[b]

Latin America (17 countries): adjusted headcount ratio (M0) of extreme poverty with different k values, around 2005 and 2012

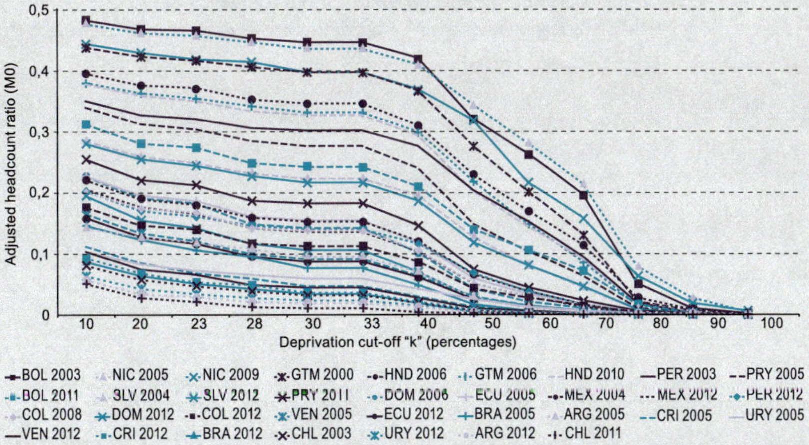

Source: Economic Commission for Latin America and the Caribbean (ECLAC).

The robustness of the index to simultaneous changes to its structure (indicators, cut-offs and weightings) and k values was then checked. Twenty-nine possible structures (specifications) were analysed, including the following:

- 14 structures were estimated for all countries and years. The structures had different weightings and sets of indicators, and seven alternative k values (of between 10% and 70%) were considered, resulting in a total of 98 variants. It was found that 85% of all possible comparisons between pairs of observations were robust to these 98 variants. When the alternatives were restricted to a narrower range of three k values, 20%, 30% and 40%, the proportion of robust pairs of combinations rose to 91%.
- the same 14 structures were also estimated for all countries and years but different monetary cut-offs (using both the poverty

Box I.5 (concluded)

line and the indigence line) and seven alternative k values (from 10% to 70%) were used, resulting in a total of 196 variants. It was found that 84% of all possible comparisons between pairs of observations were robust to these 196 variants. When the alternatives were restricted to a narrower range of three k values, 20%, 30% and 40%, the proportion of robust pairs of combinations rose to 90%.

- 29 structures were also estimated uniquely for observations without any missing indicators,[c] with k values ranging from 10% to 70% (203 alternative specifications). It was found that 81% of all possible pairs of comparisons were robust. When the alternatives were restricted to a narrower range of three k values, 20%, 30% and 40%, the proportion of robust pairs of combinations rose to 88%.

Source: Economic Commission for Latin America and the Caribbean (ECLAC).
[a] With 34 observations (17 countries at two points in time), there are 561 possible pairs of countries.
[b] The figure shows more k values close to the value actually used, 23%.
[c] The observations are: Brazil, 2005 and 2012; Colombia, 2008 and 2012; Costa Rica, 2005 and 2012; Dominican Republic, 2012; Ecuador, 2005 and 2012; El Salvador, 2004 and 2012; Guatemala, 2000 and 2006; Honduras, 2010; Mexico, 2012; Nicaragua, 2005; Paraguay, 2005 and 2011; Peru, 2003 and 2012; Plurinational State of Bolivia, 2011; and Uruguay, 2012.

Box I.6
Redundancy analysis of the indicator of income deprivations

Given that income enables the purchase of a variety of goods and services, its inclusion in the multidimensional poverty index made it necessary to ascertain whether there redundancy exists vis-à-vis non-monetary indicators of deprivation. This was determined for all possible pairs of deprivation using a correlation indicator, Cramer's V, and a measure of redundancy, the R coefficient, developed by Alkire and Ballon (2012).

The table summarizes the results of these measurements for income and other indicators. Analysis of the 34 observations (two years for each of the 17 countries under review) with Cramer's V yields a low average correlation between income deprivation and deprivation in non-monetary indicators, less than 0.25 in most cases. The lowest correlations were found in respect of deprivation in housing tenure (0.08), followed by school attendance (0.14) and schooling gap (0.15), while the highest were with deprivation in durable goods (0.25), educational attainment (0.3) and social protection (0.33).

The R coefficient indicates the degree of co-occurrence of a pair of deprivations as a proportion of the minimum marginal deprivation rate between the pair. In other words, R determines the proportion of people deprived in a given indicator "A" who are also deprived in another indicator "B" (where B is the indicator with the higher rate of deprivation). The table below shows that, in line with the findings of the correlation coefficient, the income deprivation indicator has the highest level of redundancy vis-à-vis the indicators on social protection (0.75) and durable goods (0.67). Moreover, an average R coefficient of 0.75 indicates that one in four people who are deprived in one of these indicators is not deprived in the other. These two indicators should therefore not be used simultaneously, as such people would be ignored by the poverty indicator, thus increasing the risk of failing to identify some poor individuals as poor (exclusion error).

In sum, the empirical evidence suggests that it is not redundant to include the income deprivation indicator in the multidimensional poverty index. Even when measuring deprivations which most often occur concurrently with income deprivations, excluding the income indicator would make it more difficult for the index to correctly identify people living in poverty.

Latin America (17 countries): correlation and redundancy between deprivation in income and non-monetary indicators

Income deprivation in relation to deprivation in the following indicators	Cramer's V (Correlation indicator)			R coefficient (Redundancy indicator)		
	Average [a]	Minimum	Maximum	Average [a]	Minimum	Maximum
Housing						
Housing materials	0.19	0.02	0.45	0.63	0.16	0.93
Overcrowding	0.25	0.08	0.43	0.65	0.34	0.86
Tenancy	0.08	-0.03	0.28	0.50	0.15	0.83
Basic utilities						
Drinking water	0.14	0.03	0.26	0.56	0.18	0.89
Sanitation	0.19	0.03	0.33	0.59	0.31	0.89
Energy	0.22	0.03	0.47	0.61	0.10	0.92
Education						
Educational attainment of adults	0.30	0.11	0.42	0.64	0.21	0.94
School attendance	0.14	0.03	0.24	0.57	0.11	0.87
Schooling gap	0.15	0.04	0.25	0.64	0.11	0.90
Employment and social protection						
Employment	0.15	0.06	0.25	0.52	0.30	0.83
Social protection	0.33	0.10	0.49	0.75	0.46	0.94
Living standard						
Durable goods	0.25	0.05	0.47	0.67	0.32	0.90

Source: Economic Commission for Latin America and the Caribbean (ECLAC).
[a] Simple average.

Source: Economic Commission for Latin America and the Caribbean (ECLAC).

Bibliography

Alkire, Sabina (2014), "Towards frequent and accurate poverty data", *OPHI Research in Progress series,* No. 43b [online] http://www.ophi.org.uk/wp-content/uploads/RP43a.pdf?0a8fd7.

Alkire, S. and P. Ballon (2012), "Understanding association across deprivation indicators in multidimensional poverty", paper presented at the Research Workshop "Dynamic Comparisons between Multidimensional Poverty and Monetary Poverty", University of Oxford.

Alkire, Sabina and María Emma Santos (2014), "Measuring acute poverty in the developing world: Robustness and scope of the Multidimensional Poverty Index", *World Development,* vol. 59.

___ (2010), "Acute multidimensional poverty: A new index for developing countries" [online] http://www.fundacionpobreza.cl/biblioteca-archivos/acute_multidimensional _poverty.pdf.

Alkire, Sabina and James Foster (2011), "Counting and multidimensional poverty measurement", *Journal of Public Economics,* vol. 95, No. 7–8.

___ (2007), "Counting and multidimensional poverty measurement", *OPHI Working Paper,* No. 7 [online] http://www.ophi.org.uk/wp-content/uploads/ophi-wp7.pdf.

Alkire, Sabina and others (2014), "Multidimensional poverty measurement and analysis: A counting approach", Oxford University Press, forthcoming.

Angulo, Roberto, Beatriz Yadira Díaz and Renata Pardo Pinzón (2013), "A counting multidimensional poverty index in public policy context: the case of Colombia", *OPHI Working Paper*, No. 62 [online] http://www.ophi.org.uk/a-counting-multidimensional-poverty-index-in-public-policy-context-the-case-of-colombia/.

Atkinson, Anthony and others (2002), *Social Indicators. The EU and Social Inclusion,* Oxford, Oxford University Press.

Bárcena, Alicia (2010), Opening remarks at the international seminar "Medición Multidimensional de la Pobreza en América Latina", Santiago, Chile, 13 - 14 May [online] http://www.eclac.cl/prensa/noticias/discursossecretaria /2/39502/13y14de_mayo2010DiscursoSeminarioInternMedimultidiPobrAL.pdf.

Basu, K. and J.E. Foster (1998), "On measuring literacy", *Economic Journal*, vol. 108, No. 451.

Beccaria, Luis and Alberto Minujín (1985), "Métodos alternativos para medir la evolución del tamaño de la pobreza", *Documentos de Trabajo,* No. 6, Buenos Aires, National Institute of Statistics and Censuses (INDEC).

Boltvinik, Julio (1992), "El método de medición integrada de la pobreza. Una propuesta para su desarrollo", *Comercio Exterior,* vol. 42, No. 4.

___ (1990), "Pobreza y necesidades básicas: conceptos y métodos de medición", RLA/86/004 Project, Caracas, United Nations Development Programme (UNDP).

Bradshaw, Jonathan and Naomi Finch (2003), "Overlaps in dimensions of poverty", *Journal of Social Policy*, vol. 32, No. 4.

Cecchini, Simone and Irene Azócar (2007), "Indicadores de los Objetivos de Desarrollo del Milenio en América Latina y el Caribe: una comparación entre datos nacionales e internacionales", *Estudios Estadísticos y Prospectivos series,* No. 53 (LC/L.2767-P), Santiago, Chile, Economic Commission for Latin America and the Caribeban (ECLAC).

CONEVAL (National Council for the Evaluation of Social Development Policy of Mexico) (2010), *Informe de pobreza multidimensional en México 2008* [online] http://www.coneval.gob.mx/cmsconeval/rw/resource/coneval/med_ pobreza/Informe_pobreza_multidimensional/Informe_de_Pobreza_Multidimensional_en_Mexico_2008_.pdf?view=.

Datt, G. and M. Ravallion (1992), "Growth and redistribution components of changes in poverty measures: A decomposition with applications to Brazil and India in the 1980's" *Journal of Development Economics*, No. 38.

Decancq, Koen and María Ana Lugo (2010), "Weights in Multidimensional Indices of Well-Being: An Overview" [en línea] https://lirias.kuleuven.be/bitstream/123456789/262767/1/DPS1006.pdf&gathStatIcon=truehttps://lirias. kuleuven.be/bitstream/123456789/262767/1/DPS1006.pdf&gathStatIcon=true.

Duflo, Esther, Michael Greenstone and Hanna Rema (2008), "Indoor air pollution, health and economic well-being", *Sapiens*, vol. 1, No. [online] http://sapiens.revues.org/130.

ECLAC (Economic Commission for Latin America and the Caribbean) (2014a), *Economic Survey of Latin America and the Caribbean, 2014* (LC/G.2619-P), Santiago, Chile.

___ (2014b), *Updated Economic Overview of Latin America and the Caribbean 2013* (LC/G.2605-P), Santiago, Chile.

___ (2014c), *Compacts for Equality: Towards a sustainable future* (LC/G.2586(SES.35/3)), Santiago, Chile.

___ (2013), *Social Panorama of Latin America, 2013* (LC/G.2580-P), Santiago, Chile.

ECLAC/ILO (Economic Commission for Latin America and the Caribbean/International Labour Organization) (2014), "Conditional transfer programmes and the labour market", *The Employment Situation in Latin America and the Caribbean*, Bulletin, No. 10, Santiago, Chile, May.

ECLAC/UNICEF (Economic Commission for Latin America and the Caribbean/United Nations Children's Fund) (2010), "Pobreza infantil en América Latina y el Caribe" (LC/R.2168), Santiago, Chile.

Feres, Juan Carlos and Xavier Mancero (2001), "El método de las necesidades básicas insatisfechas y sus aplicaciones en América Latina", *Estudios Estadísticos y Prospectivos series,* No. 7 (LC/L.1491-P), Santiago, Chile, Economic Commission for Latin America and the Caribbean (ECLAC).

Grosh, Margaret and Paul Glewwe (2000), *Designing Household Surveys Questionnaires for Developing Countries. Lessons from 15 years f the Living Standard Measurement Study,* vol. 1, Washington, D.C., World Bank.

Kaztman, Rubén (2011), "Infancia en América Latina: Privaciones habitacionales y desarrollo de capital humano", *Project Documents* (LC/W.431), Santiago, Chile, Economic Commission for Latin America and the Caribbean (ECLAC)/United Nations Children's Fund (UNICEF).

___ (2010), "La dimensión espacial de la cohesión social en América Latina", *La cohesión social en América Latina. Una revisión de conceptos, marcos de referencia e indicadores* (LC/G.2420), Santiago, Chile, Economic Commission for Latin America and the Caribbean (ECLAC).

___ (2001), "Seduced and abandoned: the social isolation of the urban poor", *CEPAL Review,* No. 75 (LC/G.2150-P), Santiago, Chile, Economic Commission for Latin America and the Caribbean (ECLAC).

Kaztman, Rubén and Pascual Gerstenfeld (1988), "La heterogeneidad de la pobreza: Una aproximación bidimensional" (LC/MVD/R.12/Rev.1(Sem.44/7), technical seminar on poverty research and measurement in Argentina, Brazil and Uruguay, Department of Statistics, Surveys and Censuses (DGEC)/Economic Commission for Latin America and the Caribbean (ECLAC).

Nussbaumer, Patrick and others (2011), "Measuring energy poverty: focusing on what matters", *OPHI Working Paper,* No. 42 [online] http://www.ophi.org.uk/measuring-energy-poverty-focusing-on-what-matters/.

Roche, José M. and María Emma Santos (2013), "In search of a multidimensional poverty index for Latin America", paper presented at the Society for the Study of Economic Inequality (ECINEQ) Meeting, 22-24 July [online] http://www.ecineq.org/ecineq_bari13/FILESxBari13/CR2/p170.pdf.

Ruggeri Laderchi, Caterina (1997), "Poverty and its many dimensions: The role of income as an indicator', *Oxford Development Studies,* vol. 25, No. 3.

Santos, María Emma (2013), "Measuring multidimensional poverty in Latin America: previous experience and the way forward", *OPHI Working Paper,* No. 66 [online] http://www.ophi.org.uk/measuring-multidimensional-poverty-in-latin-america-previous-experience-and-the-way-forward/.

Santos, María Emma, Pablo Villatoro, Xavier Mancero and Pascual Gerstenfeld (2015), "A multidimensional poverty index for Latin America", *OPHI Working Paper,* No. 79, University of Oxford, forthcoming.

Santos, María Emma and others (2010), "Refining the basic needs approach: a multidimensional analysis of poverty in Latin America", *Studies in Applied Welfare Analysis: Papers from the Third ECINEQ Meeting,* John Bishop (ed.), Bingley, Emerald.

Stewart, F. and others (2007), "Alternative realities? Different concepts of poverty, their empirical consequences and policy implications: Overview and conclusions", *Defining Poverty in a Developing World,* F. Stewart, R. Saith and B. Harriss-White (eds.), London, Palgrave Macmillan.

Taccari, Daniel and Pauline Stockins (2013), "Tipologías de discrepancias y medidas de conciliación estadística de los indicadores ODM. Marco general y aplicación en áreas temáticas e indicadores seleccionados", *Estudios Estadísticos series,* No. 81 (LC/L.3686), Santiago, Chile, Economic Commission for Latin America and the Caribbean (ECLAC).

Townsend, Peter (1979), *Poverty in the United Kingdom: A Survey of Household Resources and Standards of Living, 1967-1969,* Harmondsworth, Penguin Books.

UNICEF/WHO (United Nations Children's Fund/Wolrd Health Organization) (2012), "Progress on Drinking Water and Sanitation. 2012 Update" [online] http://www.unicef.org/media/files/JMPreport2012.pdf.

United Nations (2013), *Report of the Special Rapporteur on adequate housing as a component of the right to an adequate standard of living, and on the right to non-discrimination in this context* (A/HRC/25/54), New York.

Villatoro, Pablo (2007), "Hacia la ampliación del segundo Objetivo del Milenio: una propuesta para América Latina y el Caribe", *Políticas Sociales series,* No. 132 (LC/L.2712-P), Santiago, Chile, Economic Commission for Latin America and the Caribbean (ECLAC).

Whelan, Christopher, Richard Layte and Bernard Maître (2004), "Understanding the mismatch between income poverty and deprivation: A dynamic comparative analysis", *European Sociological Review,* vol. 20, No. 4.

Annex

Table I.A.1

Latin America (18 countries): poverty and indigence indicators, 1990-2013 [a]

(Percentages)

Country	Year	Poverty [b]				Indigence			
		Households	Population			Households	Population		
		Incidence (H)	Incidence (H)	Poverty gap (PG)	Poverty gap squared (FGT2)	Incidence (H)	Incidence (H)	Poverty gap (PG)	Poverty gap squared (FGT2)
Argentina [c]	1990 [d]	16.2	21.2	7.2	3.4	3.5	5.2	1.6	0.8
	1999	16.3	23.7	8.6	4.3	4.3	6.6	2.1	1.1
	2004	27.3	34.9	16.0	10.0	11.7	14.9	6.8	4.6
	2011	4.3	5.7	2.3	1.5	1.8	1.9	1.1	0.8
	2012	3.4	4.3	1.9	1.3	1.7	1.7	1.0	0.8
Bolivia (Plurinational State of)	1989 [e]	48.9	52.6	24.5	15.0	21.9	23.0	9.7	6.1
	1999	54.7	60.6	33.9	24.1	32.5	36.4	20.3	14.7
	2002	55.5	62.4	34.4	23.8	31.7	37.1	19.5	13.5
	2009	36.3	42.4	19.8	12.7	18.2	22.4	11.0	7.3
	2011	31.2	36.3	15.5	9.4	15.6	18.7	8.1	4.9
Brazil	1990	41.4	48.0	23.5	14.7	18.3	23.4	9.7	5.5
	1999	29.9	37.5	17.0	10.2	9.6	12.9	5.3	3.3
	2001	30.0	37.5	17.3	10.7	10.0	13.2	5.8	3.8
	2012	14.5	18.6	7.6	4.6	4.8	5.4	2.8	2.0
	2013	14.1	18.0	7.6	4.7	5.3	5.9	3.1	2.3
Chile	1990	33.3	38.6	14.9	8.0	10.6	13.0	4.4	2.3
	1998	17.8	21.7	7.5	3.8	4.6	5.6	2.0	1.1
	2003	15.3	18.7	6.3	3.2	3.9	4.7	1.7	1.0
	2011	9.2	10.9	3.5	1.8	3.0	3.1	1.3	0.9
	2013	6.5	7.8	2.5	1.3	2.3	2.5	1.0	0.7
Colombia	1994	47.3	52.5	26.6	17.5	25.0	28.5	13.8	9.1
	1999	48.7	54.9	25.6	15.7	23.2	26.8	11.2	6.9
	2002 [f]	42.2	49.7	21.9	12.8	14.3	17.8	6.8	3.7
	2012 [f]	26.7	32.9	12.9	7.1	8.2	10.4	3.8	2.1
	2013 [f]	24.8	30.7	11.8	6.4	7.3	9.1	3.3	1.8
Costa Rica	1990	23.6	26.3	10.7	6.5	10.0	10.1	4.8	3.4
	1999	18.2	20.3	8.1	4.8	7.5	7.8	3.5	2.3
	2002	18.6	20.3	8.4	5.2	7.7	8.2	3.9	2.7
	2012 [g]	15.4	17.8	6.9	4.0	6.3	7.3	3.1	1.9
	2013 [g]	15.6	17.7	6.9	4.0	6.4	7.2	3.1	1.9
Dominican Republic	2002	42.2	47.1	20.9	12.6	18.2	20.7	8.8	5.3
	2008	40.1	44.3	20.2	12.1	20.4	22.6	8.8	5.0
	2012	37.9	41.2	18.0	10.4	18.4	20.0	7.8	4.4
	2013	36.9	40.7	17.7	10.2	18.3	20.2	7.6	4.1
Ecuador [c]	1990	55.8	62.1	27.6	15.8	22.6	26.2	9.2	4.9
	1999	58.0	63.5	30.1	18.2	27.2	31.3	11.5	6.3
	2002	42.6	49.0	20.8	11.8	16.3	19.4	6.9	3.7
	2011	27.9	32.4	11.4	5.7	9.0	10.1	3.3	1.7
	2013	28.2	33.5	11.6	5.7	8.9	10.9	3.2	1.6
El Salvador	1995	47.6	54.2	24.0	14.3	18.2	21.7	9.1	5.6
	1999	43.5	49.8	22.9	14.0	18.3	21.9	9.4	5.8
	2001	42.9	48.9	22.7	14.0	18.3	22.1	9.5	5.7
	2012	38.9	45.3	16.7	8.4	10.9	13.5	3.9	1.7
	2013	35.5	40.9	14.9	7.4	10.1	12.5	3.5	1.5
Guatemala	1989	63.0	69.4	35.9	23.1	36.7	42.0	18.5	11.2
	1998	53.5	61.1	27.3	15.4	26.1	31.6	10.7	5.1
	2002	52.8	60.2	27.0	15.4	26.9	30.9	10.7	5.5
	2006	46.7	54.8	25.5	15.2	22.7	29.1	11.3	5.8

Table I.A.1 (concluded)

Country	Year	Poverty [b]				Indigence			
		Households	Population			Households	Population		
		Incidence (H)	Incidence (H)	Poverty gap (PG)	Poverty gap squared (FGT2)	Incidence (H)	Incidence (H)	Poverty gap (PG)	Poverty gap squared (FGT2)
Honduras	1990	75.2	80.8	50.2	35.9	53.9	60.9	31.5	20.2
	1999	74.3	79.7	47.4	32.9	50.6	56.8	27.9	17.5
	2002	70.9	77.3	45.3	31.2	47.1	54.4	26.6	16.2
	2010	63.0	69.2	39.1	26.7	39.5	45.6	22.8	14.5
Mexico	1989	39.0	47.7	18.7	9.9	14.0	18.7	5.9	2.7
	1998	38.0	46.9	18.4	9.4	13.2	18.5	5.3	2.2
	2002	31.8	39.4	13.9	6.7	9.1	12.6	3.5	1.4
	2010	29.3	36.3	12.8	6.3	9.8	13.3	4.1	1.9
	2012	29.9	37.1	12.7	6.1	10.4	14.2	4.2	1.8
Nicaragua	1993	68.1	73.6	41.9	29.3	43.2	48.4	24.3	16.2
	1998	65.1	69.9	39.4	27.3	40.1	44.6	22.6	15.1
	2001	63.0	69.4	37.1	24.5	36.5	42.5	19.2	12.0
	2009	52.0	58.3	26.1	15.2	25.1	29.5	11.7	6.3
Panama	1991 [c]	26.0	31.0	12.8	7.6	9.5	10.8	5.0	3.3
	1999 [c]	15.8	19.5	7.0	3.8	4.6	5.5	2.2	1.3
	2002	30.0	36.9	16.8	10.2	14.4	18.6	7.6	4.3
	2011	17.7	24.0	9.5	5.2	7.6	11.3	4.0	2.0
	2013	17.4	23.2	10.1	6.1	8.7	12.2	5.3	3.1
Paraguay	1990 [h]	36.8	43.2	16.1	8.0	10.4	13.1	3.6	1.5
	1999	50.3	59.0	29.1	18.4	25.0	31.8	14.1	8.6
	2001	50.7	59.7	28.7	18.0	25.2	31.3	13.7	8.2
	2012	42.1	47.3	20.6	12.1	20.4	23.6	9.7	5.5
	2013	35.2	40.7	16.6	9.3	16.8	19.2	7.1	3.9
Peru	1997	40.4	47.5	20.7	12.0	20.3	25.0	10.1	5.6
	1999	42.3	48.6	20.6	11.7	18.7	22.4	9.2	5.1
	2001 [i]	48.7	54.7	24.7	14.5	20.4	24.4	9.6	5.2
	2012 [i]	23.1	25.8	9.2	4.6	5.2	6.0	1.8	0.8
	2013 [i]	21.1	23.9	8.1	3.9	3.8	4.7	1.3	0.5
Uruguay [c]	1990	11.8	17.9	5.3	2.4	2.0	3.4	0.9	0.4
	1999	5.6	9.4	2.7	1.2	0.9	1.8	0.4	0.2
	2002	9.3	15.4	4.5	1.9	1.3	2.5	0.6	0.2
	2012	3.9	6.1	1.7	0.7	0.8	1.2	0.3	0.1
	2013	3.7	5.7	1.6	0.6	0.7	0.9	0.2	0.1
Venezuela (Bolivarian Republic of)	1990	34.2	39.8	15.7	8.5	11.8	14.4	5.0	2.4
	1999	44.0	49.4	22.6	13.7	19.4	21.7	9.0	5.5
	2002	43.3	48.6	22.1	13.4	19.7	22.2	9.2	5.7
	2012 [j]	21.2	25.4	9.1	4.9	6.0	7.1	2.7	1.7
	2013 [j]	27.3	32.1	12.1	6.7	8.8	9.8	3.9	2.5
Latin America [k]	1990	41.0	48.4	...	...	17.7	22.6	...	...
	1999	35.4	43.8	...	...	14.1	18.6	...	...
	2002	36.1	43.9	...	...	14.6	19.3	...	...
	2012	22.0	28.1	...	...	8.7	11.3	...	...
	2013	22.0	28.1	...	...	9.1	11.7	...	...

Source: Economic Commission for Latin America and the Caribbean (ECLAC), on the basis of special tabulations of data from household surveys conducted in the respective countries.

[a] H = headcount ratio; PG = Poverty gap; FGT2 = Foster, Greer and Thorbecke index.
[b] Includes households (and persons) living in indigence or extreme poverty.
[c] Urban areas.
[d] Greater Buenos Aires.
[e] Eight departmental capitals plus the city of El Alto.
[f] Figures provided by the National Administrative Department of Statistics (DANE) of Colombia, not comparable with those of previous years.
[g] Figures not comparable with those of previous years, owing to a change in the survey used.
[h] Metropolitan area of Asunción.
[i] Figures of the National Institute of Statistics and Informatics of Peru. Figures not comparable with those of previous years.
[j] Figures of the National Institute of Statistics (INE) of the Bolivarian Republic of Venezuela, not comparable with those of previous years.
[k] Estimate for 18 countries in the region plus Haiti. Weighted average.

Chapter II

Income distribution, polarization and perceptions

Introduction

One of Latin America's distinguishing features has been the uneven distribution of resources and exercise of rights. While the region is far from being the world's poorest, it stands out as the most unequal. This is strangling current well-being and the future development of its societies and economies. In a series of publications referred to as the "trilogy of equality" (2010, 2012 and 2014), ECLAC has outlined this challenge and argued that overcoming it is a prerequisite for protecting recent gains and blazing a new trail towards a virtuous circle of growth and inclusion. This chapter of *Social Panorama* tracks recent trends in income inequality, focusing on the slowing of progress in this area in recent years. It examines the degree of polarization of Latin American societies, in search of a proxy for understanding the recent manifestations of collective unrest in some of the countries in the region.

A. Income distribution: a status report

Income distribution in the region has been improving steadily for a decade now. In several countries this improvement has gained momentum in recent years but, as with poverty, the most recent data hint that the decline in inequality could be faltering.

In the early 2000s inequality began to decrease in most of the countries of the region; this trend is still holding. Between 2002 and 2013 the average Gini coefficient for the region[1] fell approximately 10%, from 0.542 to 0.486.

The dynamics of inequality reduction during the subperiod 2008-2013 did not follow the same patterns as in 2002-2008. In some countries the trend towards smaller disparities began to pick up speed up in 2008, especially in the Plurinational State of Bolivia, Uruguay, Argentina, Brazil, Mexico and Colombia. Three of these countries (the Plurinational State of Bolivia, Argentina and Brazil) also saw striking improvements in inequality in 2002-2008 (see figure II.1).

Other countries saw similar improvements (on the order of 1% per year) in both subperiods; among them were Peru, El Salvador and Chile. In the Bolivarian Republic of Venezuela, Ecuador, Paraguay and Panama, inequality fell at much higher rates between 2002 and 2008 than in the subsequent period. Panama saw a slight trend towards concentration between 2008 and 2013. In the Dominican Republic, worsening distribution in the first subperiod was followed by a partial reversal of this trend in the second. Costa Rica registered a slight improvement between 2002 and 2008 and marked concentration between 2008 and 2013, at rates in excess of 1% a year (see figure II.1).

Figure II.1 also shows the annual percentage change in the Theil and Atkinson indices (with an inequality aversion coefficient equal to 1.5) for these subperiods. In all three inequality indices there is a high degree of trend concordance, with a few exceptions. By magnitude of the reduction in inequality during the second subperiod, the Theil and Atkinson indices put Mexico and Chile in a better position than the Gini index does. The opposite happens in the case of Brazil.

Lastly, looking only at the last two estimates available (around 2012 and 2013), of 12 countries only Brazil and Ecuador show significant variations in the Gini index, which fell in the first and rose in the second. Of the other 10 countries with information available, there was a small drop in the Gini in one, little change in another five, and slight rises in the remaining four. None of these variations were large enough to be statistically significant, however.

1 On the basis of data for 15 Latin American countries around 2002 and 2013. Does not include Guatemala, Honduras or Nicaragua.

Figure II.1

Latin America (15 countries): annual variation in inequality indices,[a] 2002-2008 and 2008-2013

(Percentages)

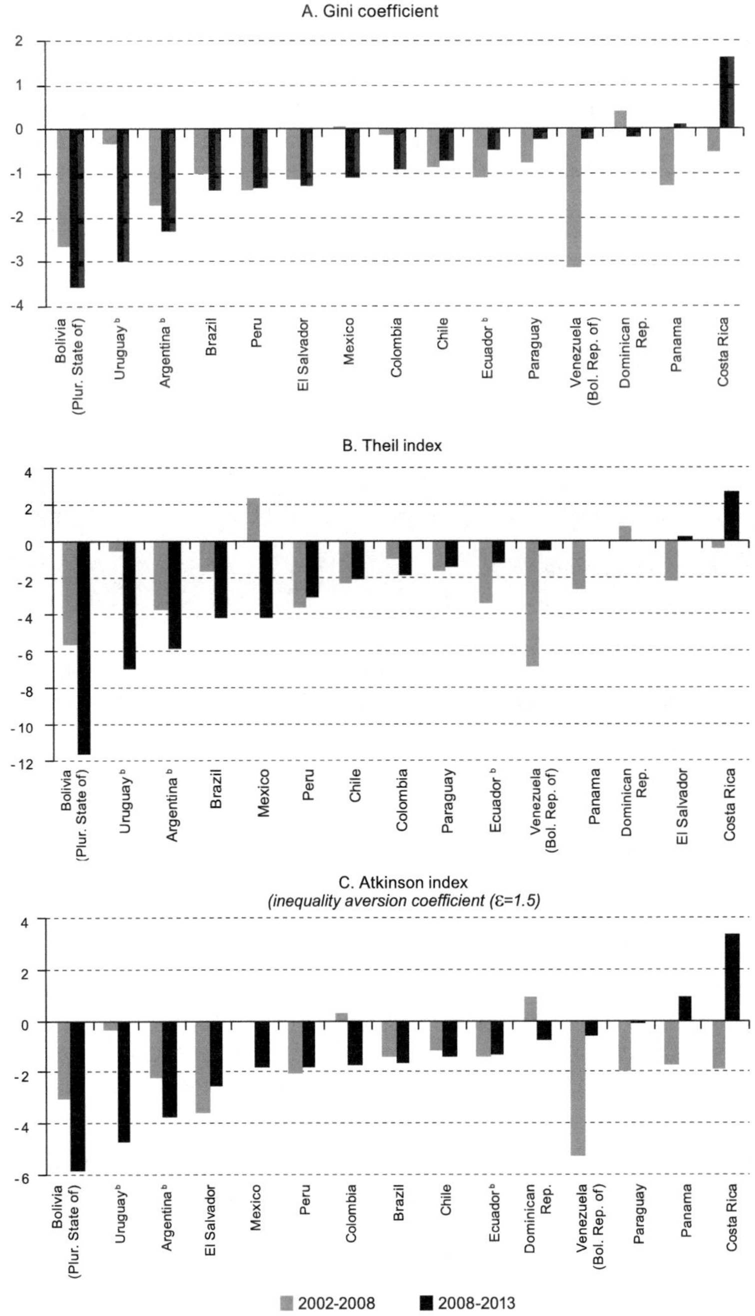

Source: Economic Commission for Latin America and the Caribbean (ECLAC), on the basis of special tabulations of data from household surveys conducted in the respective countries.

[a] Includes only countries with data available for 2011 to 2013. Countries are ordered by the magnitude of variation in the second subperiod (2008-2013).

[b] Urban areas, 2002-2008.

With regard to income distribution across population groups, the share of the poorest 20% of households increased between 2008 and 2013, from an average of 5.2% to 5.6% of the total.[2] By contrast, the same period saw the average share of the richest quintile decrease from 48.4% in 2008 to 46.7% in 2013.

2 Calculated on the basis of information from 15 countries for which the most recent data are available. Does not include Guatemala, Honduras or Nicaragua.

The share of the poorest quintile rose in 11 of the 15 countries during the period, with increases of one percentage point or more in Argentina and Uruguay. The share of the richest quintile shrank in 11 of the 15 countries reviewed, dropping by more than 4% in Uruguay, Argentina and Brazil. Costa Rica and Paraguay posted simultaneous drops in the income share of the poorest quintile and rises in the share of the richest population quintile (see figure II.2).

Figure II.2

Latin America (15 countries): share of total income of the poorest and richest quintiles, around 2008 and 2013 [a]

(Percentages)

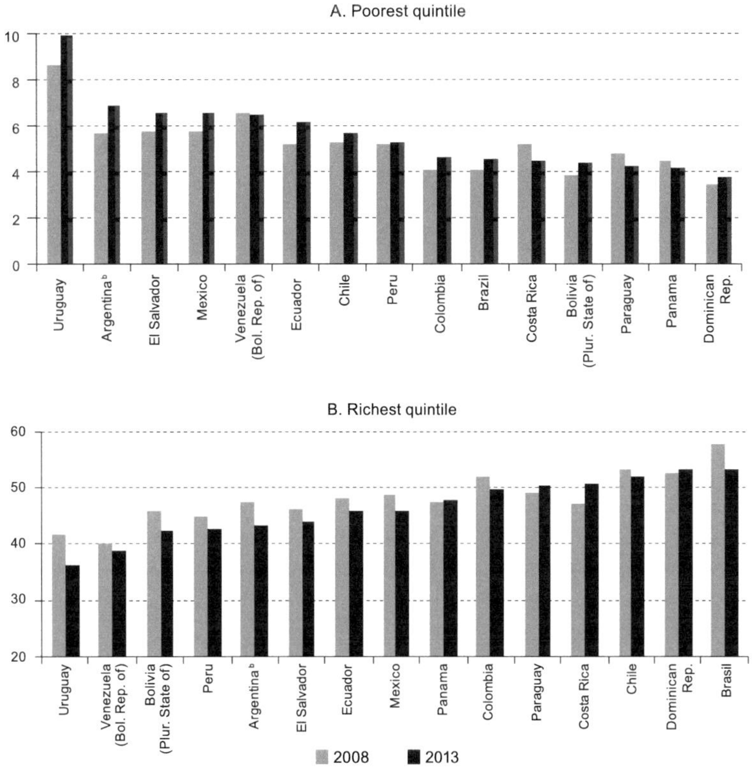

Source: Economic Commission for Latin America and the Caribbean (ECLAC), on the basis of special tabulations of data from household surveys conducted in the respective countries.

[a] Includes only countries with data available for 2011 to 2013. Countries are ordered by the magnitude of values for the second subperiod (2008-2013).

[b] Urban areas.

B. Distributive polarization

Income distribution polarization declined in most of the countries of Latin America between 2004 and 2012, especially in urban areas. Income bipolarization was down, implying that the middle sectors of the distribution expanded.

Recent years have brought conceptual and methodological developments that provide a different take on types of income distribution and their relationship to social conflict. These new developments include polarization indices, which until now have not been used much to yield a comparative description of income distribution in the countries of Latin America.[3]

This section describes and analyses trends in income distribution polarization indicators in the countries of Latin America between 2004 and 2012. First, the concepts behind the new measures of polarization are introduced, explaining how they differ from the usual indices of inequality. The second part sets out an empirical analysis covering 18 countries of the region.

1. Core concepts

Interest in distributive polarization tends to stem from concern about social cohesion and intergroup conflict management, rather than from issues of inequality per se. In the European context, this concern has been exacerbated by a weakening of middle-income groups and the emergence of strong bimodalities at the extremes of the income distribution (Gradín and Del Río, 2001).

Polarization indices add new elements for better describing income distribution, because conventional indicators are not suitable for differentiating between concentration around the mean of an income distribution or concentration around the poles of the distribution (Esteban and Ray, 1994).

Standard indicators of inequality are unable to reflect population concentration around the poles of the distribution because inequality is evaluated on the basis of the Pigou-Dalton transfer principle, according to which any redistribution of income from one person to another poorer one decreases inequality. This would mean that conventional measures of inequality would not pick up on the level of social tension associated with a distribution (Esteban, 1996).

One example would be a hypothetical distribution where average income is taken as a threshold that divides society (see distribution 1 in figure II.3). If the income of the groups below and above the average were made equal (distribution 2 in figure II.3), inequality declines but society is reconfigured into two poles, which causes greater polarization (Lasso de la Vega and Urrutia, 2002). There is also greater inequality when one individual is extremely rich and everyone else is equally poor (distribution 3 in figure II.3). But this would not be the most polarized situation: strictly speaking, polarization is highest when the population is evenly distributed in two poles (distribution 4 in figure II.3).

Polarization indices, then, are used to try to estimate the extent to which the population is clustered around a small number of poles of income. The central idea is that individuals feel *identified* with the members of their income group and feel *alienated* from those outside their group (Esteban and Ray, 1994). Alienation is shown by the distance between income for the groups; group size is a proxy for identification. The polarization approach therefore has the following properties:

(i) Individuals do not play an important role in generating social conflict. Polarization is a matter of groups.
(ii) Polarization rises along with homogeneity or within-group similarity.
(iii) Polarization increases along with heterogeneity or across-group distance.
(iv) The smaller the number of relevant groups, the greater the degree of polarization.

The last two properties are in keeping with the Pigou-Dalton transfer principle; the first two properties violate it. As for the second property, when there are two or more groups polarization increases if dispersion within the group decreases. This goes against the properties of inequality measures (Esteban and Ray, 2010).

Polarization indices have been grouped into two families. The first measures polarization based on an arbitrary number of groups. Here, the Esteban and Ray (1994), Esteban, Gradin and Ray (1999, 2007) and Duclos, Esteban and Ray (2005) indices apply. The second family comprises bipolarization indices, which take median income as the threshold. The Foster and Wolfson (2002) and Wang and Tsui (2000) indices are in this group. There are similarities and differences between the axiomatic bases of these index families (see boxes II.1 and II.2, respectively, for more details on indices and axioms).

[3] Comparative studies on Latin America (or on subgroups of countries in the region): Larrú (2013), Gasparini and others (2008) and Cruces, López Calva and Battistón (2011). Single-country studies: Violaz, Oliveri and Alejo (2009) and Groisman (2013) in Argentina; Clementi and Schettino (2013) in Brazil; D'Ambrosio and Permanyer (2010), Villalobos and Valenzuela (2012) and Modrego, Celis and Berdegué (2008) in Chile; Borraz, Gonzalez and Rossi (2013) and Gallo (2010) in Uruguay; and Aguilar (2013) in Mexico. Not all of the studies have analysed income polarization, nor have they all used the same indices.

Figure II.3

Polarization and inequality in different income distributions

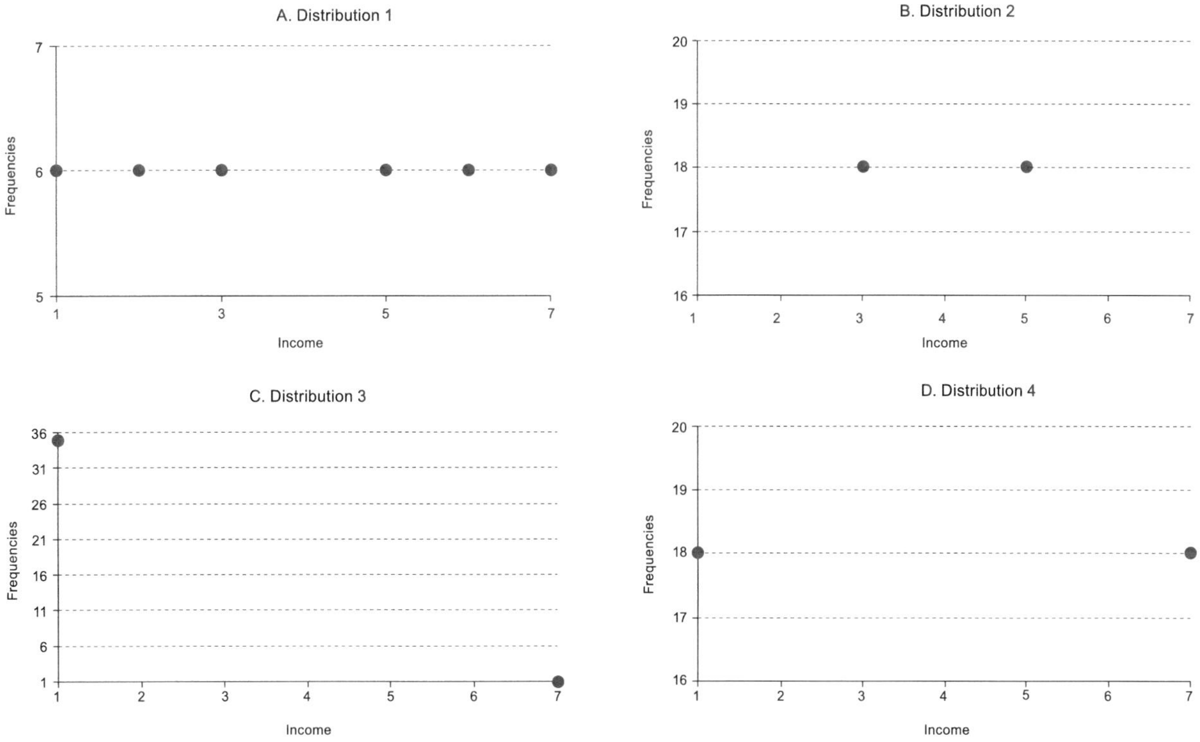

Source: Economic Commission for Latin America and the Caribbean (ECLAC).

Box II.1

Polarization indices

In the Esteban and Ray index (P^{ER}) (1994), polarization is the sum of all effective antagonisms (alienation and identification) and is estimated on the basis of the following formula:

$$P^{ER}\ p,y = K\sum_{i=1}^{n}\sum_{j=1}^{n} p_i^{1+\alpha} p_j \left|y_i - y_j\right|,\ K>0\ \ 1\le\alpha\le1.6$$

Where Pi= the proportion of group i in the population; Yi= mean income of the individuals in group i; α: polarization aversion parameter, which takes values between 1 and 1.6.

P^{ER} assumes that the population is structured ex ante in groups. In addition, the P^{ER} index has an apparent similarity to the Gini coefficient (G). But introducing polarization aversion parameter α makes P^{ER} behave very differently from G. When $\alpha = 0$, $P^{ER} = G$. The higher the value of α, the greater the difference between inequality and polarization.

In the P^{ER} index (1994), identification depends on frequency at the selected point, not at adjacent points. Consequently, two individuals with very similar incomes will belong to different groups. Thus, the pre-given discrete distribution is not an optimal grouping (Esteban, 2006).

Esteban, Gradín and Ray (P^{EGR}) (1999) proposed a solution for the problem of non-optimal grouping. P^{EGR} does not start with the assumption that the population is structured into groups, and it takes within-group dispersion into account. The starting point is a simplified representation p of a density distribution f, which produces a proxy error $e(F, p)$ that may be interpreted as lack of group identification because it indicates the degree of intragroup dispersion. In P^{EGR}, then, the global polarization of distribution *f* (extended polarization) is estimated in two steps. First, the simplified polarization (P^{ER} polarization) is measured. Then, the degree of internal heterogeneity (*e*) is discounted. The formula used is as follows:

$$P^{EGR}(\alpha,\beta) = P^{ER}(\alpha) - \beta\left[G(f) - G(\pi,\mu)\right]$$

Where P^{ER}= polarization index ^{ER}, G(f)= Gini coefficient of the original distribution; $G(\pi,\mu)$= Gini coefficient of the simplified distribution, with π being the group size vector and μ the means vector; $[G(f) - G(\pi,\mu)]$=intragroup inequality and β= free parameter that measures the weight assigned to the "measurement error" (or lack of identification).

Determining the number of groups or poles is still exogenous, but groups are located by means of an optimal grouping, ρ^*, of the original distribution. To do so, the simplification error (the difference between the inequality indices for the original distribution and the simplified distribution) is minimized.

Duclos, Esteban and Ray (*DER*) (2005) propose a solution for the problem of P^{ER} index discontinuity, given that it applies to distributions that can be described as functions of density and is based on axioms. This index is also used to try to overcome arbitrariness in setting income intervals, by means of a nonparametric estimation of group size using kernel density procedures in order to find the optimal location of the groups. The strength of group identification is measured

Box II.1 (concluded)

using the value of the density function (the relative probability of belonging to the group).

In formal terms, in *DER* a subject located at x feels alienation vis-à-vis another subject located at y. This alienation is monotonic in distance $[x-y]$. An individual located at x has a sense of identification that depends on density at x, $f(x)$. The *DER* index is written as:

$$DER(\alpha) = \iint f(x)^{1+\alpha} f(y) |y-x| dydx$$

Lastly, the Wolfson index (W) (Foster and Wolfson, 2002) is a measure of bipolarization. It was constructed to indirectly determine the weight of the middle class. W starts with partial orderings and analyses bipolarization on the basis of two groups of equal size. The median is the cut-off point. The W index can be depicted in terms of the Lorenz curve as twice the area beneath the Lorenz curve above the tangent to the inequality curve and the median of the distribution. W is written as:

$$W=2[2[0.5 - L(p=0.5) - G] \mu/M$$

Where μ= the mean of the distribution; M=the median of the distribution; L(p)= the Lorenz curve; G=the Gini coefficient.

All the indices described take values between 0 and 1.

Source: Economic Commission for Latin America and the Caribbean (ECLAC).

Box II.2

Axioms (properties) that measures of polarization must meet

Given the extent of the axiomatic literature on polarization, only a few formulations are presented here:

Esteban and Ray (1994)

Axiom 1: the joining of two population masses at their mid-point increases polarization.

Joining two small populations (masses) while keeping average distance from a third population constant increases polarization. For example, take population masses $p>0$ $q>0$, with $p>q$. Mass p has income Yo. There are two masses q, one located at level Yx and the other at level Yz such that Yo< Yx< Yz. The joining of the two masses q at their mid-point (x+z/2) increases polarization.

Axiom 2: if a population mass is moved toward another smaller and closer mass, polarization goes up.

For example, take three population masses, p, q and r. Mass p is larger than mass r. Mass q located between masses p and r is as close to the second group as to the first. If population mass q moves towards r, polarization should go up.

Axiom 3: if a population mass is shifted equally to the two sides, polarization increases.

If the population mass of the mean of the distribution is divided into two equal and discrete groups, polarization goes up. For example, take a central mass q on level Yx. Any new distribution formed by dividing the central mass q into two lateral masses, p and r, each one located d units away from Yx, should increase polarization.

Esteban and Ray (2010)

The axioms put forth by these authors are based on symmetric, unimodal and non-normalized densities, following the logic of the *DER* index. These are described below, along with adaptations of these axioms for the the Wolfson polarization index (Foster and Wolfson, 2002).

Axiom 1. If a distribution has a single basic density, then a squeeze of that basic density cannot increase polarization.

A squeeze reduces inter-individual alienation, which decreases polarization, but it raises within-group identification, which makes polarization go up.

Axiom 2. If a symmetric distribution is composed of three basic densities drawn from the same kernel, with mutually disjoint supports, then a symmetric squeeze of the side densities cannot reduce polarization.

This axiom expresses the property that polarization increases with intragroup identification and refers to a local squeeze rather than a global one (axiom 1). In this case there is a divergence from conventional measures of inequality.

For Foster and Wolfson (2002), this axiom is defined with relation to the increase in bimodal distribution. It is set out as follows: if there are two distributions F and G with the same mean and same median and distribution F is allowed to stochastically dominate G discretely at $[0;m]$ and $[m;\alpha]$, F is more polarized than G.

Axiom 3. Consider a symmetric distribution composed of four basic densities drawn from the same kernel, with mutually disjoint supports. An equal slide of the two inner densities outwards towards the outer densities makes polarization go up.

This axiom expresses the property that polarization increases with increasing intragroup identification.

In Foster and Wolfson (2002), this axiom is expressed as follows: if a distribution of the income of all individuals draws away from the median income, polarization increases.

Source: Economic Commission for Latin America and the Caribbean (ECLAC).

2. Recent trends in some indicators of polarization in Latin America

First, the findings of an empirical analysis of income distribution bipolarization for 18 countries of the region in 2004 and 2012 are set out. This exercise was based on the Wolfson and EGR indices for two groups.

For 2012, lower levels of polarization as measured by the Wolfson index were recorded in Uruguay (0.345), the Bolivarian Republic of Venezuela (0.364), El Salvador (0.378) and Peru (0.399). The highest levels of polarization were observed in Honduras (0.601), Guatemala (0.55), Colombia (0.51) and the Dominican Republic (0.50) (see figure II.4).

Figure II.4

Latin America (18 countries): Wolfson index of income distribution bipolarization, 2004 [a] and 2012 [b c]

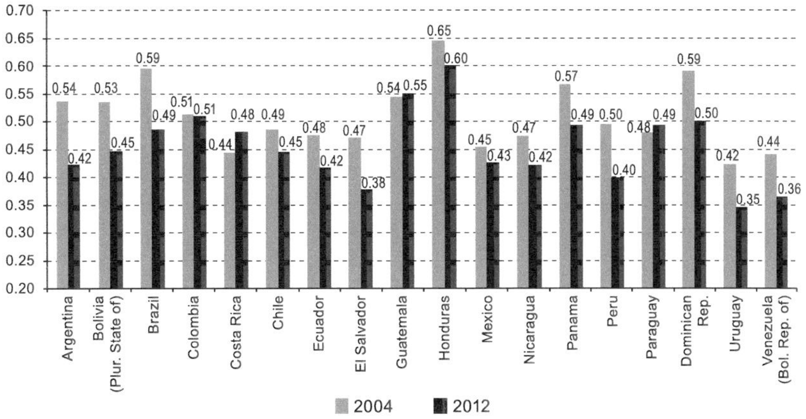

Source: Economic Commission for Latin America and the Caribbean (ECLAC), on the basis of special tabulations of data from household surveys conducted in the respective countries.

[a] Data from 2005 for Nicaragua; 2003 for Chile, Honduras, Peru and the Plurinational State of Bolivia; and 2002 for Guatemala.

[b] Data from 2011 for Chile, Paraguay and the Plurinational State of Bolivia; 2010 for Honduras; 2009 for Nicaragua; and 2006 for Guatemala.

[c] Urban areas for Argentina and the Bolivarian Republic of Venezuela in 2004 and 2012, and for Uruguay in 2004.

Tracking the Wolfson index, figure II.4 shows that the bipolarization of income declined in 15 of the 18 countries between 2004 and 2012, while it increased in only three countries (Costa Rica, Paraguay and Guatemala).[4] In terms of relative changes per year,[5] the sharpest declines in the Wolfson index were seen in Nicaragua (-2.8%), Argentina (-2.6%), El Salvador (-2.4%), Uruguay (-2.3%) and Brazil (-2.3%).

Using the EGR index for two groups paints a very similar picture. In 2012, the lowest levels of bipolarization were, again, in Uruguay (0.119), the Bolivarian Republic of Venezuela (0.123), Peru (0.137) and El Salvador (0.137). The highest levels of bipolarization were observed in Guatemala (0.214), Honduras (0.202), Brazil (0.198) and Chile (0.189) (see figure II.5).

Figure II.5

Latin America (18 countries): EGR index of income distribution bipolarization for two groups, 2004 [a] and 2012 [b c]

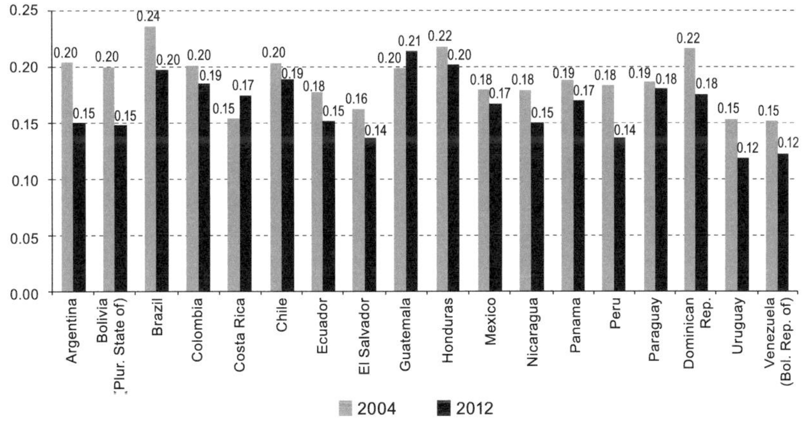

Source: Economic Commission for Latin America and the Caribbean (ECLAC), on the basis of special tabulations of data from household surveys conducted in the respective countries.

[a] Data from 2005 for Nicaragua; 2003 for Chile, Honduras, Peru and the Plurinational State of Bolivia; and 2002 for Guatemala.

[b] Data from 2011 for Chile, Paraguay and the Plurinational State of Bolivia; 2010 for Honduras; 2009 for Nicaragua; and 2006 for Guatemala.

[c] Urban areas for Argentina and the Bolivarian Republic of Venezuela in 2004 and 2012, and for Uruguay in 2004.

---

4 For Guatemala, the data are from 2002 and 2006.

5 There are differences between countries in the number of years between the baseline measurements (2004) and follow-up (2012). So it was decided to divide the relative differences in the values of the polarization index between the initial year and the final year by the number of years between the two periods. This gave the annualized relative change (ARC) for each country based on the formula ARC = ((IPas-IPab/Ipab) * 100) / AT, where Ipas = polarization value in the follow-up year; IPab = polarization value in the baseline year; AT = years elapsed between initial and final measurement.

A look at the EGR rate for two groups between 2004 and 2012 shows that income bipolarization decreased in 16 of 18 countries of Latin America. The most significant declines, measured as annualized relative changes, were in Nicaragua (-4.0%), Argentina (-3.3%), the Plurinational State of Bolivia (-3.3%), Peru (-2.8%) and Uruguay (-2.8%). Conversely, bipolarization increased in Guatemala (1.9%) and Costa Rica (1.7%) (see figure II.5).

Thus, the findings from the Wolfson and EGR indices for two groups indicate a trend toward declining bipolarization in the region between 2004 and 2012. This means growth of the middle sectors of the income distribution.

Table II.1 shows the Wolfson index values for rural and urban areas for 2004 and 2012. In 2012, the lowest levels of bipolarization in urban areas were in Peru, Uruguay, El Salvador and the Plurinational State of Bolivia. The highest were in the Dominican Republic, Costa Rica, Guatemala and Brazil. In rural areas, bipolarization was lowest in Uruguay, El Salvador, Chile and Mexico and highest in Panama, Honduras, Paraguay and the Plurinational State of Bolivia.

Table II.1

Latin America (16 countries): Wolfson index of income distribution bipolarization by area of residence, 2004 [a] and 2012 [b]

Country	Rural		Urban	
	2004	2012	2004	2012
Bolivia (Plurinational State of)	0.493	0.527	0.459	0.367
Brazil	0.509	0.513	0.579	0.473
Colombia	0.368	0.406	0.487	0.465
Costa Rica	0.409	0.420	0.425	0.481
Chile	0.377	0.356	0.481	0.453
Dominican Republic	0.511	0.437	0.610	0.516
Ecuador	0.386	0.374	0.460	0.390
El Salvador	0.396	0.347	0.419	0.349
Guatemala	0.421	0.463	0.487	0.478
Honduras	0.487	0.553	0.504	0.458
Mexico	0.416	0.368	0.423	0.396
Nicaragua	0.436	0.410	0.412	0.375
Panama	0.566	0.590	0.474	0.405
Peru	0.325	0.391	0.422	0.338
Paraguay	0.427	0.527	0.454	0.434
Uruguay		0.267		0.345

Source: Economic Commission for Latin America and the Caribbean (ECLAC), on the basis of special tabulations of data from household surveys conducted in the respective countries.

[a] Data from 2005 for Nicaragua; 2003 for Chile, Honduras, Peru and the Plurinational State of Bolivia; and 2002 for Guatemala.

[b] Data from 2011 for Chile, Paraguay and the Plurinational State of Bolivia; 2010 for Honduras; 2009 for Nicaragua; and 2006 for Guatemala.

In urban areas, polarization increased in just one country (Costa Rica) between 2004 and 2012. The most significant decreases, measured in annualized percentage changes, were in the Plurinational State of Bolivia, Brazil, Nicaragua and Peru. But in rural areas the dominant trend was toward greater polarization: 9 of the 15 countries saw increased bipolarization. The largest increases, shown in annualized percentage changes, were in Paraguay (3.4%), Guatemala (2.5%) and Peru (2.3%).[6]

In summary, falling bipolarization in most of the countries of the region between 2004 and 2012 was mainly due to what happened in urban areas. In fact, the average Wolfson index in urban areas in 15 countries (excluding Uruguay, to make the two rounds more comparable)[7] fell from 0.473 to 0.425 between 2004 and 2012, while in rural areas it increased slightly, from 0.435 in 2004 to 0.445 in 2012.

So far, the findings presented have been based on the application of bipolarization indices. The data set out below are from using polarization measurements for more than two groups: the DER index and the EGR index for three groups.

Figure II.6 shows the DER index values (alpha=0.5) for 2004 and 2012. In 2012, the lowest degrees of polarization were in Uruguay, the Bolivarian Republic of Venezuela, El Salvador and Peru. The highest levels were in Guatemala, Honduras, Brazil and Paraguay.

6 In these countries there is a large indigenous population in rural areas. In any event, there was a slight increase in bipolarization in the Plurinational State of Bolivia, a slight decrease in Ecuador and a more significant decline in Mexico.

7 In the baseline measurement there are no data for rural areas of Uruguay.

Figure II.6

Latin America (18 countries): DER index [a] of income distribution polarization, 2004 [b] and 2012 [c d]

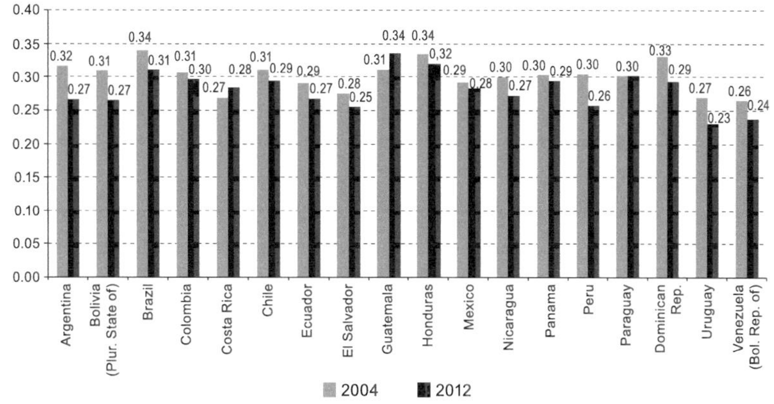

Source: Economic Commission for Latin America and the Caribbean (ECLAC), on the basis of special tabulations of data from household surveys conducted in the respective countries.

[a] Polarization aversion (alpha) = 0.5.

[b] Data from 2005 for Nicaragua; 2003 for Chile, Honduras, Peru and the Plurinational State of Bolivia; and 2002 for Guatemala.

[c] Data from 2011 for Chile, Paraguay and the Plurinational State of Bolivia; 2010 for Honduras; 2009 for Nicaragua; and 2006 for Guatemala.

[d] Urban areas for Argentina and the Bolivarian Republic of Venezuela in 2004 and 2012, and for Uruguay in 2004.

As with bipolarization, the trend is toward less income polarization in three groups or more. In 16 of 18 countries, DER index values (0.5) fell between 2004 and 2012. Nevertheless, in some countries the differences between the baseline year and the year of the last measurement are very small. One extreme case is Paraguay, where the absolute difference between the baseline year and the last measurement was only -0.1%.

As for changes in the DER index (0.5) between 2004 and 2012, the sharpest decreases, measured as annualized relative changes, were in Nicaragua, Argentina, the Plurinational State of Bolivia and Uruguay, in order of greatest change to least. Guatemala and Costa Rica once again posted an increase in income polarization.

The downtrend in polarization holds across different values for the alpha parameter for aversion to polarization (0.25 and 0.75) for the DER index, as well as for the EGR index for three groups. With the DER index (0.25), polarization decreases in 14 of 18 countries between 2004 and 2012; with the DER index (0.75), polarization decreases in 16 of 18 countries. As for the EGR index for three groups, polarization decreases in 15 of 17 countries (see table II.2). Guatemala and Costa Rica are the only countries where increasing polarization is robust to variations in parameters and indices.

Table II.2

Latin America (16 countries): DER and EGR indices of income distribution polarization, 2004 [a] and 2012 [b c]

Country	DER (alpha=0.25)		DER (alpha=0.75)		EGR (3 groups)	
	2004	2012	2004	2012	2004	2012
Argentina	0.384	0.335	0.279	0.228	0.185	0.141
Bolivia (Plurinational State of)	0.380	0.338	0.272	0.221	0.179	0.138
Brazil	0.413	0.383	0.311	0.276	0.203	0.178
Colombia	0.351	0.350	0.275	0.260	0.178	0.169
Costa Rica	0.335	0.348	0.227	0.244	0.141	0.154
Chile	0.360	0.342	0.283	0.265	-	0.165
Dominican Republic	0.390	0.351	0.298	0.252	0.191	0.163
Ecuador	0.356	0.334	0.254	0.230	0.159	0.139
El Salvador	0.340	0.300	0.233	0.219	0.140	0.128
Guatemala	0.379	0.380	0.281	0.305	0.178	0.190
Honduras	0.404	0.389	0.303	0.283	0.199	0.183
Mexico	0.366	0.343	0.259	0.250	0.159	0.152
Nicaragua	0.363	0.324	0.264	0.233	0.165	0.142
Panama	0.374	0.376	0.260	0.252	0.169	0.161
Peru	0.332	0.325	0.269	0.219	0.168	0.131
Paraguay	0.371	0.378	0.268	0.261	0.169	0.167
Uruguay	0.337	0.290	0.235	0.199	0.141	0.111
Venezuela (Bolivarian Republic of)	0.331	0.295	0.225	0.202	0.139	0.116

Source: Economic Commission for Latin America and the Caribbean (ECLAC), on the basis of special tabulations of data from household surveys conducted in the respective countries.

[a] Data from 2005 for Nicaragua; 2003 for Chile, Honduras, Peru and the Plurinational State of Bolivia; and 2002 for Guatemala.

[b] Data from 2011 for Chile, Paraguay and the Plurinational State of Bolivia; 2010 for Honduras; 2009 for Nicaragua; and 2006 for Guatemala.

[c] Urban areas for Argentina and the Bolivarian Republic of Venezuela in 2004 and 2012, and for Uruguay in 2004.

In 2012, the highest levels of polarization in urban areas, measured by the DER index (0.5), were seen in Brazil, Guatemala and Paraguay, in that order; the lowest levels were in Peru, Uruguay and El Salvador. In rural areas, the highest DER index values (0.5) were in Paraguay, Honduras and Panama, and the lowest were in Uruguay, El Salvador and Ecuador (see table II.3).

Table II.3

Latin America (16 countries): DER index [a] of income distribution polarization by area of residence, 2004 [b] and 2012 [c]

Country	Rural		Urban	
	2004	2012	2004	2012
Bolivia (Plurinational State of)	0.294	0.302	0.302	0.242
Brazil	0.306	0.294	0.340	0.313
Colombia	0.247	0.261	0.280	0.278
Costa Rica	0.255	0.267	0.260	0.276
Chile	0.280	0.278	0.299	0.278
Dominican Republic	0.297	0.275	0.319	0.279
Ecuador	0.256	0.244	0.281	0.262
El Salvador	0.261	0.237	0.261	0.241
Guatemala	0.275	0.292	0.297	0.301
Honduras	0.293	0.320	0.297	0.275
Mexico	0.298	0.264	0.289	0.268
Nicaragua	0.278	0.269	0.283	0.252
Panama	0.295	0.312	0.278	0.265
Peru	0.237	0.259	0.247	0.236
Paraguay	0.309	0.350	0.285	0.280
Uruguay		0.215		0.237

Source: Economic Commission for Latin America and the Caribbean (ECLAC), on the basis of special tabulations of data from household surveys conducted in the respective countries.

[a] Polarization aversion (alpha) = 0.5.

[b] Data from 2005 for Nicaragua; 2003 for Chile, Honduras, Peru and the Plurinational State of Bolivia; and 2002 for Guatemala.

[c] Data from 2011 for Chile, Paraguay and the Plurinational State of Bolivia; 2010 for Honduras; 2009 for Nicaragua; and 2006 for Guatemala.

As for changes in polarization between 2004 and 2012 by area of residence, in urban areas the dominant trend is towards declining polarization, as seen in 13 of 15 countries. The exceptions are Costa Rica (increase of 0.76% per year) and Guatemala (increase of 0.35% per year). In rural areas, polarization increases in 8 of 15 countries. The largest increases, measured in annualized percentage changes, are in Paraguay (1.90%), Guatemala (1.52%) and Honduras (1.35%).

One of the peculiarities of the DER index is that it makes it possible to separate the two components of polarization: distance between groups (alienation) and intragroup homogeneity (identification). As noted earlier, the greater the distance between groups and the greater the degree of intragroup homogeneity, the higher the degree of polarization.

Table II.4 shows the relative variation (unannualized) of the alienation and identification components of the DER index (0.5) for 18 countries of the region. The countries are grouped into clusters according to the joint trajectory for the alienation and identification components, in order to simplify the analysis.

Analysing changes in the alienation and identification components between 2004 and 2012 identified the following groups of countries:

(i) cluster 1, countries where alienation (distance) between groups and intragroup identification (homogeneity) both increased;

(ii) cluster 2, countries where the distance between groups decreased but there was a slight increase in intragroup identification;

(iii) cluster 3, countries where alienation decreased slightly and there was a slight increase in identification;

(iv) cluster 4, consisting of Guatemala, where the distance between groups increased and there was a sharp increase in intragroup identification.

Table II.4

Latin America (16 countries): DER index [a] of alienation and identification components, 2004 [b] and 2012 [c]

(Percentages)

Country	Alienation *(percentage variation)*	Identificacion *(percentage variation)*	Distance to cluster centre [d]
	Cluster 1 [e]		
Peru	-15.3	-6.8	3.869
Chile	-6.5	-7.2	4.942
Nicaragua	-10.3	-12.0	5.070
Brazil	-7.3	-4.0	5.148
Argentina	-17.8	-5.3	6.599
Average	-11.44	-7.06	
	Cluster 2		
Venezuela (Bolivarian Republic of)	-13.8	0.0	1.178
Bolivia (Plurinational State of)	-15.9	1.0	2.601
Dominican Republic	-11.7	-2.0	3.459
El Salvador	-11.3	5.0	4.413
Ecuador	-8.8	0.8	4.508
Uruguay	-18.3	1.6	5.028
Average	-13.30	1.07	
	Cluster 3		
Panama	-1.3	1.3	0.763
Colombia	-3.1	-0.7	2.641
Honduras	-3.5	-1.6	3.498
Paraguay	1.8	-4.6	5.911
Mexico	-4.6	6.5	6.921
Costa Rica	5.6	3.2	6.924
Average	-0.85	0.68	
	Cluster 4		
Guatemala	8.7	20.3	0.000

Source: Economic Commission for Latin America and the Caribbean (ECLAC), on the basis of special tabulations of data from household surveys conducted in the respective countries.

[a] Polarization aversion (alpha) = 0.5.

[b] Data from 2005 for Nicaragua; 2003 for Chile, Honduras and Peru; and 2002 for Guatemala.

[c] Data from 2011 for Chile, Paraguay and the Plurinational State of Bolivia; 2010 for Honduras; 2009 for Nicaragua; and 2006 for Guatemala.

[d] Urban areas for Argentina and the Bolivarian Republic of Venezuela in 2004 and 2012, and for Uruguay in 2004.

[e] Country groupings from a non-hierarchical cluster analysis. Distance to the centre of the cluster is an indicator of the extent to which the values for the countries are far from or close to the average values for the cluster (country grouping) to which they belong.

C. Social classes: perceptions and expectations

In 2011, a sense of identification with the middle class and expectations for socioeconomic achievement were higher in populations of countries with lower poverty rates. These factors should be considered when designing policies for social cohesion, especially in the face of an economic slowdown scenario.

Between 2004 and 2012, income distribution polarization decreased in most of the countries of Latin America (see the previous section). The decline in the Wolfson index of bipolarization (which means an increase in the middle sectors of the income distribution) was particularly marked. Correlatively, absolute poverty has also showed a sustained downward trend in recent years (see the first part of this chapter).

In conventional theories, declining polarization should result in less conflict (Gradín and Del Río, 2001). But Chile and Brazil, which have brought polarization and poverty down, have recently been hit by expressions of social unrest. One possibility is that in some of the countries of the region, declining polarization and poverty have boosted the sense of identification with the middle class[8] and fed higher expectations, which could lead to conflicts if not met.[9]

This study does not provide a direct test of these hypotheses, because of data limitations.[10] Instead, two more limited propositions are compared. First, in countries with less polarization and less poverty there should be a stronger sense of identification with the middle class. Second, expectations of intergenerational mobility should be higher in the groups that identify with the middle class than among those who identify with the lower class. Because of restricted data availability, the analysis is limited to 2011.

1. Identification with the middle class and associated factors

Traditionally, the middle class has been conceptualized and measured based on attributes defined externally by experts, without looking at people's perceptions.[11] Two arguments have been used to justify this practice: (a) the positions of the subjects in the socioeconomic structure are independent from their perceptions; and (b) measurements based on subjective data overstate the weight of the middle class.

However, a purely external approach to the measurement of social class turns the cognitive processes (identities and expectations) that mediate between subject positions in the socioeconomic structure and their behavioural effects (expressions of social unrest)[12] into a black box. So, what is proposed here is not a measure of class based on subjective aspects (even if a measurement including this dimension is entirely feasible). Rather, the idea is to examine the relationship between structure and perceptions.

A first step is to establish the incidence of sense of identification with the middle class in the countries of the region. In 2011, 38% of the population of Latin America reported a sense of belonging to the middle class; 31% considered themselves part of the lower-middle class and 26% reported belonging to the lower class (see figure II.7). Figure II.8 shows that the percentage of the population that feels it is part of the middle class or lower-middle class differs considerably across countries. The highest values were in Argentina, Uruguay, the Plurinational State of Bolivia and Costa Rica (85%, 82%, 80% and 79%, respectively); the lowest were in Nicaragua, Honduras, El Salvador and Guatemala (46%, 51%, 55% and 56% respectively).

A second step is to analyse the relationship between polarization and class identification. Figure II.9 shows that in 2011 the proportion of the population who felt middle-class or lower-middle class tended to be larger in countries with a less bipolar distribution of income. But the association is not statistically significant owing to the pattern in El Salvador and Nicaragua, where the population percentages with a sense of belonging to the middle class are smaller than would be expected on the basis of levels of income polarization.

---

8 The relationship between reduction of absolute poverty and growth of the middle class is not necessarily seen in measurements of social classes based strictly on relative criteria.

9 The goal is not to analyse the relationship between polarization and conflict, which would be hard to do because of the lack of data on conflict in the region. In any event, there have been some efforts along these lines (see UNDP/Fundación UNIR, 2012).

10 It would have been useful to examine changing perceptions of belonging to the middle class, in order to determine whether they have changed alongside indicators of polarization and poverty. This is impossible, though, because the Latinobarómetro survey asked about class identification only for 2011 and 2013, and (as of sign-off on this section) there is public access to the database for 2011 alone).

11 In the economic tradition, the dominant approaches have been based on monetary metrics for measuring the middle class (absolute, relative and polarization-based approaches). And there is a sociological tradition that has focused on non-monetary aspects such as occupational structure. These two traditions are not referred to here as objective approaches because perceptions can also be measured using an objective approach (notwithstanding the limitations of such an approach).

12 Marx's old distinction of class in itself and class for itself points in the direction of considering the mediating role of cognitive aspects between class structure and its behavioural consequences.

Figure II.7
Latin America (18 countries): sense of belonging to a social class in the population, 2011 [a b]
(Percentages)

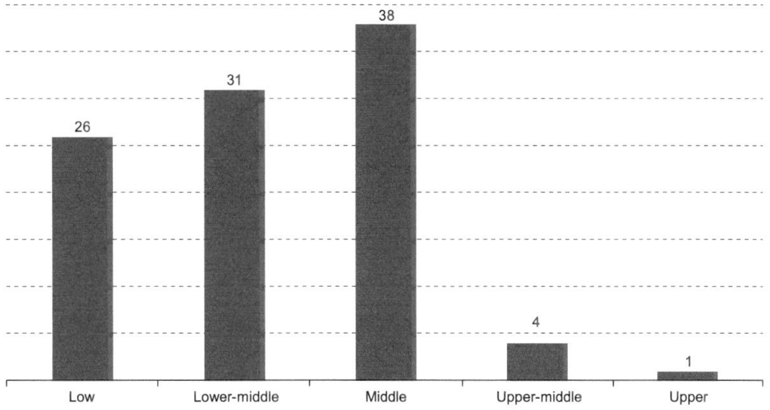

Source: Economic Commission for Latin America and the Caribbean (ECLAC), on the basis of tabulations of data from the 2011 Latinobarómetro database.
[a] Simple average for 18 countries in the region: Argentina, Bolivarian Republic of Venezuela, Brazil, Colombia, Chile, Costa Rica, Dominican Republic, Ecuador, El Salvador, Guatemala, Honduras, Mexico, Nicaragua, Panamá, Paraguay, Peru, Plurinational State of Bolivia and Uruguay.
[b] The question used was the following: "People sometimes describe themselves as belonging to a social class. Would you describe yourself as belonging to the upper, upper-middle, middle, lower-middle or lower class?"

Figure II.8
Latin America (18 countries): sense of belonging to the middle and lower-middle classes, by country, 2011
(Percentages)

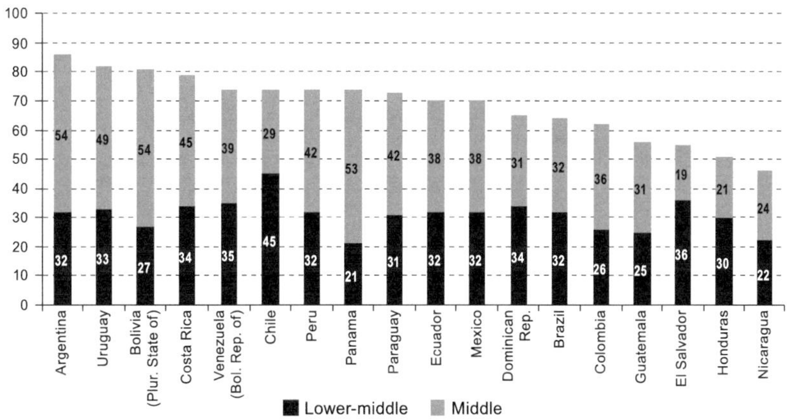

Source: Economic Commission for Latin America and the Caribbean (ECLAC), on the basis of tabulations of data from the 2011 Latinobarómetro database.

There are several ways to explain the situation in El Salvador and Nicaragua; they are not mutually exclusive. One has to do with challenges in measuring income that could lead to understatement of bipolarization in these countries. Another is that the sense of belonging to the middle class is undercaptured. Anyway, there is not enough background information to confirm or reject these hypotheses.

An alternative hypothesis is that people may tend more to define themselves as middle-class in countries with less absolute poverty. Environments with a lower incidence of poverty might increase the likelihood of people feeling that they belong to the middle class, provided that two conditions are met: (i) people believe that the middle class begins once basic subsistence needs are covered or when a certain poverty threshold is crossed; and (ii) there is a certain conceptual proximity between people's concept (and threshold) of poverty and the one used in monetary measurement.

Figure II.9
Latin America (18 countries): population identifying with the middle class [a] and bipolarization of the income distribution, [b c d] 2011
(Percentages and indices)

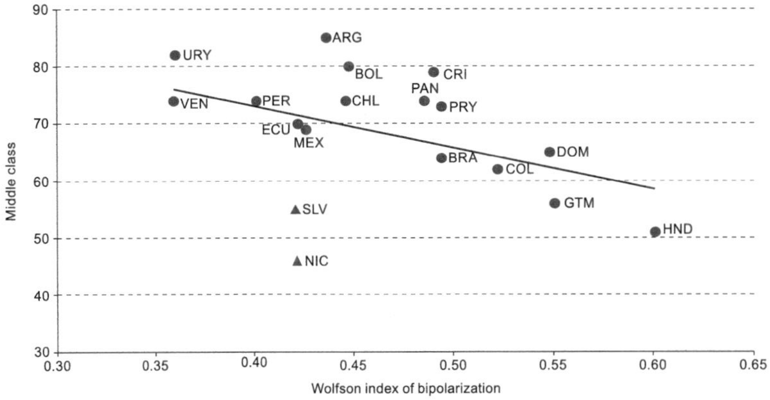

Source: Economic Commission for Latin America and the Caribbean (ECLAC), on the basis of tabulations of data from the 2011 Latinobarómetro database and from household surveys conducted in Argentina, Bolivarian Republic of Venezuela, Brazil, Chile, Colombia, Costa Rica, Dominican Republic, Ecuador, El Salvador (2010), Guatemala (2006), Honduras (2010), Nicaragua (2009), Panama, Paraguay, Peru, Plurinational State of Bolivia, Uruguay.
[a] Individuals who reported belonging to the middle class or lower-middle class are considered as middle class.
[b] The Wolfson index was calculated on the basis of the method used historically by ECLAC for aggregating income, because the new aggregations of income for 2011 were not yet available.
[c] Spearman's rho nonparametric correlation all countries=-0.373, p=0.127. Excluding Nicaragua and El Salvador, Spearman's rho =-0.689, p = 0.003**.
[d] OLS regression model all countries, p=0.080, adjusted R-squared 12.8%. Highest standardized residuals: Nicaragua=-2.5, El Salvador=-1.6.

Figure II.10 shows that the percentage of the population identifying as middle class is significantly higher in countries where the incidence of poverty is lower (such as Argentina, Uruguay and Costa Rica). This association is supported when controlling for polarization and per-capita GDP, and it is robust to changes in model specification. The countries where the observed values for identification with the middle class are farthest from the expected values are Brazil, Nicaragua, Plurinational State of Bolivia and Paraguay. In the latter two, the observed value is higher than the expected one; in the former two, the reverse occurs.

Figure II.10
Latin America (18 countries): population with a sense of belonging to the middle class and incidence of monetary poverty, [a b c d e] 2011
(Percentages)

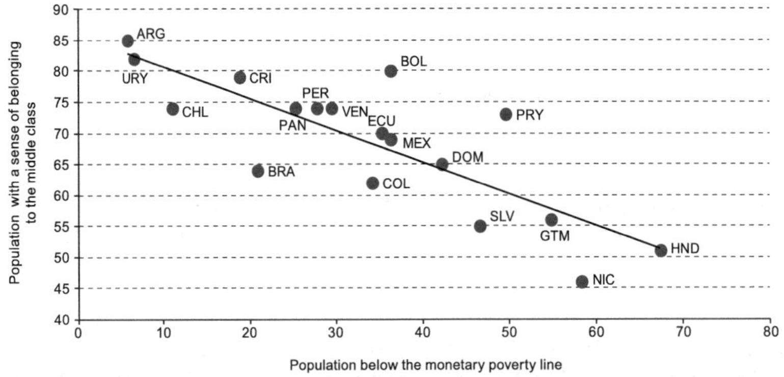

Source: Economic Commission for Latin America and the Caribbean (ECLAC), on the basis of tabulations of data from the 2011 Latinobarómetro database and from household surveys conducted in Argentina, Bolivarian Republic of Venezuela, Brazil, Chile, Colombia, Costa Rica, Dominican Republic, Ecuador, El Salvador (2010), Guatemala (2006), Honduras (2010), Nicaragua (2009), Panama, Paraguay, Peru, Plurinational State of Bolivia, Uruguay.
[a] The middle class population includes individuals who reported belonging to the middle or lower-middle class.
[b] The incidence of monetary poverty corresponds to ECLAC estimates for 2011 for 2011, except for El Salvador, Honduras and Mexico (2010), Nicaragua (2009) and Guatemala (2006).
[c] Spearman's rho non-parametric correlation=-0.767, p=0.000***. OLS regression, standardized Beta coefficient Poverty=-0.804, p=0.000***. Highest residuals: Brazil =-1.6, Nicaragua=-1.5, Paraguay=1.8, Plurinational State of Bolivia=1.9.
[d] OLS regression model controlling for polarization: poverty, p=0.000***, polarization=0.841, adjusted R-squared=60%. Durbin Watson=2.219 (independent residuals between 1.5 and 2.5), VIF (variance inflation, lowest possible value 1, values greater than 10 indicate collinearity)=1.321. Excluding Honduras and Nicaragua, poverty, p=0.013* and Wolfson, p=0.384, adjusted R-squared=44%.
[e] OLS regression model, controlling for GDP per capita: poverty, p=0.001**, GDP=0.296, adjusted R-squared=62.8%. Durbin Watson=2.255 (independent residuals between 1.5 and 2.5), VIF (variance inflation, lowest possible value 1, values greater than 10 indicate collinearity)=2.640. Excluding Mexico and Plurinational State of Bolivia, poverty, p=0.010* and GDP, p=0.565, adjusted R-squared=68%.

But these results should be evaluated with caution because of the risk of spurious correlations. And there is room for questioning the validity of a measure of the middle class based on evaluations by individuals, on the grounds that evaluations could mainly be socially desirable responses (high percentages of identification with the middle class and lower-middle class could be interpreted as reflecting this tendency). With this in mind, the conceptual proximity between the indicator for identification with the middle class and how people evaluate their own socioeconomic status was examined in order to validate the indicator, and the relationship between the sense of belonging to social classes and some commonly used measures to characterize social classes externally was examined.

Cantril's ladder question was used for the first type of analysis, asking people to rank their financial situation on an ordinal scale of poverty-wealth. In this case, the averages were not used as indicators of well-being because these are sensitive to response scale values, with the aggravating factor that different criteria for assigning values to that scale are admissible.[13] (For example, rankings of well-being based on averages should be different if, instead of using a linear scale, the scale gave more weight to levels of greater wealth.) It was therefore decided to use medians as indicators of economic well-being because they are robust to response scales, given that their value depends solely on cumulative frequency distribution.[14]

Based on this analysis scheme, in 16 of 18 countries (89%), individuals in the lower-middle class people rank their economic well-being higher than those who identify with the lower class. This percentage decreases when the medians for the middle class are compared with those for the lower-middle class (56%). In 17 of 18 countries, perceived economic well-being is greater among those who identify with the middle class (including the middle class and the lower-middle class) than in those who report belonging to the lower class (see table II.5).

Table II.5

Latin America (18 countries):[a] self-evaluation of economic well-being,[b] according to sense of belonging to a social class, by country,[c] 2011

Country	Lower class	Lower-middle class (1)	Middle class (2)	Total middle class (1+2)
Argentina	4	5	6	5
Bolivia (Plurinational State of)	3	5	5	5
Brazil	4	5	5	5
Chile	4	5	5	5
Colombia	3	4	5	4
Costa Rica	4	5	6	5
Dominican Republic	3	4	5	5
Ecuador	4	5	6	5
El Salvador	3	5	5	5
Guatemala	2	4	5	4
Honduras	3	4	5	4
Mexico	4	4	5	5
Nicaragua	2	4	5	4
Panama	4	5	5	5
Paraguay	4	5	5	5
Peru	3	5	5	5
Uruguay	4	5	5	5
Venezuela (Bolivarian Republic of)	5	5	6	5
Percentage dominance		89%	56%	94%

Source: Economic Commission for Latin America and the Caribbean (ECLAC), on the basis of tabulations of data from the 2011 Latinobarómetro database.
[a] The question used in the 2011 Latinobarómetro survey was: "Imagine a ladder with 10 steps, where the poorest people are on the first step and the richest people are on the tenth step. Where would you be?"
[b] Values shown are the respective medians.
[c] The population that self-identified as upper-middle class or upper class was excluded due to sample size restrictions.

[13] See Allison and Foster (2004) and Dutta and Foster (2011) for further detail.
[14] In any event, there are still methodological challenges, including how to deal with distances between steps. Median-based dominance analyses are not sensitive to these differences; this means, for example, that two-step differences in well-being between the middle class and the lower class (as in the Dominican Republic, El Salvador, Guatemala, Nicaragua and the Plurinational State of Bolivia) are treated the same as differences of one step.

A similar conclusion —one that is based on information from the entire distribution— emerges from a look at figure II.11, where the cumulative frequency distribution for the total middle class indicates greater economic well-being than for the lower class. This pattern is mainly seen on the first five steps of the economic well-being scale, and it is highest on the third and fourth steps. For example, the cumulative percentage of middle-class subjects on the fourth step is 37%, and it climbs to 65% among those who report belonging to the lower class.

Figure II.11

Latin America (18 countries): position on the poverty-wealth scale of individuals with a sense of belonging to the lower class or the lower-middle class, cumulative distribution,[a] 2011

(Percentages)

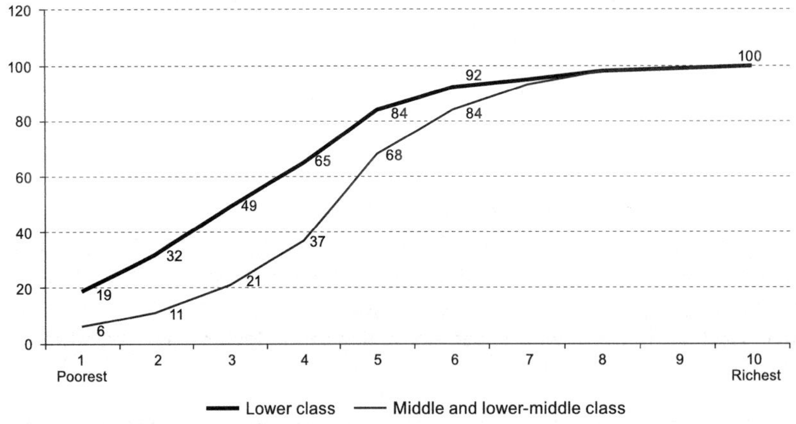

Source: Economic Commission for Latin America and the Caribbean (ECLAC), on the basis of tabulations of data from the 2011 Latinobarómetro database.

[a] The cumulative percentages are simple regional averages for 18 countries in the region: Argentina, Bolivarian Republic of Venezuela, Brazil, Colombia, Chile, Costa Rica, Dominican Republic, Ecuador, El Salvador, Guatemala, Honduras, Mexico, Nicaragua, Panama, Paraguay, Peru, Plurinational State of Bolivia and Uruguay.

As for the relationship between class identification and some measures normally used to characterize classes externally, figure II.12 shows that years of schooling increase as individuals rank their class position higher: almost half of the individuals who reported belonging to the lower class had an incomplete basic education, while only a fifth of those who reported belonging to the upper or upper-middle class had an incomplete basic education. Among those who reported belonging to the upper class or upper-middle class, 32% had an incomplete or complete higher education. This percentage drops to 4% for those who reported belonging to the lower class.

Figure II.12 also provides information on the sense of belonging to a class and occupational insertion. On average for the region, the incidence of independent or own-account work is higher among those who identified themselves as belonging to the lower class (36%) and lower among those who reported belonging to the upper or upper-middle class (29%). By contrast, the prevalence of wage workers is higher among the population reporting belonging to the upper or upper-middle class and lower among those who reported belonging to the lower class (30% and 18%, respectively). The percentage of individuals employed in unpaid domestic work is higher among those who reported belonging to the lower class (30%) and lower among those who reported belonging to the upper-middle class or upper class (19%).

Figure II.13 shows occupational situation for individuals with a sense of belonging to the middle class or lower class, disaggregated by country. Among those who identify with the lower class and reside in less developed countries, the predominant occupational status is independent or own-account. Among subjects who have a sense of belonging to the lower class but live in more developed countries, the percentage of wage workers goes up. A similar tendency is seen in the population that reported belonging to the middle class, with the difference that, overall, the percentage of wage workers rises and the incidence of own-account workers falls.

Figure II.12

Latin America (18 countries): education level and occupation, by class identification, simple average, 2011 [a]

(Percentages)

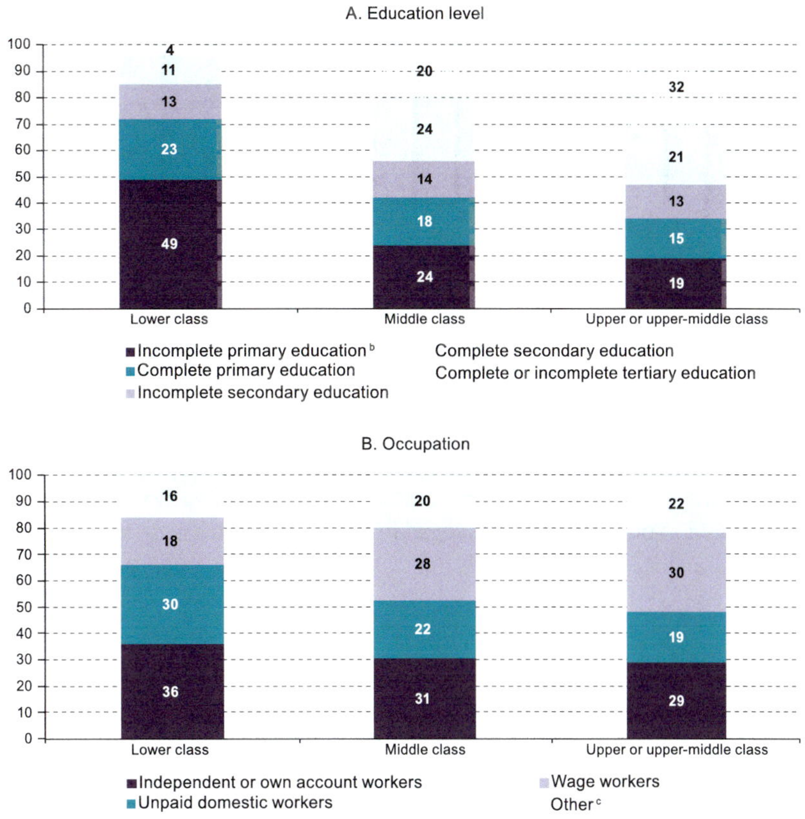

Source: Economic Commission for Latin America and the Caribbean (ECLAC), on the basis of tabulations of data from the 2011 Latinobarómetro database

[a] The cumulative percentages are simple regional averages for 18 countries in the region: Argentina, Bolivarian Republic of Venezuela, Brazil, Colombia, Chile, Costa Rica, Dominican Republic, Ecuador, El Salvador, Guatemala, Honduras, Mexico, Nicaragua, Panama, Paraguay, Peru, Plurinational State of Bolivia and Uruguay.

[b] Includes incomplete primary education, and those with no formal schooling.

[c] Includes students, pensioners and the unemployed.

Figure II.13

Latin America (18 countries): occupational situation among individuals with a sense of belonging to the middle class or lower class, by country, 2011

(Percentages)

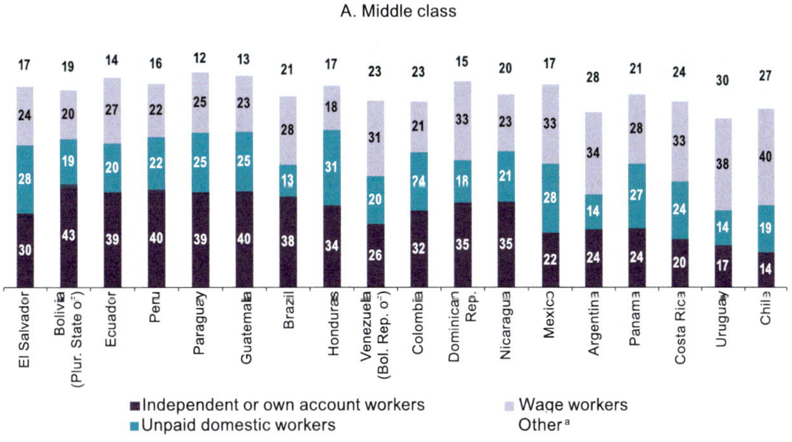

Figure II.13 (concluded)

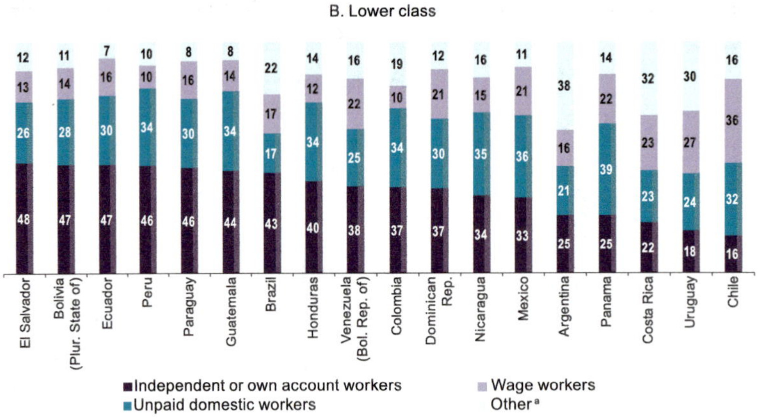

Source: Economic Commission for Latin America and the Caribbean (ECLAC), on the basis of tabulations of data from the 2011 Latinobarómetro database.
[a] Includes students, pensioners and the unemployed.

The greatest differences in occupational status among subjectively defined social classes are in the incidence of wage work and unpaid domestic work. The percentage of wage workers is, on average for the region, 1.62 times higher among individuals who self-identify as belonging to the middle class than among those who report a sense of belonging to the lower class; the proportion of individuals employed in unpaid domestic work is, on average, 1.39 times higher among those who report belonging to the lower class than among those who report belonging to the middle class.

These findings suggest that the availability of wage work is a kind of symbolic boundary used for differentiation between social classes. This might not only be due to the fact that this type of occupation generally provides a higher social status; it might also be because it provides levels of protection and security not attainable with own-account work. In turn, the incidence of unpaid domestic work (which is, in the countries of the region, performed mainly by women) might have to do, first, with deprivation of the degree of autonomy/independence required to meet basic needs, and, second, to impediments to participation and recognition in the public sphere, beyond the domestic sphere. Either way, this should be the subject of further analysis from a gender equality perspective.

2. Social class expectations and identities

It has been seen that the analysis of social classes can be enriched by incorporating subject perceptions and evaluations. In the latter sphere, standards (social mobility expectations, consumption aspirations) that individuals use to evaluate their living conditions provide basic achievement criteria against which individuals judge their socioeconomic outcomes. Failure to attain these standards could lead to expressions of social unrest.

The relationship between achievement standards and class identities can be modelled on the basis of the following assumptions: (i) in societies with an unequal distribution of resources and opportunities, segmentation of the standards for ranking living conditions is to be expected; (ii) the stringency of the standards should reflect the position that the subjects (believe they) occupy in the socioeconomic structure; accordingly, the middle classes would have more demanding standards than the lower classes because they start from a higher floor of resources and opportunities; and (iii) in societies with a greater proportion of the middle sectors and a lower incidence of lower sectors, it could be expected that, in aggregate terms, the standards would be more demanding.

Expectations of intergenerational mobility can be used as a proxy for the stringency of standards for evaluating living conditions. In societies where a portion of the population has improved its socioeconomic status, it is plausible that individuals will sustain higher expectations, either because they start from a better floor of resources or because they have observed mobility processes in their environment. However, in societies where access to opportunities is very limited and the living standards of the general population have not improved (or have improved very little), expectations should be lower.[15]

[15] There are other factors that (together with the expansion of average consumption levels) could influence the standards used by the population. One possibility is that dissemination of the rights-based approach is increasing the demand level of the standards that the population uses to rank living conditions.

Mobility expectations can be analysed by examining the difference between perception of present economic well-being and expectations for the well-being that offspring will attain. A first look at the data indicates that, on average for the region, expectations for the future well-being of offspring are placed on higher steps than those used by respondents to rank their present well-being. Thus, 42% of the respondents believe that their offspring's well-being will be above the fifth step of the poverty-wealth scale, while only 29% placed their present economic well-being above the fifth step (see figure II.14).

Figure II.14
Latin America (18 countries): present economic well-being and well-being expected for offspring in the future, 2011 [a] [b]
(Percentages)

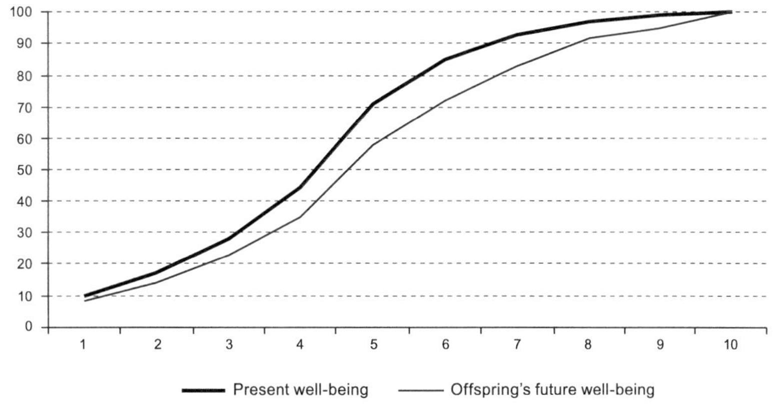

Source: Economic Commission for Latin America and the Caribbean (ECLAC), on the basis of tabulations of data from the 2011 Latinobarómetro database.
[a] The questions used in the 2011 Latinobarómetro survey were: "Imagine a ladder with 10 steps, where the poorest people are on the first step and the richest people are on the tenth step. Where would you put yourself on this ladder? And where do you think your children will be?"
[b] Simple averages for 18 countries in the region: Argentina, Bolivarian Republic of Venezuela, Brazil, Colombia, Chile, Costa Rica, Dominican Republic, Ecuador, El Salvador, Guatemala, Honduras, Mexico, Nicaragua, Panama, Paraguay, Peru, Plurinational State of Bolivia and Uruguay.

Figure II.15 shows that, on average for the region, expectations for offspring's well-being are higher among those who identify with the middle class and lower for those who reported being in the lower class. Fifty-three percent of the population reporting being in the lower class believe that the economic well-being attained by their offspring will not go above the fourth step of Cantril's ladder scale, while 47% expect that offspring's standard of living will be higher than that step. Among those who reported belonging to the lower-middle class, 37% believe that their children will attain a level of economic well-being no higher than the fourth step of the poverty-wealth scale; among those who identify with the middle class, this figure is 23% (77%).

Figure II.15
Latin America (18 countries): future well-being of offspring, by class identification, simple averages, 2011 [a]
(Percentages)

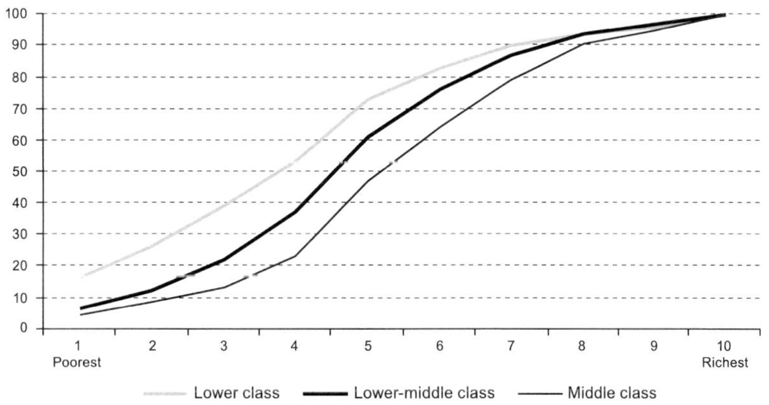

Source: Economic Commission for Latin America and the Caribbean (ECLAC), on the basis of tabulations of data from the 2011 Latinobarómetro database.
[a] Simple averages for 18 countries in the region: Argentina, Bolivarian Republic of Venezuela, Brazil, Colombia, Chile, Costa Rica, Dominican Republic, Ecuador, El Salvador, Guatemala, Honduras, Mexico, Nicaragua, Panama, Paraguay, Peru, Plurinational State of Bolivia and Uruguay.

Figure II.16 charts evaluations of present economic well-being and expectations for offspring's well-being. In 8 of 18 countries examined, expectations for the future of offspring are higher than evaluations of present well-being, and therefore express expectations of intergenerational mobility. In the other countries there is no difference, which means expectations are that position in the socioeconomic structure will be maintained (reproduced). This situation mainly refers to countries with higher poverty rates (or lower relative social development), although there are exceptions such as Uruguay.

Figure II.16

Latin America (18 countries): present economic well-being and expectations for offspring's future, 2011 [a b]

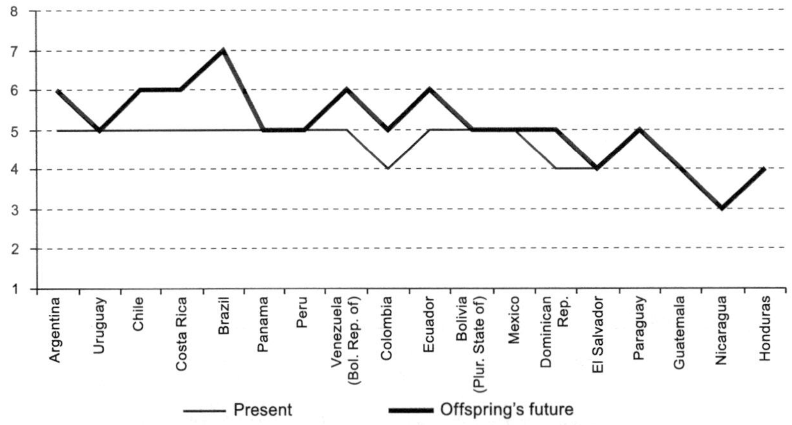

Source: Economic Commission for Latin America and the Caribbean (ECLAC), on the basis of tabulations of data from the 2011 Latinobarómetro database.

[a] Results are the median for each country. A value of 1 indicates worst level of poverty.

[b] Countries are ordered by rates of monetary poverty rate, from lowest to highest.

Brazil is the country where expectations of offspring's well-being are highest (on the seventh step of the poverty-wealth scale). Next are Chile, Argentina, Costa Rica, the Bolivarian Republic of Venezuela and Ecuador. Nicaragua simultaneously shows the lowest level of expectations for offspring's well-being and the worst evaluation of present economic well-being. Then come Honduras, Guatemala and El Salvador. In these latter four countries, with monetary poverty rates close to or above 50%, there are no differences between the median values for expectations and for present evaluation, which could be an expression of a sense of learned helplessness.

Figure II.17 charts evaluations of present economic well-being and expectations for offspring's future for different class identification groups. Strictly speaking, not all groupings of classes or countries have differences between the perception of present economic well-being and expectations about the future of offspring. In 8 of 18 countries, individuals who feel they are in the middle class believe that their children will be better off. For the lower-middle class, this is the case in just 5 of 18 countries. Regarding the population that identifies as lower class, in 10 of 18 countries expectations for offspring are better than evaluations of the present situation. Among those who defined themselves as upper or upper-middle class, in 12 of 18 countries expectations for offspring's future well-being are higher than evaluations of present well-being.

Brazil is the country with the highest expectations of intergenerational social mobility, and they cut across class identities. Such cross-cutting expectations of mobility are seen in Chile and Argentina, too. Expectations of intergenerational mobility are higher in the outlier class identification groupings (lower class and upper or upper-middle class); their incidence is lower in the lower-middle class. Among those who feel they are in the lower class, mobility expectations are higher for those living in more developed countries. This means there could be a demonstration effect at work, with expectations among sectors of the lower class rising as they observe higher consumption levels in other groups.

In short, it has been seen that in countries with less poverty and greater relative development there is a greater sense of identification with the middle class. It has also been observed that expectations of economic progress are higher among individuals who identify with the middle class than among individuals who feel they are in the lower class. All of these factors should be considered when designing policies for social cohesion, especially in the economic slowdown scenario that the countries of the region are facing.

Figure II.17

Latin America (18 countries): present economic well-being and expectations for offspring's future, by identification of social class, 2011 [a]

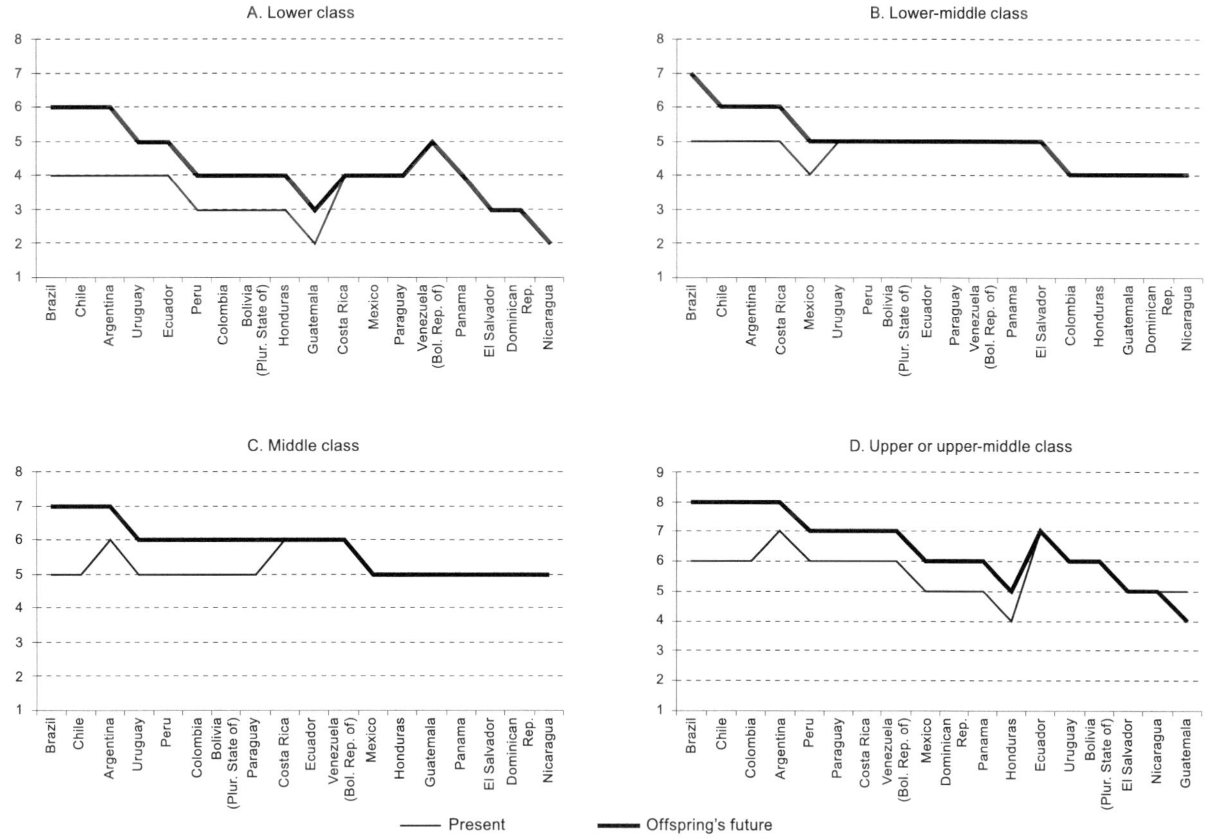

Source: Economic Commission for Latin America and the Caribbean (ECLAC), on the basis of tabulations of data from the 2011 Latinobarómetro database.
[a] Results are the median for each country. A value of 1 indicates worst level of poverty.

Bibliography

Aguilar Gutiérrez, Genaro (2013), "¿Está desapareciendo la clase media en México? Análisis de la polarización del ingreso", *Revista de Ciencias Sociales,* vol. XIX, No. 1.

Allison, Andrew and James E. Foster (2004), "Measuring health inequality using qualitative data", *Journal of Health Economics,* No. 23.

Borraz, Fernando, Nicolás González Pampillón and Máximo Rossi (2013), "Polarization and the middle class", *Latin American Journal of Economics,* vol. 50, No. 2.

Clementi, Fabio and Francesco Schettino (2013), "Income polarization in Brazil, 2001-2011: A distributional analysis using PNAD data", paper prepared for the Second AIEAA Conference "Between Crisis and Development: which Role for the Bio-Economy", Parma, Italy, 6-7 June.

Cruces, Guillermo, Luis Felipe López Calva and Diego Battistón (2011), "Down and out or up and in? Polarization-based measures of the middle class for Latin America", *Documento de Trabajo,* No. 113, Center for Distributive, Labour and Social Studies (CEDLAS) [online] cedlas.econo.unlp.edu.ar/archivos_upload/doc_cedlas113.pdf.

D'Ambrosio, Conchita and Iñaki Permanyer (2010), "Measuring social polarization with ordinal and cardinal data: an application to the missing dimensions of poverty in Chile" [online] http://www.chronicpoverty.org/uploads/publication_files/d-ambrosio_permanyer_chile.pdf.

Duclos, Jean Yves, Joan Esteban and Debraj Ray (2004), "Polarization: Concepts, measurement, estimation", *Econometrica,* No. 72.

Dutta, Indranil and James Foster (2011), "Inequality of Happiness in US: 1972-2008" [online] http://www.socialsciences.manchester.ac.uk/medialibrary/economics/discussionpapers/EDP-1110.pdf.

ECLAC (Economic Commission for Latin America and the Caribbean) (2014), Compacts for Equality: Towards a sustainable future (LC/G.2586(SES.35/3)), Santiago, Chile.

___ (2012), *Structural Change for Equality: An integrated approach to development* (LC/G.2524(SES.34/3)), Santiago, Chile.

___ (2010), *Time for Equality: closing gaps, opening trails* (LC/G.2432(SES.33/3)), Santiago, Chile.

Esteban, Joan (1996), "Desigualdad y polarización interprovincial de la renta en España", Revista de Economía Aplicada, vol. 11, No. 4.

Esteban, Joan and Debraj Ray (2010), "Comparing Polarization Measures", University of New York [online] http://www.econ.nyu.edu/user/debraj/Papers/EstRayChapter.pdf.

___ (1994), "On the measurement of polarization", *Econometrica,* vol. 62, No. 4.

Esteban, Joan, Carlos Gradín and Debraj Ray (2007), "An extension of a measure of polarization, with an application to the income distribution of five OECD countries", *Journal of Economic Inequality*, No. 5.

___ (1999), "Extensions of a measure of polarization with and application to the income distribution of five OECD countries", *Luxembourg Income Study Working Paper,* No. 218, New York, Maxwell School of Citizenship and Public Affairs, Syracuse University.

Foster, James E. and Michael C. Wolfson (2002), "Polarization and the decline of the middle class: Canada and the US", *OPHI Working Paper,* No. 31 [online] http://www.ophi.org.uk/wp-content/uploads/OPHI-wp31.pdf?92fa97.

Gallo, Mariana (2010), "Polarización de ingresos y ciclo económico: experiencia uruguaya 1999-2009", Universidad Autónoma de Barcelona [online] http://dep-economia-aplicada.uab.cat/secretaria/docrecerca/mgallo.pdf.

Gasparini, Leonardo and others (2008), "Polarización económica, instituciones y conflictos" [online] http://cieplan.lemongroup.cl/media/publicaciones/archivos/206/Anexos.pdf.

Gradín, Carlos and Coral del Río (2001), "La medición de la polarización", Universidad de Vigo [online] http://decon.edu.uy/~mito/nip/polarizacion.pdf.

Groisman, Fernando (2013), "Income polarization, the middle class and informal employment in Greater Buenos Aires, 1974-2010", *CEPAL Review,* No. 109 (LC/G.2556-P/E), Santiago, Chile, Economic Commission for Latin America and the Caribbean (ECLAC), April.

Larrú, José María (2013), "Polarización, desigualdad y ayuda al desarrollo en América Latina", *América Latina Hoy*, No. 63.

Lasso de la Vega, María and Ana Urrutia (2002), "Desigualdad y polarización de la renta a nivel mundial", Universidad del País Vasco [online] www.alde.es/encuentros/anteriores/vieea/autores/L/137.doc.

Modrego, Félix, Ximena Celis and Julio Berdegué (2008), "Polarización étnica de los ingresos rurales en el sur de Chile" [online] http://www.rimisp.org/wp-content/files_mf/136640403415_PolarizacionetnicaingresosChile_ModregoCelisBerdegue_2008.pdf.

UNDP (United Nations Development Programme)/Fundación UNIR (2012), "La protesta social en América Latina", *Cuaderno de Prospectiva Política,* No. 1, Buenos Aires, Siglo XXI.

Villalobos, Cristóbal and Juan Pablo Valenzuela (2012), "Polarización y cohesión social del sistema escolar chileno", *Revista de Análisis Económico*, vol. 27, No. 2.

Viollaz, Mariana, Sergio Olivieri and Javier Alejo (2009), "Labor income polarization in Greater Buenos Aires", *Documento de Trabajo*, No. 89, Center for Distributive, Labour and Social Studies (CEDLAS) [online] http://mpra.ub.uni-muenchen.de/42944//.

Wang, You-Qiang and Kai-Yuen Tsui (2000), "Polarization orderings and new classes of polarization indices", *Journal of Public Economic Theory*, vol. 2, No. 3.

Wolfson, Michael C. (1994), "When inequalities diverge", *American Economic Review*, vol. 84, No. 2.

Annex

Table II.A.1

Latin America (18 countries): household income distribution, 1990-2013 [a]

Country	Year	Average income [b]	Share of total income (percentages)				Ratio of average income per capita (times) [c]	
			Poorest 40%	Next 30%	20% before richest 10%	Richest 10%	$D^{10} / D^{(1\ to\ 4)}$	Q^5 / Q^1
Argentina [d]	1990 [e]	10.6	14.9	23.6	26.7	34.8	13.5	13.5
	1999	11.3	15.9	22.1	25.3	36.7	16.2	16.6
	2004	9.0	13.1	21.4	25.5	40.0	21.7	26.5
	2011	20.6	17.3	24.9	27.2	30.6	13.5	14.7
	2012	22.8	18.2	26.1	26.9	28.8	11.9	13.2
Bolivia (Plurinational State of)	1989 [f]	7.7	12.0	21.9	27.9	38.2	17.1	21.3
	1999	5.6	9.2	24.0	29.6	37.2	26.7	48.0
	2002	6.1	9.5	21.3	28.3	40.9	30.3	44.2
	2009	6.5	13.9	27.1	28.4	30.6	14.9	19.8
	2011	7.2	15.6	28.3	29.7	26.4	12.1	15.9
Brazil	1990	9.4	9.5	18.6	28.0	43.9	31.2	35.0
	1999	11.3	10.1	17.3	25.5	47.1	31.9	35.6
	2001	11.0	10.2	17.5	25.5	46.8	32.1	36.9
	2012	13.3	14.0	20.4	24.6	41.0	20.2	22.5
	2013	13.1	14.4	21.1	25.6	38.9	18.2	21.3
Chile	1990	9.5	13.2	20.8	25.4	40.6	18.2	18.4
	1998	13.7	13.0	20.5	26.6	39.9	19.1	19.7
	2003	13.6	13.7	20.7	25.5	40.1	18.8	18.4
	2011	14.2	15.0	21.5	25.9	37.6	15.1	15.0
	2013	15.0	15.3	21.8	26.7	36.2	15.0	14.5
Colombia	1994	7.7	10.0	21.3	26.9	41.8	26.8	35.2
	1999	6.7	12.3	21.6	26.0	40.1	22.3	25.6
	2002 [g]	7.2	13.0	22.5	26.6	37.9	22.0	24.1
	2012 [g]	8.3	14.2	24.4	26.9	34.5	17.5	19.8
	2013 [g]	8.6	14.4	24.1	27.0	34.5	17.8	20.0
Costa Rica	1990	9.5	16.7	27.4	30.2	25.7	10.1	13.1
	1999	11.4	15.3	25.7	29.7	29.3	12.6	15.3
	2002	11.7	14.5	25.6	29.7	30.2	13.7	17.0
	2012 [h]	11.5	14.0	24.3	29.3	32.4	14.7	16.5
	2013 [h]	11.7	13.7	23.5	29.3	33.5	14.8	16.9
Dominican Republic	2002	6.9	12.7	22.7	26.9	37.7	17.8	20.7
	2008	7.3	11.5	23.2	30.4	34.9	21.2	25.4
	2012	7.1	12.5	23.5	29.6	34.4	16.5	19.4
	2013	7.6	12.1	22.6	28.0	37.3	18.5	21.2
Ecuador [d]	1990	5.5	17.2	25.4	27.0	30.4	11.4	12.3
	1999	5.6	14.1	22.8	26.5	36.6	17.2	18.5
	2002	6.7	15.4	24.3	26.0	34.3	15.6	16.8
	2011	7.4	18.5	26.6	28.4	26.5	9.7	10.7
	2013	7.9	17.5	25.3	26.3	30.9	11.2	11.7
El Salvador	1995	6.2	15.4	24.8	26.9	32.9	14.1	16.9
	1999	6.6	13.8	25.0	29.1	32.1	15.2	19.6
	2001	6.7	13.4	24.6	28.7	33.3	16.2	20.2
	2012	5.6	19.2	26.7	26.9	27.2	9.7	10.3
	2013	6.0	18.2	26.0	26.2	29.6	10.5	11.0
Guatemala	1989	6.0	11.8	20.9	26.8	40.5	23.6	27.3
	1998	7.1	14.3	21.6	25.0	39.1	20.4	19.7
	2002	6.8	14.1	22.3	27.2	36.4	18.6	19.3
	2006	7.6	12.8	21.7	25.7	39.8	22.0	23.9

Table II.A.1 (concluded)

Country	Year	Average income [b]	Share of total income (percentages)				Ratio of average income per capita (times) [c]	
			Poorest 40%	Next 30%	20% before richest 10%	Richest 10%	$D^{10}/D^{(1\ to\ 4)}$	Q^5/Q^1
Honduras	1990	4.3	10.1	19.7	27.0	43.2	27.3	30.9
	1999	3.9	11.8	22.9	28.9	36.4	22.3	26.5
	2002	4.3	11.3	21.7	27.6	39.4	23.6	26.3
	2007	4.7	10.0	23.5	29.5	37.0	23.6	32.5
	2010	4.7	10.9	23.0	29.9	36.2	21.7	28.4
Mexico	1989	8.6	15.8	22.5	25.1	36.6	17.2	16.9
	1998	7.7	15.1	22.7	25.6	36.6	18.4	18.5
	2002	8.2	15.7	23.8	27.3	33.2	15.1	15.5
	2010	7.4	17.7	25.4	27.2	29.7	12.8	13.3
	2012	7.1	17.4	24.9	26.3	31.4	14.2	14.0
Nicaragua	1993	5.2	10.4	22.8	28.4	38.4	26.5	37.2
	1998	5.6	10.4	22.1	27.1	40.4	25.4	34.6
	2001	5.8	12.0	21.6	25.6	40.8	23.8	27.3
	2009	5.7	16.5	25.5	28.1	29.9	12.9	14.5
Panama	1991 [d]	11.1	14.1	23.8	29.4	32.7	16.8	20.2
	1999 [d]	12.9	15.6	25.2	27.8	31.4	13.9	15.9
	2002	9.8	12.1	23.6	28.0	36.3	20.1	25.8
	2011	10.9	14.5	25.1	27.0	33.4	15.7	18.6
	2013	11.6	14.3	25.7	27.4	32.6	15.6	20.2
Paraguay	1990 [i]	7.7	18.6	25.7	26.8	28.9	10.2	10.6
	1999	6.3	13.3	23.4	27.6	35.7	19.1	23.2
	2001	6.3	13.5	23.6	26.2	36.7	19.5	23.2
	2012	6.2	14.2	26.1	26.7	33.0	15.0	17.7
	2013	7.6	13.8	23.6	27.5	35.1	17.2	19.1
Peru	1997	7.5	13.4	24.6	28.7	33.3	17.9	20.8
	1999	7.5	13.4	23.1	27.1	36.4	19.5	21.6
	2001	6.4	13.4	24.6	28.5	33.5	17.4	19.3
	2012	8.8	15.9	27.3	28.6	28.2	10.9	12.7
	2013	8.9	16.3	27.9	28.5	27.3	10.8	12.3
Uruguay [d]	1990	9.9	18.9	23.2	22.6	35.3	11.0	10.5
	1999	11.9	21.6	25.5	25.9	27.0	8.8	9.5
	2002	9.4	21.6	25.4	25.6	27.4	9.5	10.2
	2012	10.7	24.7	28.4	26.4	20.5	6.7	7.3
	2013	11.1	24.4	27.6	26.2	21.8	6.7	7.2
Venezuela (Bolivarian Republic of)	1990	8.9	16.7	25.7	28.9	28.7	12.1	13.4
	1999	7.2	14.5	25.1	29.0	31.4	15.0	18.0
	2002	7.1	14.3	24.9	29.5	31.3	14.5	18.1
	2012	8.6	19.8	28.5	28.0	23.7	8.0	9.4
	2013	7.3	19.5	28.8	27.5	24.2	8.3	10.1

Source: Economic Commission for Latin America and the Caribbean (ECLAC), on the basis of special tabulations of data from household surveys conducted in the respective countries.

[a] Households nationwide ranked by per capita income.

[b] Average monthly household income in multiples of the per capita poverty line.

[c] D(1 to 4) represents the 40% lowest income households; D10 is the 10% highest income households. The same notation is used for quintiles (Q), which represent groupings of 20% of households.

[d] Urban areas.

[e] Greater Buenos Aires.

[f] Eight main cities plus El Alto.

[g] Figures not comparable with those of previous years, owing to a change in the criterion for constructing the income aggregate.

[h] Figures not comparable with those of previous years, owing to a change in the survey used.

[i] Asunción metropolitan area.

Table II.A.2
Latin America (18 countries): indicators of income concentration, 1990-2013 [a]

Country	Year	Concentration indices				
		Gini [b]	Theil	Atkinson		
				(ε=0.5)	(ε=1.0)	(ε=1.5)
Argentina [c]	1990 [d]	0.501	0.555	0.216	0.360	0.473
	1999	0.539	0.667	0.250	0.410	0.530
	2004	0.578	0.720	0.276	0.452	0.582
	2011	0.492	0.511	0.204	0.351	0.473
	2012	0.475	0.457	0.189	0.332	0.454
Bolivia (Plurinational State of)	1989 [e]	0.537	0.573	0.242	0.426	0.587
	1999	0.586	0.657	0.293	0.537	0.736
	2002	0.614	0.775	0.322	0.553	0.732
	2009	0.508	0.511	0.223	0.413	0.594
	2011	0.472	0.398	0.187	0.359	0.527
Brazil	1990	0.627	0.816	0.324	0.528	0.663
	1999	0.640	0.914	0.341	0.537	0.662
	2001	0.639	0.914	0.340	0.536	0.665
	2012	0.567	0.797	0.277	0.443	0.568
	2013	0.553	0.648	0.255	0.425	0.556
Chile	1990	0.554	0.644	0.255	0.422	0.546
	1998	0.560	0.654	0.261	0.430	0.553
	2003	0.552	0.674	0.257	0.418	0.535
	2011	0.516	0.541	0.221	0.371	0.485
	2013	0.509	0.537	0.217	0.363	0.475
Colombia	1994	0.601	0.794	0.308	0.517	0.684
	1999	0.572	0.734	0.275	0.450	0.589
	2002	0.567	0.672	0.268	0.447	0.579
	2012 [f]	0.536	0.568	0.238	0.410	0.546
	2013 [f]	0.536	0.574	0.239	0.410	0.544
Costa Rica	1990	0.438	0.328	0.152	0.286	0.412
	1999	0.473	0.395	0.179	0.328	0.457
	2002	0.488	0.440	0.193	0.349	0.491
	2012 [g]	0.504	0.481	0.209	0.372	0.511
	2013 [g]	0.512	0.487	0.213	0.380	0.520
Dominican Republic	2002	0.537	0.569	0.236	0.404	0.536
	2008	0.550	0.593	0.249	0.429	0.569
	2012	0.517	0.499	0.218	0.387	0.530
	2013	0.544	0.593	0.245	0.417	0.548
Ecuador [h]	1990	0.461	0.403	0.173	0.306	0.422
	1999	0.526	0.567	0.228	0.381	0.498
	2002	0.513	0.563	0.222	0.370	0.484
	2011	0.434	0.353	0.154	0.277	0.382
	2013	0.468	0.425	0.180	0.313	0.417
El Salvador	1995	0.507	0.502	0.213	0.376	0.520
	1999	0.518	0.495	0.224	0.414	0.590
	2011	0.525	0.527	0.232	0.423	0.599
	2012	0.437	0.368	0.159	0.284	0.389
	2013	0.453	0.444	0.176	0.303	0.406
Guatemala	1989	0.582	0.735	0.282	0.459	0.587
	1998	0.560	0.760	0.273	0.428	0.534
	2002	0.542	0.583	0.239	0.401	0.515
	2006	0.585	0.773	0.291	0.467	0.590

Table II.A.2 (concluded)

Country	Year	Concentration indices				
		Gini [b]	Theil	Atkinson		
				(Ɛ=0.5)	(Ɛ=1.0)	(Ɛ=1.5)
Honduras	1990	0.615	0.816	0.317	0.515	0.647
	1999	0.564	0.636	0.263	0.451	0.603
	2002	0.588	0.719	0.288	0.476	0.608
	2010	0.573	0.625	0.271	0.475	0.628
Mexico	1989	0.536	0.680	0.248	0.400	0.509
	1998	0.539	0.634	0.245	0.403	0.515
	2002	0.514	0.521	0.218	0.372	0.485
	2010	0.481	0.458	0.192	0.335	0.448
	2012	0.492	0.503	0.203	0.344	0.451
Nicaragua	1993	0.582	0.670	0.269	0.454	0.600
	1998	0.583	0.730	0.284	0.479	0.644
	2001	0.579	0.782	0.288	0.469	0.615
	2005	0.532	0.614	0.241	0.402	0.526
	2009	0.478	0.437	0.189	0.337	0.462
Panama	1991 [h]	0.530	0.543	0.228	0.398	0.534
	1999 [h]	0.499	0.459	0.202	0.361	0.490
	2002	0.567	0.616	0.266	0.465	0.616
	2011	0.532	0.557	0.236	0.414	0.555
	2013	0.527	0.522	0.232	0.422	0.583
Paraguay	1990 [i]	0.447	0.365	0.161	0.287	0.386
	1999	0.558	0.659	0.264	0.452	0.601
	2001	0.558	0.673	0.265	0.450	0.606
	2012	0.502	0.521	0.216	0.379	0.520
	2013	0.522	0.551	0.227	0.391	0.529
Peru	1997	0.532	0.567	0.238	0.414	0.553
	1999	0.545	0.599	0.249	0.424	0.560
	2001	0.525	0.556	0.231	0.397	0.526
	2012	0.449	0.370	0.167	0.307	0.429
	2013	0.444	0.365	0.164	0.300	0.418
Uruguay [h]	1990	0.492	0.699	0.227	0.349	0.441
	1999	0.440	0.354	0.158	0.286	0.393
	2002	0.455	0.385	0.169	0.300	0.406
	2012	0.380	0.246	0.116	0.219	0.310
	2013	0.383	0.258	0.119	0.222	0.314
Venezuela (Bolivarian Republic of)	1990	0.471	0.416	0.183	0.327	0.446
	1999	0.498	0.464	0.202	0.363	0.507
	2002	0.500	0.456	0.201	0.361	0.501
	2012	0.405	0.290	0.133	0.249	0.358
	2013	0.407	0.286	0.131	0.246	0.353

Source: Economic Commission for Latin America and the Caribbean (ECLAC), on the basis of special tabulations of data from household surveys conducted in the respective countries.

[a] Calculated on the basis of the distribution of per capita income for individuals nationwide .
[b] Includes persons with zero income.
[c] Greater Buenos Aires.
[d] Urban areas.
[e] Eight main cities plus El Alto.
[g] Figures not comparable with those of previous years, owing to a change in the criterion for constructing the income aggregate.
[h] Figures not comparable with those of previous years, owing to a change in the survey used.
[h] Urban area.
[i] Asunción metropolitan area.

Chapter III

Youth: critical areas of the agenda for development with equality

Introduction

Integrating the youth population into development processes is crucial for progress towards a more egalitarian society. The link between education and employment is one of the keys to social inclusion at this stage of life. It is important to understand the diversity of young people's current situations and life paths, which can coexist rather uneasily with inclusion difficulties specific to this age group, rather than stigmatizing them when they become separated, even if only temporarily, from both these institutions. The stereotype of violent youth also needs to be done away with, as it is a hindrance to development in equality. Understanding how social participation develops in contexts of growing violence in the region is vital for creating escape routes from these situations. Again, youth participation in designing and debating development strategies is essential if significant progress is to be made.

In recent years, ECLAC has called for equality to be viewed as the end point of development, structural change as the path and politics as the instrument for achieving it (ECLAC, 2010, 2012 and 2014a), interpreting equality in a way that looks beyond the distribution of resources such as monetary income to encompass the equalization of opportunities and capabilities. This means understanding equality as the full exercise of citizenship, with dignity and mutual recognition between actors. Progress in this direction requires policies that promote both the autonomy of subjects and protection for their vulnerabilities. It is proposed that equality in this broad, relational sense should be recognized from a rights perspective, while also bearing in mind the need for greater collective solidarity and acceptance of the diversity of groups and identities, these being crucial for a more cohesive society and sustainable development. This also means subjects having the opportunity to participate actively in decisions affecting collective development rather than just being beneficiaries of them (ECLAC, 2014b). The objective of the present chapter is to explore this perspective further from a youth-centred perspective.

Structural change involves diversifying and modifying the production structure of our economies through technological innovation and encouragement for higher-productivity sectors, intensively incorporating knowledge and technical progress. Capacity-building in the new generations is one of the basic prerequisites for progress along this path and should complement the shift in the production structure. The youth population numbers about 160 million in the region (ECLAC/OIJ/IMJUVE, 2014) and will continue to be a very substantial proportion of the population in some countries over the coming decades. What is required for that population is a higher level of education, relevant training and better preparation for lifelong learning (ECLAC/OIJ/IMJUVE, 2014). In addition to persistent structural divides, ECLAC has noted that there are inequalities in capacity-building and employment. These inequities particularly affect the young and need to be responded to if progress is to be made along the path of sustainability with equality.

The position taken in the current debate on the Post-2015 Development Agenda is that the sustainable development targets which this will have to include should centre on people and on the quest for a just and inclusive world. It is also proposed that the greatest attention should be paid to the new generations, with particular emphasis on avoiding discrimination. The main goals include the development of skills for paid work and initiatives to reduce youth unemployment and promote access to high-quality employment.

This chapter of the *Social Panorama of Latin America* looks at a number of issues with a view to analysing the link between youth and development in the region. First it reviews the education and work aspect, identified by global development agendas as the essential pillar of inclusion and equality. Second, it analyses the settings of growing insecurity and violence facing the youth of Latin America as a major obstacle to their own development processes. To conclude, it proposes that young people themselves and their demands for the debates on the development agenda should be given a hearing.

A. Opportunities and capabilities: education and work for the young

It is in youth that the link between education and work, which are among the keys to social inclusion, becomes most firmly established. More years of education mean greater job opportunities, while creating the conditions for fuller participation in democratic societies. Young people tend to work in poorer-quality jobs with lower wages and are less likely to be covered by social security and protection systems. The segment of young people who are excluded from education and paid work is diverse, with some falling out of the system temporarily and a substantial proportion of young women devoting themselves to unpaid care and domestic work. It is important for there to be a better understanding of the complexity of the situations experienced by this group so that major factors shaping young lives are not overlooked.

The relationship between education and employment is recognized as one of the main factors in social inclusion for the young (ECLAC, 2005; ECLAC/OIJ, 2004 and 2008; ECLAC/UNFPA, 2012). It is mainly at this stage in life that these two vital spheres are connected, with efforts to continue in education often coinciding with the need or desire to work and earn money. As is shown over the course of the chapter from the evidence available in the region, the new generations of young people have benefited from improvements in basic indicators of education coverage and labour force participation. Nonetheless, ECLAC has also repeatedly referred to the paradoxes and strains affecting young Latin Americans in their development processes, not least because although they now spend an unprecedented amount of time in education, they have fewer employment opportunities than adults. Furthermore, the kinds of jobs available to them are of lower quality and have less social protection (ECLAC/OIJ/IMJUVE, 2014). This spills over into other factors crucial to young people's development, such as opportunities to achieve residential and financial autonomy.

In view of all this, the present section analyses the situation of young people in the areas of education and employment and shows how this has evolved in recent years. It looks particularly closely at the circumstances of young people who are not in education or work, in an effort to understand the variety of personal histories associated with this.

1. Formal education: the main route to capacity development

Developing capacities through the formal education system is one of the main routes to social inclusion for the young, although not the only one. Having more years of education not only means greater opportunities in the labour market but also equips young people to participate more fully in today's complex, globalized, democratic societies. Education is also one of the main tools for breaking the circle of intergenerational reproduction of poverty and exclusion.

In the past 20 years, the region has made great progress with the proportion of young people completing some cycle of education. Progress in primary education has been remarkable: the proportion of young people aged 15 to 19 who had completed this cycle rose from 60% in 1990 to 94% in 2012. It is also important to mention that the improvement in this indicator has come about essentially in the past 10 years, with about 30% more young people completing some education cycle than the decade before. The situation with secondary education has also improved substantially among young people aged between 20 and 24, although there is a long way to go before this vital stage of education is universalized. In the period between 1990 and 2012, the proportion of young people completing the secondary cycle more than doubled from 26% to 59% at the end of the period. Lastly, the share of young people completing tertiary education is still very low in the region: although the proportion of those aged between 25 and 29 with a complete tertiary education has also doubled over the past two decades, only 10% of young people on average have completed this cycle (see figure III.1).

Figure III.1

Latin America (18 countries):[a] proportion of people aged 15 to 29 with complete primary, secondary and tertiary education, by age group, 1990, 2002 and 2012

(Percentages)

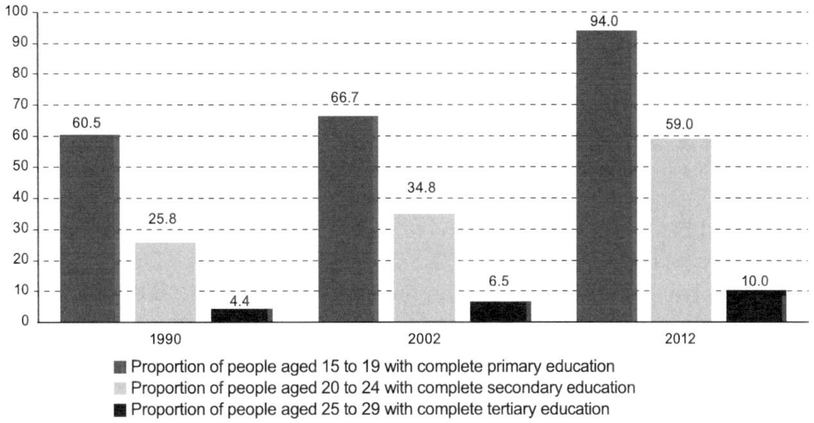

Source: Economic Commission for Latin America and the Caribbean (ECLAC), on the basis of special tabulations of data from household surveys conducted in the respective countries.

[a] Argentina (urban areas), Bolivarian Republic of Venezuela, Brazil, Chile, Colombia, Costa Rica, Dominican Republic, Ecuador, El Salvador, Guatemala, Honduras, Mexico, Nicaragua, Panama, Paraguay, Peru, Plurinational State of Bolivia and Uruguay.

Although positive at the regionwide level, developments have been heterogeneous. In fact, although the primary school completion rate was about 95% in most of the countries considered, in some it was lower, with just 62% and 73%, respectively, of the population aged 15 to 19 having completed this level of education in Guatemala and Nicaragua. In the case of people aged 20 to 24, the secondary school completion rate averages about 60% in the region, with Chile and Peru standing out for rates in excess of 80%. Conversely, the countries with the lowest secondary school completion rates are Honduras (36%), Nicaragua (36%) and Guatemala (25%) (see figure III.2). As mentioned in other editions of the *Social Panorama of Latin America* (ECLAC, 2005 and 2011), this situation is a cause for concern because a complete secondary education (about 12 years of study) is the minimum required to reduce the likelihood of remaining in poverty, while to earn more than the average for the population a minimum of 13 to 14 years of study, i.e., some amount of post-secondary education, is required in most of the countries.

Figure III.2

Latin America (18 countries): proportion of people aged 15 to 29 with complete primary, secondary and tertiary education, by age group and country, around 2012

(Percentages)

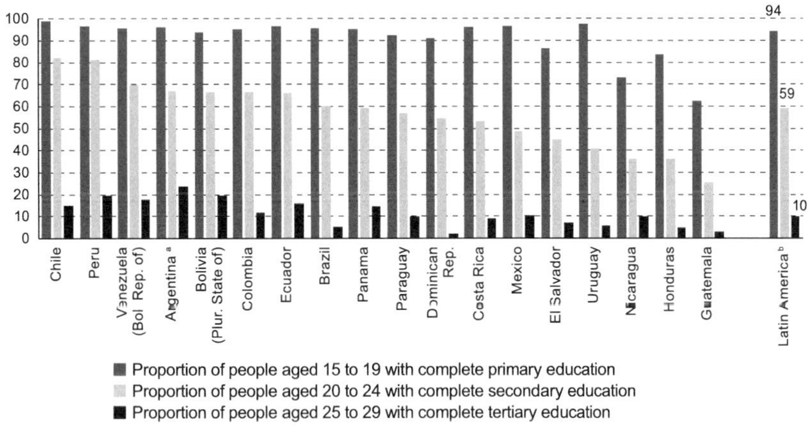

Source: Economic Commission for Latin America and the Caribbean (ECLAC), on the basis of special tabulations of data from household surveys conducted in the respective countries.

[a] Urban areas.

[b] Weighted average of results from the 18 countries included in the measurement.

The expansion of education has brought major progress with access for the region's women. In the last decade, rates of school attendance, and completion of secondary education in particular, have been higher for girls than for boys, which might be explained in part by the tendency for young men to start work at an early age, to the detriment of their present and future opportunities (ECLAC/UNFPA, 2012). Nonetheless, there are some countries (Guatemala, Paraguay, Peru and the Plurinational State of Bolivia) where girls are still at a disadvantage, particularly in contexts where there is significant inequality between ethnic groups and between rural and urban areas and they still have greater access difficulties than boys (Rico and Trucco, 2014).

Progress in educating the new generations has also meant a gradual reduction of inequality in terms of concentration of the number of years of study as measured by the Gini coefficient, both in the total population and among young people. This greater equality has been seen everywhere expect Argentina (where differences have increased slightly), and has mainly been due to expanded access and higher completion rates in secondary education, and to greater access to post-secondary education for the young. This has been critical to reducing the concentration of years of study in one population group, since adults, and particularly older adults, among whom education levels are lower in general while tertiary education is largely confined to an elite, have very little prospect of improving their situation. It is for the new generations that educational conditions are becoming more egalitarian. The highest degrees of inequity, going by the lower levels of educational attainment shown in the above charts, are found in Nicaragua and Guatemala, where concentration coefficients for the number of years' education are in excess of 0.35 (see table III.1).

Table III.1

Latin America (18 countries): Gini concentration coefficient applied to the number of years of education of the total population and those aged 15 to 29, around 2000, 2004, 2008 and 2012 [a]

	Distribution of the number of years of education in the total population		Distribution of the number of years of education among those aged 15 to 29	
	2000	2012	2000	2012
Argentina	0.373	0.388	0.178	0.230
Bolivia (Plurinational State of)	0.556	0.478	0.251	0.195
Brazil	0.550	0.442	0.328	0.223
Chile	0.443	0.361	0.221	0.171
Colombia	0.523	0.446	0.266	0.198
Costa Rica	0.517	0.406	0.277	0.225
Dominican Republic	0.496	0.440	0.257	0.199
Ecuador	0.472	0.399	0.230	0.172
El Salvador	0.599	0.500	0.315	0.234
Guatemala	0.798	0.710	0.443	0.388
Honduras	0.628	0.529	0.319	0.270
Mexico	0.463	0.430	0.224	0.173
Nicaragua	0.739	0.634	0.467	0.355
Panama	0.389	0.435	0.169	0.206
Paraguay	0.539	0.449	0.263	0.211
Peru	0.498	0.418	0.226	0.173
Uruguay	0.409	0.341	0.242	0.174
Venezuela (Bolivarian Republic of)	0.470	0.402	0.233	0.177
Simple average	**0.526**	**0.456**	**0.273**	**0.221**

Source: Economic Commission for Latin America and the Caribbean (ECLAC), on the basis of special tabulations of data from household surveys conducted in the respective countries.

[a] The years are 2000 and 2012 for Argentina, 2000 and 2012 for the Bolivarian Republic of Venezuela, 2001 and 2012 for Brazil, 2000 and 2011 for Chile, 1999 and 2012 for Colombia, 1999 and 2012 for Costa Rica, 2002 and 2012 for the Dominican Republic, 2000 and 2012 for Ecuador, 2000 and 2012 for El Salvador, 1998 and 2006 for Guatemala, 1999 and 2010 for Honduras, 2000 and 2012 for Mexico, 1998 and 2009 for Nicaragua, 2001 and 2011 for Panama, 2001 and 2011 for Paraguay, 2001 and 2012 for Peru, 2000 and 2011 for the Plurinational State of Bolivia and 2000 and 2012 for Uruguay.

Despite these major attainments in terms of education coverage and lower inequality, there are still large structural divides in capacity-building opportunities between the region's young people. Thus, for example, whereas 83% of people aged 20 to 24 in the fifth (highest-income) quintile had completed secondary education (as of about 2012), just 33% of young people in the first quintile had attained this level of education. As already mentioned, these socioeconomic inequalities are intensified when combined with other factors causing people to be discriminated against and held back, such as rural residence and ethnic origin (ECLAC, 2014a).

In addition, the guarantee of education as a social right is moving the debate towards the aspiration of equal quality. Disparities are being seen between young people who stay on in education for the secondary phase in respect of learning outcomes over their whole educational career. Thus, for example, measurements of basic learning competencies in fifteen-year-old students carried out by the Organisation for Economic Co-operation and Development (OECD) through its Programme for International Student Assessment (PISA) test, in which a number of the region's countries participate, show that most students from the first and second socioeconomic and cultural quartiles in the Latin American countries analysed do not attain the minimum levels of learning required to perform as capable citizens in the areas of reading and mathematics (Trucco, 2014). Although this only represents one very partial aspect of the right to a high-quality education, it does reflect the challenges that lie along the way.

The main problem in many of the countries is no longer exclusion from the education system but socioeducational segmentation associated with differential inclusion, whereby those living in situations of poverty and vulnerability have fewer opportunities to stay on in their educational establishment long enough to complete the education cycle and acquire an adequate level of learning. Inequalities in the education system run deep and are manifested in different dimensions, such as the quality of services, infrastructure, prestige, school size and teaching staff. The progress made is generating demands, expectations and challenges that are harder to respond to. Those who do not acquire the skills needed for the knowledge society are more likely to be socially and economically marginalized (Trucco, 2014). There is a need to design flexible strategies to give all groups of young people the opportunity to pursue educational processes that are not necessarily linear or confined exclusively to the formal system, but provide tools and develop lifelong learning capabilities while easing entry into the labour market.

2. Youth employment

Opportunities to find work during the period of youth are the other pillar of social inclusion. The move from education to employment in youth largely represents the transition from dependent to independent living (Rico and Trucco, 2014). However, the educational advances mentioned above have not been reflected in the labour market, where there are still large gaps relative to the adult population: young people have higher rates of unemployment than adults, and when they are employed it tends to be under less protected conditions.

Analysis of labour market participation and employment among young people in Latin America by age range confirms that rates for both increase with age (see figure III.3). As of around 2012, those aged between 15 and 19 presented a labour force participation rate of 39%, while the figure in the 25 to 29 age group was 80%. Meanwhile, the employment rate was 32.8% in the 15 to 19 segment and 74% in the 25 to 29 segment. These indicators certainly reflect something positive, since later entry into the labour market gives people valuable time to continue in the education system and improve their credentials (ECLAC/OIJ/IMJUVE, 2014). Unemployment, meanwhile, trends in the opposite direction to participation, as rates tend to decline up the age groups (see figure III.3).

Figure III.3

Latin America (18 countries):[a] participation, employment and unemployment rates among active persons aged 15 to 29, by age group, around 2012

(Percentages)

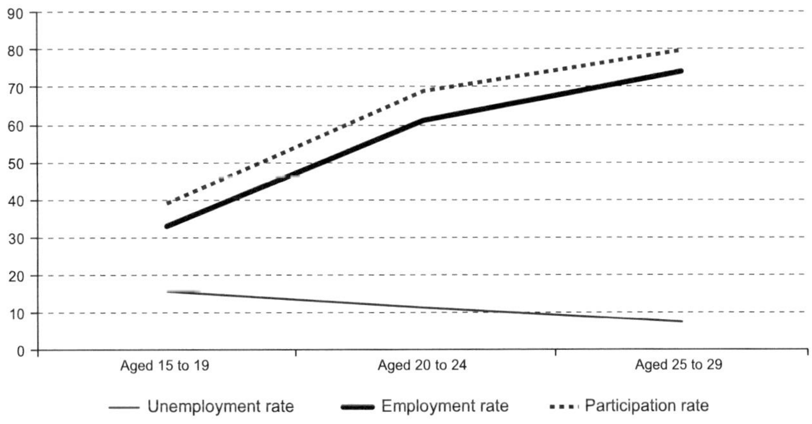

Source: Economic Commission for Latin America and the Caribbean (ECLAC), on the basis of special tabulations of data from household surveys conducted in the respective countries.

[a] Argentina (urban areas), Bolivarian Republic of Venezuela, Brazil, Chile, Colombia, Costa Rica, Dominican Republic, Ecuador, El Salvador, Guatemala, Honduras, Mexico, Nicaragua, Panama, Paraguay, Peru, Plurinational State of Bolivia and Uruguay.

Youth unemployment rates did not increase by any more than adult rates during the 2008 crisis. During the subsequent economic recovery (from 2009 to 2011), however, the employment rate increased faster for the adult population than for the young. The information available indicates that during this difficult crisis and post-crisis period in the region (between 2007 and 2011), the drop in youth employment was offset by increased time spent by the young in the education system, especially in the 15 to 19 age range, something that is also viewed positively insofar as it helped to increase the capabilities of the new generations (ECLAC/ILO, 2012).

The unemployment figures, however, also illustrate how difficult it is for the existing workforce to participate fully, since it counts all those who are not employed at a given time but are actively seeking employment (ECLAC/UNFPA, 2012). As figure III.4 shows, unemployment rates are considerably higher for the population aged 15 to 24 than for the total population in all countries of Latin America and the Caribbean. The situation in most of the English-speaking Caribbean is particularly worrying, as some countries have youth unemployment rates in excess of 30%.

Figure III.4

Latin America and the Caribbean (26 countries): unemployment rates among those aged 15 to 24 and those aged 15 and over, around 2012

(Percentages)

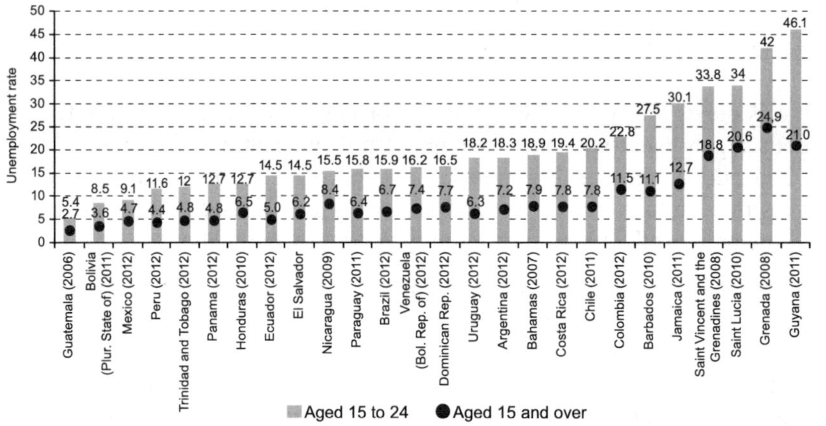

Source: Economic Commission for Latin America and the Caribbean (ECLAC), on the basis of special tabulations of data from household surveys conducted in Latin American countries. For Caribbean countries: Mónica Parra-Torrado, "Youth unemployment in the Caribbean", *Caribbean Knowledge Series*, Washington, D.C., World Bank, 2014.

However, the inequalities experienced by the young are not only age-related, as many other factors are involved, especially those associated with gender issues and the socioeconomic conditions in which they grow up and develop (ECLAC/OIJ/IMJUVE, 2014). Although unemployment rates in Latin America do not exceed 20%, analysis by per capita income quintiles reveals that it is the lowest-income strata that have the highest unemployment rates over time. Figure III.5 shows that in 2012, the population aged between 15 and 29 from households in the first quintile had an unemployment rate almost four times as high as that of the richest quintile. This pattern has not changed greatly over the last two decades. Gender gaps in employment are also marked. Females have higher unemployment rates and poorer employment conditions (Rico and Trucco, 2014), something that is reproduced when they reach adulthood, as described in chapter V.

Again, as was mentioned at the start of the section, young workers tend to be in poorer-quality jobs, with lower wages and longer working days, something that has negative long-term consequences because they are less likely to be enrolled in social protection systems (Rico and Trucco, 2014; ECLAC/OIJ/IMJUVE, 2014). The youth population, and especially those aged under 20, have less employment protection than the adult population; whereas 27.5% of wage employees aged 15 to 19 are enrolled in the social security system, the share for adults is close to 70% (see figure III.6). Enrolment rises with age, indicating that for many young people in paid work the problem of non-coverage is temporary. Nonetheless, it is clearly indicative of discrimination against young workers in the labour market.

Figure III.5
Latin America (18 countries):[a] unemployment rates for active persons aged 15 to 29, by per capita income quintile, 1990, 2002 and 2012
(Percentages)

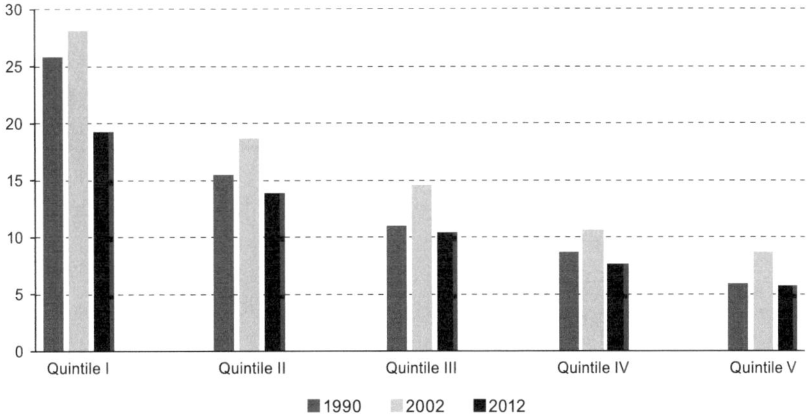

Source: Economic Commission for Latin America and the Caribbean (ECLAC), on the basis of special tabulations of data from household surveys conducted in the respective countries.
[a] Argentina (urban areas), Bolivarian Republic of Venezuela, Brazil, Chile, Colombia, Costa Rica, Dominican Republic, Ecuador, El Salvador, Guatemala, Honduras, Mexico, Nicaragua, Panama, Paraguay, Peru, Plurinational State of Bolivia and Uruguay.

Figure III.6
Latin America (18 countries):[a] wage workers enrolled in the social security system, by age group, around 2012
(Percentages)

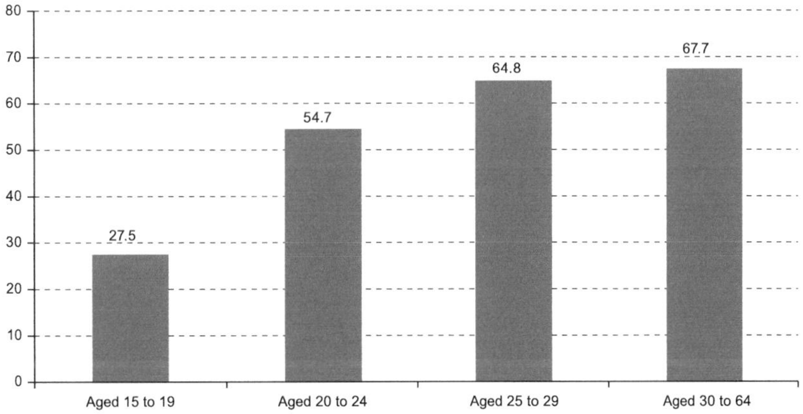

Source: Economic Commission for Latin America and the Caribbean (ECLAC), on the basis of special tabulations of data from household surveys conducted in the respective countries.
[a] Argentina (urban areas), Bolivarian Republic of Venezuela, Brazil, Chile, Colombia, Costa Rica, Dominican Republic, Ecuador, El Salvador, Guatemala, Honduras, Mexico, Nicaragua, Panama, Paraguay, Peru, Plurinational State of Bolivia and Uruguay.

The strain produced by divides in a youth population that is increasingly educated, informed and connected within a globalized society may be critical to the region's social inclusion and development processes. These barriers may result in discontent and frustration among many who are not included in the region's collective development process. Young people aspire to high-quality employment opportunities enabling them to participate fully in productive and civic development processes and achieve the conditions for personal development and well-being.

3. Young people not in education or employment

The sectoral divides described so far in relation to young people's education levels and employment types also affect their opportunities for social participation. Historically, the transition that takes place during youth has been understood as linear, with people moving from childhood to adulthood via different stages with socially and culturally defined roles (education, employment, marriage and parenthood). Increasing emancipation and autonomy became visible when young people began to gradually forego the roles associated with youth and adopt others (Filgueira, 1998, p. 12). However, the conditions and opportunities for the new generations have tended to create paths towards more heterogeneous processes of autonomy. For one thing, youth has been lengthened as certain milestones associated with its ending have shifted, with people studying for longer, delaying entry into the labour market and forming families at a later age. Consequently, life paths are being viewed not as a sequence of these life events unfolding in a linear fashion, but as a more dynamic and non-sequential process (ECLAC/OIJ, 2004; Dávila and Ghiardo, 2005, cited in ECLAC/OIJ/IMJUVE, 2014).

Some of the factors that have influenced these changes have to do with education systems, which have expanded to take in a larger share of the population, and with the requirements of more dynamic and globalized production sectors, which are demanding greater ongoing capacity-building. The increased participation of women in the labour market associated with changes in family structures has also tended to delay parenthood, so that young people are under less pressure to achieve financial independence at early ages.

However, as discussed in the latest Ibero-American youth report (ECLAC/OIJ/IMJUVE, 2014), this diversity of life paths arises not only because young people decide or wish to carry on studying in order to postpone certain functions and activities that were formerly entered upon at an earlier age, but also (and perhaps mainly) as a result of structural factors beyond the control of individuals, such as the socioeconomic conditions in which they grew up. For many of the young people who live in situations of poverty and marginalization, the linear model has tended to be replaced by irregular transitions from one condition to another; they are unable to obtain high-quality jobs because they lack educational qualifications, and so are required at some point to go back and complete their education (even if many never succeed in doing so).

This is why there is increasing concern about the young people being excluded from the institutions vital to social inclusion, namely education and employment. The aim of this section is to reach a better understanding of the situation of the 30 million or so Latin Americans aged 15 to 29 who in around 2012 were in neither one nor the other of these two institutions that are so vital for social inclusion. There has been a tendency to attach the stigmatizing label "NEETs" to young people who are not in education, employment or training. It seems best to avoid terms that imply a uniformly negative judgement on a diverse group of young people whose situation of institutional non-participation is often transitory. In the case of women, furthermore, the reason is often that they are employed without pay on domestic or care work in the home, which means that they are participating in one of society's core institutions, the family.

Thus, in the past decade a stigma has developed around the ill-termed "NEET generation", which tends to be regarded as a high-risk population made up of groups of youths with problems involving apathy, delinquency and alcohol and drug abuse. It is important to reach a better understanding of the complexity and diversity of situations experienced by this broad group of youths so that key determinants of young lives are not overlooked (Comari, 2014). For one thing, it is necessary to understand the reasons that have led to their being excluded from these institutions that are so vital to equality, but also to realize that there are other pathways to social integration being followed by this population.

It is estimated that 22% of people aged 15 to 29 in Latin America were neither studying nor in paid employment in 2012 (see figure III.7), the great majority of these being women (an average of about 70% in the subregion), predominantly from urban areas (except in some countries such as Guatemala and Honduras, where most of these young women live in rural areas). In many of the region's countries (see table III.1), the proportion of young people in this situation begins to decline with age, which means that this characteristic is dynamic and transitory for a large proportion of the group given that, as shown in the previous section, young people at the upper end of the age range (26 to 29) are more likely to be working for pay in the labour market.

Figure III.7
Latin America (18 countries):[a] activity status of young people aged 15 to 29, around 2012
(Percentages)

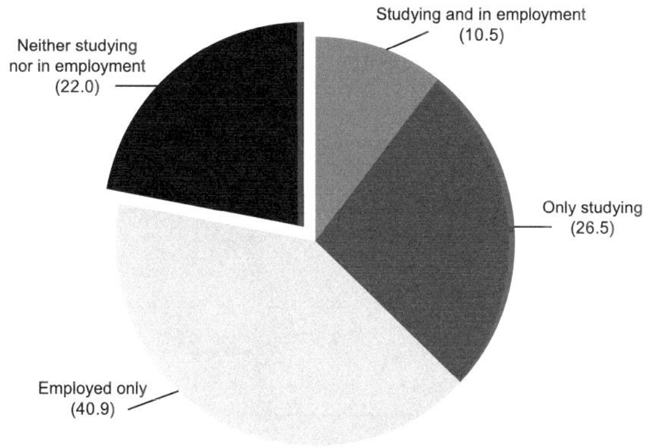

Source: Economic Commission for Latin America and the Caribbean (ECLAC), on the basis of special tabulations of data from household surveys conducted in the respective countries.

[a] Argentina (urban areas), Bolivarian Republic of Venezuela, Brazil, Chile, Colombia, Costa Rica, Dominican Republic, Ecuador, El Salvador, Guatemala, Honduras, Mexico, Nicaragua, Panama, Paraguay, Peru, Plurinational State of Bolivia and Uruguay.

When the specific activity status of this group is looked into further, it can be concluded that being outside education and employment is not synonymous with apathy or a lack of interest in participating in society. As figure III.8 shows, the great majority were engaged in unpaid care and domestic work. Furthermore, most of this group were young women (see figure III.9). This situation, which is of a piece with the tendency for adolescents to discontinue their studies at an early age, is one of the main factors preventing women from carrying on with education or training, with major costs to their opportunities for future well-being (Rico and Trucco, 2014). At the regional level, this situation affects 55% of women who are neither in education nor employment, but the figure is over 80% for women in the Central American countries (except Costa Rica), Mexico and the Plurinational State of Bolivia (see table III.2).

Figure III.8
Latin America (18 countries):[a] activity status of people aged 15 to 29 who are neither studying nor in paid employment, around 2012
(Percentages)

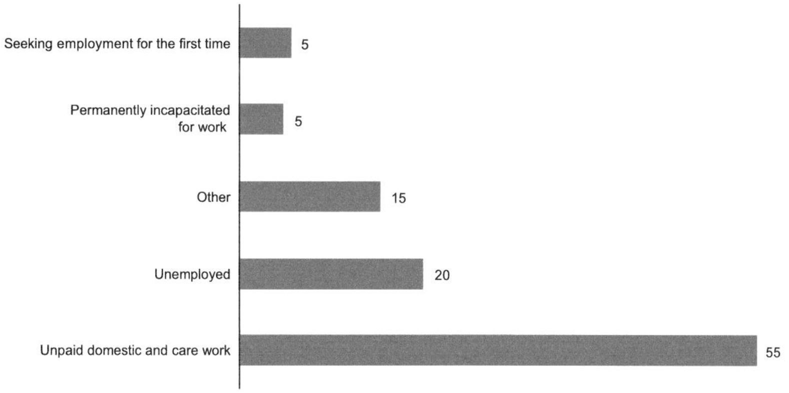

Source: Economic Commission for Latin America and the Caribbean (ECLAC), on the basis of special tabulations of data from household surveys conducted in the respective countries.

[a] Argentina (urban areas), Bolivarian Republic of Venezuela, Brazil, Chile, Colombia, Costa Rica, Dominican Republic, Ecuador, El Salvador, Guatemala, Honduras, Mexico, Nicaragua, Panama, Paraguay, Peru, Plurinational State of Bolivia and Uruguay.

Figure III.9

Latin America (18 countries):[a] activity status of young people aged 15 to 29 who are in neither education nor paid employment, by sex and age group, around 2012

(Percentages)

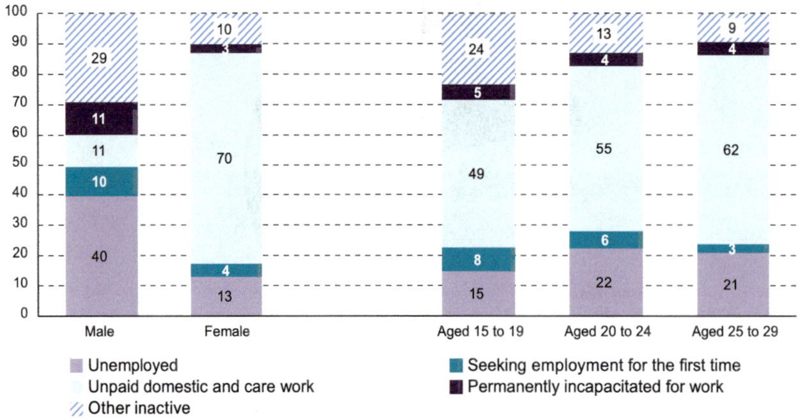

Source: Economic Commission for Latin America and the Caribbean (ECLAC), on the basis of special tabulations of data from household surveys conducted in the respective countries.

[a] Argentina (urban areas), Bolivarian Republic of Venezuela, Brazil, Chile, Colombia, Costa Rica, Dominican Republic, Ecuador, El Salvador, Guatemala, Honduras, Mexico, Nicaragua, Panama, Paraguay, Peru, Plurinational State of Bolivia and Uruguay.

The second-largest group (see figure III.8) comprises young people who are unemployed, i.e. have worked previously and are seeking and available for work. Together with those seeking a job for the first time, these made up about 25% of all young people who were neither studying nor employed at the time of measurement (as per household surveys) in the 18 countries of the region for which data were available. This is a group that finds itself temporarily in the situation described because of the difficulties young people have in finding work, as described in the previous section. The situation varies from one country to another, with levels being considerably lower in countries where a larger proportion of women are engaged in domestic work (see table III.2).

Table III.2

Latin America (18 countries):[a] people aged 15 to 29 who are inactive for unspecified reasons, by per capita income quintile, around 2012

(Percentages)

	Quintile I	Quintile II	Quintile III	Quintile IV	Quintile V
Argentina[b]	37	27	18	11	6
Bolivia (Plurinational State of)	19	16	33	17	15
Brazil	31	27	20	10	10
Chile	30	28	21	12	9
Colombia	29	25	22	14	10
Costa Rica	28	18	26	22	6
Dominican Republic	15	22	20	20	22
Ecuador	23	17	22	21	16
El Salvador	26	14	17	16	27
Guatemala	14	21	25	23	17
Honduras	14	26	14	34	12
Mexico	20	26	18	14	21
Nicaragua	18	30	22	20	10
Panama	29	25	21	15	9
Paraguay	18	16	24	23	19
Peru	22	14	27	18	20
Uruguay	47	25	14	8	5
Venezuela (Bolivarian Republic of)	31	25	22	15	7
Latin America[a]	**25**	**22**	**21**	**17**	**13**

Source: Economic Commission for Latin America and the Caribbean (ECLAC), on the basis of special tabulations of data from household surveys conducted in the respective countries.

[a] Simple average of the results for the 18 countries included in the measurement.

[b] Urban areas.

In the third place, 15% of young people who are neither studying nor in paid work are in this situation for no obvious cause (the term "other inactive" is used in these cases). This is the group that the International Labour Organisation (ILO, 2013) has singled out as the "hard core" of social exclusion in its discussion of decent work and youth in the region. It mainly includes young people at the lower end of the age spectrum and with lower per capita incomes (usually in the bottom two income quintiles) (see figure III.8 and table III.2). Some 10% of young women not in education or employment are in this group, compared to 30% of young men. They are probably the most socially marginalized young people, with no place in established social participation mechanisms. This can be put down in part to the interaction of structural factors associated with their socioeconomic origin, but also to the workings of social institutions that curtail opportunities by rejecting and discriminating against them. It is important to look at the specific life situations and paths of young people in this group in every country and local area so that suitable social participation strategies can be devised. The state of the region report for Central America (Programa Estado de la Nación, 2013) makes an effort to better understand the diversity of situations affecting these young people (see box III.1), who are the least able to exercise their rights and the most likely to become part of organizations and groups other than socially instituted ones (as will be analysed in depth in the following section).

Lastly, another group of inactive young people who need to be given greater visibility are those living with some disability that permanently incapacitates them for paid employment and often prevents them from receiving an education. Until recently, stigmatization meant that young people with disabilities were hidden away, mocked and, in many cases, subjected to violence. Information about the time spent in educational establishments by people aged 13 to 18 with disabilities reveals great disparities by country and disability type. Nonetheless, the information available indicates that in 2011 the average was no more than three years in Latin America, and only slightly more in the countries of the English-speaking Caribbean (ECLAC, 2013a).

The situation has improved somewhat thanks to certain changes in the conception of disability and the ratification of the Convention on the Rights of Persons with Disabilities by 23 countries in the region, but much remains to be done. The current approach is that society should provide resources that ensure access and inclusion, this being a responsibility for all that should be discharged through public policies. As long as young people with some disability face discrimination because of non-acceptance of differences, poverty, social isolation, prejudice, ignorance and a lack of services and support, they will be unable to exercise their rights and live life to the full. Not only does this have a negative social and economic impact on those affected, but denying them the chance to realize their full creative and productive potential also entails large costs and losses for society as a whole.

Box III.1

Educational exclusion in Central America: a qualitative approach

Social exclusion is the outcome of a process in which a variety of factors and situations in the lives of people and societies interact. To appreciate and comprehend this complexity, two studies were carried out as part of the research done in preparation for the fifth state of the region report. The first was quantitative and based on processing of national household surveys and national living condition surveys from Costa Rica, El Salvador, Guatemala, Honduras, Nicaragua and Panama for three years in the period from 2000 to 2013. The second study was qualitative and explored the life histories of 25 people aged from 16 to 24 with a sociodemographic profile similar to that obtained in the first study. The reasons leading the young people to discontinue their education, the characteristics of their households and their primary relationships were all investigated.

The main findings of the research are summarized below.

- A lack of primary relationships imbued with affection and a sense of belonging

  A number of young people came from households broken up by divorce, migration, alcoholism and family problems of various kinds. Most of them belonged to single-parent families (living with just one of the parents) or extended families (living with uncles and aunts, cousins, nieces and nephews, grandparents or other family members) and received little or no support with homework and other academic obligations. Those who were the children of migrants stated that they were very young when their parents left and had no chance to talk to them about their life plans, while internal migration meant constant changes of residence and school.

- Discontinuation of education because of poverty

  A number of the young people mentioned that they came from large families and lacked some of what they needed to carry on attending school (educational materials, food, money for transport, uniforms or shoes), which is evidence of their poverty. Some mentioned that in their households the first-born child or older children spent just a few years at school and were then taken out by their parents to help with farming and domestic work and so that younger siblings in turn could be given the opportunity to go to school and receive the school meal or snack.

- An unstimulating educational environment in the household

  Strikingly, a number of young people were unable to answer the question about what education their parents had had. Some of those interviewed were brought up by grandparents who had been through the first three grades of primary school at most. Of the 25 interviewees, just one had a university-educated mother, and only one had a sibling who had attained that level of education.

Box III.1 (concluded)

- Early motherhood and cohabitation

  After poverty, adolescent pregnancy (early motherhood) and premature cohabitation were the main reason for abandoning school. Of the 25 interviewees, 13 had one or two children and one young woman had three. In at least one case per country it was found that although the young people concerned lived with a partner, they were not self-sufficient but depended on others for their maintenance (remittances from the United States, borrowed housing or food donated by a family member). Pregnant girls mentioned that they felt uncomfortable at school because of comments and rumours among their classmates, because they had to carry on wearing their uniform or because those running the establishment were reluctant for them to carry on attending in their condition.

- Women bearing the burden of unpaid domestic work

  Although a number of male participants claimed to help their mothers or partners with housework, women spend the most time on social reproduction tasks in the home, and they very rarely (two or three cases) said that they had a job outside the household. Just two girls stated that they had jobs with a monthly wage as domestic workers without benefits. In other cases, the girls worked with their mothers or fathers, who gave them a stipend to spend on transport fares, shoes, some clothing and confectionery.

- A hostile and violent school environment

  Conflict between teachers and pupils and among the latter are one reason to leave school. Although this cannot be considered the main factor causing students to drop out, taunts and fighting among students, both in the classroom and outside of school, and negative and discriminatory attitudes towards pupils on the part of teachers affect the emotional well-being of young people and their willingness to stay on at school. By contrast, a number of young people emphasized play and recreation as the aspect that they liked best or that most attracted them during their time in education.

- Inadequate or dilapidated education infrastructure

  Half the young people interviewed had complaints about the poor condition of school infrastructure and furnishings and overcrowded classrooms. Some stated that they had to arrive very early if they wanted to get a place (seat or desk), while the few bathrooms lacked water and were ill-smelling. Excessive student numbers also meant that teachers were too overwhelmed to give them proper attention.

Lastly, it should be stressed that while most of the young people interviewed regarded education positively and were keen to return to it, their financial difficulties and the new family or work commitments they had taken on were serious obstacles to continuing with their studies. It should be noted that all the young people interviewed had a mobile phone and most had cable television and regular access to a computer and the Internet, which could mean that virtual or distance education solutions are viable.

Source: Prepared by Alberto Mora, research coordinator of *Informe Estado de la Región*, San José, Programa Estado de la Nación, 2014.

Analysis of the evidence presented brings out the complexity and diversity of youth situations and life paths in relation to the social inclusion mainstream constituted by formal education and the labour market. Education systems themselves clearly need to develop strategies to make them more inclusive, something that will require more flexible learning initiatives that suit people's financial and family dynamics and include people with different capabilities. In the labour market, too, effort needs to be concentrated on creating processes of transition from education to more suitable and better-quality work. ILO (2013) recognizes the need for measures not only to provide the young with opportunities that match their capabilities and aspirations but also to enable them to build up stable and lasting capabilities so that they can progress in life. The link between the education system and the labour market needs to be reinforced, and technical and vocational training facilities will be vital in this, particularly at the end of secondary school.

However, the analysis also makes clear the prevailing need for policies to address the demands of care and domestic work from a gender perspective. These obligations are not confined to the stage considered in this chapter, as they affect women throughout their lives. However, they are already substantial at early ages, curtailing opportunities. Progress with education coverage in the region has been very substantial, particularly for girls. However, the differences in drop-out and repetition patterns between boys and girls, especially in poorer sectors of society, are partly the result of cultural imperatives associated with gender socialization and the sexual division of labour established in households from an early age. Although boys are more likely to drop out of school than girls, the economic impact is greater among the latter, for whom dropping out of school means forfeiting a larger amount of pay (Rico and Trucco, 2014).

B. Young people and environments of violent social inclusion

The contexts of violence faced by young people in the region represent a very challenging dimension that influences their life choices. The stigmatization of youth for its supposedly violent tendencies results in a breakdown of solidarity that heightens the feeling of exclusion. Youth participation in gangs and other organized forms of urban violence has undoubtedly increased and has come about as a direct consequence of marginalization, offering an alternative form of social inclusion (inclusion in exclusion). Mechanisms are needed for communication and joint reflection on the causes of youth violence and victimization. The first step in forging a culture of peace is to internalize the basic idea that conflict is not to be denied, but can always be resolved without violence.

Paradoxically, the major advances in development that the Latin American countries have achieved in recent years and the positive effects these have had on the young now coexist with increases in indices of violence in the region, exposing the population at large, but most particularly the youth of Latin America and the Caribbean, to a context of growing violence and insecurity.

One characteristic of Latin America today that differentiates it from other regions of the world is that there is peace between States. However, there is extreme violence within civil society, to the point where the continent now has the world's highest homicide rates (UNODC, 2014, p. 22). Violence (intentional and unintentional) is the leading cause of death for the population aged 15 to 50. Furthermore, 7 of the 14 most violent countries in the world are in Latin America and the Caribbean: Belize, the Bolivarian Republic of Venezuela, Colombia, El Salvador, Guatemala, Honduras and Jamaica. Between 2000 and 2010, the homicide rate rose by 11% in the region even as it fell or stabilized in most other regions of the world. Again, robberies have almost tripled over the past 25 years in the countries for which information is available. On a typical day, furthermore, 460 people in Latin America suffer the consequences of sexual violence, most of them women (UNDP, 2013).

These issues particularly affect the youth population. Young people are frequently involved in acts of violence, whether as victims or as perpetrators. This apparently greater prevalence of violence among the young has turned the phenomenon into a stigma, so that they are seen as criminal and violent. This stigma arose in the 1980s and still persists in the collective and cultural imaginary, reinforced in large part by the messages highlighted by the media, something that influences the way certain strategies and policies towards this segment of the population are conceived. Indeed, one result has been a debate in many countries about lowering the age of criminal responsibility.

The purpose of this section is to analyse the problem of violence, understood from a multidimensional perspective, since it represents one of the most challenging contexts now facing the region's young and can have a major influence on their prospects for development and social inclusion. Particular attention is paid to the urban dimension of violence, associated with crime and drug trafficking, given the major strains and difficulties this entails for some countries and areas in the region. According to the latest report by UNODC (2014), an average of 30% of all homicides on the American continent are linked to organized crime or gangs, as compared to less than 1% in Asia, Europe and Oceania.

1. The multidimensionality of violence and its links to the young[1]

The concept of violence is a complex one to address owing to its multidimensional character, deriving from the diverse areas of people's lives in which it can manifest itself and the different causes and consequences it can have. To arrive at a better understanding of the phenomenon and its impact on the young, then, it is approached on the basis of an organizing framework constructed from the complementarity between two of the typologies of violence most used by researchers in recent years:

(i) The typology proposed by Galtung (1990), which establishes three classes based on what violence involves: direct violence (physical, verbal or psychological acts of violence intended to harm a person or group), structural violence (exclusion of certain groups by failing to provide them with opportunities to obtain food, housing, health care, employment, security, recreation, etc.) and cultural or symbolic violence (the imposition and reproduction of a system of thought and perceptions that legitimize an unequal social order).

(ii) The typology derived from the ecological model adopted by the World Health Organization (WHO) in 2002, which lays down three main categories based on the directionality of violence: self-directed violence (suicidal behaviour and self-harm), interpersonal violence (in the family towards minors, partners or the elderly and in the community, whether the perpetrator is known to the victim or not) and collective violence (social, political or economic).

The complementarity of these typologies is established by combining the types of violence defined in each. Direct violence, usually the most visible kind, is the manifestation of a problem rather than its origin. Its particular implications among the young differ depending on the category it belongs to in the ecological model. Direct self-directed violence is a very significant behavioural problem among adolescents and young people, as is direct interpersonal violence inflicted in youth by parents or a partner and violence from and towards other young people, whether strangers or otherwise. Also of great significance is direct collective violence inflicted by groups of youths upon individuals (who may or may not be young) in school or community settings.

Structural violence, usually associated with the origin of individuals, is more relevant to the analysis of multicausality and the search for potential ways of reversing it, and provides a way of identifying how fundamental rights are guaranteed or otherwise, something that is particularly important in the youth group insofar as it can shape particular conditions of exclusion, such as stigmatization. It is of particular significance among the young when it is interpersonal (mainly within the community) and collective, as it creates a situation of social exclusion that exacerbates the divides mentioned in the previous section.

Lastly, symbolic violence, which usually transcends particular manifestations and can lead to the legitimization of violence in social relationships, becomes very significant in youth populations when it takes an interpersonal form within the family (such as in the normalization of traditional gender roles and the acceptance of domestic violence) or a collective form, leading to discrimination against certain groups because they belong to some social class, an ethnic, sexual or other minority or a certain kind of youth organization (gang), exacerbating the stigma attached to young people, as mentioned above.

Thus, using the typologies to complement each other makes it easier to measure the scale of violence and identify actions to prevent it by establishing a framework for analysing dynamics within processes of violence, enabling them to be characterized as a ubiquitous phenomenon with multiple associated risk factors (at different levels) and operationalized in relation both to the perpetrator of the violent act and the subjects affected (ECLAC/OIJ, 2008; WHO, 2002).

In Latin America, there is extensive documentation reflecting the large scale of the problem of violence among young people, especially direct interpersonal violence, measured by indicators such as mortality rates, which are as high as 31 deaths for every 100,000 inhabitants in the subregion (more than twice the world average). Violence is also one of the main factors contributing to the burden of morbidity among the young, especially males (see table III.2). Comparative regionwide analysis of information on domestic and school violence is difficult, but the data generated by case studies or surveys specifically designed for this purpose reveal high levels of violence in

[1] Extracts from the "Concept Note" prepared by ECLAC for the Regional Forum of Youths of Latin America and the Caribbean 2014 held in Ecuador in May 2014.

these settings. Thus, according to the 2008 Latinobarómetro study, an average of between 25% and 30% of young people in 18 countries of the region perceived themselves as living in situations of violence at school, in the family, between gangs and among residents of the same area. Brazil is a particular case in point, with over half the young people surveyed for the study stating that they lived in contexts of violence in such immediate environments as school (see table III.3).

Table III.3

Latin America (18 countries): perceptions of violence in different settings among the population aged 16 to 29, 2008

(Percentages)

	At school	In the family	Among neighbours	Between gangs
Argentina	29	20	16	20
Bolivia (Plurinational State of)	28	32	23	28
Brazil	52	40	42	38
Chile	26	27	15	29
Colombia	33	32	25	21
Costa Rica	24	25	23	19
Dominican Republic	35	28	32	28
Ecuador	19	19	17	18
El Salvador	25	17	19	26
Guatemala	33	35	34	34
Honduras	32	28	25	24
Mexico	33	34	27	26
Nicaragua	29	22	28	30
Panama	29	32	34	28
Paraguay	20	18	18	18
Peru	28	27	20	32
Uruguay	29	21	14	21
Venezuela (Bolivarian Republic of)	29	32	31	34
Latin America [a]	**29**	**27**	**25**	**26**

Source: Economic Commission for Latin America and the Caribbean (ECLAC), on the basis of special tabulations of the 2008 Latinobarómetro Survey.

[a] Simple average of the results for the 18 countries included in the measurement.

As regards the identification of enabling factors for youth-related violence, without seeking to conduct an exhaustive analysis of the main phenomena of social change in the region, it is relevant to mention some that are often cited in the literature in order to provide an overview of the dynamic of violence and thence analyse the contemporary relationship between violence and youth. According to Imbusch, Misse and Carrión (2011), the greatest changes associated with violence in Latin America have been rapid urbanization in many countries combined with persistent poverty, inequality and political violence, inadequate social protection, the consolidation of transnational criminal organizations, the spread and trafficking of drugs, the breakdown of families and primary social networks, and the wide availability of weapons among the civilian population. The result has been a perverse reciprocal influence between structural violence and direct violence.

The joint studies prepared by ECLAC and the Ibero-American Youth Organization (OIJ) have shown that the features of social exclusion which most often seem to give rise to situations of violence in youth are urban marginalization, lack of access to channels of social mobility and consumption, the alienation from mainstream institutions of some of the young people who are neither in education nor in paid work (such as those described in the previous section as the "hard core"), socialization in aggressive and criminal behaviour from early ages (in families and local neighbourhoods) and thwarted expectations when the increased education of many young people fails to ensure greater opportunities for employment and well-being (ECLAC/OIJ, 2008).

Box III.2

The repercussions of violence on the mental health of the young

Mental health conditions have a significant impact on young people's development and directly impact their opportunities for living full lives and integrating into the economy and society. In Latin America and the Caribbean, epidemiological mental health studies among young people are few and far between and hard to compare because of differences in measuring instruments, age ranges and reference periods. However, mental illnesses are a major element in the burden of morbidity among the young. According to recent data (see table), mental health-related disability-adjusted life years (DALY) [a] make a large contribution to total DALY for the young.

Latin America and the Caribbean:main diseases, disorders and conditions contributing to the burden of morbidity among people aged 15 to 29, by sex, 2010

Male	Female
1. Violence	Unipolar depressive disorders
2. Exposure to forces of nature	Exposure to forces of nature
3. Road traffic injuries	Major depressive disorder
4. Unintentional injuries	Anxiety disorders
5. Unipolar depressive disorders	Low back pain
6. Drug use disorders	Migraine
7. Low back pain	Road traffic injuries
8. Major depressive disorder	Violence
9. Self-harm	Neck pain
10. Alcohol use disorders	Drug use disorders

Source: Institute for Health Metrics and Evaluation, *The Global Burden of Disease Study 2010*, Seattle, 2010.

Young people with mental illnesses may find it very challenging to complete their studies because of poor academic performance, discipline problems and reduced attendance, which may ultimately end in their dropping out. These difficulties leave them ill-prepared to enter the labour market, with adverse effects for their employment situation. Mental health problems during adolescence and youth can also affect the development of sound and healthy relationships with their parents and others. Lastly, it has been shown that these health difficulties affect young people's self-esteem and social interaction and may even increase the chances of their injuring and harming themselves and others (Bradshaw, O'Brennan and McNeely, 2008).

Poverty, working or living in the street and circumstances such as school bullying, traumatic events and conflict and post-conflict experiences are risk factors for young people's mental health (United Nations, 2014c). A 2010 WHO report on mental health and development highlighted the cyclical relationship between vulnerability and mental health (WHO, 2010). Similarly, the relationship between poverty and mental health conditions is cyclical: people living in poverty experience high levels of stress, trauma and social exclusion and have less access to medical care, all of which heightens the risk and severity of mental health problems. Likewise, people with mental health disorders may be more exposed to the risk of poverty because they have fewer education and employment opportunities and are subject to high medical care costs, stigmatization and social exclusion.

Dealing with the needs of young people suffering from mental illnesses requires prevention and treatment strategies that reflect their true situation. Prevention needs to aim at universality to promote mental health in the youth population, with programmes targeted on populations at higher risk of developing these disorders. Initiatives that set out to promote capabilities such as emotional regulation, social skills and conflict resolution could be very helpful. Some prevention models are oriented specifically towards the family, school, the workplace or the community, while others target different levels simultaneously.

Treatment services for young people suffering from mental disorders are usually inadequate. Problems with affordability and geographical accessibility can also restrict the use of these services by the young. Even when care programmes do exist, take-up is low, as fear of exclusion and stigmatization act as barriers. At the same time, an analysis of mental health services for young people in Latin America has concluded that the approach is mainly psychoanalytical and there is too much emphasis on severe but uncommon disorders (Belfer and Rohde, 2005).

What are required are specifically youth-centred mental health policies and programmes that are tied to a broader comprehensive health strategy for this population, encompassing the educational, social and judicial spheres as well as work with families and communities. The human rights of young people with mental health conditions also need to be safeguarded.

Source: Economic Commission for Latin America and the Caribbean (ECLAC), on the basis of M.L. Belfer and L.A. Rohde, "Child and adolescent mental health in Latin America and the Caribbean. Problems, progress, and policy research", *American Journal of Public Health*, vol. 18, No. 4/5, Washington, D.C., Pan American Health Organization (PAHO), 2005; C. Bradshaw, L.M. O'Brennan and Clea A. McNeely, "Core competencies and the prevention of school failure and early school leaving", *New Directions for Child and Adolescent Development*, vol. 2008, No. 122, Wiley, 2008; United Nations, *Mental Health Matters. Social Inclusion of Youth with Mental Health Conditions* (ST/ESA/352), New York, 2014; World Health Organization (WHO), *Mental Health and Development. Targeting People with Mental Health Conditions as a Vulnerable Group*, Geneva, 2010.

[a] According to the World Health Organization, one DALY is equivalent to a year of healthy life lost. Also known as the healthy life years (HLY) indicator, its value reflects the impact of different risks on mortality and morbidity. The sum of DALY in a population, or the burden of morbidity, represents the gap between the population's current state of health and an ideal state of health in which everyone lived to an advanced age free of disease and disability. For further information, see [online] http://www.who.int/healthinfo/global_ burden_disease/metrics_daly/en.

Apart from the general picture, it can be seen in particular that the subregion has been through its own peculiar sociohistorical processes that have caused violence to become rooted in its culture and the practices of its inhabitants, most especially post-war and post-dictatorship transition situations in which the idea of political violence begins to blur into, or rather become hybridized with, other types of violence. Certain migration-related demographic dynamics may likewise have become another factor facilitating the context of violence in some countries (see box III.3).

Box III.3

The implications of violent contexts for youth migration

In recent decades, migration, both international and internal, has become a major phenomenon in all the countries of Latin America and the Caribbean, with young people playing a prominent part in the process, either by migrating alone or with their families, or by remaining in home communities which migrant parents or close relatives have left.

Where international migration is concerned, the 2013 data from the United Nations global migration database show that one in every five emigrants from Latin American and Caribbean countries is aged between 15 and 29. In the case of internal migration, the studies available show that the young migrate most, especially from the countryside, and are practically the only age group to still be attracted by large cities, albeit in a segmented fashion, usually in search of work in the case of individuals from the low socioeconomic strata and educational opportunities in the case of those from the medium and high strata (Rodríguez, 2008).

Young people have a greater propensity to migrate owing, first, to the particular features of the stage in the life cycle they are going through, ranging from personal considerations (such as socioeconomic circumstances) to situations of conflict and violence, persecution and risk from localized threats (ECLAC/OIJ, 2008). Another influence has been the facilitation of human movement resulting both from the availability of cheaper and faster transport and from the development and mass take-up of information and communication technologies (ICTs), with young people usually being the greatest users of these. For example, Internet-based social networks have played a key role in facilitating the migration of young people by providing information about jobs and conditions in the migration destination chosen, or by allowing frequent contact with their home communities and thus helping them to cope with the challenges of adapting to their new environment (United Nations, 2013).

The impact of migration on young people and their families is very significant and sometimes positive, whether because it gives people opportunities to increase their education and earnings or as an important stage in the transition to adulthood. It often also benefits non-accompanying family members whose incomes are increased by the remittances young people send, which can mean increased access to education and health care or provide a buffer against economic and other shocks. In some cases, it can benefit the whole community by enabling basic infrastructure projects to be implemented, so that local development in the countries of origin is enhanced. Migration can also strengthen the decision-making authority of young women vis-à-vis their families and communities, contributing to greater gender equality.

However, the adverse effects of migration, chiefly of the cross-border variety, can be critical for the lives of young migrants, since in undertaking their journey they may face situations of danger and violence on their way to the destination country, and upon arrival may experience restrictions on their rights and be exposed to abuses by employers, poor access to services and situations of discrimination and marginalization. For the communities of origin, an exodus of skilled young people is a challenge that can constrain their development, at least temporarily.

The positive and negative effects of migration by young people are influenced by specific factors such as the motivations and category of migrants, but above all by programmatic policies and interventions in the places of origin, transit and destination. Because of this, there is a need to pursue initiatives to safeguard the rights of young migrants at every stage in the process so that the benefits of migration for individuals, families and communities can be reaped to the full.

Migration to the United States

The case of migration to the United States is particularly important because it is the main destination for emigrants from the countries of Latin America and the Caribbean. According to the 2010 census, 21.2 million people born in some country of the region were resident in the United States, of whom 55.2% were of Mexican origin, 14.3% Central American, 12.8% South American and 17.5% Caribbean. The Central American share is greatest if the population living in the United States is compared with the total population of certain countries (for example, 1 in 5 Salvadorans, 1 in 10 Mexicans and 1 in 15 Hondurans reside in the United States). A fifth of these emigrants are young people aged between 15 and 29.

Changes in United States migration policy resulting from the regrettable events of 11 September 2001 have slowed the flow of migrants into the country, particularly in the young age group (the proportion of Mexican migrants aged 15 to 29 dropped from 31.4% in 2005 to 21.8% in 2013, so that this group's share was outstripped by that of the 45 to 64 age group), while also exacerbating the adverse effects of migration from the countries of Latin America and the Caribbean, both because of the increased difficulty of entering the country and because of the rise in the number of people expelled (by a court order resulting in a criminal record) or returned (stopped while trying to cross the border and sent back without a court order resulting in a criminal record).

These circumstances are very important in a context where one in every two immigrants from Latin America and the Caribbean in the United States are estimated to be living there without authorization or irregularly, particularly given the scale of the migration flows of the last 30 years, resulting in illegal immigrants living side by side with second- and even third-generation family members born in the United States. This creates a difficult situation for people who are returned to their countries, owing to the family break-up and breakdown resulting from these deportations, and for family members who stay on in the United States with levels of social protection that differ according to the legality of their migration status.

A substantial portion of Central American youth, mainly from El Salvador, Guatemala and Honduras, continue to undertake hazardous migration journeys to the north of the continent in

Box III.3 (concluded)

search of better living conditions, driven out by the violence in their own countries. When deported, these young people return to contexts of economic, social and even political insecurity. The number of deportations from the United States has increased in recent years. In 2011, for example, there were 1,200 expulsions a month to El Salvador. Although most of those deported have no criminal history, some do, and they fall on "fertile ground" when they return to their countries of origin, as there they find a society that excludes them (few prospects of entering the education system and labour market), little social capital (almost no friends or family), difficulty communicating in Spanish, and discrimination of every kind.

In this situation, it could be argued that the so-called "transculturation" produced by migration and deportation processes has specific characteristics in the cases of El Salvador, Guatemala and Honduras. This specific transculturation is instrumental in developing (and in some cases strengthening) violent behaviour patterns that are manifested in family relationships, gangs and society at large. The United Nations Development Programme speaks of the "contagious effect of migrants' return": "young people deported from the United States in the 1980s and belonging to one of these two groups (the Mara Salvatrucha or the Calle 18 gang) returned to countries such as Guatemala, El Salvador and Honduras to find poverty-stricken societies torn apart by violent, patriarchal cultures, with States incapable of providing them with opportunities. In this environment, both gangs are expanding their territories" (UNDP, 2012).

Source: Economic Commission for Latin America and the Caribbean (ECLAC), "Long Term Population Estimates and Projections 1950-2100", Santiago, Chile, 2013 [online] http://www.cepal.org/celade/proyecciones/basedatos_bd.htm; Economic Commission for Latin America and the Caribbean (ECLAC)/Ibero-American Youth Organization (OIJ), *Juventud y cohesión social en Iberoamérica: Un modelo para armar* (LC/G.2391), Santiago, Chile, October 2008; National Population Council (CONAPO)/Fundación BBVA Bancomer, *Anuario de migración y remesas México 2014*, Mexico City, 2014 [online] https://www.fundacionbbvabancomer.org/imagenes/Docs/Anuario_Migracion_y_Remesas_2014.pdf; C. Grieco and others, "The Foreign-Born Population in the United States: 2010", United States Census Bureau, 2012 [online] http://www.census.gov/prod/2012pubs/acs-19.pdf; Migration Policy Institute (2012), "Countries of Birth for U.S. Immigrants, 1960-2012" [online] http://migrationpolicy.org/programs/data-hub/charts/immigrants-countries-birth-over-time; Jorge Rodríguez, "Migración interna de la población joven. El caso de América Latina", *Revista Latinoamericana de Población*, vol. 2, No. 3, Latin American Population Association, 2008; United Nations, *World Youth Report. Youth and Migration* (ST/ESA/338), New York, 2013. United Nations publication, Sales No. E.12.IV.6; United States Census Bureau, "Current Population Survey", 2012 [online] http://www.census.gov/population/foreign/data/cps2012.html; United Nations Development Programme (UNDP), *Informe Nacional de Desarrollo Humano 2011-2012 Guatemala*, Guatemala City, 2012.

The enabling factors described above, which have helped shape today's situations of violence, mean there is a need for youth-focused multidimensional analysis of violence to look into the existence of a close relationship with social exclusion processes for both victims and perpetrators, where violence and context feed upon and into each other, so that social, territorial and family settings can end up encouraging the young to seek violent solutions (ECLAC/OIJ, 2008). Social exclusion is understood to mean the absence of recognition or of mechanisms for enforcing the rights of the young, so that a particular group is marginalized by being denied the possibility of participating in the social, economic and political spheres. The subjective reaction to exclusion derives from the lack of a sense of belonging. Thus, it is impossible to dissociate the analysis of violence from an analysis of the social context shaping the prevailing contexts of violence.

2. Violence and the social context: fear and stigmatization

In recent years, the region has gone from a situation of collective violence (in a context of dictatorships and civil wars) to one in which interpersonal violence appears to have been garnering greater prominence in the media and greater attention as a subject of study (Imbusch, Misse and Carrión, 2011, p. 98). This attention has essentially focused on the concept of crime, which is hard to define, and the stigmatization of people living in sectors beset by violence. In the first place, crime is a phenomenon delineated by the criminal law, meaning that behaviour which is treated as a crime in one context may be considered reprehensible but not criminal in another. Gender violence is a clear example of changes in the delimitation of a criminal act, owing to the operation of a culture that legitimizes violence. Violence of this type has long been tolerated in the region (Imbusch, Misse and Carrión, 2011, p. 100). Although indicators of violence usually show males as worst affected, some violence against young women is rendered invisible because it is associated with subjects society is reluctant to address directly. However, it represents a heavy public health burden for the region (ECLAC/OIJ, 2008). Different social, legislative, judicial and political initiatives have sought to bring about a cultural shift so as to make such violence not just reprehensible but punishable under the criminal law (see box III.4 for an analysis of gender violence and youth).

Again, the territorial distribution of violence is uneven, with its manifestations being differentiated particularly in urban areas, where deprived sectors become the setting for violence. Shanty towns and some slum areas are characterized not only by poverty but by violence, and this is a burden that reproduces and exacerbates social exclusion. The stigmatization of the young in these areas for their supposedly violent way of life represents a breakdown in solidarity and a denial of dignity.

Box III.4

Gender violence and youth

The evidence on gender violence has revealed striking differences in the nature and scale of violence perpetrated or suffered depending on whether it is men or women who are analysed. Nonetheless, given that the youth group is among those most directly involved in the manifestations and impact of violence, analysis of the convergences between gender, youth and violence has been confined to two hypotheses of great importance: (i) young people's sex can be considered a differential risk factor for the likelihood of falling victim to violence, and (ii) being a young person can be a differentiating factor for the perpetration of gender violence.

There is statistical information that can yield some partial conclusions on the first of these hypotheses, particularly for some types and manifestations of violence. For example, figures estimated from administrative records by the Global Health Observatory for 2012 show that mortality from intentional injuries in Latin America and the Caribbean is 8.5 times higher among young men (aged 15 to 29) than among women in the same age range. Conversely, although men commit suicide more than women in absolute terms, with the figures showing a ratio of three suicides by young men to every one by a young woman, in relative terms suicide bulks larger in female mortality, as the percentage of suicides in total deaths from intentional injury is twice as great among young women as among young men. This is evidence of the need to analyse direct violence affecting young people more thoroughly by sex to account for the differences observed.

In the case of direct violence deriving from criminal acts that do not lead to death but cause injuries and harm of various kinds, information from the Barometer of the Americas 2012 produced by the Latin American Public Opinion Project (LAPOP) shows that young women in the Latin American countries selected are three times as likely to fall victim to rape or sexual assault as women of other ages and seven times as likely as young men. The data from this source also show that young women are twice as likely to be abducted as young men.

Where manifestations of violence associated with direct victimization of women are concerned, information from the demographic and health surveys of some countries in Latin America shows that, while young women are no more likely than those of other ages to be pushed or struck by their partners, they are more likely to fall victim to attacks by people other than their partners. The data also show that young women are more likely than those of other ages to be subject to attacks of a sexual nature, particularly for forced sex.

There is not enough information available to analyse other manifestations of violence for the region as a whole, such as violence associated with human trafficking (including sexual and psychological violence), ill-treatment of children by their parents, school violence or community violence, like that perpetrated against sexual minorities. However, qualitative or quantitative studies carried out in some countries by means of ad hoc surveys provide enough information to indicate that the difference is there and further analysis is required.

With regard to the possible influence of an individual's sex on the tendency to perpetrate acts of violence, an important consideration is that the data sources available do not usually include information about the perpetrator, so that it is not possible to determine whether an individual's sex might be a determinant of the propensity to perpetrate some type of violence. This is particularly the case with data on homicides, among other crimes. Where surveys of women who have fallen victim to violence are carried out, their purpose is to determine whether they are being subjected to any violence by their partners and there is usually only evidence of male perpetrators. This is explained by a general conclusion from qualitative studies of gender violence that violence against women is perpetrated by men in the great majority of cases, irrespective of age group. Because of this, the hope is that the indices of gender violence can be brought down by a generational cultural shift whereby men are made aware that violence against women is unacceptable and women cease to put up with this type of violence. To achieve this goal, young people will have to be treated as the main actors in the process.

Source: Economic Commission for Latin America and the Caribbean (ECLAC), on the basis of Latin American Public Opinion Project (LAPOP), Barometer of the Americas 2012; Global Health Observatory Data Repository, 2013; and World Health Organization (WHO), *World Report on Violence and Health*, Washington, D.C., Pan American Health Organization (PAHO), 2012.

In these circumstances, the involvement of young people and adolescents, many of them part of the "hard core" of exclusion, in different criminal practices directed by adults, who use them in the service of their own interests in the knowledge that minors cannot be held criminally responsible, has become a matter of growing public concern. Since the 1980s, the gangs operating in cities right across the continent have become associated with an expression of youth identity linked to violence, substance abuse and illegal acts such as robbery. In this way, young people, including under-eighteens, have come to form part of the situations that go to form the complex universe of Latin American law-breaking and the economy of crime: not only are they involved in adult-led criminality, but they have their own forms of integration associated with law-breaking.

All this matches people's perception of the contexts of insecurity they face. According to figures gathered by the Latin American Public Opinion Project (LAPOP), in 2012 some 20% of young people and 16% of the adult population in the subregion claimed to have been the victims of some crime (see figure III.10). The situation varies by country and the youth population is not always disproportionately affected, although it does tend to be more involved where crime is particularly rife.

According to the figures gathered in the LAPOP study, most of the crimes declared take place in the respondents' own local areas. Among the young people stating they had been victims of crimes in the last year, just a quarter of these were committed outside their own municipality, while the figure for the adult population was only a fifth (see figure III.11). A larger proportion of adults stated that they had been affected inside their own homes (34%, as against 21% for young people), while the young tend to experience crime mainly in their own municipalities, within their local area or community (54%, as against 47% for adults).

Figure III.10
Latin America and the Caribbean (18 countries): population claiming to have been the victim of crime in the last 12 months, by age group, 2012
(Percentages)

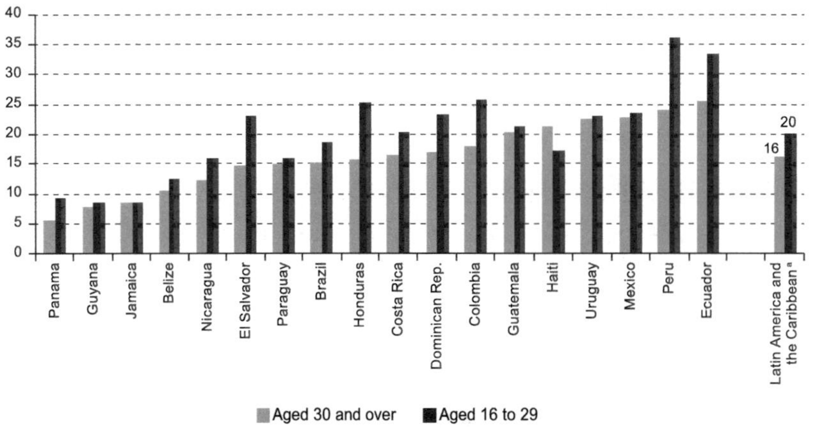

Source: Economic Commission for Latin America and the Caribbean (ECLAC), on the basis of special tabulations of the biannual survey of the Latin American Public Opinion Project (LAPOP), 2012.
[a] Simple average of the results for the 18 countries included in the measurement.

Figure III.11
Latin America and the Caribbean (18 countries): [a] distribution of crime in the last year, by victim's location and age group, 2012
(Percentages)

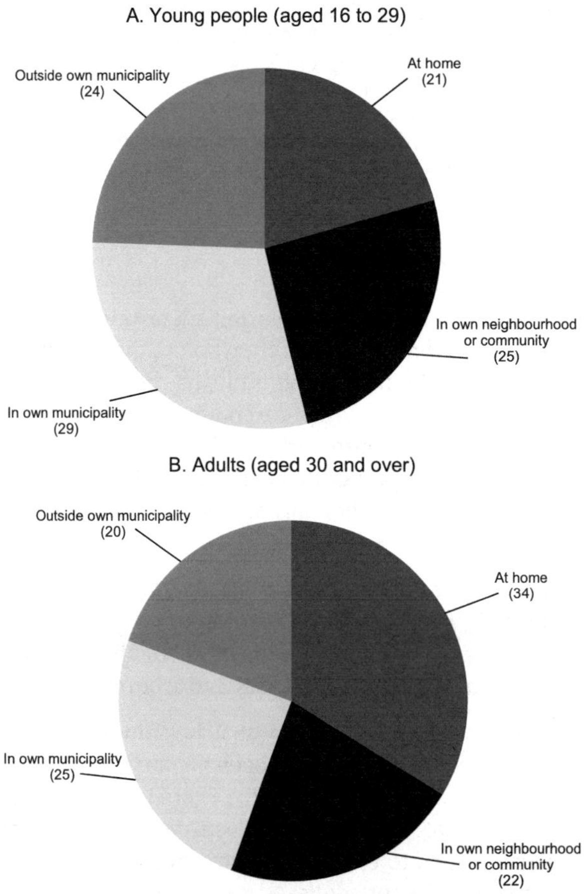

Source: Economic Commission for Latin America and the Caribbean (ECLAC), on the basis of special tabulations of the biannual survey of the Latin American Public Opinion Project (LAPOP), 2012.
[a] Simple averages of the results from the 18 countries included in the measurement.

Being a crime victim does not always mean suffering a situation of violence, although the figures indicate that they tend to go together. According to the Latinobarómetro Study (2013), a majority on average of young people stating that they or a family member had been the victim of some crime during the past year said that the crime involved violence (see figure III.12). The situation varied by country, however. Those with the highest figures for violent crime and the number of victims in general were Mexico, Peru, the Plurinational State of Bolivia and Colombia. These studies show high crime figures, indicating that young people are living in societies where violence is strongly present and which are fractured by perceptions of insecurity and a lack of feelings of solidarity and cohesion.

Figure III.12
Latin America (18 countries): people aged 16 to 29 stating they have been victims of violent and non-violent crime in the past 12 months, 2013
(Percentages)

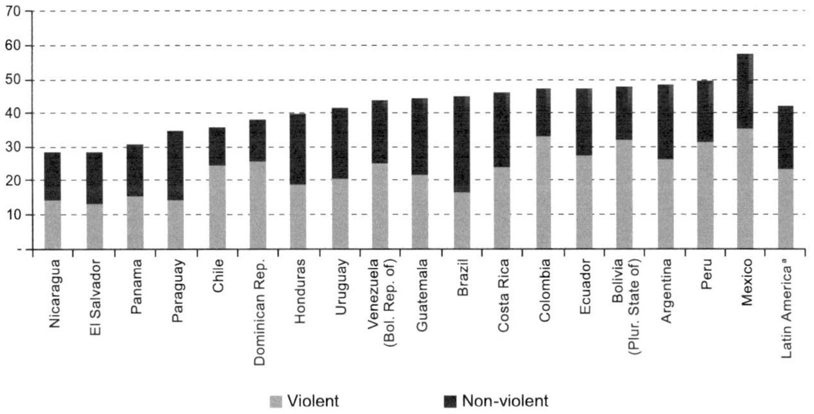

Source: Economic Commission for Latin America and the Caribbean (ECLAC), on the basis of special tabulations of the 2013 Latinobarómetro Survey.
[a] Simple average of the results for the 18 countries included in the measurement.

Fear, the immediate expression of insecurity and weakened social cohesion, permeates contemporary society, which is less and less able to generate cohesion. Although the feeling of living in an unsafe country has decreased in the past decade, according to the Latinobarómetro figures, even in 2011 the proportion of citizens considering their country to have become less safe was over 50%, with figures of 58% in the youth population and 54% in the adult one (see figure III.13). Perceptions of insecurity declined most between 2003 and 2011 in Nicaragua, El Salvador, Brazil and Argentina. The countries where the perception of insecurity was most widespread were the Bolivarian Republic of Venezuela and Guatemala, whose levels of violence were among the highest in the world. Costa Rica is a striking case, for although the level of violence there was at a historic low, the population, and young people especially, perceived insecurity as being on the rise.

Throughout history, every society has at some point made a particular group the repository for its deep-seated fears, usually a population that is stigmatized and thus rejected and excluded. Young people are now that population, especially those living in the extensive areas of poverty found in Latin American cities. The stigma has arisen on the basis of a symbolism that is very easily transferred from poor youth to criminal youth, closing yet more doors to inclusion. The *marero* (Central American gang member), tattooed up to the face and with an extremely aggressive attitude, is the ultimate embodiment of the archetype that provokes urban panic: the young man from the slums bursting with defiance, threatening the peace on every corner. This figure and the use it has been put to by the global media are revealing of the stigma now attached to this population, on to which today's society projects its fear of insecurity. This judgement is not necessarily based on the real evidence of the facts.

Figure III.13

Latin America (18 countries): people stating that their country is becoming more and more unsafe, by country and age group, 2003 and 2011

(Percentages)

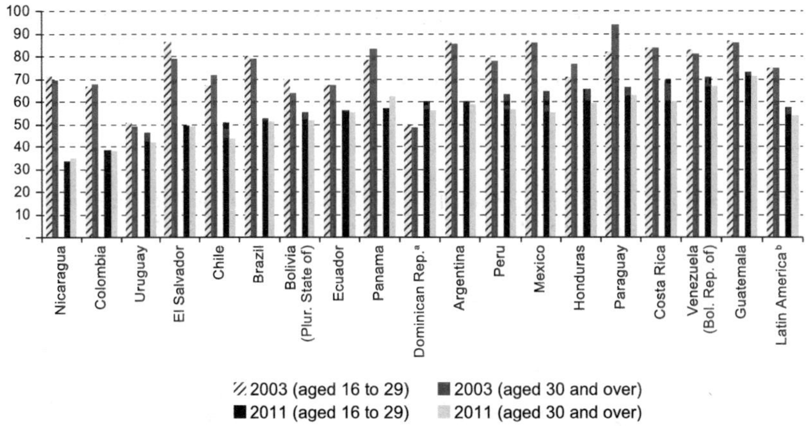

Source: Economic Commission for Latin America and the Caribbean (ECLAC), on the basis of special tabulations of the 2003 and 2011 Latinobarómetro Surveys.
[a] Data for 2007 and 2011.
[b] Simple average of the results for the 18 countries included in the measurement.

Little is known about the perpetrators of violence and their age distribution. Statistics are few and hard to find, and record-keeping is deficient, partly because so much crime goes unpunished in many of the region's countries. For example, in Mexico, according to the published data,[2] the conviction rate for homicide in 2008 was fairly similar for young people aged 16 to 29 (10.7 per 100,000 inhabitants) and adults aged between 30 and 44 (9.6 per 100,000 inhabitants), dropping substantially for the group of adults aged 45 to 59 (5.2 per 100,000 inhabitants). A more general approach to gauging participation in acts of violence are the figures for victims of extreme violence, such as homicide, the assumption being that the risk of falling victim to them rises with the degree of participation in violent organizations. When these figures are analysed, the supposedly predominant role of the young is called into question. As always happens with stigmas, reality and fantasy are intermingled. In the case of death rates from interpersonal violence involving assaults with firearms, blades and other weapons, for example, the data for Latin America and the Caribbean between 1990 and 2010 do not suggest that violent deaths among young people are significantly different in nature to those among people aged 30 to 44 (see figure III.14). The two curves are roughly equal, and while the proportion of adults fell between 1995 and 2005, the differences were not enough to be statistically significant.

Figure III.14

Latin America and the Caribbean (33 countries): rate of mortality from interpersonal violence, by age group, 1990-2010

(Deaths per 100,000 inhabitants)

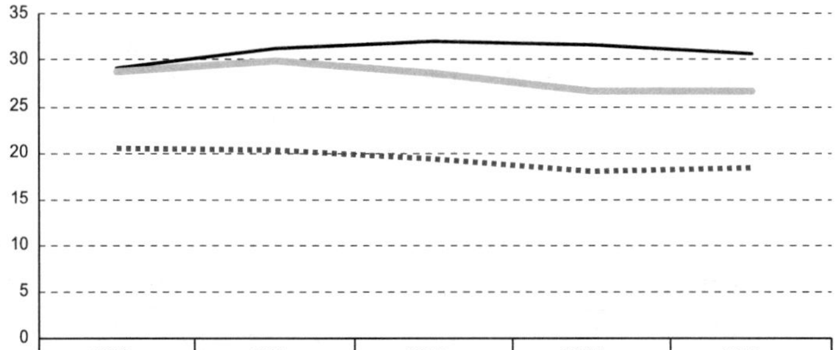

	1990	1995	2000	2005	2010
Aged 15-29	29	31	32	32	31
Aged 30-44	29	30	29	27	27
Aged 45-59	20	20	19	18	18

Source: Institute for Health Metrics and Evaluation [online] http://vizhub.healthdata.org/gbd-compare/.

2 Judicial crime statistics available from the website of the National Institute of Statistics and Geography (INEGI).

If this information is analysed at the national level, taking the countries worst affected by waves of violence in recent years (with rates in excess of 27 homicides per 100,000 inhabitants), it can be seen that the behaviour of the youth population is variable. There is no general rule that young people are the main victims of homicide; rather, the situation depends on the country, the time period and the general context of violence facing each society. For example, the rate of mortality from homicide by age group in the Bolivarian Republic of Venezuela, Brazil and Colombia (the three countries in the South American subcontinent with a higher level of violence) shows that the bulk of those affected in the last two decades were young (see figure III.15).

Figure III.15

Bolivarian Republic of Venezuela, Brazil and Colombia: rate of mortality from interpersonal violence, by age group, 1990-2010 [a]

(Deaths per 100,000 inhabitants)

A. Brazil

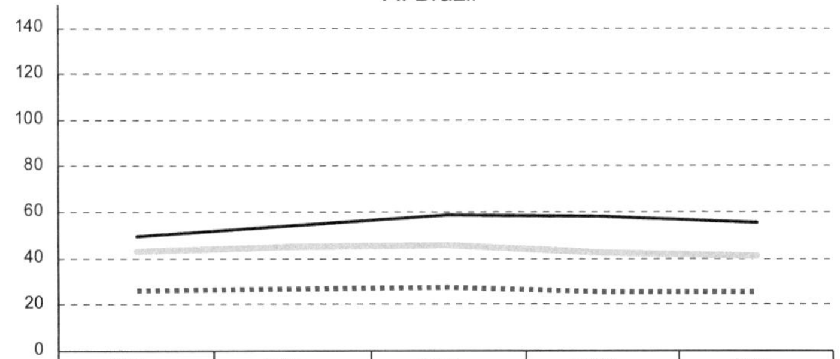

	1990	1995	2000	2005	2010
Aged 15-29	49	54	59	58	56
Aged 30-44	43	45	46	43	41
Aged 45-59	26	27	27	26	25

B. Colombia

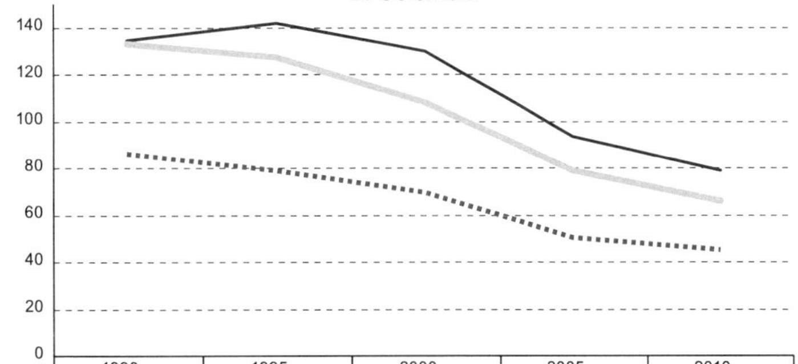

	1990	1995	2000	2005	2010
Aged 15-29	135	142	130	94	79
Aged 30-44	133	127	108	79	66
Aged 45-59	86	79	70	51	45

C. Bolivarian Republic of Venezuela

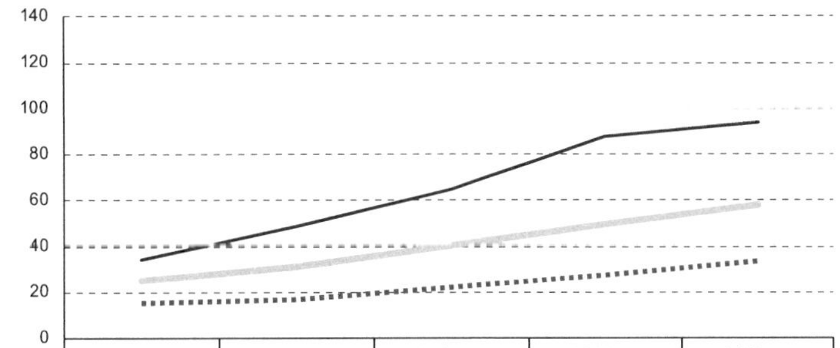

	1990	1995	2000	2005	2010
Aged 15-29	34	48	65	88	93
Aged 30-44	25	31	41	49	58
Aged 45-59	15	17	22	27	34

Source: Institute for Health Metrics and Evaluation [online] http://vizhub.healthdata.org/gbd-compare/.

[a] The differences between age groups are statistically significant except for the difference between the 15 to 29 and 30 to 44 groups in Colombia.

The social context of these countries also reflects the presence of organized and powerful violent actors associated with the dynamics of drug trafficking and criminal organizations. Nonetheless, violent territorial fiefdoms (drug traffickers in Rio de Janeiro in Brazil, or guerrillas in Colombia) are not enough to explain the situation. The case of Central America bears this out. Increased violence linked to the presence of these actors does not imply a higher level of youth involvement in homicide, as would be expected from the stigma. The cases of El Salvador, Guatemala, Honduras and Mexico confirm this (see figure III.16): up until 2000, young adults (aged 30 to 44) displayed a slightly higher level of participation, although the difference was not statistically significant. In the last decade, a time when general violence has been on the increase, segments of the youth population have participated on a more equal footing.

Figure III.16

El Salvador, Guatemala, Honduras and Mexico: rate of mortality from interpersonal violence, by age group, 1990-2010 [a]

(Deaths per 100,000 inhabitants)

A. El Salvador

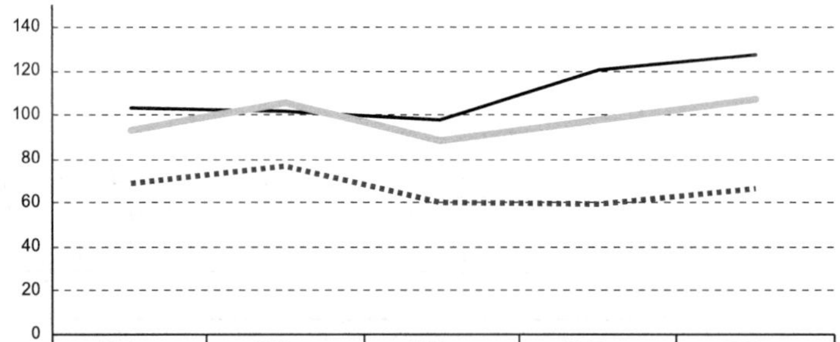

	1990	1995	2000	2005	2010
Aged 15-29	103	102	98	121	127
Aged 30-44	93	106	89	98	107
Aged 45-59	69	77	60	59	67

B. Guatemala

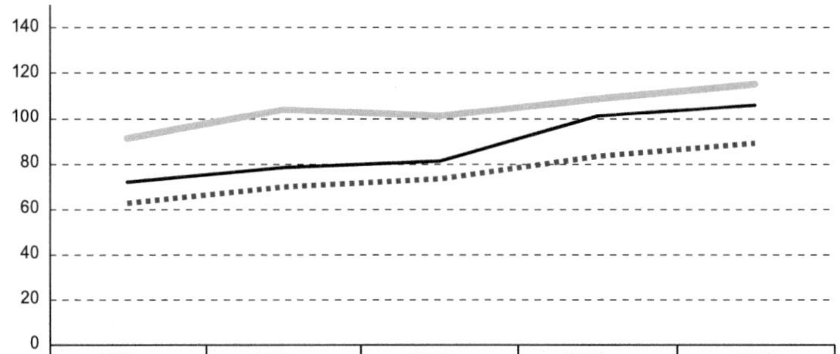

	1990	1995	2000	2005	2010
Aged 15-29	72	78	81	101	106
Aged 30-44	91	104	101	109	115
Aged 45-59	63	70	73	83	89

C. Honduras

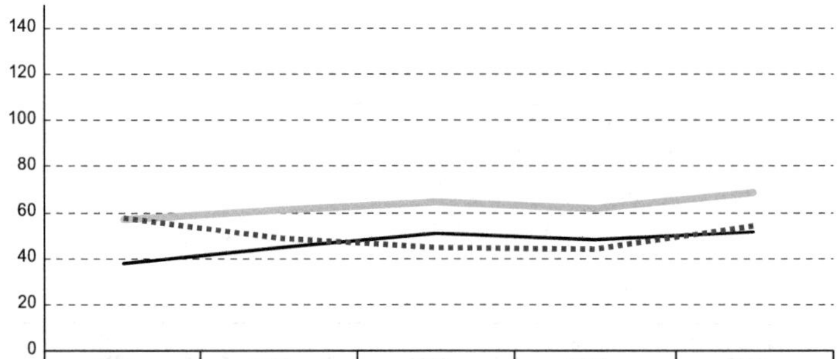

	1990	1995	2000	2005	2010
Aged 15-29	38	45	50	48	51
Aged 30-44	57	61	65	62	69
Aged 45-59	58	49	45	44	54

Figure III.16 (concluded)

D. Mexico

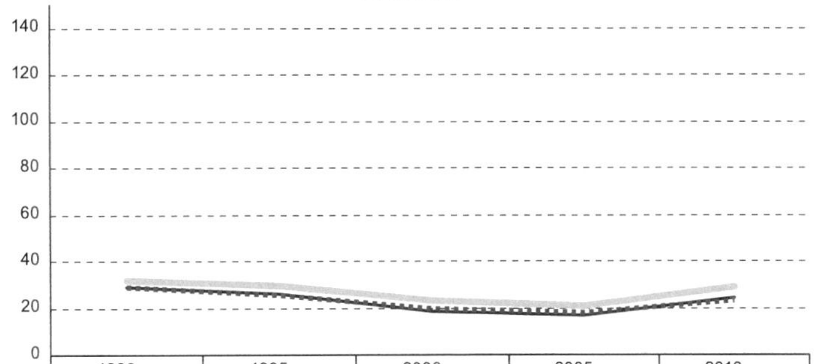

	1990	1995	2000	2005	2010
Aged 15-29	29	26	19	17	25
Aged 30-44	32	30	23	21	29
Aged 45-59	29	25	20	18	23

Source: Institute for Health Metrics and Evaluation [online] http://vizhub.healthdata.org/gbd-compare/.
[a] Differences in young people's mortality rates are not statistically different from those of other age groups in any of the countries.

Thus, while more young people die from violent causes in the more violent countries of South America, in the nations with the same characteristics in the centre of the continent it is adults who are most affected. It should be stressed that there is a considerable difference in homicide rates between the two subcontinents, with a figure of 37 for Central America and 16 for South America (UNODC, 2012). Thus, the theory that the young are disproportionately involved in acts of violence is unsupported, as the adult population segment above them is similarly involved. Nonetheless, the context for youth integration is clearly a very difficult one in some of the region's cities.

3. Organized participation in violence: gangs and drug trafficking

The statistical approach to gauging the extent of involvement in violent behaviour based on victim figures indicates that the stigma attaching to violent youth derives not so much from the scale of their participation in acts of violence as in the way they participate. What the mass media most highlight are organized forms of urban violence among the young (usually males) in gangs going by the name of *pandillas*, *maras*, *clicas* or *combos*, depending on the country. Young people of this type are categorized in the collective imaginary as "deviants" or "misfits".

The information collected in the LAPOP 2012 study (see table III.4) shows that around a third of the population perceive their local areas as being affected by organizations of this kind, with the proportion being somewhat higher among the young (an average of 35%, as against 31% for adults). It should be pointed out that citizens of the countries of the triangle in the north of Central America (El Salvador, Guatemala and Honduras), where *maras* are a strong presence in the main cities, are not the ones where gangs are considered most prevalent. There is greater awareness of them in other countries in the area, such as Panama and particularly the Dominican Republic, where this perception has been growing in recent years.

The rise of youth involvement in different forms of organized urban violence in the region is undeniable. The territorial role of gangs within cities is one of the things that do most to create a feeling of insecurity among the population at large, as it directly affects community life. The figure of the gang member standing on a corner, alienated from the institutions he should be participating in at his stage of the life cycle (traditionally school or work), feeds the stigma of the violent youth representing a threat to civic order and the city as a cultural project because his sovereignty is based on the local district or *barrio* (Perea, 2008). The territorialization of organized criminal power is associated with the high levels of segregation and "ghettoization" in many Latin American cities (see chapter V).

Table III.4

Latin America and the Caribbean (18 countries): residents' perception of the incidence of gangs or *maras* in their local area, by country and age group, 2012

(Percentages)

Country	Aged 16 to 29	Aged 30 and over
Guyana	19	14
Haiti	20	19
Jamaica	25	20
Belize	28	27
Nicaragua	28	24
Paraguay	30	24
Honduras	31	26
Mexico	33	35
Guatemala	36	31
Uruguay	37	35
Brazil	37	40
El Salvador	38	32
Costa Rica	39	32
Peru	40	35
Ecuador	41	38
Colombia	42	33
Panama	43	45
Dominican Republic	55	48
Latin America and the Caribbean [a]	**35**	**31**

Source: Economic Commission for Latin America and the Caribbean (ECLAC), on the basis of special tabulations of the biannual survey of the Latin American Public Opinion Project (LAPOP), 2012.

[a] Simple averages of the results from the 18 countries included in the measurement.

Gangs have emerged as a direct effect of what has been described as structural violence, people's exclusion and marginalization from the development of society. Specialists in youth issues have been arguing for decades that gangs are organizations that provide some Latin American youths with a form of social inclusion; when all there is are poverty, very limited employment options and a near-absence of the State and institutions in general, then the only thing left to give a sense of future to many young people's lives is their peer group in the *barrio*. Gangs give them power, cash incomes, a space and a feeling of belonging that no other social institution provides. As ECLAC/OIJ (2008) put it before, belonging to a gang operates as a form of "inclusion within exclusion"; many gangs act as microsystems of social integration that reflect, compensate for and reinforce lack of integration into society. However, Reguillo (Perea, 2008) notes that organizations of this type have changed in recent years from a core space of belonging to one of survival: "Youth groupings in contexts of exclusion and poverty seem to operate for many of their members as a setting that provides a minimum of security and trust, however precarious."

This phenomenon cannot be grasped without understanding the sociopolitical and cultural history of each territory in which these organizations emerge. These parameters influence the way they organize, the power criminal organizations have to recruit young people and the type of territorial dominance they exercise. It is important to analyse membership of these groups and the levels of violence that some of their efforts to assert this dominance result in, set as they are within a multiplicity of social processes that facilitate this kind of alternative social inclusion for some of the region's young people. The literature has identified many risk factors associated with the incorporation of certain sections of youth into violent territorial groups. They include the weakening of the social fabric, the aftermath of a history of civil violence, the availability of firearms, processes of increasing inequality and marginalization, the alienation of some groups of young people from institutions, and education systems that reject and discriminate against them, among other things.

However, there is one thing that it is important to highlight, as it is common to a number of the region's countries (particularly those that have suffered from alarming cycles of violence) and is also particularly characteristic of the region: cocaine trafficking, which in the past few decades has become the dominant illegal market in cities marked by violence, such as Medellín in Colombia, Rio de Janeiro in Brazil, Ciudad Juárez in Mexico and, recently, cities in the northern triangle of Central America comprising El Salvador, Guatemala and Honduras. It is a market which provides large profit margins and around which another set of illegal activities is organized (Perea, 2014). In many of these cities, there is no prospect whatever of the legal market, much less the State, creating economically competitive forms of employment for young people from marginalized populations. In some countries, such as those of Central America and Mexico, the cartels are increasingly tending to use gangs to "outsource" abduction and contract killing activities, particularly when they come into conflict with one another and have to find more recruits quickly and at lower cost. Cocaine trafficking in the region has played a key role as a driver of conflict and a multiplier of violence.

The crisis being experienced by countries with more fragile States, such as those of the northern triangle of Central America, is plain to see. They have been most affected by changes in cocaine trafficking routes into the United States since Colombia ceased to be the epicentre. The way these organizations embed themselves in each city and each country depends greatly on institutions and the social fabric, and on the power structures of the criminal organizations themselves. These same factors determine the way they interact with society on the ground and the extent to which local youths are involved. Nonetheless, drug trafficking is one of the central factors in the crises of violence, and the Latin America and Caribbean region needs to respond as a bloc vis-à-vis the world, which also means tackling consumption (most of which takes place in countries outside the region). As Perea says, this vastly wealthy activity privatizes power and further undermines the justice system in many countries. It also heightens inequality and segregation and serves to increase the stigmatization of poor young people and citizen insecurity (Perea, 2014).

4. Prospects for dealing with contexts of urban violence and youth

Describing young people from the perspective of the stigma of violence distorts appreciations of the roots of the problem and opens the way to alarmist and exaggerated proposals for preventing and solving it. The stigma constrains our understanding of the different situations and contexts experienced by most young people and is used to justify policies that treat aggressive behaviour by some groups of individuals as part of growing up. As has been seen throughout this chapter, the causes are manifold, and those underlying the most extreme urban violence are associated with types of behaviour that are often directed from the adult world and form part of a context of large-scale law-breaking and crime. What is taking place reveals a society that is proving incapable of including its new generations.

It is clear that State policies or strategies of over-criminalization, repression, non-adherence to the law, criminal responsibility for adolescents and others that were vigorously pursued in the 2000s proved counterproductive, as levels of violence kept on rising. It is important to grasp the sociocultural factors that have come into play in each of the territories where violence has broken out most strongly and where young people are involved. Territorial inequality in a city makes criminal organizations very attractive for the part of the population that is being excluded from established mechanisms of social participation. To be able to solve this problem, it is important to understand the corrupt ties that criminal organizations have developed with the various State political, police and judicial authorities, but also the links they establish with local communities themselves and the degree of support and protection they receive from the population where they hold sway (Perea, 2014).

There is a need for mechanisms of communication and shared reflection on the causes of youth victimization and violence. The first step in forging a culture of peace is to internalize the basic idea that conflict is not to be denied, but can always be resolved without violence. Peaceful negotiation and resolution should be part of formal and non-formal education, as this would give the new generations tools for relating, understanding the other and resolving disagreements without resorting to violence. The State needs to be capable of transmitting models of a culture of peace through policies, judicial systems, transparency, support for the community, and its institutions in general.

The need to move in this direction in the countries of Latin America and the Caribbean is plain. For example, the idea that law enforcement should itself be law-abiding is not universally established in the social imaginary of the population. According to figures from the LAPOP 2012 survey, some 37% of the youth population believe that the authorities can act outside the law to catch criminals, a share that falls to 33% among the adult population (see figure III.17). In countries such as Ecuador and Honduras, about half the youth population is supportive of the authorities acting outside the law. Similarly, many young people in the region think that the police are involved in crime (an average of 43%). Mistrust of the security forces is at an alarming level in countries such as Belize, the Dominican Republic, Guatemala and Honduras, where over 60% of young people believe that the police are part of the problem of crime and do not discharge their responsibility of protecting the population (see figure III.18). These countries are also characterized by high levels of violence in general.

Figure III.17

Latin America and the Caribbean (18 countries): people considering that the authorities can sometimes act outside the law to catch criminals, by country and age group, 2012

(Percentages)

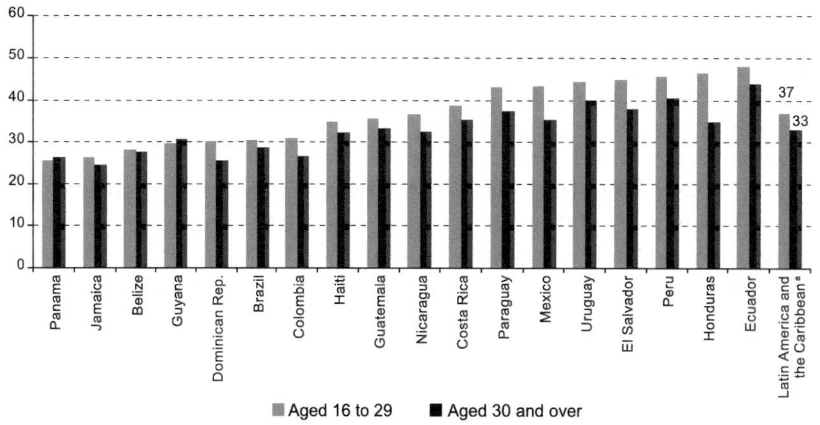

Source: Economic Commission for Latin America and the Caribbean (ECLAC), on the basis of special tabulations of the biannual survey of the Latin American Public Opinion Project (LAPOP), 2012.

[a] Simple averages of the results from the 18 countries included in the measurement.

Figure III.18

Latin America and the Caribbean (18 countries): perceptions of the role of the police in the respondent's district or town of residence, population aged 16 to 29, by country, 2012

(Percentages)

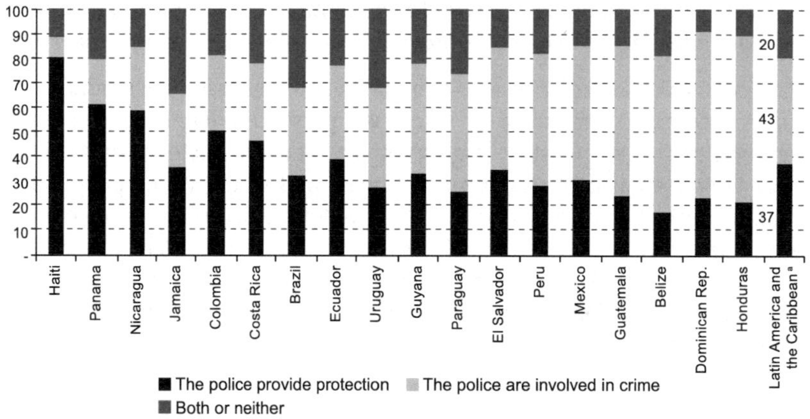

Source: Economic Commission for Latin America and the Caribbean (ECLAC), on the basis of special tabulations of the biannual survey of the Latin American Public Opinion Project (LAPOP), 2012.

[a] Simple averages of the results from the 18 countries included in the measurement.

The system of justice needs to be more effective and equitable so that the relationship between actions and punishment is more clearly defined and perceptions of security improve. Looking ahead, there is a need for reconstruction mechanisms to transmit capabilities and create opportunities, as discussed in the previous section. Many of the strategies intended to promote social inclusion for the young have been unsuccessful because of their conception of these as nothing more than beneficiaries of policies to prevent high-risk behaviour (Rodríguez, 2013). Recognizing the young as strategic actors who possess rights would make it possible to move towards more relevant models of development and enhance this population segment's feeling of social cohesion and belonging. The following chapter describes some of the main changes demanded by the young of the region as being essential for their own development.

C. Youth and the development agenda

Support for political participation by the young, with consideration of their diversity, is essential to strengthen their commitment to the development of public policies that can overcome the persistent inequalities of Latin America and the Caribbean. The priority development areas for the young are education, work, health, peace, personal security, good governance and participation.

In 2013, the Secretary-General of the United Nations appointed an Envoy on Youth to enhance the commitment of the United Nations to the young. He also set up a working group tasked with developing a System-wide Action Plan on Youth that would bring together different United Nations bodies and set global and regional working priorities. These efforts have improved our knowledge and understanding of the challenges and problems now faced by the young. Two challenges are identified for society as a whole: one is to respond to the demands of the young, in a way that guarantees their rights, in the different areas where their voices go unheard, and the other is the importance of treating young people as key development actors.

The inter-agency group for Latin America and the Caribbean has been very active in this context, and in 2014 it held a forum with young people and other critical actors with a view to drawing up recommendations for the youth development agenda and its inclusion in the Post-2015 Development Goals. As stated in the concept notes for the event (United Nations, 2014b), the region is in debt to the young, who often do not feel represented in traditional political discourses, spaces and mechanisms and do not participate in decision-making processes or in debates on key socioeconomic and political issues, even though they are considered to be sensitive to demands for equity and social justice, environmental protection and cultural diversity. To conclude this chapter, we shall try to incorporate what young people themselves have said in the different forums for debate on the forthcoming development targets.

1. Priority issues for the young

In recent years, different youth participation forums have been held in connection with the worldwide debate on the new development targets, with a view to identifying the main challenges facing them in the region. Their priorities are as diverse as the groups represented, although they have come together on certain issues regarded as essential and critical to the full development of youth in the region. These match the prioritization areas agreed as a result of the Global Youth Call,[3] an unprecedented exercise in consensus-building over the priorities of the young themselves in the Post-2015 Development Agenda. Some 1.3 million young people voted in the My World 2015 survey, which was prepared by youth from all countries on the online crowdsourcing platform. The findings of this survey are being taken into account in proposals for sustainable development goals. The priority areas are: education; employment and entrepreneurship; health; peace and personal security; and good governance and participation.

In a number of the forums, young people have argued that education is essential to development. Accordingly, they have recommended that the region's States should guarantee the right to an accessible, free and high-quality education. They value the central role played by education in improving employment options and rising above the poverty threshold. However, they suggest that it should be linked to development models that promote decent work. They also propose that technical training should be strengthened at all levels, together with other non-formal methods of training as local needs require.

Education is regarded as a socializing space where young people should receive a broad preparation based on secular values, without discrimination and with support for diversity. Thus, participants have argued for the need to achieve qualitative improvements through an intercultural and gender approach, with a broad, high-quality curriculum that includes education in the arts, ethics and civics and promotes cultures of peace. Although reasonably satisfied with the education they receive,

[3] See [online] http://www.un.org/en/ecosoc/youth2014/pdf/summary.pdf.

they believe more work is needed on inclusion, sex education, retention in the education system and help with access. Young people have high expectations of education, as they have greater aspirations than their elders, especially in the contexts of economic growth and human development advances achieved in the region in recent years. Young people's trust in teachers and educational institutions is fairly high by comparison with other types of institution.

In the area of work, they argue that it is important to create a consistent legal framework capable of guaranteeing decent working conditions, especially for all young women and for indigenous and Afro-descendent people. It should also provide adequate opportunities for autonomy and full emancipation, including people with different capabilities. The global consensus is that the following goals need to be included in the Post-2015 Development Agenda: expanding access to decent work and opportunities to earn a livelihood, promoting access to financial and non-financial resources that are essential for increasing opportunities for enterprise, and developing public-private partnerships with a view to stimulating job creation for the young.

In young women's forums,[4] there has been discussion of the difficulties these have in reconciling opportunities for work and motherhood. Here, youth forums have brought up the need to recognize unpaid domestic work and the care economy and to introduce policies to promote shared responsibility for men and women in this area and support the work-life balance for both sexes. Another demand is for measures to promote protected jobs with contracts and fair conditions for the young, from a rights perspective. A number of forums have called for strengthened protection of employment rights, including the right to join a union and to strike.

Regarding the youth development agenda, it has also been proposed that States should provide universal access to affordable, high-quality health services, including access to sexual and reproductive health and education services for the young. It is recommended that the necessary mechanisms should be established to ensure that the right to health can be exercised via social protection, with adequate and sustainable budgets. The importance of food security and a healthy environment has also been raised.

Young people regard sexual and reproductive rights as especially important. They realize that it is necessary for a comprehensive sex education to be provided and for there to be proper information about women's right to make decisions about their bodies and their ideas of motherhood, for respect for sexual diversity to be guaranteed and for those obstructing or refusing to tolerate this to be punished. In addition, there is a need to bring about change in the hegemonic cultural patterns associated with sexuality, particularly to prevent gender roles and sexual violence from being reproduced (see box III.5). Similarly, there is recognition of the particular needs of young people when it comes to information about and prevention and treatment of HIV/AIDS and other sexually transmitted diseases, ensuring that there is a multisectoral response and access to inputs.

Box III.5

Sexual and reproductive health education in Latin America and the Caribbean

In the development of young people and adolescents, sexuality plays a vital role in defining personality and individual identity. As Castellanos and Falconier (2001, p. 15) put it, "one of the determinants in the development of human personality and individual identity is the fact of being a man or a woman in a particular historical epoch and in the spaces of a particular culture". In the same publication, the authors highlight the need to use education to promote new ways of feeling and experiencing sexuality in a way consistent with human rights, thus giving young people the opportunity to take free, responsible decisions about their sexual and reproductive behaviour.

The concept of sexual and reproductive health as a public policy matter came out of the International Conference on Population and Development (ICPD) of 1996. It centres on lifelong health, with emphasis on the promotion of free, responsible, informed decision-making about sexuality and reproduction, including the formation of couples and families.

In the context of growth and development for adult life and of the rights of young people, sexual and reproductive health needs to be addressed by emphasizing the reduction of health risks during this early stage in the sexual and reproductive function (ECLAC/OIJ, 2004). In the case of Latin America and the Caribbean, it needs to be borne in mind that young people and adolescents in developing countries are particularly vulnerable to a number of reproductive health problems, such as teenage pregnancy, infertility, genital mutilation, high-risk abortions, sexually transmitted infections (including HIV) and gender violence, not to mention harassment and rape (WHO, 2009). For example, 18% of births in the region are to teenage mothers (WHO, 2012), which affects the latter's opportunities, educational performance, school completion rates and future position in the labour market (World Bank, 2011; Rico and Trucco, 2014). This problem-can amplify inequalities, since the statistics show that the largest proportion of pregnancies is still concentrated in the sectors with the lowest incomes and education levels (ECLAC, 2013b). Again, it is estimated that there were 68,000 adolescents (aged 10 to 19) with HIV in Latin America in 2012 (UNAIDS, 2012).

Discussion of sexual and reproductive rights in adolescence is vital for the development of inclusive policies that can reduce the youth population's vulnerability to these problems. Gender

[4] Declaration of Young Women of Latin America and the Caribbean (Panama City, 23 to 25 November 2012) (UN-Women, 2012).

Box III.5 (concluded)

discrimination also needs to be considered, with further analysis being required so that young women always have the information they need to take informed decisions and the freedom to act on their desires regarding motherhood. Thus, sexuality education is essential for providing tools to help young people achieve full development.

Sexuality education is one of the policies needed to work on prevention of the problems arising from the exercise of sexuality, while it is also part of "children and adolescents' right to knowledge and building the skills required to develop responsible behaviours and live life fully" (UNFPA, 2005). By exercising this right to education, young people acquire the resources to take decisions freely in their adolescent and adult lives. Thus, for example, the positive impact of education programmes in the syllabus for preventing sexually transmitted infections and teenage pregnancy has been demonstrated (Bearinger and others, 2007, cited in WHO, 2009).

In Latin America and the Caribbean, the earliest sexuality education initiatives date from the 1990s, being associated with educational reforms and global conferences organized by the United Nations, particularly the 1994 International Conference on Population and Development (ICPD). According to studies carried out by Castellanos and Moyano in 2001, five of the region's countries had sexuality education policies at that time: Chile (Sexuality Education Policy), Costa Rica (Policies for Comprehensive Education in Human Sexuality), the Dominican Republic (National Adolescence and Youth Policy), Nicaragua (National Population Policy and Population Policy Action Plan) and Peru (National Population Policy).

The following table details the situation in some of the region's countries. It can be seen that a specific sexuality education syllabus is followed only in a very few. While such education is usually provided for in laws and decrees, in practice there are large differences in the way it is imparted.

Sex education in Latin America and the Caribbean

Argentina	The National Sexuality Education Act of 2006 coordinates the design, implementation and evaluation of activities in the curriculum with a view to bringing in comprehensive sex education at all levels of education. There is also a national comprehensive sex education syllabus.
Brazil	The National Education Plan 2001-2011 Act provides that curricular guidelines for teacher training must include subjects relating to issues dealt with transversally such as gender, sex education, plurality and the environment, among others. There are no specific syllabuses.
Chile	The sexuality education policy agreed upon on an inter-agency basis and approved in 1993 provides a framework for including sex education issues in reformed curricula. There are no syllabuses. Material and tools for sexuality, emotional and gender education are provided.
Colombia	General Education Act no. 115 (1994). Education Syllabus for Sexuality and the Construction of Citizenship.
Costa Rica	Policy on Comprehensive Education in the Expression of Human Sexuality, approved by the Higher Council on Education in 2001. The creation, also in 2001, of the Department of Comprehensive Sexuality Education in the Ministry of Public Education. Syllabus on comprehensive education in the expression of human sexuality.
Cuba	Syllabus on sexuality education with a gender and sexual rights approach, to be applied in the school curriculum and in teacher training institutions (Ministry of Education Resolution no. 139 of 1 June 2011).
Ecuador	The National Intersectoral Strategy for Family Planning and Prevention of Adolescent Pregnancy (ENIPLA) is designed to reduce unwanted pregnancies and maternal mortality and to lower the proportion of adolescent pregnancies nationally.
Guatemala	Decree 42-2001, Social Development Act. There is no specific syllabus. Some subjects have been included in the curriculum.
Honduras	HIV/AIDS Prevention Act (1999), incorporating sex education as a compulsory subject in formal education syllabuses.
Mexico	The 1993 curricular reform includes sex education as a subject. There is no particular syllabus, although one of the goals in the 2013-2018 sectoral education programme is to strengthen sexuality education.
Nicaragua	National Population Policy and Population Policy Action Plan. Implementation of sex education via the curriculum. There is no specific syllabus, and it is not compulsory.
Paraguay	There is no specific syllabus, but the Jaikuaa project currently under way is designed to protect and promote young's people's right to health and their sexual and reproductive rights.
Peru	National Population Policy. There is no specific syllabus. The functions of the Department of Educational Tutorship and Guidance of the Ministry of Education, created in 2006, include proposing sex education policies and strategies.
Uruguay	Sex education syllabus developed in 2006 with a view to introducing this type of education progressively into schools.

To evaluate the quality and type of sex education provided, syllabuses need to be reviewed more thoroughly. As noted in UNFPA (2005), a detailed syllabus analysis shows that the approach is often confined to information initiatives. The best way to provide sexuality education is the subject of a wide-ranging debate involving numerous supporters and detractors of the two main tendencies: the cross-cutting approach, and the teaching of content in a specific course. Irrespective of the advantages and disadvantages of each system, Castellanos and Moyano (2005) highlight the need to fill out the content of this education with "philosophical, sociological, psychological and pedagogical underpinnings in the curriculum and the curricular model adopted" (UFNPA, 2005). At the same time, they highlight the importance of the teaching profession in this discussion, as there can be no progress with sexuality education unless the practices of teachers match the message to be conveyed.

In Latin America and the Caribbean, there has been progress in debating and implementing sexuality education syllabuses, but much remains to be done. Sexual and reproductive health is a right and young people need to be acquainted with the subject so that they can take informed, independent and responsible decisions.

Source: Economic Commission for Latin America and the Caribbean (ECLAC), on the basis of Leticia Benedet, "La educación sexual en el sistema educativo formal uruguayo durante el período 2005-2009. Análisis desde un enfoque de género y de política pública", thesis, 2014; World Bank, *Embarazo adolescente y oportunidades en América Latina y el Caribe. Sobre las decisiones de fecundidad adolescente, la pobreza y los logros económicos*, Washington, D.C., 2011; Beatriz Castellanos and Martha Falconier de Moyano, *La educación de la sexualidad en países de América Latina y el Caribe*, Mexico City, United Nations Population Fund (UNFPA), December 2001; Economic Commission for Latin America and the Caribbean (ECLAC)/Ibero-American Youth Organization (OIJ), *La juventud en Iberoamérica. Tendencias y urgencias* (LC/L.2180), Santiago, Chile, October 2004; Economic Commission for Latin America and the Caribbean (ECLAC), "La maternidad en adolescentes. La desigualdad en distintas dimensiones", *Notas para la Igualdad*, No. 8, Santiago, Chile, Gender Equality Observatory for Latin America and the Caribbean, 2013; World Health Organization (WHO), *Promoting Adolescent Sexual and Reproductive Health through Schools in Low Income Countries. An Information Brief* (WHO/FCH/CAH/ADH/09.03), Geneva, 2009; United Nations Population Fund (UNFPA), *Background, Current Situation and Challenges of Sexuality Education in Latin America and the Caribbean*, Mexico City, Country Support Team for Latin America and the Caribbean, 2005.

Meanwhile, the opportunity to live in settings free of violence is very important for the lives and development of young people in the region. It has been argued that public policies are needed to raise youth awareness of the culture of peace and to eliminate all forms of violence against women via prevention and education programmes and processes aimed at men and women at every stage of their lives, and that femicide should be recognized as the ultimate manifestation of violence against women and as a crime that should be specifically legislated for (United Nations, 2014a). What young women have mainly called for are increased fiscal spending to prevent and combat gender violence, easier access to the health-care and security system in the event they are assaulted, reparation programmes and laws on discrimination and racism, among other things.

Another important issue for many young people is protection against violence in virtual spaces, such as bullying and harassment on the Internet and social networks. Some forums have also advocated that States should move forward with a security paradigm that protects young people rather than acting repressively against them, which means avoiding institutional violence of any kind and fully guaranteeing their rights. The global consensus is that young people recognize the importance of their own role in conflict prevention and resolution, appreciating that this is an indispensable condition for the development of peaceful, inclusive and safe societies.

On the whole, young people consider that the best way of bringing about social change is through political participation. They also perceive that the best way to do this is through social movements and youth organizations, which will be discussed more fully in the next section. Likewise, they consider that there need to be more opportunities for them to influence the political agenda, which ought to include positive discrimination initiatives. They believe there is a need for specific mechanisms to remove obstacles to participation, for example by introducing quotas for young people, reducing the minimum age for seeking public office and creating consistent legal frameworks to regulate re-election so that power can be transferred between generations. To ensure good governance, young people have argued for the need to guarantee institutional transparency and the full enforcement of rights, and to pursue the fight against corruption and impunity.

2. New forms of participation: the role of social networks

The ways in which the new generations participate have been transformed. It may well be that many young people today do not share the same imaginary of far-reaching social or political change as the young of three of four decades ago, who saw party politics as the primary field in which to commit their energies. For some time now, the young have seemed to be more detached from the political system and electoral competition. In all the region's countries without exception, they are showing less willingness to vote (UNDP, 2013). There is more and more evidence that young people's levels of participation are falling, not just in elections, political parties and traditional social organizations, but also in the important process of public policy generation. The publications of the United Nations Educational, Scientific and Cultural Organization (UNESCO) have pointed out that the vast majority of young people in Latin America and the Caribbean stand outside existing youth associations and movements (between 5% and 20% participate, depending on the country, with sporting and religious organizations accounting for the overwhelming majority), in what could be seen as a transition to new forms of youth participation and new understandings of civic engagement or action (United Nations, 2014b).

Globally, however, youth-led social movements have been prominent in recent years, which should alert us to their interest in being listened to and participating actively in the development of their societies. Thus, new forms of youth mobilization and organization are emerging, in which a key element is technology, particularly social networks. These are among the Internet platforms most favoured in Latin America: of the 12 countries in the world where most time is spent on social networks, 5 are in the region. Users are mainly adolescents and young people. The communication model offered by social networks is opposed to that of the traditional mass media, which transmit a unitary message to an undefined group of individuals. With social networks, conversely, it is users who are in a position to create and disseminate messages, and this interactivity is heightened by their ability to create networks and establish contacts. This model involves a substantial change in the way people interact, both among themselves and with institutions, whether individually, in communities or in movements (Pavez, 2014).

As described in the analysis by Pavez (2014), social networks are playing an increasingly prominent role in the way adolescents and young people exercise influence and raise concerns and ideas, opening the way to new forms of organization that have spawned both social movements and communities (UNDP, 2013). One example that may be cited is the case of young Chileans, whose low electoral turnout has been unchanged in recent years. Thanks to the progressive spread of the Internet, they are using other platforms to express their discontent, approval or rejection on issues affecting the country, and to organize themselves. This participation has taken place both in web-based campaigns and through the creation of virtual groups or communities.

This new technology has opened the way to social movements that have mainly catalysed discontent, as has been seen in the so-called Arab Spring, prompting a number of researchers to study the link between the use made of social networks and the expression of political views (Allagui and Kuebler, 2011; Faris, 2013, and Valenzuela, 2013, cited in Pavez, 2014). In Latin America and the Caribbean, young people have joined in these demonstrations of social discontent, organizing through networks and capturing the attention of both the mass media and their Governments. One of the most striking instances in recent years was led by young Mexicans with the #yosoy132 movement, organized by university students amid the 2012 presidential campaign. Brazil is another country that has seen this type of social discontent, expressed and organized via the Internet. Since June 2013, the media have reported on movements with tens of thousands of participants, most of them university students and other young people, who have come out on matters such as high public transport prices and the cost of the football World Cup, resulting in one of the largest waves of protests seen in the country for many years. This too is a movement that has been organized through social networks, mainly Facebook. As with the Mexican movement, participants say that it is a horizontal organization and pride themselves on having no party affiliations or defined leaderships (Pavez, 2014).

Supporting political participation by the young, with regard to their diversity, is essential for strengthening their contribution and access to public policymaking with a view to overcoming the inequalities that persist in Latin America and the Caribbean. Misrepresentation or under-representation of the young in all their plurality affects the democratic quality of institutions. This situation has facilitated the emergence of non-traditional social movements, campaigns and organizations like those described, in which young people exercise crucial leadership and which are characterized by new forms of communication, outreach and participation. The recommendation from the youth forums is to ensure that adolescents and young people are present and involved in the formulation, implementation, oversight and validation of multisectoral public policies at all levels, with sustainable budgets and an awareness of particular contexts and situations. Policies that are inappropriate for the young have significant costs for all, both because they worsen the problems described in the earlier sections and because of the consequences of failing to include this population properly in economic development efforts and thereby sacrificing their creativity and energy. In other words, a virtuous circle is foregone and a vicious circle is entrenched.

"Young people today are the present for change in an unequal Latin America. We are social and political subjects of rights with different ways of thinking and living, and we are changing the world around us. We are fighting for a fairer and more democratic, sustainable, respectful, diverse and equitable world in which every young person will have a voice" (Juventud con Voz, 2013).

Bibliography

Alonso, Jorge (2013), "Cómo escapar de la cárcel de lo electoral: El movimiento #Yosoy132", *Desacatos*, vol. 42, May.

Bearinger, L.H. and others (2007), "Global perspectives on the sexual and reproductive health of adolescents: patterns, prevention, and potential", *The Lancet*, Elsevier.

Belfer, Myron Lowell and Luis Augusto Rohde (2005), "Child and adolescent mental health in Latin America and the Caribbean. Problems, progress, and policy research", *Pan American Journal of Public Health*, vol. 18, No. 4/5, Washington, D.C., Pan American Health Organization (PAHO).

Benedet, Leticia (2014), "La educación sexual en el sistema educativo formal uruguayo durante el período 2005-2009. Análisis desde un enfoque de género y de política pública", thesis, Master in Gender, Society and Policies.

Bradshaw, Catherine P., Lindsey M. O'Brennan and Clea A. McNeely (2008), "Core competencies and the prevention of school failure and early school leaving", *New Directions for Child and Adolescent Development*, vol. 2008, No. 122, Wiley.

Castellanos, Beatriz and Martha Falconier de Moyano (2001), *La educación de la sexualidad en países de América Latina y el Caribe*, Mexico City, United Nations Population Fund (UNFPA), December.

Comari, Claudio (2014), "La generación de los *nini* ¿existe? Una desmentida desde la demografía mediante un enfoque dinámico. Avance de tesis para doctorado en demografía".

CONAPO (National Population Council)/Fundación BBVA Bancomer (2014), *Anuario de migración y remesas México 2014*, Mexico City [online] https://www.fundacionbbvabancomer.org/imagenes/Docs/Anuario_Migracion_y_Remesas_2014.pdf.

Dávila, Oscar and Felipe Ghiardo (2005), "Trayectorias, transiciones y condiciones juveniles en Chile", *El futuro ya no es como antes. Ser joven en América Latina*, Nueva Sociedad.

ECLAC (Economic Commission for Latin America and the Caribbean) (2014a), *Guaranteeing indigenous people's rights in Latin America: progress in the past decade and remaining challenges*. Summary (LC/L.3893), Santiago, Chile.

___ (2014b), *Compacts for Equality: Towards a Sustainable Future* (LC/G.2586(SES.35/3)), Santiago, Chile, April.

___ (2013a), *Social Panorama of Latin America 2012* (LC/G.2557-P), Santiago, Chile. United Nations publication, Sales No. E..13.II.G.6.

___ (2013b), "La maternidad en adolescentes. La desigualdad en distintas dimensiones", *Notas para la Igualdad*, No. 8, Santiago, Chile, Gender Equality Observatory for Latin America and the Caribbean.

___ (2013c), "Long Term Population Estimates and Projections 1950-2100", Santiago, Chile [online] http://www.cepal.org/celade/proyecciones/basedatos_bd.htm.

___ (2012), *Structural Change for Equality: An Integrated Approach to Development* (LC/G.2524(SES.34/3)), Santiago, Chile.

___ (2011), *Social Panorama of Latin America 2010* (LC/G.2481-P), Santiago, Chile. United Nations publication, Sales No. E.11.II.G.6.

___ (2010), *Time for equality: closing gaps, opening trails* (LC/G.2432(SES.33/3)), Santiago, Chile.

___ (2009), *Social Panorama of Latin America 2008* (LC/G.2402-P), Santiago, Chile. United Nations publication, Sales No. E.08.II.G.89.

___ (2005), *Social Panorama of Latin America 2004* (LC/L.2259-P), Santiago, Chile. United Nations publication, Sales No. E.04.II.G.148.

ECLAC/OIJ (Economic Commission for Latin America and the Caribbean/Ibero-American Youth Organization) (2008), *Youth and Social Cohesion in Ibero-America: A Model in the Making* (LC/G.2391), Santiago, Chile, October.

___ (2004), *La juventud en Iberoamérica. Tendencias y urgencias* (LC/L.2180), Santiago, Chile, October.

ECLAC/OIJ/IMJUVE (Economic Commission for Latin America and the Caribbean/Ibero-American Youth Organization/Mexican Youth Institute) (2014), *Invertir para transformar. La juventud como protagonista del desarrollo*, Madrid, September.

ECLAC/ILO (Economic Commission for Latin America and the Caribbean/International Labour Organization) (2012), "Youth employment: crisis and recovery", *The Employment Situation in Latin America and the Caribbean*, No. 7, Santiago, Chile, October.

ECLAC/UNFPA (Economic Commission for Latin America and the Caribbean/United Nations Population Fund) (2012), *Regional Population Report in Latin America and the Caribbean 2011. Investing in Youth in Latin America and the Caribbean: A Rights Imperative and Inclusion*, Santiago, Chile.

Filgueira, Carlos (1998), "Emancipación juvenil. Trayectorias y destinos" (LC/MVD/R.154.REV.2), Montevideo, ECLAC office in Montevideo.

Galindo Cáceres, Jesús and José Ignacio González-Acosta (2013), #YoSoy132: *La primera erupción visible*, Global Talent University Press.

Galtung, Johan (1990), "Cultural violence", *Journal of Peace Research*, vol. 27, No. 3, Sage.

Goche, Flor (2012), "Yo Soy 132, movimiento del siglo XXI", *Contralínea* [online] http://contralinea.info/archivo-revista/index.php/2012/09/11/yo-soy-132-movimiento-del-siglo-xxi/

González, Luis Josué (2012), "#YoSoy132. Participación política 2.0 en México", *Diálogo Político*, No. 2.

Grieco, C. and others (2012), "The Foreign-Born Population in the United States: 2010", United States Census Bureau [online] http://www.census.gov/prod/2012pubs/acs-19.pdf.

"Hacia una participación inclusiva e integral de las Juventudes de América Latina y el Caribe" (2013) [online] http://www.juventudconvoz.org/archivos/brasilia/hacia-una-participacion-inclusiva-e-integral-de-las-Juventudes.pdf.

ILO (International Labour Organization) (2013), *Trabajo decente y juventud en América Latina. Políticas para la acción*, Lima, ILO Regional Office for Latin America and the Caribbean.

Imbusch, Peter, Michel Misse and Fernando Carrión (2011), "Violence research in Latin America and the Caribbean: a literature review", *International Journal of Conflict and Violence*, vol. 5, No. 1.

Juventud con Voz (2013), *Recomendaciones para el desarrollo integral, inversión social y el buen vivir de las juventudes de América Latina y el Caribe*.

Migration Policy Institute (2012), "Countries of Birth for U.S. Immigrants, 1960-2012" [online] http://migrationpolicy.org/programs/data-hub/charts/immigrants-countries-birth-over-time.
PAHO (Pan American Health Organization) (2012), "The International Day of the Girl Child, celebrated today, advocates to end child marriage, which causes early and unintended pregnancies" [online] http://www.paho.org/hq/index.php?option=com_content&view=article&id=7322%3Ael-18-de-los-nacimientos-son-de-madres-adolescentes-en-america-latina-y-el-caribe&catid=1443%3Anews-front-page-items&lang=en&Itemid=1926.
Pavez, María Isabel (2014), "Los derechos de la infancia en la era de Internet. América Latina y las nuevas tecnologías, *Políticas Sociales series*, No. 210 (LC/L.3894), Santiago, Chile, Economic Commission for Latin America and the Caribbean (ECLAC), September.
Perea Restrepo, Carlos (2014), "La muerte próxima. Vida y dominación en Río de Janeiro y Medellín", *Análisis Político*, vol. 27, No. 80.
___ (2008), *¿Qué nos une? Jóvenes, cultura y ciudadanía*, Medellín, La Carreta.
Programa Estado de la Nación (2013), *Decimonoveno Informe Estado de la Nación en Desarrollo Humano Sostenible*, San José.
Rico, María Nieves and Daniela Trucco (2014), "Adolescentes. Derecho a la educación y al bienestar futuro", *Políticas Sociales series*, No. 190 (LC/L.3791), Santiago, Chile, Economic Commission for Latin America and the Caribbean (ECLAC).
Rodríguez Vignoli, Jorge (2013), "Migración interna y jóvenes. Hechos estilizados e implicaciones de política", document presented at the Seminario Temático de Análisis de los Resultados de la Ronda de Censos de 2010.
___ (2008), "Migración interna de la población joven. El caso de América Latina", *Revista Latinoamericana de Población*, vol. 2, No. 3, Latin American Population Association.
Rovner, Helena (s/f), "¿Qué y cómo piensan los jóvenes en América Latina y el Caribe?", [online] http://www.juventudconvoz.org/2-uncategorised/18-que-y-como-piensan-los-jovenes-en-america-latina-y-el-caribe.
Trucco, Daniela (2014), "Educación y desigualdad en América Latina", *Políticas Sociales series*, No. 200 (LC/L.3846), Santiago, Chile, Economic Commission for Latin America and the Caribbean (ECLAC), June.
UNAIDS (Joint United Nations Programme on HIV/AIDS) (2012), "Young people living with HIV in Latin America make their voices heard" [online] http://www.unaids.org/en/resources/presscentre/featurestories/2012/october/20121018npyconsultation.
UNDP (United Nations Development Programme) (2013), *Human Development Report for Latin America 2013-2014. Citizen Security with a Human Face: Evidence and Proposals for Latin America*, New York, November.
UNFPA (United Nations Population Fund) (2005), *Background, Current Situation and Challenges of Sexuality Education in Latin America and the Caribbean*, Mexico City, Country Support Team for Latin America and the Caribbean.
United Nations (2014a), "ECOSOC Forum on Youth 2014. #Youth2015: Realizing the Future They Want" [online] http://www.un.org/en/ecosoc/youth2014/pdf/background_note.pdf.
___ (2014b), "Regional Youth Forum for Latin America and the Caribbean".
___ (2014c), *Mental Health Matters. Social Inclusion of Youth with Mental Health Conditions* (ST/ESA/352), New York.
___ (2013), *World Youth Report. Youth and Migration* (ST/ESA/338), New York. United Nations publication, Sales No. E.12.IV.6.
United States Census Bureau (2012), "Current Population Survey" [online] http://www.census.gov/population/foreign/data/cps2012.html.
UNODC (United Nations Office on Drugs and Crime) (2014), *Global Study on Homicide 2013. Trends, Contexts, Data*, Vienna.
___ (2012), *World Drug Report 2012*, New York.
UN-Women (United Nations Entity for Gender Equality and the Empowerment of Women) (2012), "Declaration of young women of Latin America and the Caribbean", Regional Forum of Latin America and the Caribbean "Young Women, Leadership and Governance: Sharing Experiences Worldwide".
WHO (World Health Organization) (2010), *Mental Health and Development. Targeting People with Mental Health Conditions as a Vulnerable Group*, Geneva.
___ (2009), *Promoting Adolescent Sexual and Reproductive Health through Schools in Low Income Countries. An Information Brief* (WHO/FCH/CAH/ADH/09.03), Geneva.
___ (2002), *World Report on Violence and Health*, Washington, D.C., Pan American Health Organization (PAHO).
World Bank (2011), *Teenage Pregnancy and Opportunities in Latin America and the Caribbean. On Teenage Fertility Decisions, Poverty and Economic Achievement*, Washington, D.C.
#YoSoy132 Media (n/d), "¿Quiénes somos?" [online] http://www.yosoy132media.org/quienes-somos/.

Annex

Table III.A.1

Latin America (18 countries): people aged 15 to 29 who are in neither education nor paid employment, by country, sex, area of residence and age group, selected years between 2006 and 2012

(Percentages)

Country	Year	Proportion of young people in neither education nor employment	Sex		Geographical area of residence		Age group		
			Male	Female	Urban	Rural	15 to 20	21 to 25	26 to 29
Argentina	2012	19.3	32.9	67.1	-	-	26.5	40.2	33.3
Bolivia (Plurinational State of)	2011	28.6	32.2	67.8	82.5	17.5	50.3	30.7	19.0
Brazil	2012	20.8	29.7	70.3	83.9	16.1	25.5	38.2	36.3
Chile	2011	21.8	59.3	40.7	87.6	12.4	8.4	40.0	51.6
Colombia	2012	22.7	27.3	72.7	72.6	27.4	31.7	38.2	30.1
Costa Rica	2011	18.6	28.4	71.6	52.6	47.4	29.0	35.8	35.2
Dominican Republic	2012	23.6	32.3	67.7	63.9	36.1	27.3	40.0	32.6
Ecuador	2012	17.7	27.4	72.6	68.2	31.8	28.1	40.9	31.1
El Salvador	2012	24.8	21.8	78.2	52.8	47.2	31.2	40.7	28.1
Guatemala	2006	25.7	9.2	90.8	39.3	60.7	33.9	36.2	29.9
Honduras	2010	27.3	19.0	81.0	40.0	60.0	36.9	36.5	26.6
Mexico	2012	20.5	21.1	78.9	56.7	43.3	32.1	35.3	32.6
Nicaragua	2009	28.4	22.9	77.1	54.0	46.0	36.9	34.3	28.8
Panama	2011	22.3	22.6	77.4	60.6	39.4	26.3	38.2	35.4
Paraguay	2011	17.8	25.1	74.9	48.0	52.0	29.7	39.0	31.3
Peru	2012	19.8	36.1	63.9	80.5	19.5	44.7	32.1	23.3
Uruguay	2011	16.4	35.0	65.0	92.3	7.7	38.4	33.6	28.0
Venezuela (Bolivarian Republic of)	2012	20.5			-	-	28.6	37.9	33.5
Latin America [a]		**22.0**	**28.3**	**71.7**	**64.7**	**35.3**	**31.4**	**37.1**	**31.5**

Source: Economic Commission for Latin America and the Caribbean (CEPAL), on the basis of special tabulations of data from household surveys conducted in the respective countries.

[a] Simple averages of the results from the 18 countries included in the measurement.

Table III.A.2

Latin America (18 countries): people aged 15 to 29 who are in neither education nor paid employment, and country, sex and activity status

(Percentages)

Country	Year	Male						Female					
		Unemployed	Seeking employment for the first time	Pensioners	Unpaid domestic or care work	Permanently incapacitated for work	Other inactive	Unemployed	Seeking employment for the first time	Pensioners	Unpaid domestic or care work	Permanently incapacitated for work	Other inactive
Argentina	2012	35.6	7.8	2.7	11.2	4.6	38.1	16.1	3.3	1.9	62.9	1.0	14.6
Bolivia (Plurinational State of)	2011	20.2	20.4	0.0	9.1	16.7	33.7	5.8	4.7	0.0	82.2	3.2	4.2
Brazil	2012	24.2	9.1	7.9	19.4	0.0	39.4	12.1	6.8	10.3	64.0	0.0	6.7
Chile	2011	37.3	6.0	1.2	3.2	7.7	44.6	17.2	4.4	0.4	29.0	3.1	46.0
Colombia	2012	50.0	9.9	0.0	9.5	4.1	26.5	24.5	5.9	0.0	62.2	0.7	6.7
Costa Rica	2011	45.7	6.9	4.1	25.3	3.8	14.1	15.9	4.3	1.2	75.4	0.7	2.0
Dominican Republic	2012	54.4	13.8	0.3	0.4	15.1	16.0	33.0	7.0	0.0	43.2	9.3	7.3
Ecuador	2012	50.1	0.0	0.0	1.2	17.7	30.7	13.4	0.0	0.0	72.1	4.6	9.9
El Salvador	2012	51.0	12.5	0.1	6.8	17.2	12.4	6.4	3.0	0.0	86.2	3.0	1.4
Guatemala	2006	29.6	6.3	0.1	12.2	24.1	27.7	2.8	0.8	0.0	93.9	1.7	0.9
Honduras	2010	27.8	6.1	0.2	23.8	8.2	33.7	5.0	2.5	0.1	87.1	1.1	4.3
Mexico	2012	71.6	0.0	0.0	10.8	8.0	9.5	8.0	0.0	0.0	89.9	0.9	1.1
Nicaragua	2009	41.3	11.1	0.0	9.5	8.2	29.9	6.1	3.2	0.0	86.7	1.8	2.1
Panama	2011	38.8	15.0	0.0	10.3	4.3	31.6	7.0	3.4	0.0	84.3	0.7	4.6
Paraguay	2011	29.5	9.9	0.0	2.5	19.2	38.9	11.6	5.4	0.0	41.9	5.0	36.1
Peru	2012	26.5	5.0	0.0	31.6	10.6	26.2	12.7	3.6	0.0	72.5	3.6	7.6
Uruguay	2011	37.8	6.3	3.5	5.0	8.3	38.9	22.3	4.4	2.0	47.3	3.6	20.2
Venezuela (Bolivarian Republic of)	2012	47.0	8.1	0.0	3.5	5.9	35.6	13.3	4.6	0.0	71.9	1.7	8.4
Latin America [a]		**39.9**	**9.6**	**1.1**	**10.9**	**10.8**	**29.3**	**13.0**	**4.2**	**0.9**	**69.6**	**2.7**	**10.2**

Source: Economic Commission for Latin America and the Caribbean (CEPAL), on the basis of special tabulations of data from household surveys conducted in the respective countries.
[a] Simple averages of the results from the 18 countries included in the measurement.

Chapter IV

Gender inequality in the labour market and its impact on socioeconomic inequality: what gains could be made?

Introduction

In recent years, ECLAC has placed the issue of equality front and centre on the region's agenda, setting forth a broad concept of equality whose scope extends beyond distributive justice to include subjects' demands for recognition, dignity and autonomy (ECLAC, 2014). The autonomy of individuals is dependent on the range of options and resources that society makes available to them (Lechner, 2002). ECLAC has also highlighted the issue of equality between men and women, with an emphasis on the unpaid work performed by women within households, its economic value and how these activities prevent women from achieving economic autonomy and full integration into the labour market (ECLAC, 2013). In this context, a gender perspective is indispensable to analysing prevailing societal inequalities, and their interlinkages, as such an approach shines a spotlight on issues and stances that more traditional approaches hide under a "conceptual silence" (Bakker, 1999). This breaks down the resistance to acknowledging that the labour market is a social space marked by asymmetries between men and women and one that reflects and perpetuates those same asymmetries (Rico and Marco, 2006). What is more, it also bestows conceptual and political significance on gender relations in terms of the functioning of the economy in general and the labour market in particular. Several studies have argued that the absence of a gender perspective impedes an understanding of the different positions of men and women as economic agents and subjects of economic policies (Giosa and Rodríguez, 2010), while also masking the role of unpaid domestic work as a factor that both conditions and sustains the labour market.

Inequalities are generated in various dimensions of the market, in connection with variables such as income, participation and access to different occupations. Not only does the labour market offer an unparalleled space for social relations, mutual recognition and building autonomy and identity, it is also one of the arenas in which the struggle to overcome poverty and extend citizenship plays out, making it a crucial sphere for advancing towards the goal of equality. Several studies on the region's labour markets (for example, ECLAC/FAO/UN-Women/UNDP/ILO, 2013) show significant changes in female labour force participation in recent decades. However, these changes have taken place at different rates in each country, and even among women in the same country, depending on their socioeconomic status, their education level and the number of dependent minors in their households, among other factors. In the last decade, most countries have narrowed their gender gaps in labour participation and employment; yet these remain wide despite the fact that in the same period women overcame the educational disadvantages that were long considered the reason for their limited and poor labour market integration. With respect to income gaps and occupational segregation, the picture is more diverse across the countries and cannot be painted as one of progress for the region as a whole (ECLAC, 2014).

It is clear then that the labour market and its flip side, unpaid work, constitute a single, complex issue, and that moving towards the horizon of equality put forward by ECLAC calls for the prompt implementation of a number of changes on this front (ECLAC, 2010a, 2012a and 2014). In this context, it is necessary to reduce gaps in participation, employment and income, and to introduce policies for reconciling work and family life for men and women, as doing so will have positive effects at different levels. For one, there will be productivity gains, higher household income and, as shown in this chapter, lower levels of socioeconomic inequality and household poverty. But it will also give impetus to equality in other spheres, such as the full exercise of autonomy, the development of individual capacities and potential, access to contributory social protection and broader participation in society beyond the household. All of these are central issues on the region's equality and rights agenda.

Against this backdrop, this chapter links the gender inequalities in labour market integration and the household income inequalities prevalent in the region's economies. It examines the impact of women's employment on household well-being, measured in terms of their income and the distribution of that income.

It carries forward the line of research taken in previous editions of the *Social Panorama of Latin America* (ECLAC, 2010b and 2013), which looked at the division of labour within households and the role of the care economy in the region, and pursues further the analysis presented in *Compacts for Equality: Towards a Sustainable Future* (ECLAC, 2014) regarding gender differences and inequalities in the world of work. The chapter begins by presenting the interlinkages between paid and unpaid work (section A), then addresses female labour market engagement (section B), the importance of women's labour income (section C) and its impact on inequality and poverty (section D). This last section seeks to illustrate the levels of inequality and poverty that would prevail in the region under two desirable scenarios: (i) if the labour force participation gap between men and women were closed; and (ii) if women were paid the same as their male counterparts with the same qualifications for work of equal value.

Seeking to make progress on closing these gaps is not a utopian exercise. The fact that these gender-based disparities are ingrained in multiple mechanisms of discrimination and cultural reproduction makes them difficult, but not impossible, to reverse. Public policies on employment, care and gender equality have much to contribute in these areas, as shown by international experience and as reflected in the actions and regulations that are beginning to take shape in some countries in the region.

A. Interlinkages between paid and unpaid work

Work can be defined as the physical or mental effort that people make with the aim of generating wealth. When this work is carried out in the market in exchange for pay, it is referred to as employment. Unpaid domestic work, done mostly by women, is excluded from countries' labour statistics and accounts of economic activity. Women's opportunities for entering the labour market in good-quality jobs and generating independent income are closely tied to the current sexual division of labour. The large amount of time that women devote to unpaid work and the almost complete lack of male involvement in domestic and care work prevent women from entering the labour market on equal terms.

Before analysing the labour markets in the countries of the region it is important to focus on the distinction between work and employment, as these concepts are fundamental to understanding the inequalities between men and women, and to measuring the overall economic contribution of individuals.

Work can be defined as the physical or mental effort that people make with the aim of generating wealth. When this work is carried out in the market in exchange for pay, it is referred to as employment, whether carried out in the public or private sector, on a wage or own-account basis, on formal or informal terms, and in any of the many sectors of economic activity. Employment is valued socially and economically, measured in statistics and included in national accounts.

One special case is unpaid employment, that is, work carried out within the scope of the market without pay. This group includes individuals who work for a company or business, regardless of whether they are related to the owner, without receiving any pay. They are considered to be employed for the purposes of labour statistics. Also, this category of unpaid work is included in the system of national accounts and is incorporated in the calculation of GDP. This type of employment is more prevalent among women, and is particularly common in some countries of the region. The activities usually included in this category are subsistence activities in rural areas, running family businesses, and apprenticeships or traineeships. This category should not be confused with unpaid work in a wider sense, which extends to domestic and care work in households and communities.

Unpaid domestic work, done mostly by women, is not included in countries' labour statistics and accounts of economic activity. Nevertheless, 30% of women in the region report devoting all of their time to housework, which is associated with lower participation in the labour market. Some countries in the region are making efforts to assign a value to this work in order to incorporate it into national statistics through the calculation of satellite accounts (see box IV.1). Those women who do not work for pay, but who devote many hours to unpaid domestic work in their homes, are counted as inactive in economic statistics. However, the two types of work are strongly interlinked and both are productive, the only difference is that in one case the production is market-oriented and in the other it is destined for the home and community. In statistics, households are considered primarily as consumer units, even though they are also the site of production of goods and services that meet the needs of individuals, and this requires work, especially care work. Similarly, the work carried out in the community to improve the lives of children, older persons and the poor, to fulfil needs that public policies do not meet, is often unpaid and carried out outside the market (Espino, 2010). All of these activities, which include tasks such as shopping, preparing meals, washing clothes, caring for the sick, children and persons with disabilities, are carried out for members of the family or community and are excluded from national accounts and employment statistics.

Box IV.1

Assigning a value to unpaid domestic work

Feminist economists argue that assigning a value to unpaid work would reveal the gender bias in who is carrying out such work, make visible part of the economy that remains hidden despite being of vital importance to the reproduction of the workforce, and help to better understand the links with paid work (Durán, 2006; Gómez Luna, 2008; Salvador, 2009).

However, in the traditional System of National Accounts (SNA) used by countries to generate economic statistics, the production activities of households, whose outputs are not traded in the market and therefore do not have a monetary value, are excluded from the national accounts.

Satellite accounts of household production are a statistical tool that allow for the valuation of unpaid work within the SNA framework. The concept of satellite accounts was introduced in the SNA review conducted in 1993 in order to accommodate complementary or alternative concepts, thus extending the bounds of national accounts. Although satellite accounts are separate from the traditional national accounts, they are conceptually consistent with the system, enabling a flexible expansion of the analytical capacity of the national accounts without overburdening or disrupting the central system. Thus, the satellite account of unpaid work can include the production of domestic and personal services consumed within the same household, such as food preparation, child care, cleaning and repairs, among other activities.

In methodological terms, there are two possible ways to measure and assign a value to this production. One is the input approach, which measures and valuates the costs of production. The main production cost is associated with labour and there are two ways of calculating its value: one is to consider the replacement cost, that is, the wage paid in the market for performing a similar activity; the other is to consider the opportunity cost, which is the potential wage that the person carrying out the unpaid work could earn in the labour market. The second method of valuing household production is the output approach. It consists in multiplying the volume of household production in each activity by its equivalent market value. Subtracting the value of the intermediate inputs from that sum gives the value added of household production. Previous experiences of assigning value to unpaid work have tended to be based on the more advanced input method (see Eurostat, 2003; Salvador, 2009).

Developing a satellite account to measure unpaid household work is a complex task. For example, in some countries of the region the national accounts are not disaggregated by institutional sector, which makes it much more difficult to construct a satellite account. Furthermore, it can be difficult to compare the data from satellite accounts owing to the different methodologies that can be used for estimating the value of unpaid work.

The valuation of unpaid work in developed countries presented by Durán (2006) recognizes the importance of household production. The gross value added of domestic production that is not included in the SNA is worth between 15% of GDP for Japan in 1996 and 67% of GDP in Germany in 1992 (see table).

Gross value added of domestic production not included in the System of National Accounts, according to the input and replacement cost method

(Percentages of GDP)

Country	Year	Percentages of GDP
Australia	1992	54
	1997	43
Canada	1992	41
	1997	34
Denmark	1987	37
Finland	1990	45
France	1975	31
Germany	1992	67
Japan	1996	15
New Zealand	1991	42
	1999	39
Norway	1990	38
Switzerland	1997	41
United States	1976	32

Source: M. Durán, *La cuenta satélite del trabajo no remunerado en la comunidad de Madrid*, Madrid, Consejería de Empleo y Mujer, Dirección General de la Mujer, 2006.

Since the mid-2000s, several countries in the region have introduced specific legislation aimed at generating statistics on the value of unpaid work (Argentina, Brazil, Chile, Colombia, Costa Rica, Ecuador, El Salvador, Honduras, Mexico, Peru, Plurinational State of Bolivia, Trinidad and Tobago and Uruguay) (INMUJERES, n/d) and even calculating satellite accounts on unpaid household work (for example, Colombia, Ecuador, Mexico and Peru). In other cases, progress has been made towards introducing such legislation.

In Mexico, for example, the National Institute of Statistics and Geography (INEGI) began to study the economic value of

Box IV.1 (concluded)

unpaid work in 2009 and has been publishing a satellite account of unpaid household work since 2011. The data available for 2012 indicate that the economic value of unpaid household work represents approximately 19.5% of Mexico's GDP and that women carry out 76% of that work.

In Colombia, the National Administrative Department of Statistics (DANE) carried out a valuation of unpaid domestic work in households and found that it was equivalent to 19.3% of GDP in 2012. In 2013, Ecuador developed a satellite account of unpaid work. In Peru, a law was passed recently establishing that a satellite account of unpaid domestic work is to be designed and developed by the National Institute of Statistics and Informatics (INEI).

In other countries, even when official estimates of the value of unpaid work have not been calculated as part of the national statistics system, individual researchers have sometimes carried out such valuations. For example, the economic value of unpaid domestic work in Uruguay was estimated at about 21% of GDP in 2007 (Salvador, 2009). In Argentina, Esquivel (2008) put the economic value of unpaid work in the city of Buenos Aires at between 7% and 12% of GDP, depending on the estimation method used. In El Salvador, the United Nations Development Programme (UNDP, 2008) estimated that the economic value of unpaid work was 31.8% of GDP in 2005, of which men accounted for 4.5 percentage points and women 27.3 percentage points.

Source: INMUJERES (National Women's Institute) (n/d), Medir el trabajo no remunerado (TnR) y el uso del tiempo (UdT). Visibilizar la contribución de las mujeres a la economía y la sociedad [online] http://cedoc.inmujeres.gob.mx/cendoc//documentos_download/TnR_UdT.pdf; M. Durán, La cuenta satélite del trabajo no remunerado en la comunidad de Madrid, Madrid, Consejería de Empleo y Mujer, Dirección General de la Mujer; V. Esquivel, "The political and social economy of care: Argentina", Research Report, No. 2, Geneva, United Nations Research Institute for Social Development (UNRISD), 2008; Eurostat, Household Production and Consumption: Proposal for a Methodology of Household Satellite Accounts, Luxembourg, European Commission; M.E. Gómez Luna, "Cuentas satélite de los servicios no remunerados de los hogares: Una aproximación para México", La economía invisible y las desigualdades de género. La importancia de medir y valorar el trabajo no remunerado, Washington, D.C., Pan American Health Organization (PAHO), 2008; National Institute of Statistics and Geography (INEGI), "Cuenta satélite del trabajo no remunerado de los hogares de México 2007-2011", Boletín de Prensa, No. 174/13, Aguascalientes, 2013; United Nations Development Programme (UNDP), Informe sobre desarrollo humano El Salvador 2007-2008, San Salvador, 2008; S. Salvador, Aportes para la elaboración de una cuenta satélite del trabajo no remunerado en Uruguay, Montevideo, Interdisciplinary Centre for Development Studies, 2007; and "La valorización económica del trabajo no remunerado", Las bases invisibles del bienestar social, Montevideo, United Nations Development Fund for Women (UNIFEM), 2009.

Distinguishing between work and employment is important for at least three reasons. First, because the interaction between the two types of activity conditions the lives of men and women in different ways. Second, because the distinction helps to identify individuals', and in particular women's, overall economic contribution, beyond whether the task performed is paid or not. And third, because in order to analyse female employment, its contribution to countries' development and the benefits and rights derived therefrom, it is essential to relate the two concepts. A full examination of the issues surrounding women's labour market participation and gender inequalities requires an acknowledgement that people's contribution to the economy consists of market and non-market work. According to Picchio (2005), the tension between goods production and human reproduction is at the very core of the wage labour market, which constitutes a particular historical model for the exchange of labour and means of subsistence. The key point is that, in order for a supply of wage workers to be available, someone has to undertake the social reproduction work that is overlooked by conventional economic analysis.

Highlighting the sexual division of labour and the links between the spheres of production and reproduction provides insight into the origin of gender inequalities in various areas. The rules governing the division of labour within the family operate not only in the private sphere, but also determine women's access to the public space, thus freeing up men for market production (Guzmán, 2003) and for roles in society and politics. Women's opportunities for entering the labour market in good-quality jobs and generating independent income are closely tied to the current sexual division of labour. The large amount of time that women devote to unpaid work and the almost complete lack of male involvement in domestic and care work prevent women from entering the labour market on equal terms.

The uneven gender distribution of productive and reproductive work assumes the economic subordination of women, as reflected in their being excluded from or encountering problems entering the labour market. The main obstacles are poor quality jobs, horizontal and vertical occupational segregation and lower pay than men for the same work. Furthermore, the unequal economic and social value assigned to the tasks they perform results in unequal access to productive resources and fewer opportunities to participate in decision-making and to exercise economic and social rights. Their more restricted access to resources undermines women's autonomy, which adversely affects their opportunities and quality of life. It cannot be ignored that women's labour market situation is affected by certain factors associated with discrimination prior to their entering that market (for example, in the household and the education system), which are then subsequently compounded by discrimination in the labour market (Espino, 2010). Both types of discrimination are the result of the naturalization of women's domestic work and caregiving roles, and of cultural conditioning and male and female stereotypes, with traditionally female roles being assigned little value in the market. The following sections analyse in detail the impact of these forms of discrimination, which are reflected in female labour force participation and highlight the tension between production and reproduction, and conflicts in the organization of social time (Carrasco and Mayordomo, 2006).

B. Female labour force participation

There are wide differences between men and women in terms of participation, employment, unemployment and income, even though the gaps have narrowed in the last decade. The primary structural features of segregation and the concentration of female employment in low-productivity sectors persist. The gender gap in labour force participation decreases among men and women with higher levels of education, and varies significantly with household composition. When childcare demands are high, the participation rate (or economic activity rate) for women represents only 60% of the male rate.

1. Participation, employment and unemployment

In the last decade, the overall participation rate in Latin America has held relatively steady, notwithstanding small fluctuations in different countries. The female participation rate, despite losing some momentum in relation to previous decades, continued to show moderate growth in some countries. Yet even with those increases in labour force participation, a third of working-age women still have no income of their own (Gender Equality Observatory for Latin America and the Caribbean, n/d) and are classified for statistical purposes as economically inactive, regardless of their high workloads associated with their domestic responsibilities. Meanwhile, the growth in labour force participation rates for men has been less pronounced (see figure IV.1).

Figure IV.1
Latin America (18 countries): female and male labour force participation rates, around 2002 and 2012
(Percentages)

A. Women

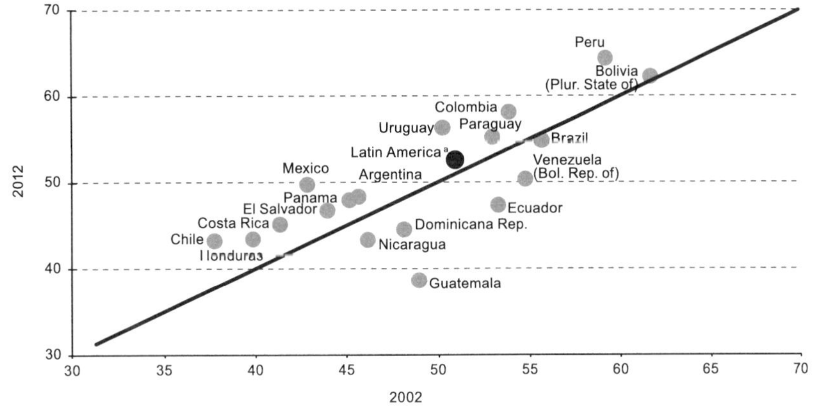

Figure IV.1 (concluded)

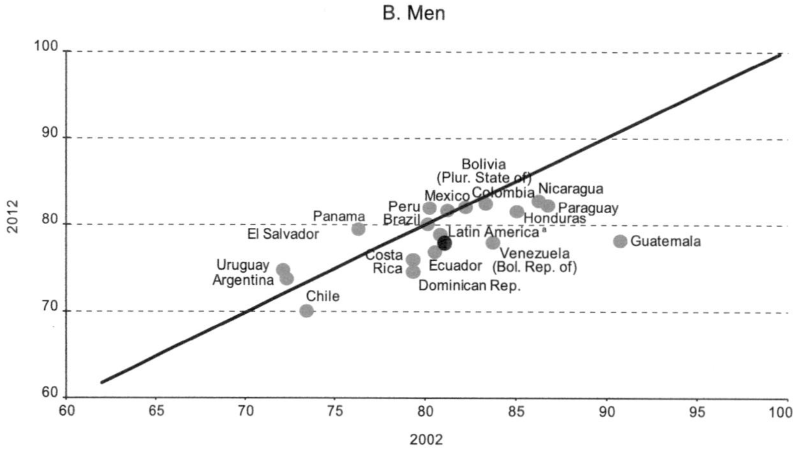

Source: Economic Commission for Latin America and the Caribbean (ECLAC), on the basis of special tabulations of data from household surveys conducted in the respective countries.
[a] Weighted average.

On the back of these developments, the gender participation gap has narrowed in most countries, (ECLAC, 2014) (see figure IV.2). In 2002, the weighted average female participation rate was 63% of the rate for men, rising to 67% in 2012. Although the gap has narrowed, it nevertheless remains significant (see figure IV.3). For example, the female participation rate in Guatemala, Honduras and Nicaragua is on average half the male rate, and even in countries where the gap is smaller, the participation rate for women falls short of 80% of the rate for men (this is the case in Peru, the Plurinational State of Bolivia and Uruguay). This means that, despite the considerable differences between the countries, there remains broad scope for increasing women's labour market participation in all cases.

Figure IV.2
Latin America (18 countries): female-to-male participation ratio, around 2002 and 2012

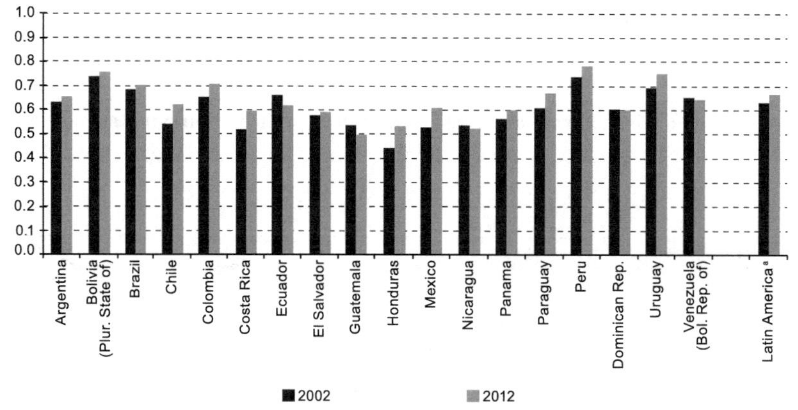

Source: Economic Commission for Latin America and the Caribbean (ECLAC), on the basis of special tabulations of data from household surveys conducted in the respective countries.
[a] Weighted average.

Figure IV.3

Latin America (18 countries): female and male participation rates, around 2012

(Percentages)

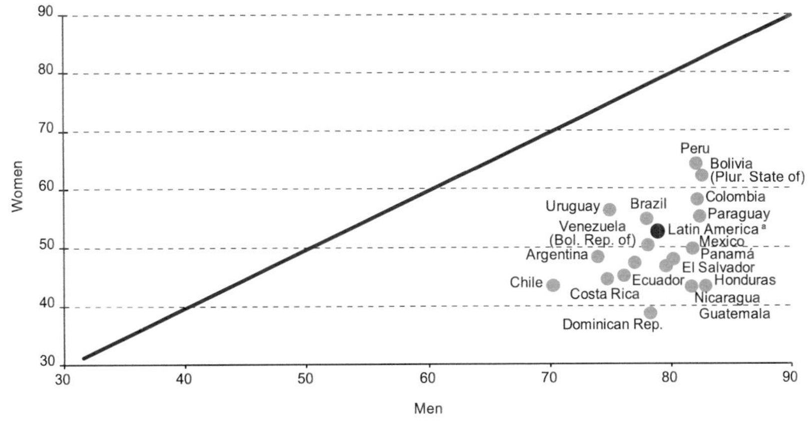

Source: Economic Commission for Latin America and the Caribbean (ECLAC), on the basis of special tabulations of data from household surveys conducted in the respective countries.

[a] Weighted average.

The English-speaking Caribbean countries are no exception to the rule and their participation rates are also lower for women than for men (see table IV.1). However, the gap is smaller in most of the Caribbean countries for which information is available than in many of the Latin American countries. In the Bahamas, Barbados and Saint Lucia the ratio of the female to male participation rates is over 80% —making the gap considerably smaller than in any country in Latin America. It is also noteworthy that a substantially higher proportion of households are headed by women in the Caribbean and their subsistence therefore depends entirely on female employment.

Table IV.1

The Caribbean (9 countries): female and male participation rates, 2009, 2010 and 2011

(Percentages and ratio)

Country	Men *(percentages)*			Women *(percentages)*			Female-to-male ratio		
	2009	2010	2011	2009	2010	2011	2009	2010	2011
Bahamas	79.3	79.4	79.3	69.2	69.3	69.3	0.87	0.87	0.87
Barbados	76.3	76.3	76.2	64.8	64.8	64.8	0.85	0.85	0.85
Belize	81.6	81.8	81.8	47.4	48.0	48.3	0.58	0.59	0.59
Guyana	80.1	79.6	79.1	40.8	41.3	41.8	0.51	0.52	0.53
Jamaica	73.1	72.0	71.8	56.7	56.0	56.0	0.78	0.78	0.78
Saint Lucia	76.7	77.0	77.3	63.5	63.9	64.2	0.83	0.83	0.83
Saint Vincent and the Grenadines	78.4	78.5	78.4	55.2	55.5	55.7	0.70	0.71	0.71
Suriname	68.5	68.7	68.7	39.7	40.1	40.5	0.58	0.58	0.59
Trinidad and Tobago	77.7	78.0	78.3	54.3	54.6	54.9	0.70	0.70	0.70

Source: Commonwealth Secretariat, *Small States: Economic Review and Basic Statistics*, vol. 17, London.

The moderate economic growth in the last decade has led to declines in the unemployment rate for both men and women (see figure IV.4). In aggregate terms for the region, the female-to-male unemployment ratio held relatively steady, although there are significant variations between countries in a context of low regional unemployment rates (see figure IV.5). However, in all countries of the region unemployment rates are significantly higher for women than for men (see figure IV.6).

Figure IV.4
Latin America (18 countries): variation in female and male unemployment rates between 2002 and 2012
(Percentages)

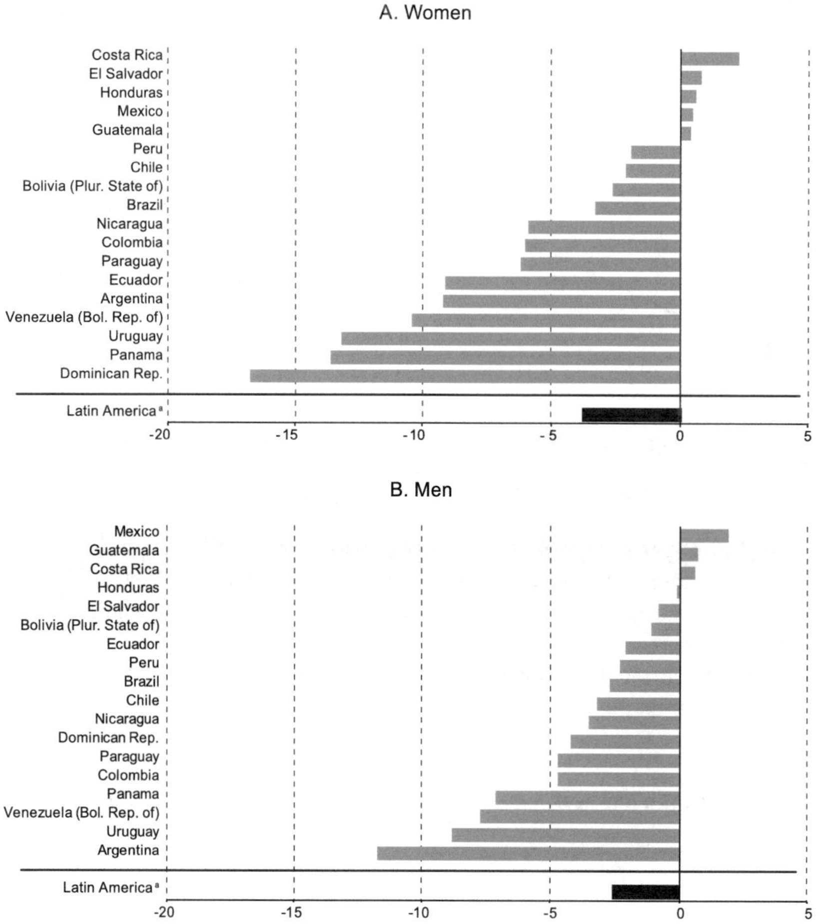

Source: Economic Commission for Latin America and the Caribbean (ECLAC), on the basis of special tabulations of data from household surveys conducted in the respective countries.
[a] Weighted average.

Figure IV.5
Latin America (18 countries): female-to-male unemployment ratio, around 2002 and 2012

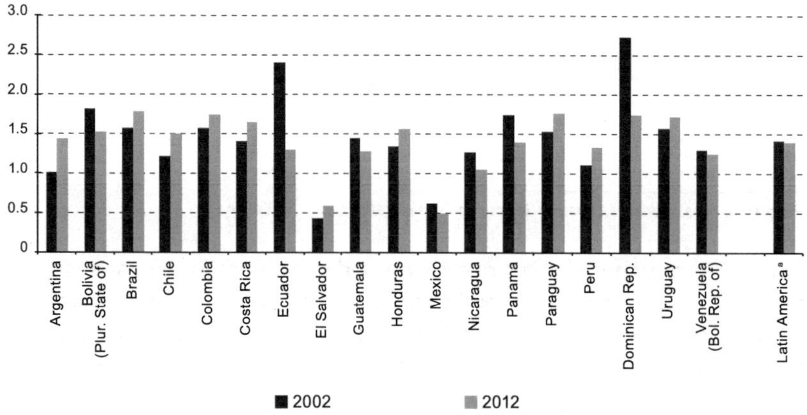

Source: Economic Commission for Latin America and the Caribbean (ECLAC), on the basis of special tabulations of data from household surveys conducted in the respective countries.
[a] Weighted average.

Figure IV.6

Latin America (18 countries): female and male unemployment rates, around 2012

(Percentages)

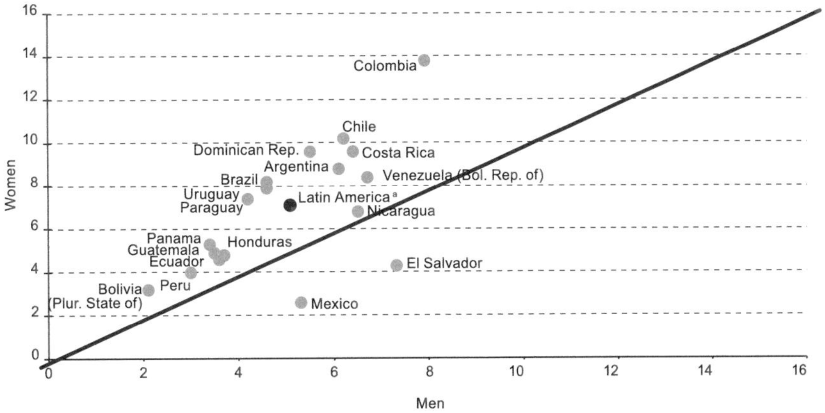

Source: Economic Commission for Latin America and the Caribbean (ECLAC), on the basis of special tabulations of data from household surveys conducted in the respective countries.

[a] Weighted average.

Most countries of the region saw a rise in the overall employment rate over the decade. While the employment rate for women expanded in all countries except Ecuador and Guatemala, the male employment rate fell in several countries (see figure IV.7).

Figure IV.7

Latin America (18 countries): female and male employment rates, around 2002 and 2012

(Percentages)

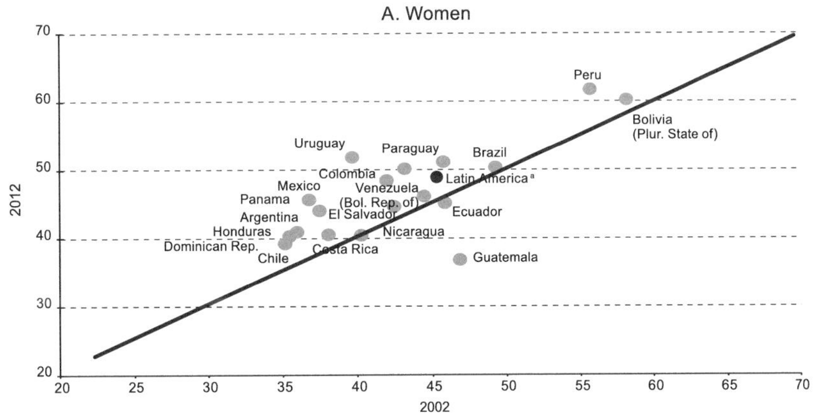

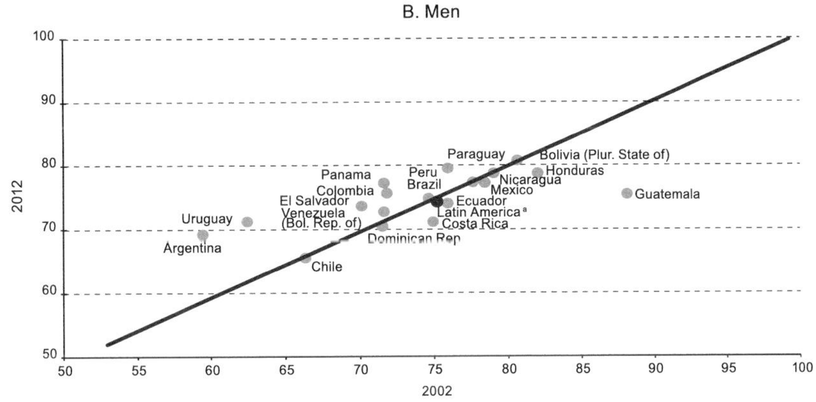

Source: Economic Commission for Latin America and the Caribbean (ECLAC), on the basis of special tabulations of data from household surveys conducted in the respective countries.

[a] Weighted average.

As a result of these developments, the gender gap in employment between men and women has narrowed significantly, although broad differences still remain in all countries, as is the case for participation (see figures IV.8 and IV.9). On average for the region, the female employment rate stood at 65% of the male employment rate in 2012, compared with 61% in 2002. The largest gender gaps in employment were found in Guatemala, Honduras and Nicaragua.

Figure IV.8
Latin America (18 countries): female-to-male employment ratio, around 2002 and 2012

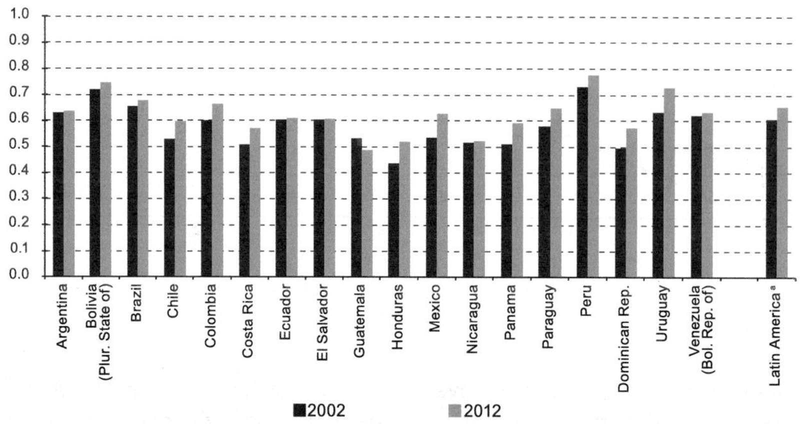

Source: Economic Commission for Latin America and the Caribbean (ECLAC), on the basis of special tabulations of data from household surveys conducted in the respective countries.
[a] Weighted average.

Figure IV.9
Latin America (18 countries): female and male employment rates, around 2012
(Percentages)

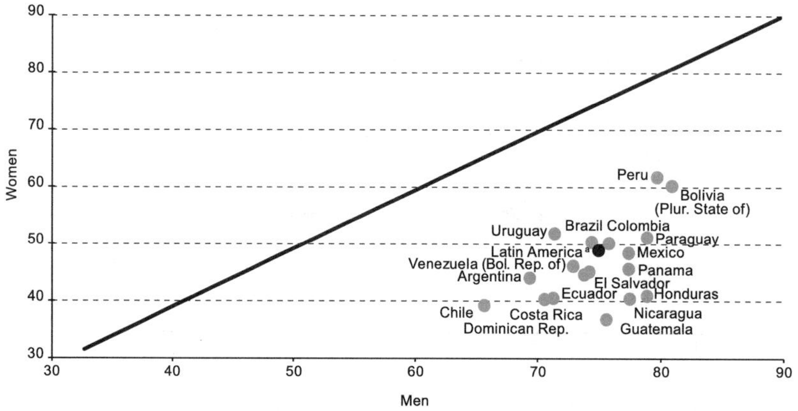

Source: Economic Commission for Latin America and the Caribbean (ECLAC), on the basis of special tabulations of data from household surveys conducted in the respective countries.
[a] Weighted average.

2. The labour market outlook in the current climate

There was good news for the key labour market indicators in the 2000s, especially in the second half of the decade. However, today, a new economic scenario is taking shape in the region. The most recent projections forecast modest growth and an economic slowdown, with a corresponding loss of momentum in the labour market indicators (ECLAC/ILO, 2014). First, for Latin America as a whole, the participation rate has declined for men and has remained constant for women in the last year, bringing to a halt the recent expansion in the proportion of women in the workforce. In all countries of the region, except Jamaica and the Bolivarian Republic of Venezuela, the participation rate for men fell between 2012 and 2013, while the variations in women's labour force participation have been different for each country.

Second, the unemployment rate for the entire region has continued to fall, although much more slowly: in 2012 it stood at 6.4% and in 2013 6.2%. In addition to the gender gaps in the labour markets —which are discussed in this chapter as a structural feature of these markets— the situation of young people is also worrying. The unemployment rate of young people aged 15 to 24 years has edged up from 14.0% in 2012 to 14.3% in 2013. As discussed in the previous chapter, this rise in unemployment should be analysed in conjunction with an assessment of young people's performance in the education system.

Third, although the total number of employed persons has increased in all countries, job creation is beginning to slow. In fact, in some countries that increase is attributable to own-account employment rather than wage employment, contrary to the trend in previous years. Registered employment has also lost momentum, with signs of stagnation beginning to show with respect to the pace of job formalization in successive years previously.

Lastly, with regard to income, in 2013 average wages continued to grow in real terms in a context of low unemployment and moderate inflation. Indeed, with the exception of the Bolivarian Republic of Venezuela, overall wages in the region have grown in real terms, although that growth was very modest in Mexico and Nicaragua. The minimum wage, meanwhile, rose by 2.2% in real terms last year in the region (ECLAC/ILO, 2014).

In view of this change in the region's economic outlook, the question is whether men and women will be affected differently by the new economic cycle. Experience in the region shows that changes in economic cycles and periods of crisis or recession often affect the labour market position of men and women in different ways, as shown in the next section.

3. Economic cycles and differential gender impacts

Throughout its history, Latin America has endured a series of crises that have dampened the performance of the main macroeconomic variables. Indeed, a striking feature of the countries of the region has been the volatility of their economic cycles, which has had a knock-on effect on social stability, companies, institutions and policies, and has also exacerbated the economic insecurity affecting much of the population (Bértola and Ocampo, 2012).

Workers suffer when economic activity contracts as it leads to diminished earnings and job losses. Given the differential inclusion of men and women in the labour market and the unequal amount of time they spend on unpaid work, it is logical to expect different outcomes by sex during periods of downturn. Economic theory posits that labour supply reacts in one of two ways in an economic crisis. The first is a countercyclical approach, which seeks to increase labour participation in response to a decline in economic activity, often referred to as the added worker effect. This essentially involves an extra member of the household entering the job market. The alternative is a procyclical approach, which consists in a fall in labour participation to match the slump in economic activity. This is known as the discouraged worker effect and it occurs when individuals cease to participate in the labour market because they have lost hope in finding work. Several studies have suggested that the first of these effects tends to predominate among women and the second among men (Espino, 2012; Antonopoulos, 2009; Arroyo and others, 2010). It should be noted that these effects are influenced by many factors and they may even occur simultaneously in certain groups of men and women. For example, it has been suggested that the added worker effect is more prevalent among older, less educated women, while the discouraged worker effect is more common among younger, more educated women (Sabarwal, Sinha and Buvinic, 2012).

In order to analyse the impact of crises on key labour market indicators, five countries that have reported major declines in economic activity at some point in recent decades were selected. Brazil's GDP fell by 4.4% between 1989 and 1990. In Paraguay and the Bolivarian Republic of Venezuela GDP fell by 4.0% and 3.2%, respectively, between 2008 and 2009. Economic activity fell even more sharply in Argentina and Uruguay where GDP dropped by 11.0% and 10.9%, respectively, between 2001 and 2002, constituting true economic crises (see figure IV.10).

An analysis of labour market indicators for the five countries considered here shows that in recessive phases of the economic cycle, the female participation rate has increased and the male participation rate has decreased (see table IV.2). This evidence appears to support the hypothesis that female labour supply expands in crisis situations owing to the added worker effect and that male labour supply diminishes owing to the discouraged worker effect. The fact that the female participation rates did not subsequently fall as the economy picked up again suggests that women who enter the labour market in times of crisis tend to stay there even after the crisis is over (Montaño and Milosavljevic, 2010).

Figure IV.10

Latin America (5 countries): [a] **annual GDP growth at constant prices, 1990-2010**

(Percentages)

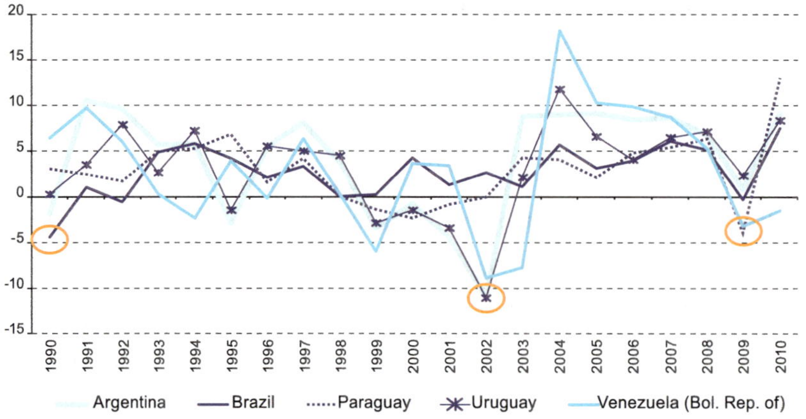

Source: Economic Commission for Latin America and the Caribbean (ECLAC), CEPALSTAT database.

[a] The five countries selected reported major declines in economic activity at some point in recent decades.

Table IV.2

Latin America (5 countries): [a] **cumulative variation in GDP and in the main labour market indicators**

(Percentages)

	GDP	Participation rate		Unemployment rate		Employment rate	
		Women	Men	Women	Men	Women	Men
Brazil (1989-1990)	-4.4	1.0	-1.1	3.7	20.2	0.8	-1.1
Argentina (2000-2002)	-14.8	2.5	-1.8	9.7	30.4	0.5	-6.5
Uruguay (2000-2002)	-14.0	0.2	-1.9	24.9	24.4	-4.4	-4.4
Paraguay (2008-2009)	-4.0	2.5	-0.2	7.6	26.8	1.9	-1.5
Venezuela (Bolivarian Republic of) (2008-2009)	-3.2	1.8	-0.3	6.0	6.3	0.8	-1.1

Source: Economic Commission for Latin America and the Caribbean (ECLAC), on the basis of special tabulations of data from household surveys conducted in the respective countries, and information from the Centre for Distributive, Labour and Social Studies (CEDLAS).

[a] The five countries selected have reported major declines in economic activity at some point in recent decades.

While unemployment rates have historically been higher among women than men, the rise in unemployment was much greater for men during the periods of economic slowdown in three of the five countries that were analysed. Uruguay and the Bolivarian Republic of Venezuela were the exceptions, recording a similar increase in unemployment for both sexes. Lastly, certain differences were seen in the employment rate between countries, but to a greater or lesser extent, the female employment rate rose and the male employment rate fell in all of the countries, except Uruguay.

An economic depression can drive down real wages for men and women. If men's wages fall by more than women's wages, it narrows the gender pay gap, however, that should not be interpreted as progress towards equality. The evidence regarding the differential income trends for men and women during crises indicates that the income gap between the sexes tends to narrow as men's earnings deteriorate by more than women's earnings (Montaño and Milosavljevic, 2010).

The financial crisis of 2008 and 2009 had a significant impact on the Caribbean countries, resulting in higher food prices, falling production and rising informal employment and unemployment. However, as argued in ECLAC (2010b), the analyses of the crisis have tended to be gender neutral and have not examined the possible differential impacts on men and women, despite some indicators reflecting inequalities. As was the case during the economic crises discussed in the preceding paragraphs, in the Caribbean, the financial crisis caused the male participation rate to fall sharply, while the female rate declined to a lesser extent and even increased in some countries.

4. Traits associated with male and female labour market insertion

The gender differences in the key labour market indicators that are revealed by comparing the aggregate averages for each country mask other more specific patterns that are clearly repeated in all of the economies. For example, the gender gap in participation rates is narrower for men and women with higher education levels: more educated men and women display more similar labour market behaviour. Thus, in the region the female-to-male ratio for the participation rate among workers with incomplete primary education is 54%, compared with 87% for workers with secondary or higher education (see figure IV.11).

Figure IV.11

Latin America (18 countries):[a] female and male participation rates by educational level, around 2012

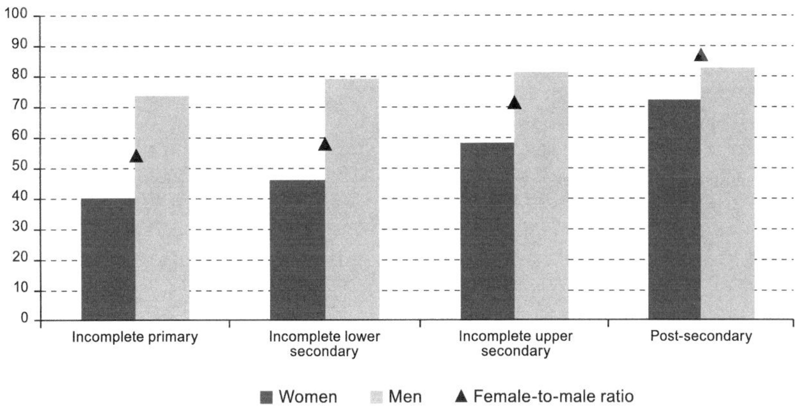

Source: Economic Commission for Latin America and the Caribbean (ECLAC), on the basis of special tabulations of data from household surveys conducted in the respective countries.

[a] Weighted average.

Gender differences in labour force participation also vary with the workers' household composition. When there are children aged 6 years or under in the household, that is, when care demands are very high, women's participation rates are equivalent to 60% of those of men. When the youngest child in the household is between 6 and 14 years, the ratio rises to 75% and if there are no young children in the household the ratio goes up to 80% (see table IV.3). The differences are much more pronounced in the poorest households in the first quintile than in households in the wealthiest quintile. Indeed, the pattern described above of a smaller gap between men and women in households without children than in households with children is not seen in the highest income quintile. The greatest scope for increasing female labour participation is therefore among women with lower education levels who have household responsibilities. The specific public policy efforts required to target this segment should focus on education and training, care services and active employment. Probability model estimates on the female participation rate showed very consistent results for all countries in the region (see box IV.2).

Table IV.3

Latin America (18 countries):[a] female and male participation rates by household composition and income quintile, around 2012

(Percentages)

		Youngest child aged under 6 years	Youngest child aged 6-14 years	No children
Total	Women	54.3	60.9	64.2
	Men	90.0	81.3	80.0
	Female-to-male ratio	60.3	74.9	80.3
Quintile I	Women	39.9	45.0	41.2
	Men	85.5	74.7	63.7
	Female-to-male ratio	46.7	60.2	64.7
Quintile V	Women	73.5	74.1	70.2
	Men	93.8	83.5	85.0
	Female-to-male ratio	78.4	88.7	82.6

Source: Economic Commission for Latin America and the Caribbean (ECLAC), on the basis of special tabulations of data from household surveys conducted in the respective countries.

[a] Weighted average.

Box IV.2

The determinants of women's labour market participation in Latin America

With a view to analysing in greater depth the determinants of female labour participation, a probit model was estimated where the dependent binary variable was equal to 1 if a woman was economically active and 0 if not. The model was estimated for women aged 14 to 65 years, for the 18 countries of the region, using data from the 2012 round of household surveys. The determinants included personal characteristics (age, education level and whether the woman lived with a partner) and a number of variables relating to the characteristics of the household (income quintile, household size, presence of children under 6 years old, presence of children aged 6 to 14 years, age of the youngest person in the household, the proportion of household members aged 15 to 65 years who were not economically active and the proportion of men and women who were not economically active).

In all countries, the coefficients associated with these variables were significant and presented a very consistent pattern. In general terms, the probability that a woman is economically active:

- Increases with age (albeit at an ever slower pace) and education level. Higher levels of education lead to higher expected returns from work and a greater value is thus assigned to working, which increases the probability of an individual working. At older ages, women leave the education system and enter the job market.
- Is lower for women living with a partner than for those who do not.
- Increases with household income: women in higher income quintiles participate to a greater extent in the workforce. This results in reciprocal causality, since women who work generate a higher income for the household, which can push the household into a higher income quintile. Also at play are different cultural norms and incentives in keeping with the socioeconomic status of households, which is reflected in their income quintiles.
- Decreases with the presence of children in the household and in line with the age of the youngest member of the household. The costs associated with care can mean that the household income is lower as result of women going to work (Immervoll and Barber, 2005). These costs can be high enough to constitute a barrier to women's entry to the labour market (Deutsch, 1998). Childcare costs are especially high for families with children aged under 6 years for two reasons: first, the care required by these children is more labour-intensive and therefore more expensive than for school-age children; second, for children over 6 years old, lower cost care options are generally available in the public system, at least part time (Klerman and Leibowitz, 1990).
- Decreases with the presence of other economically inactive adults in the household. The presence of other inactive adults can have one of two opposite effects. Either they can help with childcare in the household, providing a free or low-cost alternative to maternal care and enabling the woman to participate in the labour market. Or these non-working adults may require care themselves and thus decrease the likelihood that the working-age woman in the household will join the labour market. According to the estimates, the latter effect outweighs the former.
- Increases with household size. After controlling for the other determinants, a larger household increases the probability of labour market participation owing to the need to generate more income to support more numerous households.

Source: Economic Commission for Latin America and the Caribbean (ECLAC), on the basis of R. Deutsch, "Does child care pay? Labor Force Participation and Earnings: Effects on Access to child care in the favelas of Rio de Janeiro", *Working Paper,* No. 384, Washington, D.C., Inter-American Development Bank, 1998; H. Immervoll and D. Barber, "Can parents afford to work? Childcare costs, tax-benefit policies and work incentives", *OECD Social, Employment and Migration Working Papers,* No. 31, OECD Publishing, 2005; J.A. Klerman and A. Leibowitz, "Child care and women's return to work after childbirth", *American Economic Review,* vol. 80, No. 2, Nashville, Tennessee, American Economic Association, 1990.

A comparison of employed men and women reveals differences in several areas. Women work considerably fewer hours per week in the labour market than men (37 hours for women compared with 45 hours for men) (see figure IV.12) in all countries. This very significant gap is linked to women's unpaid work responsibilities, especially care within households. As has been widely documented, when total work hours, including paid and unpaid work, are taken into account, women shoulder a heavier overall burden than men in most countries (see, for example, ECLAC, 2014). The latest information from the Gender Equality Observatory for Latin America and the Caribbean indicates that women have a heavier total workload than men in 9 of the 11 countries for which data are available.[1]

Another recognized feature of female labour force participation is the high concentration of women in certain occupations and sectors, otherwise known as occupational segregation. Large differences are seen in the sex distribution by sector and, to a lesser extent, by occupational category (see figure IV.13). The concentration of women in specific sectors is much more marked than for men: almost 70% of women worked in social services and commerce in 2012, while the top two sectors for men, agriculture and commerce, accounted for about 40% of male workers. In terms of occupational categories, a smaller proportion of women are private-sector employees and employers and 18% of women are domestic workers or unpaid workers. Approximately 25% of employed women in the region are self-employed, an occupational category that encompasses a broad range of situations (see box IV.3).

1 See [online] http://www.cepal.org/oig/WS/getRegionalIndicator.asp?language=english&page=13.

Figure IV.12
Latin America (18 countries): average hours worked in the labour market per week by sex, around 2012
(Number of hours)

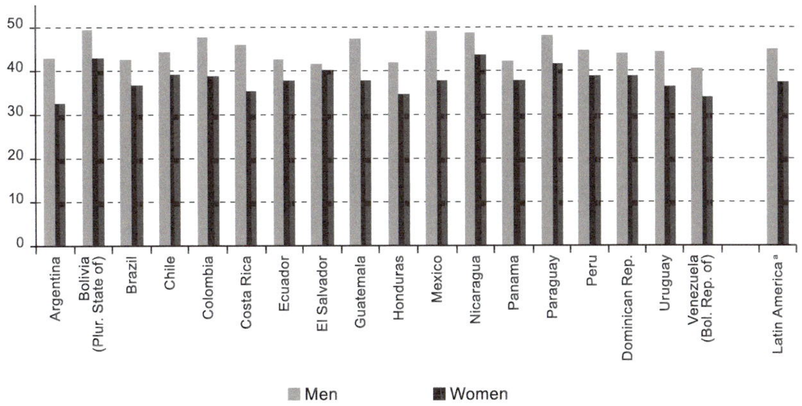

Source: Economic Commission for Latin America and the Caribbean (ECLAC), on the basis of special tabulations of data from household surveys conducted in the respective countries.

[a] Weighted average.

Figure IV.13
Latin America (18 countries):[a] distribution of men and women by sector and occupational category, around 2012
(Percentages)

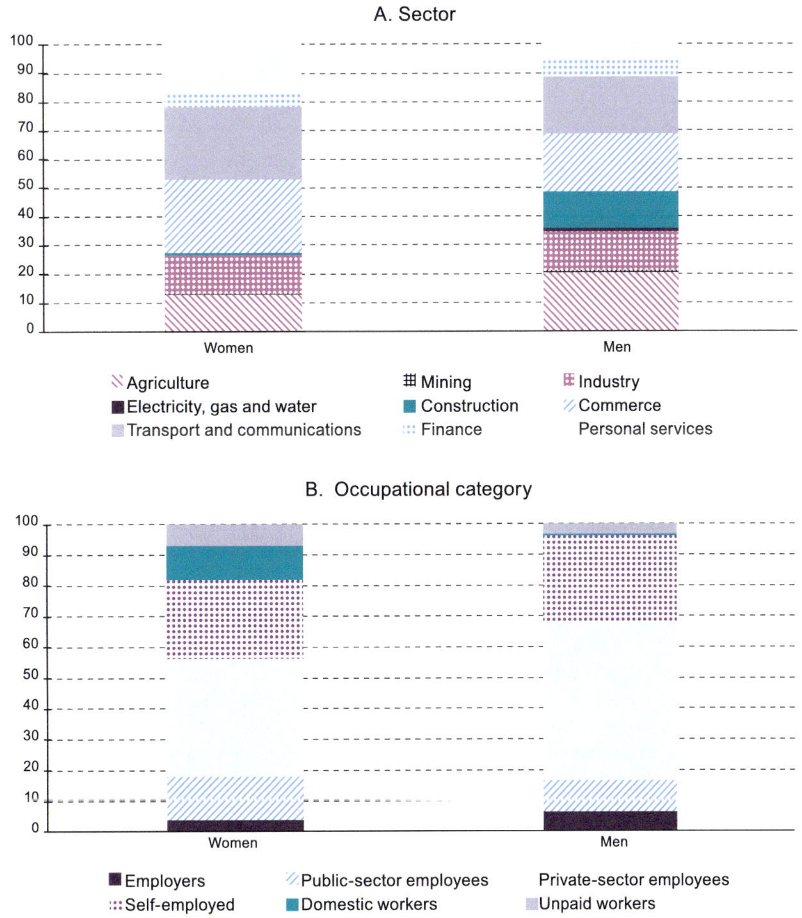

Source: Economic Commission for Latin America and the Caribbean (ECLAC), on the basis of special tabulations of data from household surveys conducted in the respective countries.

[a] Weighted average. The surveys conducted in Costa Rica and Nicaragua do not distinguish between public-sector employees and private-sector employees. For the purposes of this figure, therefore, all employees from these two countries were counted as private-sector employees.

Box IV.3

Who are the self-employed women of Latin America?

A total of 25% of working women in the region are self-employed, but this average masks substantial differences between countries. There is a clear association between the country's income level and the proportion of women in self-employment. In Honduras, Colombia and Nicaragua, over 40% of women are self-employed, while in Chile, Uruguay, Costa Rica and Argentina this figure is less than 20% (see figure).

Latin America (18 countries): proportion of employed women in own-account work, around 2012

(Percentages)

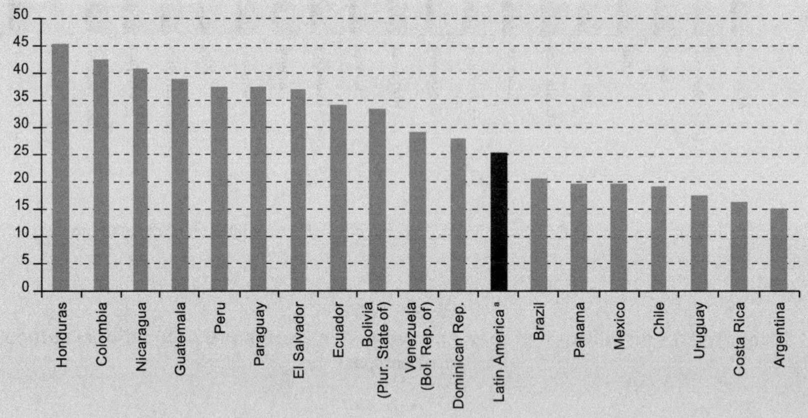

Source: Economic Commission for Latin America and the Caribbean (ECLAC), on the basis of special tabulations of data from household surveys conducted in the respective countries.

[a] Weighted average.

On average in Latin America, one in four women is self-employed, with the majority working in commerce and services (low-productivity sectors) owing to lower initial capital requirements. Female own-account workers include women entrepreneurs who have been driven to set up microenterprises by the lack of opportunities in the wage labour market and the need for an income of their own. Gender issues also weigh on the accumulation of assets and human capital and on the intrahousehold allocation of resources and parenting responsibilities.

Given the large share of female workers in this occupational category in the region, it is interesting to analyse in depth the profile of these women who, either by choice or lack of an alternative, pursue own-account work. To this end, a measure of relative risk is calculated, whereby the level of risk is deemed higher if a working woman is more likely to be self-employed than a wage worker. It is calculated by quantifying, for a group of women who share a specific feature, the number of times by which the proportion of self-employed women exceeds the proportion of female wage workers. A ratio of 1 means that the women with that specific feature are equally as likely to be self-employed as engaged in wage work; a ratio of more than 1 indicates that women in this group are more likely to be self-employed and if it is less than 1 it indicates a greater propensity for wage work.

The findings show that women in rural areas are more than twice as likely to be own-account workers than urban women, although the difference between these groups diminished somewhat between 2002 and 2011 (see table). Women living in poverty are more than twice as likely to work on their own account, an effect that grew stronger between 2002 and 2011.

The likelihood of being self-employed increases with age for women. Among women aged 50 to 60 years, who are nearing the end of their period of childrearing responsibilities, there are four self-employed women per female employee. Older women are more likely to work independently, especially those at retirement age (aged over 60 years). This is related to the difficulties that women face in accessing a pension on which they can subsist at the end of their working lives. Women who have not made the required pension contributions are forced to continue working on their own account in order to make ends meet in old age.

The association between education level and own-account work is also clear. An education consisting of fewer than four years of basic schooling is strongly associated with self-employment: 2.6 times more women with that level of schooling are self-employed than women with more schooling.

Married women and widows are more likely to be self-employed than single or separated women. In fact, married women are 2.3 times more likely than other women to be own-account workers and the figure for widows is very similar (2.2 times).

The probability of being self-employed decreases with the number of hours worked per week. Thus, women who work fewer than 8 hours a week are 3.2 times more likely to be self-employed than women who work longer hours. This probably reflects their need for greater flexibility in order to balance paid work with their domestic responsibilities.

Box IV.3 (concluded)

Latin America (18 countries): [a] relative risk of female workers being engaged in own-account work compared with wage work [b] by selected characteristics, around 2002 and 2011

Variable	Characteristic	2002	2011
Geographical area	Rural area	2.31	2.08
Poverty status	Poor	1.48	1.67
Age	50-60 years	4.65	4.28
	61 years and over	4.89	4.57
Years of schooling	Between 0 and 3 years	2.39	2.64
	Between 4 and 8 years	1.29	1.65
Civil status	Married/cohabiting	1.94	2.26
	Widow	3.84	2.17
	Single	1.33	0.96
Type of household	Single-person	1.44	1.39
	Two-parent	1.05	0.97
	Single-parent	0.77	0.82
	Extended	1.32	1.24
Working week	1 to 7 hours	4.26	3.16
	8 to 16 hours	2.94	2.60
	17 to 34 hours	1.71	1.80
	35 to 48 hours	0.38	0.41
	More than 49 hours	1.51	1.49

Source: Economic Commission for Latin America and the Caribbean (ECLAC), on the basis of special tabulations of data from household surveys conducted in countries in the region.

[a] Weighted average.

[b] Calculated by quantifying, for a group of women who share a specific feature, the number of times by which the proportion of self-employed women exceeds the proportion of female wage workers.

Source: Economic Commission for Latin America and the Caribbean (ECLAC).

The share of unpaid workers in the labour market is relevant to the analysis presented below. As defined in section A, these workers are engaged by a business, but receive no income for their work. In some countries of the region female unpaid workers make up a large proportion of women in the labour market: in the Plurinational State of Bolivia 31% of employed women are unpaid, while in Peru and Ecuador this figure equates to 17% and 15%, respectively (see table IV.4). Unpaid work is associated with rural areas: in all three of the aforementioned countries, the majority of unpaid workers are found in rural zones (72% of unpaid workers are rural workers in the Plurinational State of Bolivia, 61% in Ecuador and 60% in Peru). In turn, indigenous workers account for a large proportion of unpaid workers: 23% in the Plurinational State of Bolivia, 20% in Ecuador and 36% in Peru. In Guatemala, Honduras and Nicaragua this occupational category also accounts for a large share of workers, but in these cases the situation of men and women is relatively similar. In countries where a large proportion of employed women are engaged in unpaid work, a simulation shows that a significant improvement in household well-being could be achieved by closing the income gap (see section D).

Table IV.4

Latin America (18 countries): share of unpaid work in the labour market by sex, around 2012

(Percentages)

Country	Women	Men	Total
Argentina	0.8	0.3	0.5
Bolivia (Plurinational State of)	30.6	8.4	18.2
Brazil	4.1	1.9	2.8
Chile	0.6	0.3	0.4
Colombia	7.4	2.7	4.7
Costa Rica	1.8	1.2	1.4
Dominican Republic	2.5	1.4	1.8
Ecuador	15.4	4.8	9.0
El Salvador	8.5	8.9	8.7
Guatemala	11.4	8.4	9.4
Honduras	11.2	10.1	10.5
Mexico	7.8	4.6	5.9
Nicaragua	8.7	12.8	11.3
Panama	7.2	3.3	4.8
Paraguay	7.6	7.2	7.4
Peru	17.6	5.7	11.1
Uruguay	1.9	0.7	1.2
Venezuela (Bolivarian Republic of)	1.1	0.5	0.8
Latin America [a]	6.8	3.3	4.8

Source: Economic Commission for Latin America and the Caribbean (ECLAC), on the basis of special tabulations of data from household surveys conducted in the respective countries.

[a] Weighted average.

ECLAC (2014) analysed the changes in an index of occupational segregation for the countries of the region over the last decade and concluded that even though gender gaps had narrowed in a number of areas, there was no overall improvement in occupational segregation. The more structural characteristics of female labour force participation had not appeared to change during this period. The prevailing high levels of segregation may be due largely to attitudes on the part of employers or of workers themselves regarding which occupations are appropriate for women and men, based on a learned social construct that is reproduced in households, the education system, the media and the labour market. In turn, labour discrimination can influence decisions taken by individuals, and especially women, before entering the labour market. What is more, in some cases occupational segregation can follow on from educational segregation, which to some extent reflects women's choices and preferences, but can also stem from social norms and learned behaviour (ECLAC, 2014). Indeed, even though the proportion of female students in tertiary education has increased in the region, they are less likely to enrol on courses relating to science and technology, which are the fields that the labour market tends to value more highly and thus reward more handsomely (Rico and Trucco, 2014). This segregation is associated with attitudes and achievements over the course of a person's education and socialization. Subject and career choices are influenced by the roles played out in households, which in turn are the result of cultural gender mandates. It has also been suggested that girls may be more likely to choose less competitive careers with intrinsic rewards in fields involving more social cooperation, such as care-related roles (Rico and Trucco, 2014).

In terms of the quality of employment, the rates of social security affiliation for men and women increased between 2002 and 2012, and the prevailing rates of formal employment are similar for men and women (see figure IV.14). ECLAC (2013) presented a multivariate analysis showing no clear association between gender and social security affiliation, and that the probability of affiliation is linked primarily to the nature of the job. Previous studies had showed that countries with large gender gaps in employment rates tended to post smaller differences in contribution rates, with women even posting higher affiliation rates (see ECLAC, 2014). This suggests that, in these countries, the women who manage to enter the labour market, despite low female-to-male employment ratios, are very likely to pay social security contributions. This is because only women with higher education levels are able to enter the labour market, in contrast with men from the full educational spectrum. The contribution levels of these relatively more educated women are therefore higher on average than those of employed men (ECLAC, 2014).

Figure IV.14
Latin America (16 countries): male and female social security affiliation, around 2012
(Percentages)

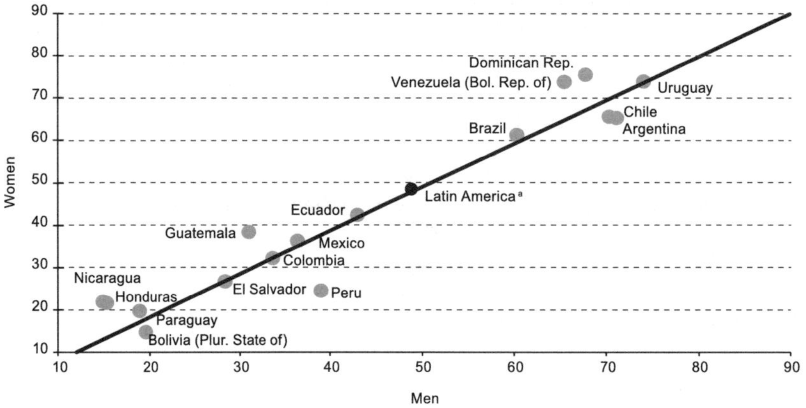

Source: Economic Commission for Latin America and the Caribbean (ECLAC), on the basis of special tabulations of data from household surveys conducted in the respective countries.
[a] Weighted average.

5. Heterogeneity in the production structure and gender inequality

One of the distinguishing features of the region's economies is the striking heterogeneity of their production structures, manifested in sharp differences in worker productivity. One way of analysing this structural heterogeneity is to take a sectoral approach and to focus on the productivity differentials between sectors or branches of economic activity. In this context, it is also interesting to compare the employment of men and women in sectors with different productivity levels. To this end, the sectors were divided into three groups on the basis of their average labour productivity (at purchasing power parity 2005 dollars): the low-productivity sector, which includes agriculture, commerce and services; the medium-productivity sector, which covers construction, manufacturing and transport; and the high-productivity sector, encompassing finance, electricity and mining. As indicated in ECLAC (2014), output per worker is 5.8 times higher in the high-productivity sector than in the low-productivity sector, which illustrates the huge difference in productivity between sectors in the region. Workers employed in low-productivity sectors receive lower wages, have lower education requirements and face greater job instability, limited social security coverage and often have no employment contract (ECLAC, 2012b). As shown below, women make up a larger proportion of workers in the low-productivity sector than in other sectors; and, furthermore, this sector employs the bulk of women in the region.

In 2012, women represented 41% of the employed population in the region. However, they made up 49% of those employed in low-productivity sectors (see table IV.5). The medium-productivity sectors were mostly male-dominated since men represented 77% of all workers in construction, manufacturing and transport. In the high-productivity sectors, women represented only 37% of all workers. There was little change in the distribution of employment between men and women according to productivity level between 2002 and 2012, except for a slight increase in the participation of women in the low- and high-productivity sectors.

Table IV.5

Latin America (18 countries):[a] distribution of workers by sex and productivity level, around 2002 and 2012

(Percentages)

	Men		Women	
	2002	2012	2002	2012
Low productivity	53.4	50.5	46.6	49.5
Medium productivity	76.6	77.7	23.4	22.3
High productivity	67.2	62.7	32.8	37.3
Total	60.2	58.6	39.8	41.4

Source: Economic Commission for Latin America and the Caribbean (ECLAC), on the basis of special tabulations of data from household surveys conducted in the respective countries.

[a] Weighted average.

A sectoral analysis shows that 1 in 10 employed women in the region works in agriculture. In Ecuador, Paraguay and Peru that ratio is one in every five and in the Plurinational State of Bolivia, one in three. A large proportion of women employed in agriculture are unpaid family workers, putting them in an unfavourable position since not getting paid for their activities often results in cycles of economic dependence. The services sector employs the largest number of Latin American women. This sector includes domestic work, an almost completely feminized area of employment with some of the worst working conditions. Of the women working in social, personal and community services, 27% are domestic workers in private households and in most countries in the region they are not covered by labour legislation, social security affiliation or protection through unionization.

Figure IV.15

Latin America (18 countries):[a] sectoral distribution of workers by sex, around 2012

(Percentages)

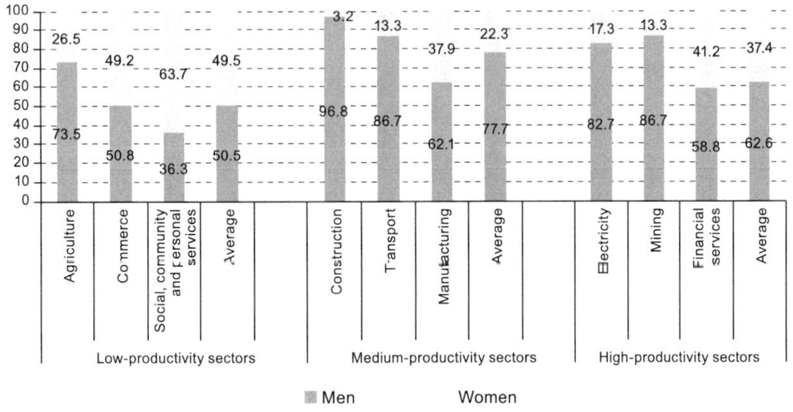

Source: Economic Commission for Latin America and the Caribbean (ECLAC), on the basis of special tabulations of data from household surveys conducted in the respective countries.

[a] Weighted average.

Women in El Salvador, Guatemala and Honduras have a greater presence in the medium-productivity sectors, since in these countries more than 15% of women work in manufacturing. In Costa Rica, women's participation in the high-productivity sectors is higher than the regional average because 12.3% of women are employed in the financial sector.

A look at the occupational categories within each sector reveals that a large proportion of women work in the low-productivity sectors as employees (37.6% of all working women), own-account workers (20.2%) or domestic workers (10.7%). While the proportion of female wage workers in each category increases with the level of productivity, in absolute terms only a small number of women obtain paid employment in the high-productivity sectors (see table IV. 6).

Table IV.6

Latin America (18 countries): [a] occupational category by sectoral productivity level, around 2012

(Percentages)

Sectoral productivity level		Occupational category				
		Employer	Employee	Domestic worker	Own-account worker	Unpaid worker
Low	Men	7.5	56.9	0.9	29.4	5.2
	Women	4.1	48.3	13.7	26.0	7.9
	Total	5.8	52.7	7.3	27.7	6.6
Medium	Men	4.9	68.4	0.1	25.8	0.8
	Women	3.3	62.6	2.3	26.8	5.0
	Total	4.5	67.1	0.6	26.0	1.8
High	Men	4.7	76.0	0.0	19.0	0.3
	Women	2.4	77.7	0.0	18.9	1.0
	Total	3.8	76.6	0.0	19.0	0.6

Source: Economic Commission for Latin America and the Caribbean (ECLAC), on the basis of special tabulations of data from household surveys conducted in the respective countries.

[a] Weighted average.

In terms of GDP, in 2012 the low-productivity sector generated 39% of GDP in Latin America, compared with 28% of GDP for the high-productivity sector (see figure IV.16). As for employment, the low-productivity sector accounted for 66% of total employment and the high-productivity sector for 7%. It is not possible to calculate, using the statistical information available, the share of GDP generated by each sex, but it is possible to approximate the total labour income attributable to men and women. Of female labour income, 71% is generated in the low-productivity sector, compared with 53% of male labour income. There is marked difference in the distribution of men and women in the different sectors according to productivity level: while 57% of male workers are employed in the low-productivity sector, this is the case for 79% of employed women.

Figure IV.16

Latin America (18 countries):[a] GDP,[b] labour income and employment by sex and sectoral productivity level, around 2012

(Percentages)

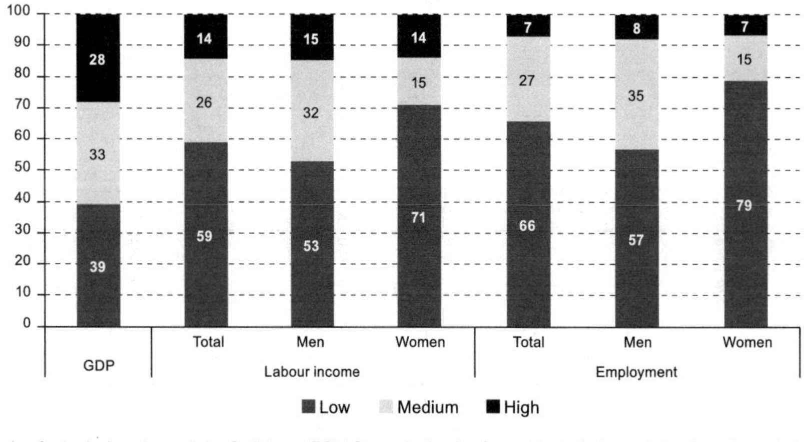

Source: Economic Commission for Latin America and the Caribbean (ECLAC), on the basis of special tabulations of data from household surveys conducted in the respective countries.

[a] Weighted average.

[b] Constant dollars.

This information indicates that structural heterogeneity, which is key to understanding the high levels of income inequality in the region, is closely linked to women's labour participation and gender inequalities in the labour market. The majority of women find themselves working in low-productivity sectors, while men are more likely than women to be employed in medium-productivity sectors. What is needed are policies to close the productivity gap by increasing capabilities, pursuing production policies, fostering industry and innovation, and building labour institutions to actively promote decent work for men and women (ECLAC, 2014).

C. Labour income of women and men

The differences in participation rates, employment and wages between men and women combine to set a scenario in which female earnings contribute significantly less to household income than male earnings. Indeed, women consistently account for less than half of total household labour income. They make the largest proportional contribution in Uruguay, furnishing 39% on average of total household earnings, and the smallest in Dominican Republic, where their share is 26%.

A persistent feature of the region's labour markets is the systematic discrepancy between the average wages earned by men and women. In all countries of the region, women's average monthly earnings are lower than men's (see figure IV.17). The differences by sex for the employed population as a whole are also observed for the individual occupational categories (see box IV.4). The gaps vary significantly between countries: in the Plurinational State of Bolivia and Peru men earn on average over 50% more per month than women, but in El Salvador, Honduras and Panama this difference is less than 10%. This gap may in part be attributable to the lower number of hours that women devote to paid work per month compared with men. Indeed, in 2012 men spent an average of 8 hours per week more than women on paid work. But even when this factor is taken into account, there remains a considerable difference in average earnings by sex in most countries, although the gap does narrow somewhat. As in the case for monthly earnings, the largest gaps in hourly earnings to the detriment of women are seen in the Plurinational State of Bolivia and Peru. In some countries, such as Argentina, Costa Rica, El Salvador, Honduras and Nicaragua, wage differentials tend to disappear when controlling for hours worked. This means that in these countries, women's average hourly earnings are not lower than men's (and are even higher in some cases).

Figure IV.17

Latin America (18 countries): difference between average wages for men and women, around 2012

(Percentages of female income)

A. Monthly income

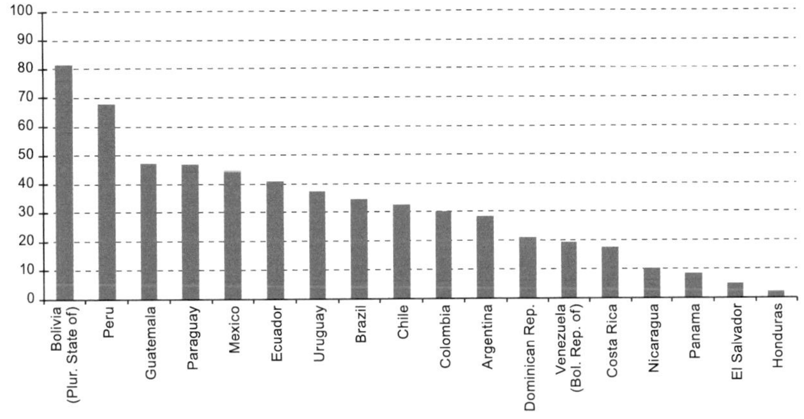

Chapter IV

Figure IV.17 (concluded)

B. Hourly income

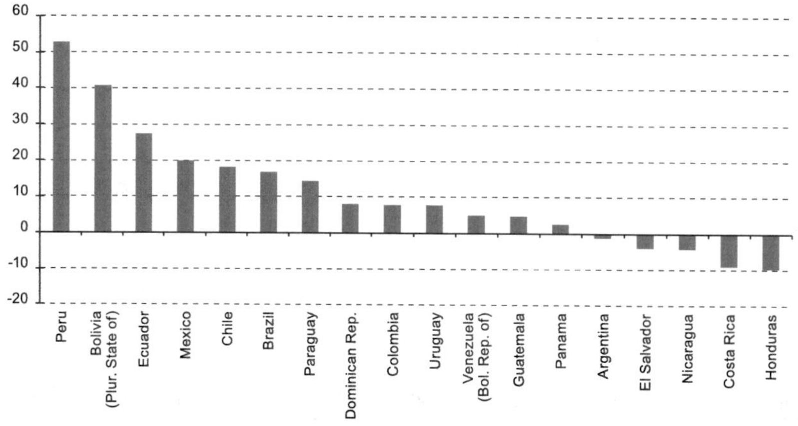

Source: Economic Commission for Latin America and the Caribbean (ECLAC), on the basis of special tabulations of data from household surveys conducted in the respective countries.

Box IV.4
The gender wage gap in specific occupational categories

The gender pay gap narrowed for both employees and the self-employed between 2000 and 2011, albeit for different reasons. The income of self-employed women, regardless of the number of years of study, held steady over the period. The earnings of self-employed men varied, with the greatest deterioration in the income of those with 12 or more years of education. Therefore, the narrower gender pay gap for own-account workers was prompted by a drop in men's earnings as women's earnings stagnated.

There is a more dramatic difference between the earnings of wage earners and own-account workers among women than men. Self-employed men earn the equivalent of 52% of the earnings of male employees, while self-employed women make 30% of the income of female wage workers.

Latin America (17 countries):[a] income from wage work and own-account work by sex and years of schooling, around 2002 and 2011

(Poverty lines)

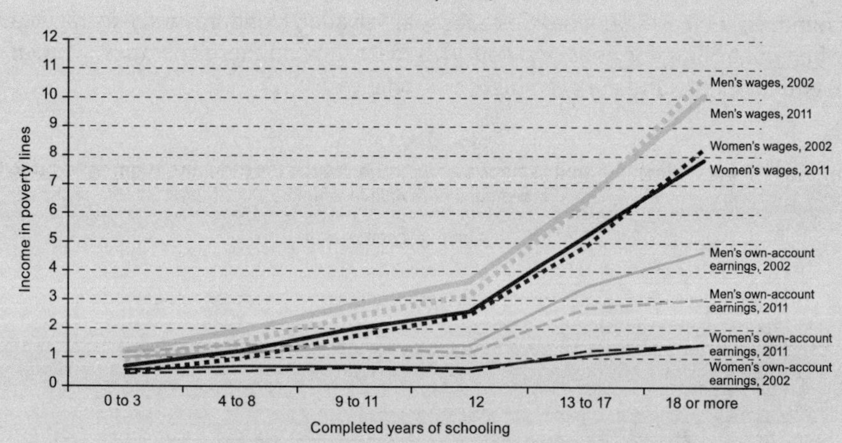

Source: Economic Commission for Latin America and the Caribbean (ECLAC), on the basis of special tabulations of data from household surveys conducted in the respective countries.

[a] Weighted average. Does not include Peru.

Source: Economic Commission for Latin America and the Caribbean (ECLAC).

As discussed in ECLAC (2014), female participation and employment rates have a negative association with the average gender wage gap for the countries. For example, the countries of Central America, which have wider participation and employment gaps between women and men, show fewer gender differences in earnings on average. As analysed above in connection with social security contributions, the explanation for this finding lies in the selection process that women undergo to gain entry to the labour market. It is the women with better education levels who are more likely to participate actively in the labour market and get jobs, while employment among men is more widespread. A comparison of the average income of male and female workers in Central America does not reveal the same income penalty for women that is detected in other countries. The correlation between the gender employment gap and the hourly earnings gap is -0.27, reinforcing the idea that countries with a wider employment gap between men and women tend to post a smaller average pay gap.

Since the differences between average male and female earnings may be due to the specific characteristics of the workers, it is more accurate to analyse these income differences controlling for the age and education levels of men and women, in order to compare individuals with similar characteristics. When this exercise is performed, the gender gap in hourly earnings becomes positive for all countries, indicating a wage premium for men. Figure IV.18 shows the coefficient of the binary variable that distinguishes between men and women in a wage equation (equal to 1 for men); this coefficient is positive and statistically significant in all countries except in Guatemala and Honduras.[2] The countries whose average income differences disappeared when considering hourly earnings now show a significant penalty for women, and this is because although on average women do not earn less than men, they do when comparing men and women with similar characteristics in terms of education and age.

Figure IV.18

Latin America (18 countries): differences in hourly wages between men and women, expressed as the gender binary variable coefficient in wage equations, around 2012

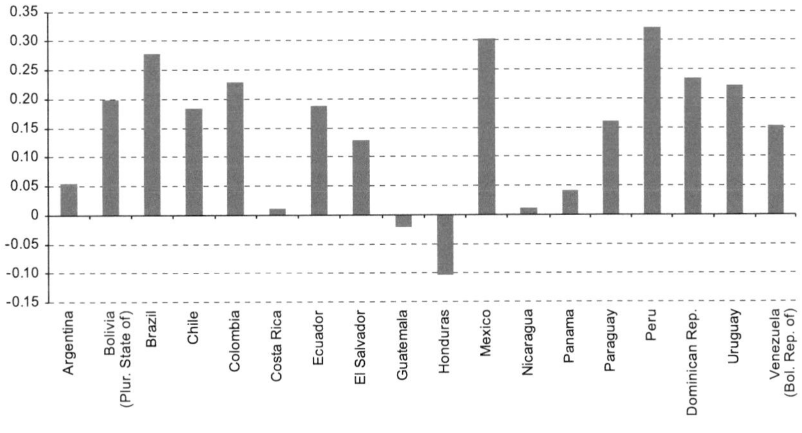

Source: Economic Commission for Latin America and the Caribbean (ECLAC), on the basis of special tabulations of data from household surveys conducted in the respective countries.

Despite the relative paucity of data for the region, a gender gap in participation rates has also been detected in the highest income groups in society. Capital income is concentrated in the richest top 1% and most of the earners in this category are men (see box IV.5).

2 The coefficient presented is calculated by estimating wage equations for men and women, controlling for selection bias using the method proposed by Heckman (1979). The gender binary variable equals 1 for men, meaning that a positive coefficient indicates a wage penalty for women.

Box IV.5

Gender inequalities among high earners

In the last decade, a number of researchers have used tax records to study high earners (Piketty, 2002; Atkinson, Piketty and Saez, 2011; Alvaredo and Londoño, 2013). The enormous potential for this area of research to examine gender differences in greater depth is demonstrated in the example given here, based on a study conducted in Uruguay.

According to that study, while the aggregate inequality indices fell between 2009 and 2012, whether calculated using information from the tax records database or from household surveys, the share of the top 1% of earners held steady at about 12% or 14% of total income, depending on the methodology applied. Disaggregated by sex, the top 1% of male earners accounted for 17% of total male income and the top 1% of female earners accounted for 7.2% of women's income. With respect to capital income, 65.2% is concentrated in the hands of the richest 1%. That proportion is as high as 73.9% for men and 46.9% for women (see figure 1).

Figure 1

Uruguay: concentration of total income and capital income in the hands of the richest 1% and by sex, 2012

(Percentages)

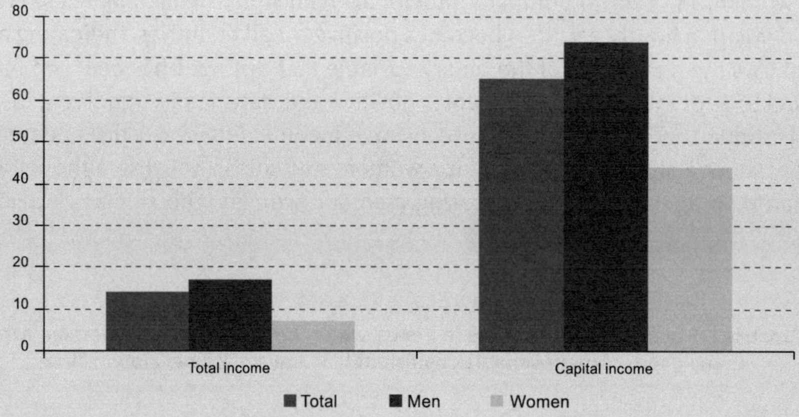

Source: Gabriel Burdín, Mauricio Da Rosa and Andrea Vigorito, "Sectores de altos ingresos en Uruguay: participación relativa y patrones de movilidad en el período 2009-2012. Informe del Convenio Facultad de Ciencias Económicas y de Administración", Montevideo, Centre for Fiscal Studies, University of the Republic (UDELAR), 2014.

Extensive studies have been carried out into the connection between women's more limited access to high income and inequality and segregation in the labour market. However, there has been less of a focus on women's more limited access to capital income. More information on wealth is needed to be able to understand in greater detail the causes of these marked disparities in capital income. A first look at this income, separating property income from corporate profits, shows that the gender difference is attributable to the latter since the distribution of income from property rentals is similar for men and women (see figure 2).

Figure 2

Uruguay: capital income density for men and women by source of income, 2012

A. Corporate profits

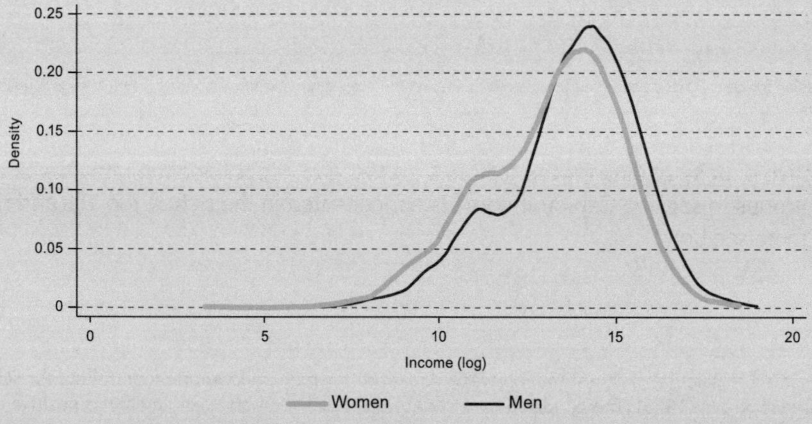

Box IV.5 (concluded)

Figure 2 (concluded)

B. Rental income

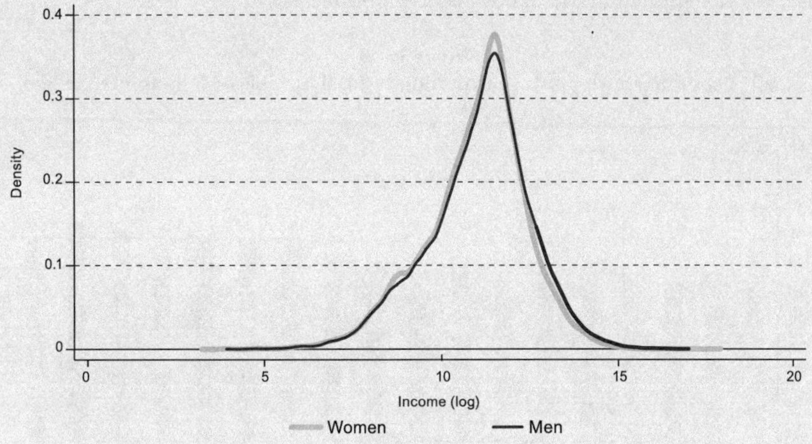

Source: Economic Commission for Latin America and the Caribbean (ECLAC), on the basis of Gabriel Burdín, Mauricio Da Rosa and Andrea Vigorito, "Sectores de altos ingresos en Uruguay: participación relativa y patrones de movilidad en el período 2009-2012. Informe del Convenio Facultad de Ciencias Económicas y de Administración", Montevideo, Centre for Fiscal Studies, University of the Republic (UDELAR), 2014.

The wage gap between men and women is also reflected in the tax records. Women are overrepresented in the lower income deciles and their share decreases consistently with each income group, reaching its minimum in the highest income stratum. Women make up 40% of the richest decile (the top 10%), 29% of the richest 1% and 14% of the top 0.1% (see figure 3). This pattern holds true for both labour income and capital income.

Figure 3

Uruguay: women as a proportion of total earners by pre-tax income bracket, 2009-2012

(Percentages)

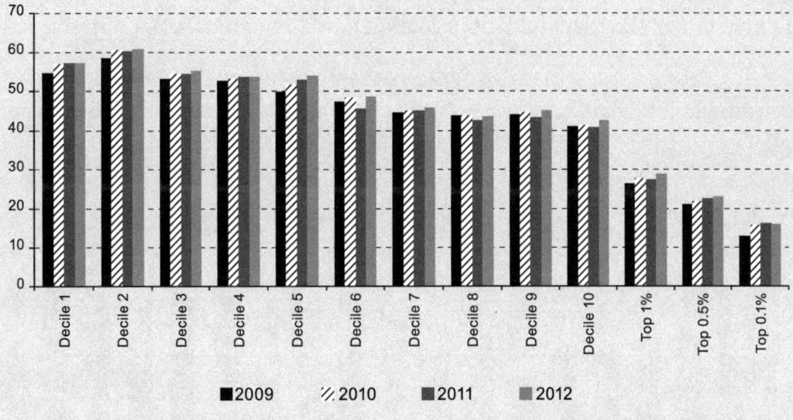

Source: Gabriel Burdín, Mauricio Da Rosa and Andrea Vigorito, "Sectores de altos ingresos en Uruguay: participación relativa y patrones de movilidad en el período 2009-2012. Informe del Convenio Facultad de Ciencias Económicas y de Administración", Montevideo, Centre for Fiscal Studies, University of the Republic (UDELAR), 2014, on the basis of National Institute of Statistics (INE), continuous household survey (ECH); Latin American and Caribbean Demographic Centre (CELADE)-Population Division of ECLAC, population projections of CELADE-Population Division of ECLAC and records of the Tax Administration Department (DGI), Uruguay.

Source: Economic Commission for Latin America and the Caribbean (ECLAC), on the basis of Gabriel Burdín, Mauricio Da Rosa and Andrea Vigorito, "Sectores de altos ingresos en Uruguay: participación relativa y patrones de movilidad en el período 2009-2012. Informe del Convenio Facultad de Ciencias Económicas y de Administración", Montevideo, Centre for Fiscal Studies, University of the Republic (UDELAR), 2014.

The differences in participation rates, employment and wages between men and women combine to set a scenario in which female earnings contribute significantly less to household income than male earnings (despite the positive correlation between the two within households, as shown in box IV.6). Indeed, women consistently account for less than half of total household labour income. In fact, that proportion fell short of 40% in all of the countries in the region in 2012. Women make the largest proportional contribution in Uruguay, furnishing 39% on average of total household earnings, and the smallest in Dominican Republic, where their share is 26% (see figure IV.19). It is important to bear in mind that this indicator overlooks the economic value of unpaid domestic work, which, as explained in section A, is not included in the accounts of economic activity.

Figure IV.19

Latin America (18 countries): women's contribution to total household labour income, around 2012

(Percentages)

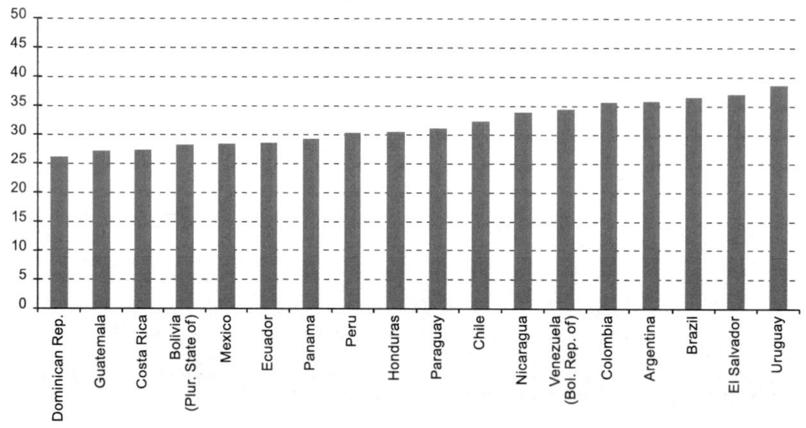

Source: Economic Commission for Latin America and the Caribbean (ECLAC), on the basis of special tabulations of data from household surveys conducted in the respective countries.

Even greater heterogeneity is detected in the region regarding women's contribution to total household labour income in the lowest income quintile in each country. Women's share of household labour income in the lowest quintiles ranges between 9% and 34%, averaging 26%. Meanwhile, in the highest income quintile in each country, women's contribution exceeds 29% in all cases and averages 36% (see figure IV.20). The significantly smaller share in the lowest quintile may reflect the reduced labour market participation of women in this economic stratum.

Figure IV.20

Latin America (18 countries): women's contribution to total household labour income in the first and fifth income quintiles, around 2012

(Percentages)

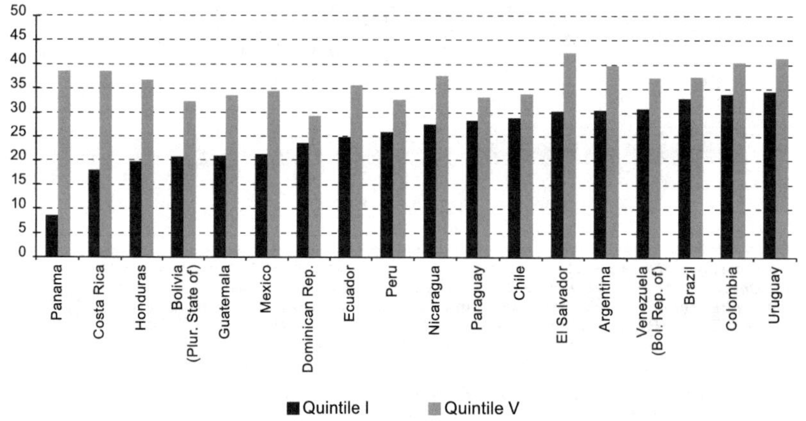

Source: Economic Commission for Latin America and the Caribbean (ECLAC), on the basis of special tabulations of data from household surveys conducted in the respective countries.

There is therefore scope for increasing women's contribution to household income, either by expanding their labour market participation or eliminating wage discrimination. Depending on the starting position of each country, the greatest gains can be achieved by advancing on one of these two fronts, although they are obviously not mutually exclusive. The next section examines the potential gains to be made, with the aim of promoting the formulation of public policies that are conducive to greater equality. The two scenarios taken into consideration would lead to advances in development for the countries and in the exercise of women's rights.

Box IV.6

Income associations within couples

An important factor in household income and the resulting levels of inequality in society is the association between the income of spouses in two-parent households. The fact that spouses have similar incomes —a positive association between partners' income levels— has been identified as a relevant factor in determining household income inequality (Nieuwenhuis, Need and Van der Kolk, 2013; Pasqua, 2002; Burtless, 1999; Harkness, 2013; among others). A strong positive income correlation between spouses widens income inequality between households, whereas a negative correlation would mitigate income inequality between households (correlation coefficients range from -1 to 1).

The positive correlation between spouses' income suggests the existence of selective mating in working couples (Harkness, 2013), which in extreme cases could arrest social mobility. Educational homogamy is one of the key factors explaining the high correlation of income between spouses: more educated women usually marry more educated men, with both partners likely to earn high incomes. The same pattern is true for less educated men and women, who receive lower incomes. Several studies in developed countries show assortative mating at all educational levels, which largely accounts for income inequality between households (Eika, Mogstad and Zafar, 2014).

According to the evidence provided by Harkness (2013) on the correlation coefficients of spousal income in developed countries, the highest values are found in the countries of south-east Europe, in particular Greece, which has a correlation coefficient of about 0.46. The English-speaking countries, particularly the United States, have the lowest coefficients (in the United States it is close to 0.03). The highest correlation coefficient for the Nordic countries is 0.25 and the lowest value corresponds to Norway (0.15). In the rest of Europe, the situation is more heterogeneous, with countries whose coefficients exceed 0.30 and others, such as Germany and the Netherlands, with a very low value of about 0.025. The study posits a number of hypotheses to explain the differences in this indicator between countries. In countries where the female employment rate is high, such as the Netherlands, women's wages are often lower because they spend less time on paid work. In countries such as Spain, by contrast, women are less likely to work, but those who do devote more hours to paid work, and their wages are therefore higher. This is a possible explanation for the difference between the correlation coefficient of 0.025 for the Netherlands and 0.361 for Spain.

In the countries of Latin America, the correlation coefficient of spousal income, calculated on the basis of primary monthly labour income and for the universe of households comprising couples with or without children where both partners are employed, ranged between 0.15 and 0.60 in 2012. If instead the correlation coefficient was calculated on the basis of hourly income, a lower correlation of between 0.10 and 0.45 was found for most countries.

Figure 1

Latin America (18 countries): correlation coefficient of spousal income, around 2012

A. Monthly income

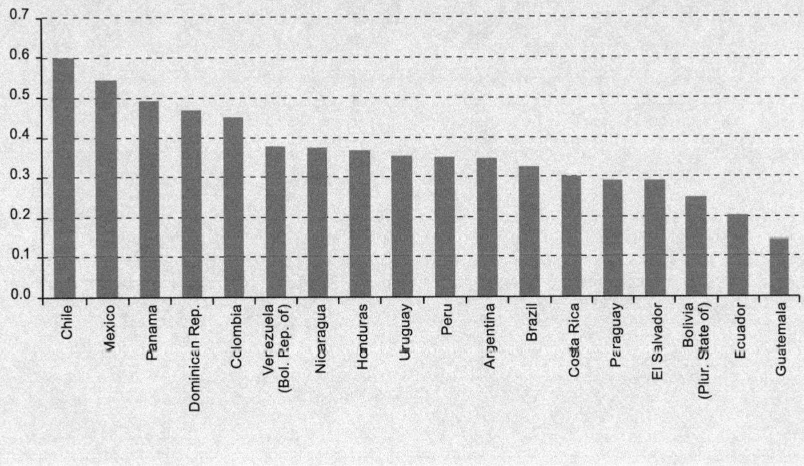

Box IV.6 (concluded)

Figure 1 (concluded)

B. Hourly income

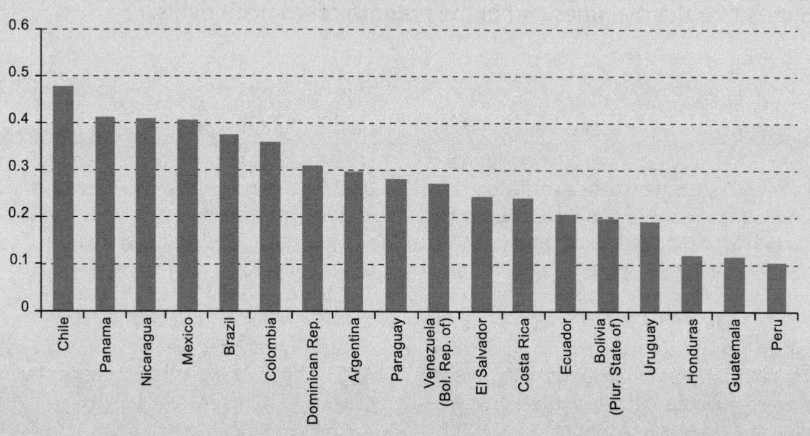

Source: Economic Commission for Latin America and the Caribbean (ECLAC), on the basis of special tabulations of data from household surveys conducted in the respective countries.

It is interesting to confirm the very high correlation of spousal education levels (measured by years of schooling) within a set of households. This correlation ranges from 0.76 in Ecuador to 0.58 in the Bolivarian Republic of Venezuela, as shown in the figure below, reflecting a high level of educational homogamy in the region.

Figure 2

Latin America (18 countries): correlation coefficient of spousal education levels, around 2012

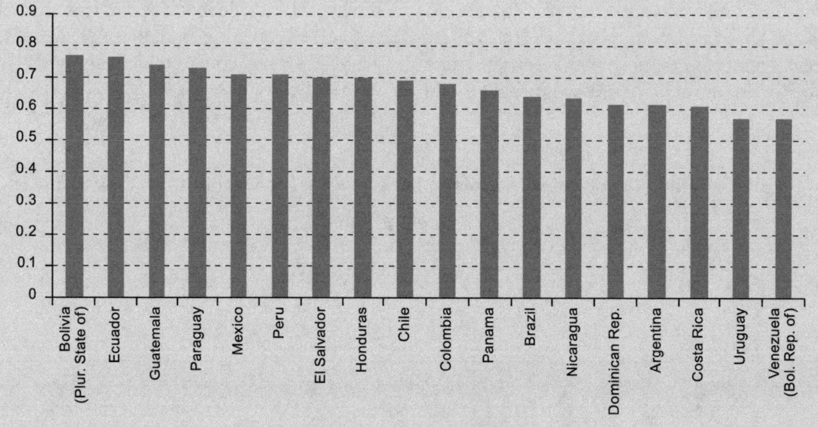

Source: Economic Commission for Latin America and the Caribbean (ECLAC), on the basis of special tabulations of data from household surveys conducted in the respective countries.

Source: Economic Commission for Latin America and the Caribbean (ECLAC), on the basis of special tabulations of data from household surveys conducted in the respective countries; G. Burtless, "Effects of growing wage disparities and changing family composition on the U.S. income distribution", *CSED Working Paper*, No. 4, Center on Social and Economic Dynamics, 1999; L Eika, M. Mogstad and B. Zafar, "Educational assortative mating and household income inequality", *Staff Reports*, No. 682, New York, Federal Reserve Bank of New York, 2014; S. Harkness, "Women's employment and household income inequality", *Income Inequality: Economic Disparities and the Middle Class in Affluent Countries*, J. Gornick and M. Jantii (eds.), Stanford, California, Stanford University Press; R. Nieuwenhuis, A. Need and H. van der Kolk, "Women's Earnings: Trends in earnings inequality within and between couple households in 18 OECD countries, 1981-2005", *LIS Working Paper Series*, No. 598, Luxembourg Income Study (LIS), 2013; and S. Pasqua, "Wives' work and income distribution in European Countries", *CHILD Working Paper*, No. 1, 2002.

D. Women's labour income and its effects on inequality and poverty

If women were to participate in the labour market in the same way as men, levels of poverty and inequality in the countries of the region would be reduced significantly. The countries with the widest gender gap in participation rates would gain the most in terms of average household income if those participation gaps disappeared. Inequality and poverty indicators would also improve substantially if women earned the same as their male counterparts with the same qualifications.

The previous sections have examined the profound differences and inequalities in the employment and earnings of men and women, showing that there is scope for improvement in terms of greater equality in these two dimensions, which will result in increased household well-being, and a more level playing field for men and women with regard to resource availability and economic capacities, and in the exercise of their social and economic rights. This section attempts to quantify the progress that could be made on some basic well-being indicators (namely the levels of socioeconomic inequality and poverty) if advances in gender equality were made in the region's labour markets.

In particular, it sets out to ascertain what the levels of income inequality and poverty would be in the region in two scenarios: (i) if the participation gap between men and women were closed; and (ii) if women earned the same as men (with the same qualifications). The aim is to reflect on what the contribution of female earnings to overall household well-being could be if women's labour participation increased or the wage gap narrowed. The simulations are based on the latest information available from household surveys conducted in the respective countries, which in most cases corresponds to 2012.

Setting out to close these gaps is not a utopian exercise. The fact that these disparities are ingrained in multiple mechanisms of cultural reproduction may make them difficult to reverse, but international experience has showed that public policies on labour and care have much to contribute in these areas (see box IV.7).

1. Closing the participation gap

The first analysis looked at what would happen if the participation rate for women in the intermediate age group (14-65 years) was similar to that for men. The first step was to develop a model of the female participation rate in order to better understand the variables determining women's participation and to be able to predict the probability of each woman actively entering the labour market.[3] The exercise essentially consisted in simulating the incorporation of inactive women into the labour market, sorting them according to the probability predicted using the estimated model of labour force participation, and matching the female participation rates to the male rates by age group.[4] That is, the women simulated as entering the labour market were those of the inactive group who were deemed most likely to become active. Once the participation gap had been closed, the probability of these newly active women being employed or unemployed was predicted, assuming a constant rate of female unemployment (that is, the percentage of unemployed women as a share of active women did not vary).[5] A labour income was calculated for the women who were simulated as gaining employment, similar to the earnings of other women with the same characteristics (age

3 A probit model was estimated using the female participation rate as the dependent binary variable.

4 The following age groups were considered: 15-24 years, 25-49 years, 50-65 years. The labour force participation of women aged 65 years and older is not altered (that is, if they were originally active, they remain so).

5 A second scenario was estimated matching both the participation rates and unemployment rates for men and women, thus closing the employment gap. As the results were very similar (although slightly higher) to those for the scenario of closing the participation gap, a decision was taken not to present them. The finding was attributable mainly to the low levels of unemployment recorded in the baseline year used for the simulation (2012).

and education level). A new vector of female earnings and household income was thus obtained, having knock-on effects on levels of household income, poverty and inequality.

The simulation introduced significant changes in the participation rates for women by age group (see table IV.7), almost closing the participation gaps between men and women (see figure IV.21).

Table IV.7
Latin America: observed and simulated female participation rates by age group, around 2012
(Percentages)

Country	15-24 years		25-49 years		50-65 years	
	Observed	Simulated	Observed	Simulated	Observed	Simulated
Argentina	32	49	68	95	53	84
Bolivia (Plurinational State of)	45	61	74	97	71	93
Brazil	51	67	71	93	45	76
Chile	29	42	64	92	43	85
Colombia	47	65	74	97	54	87
Costa Rica	36	56	62	95	40	83
Dominican Republic	28	53	61	92	44	83
Ecuador	31	52	63	96	51	89
El Salvador	32	62	63	96	47	87
Guatemala	30	64	48	91	40	85
Honduras	31	71	56	93	46	90
Mexico	39	66	63	96	48	85
Nicaragua	30	71	57	96	44	87
Panama	32	61	64	97	49	85
Paraguay	47	69	68	96	54	87
Peru	52	65	78	95	68	91
Uruguay	45	60	81	96	61	82
Venezuela (Bolivarian Republic of)	28	53	69	95	48	83

Source: Economic Commission for Latin America and the Caribbean (ECLAC), on the basis of special tabulations of data from household surveys conducted in the respective countries.

Figure IV.21
Latin America (18 countries): participation rates for men (observed) and women (observed and simulated), around 2012
(Percentages)

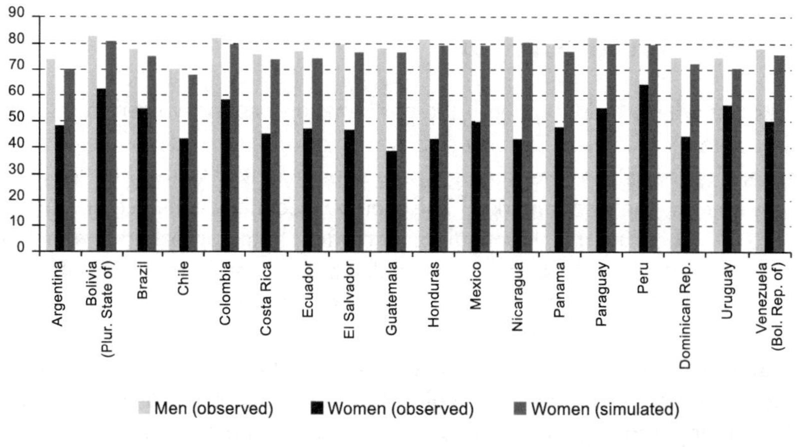

Source: Economic Commission for Latin America and the Caribbean (ECLAC), on the basis of special tabulations of data from household surveys conducted in the respective countries.

Such a rise in the female participation rate would lead to an increase in average household income ranging from 3% to 4% in Argentina, Brazil, Colombia, Mexico and Uruguay, and reaching over 10% in El Salvador, Honduras, Nicaragua and Peru. The countries with the largest gender gap in participation rates would gain the most in terms of average household income if those participation gaps disappeared. Evening up the rates of female and male participation would reduce poverty and inequality in the countries. The massive incorporation of women into the labour market could be expected to lead to declines in the poverty rate ranging from 1 percentage point in Argentina and Uruguay to over 10 percentage points in El Salvador and Nicaragua (see table IV.8 and figure IV.22). In addition, if more women were to enter the labour market it would help reduce inequality, measured using the Gini index, by 4 percentage points in Nicaragua and Panama, and by 3 percentage points in the Dominican Republic, Ecuador, El Salvador, Honduras and Paraguay. The Theil index would drop sharply in some countries (6 to 8 percentage points in Guatemala, Honduras, Nicaragua, Panama and Paraguay) because this measure of inequality is particularly sensitive to movements in the lower income segments and these countries would see a large increase in the proportion of women with lower levels of education entering the labour market.

Table IV.8

Latin America (18 countries): changes in poverty rates and inequality indicators as a result of closing the labour participation gap

(Percentage points)

Country	Poverty	Gini index	Theil index
Argentina	-1	-2	-4
Bolivia (Plurinational State of)	-5	-1	-3
Brazil	-3	-2	-5
Chile	-3	-2	-5
Colombia	-4	-2	-3
Costa Rica	-4	-2	-4
Dominican Republic	-6	-3	-5
Ecuador	-9	-3	-5
El Salvador	-12	-3	-5
Guatemala	-5	-2	-6
Honduras	-7	-3	-8
Mexico	-4	-1	-2
Nicaragua	-12	-4	-7
Panama	-7	-4	-8
Paraguay	-6	-3	-6
Peru	-6	-1	-1
Uruguay	-1	-1	-1
Venezuela (Bolivarian Republic of)	-4	-2	-2

Source: Economic Commission for Latin America and the Caribbean (ECLAC), on the basis of special tabulations of data from household surveys conducted in the respective countries.

Figure IV.22

Latin America (18 countries): poverty and inequality levels as a result of closing the labour participation gap compared with a baseline scenario

(Percentages)

A. Poverty

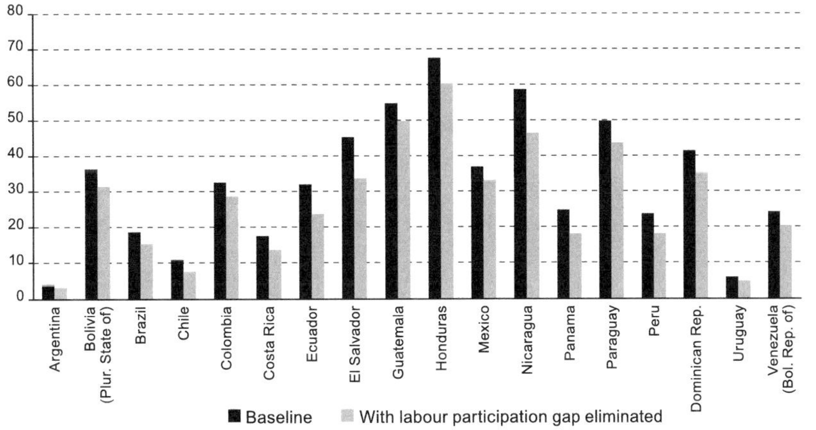

Figure IV.22 (concluded)

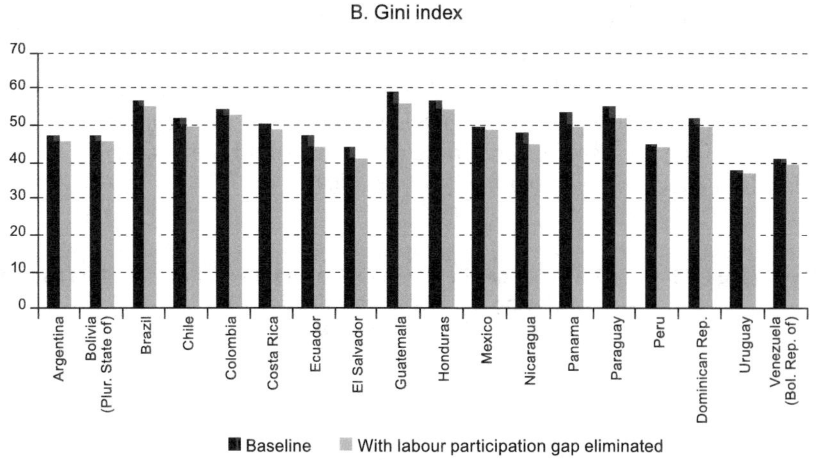

Source: Economic Commission for Latin America and the Caribbean (ECLAC), on the basis of special tabulations of data from household surveys conducted in the respective countries.

The above findings show that if more women were to enter the labour market, great strides would be made in reducing poverty and inequality, with the most substantial progress being seen in the countries with the widest participation gaps, such as those in Central America. It is clear, however, that even the massive incorporation of women into the labour market would not eliminate poverty in Latin America owing to the structural characteristics of the region's labour markets. The income that these women would earn would help to improve their situation, but only to some extent. Nevertheless, some countries would register very significant progress, especially with regard to inequality. Even more importantly, the entry of women into the labour market would have a profound impact in terms of the full exercise of autonomy, the development of capacities and personal potential, access to contributory social protection and broader participation in society beyond the household.

Box IV.7

Norway's social policy experience

Norway has a system of care for people with some level of dependency (children, older persons and persons with disabilities), in which the State plays a leading role. It operates on the basis that providing protection against the social risks to which individuals are exposed is a public responsibility and that the corresponding services should be available to the entire population. To that end, the State is committed to solving many of the problems that restrict development and prevent individuals from taking advantage of their opportunities and capacities, including lack of technical training, health problems, unemployment and care responsibilities.

The current Norwegian welfare State is built on high employment rates for working-age men and women. Paid work not only provides a significant source of financing for the care system through taxes, but is also considered a right in connection with the pursuit of self-fulfilment. In order to ensure that this age group can be as active as possible in the labour market, the State participates in the care of household members, including dependents.

The Norwegian care system has been developed gradually since the nineteenth century. By the mid-nineteenth century, a public, compulsory education system had been established, provided by the local community. The system was compulsory through to the completion of primary education, thus ensuring that the vast majority of Norwegians were literate. In response to expanding industrialization, the growth of cities and the health problems caused by population density, the State added medical care to its list of responsibilities. The early establishment of minimum educational coverage and universal health care, which laid the foundations for a highly productive workforce, would prove to be extremely important for the subsequent development of the Norwegian welfare State.

In the late nineteenth century, the first labour laws were passed in Norway. By the first decade of the twentieth century, legislation was already in place on insurance against accidents and unemployment. Initially, the rights were limited to certain groups, such as industrial workers or members of some unions, but over time their coverage was extended. By contrast, when health insurance was introduced in the first decade of the twentieth century, it covered, from the outset, not only workers, but also their spouses and children (the first of its kind in the world).

In the post-war period, progress was made towards universal benefits. This process encouraged greater equality between people, eliminating the discrimination between recipients and non-recipients. It also brought down the costs associated with the selection of beneficiaries since the vast majority of the population was now considered eligible. In just three years, legislation was passed on workplace accident insurance for all sectors, health insurance coverage was expanded to the entire population and a universal pension was introduced that was not linked to past earnings. Education coverage

Box IV.7 (concluded)

was also extended to include higher education. Thus, since the 1960s the Government of Norway has been providing public health care, education and pensions to all its citizens, as well as relatively generous economic assistance to the unemployed and persons with disabilities (Dølvik and Fafo, 2007; Sønneland, 2013).

Since then, the State has focused on strengthening childcare policies. Parents' labour rights have been extended (to allow mothers and fathers to spend more quality time with their children) and public care services have been provided (allowing both parents to pursue their labour activities). Currently, the State makes cash transfers to families with children under 1 year old and grants leave for one year at full pay, which is split between the parents for the purposes of caring for the child. Each parent is required to use a minimum period of the leave and to that end a certain number of days are reserved exclusively for each parent, which seeks to reduce inequality in the provision of care within the family. The State also contributes directly to the care of children through public kindergartens for children aged under 6 years (Dølvik and Fafo, 2007; Kitterød and Rønsen, 2013; Sønneland, 2013).

The various benefits provided by the State for the care of dependents in households enable people who are able to work to focus on their careers. This is reinforced by the provision of technical training and medical care by the Norwegian State to individuals, in order to ensure that they are qualified and physically able to do their job. Indeed, Norway is one of the countries that is best placed in comparative rankings of productivity and that has made the most progress in this regard in recent years (Barth, Moene and Willumsen, 2014). The State also provides for those who are unable to work either temporarily or permanently in the form of an income that allows them to live with dignity.

Source: E. Barth, K.O. Moene and F. Willumsen, "The Scandinavian model: an interpretation", Journal of Public Economics, vol. 117, Amsterdam, Elsevier, 2014; G. Botten, K.T. Elvbakken and N. Kildal, "The Norwegian welfare state on the threshold of a new century", Scandinavian Journal of Public Health, vol. 31, 2, 2003; J.E. Dølvik, "The Nordic regimes of labour market governance: from crisis to success-story", Fafo-Paper, No. 7, 2007; J.E. Dølvik, "The Nordic model of collective bargaining and trade unionism", Fafo, 2007 [online] http://h24-files.s3.amazonaws.com/62061/154367-wsHHZ.pdf; R.H. Kitterød and M. Rønsen, "Opting out? Who are the housewives in contemporary Norway?", European Sociological Review, vol. 29, No. 6, 2013; S. Kuhnle and S.E. Hort, The Developmental Welfare State in Scandinavia: Lessons for the Developing World, Geneva, United Nations Research Institute for Social Development (UNRISD), 2004; A.M. Sønneland, "El sistema de protección social en Noruega", internacional seminar "Políticas públicas para la igualdad: hacia sistemas de protección social universal", Montevideo, 2013.

Accelerating changes in the proposed sense would clearly not be possible without active, resolute policies that promote and encourage such changes, including policies on care. The region has much ground to cover in this respect, because although progress has been made on a legal and regulatory front, scant substantial changes have been seen. Care services generally have low coverage and operate in a weak institutional framework, thus failing to meet the growing needs of societies. Nevertheless, several countries have incorporated the issue into their policy agendas and have made different degrees of progress (ECLAC, 2012a). Active labour market policies can encourage greater participation by women in the labour market by helping to ensure that they are properly qualified and by facilitating their labour market integration. Of course, there are other policies that can influence the female participation rate, such as the provision of preschool education and extended schooldays at the primary stage. Lastly, as ECLAC has highlighted in several studies, what is needed is a new gender compact that involves a more equitable distribution of roles within the household and is thus conducive to female labour force participation.

2. Closing the income gap

The second question addressed was what would happen to poverty and inequality in the region if the income gap between men and women disappeared. In the simulations carried out for this purpose, a decision was taken to eliminate the monthly income gap between men and women, which also effaced the differences in hours worked. The first step was to estimate wage equations for employed men. The monthly earnings of women were then predicted using the coefficients of these equations. This calculation removed the gender differences in labour market returns and assumed that men and women receive equal pay in the market according to their education level and age.

Closing the gender income gap would lead to milestone achievements in poverty reduction in countries such as the Plurinational State of Bolivia and Peru (see table IV.9 and figure IV.23) by significantly boosting household income. As noted above, a significant percentage of women in these countries are employed but not paid, which explains the dramatic changes that would take place if these women were to receive a similar income to men with the same level of education and work experience. The changes to the poverty level in Colombia, Ecuador and Nicaragua would also be very significant. The Gini index would fall by between 2 and 8 percentage points, depending on the country, and the Theil index would mark an even larger decline in inequality, being more sensitive to the changes that occur in lower income households.

Table IV.9
Latin America (18 countries): changes in poverty rates and inequality indicators as a result of closing the gender income gap
(Percentage points)

Country	Poverty	Gini index	Theil index
Argentina	-1	-3	-5
Bolivia (Plurinational State of)	-14	-8	-12
Brazil	-6	-4	-13
Chile	-2	-4	-8
Colombia	-9	-5	-12
Costa Rica	-4	-3	-7
Dominican Republic	-5	-3	-6
Ecuador	-8	-4	-8
El Salvador	-6	-3	-5
Guatemala	-4	-2	-7
Honduras	-1	-2	-6
Mexico	-5	-3	-6
Nicaragua	-8	-4	-8
Panama	-6	-4	-10
Paraguay	-7	-5	-12
Peru	-8	-5	-8
Uruguay	-2	-3	-4
Venezuela (Bolivarian Republic of)	-4	-2	-3

Source: Economic Commission for Latin America and the Caribbean (ECLAC), on the basis of special tabulations of data from household surveys conducted in the respective countries.

Figure IV.23
Latin America (18 countries): poverty and inequality levels as a result of eliminating the gender income gap compared with a baseline scenario
(Percentages)

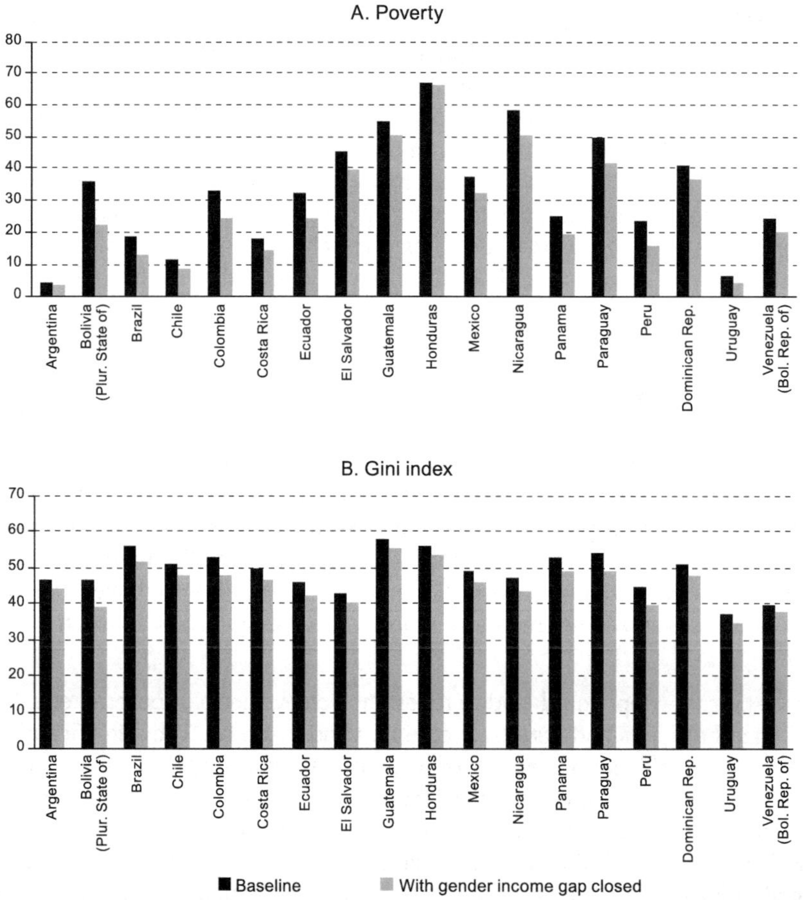

Source: Economic Commission for Latin America and the Caribbean (ECLAC), on the basis of special tabulations of data from household surveys conducted in the respective countries.

Again, the quest for progress on this front calls for public policy. Governments in the region have ratified international agreements and passed domestic legislation to endorse the principles of equal opportunity and non-discrimination between women and men. However, the figures indicate that these actions alone are insufficient to ensure the eradication of gender discrimination in the labour market. Once specific legislation on equal pay has been enacted, labour market institutions can play a role in helping to close gaps. Expanding the coverage of collective bargaining to include workers in traditionally excluded sectors, such as domestic workers, rural workers and homeworkers, can help to narrow the gender income gap. Another approach is to address issues relating to the protection of maternal and paternal labour rights (see Maurizio, 2010). Improving labour inspections can also help to eliminate discriminatory practices. Furthermore, as several studies have indicated that occupational segregation is responsible for a significant part of the gender wage gap (for example, Macpherson and Hirsch, 1995; Miller, 2009), policies to address occupational segregation, for example, by training women for occupations that are not considered typically female, would narrow the wage gap. Similarly, little progress has been made to date on extending training to men for occupations that have traditionally been considered female with a view to eliminating the stereotypes and prejudices that also translate into wage discrepancies.

E. Concluding remarks

ECLAC has consistently promoted and reiterated the idea that the region should move towards the horizon of equality, understood in a broad sense. To this end, strategies must be implemented for achieving gender equality in various areas and for advancing towards the mutual recognition of men and women. In addition to fulfilling policy requirements, achieving greater gender equality, whether by expanding women's labour force participation or by eliminating occupational segregation and wage discrimination, can help boost the productivity levels of these economies and enhance growth.

This chapter has detailed the various spheres in which gender inequalities occur and showed how they are reflected and reproduced in the labour market, despite originating in forms of discrimination that predate the labour market and are related to sociocultural conditioning. The simulation exercises conducted have showed that eliminating the participation gap between men and women and closing the gender pay gap can result in significant improvements in household well-being, leading to higher household income and lower poverty and socioeconomic inequality levels. The potential for progress varies between countries and is greater in the countries where the gaps are more pronounced. Nevertheless, significant changes could be attained for the whole region. Specific labour market policies and care policies can directly influence both women's labour market participation and income discrimination.

Crucially, policies to promote gender equality in the labour market must be fully integrated by countries into their public agendas. Those policies should be associated with legislation and programmes that facilitate and encourage a balance between the work and family demands of male and female workers. They should also seek to strengthen women's autonomy and involve society as a whole in providing for the care needs of the population. Equality and structural change call for compacts to boost and improve women's participation in the region's economic development, overcome discrimination in the labour market and consolidate the guarantee of rights.

Bibliography

Alvaredo, F. and J. Londoño (2013), "High incomes and personal taxation in a developing economy: Colombia 1993-2010", *Working Paper*, No. 12, Commitment to Equity, March. Antonopoulos, R. (2009), "The current economic and financial crisis: a gender perspective", *The Levy Economics Institute of Bard College*, No. 562, May.

Arroyo, L. and others (2010), "Los efectos de la crisis sobre las mujeres: Empleo, segregación ocupacional y modelo productivo", *Informes de la Fundación*, Madrid, March.

Atkinson, A., T. Piketty and E. Sáez (2011), "Top incomes in the long run of history", *Journal of Economic Literature*, vol. 49, No. 1.

Bakker, I. (1999), "Dotar de género a la reforma de la política macroeconómica en la era de la reestructuración y el ajuste global", *Mujeres y economía: Nuevas perspectivas para viejos y nuevos problemas*, C. Carrasco, Barcelona, Editorial Icaria.

Bértola, L. and J.A. Ocampo (2012), *The Economic Development of Latin America since Independence*, Oxford University Press.

Carrasco, C. and M. Mayordomo (2006), "Trabajo y condiciones de vida: Una mirada no androcéntrica", *Documentación Social*, No. 143, Madrid, Cáritas Española.

ECLAC (Economic Commission for Latin America and the Caribbean) (2014), *Compacts for Equality: Towards a Sustainable Future* (LC/G.2586(SES.35/3)), Santiago, Chile, April.

___(2013), *Social Panorama of Latin America 2013* (LC/G.2580), Santiago, Chile. United Nations publication, Sales No. E.14.II.G.6.

___(2012a), *Structural Change for Equality: An Integrated Approach to Development* (LC/G.2524(SES.34/3)), Santiago, Chile.

___(2012b), *Social Panorama of Latin America 2011* (LC/G.2514-P), Santiago, Chile. United Nations publication, Sales No. E.12.II.G.6.

___(2010a), *Time for equality: closing gaps, opening trails* (LC/G.2432(SES.33/3)), Santiago, Chile.

___(2010b), *Social Panorama of Latin America 2009* (LC/G.2423-P), Santiago, Chile. United Nations publication, Sales No. E.09.II.G.135.

ECLAC/FAO/UN-Women/UNDP/ILO (Economic Commission for Latin America and the Caribbean/Food and Agriculture Organization of the United Nations/United Nations Entity for Gender Equality and the Empowerment of Women/ United Nations Development Programme/International Labour Organization) (2013), *Trabajo decente e igualdad de género. Políticas para mejorar el acceso y la calidad del empleo de las mujeres en* América *Latina y el Caribe*, Santiago, Chile.

ECLAC/ILO (Economic Commission for Latin America and the Caribbean/International Labour Organization) (2014), "Conditional transfer programmes and the labour market", *The Employment Situation in Latin America and the Caribbean*, No.10 (LC/L.3815), Santiago, Chile.

___(2011), "Countercyclical policies for a sustained recovery in employment", *The Employment Situation in Latin America and the Caribean*, No. 5, Santiago, Chile.

___(2009), "Impact of the financial crisis on women in the Caribbean" (LC/CAR/L.243), Port of Spain, ECLAC subregional headquarters for the Caribbean.

Espino, Alma (2012), "La dimensión de género de la crisis. ¿Existe una agenda feminista?", *Nueva Sociedad*, No. 237, January/February.

___(2010), "Economía feminista: Enfoques y propuestas", *Working Paper*, No. 5/10, Montevideo, Institute of Economics, University of the Republic.

Gender Equality Observatory for Latin America and the Caribbean (n/d) [online] http://www.cepal.org/oig/default.asp?idioma=IN/.

Giosa, Z. and C. Rodríguez (2010), "Estrategias de desarrollo y equidad de género: Una propuesta de abordaje y su aplicación al caso de las industrias manufactureras de exportación en México y Centroamérica", *Mujer y Desarrollo series*, No. 97 (LC/L.3154-P), Santiago, Chile, Economic Commission for Latin America and the Caribbean (ECLAC). United Nations publication, Sales No. S.09.II.G.127.

Guzmán, V. (2003), "Gobernabilidad, democracia y género, una articulación posible", *Mujer y Desarrollo series*, No. 48 (1962-P), Santiago, Chile, Economic Commission for Latin America and the Caribbean (ECLAC). United Nations publication, Sales No. S.03.II.G.119.

Heckman, J. (1979), "Sample selection bias as a specification error", *Econometrica*, vol. 47, No. 1.

Lechner, N. (2002), *Las sombras del mañana. La dimensión subjetiva de la política*, Santiago, Chile, Editorial Lom.

Macpherson, D.A. and B.T. Hirsch (1995), "Wages and gender composition: why do women's jobs pay less?", *Journal of Labor Economics*, vol. 13, No. 3, Chicago, University of Chicago Press.

Maurizio, R. (2010), "Enfoque de género en las instituciones laborales y las políticas del mercado de trabajo en Argentina", *Macroeconomía del Desarrollo series*, No. 104 (LC/L.3230-P), Santiago, Chile, Economic Commission for Latin America and the Caribbean (ECLAC). United Nations publication, Sales No. S.10.II.G.34.

Miller, P. (2009), "The gender pay gap in the US: does sector make a difference?", *Journal of Labor Research*, vol. 30, No. 1, Springer.

Montaño, S. and V. Milosavljevic (2010), "La crisis económica y financiera. Su impacto sobre la pobreza, el trabajo y el tiempo de las mujeres", *Mujer y Desarrollo series*, No. 98 (LC/L.3168-P), Santiago, Chile, Economic Commission for Latin America and the Caribbean (ECLAC). United Nations publication, Sales No. S.09.II.G.141.

Picchio, A. (2005), "La economía política y la investigación sobre las condiciones de vida", *Por una economía sobre la vida. Aportaciones desde un enfoque feminista*, Gemma Cairó i Céspedes and Maribel Mayordomo Rico (comps.), Barcelona, Icaria.

Piketty, T. (2003), "Income inequality in France, 1901–1998", *Journal of Political Economy*, vol. 111, No. 5.

Rico, M.N. and D. Trucco (2014), "Adolescentes. Derecho a la educación y al bienestar futuro", *Políticas Sociales series*, No. 190 (LC/L.3791), Santiago, Chile, Economic Commission for Latin America and the Caribbean (ECLAC).

Rico, M.N. and F. Marco (2006), "Las mujeres en el empleo sectorial de América Latina", *Mujer y empleo. La reforma de la salud y la salud de la reforma en Argentina*, M.N. Rico and F. Marco (coords.), Buenos Aires, Siglo XXI Editores.

Sabarwal, S., N. Sinha and M. Buvinic (2012), *How Do Women Weather Economic Shocks? What We Know?*, Washington, D.C., World Bank.

Chapter V

Residential segregation and the reproduction of inequalities

Introduction

Socioeconomic groups generally exhibit distinctive location patterns within cities. If these patterns involve physical distances that hinder or prevent interaction, recognition and cooperation between these groups, social cohesion and city governance are likely to be weakened. Where the location pattern of socioeconomic groups contributes to perpetuating social inequalities in the city (either by blocking the upward social mobility of disadvantaged groups, by creating privileges and rents for affluent groups, or by segmenting and excluding the poor from the circuits through which the different kinds of capital flow), socioeconomic residential segregation ensues, posing a fundamental challenge for the development of inclusive and sustainable cities.

This chapter looks at socioeconomic residential segregation in the region's largest cities and examines the changes that have occurred in the past decade, on the basis of information provided by the latest population and housing censuses in 10 Latin American countries.[1]

Socioeconomic residential segregation causes concern to authorities, experts and social actors because of its connections with other issues on the region's public agenda, including the reproduction of poverty and social inequality, the weakening of social cohesion, and sustainability and governance problems. The distribution of the population within cities is not random and for various reasons usually favours the most affluent groups, who tend to be found closer —and with easier access— to jobs and services. They also benefit from better public facilities, more social and private infrastructure and investment, and better funded and more capable local government, and are less exposed to crime and environmental problems. The advantageous location of these groups tends to consolidate their well-being and therefore reproduce wealth. Conversely, the disadvantageous location of groups whose socioeconomic status is lower tends to further compound their already poor living conditions, which helps perpetuate poverty. A number of well-grounded arguments suggest that socioeconomic residential segregation contributes to the reproduction of inequality and undermines social cohesion, environmental sustainability and governance (ECLAC, 2014).

The high and increasing urbanization of the region —80%, the world's highest level after North America (United Nations, 2014, page 8)— is also a factor in placing urban matters on the public agenda. The fact that about one third of the region's population resides in large cities (those with over 1 million inhabitants) increases the visibility and the significance of segregation, which is usually more pronounced in these metropolises.

In light of the above, there is a need for up-to-date knowledge on recent trends in socioeconomic residential segregation and their potential consequences for metropolitan areas, cities, neighbourhoods, households and individuals. With that in mind, this chapter takes a systematic approach to various indicators of socioeconomic residential segregation in some 20 large Latin American cities. The effect of internal migration on trends in socioeconomic residential segregation is also estimated, considering that changes in residence might be the factor with the fastest and most direct impact on the phenomenon.

First, this chapter reviews the causes of socioeconomic residential segregation in the context of the debate over how cities are changing and being reconfigured. Next, trends in socioeconomic residential segregation are examined along with the effects of migration and its consequences; and a closer look is taken at other types of segregation, particularly that of ethnic groups and international immigrants. The chapter closes with a brief overview of the outcomes of interventions aimed at reducing socioeconomic residential segregation, followed by a set of policy guidelines.

1 Argentina, Bolivarian Republic of Venezuela, Brazil, Costa Rica, Dominican Republic, Ecuador, Mexico, Panama, Peru and Uruguay. The Argentine and Peruvian cities included in this chapter (Buenos Aires and Lima), are only considered for a small number of indicators, and it is ultimately the selected cities of the other eight countries that are the focus of this research and the data presented in the figures and tables on trends in socioeconomic residential segregation.

A. The problem of socioeconomic residential segregation in Latin America

Until the late twentieth century there was relative consensus, albeit little supporting evidence, that socioeconomic residential segregation was increasing in Latin American cities. There are doubts over whether this is still the case, especially because of social diversification in city peripheries, owing to non-traditional movements to these areas or because of rising living standards there.

There are a number of dimensions to socioeconomic residential segregation (Massey and Denton, 1988); in Latin America they are largely reflected in the uneven territorial distribution of socioeconomic groups within cities. During the twentieth century, this uneven distribution took the form of a stark contrast between affluent areas where the high- and upper-middle-income population was concentrated[2] (after originally locating in central and pericentral areas and then moving toward the outer ring in varying directions depending on the city) and the rest of the metropolitan area inhabited by medium- and low-status socioeconomic groups. The non-affluent areas exhibited certain typical features: the dilapidation of central and pericentral areas and the development of informal and makeshift housing in much of the periphery (ECLAC, 2012; Jordán, Rehner and Samaniego, 2010; Torres, 2008; Borsdorf, 2003; Romero, 1976; Herrera, Pecht and Olivares, 1976).[3]

This contrast was certainly not absolute; exceptions to the rule could be found in all large cities, such as poor neighbourhoods within affluent districts, socially mixed areas, and high-income neighbourhoods located in poor peripheral areas. Some of the region's military dictatorships —of which there were several during the twentieth century— carried out "urban surgeries" (Lombardi and Veiga, 1989) which helped to reinforce patterns of socioeconomic residential segregation and to diminish social heterogeneity in the municipalities and neighbourhoods of large cities, especially by displacing poor settlements from high-income areas towards the periphery. Residential segregation intensified during the 1980s and 1990s as the external debt crisis and economic adjustment processes led to soaring urban poverty, limiting States' capacity to develop city edges and weakening institutions that underpin social integration, such as State schools. The same period saw a decline in the community organizations and political and social movements that were active in low-income areas of major cities, leading to the loss of vehicles for coordination and integration in these districts. Socioeconomic residential segregation thus emerged as a cause for concern, but was not deemed a public policy priority owing to the intensification of other social problems such as rising poverty and deteriorating basic services, government institutions, infrastructure, public transport and the urban environment (due to increased congestion, pollution and crime).

Confining the poor to the periphery, where they suffered from social deprivation and limited access to public services and jobs, coincided with the concept of the "dual city", which was in vogue the early 1990s. In spatial terms, this meant that cities were split into two large, clearly separate areas, one "rich" and the other "poor", creating

---

2 This settlement pattern of groups with higher socioeconomic status, which some texts on models of the Latin American city (Borsdorf, 2003) describe as a "high-income cone", was applicable in some cases, but not all. As this chapter will show, its validity is under discussion.

3 This situation contrasts with the pattern of ethnic residential segregation in the metropolitan areas of the United States, which is marked by concentrations of poor ethnic minorities in relatively central districts, and the exodus of high- and middle-income "non-Hispanic whites" to the suburbs (Fosset, 2004). This is one reason why some of the dimensions of socioeconomic residential segregation identified by Massey and Denton (1988), such as centralization, are not relevant to the cities of Latin America. Similarly, some of the stylized facts applied to the metropolitan dynamics of developed countries (Ingram, 1998) do not always correspond to the reality in Latin America and the Caribbean.

large-scale residential segregation owing to the distances between them (Smets and Salman, 2008; Ribeiro and Telles, 2000; Mollenkopf and Castells, 1991; Sassen, 1991).[4]

The close of the twentieth century and the first decade of the twenty-first were, however, characterized by more complex urban processes that have given rise to two opposing explanatory hypotheses: one that socioeconomic residential segregation is rising, the other that it is on the wane. While households of low socioeconomic level did flow from well-off central areas towards the low-income periphery, this was not the result of "urban surgery", but mainly the consequence of urban land market pressures and housing policies. Owing to high building and rental costs in central and pericentral areas, as well as zoning regulations and public housing policies, social housing has been built on the cheapest land, often without city-building in the proper sense of the term. This endogenous centrifugal flow coexists with traditional migration from rural to urban areas, most of which ends up in the peripheral belt, which has lower had costs and fewer regulations. In many urban areas, intrametropolitan migration has begun to outpace (sometimes considerably) flows of external migrants and has become a driver of the periphery's demographic, geographical and housing expansion (Chávez and others, 2013).

Another trend observed in recent decades, albeit on a smaller scale and only in certain areas, is that city centres have regained their appeal as places to live, thanks to urban renewal and repopulation policies. These programmes generally attracted middle- and high-income residents to previously run-down areas, setting off gentrification. One typical feature of this phenomenon is the departure of the former residents, who usually belong to low-income groups (Pacione, 2009, pages 211-212). Taken together, these processes are likely to lend weight to the hypothesis that socioeconomic residential segregation has increased in recent decades.

By contrast, in the 1990s middle- and high-income households began to relocate to those parts of the periphery situated in the vicinity of (or at least well connected with) the traditional habitat of the highest socioeconomic segments. These households also moved to areas further afield, to historically poor districts or those with rural characteristics (ECLAC, 2012; Rogers, Beall and Kanbur, 2012; Arroyo, 2001). Such movements, especially towards gated communities (Ribeiro, 2013; ECLAC, 2012; IDB, 2011; De Mattos, 2010; Roberts and Wilson, 2009; Sabatini and Cáceres, 2004) fragment the spatial distribution of this socioeconomic group and diversify the socioeconomic make-up of destination areas in the periphery, which actually helps reduce standard indicators of socioeconomic residential segregation. Yet there is some debate over whether this type of settlement could undermine the potential for social interaction associated with the residential coexistence of different socioeconomic groups, "between whom there is neither interaction nor any form of social cohesion" (Aguilar and Escanilla, 2011, page 6). In other words, "nothing guarantees that potential contact coming from spatial propinquity is not hindered by these social and cultural barriers" (Flores, 2008 page 22).[5]

To complete this overview, the construction of large social and private housing developments aimed at middle-income groups has gradually consolidated formal housing in city peripheries. Coupled with this, the economic boom of the 2000s and broader State intervention, for example through neighbourhood improvement programmes, the expansion of basic infrastructure and the provision of public facilities (particularly in education and health), were conducive to better housing conditions and helped enhance the living standards of residents. Improvements were noted across a number of housing and social indicators, especially in terms of socioeconomic diversity, which should support the hypothesis that residential segregation is decreasing.

On top of the controversy surrounding trends in socioeconomic residential segregation comes the debate as to its consequences. The mere term carries a connotation of adversity. Yet there are other forms of territorial grouping that can be described in terms of functionality or identity: other expressions should be used for such cases. One example is the grouping of ethnicities in specific parts of cities, which may have its roots in shared cultural aspects, such as

---

[4] Polese and Stren (2000, pages 308 and 309) neatly capture the prevailing opinion of the time: "Many modern students of the city (...) appear to sense, if only intuitively, the emergence of a new, more brutal, form o spatial polarization. The modern city offers new possibilities for physically, politically, and socially isolating (excluding) certain groups".

[5] While this debate is certainly challenging and significant, it is nevertheless beyond the scope of this chapter, at least in terms of measurement, because all of the indices used seek to quantify the geographical facet of socioeconomic residential segregation. The type of social relations established by the various groups that cohabit city neighbourhoods therefore cannot be directly extrapolated from the identified trends in socioeconomic residential segregation.

language. Such instances may be described as communities establishing their location on the basis of cultural identity. Of course, if such concentrations are imposed —as in cases of ethnic discrimination— then the term segregation would indeed be appropriate. Even if concentration is not imposed but is, instead, related to adverse living conditions in specific enclaves, it is the most suitable term.

In any case, it is generally accepted that physical separation and a lack of socioeconomic heterogeneity in a given habitat (which are dimensions of socioeconomic residential segregation) in principle hamper interaction between different groups. However, this is a probability rather than a causality (Andrade and Silveira, 2013). Socially mixed residential spaces do not ensure interaction between different social groups, nor do they ensure symmetrical and functional relations between them. On the other hand, neither is physical distance between social groups an insurmountable barrier to their social interaction, since this may take place elsewhere (for example, public squares, schools and workplaces).

The following sections seek to determine segregation trends in cities of over 1 million inhabitants[6] in the 10 countries mentioned above, based on the most recent available census information (from the 2000 and 2010 rounds). Some of the causes and consequences of socioeconomic residential segregation will also be examined, taking into account at least three variables to define socioeconomic groups.[7]

B. The social composition of large cities and population growth in the 2000s: some trends

All of Latin America's large cities have expanding populations, though growth rates are slowing. The fastest population growth and the lowest socioeconomic indicators are still to be found in city peripheries, but peripheries are witnessing a rise in socioeconomic diversity.

The first finding to emerge from an analysis of demographic and social indicators for cities is that while population growth remains in positive territory in all metropolitan areas, it is slowing. At present, most cities are experiencing average annual population growth of less than 2%, compared with 4% in many cases until the 1980s (ECLAC, 2012). While all of these metropolitan areas are undergoing demographic expansion and their governments and institutions must meet the requirements arising from this process, rapid population growth is no longer a defining feature of the cities studied.

Another notable dimension is the persistence of clear contrasts between central and peripheral areas of cities, both in terms of demographic growth (which remains much slower in centres) and in terms of social composition (socioeconomic and education levels remain lower in peripheral districts). These patterns are particularly apparent in maps V.1 and V.2, in which the borders of the central minor administrative division (MIAD)[8] are highlighted. Map V.1

6 With the exception of Cuenca, Ecuador, which has a population of fewer than 500,000 people.

7 A technical note in annex 1 lists the cities studied and describes the variables and data sources used, as well as the three geographical areas used: broad urban areas, MIADS and subMIADS.

8 Minor administrative divisions (MIADs) are usually municipalities or their equivalent, depending on the country. In the cities in maps V.1 and V.2, the MIADs are the borough of Cuauhtémoc in Mexico City, the municipalities of São Paulo and Santo Domingo, and the canton of San José. In some cities these central MIADs refer to the entire "greater" downtown area, but in others are only a component part of it (see definitions of "broad urban areas" used for each city in annex 1).

contrasts the proportion of heads of household with higher education in the MIADs of 4 of the 20 selected cities.[9] In these four cities, the third of MIADs with the highest proportion was located in or around the downtown area, or in the MIADs comprising the "gentrified periphery". The third of the MIADs with the lowest proportion of heads of household with higher education was usually located in the periphery. As such, while the development of gentrified peripheries effectively implies an increase in social diversity, the periphery remains the area of lowest socioeconomic level in most cities.

Map V.1

Mexico City, São Paulo (Brazil), San José and Santo Domingo: minor administrative divisions (MIADs), by proportion of heads of household with higher education, 2010 census round [a]

(Percentages)

A. Mexico City: heads of household with higher education, by municipality and delegation, 2010 census

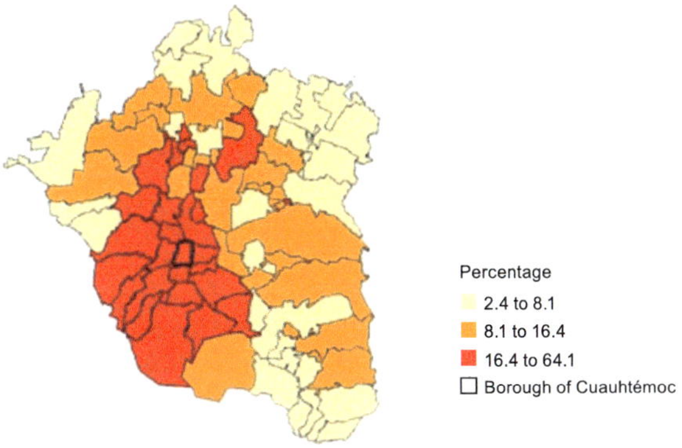

B. São Paulo: heads of household with higher education, by municipality, 2010 census

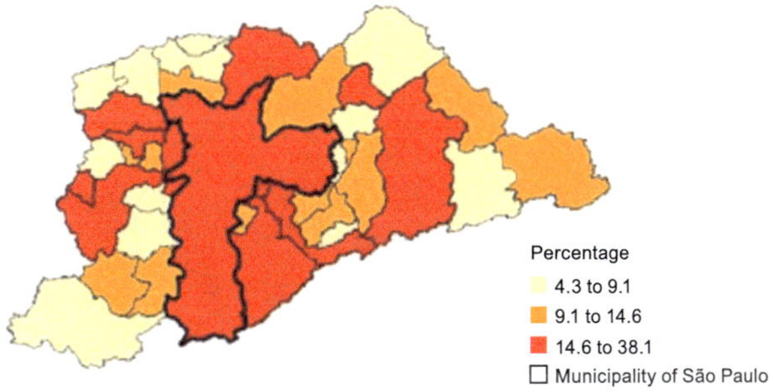

C. San José: heads of household with higher education, by canton, 2011 census

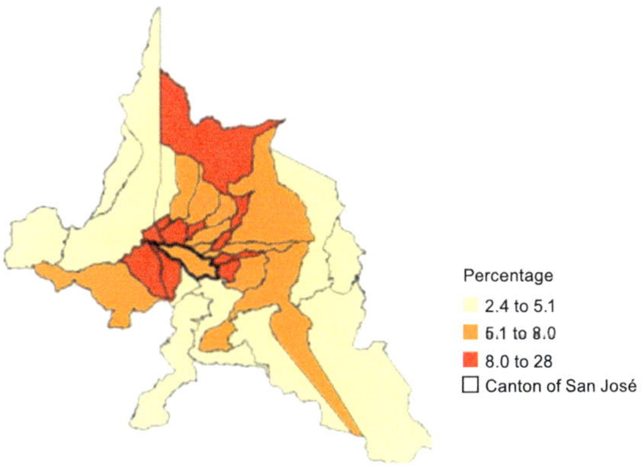

9 Cities were chosen in keeping with the limited scope of this chapter and a number of selection criteria; notably, the representation of different city types (megalopolises and smaller cities), cities in different countries (with a maximum number of cities per country) and the number of constituent MIADs (priority was given to cities with nine MIADs or more).

Map V.1 (concluded)

D. Santo Domingo: heads of household with higher education, by municipality, 2010 census

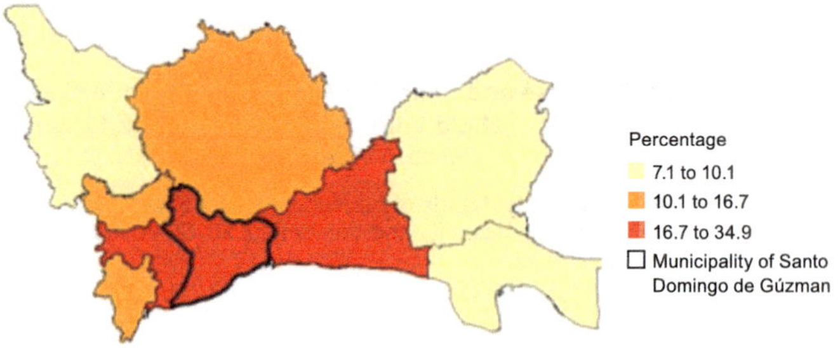

Source: Economic Commission for Latin America and the Caribbean (ECLAC), on the basis of special processing of census microdata.

[a] The categories used in each map refer to terciles of the distribution of municipalities or boroughs, according to the percentage of heads of household with higher education. Borders outlined in bold denote the central minor administrative division (MIAD).

Map V.2

Mexico City, São Paulo (Brazil), San José and Santo Domingo: minor administrative divisions (MIADs) by population growth rate, 2000-2010 [a]

(Average annual percentage rate)

A. Mexico City: overall population growth rate, by municipality and delegation, 2000-2010

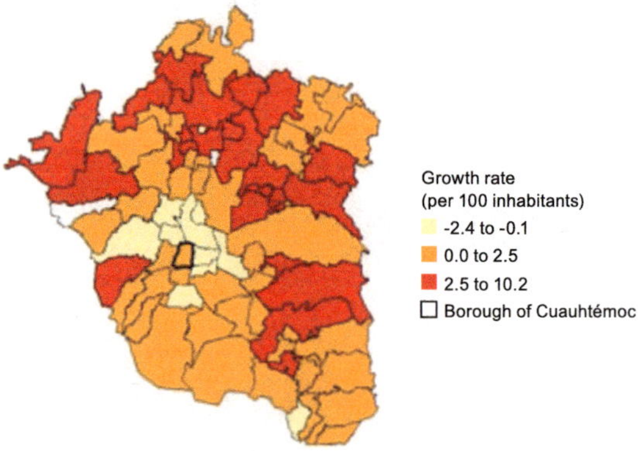

B. São Paulo: overall population growth rate, by municipality, 2000-2010

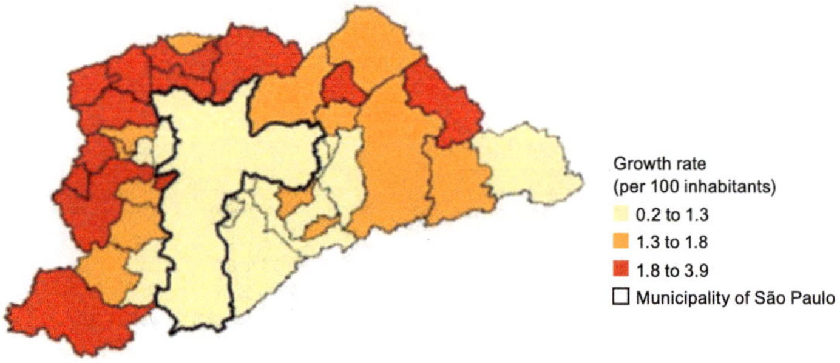

Map V.2 (concluded)

C. San José: overall population growth rate, by canton, 2000-2011

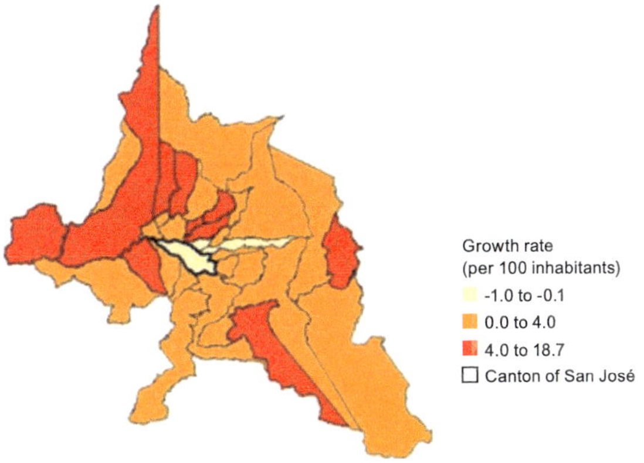

D. Santo Domingo: overall population growth rate, by municipality, 2002-2010

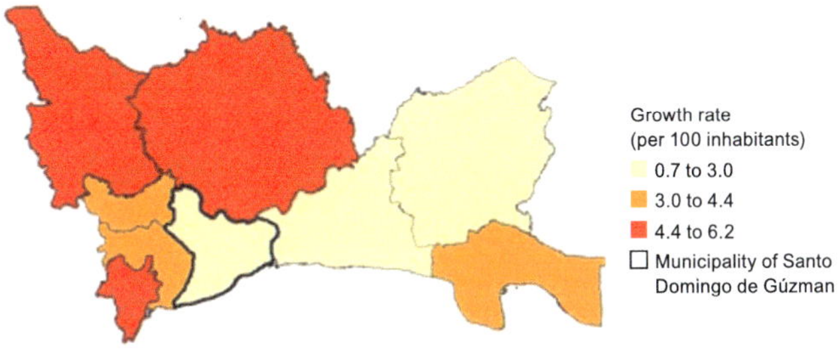

Source: Economic Commission for Latin America and the Caribbean (ECLAC), on the basis of special processing of census microdata.
[a] The categories used in each map refer to terciles of the distribution of municipalities or boroughs, according to the population growth rate. Borders outlined in bold denote the central minor administrative division (MIAD).

As map V.2 shows, the population in central MIADs is growing very slowly or even decreasing, while peripheral MIADs continue to post growth rates above 2%. However, population growth varies greatly both in the periphery (where the fastest rate of growth is not always to be found in the most outlying MIADs) and in central areas. This is certainly true of Mexico City, where some boroughs of the Federal District have returned to positive rates of population growth.

Another stand-out feature is the rise in populations' education levels (specifically, those of heads of household), although again there were striking variances between cities (see table V.A2.1 of annex 2). For example, the improvement in education levels is much more pronounced in Brazilian cities than in Mexican ones.[10] The metropolitan area of Caracas showed improved education indicators at the base level (with a decreasing percentage of heads of household with a low level of education) but made little progress in terms of the percentage of heads of household with higher education.

Lastly, differences in levels of well-being have narrowed across urban spatial categories. This is because the most rapid socioeconomic and educational advances among the resident population are being achieved in the periphery, while progress in central areas is slower. It should be noted that differences in baseline levels have an impact on this finding.

[10] This finding is not so unexpected, considering the contrasting socioeconomic trends in these two countries during the 2000s (much stronger in the case of Brazil).

C. Migration in large cities and socioeconomic profile: developments in the 2000s

Large cities are becoming less of a draw for migrants; some are even experiencing net emigration though most continue to post net immigration. Without exception, they still attract the young. City peripheries still have the strongest migrant draw, while central districts continue to push out population, albeit with signs that this trend is slowing. In several cities, flows towards the periphery have diversified, both in terms of their origin (especially in the case of intrametropolitan migrants) and social composition, as high- and middle-income households relocate to the periphery.

Recent census information on net migration and net migration rates in metropolitan areas point to at least two significant stylized facts. First, the weakening draw for migrants —in some cases leading to net emigration— is contributing to the slowdown in cities' population growth. However, most cities posted positive net migration, suggesting that major cities still have a number of pull factors.

Second, metropolitan areas differ in terms of their draw for migrants in different age groups. That they are a magnet for young people (aged 15 to 29) is clearly apparent in cities with negative net migration overall but positive net youth migration. One consequence of this phenomenon —associated with a greater supply of educational establishments, workplaces and recreational facilities for adolescents and young people in large cities— is that migration tends to "rejuvenate" cities and thereby contribute to their growth.[11]

As for the impact of education levels on migration, the findings do not reveal definite patterns but rather suggest that some cities with net immigration, especially in Mexico, are a particularly strong draw for heads of household with high levels of schooling, which might boost their supply of qualified human resources. However, the opposite occurs in other cities with similar trends, notably in Ecuador. The use of ad hoc procedures to estimate the impact of migration on the educational composition of the population in a smaller sample of cities suggests that internal migration tends to slightly reduce the educational level of large cities, fundamentally through the emigration of groups with high and medium levels of education (Rodríguez, 2013).

This evidence indicates that migration between major cities and other settlements in the same country could be losing importance as a factor in the demographic and territorial growth of large cities. By contrast, intrametropolitan migration is crucial to differential population growth between areas. Figure V.1 shows the marked contrast between trends in city centres (as migration senders) and in peripheries (as receivers). Average annual net immigration rates continue to exceed 20 per thousand in the peripheries of several cities, whereas most downtown areas are posting net emigration. However, there are signs that these contrasting patterns are weakening. In the 2000s, few cities witnessed any intensification in the trend for central areas to lose population, with net emigration rates falling in most cases. Meanwhile, very few cities posted an increase in net immigration to their peripheries, whose pull appeared to have diminished sharply in many instances. The periphery's declining pull for migrants may be the result of several factors, but is unlikely to be driven by specific policies and programmes (other than as an indirect consequence of programmes to repopulate central areas) since to date very few cities in the region have applied effective measures to limit their horizontal expansion. It might

[11] This outcome is compatible with the findings of Rodríguez (2013, table 20), who applies a synthetic procedure to estimate the effect of internal migration on the population make-up of a smaller group of large cities.

even be due to the territorial definitions used for cities, since in some cases migration is shifting to more distant outlying areas that are not defined as part of the periphery.[12]

Figure V.1

Latin America (17 selected cities): net migration rates of city centres and peripheries, five-year periods prior to the 2000 and 2010 census rounds [a]

(Per 1,000 inhabitants)

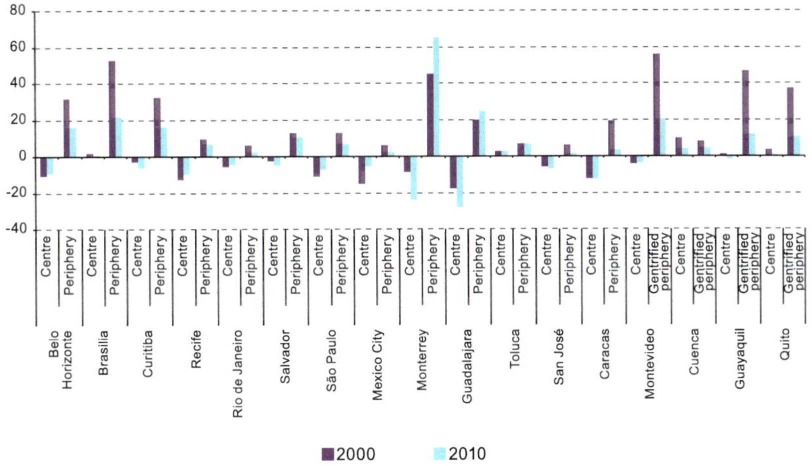

Source: Economic Commission for Latin America and the Caribbean (ECLAC), on the basis of special processing of census microdata.

[a] The centre usually comprises several MIADs and forms a single category, as defined in annex 1 (see table V.A1.1). The "periphery" category, which also comprises several MIADs, refers to the "traditional periphery" unless otherwise indicated (as with Montevideo and cities in Ecuador); this category is also definied in annex 1.

Map V.3 illustrates the situation at the MIAD level for four cities. Clearly, while peripheral tend to pull in migrants, central ones have a push effect.[13] Even so, a variety of migration patterns were observed in both central and peripheral areas, a diversity that is likely to be increasing in several cities. For example, in Mexico City, the central urban area went from a uniformly high emigration rate according to the 2000 census, to a more diverse pattern, with some boroughs drawing in migrants, in 2010. However, as in the other cities, these shifts in migration towards central areas are still incipient and have not yet reversed the overall trend for population loss.

Map V.3

Mexico City, São Paulo (Brazil), San José and Santo Domingo: minor administrative divisions (MIADs) by average annual net migration rate, five-year period prior to the 2010 census round [a]

(Per 1,000 inhabitants)

A. Mexico City: net internal migration rate, by municipality, 2005-2010

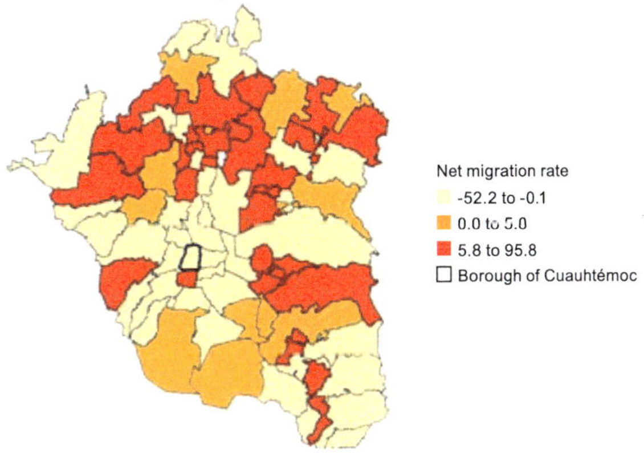

[12] This situation varies from one city to the next and depends on the definitions of traditional periphery and far periphery (for more details, see annex table V.A1.1). The respective data are not included owing to space restrictions, but are available to interested parties on request.

[13] Since the push from central districts is selective, migration not only affects the growth of downtown areas, but also reshapes their demographic and socioeconomic structure and thus has a direct impact on levels and patterns of socioeconomic residential segregation.

Map V.3 (concluded)

B. São Paulo: net internal migration rate, by municipality, 2005-2010

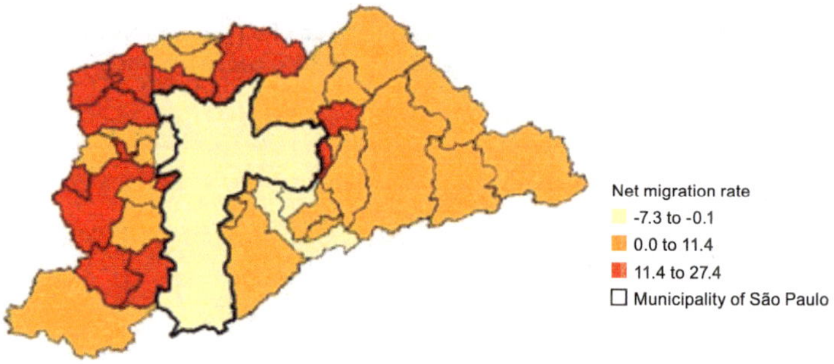

C. San José: net internal migration rate, by canton, 2006-2011

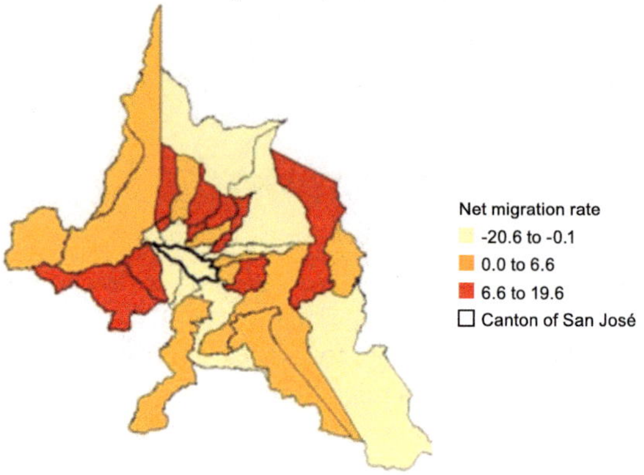

D. Santo Domingo: net internal migration rate, by municipality, 2005-2010

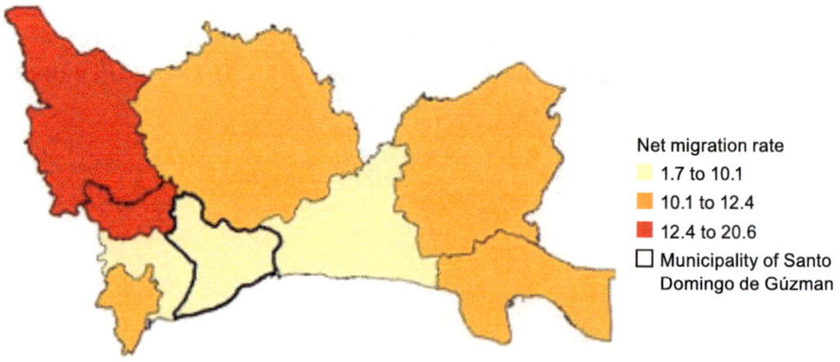

Source: Economic Commission for Latin America and the Caribbean (ECLAC), on the basis of special processing of census microdata.

[a] The categories used in each map refer to terciles of the distribution of municipalities or boroughs, according to population growth rate. Borders outlined in bold denote the central MIAD.

D. Socioeconomic residential segregation: levels and trends

Socioeconomic residential segregation, measured by indices of dissimilarity and exposure, diminished during the 2000s. This is especially due to the downtrend in Brazilian cities, since several cities in other countries recorded increases in socioeconomic residential segregation. The dissimilarity indicator was highest among the upper socioeconomic groups, which confirms that socioeconomic residential segregation is related to the intergenerational reproduction of wealth as well as poverty.

Socioeconomic residential segregation, its trends, consequences and links to the ethnic characteristics of the population and migration, are phenomena which may be analysed on the basis of available census information, using methodological proposals (see box V.1 and annex 1). The following section highlights four key findings that describe the situation in the subject Latin American cities.

Box V.1

Measures of socioeconomic residential segregation

Index of dissimilarity

This is the most frequently used indicator for measuring socioeconomic residential segregation. Popularized by Duncan in the 1950s, it was originally utilized to measure racial residential segregation. While its limitations are well documented (Reardon and O'Sullivan, 2004, Massey and Denton, 1988), it is a relatively robust tool that is useful and easy to understand and calculate. To provide a relatively comprehensive and rigorous picture of socioeconomic residential segregation trends, three socioeconomic variables will be used: the education level of heads of household; the socioeconomic status of households, measured using an ad hoc index (for more details see annex 1); and per capita income (in countries whose censuses record this variable). The latter two indicators make it possible to estimate their distribution in the form of deciles. The top and bottom deciles (in other words, the deciles with the highest and lowest socioeconomic status) are used as a "minority group" when calculating the index of dissimilarity. These deciles correspond to the distribution in each city (see annex 1). Working with groups that maintain their relative proportion of the population during the study period has methodological advantages, because it prevents the measurement of socioeconomic residential segregation over time from being skewed by changes in the relative weight of these groups. This does not occur with the socioeconomic fragmentation variable that deals with the education level of heads of household, whose categories change over time in terms of relative weight within the population. However, working with deciles does not guarantee that the distance between them will stay the same over time, which depends on the heterogeneity of the distribution. To offer a more rigorous spatial analysis, two geographical levels will be used: minor administrative divisions (MIADs: normally municipalities or their equivalent) and even smaller census or administrative divisions (subMIADs: their names and geographical sizes vary from one country to the next, but they include weighting areas in Brazil, with an average population of 32,000 people in the case of São Paulo, and census tracts in Cuenca (Ecuador), with an average population of 1,400 inhabitants). Furthermore, to add rigour to the methodology and to control the exogenous effects of changes in the age structure with regard to the education variable, the study will control for age so as to verify whether the overall trend for all heads of household will remain the same when these are broken down into age groups.

The index of dissimilarity (D) estimates segregation as the "differential spatial distribution" of a particular "interest group" (often termed a "minority"), compared with a reference population, or "the rest of the population". In the United States, where the main object of measurement and monitoring is usually racial segregation, the majority (or reference) group is usually *not* "the rest of the population" but rather the "non-Hispanic white" population (for further details, see [online]: www.census.gov/housing/patterns/data/). Some authors (Martori and Hoberg, 2004) suggest that the first index be referred to as the index of segregation and the second as the index of dissimilarity, though there is not yet a standardized usage in this regard. The index used in this chapter adheres to the following formula:

$$D = \frac{1}{2}\sum\left|\frac{N_{1i}}{N_1} - \frac{N_{2i}}{N_2}\right| \quad (1)$$

where N_1 is the subject group ("the minority"), N_2 the remainder of cases, and i the territorial divisions of the city. The range of this measurement is from zero to one. A score of zero signifies the absence of segregation, because the compared groups have an identical territorial distribution. A score of one denotes maximum segregation, because the two groups are so dissimilar in their distribution that there are no territorial divisions in which both

Box V.1 (concluded)

populations are represented. The value of the index is interpreted as the proportion of the minority group that would have to be redistributed among the territorial divisions of the city in order to achieve zero segregation, which occurs when both groups (the minority and the rest) are equally distributed. This is a technical interpretation that quantifies the magnitude of the redistribution required to arrive at a situation of zero segregation, and is not a practical suggestion for vertical action or intervention. In fact, any attempt to redistribute population within cities should be promoted through incentives and rules that take people's rights into account, while coercive relocation measures must be ruled out. On the other hand, the value of the index is valid for the urban area as a whole, and does not indicate segregated areas, which must be identified by examining distributions, and are potentially those areas in which groups with the lowest socioeconomic status are overrepresented.

Given that dissimilarity is only one of the five dimensions of socioeconomic residential segregation identified in the literature (Massey and Denton, 1988), it may be necessary to include another dimension, linked to the probability of living in the same spatial area (municipality or neighbourhood) with residents from the same and other social groups. The most frequently used indicators for measuring this "exposure" dimension of socioeconomic residential segregation are:

The interaction index (xP*y): the likelihood that an average member of the minority is exposed to interactions with members of the majority in a determined space. The range of the index is from zero to one; the lower the index level the greater the degree of segregation.

$$(2)\quad xP^*y = \sum_{i=1}^{n}\left(\frac{x_i}{X}\right)\left(\frac{y_i}{t_i}\right)$$

Where x_i is the minority population in zone i, X is the total population of the minority in the city, yi= is the majority population zone i, and t_i is the total population in i.

The isolation index (xP*x): the likelihood that an average member of the minority is exposed to interactions with other members of the minority in a determined space. The range of the index is from zero to one; the higher the index level the greater the degree of segregation.

$$(3)\quad xP^*x = \sum_{i=1}^{n}\left(\frac{x_i}{X}\right)\left(\frac{x_i}{t_i}\right)$$

When only two groups are compared, as is the case in this study, which also uses deciles that retain their relative weight in the population, the values of these indices are complementary (xP*y + xP*x = 1). (Massey and Denton, 1988, pages 288-289).

Global Moran's I index

Residential segregation includes an element of geographical agglomeration in territories whose populations share certain socioeconomic attributes. This dimension may be measured by the global Moran's I index, which reveals "spatial dependence", i.e. whether the concentration of observation units according to the variable studied (ad hoc socioeconomic status) makes a statistically significant departure from a random distribution of observation units (which is obtained through simulations).

Moran's index is defined using the formula below:

$$(4)\quad I = \frac{n}{\sum_i\sum_j w_{ij}}\;\frac{\sum_i\sum_j w_{ij}(x_i-\bar{x})(x_j-\bar{x})}{\sum_i\sum_j (x_i-\bar{x})^2}$$

Where n is the number of zones, w_{ij} is a contiguity matrix and x_i are the observations of the variable of interest. Moran's I index has a statistical range from -1 to 1. Values close to 1 represent a positive spatial correlation, those close to -1 indicate a negative spatial correlation and those around -1/(n-1) suggest a random spatial distribution.

Source: Economic Commission for Latin America and the Caribbean (ECLAC).

(i) **Socioeconomic residential segregation, measured as the average of the index of dissimilarity for the cities studied, diminished** during the study period (see figure V.2 and tables V.A2.3a, V.A2.4a and V.A2.5a). However, segregation processes varied greatly between countries, with the outcome almost entirely dependent on the decreases in Brazilian cities (down between 8% and 46% in education, and between 8% and 22% in the top and bottom deciles of the socioeconomic index).[14] In fact, if the average of the sample is calculated for all countries excluding Brazil, not only is the overall downtrend much less pronounced, but is actually reversed in the cases of the least educated group and the group with the lowest socioeconomic status, at least at MIAD level. Although this finding may seem striking, it shouldn't be, according to the specialized literature on the region which, as noted previously, supports the theory that socioeconomic residential segregation is decreasing, at least at aggregate geographical levels such as minor administrative divisions. This finding remains valid even for more disaggergated geographical scales, although unfortunately time comparisons on a such scales are not possible for several of the cities studied, and therefore have not been included in this chapter.

14 These figures are compatible with the findings of recent research in that country; for example, Carvalho and others (2013). Specific analyses on Brazilian cities are available from the Observatory of the Metropolis, see [online] http://www.observatoriodasmetropoles.net/.

Figure V.2

Latin America (selected cities): index of dissimilarity by education group, highest and lowest socioeconomic deciles, and highest and lowest deciles of the household income distribution, including and excluding cities in Brazil, 2000 and 2010 censuses

(Simple averages)

A. Latin America (22 selected cities):[a] index of dissimilarity (at the level of minor administrative divisions) of three education groups, including and excluding Brazilian cities, 2000 and 2010 censuses

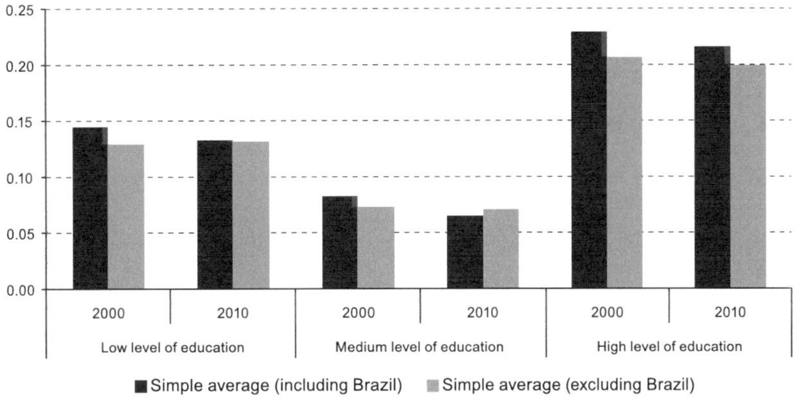

B. Latin America (17 selected cities):[b] simple average of the index of dissimilarity (at the level of minor administrative divisions) of the top and bottom socioeconomic deciles, including and excluding Brazilian cities, 2000 and 2010 censuses

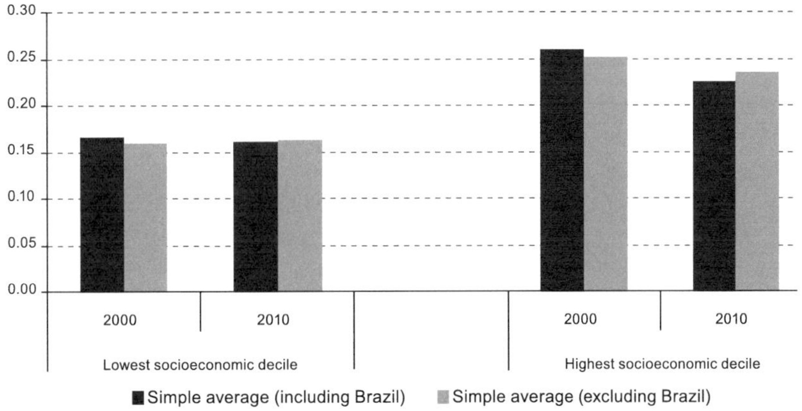

C. Latin America (8 selected cities):[c] simple average of the index of dissimilarity (at the level of minor administrative divisions) of the top and bottom deciles of the per capita household income distribution, 2000 and 2010 censuses

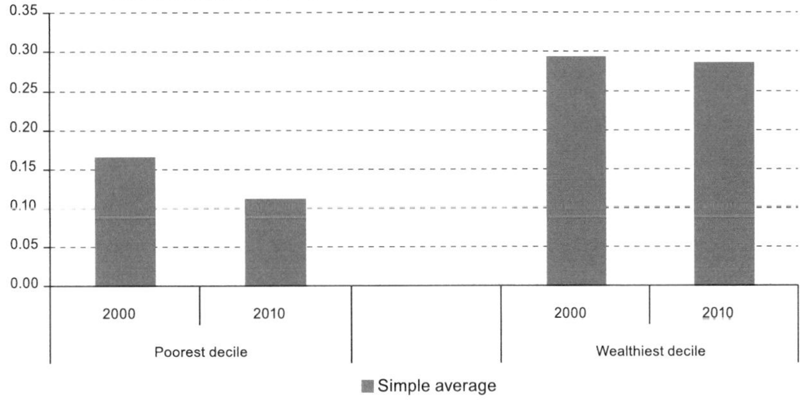

Source: Economic Commission for Latin America and the Caribbean (ECLAC), on the basis of special processing of census microdata.

[a] Buenos Aires (Argentina), Caracas, Maracaibo (Bolivarian Republic of Venezuela), Belo Horizonte, Brasilia, Curitiba, Recife, Rio de Janeiro, Salvador, São Paulo (Brazil), San José (Costa Rica), Santo Domingo (Dominican Republic), Cuenca, Guayaquil, Quito (Ecuador), Guadalajara, Mexico City, Monterrey, Toluca (Mexico), Panama City (Panama), Lima (Peru), Montevideo (Uruguay).

[b] Caracas, Maracaibo (Bolivarian Republic of Venezuela), Belo Horizonte, Brasilia, Curitiba, Recife, Rio de Janeiro, Salvador, São Paulo (Brazil), San José (Costa Rica), Santo Domingo (Dominican Republic), Guadalajara, Mexico City, Monterrey, Toluca (Mexico), Panama City (Panama), Montevideo (Uruguay).

[c] Brazil (Belo Horizonte, Brasilia, Curitiba, Recife, Rio de Janeiro, Salvador, São Paulo) and Panama (Panama City).

The downtrend in socioeconomic residential segregation is also seen in the exposure indicators (see figure V.3 and table V.A2.6).[15]

Figure V.3

Latin America (14 selected cities):[a] interaction and isolation indices, at the level of minor administrative divisions, for the top and bottom deciles of the ad hoc socioeconomic status variable, 2000 and 2010 censuses

(Simple average)

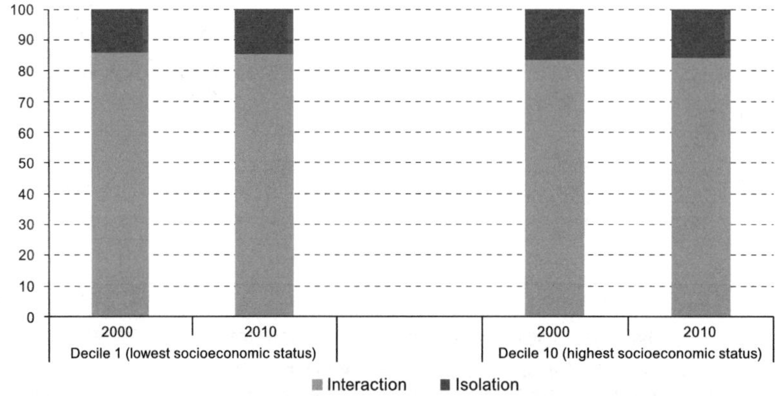

Source: Economic Commission for Latin America and the Caribbean (ECLAC), on the basis of special processing of census microdata using REDATAM.
[a] Belo Horizonte, Brasilia, Curitiba, Recife, Rio de Janeiro, Salvador, São Paulo (Brazil), San José (Costa Rica), Santo Domingo (Dominican Republic), Guadalajara, Mexico City, Monterrey, Toluca (Mexico) and Panama City (Panama).

(ii) **Socioeconomic residential segregation is invariably greater among groups with higher socioeconomic status,** which reflects how strongly they are influenced by mechanisms that perpetuate residential exclusion and the desire for territorial distinctiveness and exclusivity (see figure V.2 and, in annex 2, tables V.A2.3 and V.A2.4). The simple average of the index of dissimilarity at the MIAD level in the cities studied is greater than 0.2 for the most educated group and for the top socioeconomic decile. This means that a fifth of the population is thought to be residing in areas in which it is underrepresented in comparison with the spatial distribution of the rest of the population. Again, this is a technical interpretation that quantifies the magnitude of socioeconomic residential segregation and is in no way a suggestion that population redistribution within cities should be imposed. By contrast, the simple average of the index of dissimilarity is in the region of 0.15 for the group with the lowest education and the lowest socioeconomic status.

(iii) **The exposure indices for the top and bottom deciles and the rest of the population paint a picture of socioeconomic residential segregation that is less intense** at MIAD level, with the interaction index for the latest censuses yielding values of above 0.80 (see figure V.3). However, where the calculations consider only the extreme groups (wealthiest and poorest deciles), the exposure indices reveal much greater segregation. For example, in Mexico City the interaction index of the top and bottom deciles was lower than 0.50 in 2010, suggesting that on average one in two individuals from the poorest decile resides in a MIAD where the wealthiest decile is not present among the population. In São Paulo, also in 2010, the isolation index on the smallest geographical scale (subMIAD) stood at 0.73 for the upper socioeconomic decile, suggesting that on average almost three out of four people lived in neighbourhoods with people of the same socioeconomic status, and only one in four lived with somebody of a different status.

(iv) **Notwithstanding the average trend, several of the studied cities registered increases in socioeconomic residential segregation for either the top, the bottom or both the extreme socioeconomic deciles** in one or both of the socioeconomic variables (see tables V.A2.3 and V.A2.4 in annex 2).

15 The only indicator of socioeconomic residential segregation to register a different trend is the Global Moran's I index. However, a detailed examination of the cities where this index presents an increase revealed a wide variety of situations, preventing the identification of a common pattern.

In short, the finding that socioeconomic residential segregation is in decline seems to be confirmed, since a number of different measurements support this. However, this general observation masks the fact that socioeconomic residential segregation is increasing in several of the cities considered. Meanwhile, there is no robust evidence to determine which socioeconomic group is experiencing the steepest fall in segregation. All of the above points to the existence of fairly heterogeneous processes in the region, and thus the need to study each city in greater detail and on its own merit, to understand the specific factors behind socioeconomic residential segregation trends.

E. Impact of internal migration on socioeconomic residential segregation in large cities in the region

New procedures were applied to quantify the effect of internal migration, including intrametropolitan migration, on the educational make-up of different areas of cities and their socioeconomic residential segregation. Significant impacts were discovered in several cases, notably increased education levels in peripheral areas that received immigration from high and medium socioeconomic groups, mostly from within the same city. However, migration was not found to systematically diminish residential segregation, meaning that its decrease must be due to other factors.

To gain a deeper understanding of residential segregation and its evolution over the past decade, this section analyses the impact of internal migration on changes in the age and education composition of central and peripheral areas of cities.[16]

In terms of age structure, considering only the results of the 2010 census (see table V.1), migration is pushing down the percentage of children (aged 15 and under) in central areas in the selected cities.[17] In peripheral areas, the main effect of migration is to reduce the percentage of older adults (aged 60 and over).[18]

In education, again considering only the results of the 2010 census (see table V.1), the picture is less stylized, since the consequences of migration differ considerably from one city to the next. In most of them, migration tends to reduce the proportion of heads of household with low levels of education, owing to the fact that migrants to the periphery[19] are less likely to be concentrated in the "least educated" group than those who already reside there.

---

16 As explained in other studies (Rodríguez, 2010 and 2012), dissimilarity trends might reflect changes in the composition of neighbourhoods with little mobility (for example, because of socioeconomic ups and downs that create a more symmetrical territorial distribution) or patterns of spatial mobility (intra- and extra-metropolitan migration) that are socioeconomically and territorially selective (or a combination of both processes although they could have opposite effects). Either way, the two cases differ greatly in theoretical and, above all, political terms.

17 This is because children are overrepresented in population outflows from downtown areas, where emigration is the predominant pattern (see figure V.1), owing to the departure of households in the early stages of family life. Meanwhile, inflows contain few children since central districts primarily attract young people and childless adults.

18 In population flows to peripheral areas, where immigration is the prevailing trend (see figure V.1), young adults are overrepresented and older adults are underrepresented, since many of the households that migrate to the periphery are in the initial and intermediate stages of the family life cycle.

19 Since the periphery is a draw, the effect of immigration on its educational make-up largely depends on the volume and education level of immigrants.

In some cities, migration has a stronger positive effect on education levels because it also raises the proportion of heads of household with higher education. This is true of most Mexican cities, though not the capital. In most cities, the centre is trending toward education-based dualization because of migration, which increases the proportion of heads of household in the lowest educational category. This is because the emigration of those with medium education levels, raises proportionally the share of heads of household with a low education level, at the same time as the immigration of young, highly qualified population segments generally raises the percentage of heads of household with high levels of education. Lastly, table V.1 shows that, without exception, migration reinforces the characteristics of gentrified peripheries by significantly boosting their education levels. In relation to these neighbourhoods, the calculations given in table V.1 estimate a coefficient for the relatively well-known processes that have been described in recent literature on changes in the peripheries of large cities in the region (Aguilar and Escanilla, 2011; ECLAC, 2012; De Mattos, 2010). The results show that the socioeconomic profile of the "gentrified periphery" is undergoing a rapid transformation in its owing to massive migration of highly educated individuals and households, many including young families.

Table V.1

Latin America (18 selected cities): effect of total internal migration on the age and educational composition of populations living in central and peripheral urban areas, 2000 and 2010 censuses [a]

(Percentages)

Metropolitan area	Broad urban area	2000 census round				2010 census round			
		Children	Older adults	Heads of household with low education level	Heads of household with high education level	Children	Older adults	Heads of household with low education level	Heads of household with high education level
Belo Horizonte	Centre	-3.03	2.29	-1.78	4.91	-3.61	1.45	-1.12	1.70
	Periphery	0.28	-5.11	-0.19	-2.40	-0.24	-2.66	-0.37	-0.19
	Gentrified periphery	-0.26	-3.84	-2.88	29.81	-0.94	-2.38	-5.11	18.24
Brasilia	Centre	-2.99	-2.76	-3.13	8.44	-3.63	-1.56	-1.72	3.78
	Periphery	-2.43	-11.09	-0.13	-5.64	-1.48	-3.31	-0.78	2.35
Curitiba	Centre	-3.11	0.08	-1.78	3.63	-3.57	0.65	-1.18	2.41
	Periphery	-0.09	-6.25	-1.69	11.00	-1.48	-2.61	-1.56	8.41
Recife	Centre	-0.69	2.62	0.60	1.37	-0.69	2.03	0.24	1.30
	Periphery	-0.26	-0.35	-1.23	5.74	-0.36	-0.25	-0.28	-1.53
Rio de Janeiro	Centre	-1.01	-0.52	0.43	0.26	-1.17	-0.65	0.30	-0.20
	Periphery	-0.17	-0.91	-0.11	-0.37	-0.13	-0.17	0.26	-1.20
	Gentrified periphery	-2.25	-3.35	-7.11	21.44	1.86	-3.71	-6.05	12.65
Salvador	Centre	-1.32	0.48	-0.01	0.46	-0.85	0.59	0.29	-1.12
	Periphery	-1.08	1.34	-0.78	11.64	-0.19	-0.91	-0.87	0.75
	Gentrified periphery	-4.54	-4.01	-7.71	33.94	-4.00	-1.53	-5.77	16.73
São Paulo	Centre	-2.13	-0.17	-0.21	1.62	-2.38	-0.27	-0.00	0.87
	Periphery	-0.82	-2.99	-1.37	2.15	-1.11	-1.80	-0.35	1.25
	Periphery elitizada	-0.58	-3.36	-0.24	5.85	-0.68	-1.11	-0.51	3.75
San José	Centre	-1.9	1.2	0.83	-0.60	-1.99	1.12	-0.31	0.02
	Near periphery	-0.8	-0.8	-0.62	1.25	-1.34	-0.31	-0.87	2.00
	Far periphery	-0.3	-2.3	-1.84	8.16	-0.09	-0.82	-2.04	5.09
Santo Domingo	Centre	-2.2	0.6	0.14	0.17	-1.66	-0.06	0.05	0.31
	Near periphery	-1.7	0.1	0.17	0.15	-1.19	1.99	-0.25	0.32
	Far periphery	-1.2	-0.2	-0.01	0.22	-1.45	-0.52	-0.43	1.63

Table V.1 (concluded)

Metropolitan area	Broad urban area	2000 census round: Children	2000 census round: Older adults	2000 census round: Heads of household with low education level	2000 census round: Heads of household with high education level	2010 census round: Children	2010 census round: Older adults	2010 census round: Heads of household with low education level	2010 census round: Heads of household with high education level
Cuenca	Centre	-2.4	-3.2	1.6	-2.20	-2.20	-1.39	1.09	-1.57
	Periphery	-0.9	-2.7	-0.7	4.75	-0.07	-1.27	-0.27	2.23
Guayaquil	Centre	-1.0	1.0	2.47	-2.35	0.04	-1.87	1.19	-3.33
	Periphery	-2.9	-2.8	-0.62	11.52	-0.03	0.32	-0.99	-6.23
Quito	Centre	-2.7	-1.6	2.03	-2.61	-1.88	-0.71	0.74	-0.66
	Periphery	-2.3	-5.7	-4.71	7.93	-0.95	-2.62	-0.41	0.07
Guadalajara	Centre	-2.1	5.6	2.86	-2.83	-5.10	9.52	7.67	-5.11
	Periphery	-0.7	-4.3	-4.82	9.09	-0.71	-4.58	-8.20	15.73
Mexico City	Centre	-4.5	3.1	-0.2	3.1	-3.53	0.23	-1.54	3.75
	Periphery	-0.3	-0.6	-0.7	-0.4	-0.20	-0.57	-0.75	-1.04
Monterrey	Centre	-2.0	3.1	2.37	1.28	-4.99	10.03	8.31	3.80
	Periphery	-1.4	-11.6	-4.57	16.03	0.90	-20.07	-11.78	16.26
Toluca	Centre	0.3	1.5	-1.07	3.19	-0.61	0.52	-2.45	7.62
	Periphery	-0.0	0.9	-0.48	4.69	-0.29	-5.48	-4.15	9.80
Montevideo	Centre	-2.3	-0.5	0.43	-0.24	-2.65	-0.53	0.20	0.16
	Gentrified periphery	0.4	-8.9	-4.56	2.89	-1.54	-3.12	-5.77	7.23
	Poor periphery	0.7	-3.1	-0.42	-0.02	0.98	-0.91	0.22	-4.97
Caracas	Centre	-1.2	3.0	1.91	-3.90	-1.19	2.99	1.91	-3.90
	First ring	-1.1	-1.6	-1.90	2.41	-1.15	-0.57	-1.90	2.41
	Inner periphery	-0.9	-1.4	-1.27	1.65	-0.94	-0.77	-1.27	1.65
	Outer periphery	-0.1	-4.2	-1.11	1.66	-0.05	-0.55	-1.11	1.66

Source: Economic Commission for Latin America and the Caribbean (ECLAC), on the basis of special processing of census microdata.
[a] The "periphery" category in the above table refers to one of the types of periphery that make up the "broad urban areas"; unless otherwise indicated it refers to the "traditional periphery".

This calculation does not permit the estimation of the effect of migration on socioeconomic residential segregation, since the latter is measured on a more disaggregated scale than that of "broad urban areas" (see item (vi) in annex 1) —generally at the MIAD level, because this is the most disaggregated scale on which migration is measured in censuses. Moreover, this effect does not depend only on developments in the centre and at the periphery, but on what occurs throughout the metropolitan area. Table V.2 therefore applies the procedure devised by the Latin American and Caribbean Demographic Centre (CELADE)-Population Division of ECLAC to estimate the effect of migration on socioeconomic residential segregation. The figures in the table refer to the percentage change in the index of dissimilarity as a result of migration. If the values are negative, it means that migration caused a drop in the index and therefore in socioeconomic residential segregation, while positive values mean that migration caused the index to rise, thereby driving up socioeconomic residential segregation. The results do not permit a general conclusion for all of the region's cities, since the effects of any increase or decrease are shared between them. According to an examination of the five-year period prior to the latest census, it would be premature to say that internal migration plays a decisive role in reducing segregation. One need only look at Brazil to realize that, while the index of dissimilarity is falling for all cities and for all three education groups, migration exerts a positive influence on the index in numerous cases (cities or education groups). In fact, in most Brazilian cities, internal migration tended to increase the index of dissimilarity.

Table V.2

Latin America (18 selected cities): change in the index of dissimilarity due to internal migration (including intrametropolitan migration) for three education groups, at the level of minor administrative divisions (MIADs), 2000 and 2010 censuses

(Percentages)

City		Total 2000	Intrametropolitan 2000	Total 2010	Intrametropolitan 2010
Belo Horizonte	Heads of household with basic education	4.3	3.2	0.8	0.6
	Heads of household with secondary education	3.1	1.6	(1.4)	(4.0)
	Heads of household with higher education	7.0	5.6	3.5	3.0
Brasilia	Heads of household with basic education	16.2	12.2	5.2	2.9
	Heads of household with secondary education	11.1	10.0	(3.2)	(1.3)
	Heads of household with higher education	19.9	15.8	7.2	5.6
Curitiba	Heads of household with basic education	3.4	1.4	(0.5)	(1.6)
	Heads of household with secondary education	(3.2)	(3.3)	(2.7)	(2.2)
	Heads of household with higher education	7.6	4.8	2.3	0.6
Recife	Heads of household with basic education	(6.0)	(5.7)	(3.8)	(1.6)
	Heads of household with secondary education	(3.6)	(2.1)	13.4	10.9
	Heads of household with higher education	(2.5)	(2.7)	1.7	1.5
Rio de Janeiro	Heads of household with basic education	0.9	1.3	0.2	0.6
	Heads of household with secondary education	(2.4)	(2.3)	3.8	3.2
	Heads of household with higher education	4.2	3.0	1.9	1.4
Salvador	Heads of household with basic education	0.7	(3.6)	(3.1)	(3.8)
	Heads of household with secondary education	1.0	(4.7)	(5.3)	(4.9)
	Heads of household with higher education	(0.4)	(2.6)	3.4	1.3
São Paulo	Heads of household with basic education	5.3	2.9	0.7	(0.2)
	Heads of household with secondary education	2.7	1.7	12.9	7.3
	Heads of household with higher education	7.5	4.5	3.7	1.8
San José (expanded)	Heads of household with basic education	(2.3)	(3.4)	0.0	(1.6)
	Heads of household with secondary education	(1.3)	(1.3)	2.7	4.4
	Heads of household with higher education	(1.0)	(2.2)	1.9	0.6
Santo Domingo	Heads of household with basic education	3.1	(0.5)	0.3	(0.7)
	Heads of household with secondary education	(3.4)	(0.5)	5.3	1.1
	Heads of household with higher education	1.9	(0.3)	0.1	(1.0)
Cuenca	Heads of household with basic education	(3.6)	(1.1)	(0.8)	(0.4)
	Heads of household with secondary education	(2.2)	(0.6)	(0.6)	(0.4)
	Heads of household with higher education	(2.8)	(0.7)	(0.5)	(0.1)
Guayaquil	Heads of household with basic education	(8.1)	(7.3)	1.7	(0.3)
	Heads of household with secondary education	3.6	1.4	12.2	7.3
	Heads of household with higher education	(3.1)	(5.7)	8.2	5.8
Quito	Heads of household with basic education	(12.2)	(10.8)	0.5	(0.3)
	Heads of household with secondary education	9.0	12.0	3.0	2.6
	Heads of household with higher education	(1.7)	(3.4)	6.4	1.2
Guadalajara	Heads of household with basic education	(9.7)	(11.8)	(24.0)	(19.9)
	Heads of household with secondary education	6.2	(9.0)	74.1	54.0
	Heads of household with higher education	7.3	4.3	3.3	0.7
Mexico City	Heads of household with basic education	(2.9)	(3.6)	4.4	3.6
	Heads of household with secondary education	8.3	7.9	12.5	12.5
	Heads of household with higher education	4.0	2.6	4.1	3.5
Monterrey	Heads of household with basic education	20.0	15.8	20.0	21.3
	Heads of household with secondary education	20.6	21.5	40.5	39.4
	Heads of household with higher education	1.3	(0.2)	2.8	0.4
Toluca	Heads of household with basic education	(0.5)	(0.9)	(0.2)	(1.3)
	Heads of household with secondary education	(6.2)	(2.8)	6.8	(3.3)
	Heads of household with higher education	(1.1)	(2.7)	3.7	(0.2)
Panama City	Heads of household with basic education	(25.9)	(22.6)	(16.9)	(16.2)
	Heads of household with secondary education	(0.3)	(17.3)	(4.0)	(4.2)
	Heads of household with higher education	(21.0)	(24.6)	(5.1)	(6.0)
Lima	Heads of household with basic education			3.6	3.1
	Heads of household with secondary education			9.2	7.1
	Heads of household with higher education			6.0	4.7
Montevideo	Heads of household with basic education			18.9	13.3
	Heads of household with secondary education			27.7	12.2
	Heads of household with higher education			15.3	11.6

Source: Economic Commission for Latin America and the Caribbean (ECLAC), on the basis of special processing of census microdata.

So why did this increase not ultimately occur? Not counting the limitations of measuring migration in censuses, and in the applied methodology,[20] the explanation is found in the other proximate determinants of segregation, especially the increase in the education levels of the population as a whole and in the municipalities or neighbourhoods with lower education levels,[21] which was the prevailing trend in the region and especially in Brazil during a decade of well-documented social and educational improvements (ECLAC, 2014). The fall in socioeconomic residential segregation would therefore be circumstantial and not attributable to specific policies, which largely function by providing incentives for relocation, intended to improve socioeconomic diversity in certain urban areas. Considering that the downtrend is situational, there is no certainty that it will continue, so subsequent decreases will probably require more targeted and explicit public action, which should take into account the experiences gained in the field, which will be discussed in the final section of this chapter.

F. Effects of residential segregation on cities, communities, households and individuals

Socioeconomic residential segregation, operating through a number of mechanisms, tends to reproduce existing socioeconomic inequalities in cities. The "neighbourhood effect" adds to the disadvantages facing young people in segregated areas, as is reflected by the increased likelihood of teenage pregnancy among residents. And inequalities in municipal budgets illustrate the neglect of poor areas in terms of local resources and private investment.

In the aforementioned debate over the effects of socioeconomic residential segregation, the specialized literature generally takes the view that the phenomenon has a negative impact on people and communities —especially segregated communities— and also on the governance and functioning of cities. This view is based on the conviction that a person's place of residence influences his or her life path because: (i) it is crucial for building social networks (social capital) and for learning patterns of behaviour, codes and knowledge that are important for social performance; (ii) it is linked to the quality and quantity of available public goods, essential institutions (such as schools), government and local budgets, and private investment and jobs; (iii) it is related to exposure to various types of risk (safety, sanitation or natural disasters); and (iv) it is associated with stigma and social status (Sampson, 2012; Katzman, 2009; Zubrinsky, 2003).

From this perspective, socioeconomic residential segregation creates adversity for the people and areas that are segregated through various mechanisms, including socialization and instrumental mechanisms. Socialization mechanisms are related to social learning and its effect on the reproduction of behaviours, and they mainly affect children, adolescents and young adults. Instrumental mechanisms basically impact adults and deal with access to the resources[22] associated with territorial location and its physical, social, political and symbolic dimensions.

[20] For a more detailed examination of these limitations, see Rodríguez (2011).

[21] This may also have occurred with the other two variables used to measure segregation in this chapter. However, the nature of these variables (whose values may change during the reference period, including as a direct result of migration) means that the procedure used with education levels cannot be applied to them (Rodríguez, 2011). In fact, the procedure used with education levels was only applied to the population of heads of household aged over 24, in order to comply with the assumption of constant education levels over the last five years.

[22] Or capital, in its various forms according to the definition by Bourdie (1986, pages 46-47).

The socialization mechanism incorporates a variety of theoretical models that emphasize specific channels of influence. At least six models have been identified in the English-language literature,[23] while Latin American research focuses above all on daily peer-to-peer exchange as a process of acquiring codes, naturalizing practices and reproducing behaviours (imitation); collective socialization, which depends on adult role models and normative effectiveness, and institutional socialization, particularly through the influence of school.

As regards instrumental mechanisms, research conducted in English-speaking countries mentions at least three models.[24] The main ones identified in Latin America and the Caribbean are those of the opportunity structure[25] —in terms of public goods, relevant institutions and the networks, knowledge and skills needed for the labour market—, and "stigma". According to the second of these models, people who live in segregated and stigmatized neighbourhoods suffer discrimination in terms of access to the labour market, transport services and credit, as well as bias on the part of the police, the judiciary and the State in general (including teachers and basic service providers).

Empirical support for these ideas, which describe the adversity brought about by socioeconomic residential segregation, is largely provided by the research carried out in developed countries, particularly the United States (Kaztman, 2007; Zubrinsky, 2003). Research studies carried out in Latin America during the 2000s also offer support for this hypothesis (see box V.2).

Box V.2

Selected research on the neighbourhood effect in Latin America, 2000-2014

In Latin America, few studies have investigated the effects of urban residential segregation on the expectations and behaviours of residents in socially homogenous neighbourhoods. The little research that does exist refers to a "neighbourhood effect" in terms of educational achievement, unemployment, job quality and teenage motherhood. The studies on spatial segregation and employment are descriptive, and usually suggest that the residents of uniformly poor neighbourhoods find it harder to gain employment, owing to difficulties in reaching their workplaces, the want of job opportunities in their own neighbourhoods, and a lack of information and contacts that would help them find and secure positions (Gómez and Amitrano, 2005). A study on Montevideo confirmed that there were positive correlations between the level of social homogeneity of poor neighbourhoods, unemployment rates, the proportion of the economically active population (EAP) working informally without social protection, and the proportion of young people not in education or seeking employment (Kaztman and Retamoso, 2005). Several studies describe significant associations between the characteristics of neighbourhoods and risky behaviours among children and adolescents, which help perpetuate urban inequalities and drive the mechanisms whereby poverty is reproduced from one generation to the next. One such example is the neighbourhood effect on the reproductive behaviours of adolescents (Sabatini, Cáceres and Cerda, 2001). Another type of research examines the consequences of residing in certain neighbourhoods on academic performance variables, such as evaluations of learning performance, school dropout rates among adolescents, over-age students, and average years of schooling completed, among others. Lastly, some studies look at the relationship between the social characteristics of the neighbourhood and the average number of young people not in work, looking for work, or enrolled in education. Generally speaking, the risk inherent to the above-mentioned behaviours (early reproduction, falling behind at school, dropping out, unemployment and discouragement) is that they prevent individuals from acquiring the assets they need for full social integration through the market, society and the State; they also constitute an infringement of basic rights, such as the right to timely and appropriate sexual and reproductive health, to good-quality schooling and to decent work.

There has also been a wave of more recent studies using data from the 2000 round of censuses, specialized surveys and rather more qualitative methodologies (ethnographies) (Andrade and Silveira, 2013; Solís and Puga, 2011; Ribeiro and others, 2010; Ribeiro and Koslinksi, 2009, Roberts and Wilson, 2009). This body of research demonstrates the persistence of adverse effects associated with residence in segregated areas. For example, one study (Solís and Puga, 2011, page 233) proposed to test how the socioeconomic status of residential areas affected eight educational and occupational outcomes, and found that the effects were significant in five of the eight outcomes. Similarly, Andrade and Silveira (2013, page 385) summarized recent research on the favelas of Brazil, according to which, based on the same parameters of comparison and controlling for variables such as age, years of schooling, sex and occupation, favela residents are always outperformed by non-favela residents.

Source: R. Kaztman, "La calidad de las relaciones sociales en las grandes ciudades de América Latina: viejos y nuevos determinantes", *Pensamiento Iberoamericano*, No. 1, Madrid, 2007, page 195 and Economic Commission for Latin America and the Caribbean (ECLAC).

[23] Epidemic, collective socialization, institutional, linguistic isolation, oppositional culture and relative deprivation (Small and Newman, 2001, cited in Andrade and Silveira, 2013).

[24] The networks isolation model, the resources model, and the limitation of political alliances model (Small and Newman, 2001, cited in Andrade and Silveira, 2013).

[25] Defined by Kaztman (1999) in his seminal work.

This section contains an empirical analysis of the some of the mechanisms that drive socioeconomic residential segregation. One such mechanism is the "neighbourhood effect" on the behaviours of children and adolescents, especially with regard to their likelihood of becoming a teenage mother. Figure V.4 and table V.3 show an approximation of this effect in the case of Brazil.[26] In figure V.4, it is shown that the probability of a Brazilian woman becoming a mother by the age of 19 is invariably higher for favela residents, even after controlling for per capita household income and filtering only those women that have always resided in the same municipality.

Figure V.4

Brazil: women aged 19 who are mothers and who have always resided in the same municipality, by per capita household income and favela residence or non-residence, 2000

(Percentages and multiples of the minimum wage)

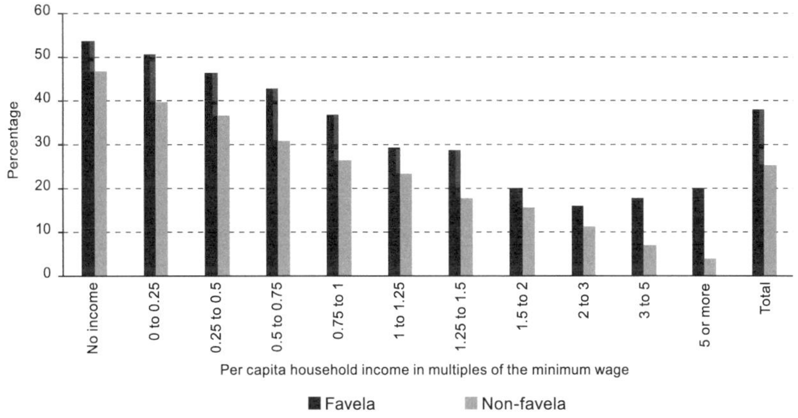

Source: Economic Commission for Latin America and the Caribbean (ECLAC), on the basis of special processing of 2000 census microdata.

Table V.3

Rio de Janeiro (Brazil): women aged 19 and 20 who have always resided in the same municipality and who live with heads of household who have completed secondary or higher education, by income level and neighbourhood of residence, 2010 census

(Total number of women, number of mothers, and percentage of mothers)

	Area	Total	Mothers	Percentage of mothers
Per capita income over 1.25 times the minimum wage	Total city	49 758	3 674	7.4
	Favela Rocinha	148	33	22.3
	Favela Complexo do Alemão	209	24	11.5
	Favela Maré	462	149	32.3
	Three favelas combined	819	206	25.2
	Tijuca	1 414	23	1.6
Per capita income equal to or less than 0.75 times the minimum wage	Total city	63 049	20 644	32.7
	Favela Rocinha	354	147	41.5
	Favela Complexo do Alemão	965	365	37.8
	Favela Maré	910	285	31.3
	Three favelas combined	2 229	797	35.8
	Tijuca	264	73	27.7

Source: Economic Commission for Latin America and the Caribbean (ECLAC), on the basis of special processing of 2010 census microdata.

26 Brazilian census data are especially useful for this estimate, because (i) they include a module on migration that identifies individuals who have never moved from their municipality; (ii) the 2000 census contains a variable that identifies all housing units located in favelas, so that these can be used as examples of segregated neighbourhoods; (iii) the long-form census questionnaire contains several questions on social performance; (iv) in the 2010 census, the long-form questionnaire does not include the questions on social performance (a few such questions are included in the short-form questionnaire) but it is possible to identify specific favelas using the names and codes of weighting areas, the smallest territorial units of the sample to which the long-form questionnaire is applied. Using both censuses, results were obtained that suggested a neighbourhood effect, in this instance a "favela effect", as may be observed in figure V.4 and table V.3.

Table V.3 shows the stark contrast between segregated and exclusive neighbourhoods. Based on 2010 census data, the table compares women aged 19 and 20 living in three densely-populated favelas of Rio de Janeiro with women of the same age residing in the city's prosperous Tijuca neighbourhood. To control for income, two groups were used. Of the women who lived in households with a per capita income of more than 1.25 times the minimum wage, 25.2% of those living in the three selected favelas were mothers, compared with just 1.6% of their counterparts in Tijuca. In the case of women whose per capita household income was less than 0.75 times the minimum wage, 35.8% of favela residents were mothers, compared with 27.7% of their counterparts in Tijuca.

Another mechanism linked with socioeconomic residential segregation is the availability of resources for segregated areas. Disparities in local income continue to feed back into territorial inequalities and amplify the effects of segregation. By way of illustration, figure V.5 presents the per capita municipal budgets of Mexico City and São Paulo, broken down by broad urban areas. In São Paulo, both the central area (the municipality of São Paulo) and the gentrified periphery have higher than average budgets, while the traditional poor periphery is allocated a budget that is well below the average for the city. A similar pattern prevails in Mexico City, although in 2010 the municipal income of the far periphery shot up, overtaking the average level for the city.

Figure V.5

Mexico City and São Paulo: per capita municipal income, by broad urban area, 2000 and 2010

(Whole city=100)

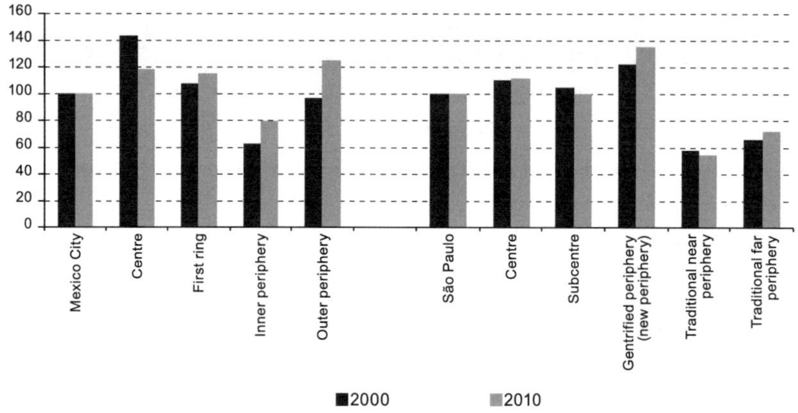

Source: For municipalities of Mexico City: National Institute of Statistics and Geography (INEGI), "Ingresos Brutos Municipales, 2000-2012", *Estadística de Finanzas Públicas Estatales y Municipales* [online] http://sc.inegi.org.mx/sistemas/cobdem/index.jsp; for boroughs of Mexico City: INEGI, "Finanzas públicas de las delegaciones del Distrito Federal 1999-2012", *Estadística de Finanzas Públicas Estatales y Municipales* [online] http://www.inegi.org.mx/est/lista_cubos/consulta.aspx?p=adm&c=2; for São Paulo: Ministry of Finance, Secretariat of the Treasury, "Rec Orçamentária" = Receitas correntes + Receitas de Capital + Deduções da Receita Corrente + Receitas Correntes Intra-Orçamentárias + Receitas de Capital Intra-Orçamentárias", FINBRA – *Finanças do Brasil – Dados Contábeis dos Municípios*, 2000, 2010 [online] www.tesouro.fazenda.gov.br/contas-anuais.

G. Ethnic segregation and international inmigrants

Indigenous migrants and international immigrants also display distinctive localization patterns in cities. Frequently, they cluster in specific areas whose functions are conducive to the newcomers' integration and performance. However, on examining these areas, shortcomings of various kinds become apparent, suggesting that these groups suffer from a number of persistent exclusion mechanisms in large cities.

1. Indigenous peoples

The indigenous peoples of Latin America are not immune to the territorial processes that are shaping the region, particularly rapid urbanization and the preference for living in large towns and cities (metropolises and megalopolises). Recent information from countries with available data from the 2010 census round revealed that slightly more than 50% of the indigenous population now lives in urban areas. Addressing this situation presents a considerable public policy challenge.

Several studies have suggested that the increasing urbanization of indigenous peoples poses some major concerns, especially a potential loss of identity and culture. To counter the risk, indigenous peoples deploy a variety of strategies in an attempt to maintain their sociocultural system and retain their ties with their communities of origin. Some of these strategies are related to their choice of neighbourhood (Camus, 2002; Del Popolo and others, 2007). Studies have also provided evidence to suggest that, for many indigenous people, moving to urban areas has exacerbated the poverty in which they live, since they often inhabit marginal, precarious areas, subject to environmental and social risks and a lack of security; these areas often lack access to decent jobs and basic services such as health and education. Indigenous migrants also run the constant risk of trafficking and exploitation, among other factors that threaten the exercise of their rights in the urban environment (ECLAC, 2007 and 2014).

For indigenous peoples, cultural factors and symbolic dimensions —such as the preservation and strength of links with their ancestral territories and original sociocultural systems— mediate certain aspects of the urban relocation process, including the social and economic motivations for migration, physical location within the cities themselves, and relationships with the urban environment. As a result, indigenous populations in cities assume a complex structure of spatial relations that varies between countries, cities, peoples and even generations.

The urbanization of the indigenous population is a dynamic phenomenon that has diverse and multifaceted implications, some of which are favourable to the population in question. In this respect, León (2003) recognizes that, "(...) indigenous urbanization processes have been crucial for social mobility [among the indigenous population] in its various dimensions (professional, political, economic and intra- and intergenerational)." According to Yanes (2004), "it is not just that cities are transforming indigenous peoples, but that indigenous peoples are also transforming cities", shaping a process of what has been termed "ethnicization"; a process whereby indigenous peoples give urban centres "a distinct social composition, producing new cultural and political dynamics".

On arrival in the region's cities, indigenous and Afro-descendant populations typically establish their residence in quarters characterized by substandard housing and poor access to basic services. They therefore find themselves in a situation of social and spatial segregation that is similar to or greater than that of the urban population as a whole. This phenomenon has not been empirically verified to the required extent, although disaggregated census data on ethnic self-recognition allows for some progress in this direction. Evidence is given below on certain characteristics of urban migration among indigenous and Afro-descendant people, with social and spatial segregation examined in 12 of the region's cities: Caracas and Maracaibo in the Bolivarian Republic of Venezuela; Belo Horizonte, Rio de Janeiro, Salvador and São Paulo in Brazil; San José in Costa Rica, Quito and Guayaquil in Ecuador; and Mexico City, Panama City and Montevideo.

The index of dissimilarity offers an initial approach for analysing how equidistributed indigenous or Afro-descendant individuals are throughout the population of a city.[27] One notable aspect is that the segregation of the indigenous population is generally greater than that of the Afro-descendant population. For example, in Quito indigenous people are 40% more concentrated than if they had an even spatial distribution, almost double the figure for the Afro-descendant population (22%). Exceptions to this rule were noted in Colón (Panama) and San José, while other cities (such as Salvador and Montevideo) showed no significant differences.

The cities where, according to the index, the indigenous population is most segregated, are those of Maracaibo (Bolivarian Republic of Venezuela), Limón (Costa Rica) and Guaranda (Ecuador), with concentrations that exceed the random distribution by 60%, followed by Belo Horizonte, Fortaleza, Guayaquil, Rio de Janeiro and São Paulo (between 40% and 50%). The highest levels of segregation among the Afro-descendant populations are below 30%, with the sole exception of Guaranda (Ecuador), which is unique in that both indigenous and Afro-descendant citizens are highly concentrated in certain parts of the city.

Table V.4

Latin America (21 selected cities): index of dissimilarity, at the subMIAD level,[a] for indigenous and Afro-descendant populations, 2010 census round

Country and census date	City	Type of subMIAD	Ethnic group	
			Indigenous population	Afro-descendant population
Brazil, 2010	Belo Horizonte	Weighting area	0.4249	0.2375
	Fortaleza	Weighting area	0.5648	0.1337
	Rio de Janeiro	Weighting area	0.4197	0.2312
	Salvador	Weighting area	0.2551	0.2469
	São Paulo	Weighting area	0.4636	0.2789
Costa Rica, 2011	Limón	District	0.6578	0.2853
	San José	District	0.1500	0.1726
Ecuador, 2010	Esmeraldas	Census zone	0.3372	0.1768
	Guaranda	Census zone	0.6350	0.5117
	Guayaquil	Census zone	0.4652	0.2582
	Otavalo	Census zone	0.2120	0.1433
	Quito	Census zone	0.3967	0.2235
Mexico, 2010	Ciudad de México	Municipality	0.1803	...
Panama, 2010	Changuinola	Corregimiento	0.3145	0.3004
	Ciudad de Panamá	Corregimiento	0.3508	0.1671
	Colón	Corregimiento	0.1917	0.2591
	David	Corregimiento	0.2966	0.0677
Uruguay, 2011	Montevideo	Locality	0.0612	0.0484
Venezuela (Bolivarian Republic of) 2011	Caracas	Parish	0.1619	0.1138
	Maracaibo	Parish	0.6025	0.1071
	Puerto Ayacucho	Parish	0.0588	0.0263

Source: Economic Commission for Latin America and the Caribbean (ECLAC), on the basis of special processing of census microdata.
[a] A division smaller than a minor administrative division (MIAD).

The analysis of ethnic segregation using Moran's index yielded statistically significant results for three cities (Maracaibo, Panama City and San José), but not for Caracas or Mexico City. In the latter, as with the index of dissimilarity, this may have been because its internal divisions are too large for the purposes of this analysis.

Maracaibo, Panama City and San José provided examples of areas of high concentration of indigenous population in central and peripheral parts of the city. This may be related to the time period in which migrants arrive in cities, the strength of cultural links with their communities, and their integration in various urban activities. As a result, some indigenous groups tend to settle on city edges, while others establish themselves near commercial districts.

In terms of living conditions, indigenous and Afro-descendant populations were often more concentrated in places with housing and education deficits. Afro-descendant populations tend to be even more segregated in these precarious parts of the city.

[27] Calculations are made at the subMIAD level where possible. While some cities have more detailed data available for other levels of disaggregation, the subMIAD level provides a broader overview.

2. International inmigrants

There is a marked historical trend for international immigrants to concentrate in cities. Migrants frequently occupy a disadvantaged position in the host society, generating a need for palliative and corrective measures to socially integrate these populations and prevent their exclusion (Bayona, 2007).

Specialized studies warn of certain scenarios and aspects that are masked by this direct association between the clustering of international immigrants and segregation (Mera, 2008, 2009 and 2011; Kaminker, 2011):

- The risk of naturalization of differences. While certain migrant groups tend to suffer from specific disadvantages, exclusion, xenophobia, racism and discrimination, associated with their status as foreigners, immigrants do not necessarily form "ethnic groups" with homogeneous social and cultural features. They also differ from the supposedly homogeneous destination society.
- The need to overcome the risks of methodological nationalism, and therefore the need for caution in the exclusive use of categories that highlight and differentiate according to nationality or country of birth. Such categories occasionally result in an oversimplified approach to integrating immigrants into society, cancelling out their differences and constructing subordinations that reproduce inequality.
- The need to consider that in the settlement patterns of international immigrants, internal decision-making factors (associated with the shaping of social networks, labour market entry, and even the adoption of community strategies) are often interrelated with prospects for overcoming the inequalities inherent to the host society, especially in access to employment and housing.

There are few studies on the spatial segregation of immigrants in Latin American cities. In Uruguay, Macadar and others (2002, page 19) concluded that Montevideo resembles Buenos Aires in that it has "low levels of spatial segregation among immigrant groups, and is therefore among the least ethnically segregated cities in the world". Brenes (2003 and 2004, cited in Morales, 2008) asserted that the spatial segregation of Nicaraguans in Costa Rica was relatively modest and was very similar to that of Hispanic immigrants residing in urban areas of the United States, while much lower than that of the Afro-descendant population of that country. In Chile, Arriagada (2011, pages 217-218) concluded that "ethnic ghettos do not exist in Santiago, insofar as no habitats have been identified that are exclusively or predominantly inhabited by foreigners".

Generally, these studies draw attention to certain vulnerabilities among immigrant groups. They also quantify demands and define priorities for policy interventions, some of which are governed by the general idea of the need for integration and which agree on preventing exclusion (for example, in the real estate market).

According to census information, one feature of international immigrants' location within large cities is that they cluster in central areas. It is likely that this reflects a desire to take advantage of support networks and other location-related benefits such as access to jobs, services and public transport. However, the living conditions that immigrants face in these central areas are usually rather insecure, which somewhat diminishes the benefits of this location. Map V.4 illustrates this for the location of Colombian women living in Panama City.

Map V.4
Panama City: Colombian women as a proportion of the total, by corregimiento, 2010 census
(Percentages)

Source: Economic Commission for Latin America and the Caribbean (ECLAC), on the basis of special processing of 2010 census microdata.

H. Public policies: experiences and general guidelines for the region

While many policies may have some impact on socioeconomic residential segregation, few are available to reduce it in a direct and explicit fashion. Most experiences in this regard have occurred in developed countries and are comparatively rare in the region. Those responsible for public initiatives must be aware of the segregating effects that they produce, and take steps to prevent them. At the same time, policies must curb the effects of socioeconomic residential segregation, for example by increasing public investment in segregated areas and promoting a better social mix across urban areas and in key institutions (particularly schools), through incentives and specific regulations.

In Latin America, few policies and programmes are intended to directly reduce socioeconomic residential segregation. In addition, some of the policy instruments deployed by developed countries (see box V.3) are unavailable or are, in practical terms, ineffective in the region. The very notion of social housing —in the sense of publicly owned real estate set aside to meet the housing requirements of vulnerable or special-needs households— is non-existent in the region. In Latin America, social housing is that which is provided to the poor, either free or at subsidized prices. The focus is therefore on reducing housing costs, which incentivizes the construction of massive social housing projects at the urban edge, creating new neighbourhoods whose inhabitants remain poor and who suffer from a lack of public facilities and accessibility. It is well documented that this model may accentuate socioeconomic residential segregation (ECLAC, 2014, 2012 and 2010; Aguilar and Escanilla, 2011). Moreover, once the housing has been handed over, the State is no longer able to use it as part of schemes to reduce socioeconomic residential segregation, although it could certainly regulate their sale to contain, at least partially, the market processes that exacerbate the phenomenon.

The absence of instruments to ensure that low-income housing is built in middle- or upper-class neighbourhoods makes it impossible to break the pattern of market selection determined by land prices And weaknesses of the State school system considerably limit the options for reducing socioeconomic residential segregation by supporting the upward social mobility of families (or by attracting middle- and upper-class families) in poor neighbourhoods with good schools (ECLAC, 2014; Rosetti, 2014). Serious public budget constraints and a lack of mechanisms for the territorial redistribution of local revenues make it difficult for local governments to balance inequalities between rich and poor neighbourhoods.

The Economic Commission for Latin America and the Caribbean (ECLAC) has proposed lines of action to deal with urban deprivation that may help reduce socioeconomic residential segregation by making structural changes to habitats. These include: (i) improving the quality of housing and building new housing units; (ii) creating and improving access to land; (iii) providing basic infrastructure services and ensuring access; (iv) providing and improving neighbourhood public spaces; (v) providing spaces for productive activities and job and income creation. In this context, strategic changes have been posited that may offer a comprehensive approach to tackling socioeconomic residential segregation. One such change is the proposal for a redesign or refocusing of urban and housing policy in the countries of the region, involving a shift from the perception of housing as a commodity provided by the market, to the recognition that homes, notwithstanding their economic value, have a greater social, cultural and family significance, which emerges from the right to a housing choice that accords with the means and the needs of each household (Jordán and Martínez, 2009). Recent ECLAC studies investigated the links between school segregation (which is increasing) and residential segregation, and suggested that the issue of segregation goes beyond housing, and that analysis and policies should consider the other expressions of segregation that exist in Latin American cities (ECLAC, 2014; Rossetti, 2014).

Box V.3

Policies for reducing socioeconomic residential segregation: comparison of international experiences

Positive territorial discrimination —especially by compensating for neighbourhoods' deficiencies in public services and jobs— has been one of the main instruments deployed to mitigate the effects of socioeconomic residential segregation and reduce it over the long term. Governments' political orientations have an impact on how this positive discrimination is conceived and implemented. For example, France's socialist government of the early 1980s set up priority education zones (*zones d'éducation prioritaires*, ZEP) to strengthen public services in segregated areas. Fifteen years later, a conservative administration launched the Urban Regeneration Pact (Pacte de Relance pour la Ville) which sought to boost employment through the creation of urban free zones (*zones franches urbaines*, ZFU), which offered benefits and compensation for enterprises that created jobs in these areas.

For some authors, housing policy represents the most important tool for addressing socioeconomic residential segregation although it has often tended to exacerbate the situation. Torres (2004, pages 50-51) asserts that housing policy is one of the few social policies that might be consistently used to combat residential segregation —even though it might also increase it. In France, after the Second World War it was decided to build large-scale developments designed for different social groups, including low-cost housing (*habitation à loyer modéré*, HLM) for poor or vulnerable families. However, eventually most of these developments became less socially diverse and were stigmatized as dwellings for the poor and the State-dependent. Even worse, sociological and anthropological research found that social diversity in these spaces did not necessarily lead to more integrated or harmonious social relations. Jaillet, Perrine and Ménard (2008, page 31) cite an article published by J.C. Chamboredon and M. Leamire in 1970, in which it was shown that proximity (that is, mixing) can sometimes heighten perceptions of social differences. Another measure employed in France was the introduction of social housing quotas in municipalities and urban districts (*arrondissements*). For example, the Town Planning Act of 1991 (*loi d'orientation pour la ville*, LOV), also known as the anti-ghetto law, forced some local authorities to set aside a minimum of 20% social housing, planned specific public construction programmes, imposed fines for failure to meet quotas and gave the State the power to veto private housing projects unless the quotas were met. Encouraging the middle class to relocate or return to low-income neighbourhoods, usually in good locations, was also a tactic used under the Urban Regeneration Pact (1996) and the Urban Planning and Renewal Act (*loi d'orientation et de programmation pour la ville et la renovation urbaine*, the "Borloo" law) of 2003. Meanwhile, a National Urban Renewal Agency (ANRU) was set up to improve the demolition and construction cycle.

In the Netherlands, one of the countries with lower levels of socioeconomic residential segregation (albeit higher rates of ethnic residential segregation), housing policy has been crucial, because: (i) it guaranteed the universal right to a dwelling, (ii) it acted early in conjunction with housing corporations that prioritized the protection of vulnerable groups over maximizing profits or minimizing expenditure; (iii) it adopted parameters including minimum social housing thresholds, guaranteed or promoted through the active involvement of municipalities in the real-estate market; (iv) it intervened forcefully in the housing market, setting maximum rental and sale prices; (v) it carried out politically and geographically coordinated urban planning and management (using the concept of "clusters", in which all new developments had to be comprehensive, not merely residential, with urban services and infrastructure forming part of housing schemes); and (vi) it promoted political and citizen control of urban renewal processes so that poor households would not be driven out. Despite these measures, rates of socioeconomic residential segregation have climbed in the Netherlands in recent years, partly owing to a new public policy approach that gives precedence to the recovery of run-down areas over the continued residence of the local population, and is unconcerned with ensuring the social mix of newcomers (Smets and Salman, 2008).[a]

In the United States, various policies have been applied, most intended to eradicate racial residential segregation. Initiatives have been rolled out to expand the spatial dispersion of poor people, especially by relocating low-income households from segregated neighbourhoods to more prosperous parts of the city. Such schemes include Moving to Opportunity and HOPE VI, which allocate subsidies to poor households so that they can rent private housing in neighbourhoods with low poverty rates. Steps have also been taken to regenerate troubled districts, including measures to improve social services and local programmes relating to issues such as security, the fight against crime and territorial stigma, and the demolition of rundown housing and its replacement with better quality accommodation for the original residents and middle-class incomers. In the United Kingdom, another strategy to promote the social mix in urban spaces takes the form of housing regulations that set minimum social diversity thresholds in order to secure the approval of and access to funding. These regulations allow local authorities to negotiate a percentage of affordable housing units with real-estate developers in exchange for planning permits (Feitosa and others, 2012).

These experiences do not necessarily mean that there is consensus as to the effectiveness of housing policies. As Feitosa and others point out (2012, pages 1,133 and 1,134): "There are many diverging opinions regarding the impact of policies for minimizing segregation. Some studies identify accomplishments and judge many policies to be successful (Feins and Shroder, 2005), while others focus on their failure and the need for restructuring (Smets and den Uyl, 2008). These divergences highlight the importance of constantly monitoring and adjusting policies to attain the expected results. Most significantly, the design of these policies must consider the peculiarities of cities, which differ in segregation patterns, population composition, levels of deprivation, culture, housing market structure, and many other features that demand specific approaches".

Source: Economic Commission for Latin America and the Caribbean (ECLAC), on the basis of M. Jaillet, F. Perrin and F. Menard, "Divesité sociale, segregation, mixité", *Recherches*, No. 180, Paris, PUCA, 2001; P. Smets and T. Salman, "Countering urban segregation: theoretical and policy innovations from around the globe", *Urban Studies*, vol. 45, No. 7, 2008; and F. Feitosa and others, "Countering urban segregation in Brazilian cities: policy-oriented explorations using agent-based simulation", *Environment and Planning B: Planning and Design*, vol. 39, No. 6, 2012.

[a] However, some analysts believe that these measures could reduce socioeconomic residential segregation (Kamal-Chaoui and Sanchez-Reaza, 2012).

One frame of reference for public action in this area is Brazil's "City Statute" (2001). Innovative in several ways (for example, by defining and regulating constitutional principles relating to the social function of land and property), it created new institutional arrangements (the Ministry of Cities in 2003, and the National Social Housing System under Law No. 11,124/05 of 2005) and provides tools for urban planning and management based on pillars designed to reduce segregation: the formulation of comprehensive policies; the democratic management of cities; the influence and participation of social movements in formulating urban policies; guarantees of the social function of land; and the decentralization of administrative responsibilities for precarious settlements, and their formalization through the creation of "special social interest zones" (*Zonas Especiais de Interesse Social*, ZEIS). While the City Statute has some potential and has earned the approval of urban specialists, its practical outcomes remain far from satisfactory (Ribeiro, 2013; Rolnik and Klink, 2011).

Reports by the Organization for Economic Co-operation and Development (OECD) have called attention to the Habitat programme of the Secretariat of Social Development (SEDESOL) of Mexico, which "allocates federal subsidies to support works and actions in marginalized urban areas and those areas suffering from poverty, insecurity or social violence, to introduce or improve basic urban infrastructure and facilities; to improve the physical environment; to build or improve centres for community development, and to support individual and community capacity-building initiatives, among others" (Kamal-Chaoui and Sanchez-Reaza, 2012).[28] However, the focus of these policies was to improve neighbourhoods rather than to combat socioeconomic residential segregation. Schemes to repopulate city centres, which have achieved some progress during the first decade of the twenty-first century, have not been analysed with due attention in terms of their impact on socioeconomic residential segregation (Salazar and Sobrino, 2010).

It is well documented that Chile's housing policy has made great strides in reducing the country's housing deficit since the 1990s. This success was tempered by the segregating effect of the policy, specifically due to the mass construction of subsidized housing in city peripheries. This resulted in the wholesale relocation of poor households to city edges, where precarious living conditions led to the emergence of metropolitan ghettos (Sabatini, Mora and Polanco, 2013). The early 2000s saw a revival of neighbourhood improvement initiatives, while mechanisms for social housing quotas were initially examined but never actually materialized. An attempt was made to prevent the departure of subsidized housing beneficiaries by building housing projects in the municipalities where the beneficiaries resided.

Segregation is entrenched in Chile and causes plenty of concern. A broad range of measures have been put forward as part of the most recent proposals, many of which are not aimed at promoting residential social diversity but at improving living conditions in poor and segregated neighbourhoods, albeit under a concept of urban restructuring that implies some larger changes.[29] Thus, Aravena, de Gregorio and Poduje (2013) point out four key ideas for containing and mitigating socioeconomic residential segregation: (i) switch investment support from people to places, through public investment that is well targeted, designed and maintained over time; (ii) focus on territories with high segregation rates, which must be selected on the basis of indicators and participatory processes involving municipalities and affected residents; (iii) integrate the periphery into the modern city, bringing it closer through high-quality corridors, while also taking the modern city to the periphery; (iv) coordinate, breaking with sectoral, centralist logic, without waiting for a new institutional framework to be developed. The authors also advance nine near-term proposals.

(i) Create a "government for cities"
(ii) Set up "Areas of Territorial Equity" (*zonas de equidad territorial*, ZET)
(iii) Create a short-term task force for these areas
(iv) Transfer resources to municipalities to pay for projects
(v) Open up major avenues
(vi) Take part of the modern city to the segregated periphery
(vii) Create a discounted transport fare for vulnerable groups
(viii) Set up a public land bank, and
(ix) Establish social housing quotas and incentives

28 See also SEDESOL [online] http://www.sedesol.gob.mx/.
29 In the words of the authors, "taking the modern city to the periphery" (Aravena, de Gregorio and Poduje, page 23).

Sabatini, Mora and Polanco (2013, page 26) propose three policy vectors for reducing segregation in Santiago, Chile: (i) keep low-income groups in well-located, socially diverse areas; (ii) disperse affordable housing (relocating low-income households to well-established neighbourhoods); and (c) improve the quality of life in low-income neighbourhoods (attracting or retaining middle- and upper-class households in lower-income neighbourhoods and developments).

Policy lines aimed at reducing or containing socioeconomic residential segregation are limited.[30] Preventing the phenomenon, or at least containing it, requires housing programmes that help disperse housing for different social groups throughout urban areas, ensuring a minimum number of units for each group in each part of the city. It has been stressed that public policies to promote and facilitate non-segregated residential patterns should include mechanisms for social integration and exchange, as well as measures to minimize or offset market-driven impacts on housing prices as a result of social and residential diversity. Conversely, when socioeconomic residential segregation is already entrenched, effective short-term actions necessarily entail promoting the relocation of the population, either by situating social housing in middle-class and affluent neighbourhoods (using some of the existing housing stock for this purpose), or by attracting middle-class families and individuals to poor neighbourhoods (Kamal-Chaoui and Sanchez-Reaza, 2012, pages 127-129).

I. Final comments

This chapter has spotlighted certain key aspects of the debate on socioeconomic residential segregation in Latin America's large cities.

First, it is confirmed that there is a higher level of residential segregation among the upper socioeconomic strata. The territorial distribution of high-income groups is more strongly differentiated, in that they tend to concentrate in a small number of metropolitan enclaves where they generally form a majority. Lacking verifiable empirical reference points, it is probable that this pattern interactively combines a *habitus* in which these groups defend and protect their capital, attitudes and self-image, with urban rules and interventions and market signals (land and housing prices).

Second, while the majority of cities, expressed as the simple average for the region, are currently experiencing a downswing in socioeconomic residential segregation, the trend is sensitive to the measurement variable. The downtrend is particularly dependent on the pattern in Brazil, where residential segregation is in broad decline. In fact, in other Latin American countries the prevailing trend is for segregation to increase among the poorest population groups (the least educated or the bottom socioeconomic decile). In other words, processes differ depending on the city, the interest group and the socioeconomic variable used.

A third noteworthy aspect is the geographical scale adopted for measurement purposes. The theory that the fall in segregation would be more sustained if it were measured on a smaller geographical scale, particularly for the uppermost socioeconomic group, seems to be clearly confirmed. However, Brazil is again thought to weigh decisively on the outcome (in terms of direction and magnitude). But the comparability of minor administrative divisions (MIADs) over time is not guaranteed in that country, introducing a distortion that cannot be controlled for and raising doubts over the validity of this outcome.

Fourth, the hypothesis that internal migration could play a significant role in reducing segregation was disproved in the case of most cities, through empirical analysis.

A fifth aspect, relating to active policies designed to curb or mitigate segregation, is that a review of experiences in the region revealed a degree of progress, albeit with the focus generally more on mitigating poverty and housing vulnerability than on tackling the segregation of populations. Only recently does residential segregation seem to have appeared on the public agenda, and profound challenges remain if it is to become a housing and urban policy focus in the region.

30 There are those who do not perceive socioeconomic residential segregation to be a serious problem, or rather view it as an intractable issue. Consequently, Van Kempen (2007, pages 13-31 and 14-15) holds that "cities consist, almost by definition, of various neighbourhoods, each with its own function, nature, architectural style, attraction, and advantages and disadvantages for various residents and visitors. In other words, the undivided city is a myth and a utopia at the same time." Barbosa (2001, p.6) cites the work of previous authors, noting that "sharing the universal nature of the larger differentiation process, urban spatial segregation proves to be a structural invariant. The idea of eradicating it, despite the good intentions, is an ideological view (Lefebvre 1972, p. 99). Nevertheless, even though it has always been present in urban context, it takes on different historical forms over time. Knowing the invariants and variables according to Bourdieu, is exactly what sociology "can and must do" (Bourdieu, 1996, page 28) and this is one of its contributions to the understanding of spatial segregation."

Bibliography

Aguilar, G. and I. Escanilla (2011), *Periurbanización y sustentabilidad en grandes ciudades*, Mexico City, National Autonomous University of Mexico (UNAM)-Porrúa,

Andrade, L. and L. Silveira (2013), "Efeito-território. Explorações em torno de um conceito sociológico", *Civitas*, vol. 13, No. 2, Porto Alegre.

Aravena, A., J. de Gregorio and I. Poduje (2013), "Vía rápida para reducir la desigualdad propuestas para revertir la segregación urbana en nuestras ciudades", *Informe de Políticas Públicas*, No. 2.

Arriagada, Camilo (2011), "Segregación residencial según dos modelos de urbanización y bienestar: estudio comparado de las áreas metropolitanas del Gran Santiago, Toronto y Vancouver", *Notas de Población*, No. 91 (LC/G.2484-P), Santiago, Chile, Economic Commission for Latin America and the Caribbean (ECLAC).

Arroyo, M. (2001), "La contraurbanización: un debate metodológico y conceptual sobre la dinámica de las áreas metropolitanas", *Papeles de Población*, vol. 7, No. 30, Toluca, Centro de Investigación y Estudios Avanzados de la Población, Universidad Autónoma del Estado de México.

Barbosa, E. (2001), "Urban Spatial Segregation and Social Differentiation: Foundation for a Typological Analysis", paper presented at the International Seminar on Segregation in the City, Lincoln Institute, 26-28 July [online] https://www.lincolninst.edu/education/83/International-Seminar-on-Segregation-in-the-City.

Bayona, Jordi (2007), "La segregación residencial de la población extranjera en Barcelona: ¿una segregación fragmentada?", *Scripta Nova*, vol. XI, No. 235 [online] http://www.ub.edu/geocrit/sn/sn-235.htm.

Borsdorf, A. (2003), "Cómo modelar el desarrollo y la dinámica de la ciudad latinoamericana", *EURE*, vol. 29, No. 86 [online] http://dx.doi.org/10.4067/S0250-71612003008600002.

Bourdie, P. (1986), "The forms of capital", *Handbook of Theory of Research for the Sociology of Education*, J. E. Richardsun (ed.), Grenwood Press [online] http://econ.tau.ac.il/papers/publicf/Zeltzer1.pdf

Camus, M. (2002), *Ser indígena en la ciudad de Guatemala*, Guatemala City, Latin American Faculty of Social Sciences (FLACSO).

Carvalho, A. and others (2013), "Um estudo das metodologias e funcionalidades dos índices de segregação", *Revista Brasileira de Estudos da Populacão* (REBEP), vol. 30, No. 2.

Chávez, A. and others (2013), "Nouvelles tendances de la migration métropolitaine en Amérique Latine: est-ce que les aires métropolitaines gagnent ou perdent population à cause de la migration interne", paper presented at the session 091 "Internal migration and urbanization: Overview", XXVII Conference of the International Union for the Scientific Study of Population (IUSSP), Pusan, Republic of Korea [online] www.iussp.org/en/event/17/programme/paper/2698.

De Mattos, C. (2010), "Globalización y metamorfosis metropolitana en América Latina: De la ciudad a lo urbano generalizado", *Revista de Geografía Norte Grande*, No. 47.

Del Popolo, Fabiana and others (2007), "Indigenous people and urban settlements: spatial distribution, internal migration and living conditions", *Población y Desarrollo series*, No. 78 (LC/L.2799-P), Santiago, Chile, Economic Commission for Latin America and the Caribbean (ECLAC), July.

ECLAC (Economic Commission for Latin America and the Caribbean) (2014), *Compacts for Equality: Towards a sustainable future* (LC/G.2586(SES.35/3)), Santiago, Chile.

___ (2012), *Population, Territory and Sustainable Development* (LC/L.3474(CEP.2/3), Santiago, Chile [online] http://www.cepal.org/celade/noticias/paginas/0/46070/2012-96-Poblacion-WEB.pdf.

___ (2010), *Time for Equality: Closing gaps, opening trails* (LC/G.2432(SES.33/3)), Santiago, Chile.

___ (2007), *Social Panorama of Latin America, 2007* (LC/G.2351-P), Santiago, Chile.

Feitosa, F. and others (2012), "Countering urban segregation in Brazilian cities: policy-oriented explorations using agent-based simulation", *Environment and Planning B: Planning and Design*, vol. 39, No. 6.

Flores, C. (2008), "Residential segregation and the geography of opportunities: a spatial analysis of heterogeneity and spillovers in education", PhD thesis, The University of Texas at Austin [online] http://repositories.lib.utexas.edu/bitstream/handle/2152/3843/floresc32578.pdf?sequence=2.

Fosset, M. (2004), "Racial Segregation in American Cities: A Brief Introduction to Theoretical Perspectives", Department of Sociology and Racial and Ethnic Studies Institute, Texas A&M University, College Station, Texas.

Gómez, S. and C. Amitrano (2005), "Local da moradia na metropole e vulnerabilidade ao (emprego e) desemprego", *São Paulo: segregacão, pobreza e desigualdade sociais,* E. Marques and H. Torres (orgs.), São Paulo, SENAC.

Herrera, L., W. Pecht and F. Olivares (1976), "Crecimiento urbano en América Latina", Serie E, No. 22, Santiago, Chile, Latin American and Caribbean Demographic Centre (CELADE)/Inter-American Development Bank (IDB).

IDB (Inter-American Development Bank) (2011), *Urban Sustainability in Latin America and the Caribbean,* Washington, D.C. [online] http://idbdocs.iadb.org/wsdocs/getdocument.aspx?docnum=35786014.

Ingram, G. (1998), "Patterns of metropolitan development: What have we learned?", *Urban Studies*, vol. 35, No. 7, Edinburgh.

Jaillet, M., E. Perrin and F. Menard (2008), "Divesité sociale, segregation, mixité", *Collection Recheches*, No. 180, Paris, PUCA

Janoschka, M. (2002), "El nuevo modelo de la ciudad latinoamericana: fragmentación y privatización", *EURE*, No. 28, Santiago, Chile.

Jordán, R. and R. Martínez (2009), "Pobreza y precariedad urbana en América Latina y el Caribe. Situación actual y financiamiento de políticas y programas", *Project Document*, No. 245 (LC/W.245), Santiago, Chile, Economic Commission for Latin America and the Caribbean (ECLAC).

Jordán, R., J. Rehner and J. Samaniego (2010), "Regional Panorama. Latin America: Megacities and Sustainability", *Project Document* (LC/W.289), Santiago, Chile, Economic Commission for Latin America and the Caribbean (ECLAC).

Kamal-Chaoui, L. and J. Sanchez-Reaza (eds.) (2012), "Urban Trends and Policies in OECD Countries", *OECD Regional Development Working Papers*, No. 2012/01, Paris, OECD Publishing [online] http://dx.doi.org/10.1787/5k9fhn1ctjr8-en.

Kaminker, Sergio Andrés (2011), "La dimensión racial en el análisis de la segregación residencial urbana en Puerto Madryn, Chubut", *Papeles de Trabajo del Centro De Estudios Interdisciplinarios en Etnolingüística y Antropología Sociocultural,* No. 22 [online] http://www.scielo.org.ar/scielo.php?script=sci_arttext&pid=S1852-45082011000200004&lng=es&nrm=iso.

Kaztman, R. (2009), "La dimensión espacial de la cohesión social en las grandes ciudades de América Latina", Santiago, Chile, Economic Commission for Latin America and the Caribbean (ECLAC) [online] www.eclac.cl/deype/noticias/noticias/1/36981/2009_08_sem_cohesion-social_Ruben_Kaztman.pdf.

___ (2007), "La calidad de las relaciones sociales en las grandes ciudades de América Latina: viejos y nuevos determinantes", *Pensamiento Iberoamericano*, No. 1.

___ (2001), "Seduced and abandoned: the social isolation of the urban poor", *CEPAL Review*, No. 75 (LC/G.2150-P/E), Santiago, Chile, Economic Commission for Latin America and the Caribbean (ECLAC).

___ (1999) (coord.), "Activos y estructuras de oportunidades. Estudios sobre las raíces de la vulnerabilidad social en Uruguay" (LC/MVD/R.180/E), Montevideo, ECLAC office in Montevideo.

Kaztman, R. and A. Rematoso (2005), "Spatial segregation, employment and poverty in Montevideo", *CEPAL Review*, No. 85 (LC/G.2266-P/E), Santiago, Chile, Economic Commission for Latin America and the Caribbean (ECLAC).

Kempen, R., van (2007), "Divided cities in the 21st century: challenging the importance of globalization", *Journal of Housing and the Built Environment*, vol. 22, No. 1.

León, Guadalupe (2003), "Ecuador. Etnicidad, pobreza y exclusión de los indígenas inmigrantes en Quito, Guayaquil y Tena", *Exclusión Social y estrategias de vida de los indígenas urbanos en Perú, México y Ecuador*, Washington, D.C., World Bank.

Lombardi, M. and D. Veiga (1989), *Las ciudades en conflicto. Una perspectiva latinoamericana*, Montevideo, Centro de Informaciones y Estudios del Uruguay (CIESU).

Macadar, Daniel and others (2002), "Proyecto segregación residencial en Montevideo: ¿Un fenómeno creciente?", Montevideo, Comisión Sectorial de Investigación Científica (CSIC), Universidad de la República, unpublished.

Marpsat, M. (1999), "La módelisation des "effets de quartier" aux États-Unis. Une revue des travaux récents", *Population*, vol. 54, No. 2.

Martori, J. and K. Hoberg (2004), "Indicadores cuantitativos de segregación residencial. El caso de la población inmigrante en Barcelona", *Geo Crítica. Revista Electrónica de Geografía Y Ciencias Sociales*, vol. VIII, No. 169, University of Barcelona [online] www.ub.edu/geocrit/sn/sn-169.htm.

Massey, D. and N. Denton (1988), "The dimensions of residential segregation", *Social Forces*, vol. 67, No. 2.

Matas, J. (1975), *Aspectos del diseño de ciudades en la historia*, Santiago, Chile, Pontificia Universidad Católica de Chile, Centro de Información y Documentación Universitaria (CIDU).

Mera, Gabriela (2011), "Pensar las categorías, pensar al Estado. Reflexiones en torno al concepto de segregación espacial de los inmigrantes", *Migraciones Internacionales Contemporáneas: Estudios para el debate,* Cynthia Pizarro (coord.), Ediciones CICCUS.

___ (2009), "De problema estatal a problema sociológico. Políticas migratorias y discursos científicos en torno a la distribución espacial de los inmigrantes en las ciudades", *Temáticas migratorias actuales en América Latina: remesas, políticas y emigración*, Montevideo, Latin American Population Association (ALAP) [online] http://paraguay.sociales.uba.ar/files/2011/07/Mera_01.pdf.

___ (2008), "Pensar las categorías, pensar al Estado. El concepto de "segregación espacial" de los inmigrantes en los estudios migratorios" [online] http://webiigg.sociales.uba.ar/pobmigra/archivos/mera_segregacion.pdf.

Metzger, John T. (2000), "Planned abandonment: the neighborhood life-cycle theory and national urban policy", *Housing Policy Debate*, vol. 11, No. 1.

Mollenkopf, J. H. and M. Castells (eds.) (1991), *Dual City. Restructuring New York*, New York, Russel Sage Foundation.

Morales, Abelardo (2008), "Inmigración en Costa Rica: características sociales y laborales, integración y políticas públicas", *Población y Desarrollo series*, No. 85 (LC/L.2929-P), Santiago, Chile, Economic Commission for Latin America and the Caribbean (ECLAC) [online] http://www.cepal.org/publicaciones/xml/0/34570/lcl2929-P.pdf.

Musterd, S. (2005), "Social and ethnic segregation in Europe: levels, causes, and effects", *Journal of Urban Affairs*, vol. 27, No. 3.

OECD (Organization for Economic Cooperation and Development) (2012), *Compact City Policies: A Comparative Assessment*, OECD Green Growth Studies, Paris, OECD Publishing.

Pacione, M. (2009), *Urban Geography. A Global Perspective*, New York, Routledge.

Polese, M. and R. Stren (2000), *The Social Sustainability of Cities*, University of Toronto Press.

Reardon, S. and D. O'Sullivan (2004), "Measures of spatial segregation", *Sociological Methodology*, vol. 24, No. 1.

Ribeiro, L. (2013), "Transformações na Ordem Urbana na Metrópole Liberal-Periférica: 1980/2010. Hipóteses e estratégia teórico -metodológica para estudo comparativo", Rio de Janeiro, Observatório das Metrópoles/Instituto Nacional de Ciência e Tecnologia [online] http://observatoriodasmetropoles.net/index.php?option=com_k2&view=item&id=818&Itemid=164.

Ribeiro, L. and M. Koslinksi (2009), "Efeito-metrópole e acesso às oportunidades educacionais", *EURE*, vol. 35, No. 106, Santiago, Chile.

Ribeiro, L. and E. Telles (2000), "Rio de Janeiro: emerging dualization in a historically unequal city", *Globalizing Cities: A New Spatial Order?*, P. Marcuse and R. Kempen, London, Blackwell.

Ribeiro, L., J. Rodrigues and F. Corrêa (2010), "Segregação residencial e emprego nos grandes espaços urbanos brasileiros", *Cadernos Metrópole*, No. 23, São Paulo.

Roberts, B. and R. Wilson (eds.) (2009), *Urban Segregation and Governance in the Americas,* New York, Palgrave-Macmillan.

Rodgers, D., J. Beall and R. Kanbur (2012), *Latin American Urban Development into the Twenty First Century Towards a Renewed Perspective on the City*, Palgrave Macmillan.

Rodríguez, J. (2013), "La migración interna en las grandes ciudades ciudades en América Latina: efectos sobre el crecimiento demográfico y la composición de la población", *Notas de Población*, No. 96 (LC/G.2573-P), Santiago, Chile, Economic Commission for Latin America and the Caribbean (ECLAC).

___ (2012), "¿Policentrismo o ampliación de la centralidad histórica en el Área Metropolitana del Gran Santiago? Evidencia novedosa proveniente de la encuesta Casen 2009", *EURE,* No. 38, Santiago, Chile.

___ (2011), "Migración interna en ciudades de América Latina: Efectos en la estructura demográfica y la segregación residencial", *Notas de Población*, No. 93 (LC/G.2509-P), Santiago, Chile, Economic Commission for Latin America and the Caribbean (ECLAC).

___ (2009a), "La captación de la migración interna mediante censos de población: la experiencia de la ronda de 2000 y sus lecciones para la ronda de 2010 en América Latina y el Caribe", *Notas de Población*, No. 88 (LC/G.2409-P), Santiago, Chile, Economic Commission for Latin America and the Caribbean (ECLAC).

___ (2009b), "Dinámica demográfica y asuntos urbanos y metropolitanos prioritarios en América Latina: ¿qué aporta el procesamiento de microdatos censales?", *Notas de Población*, No. 86 (LC/G.2349-P), Santiago, Chile, Economic Commission for Latin America and the Caribbean, (ECLAC).

___ (2001), "Segregación residencial socioeconómica: ¿qué es?, ¿cómo se mide?, ¿qué está pasando? ¿importa?", *Población y Desarrollo series*, No. 16 (LC/L.1576-P), Santiago, Chile, Economic Commission for Latin America and the Caribbean (ECLAC).

Rolnik, R. y J. Klink (2011), "Crescimento economico e desenvolvimento urbano: por que nossas cidades continuam tão precárias?", paper presented at the "XIV Encuentro nacional de la Asociación Nacional de Posgrado e Investigación en Planificación Urbana y Regional (ANPUR)", Rio de Janeiro [online] www.observatoriodasmetropoles.net/download/raquelrolnik.pdf.

Romero, J.L. (1976), *Latinoamérica, las ciudades y las ideas*, Buenos Aires, Siglo XXI.
Rossetti, M. (2014), "La segregación escolar como un elemento clave en la reproducción de la desigualdad", *Políticas Sociales series,* No. 199 (LC/L.3845), Santiago, Chile, Economic Commission for Latin America and the Caribbean (ECLAC).
Sabatini, F. and G. Cáceres (eds.) (2004), *Barrios cerrados en Santiago, Chile: entre la exclusión y la integración social,* Santiago, Chile, Lincoln Institute, Pontificia Universidad Católica.
Sabatini, F., P. Mora and I. Polanco (2013), "Control de la segregación socio-espacial: Rebatiendo mitos, construyendo propuestas", *Espacio Público,* No. 7.
Sabatini, F., G. Cáceres and J. Cerda (2001), "Segregación residencial en las principales ciudades chilenas: tendencias de las tres últimas décadas y posibles cursos de acción", *EURE*, vol. 27, No. 82, Santiago, Chile, Pontificia Universidad Católica de Chile.
Salazar, C. and J, Sobrino (2010), "La ciudad central de la Ciudad de México: ¿espacio de oportunidad laboral para la metrópoli?", *Estudios Demográficos y Urbanos*, vol. 25, No. 3.
Sampson, R. (2012), *Great American City: Chicago and the enduring neighbourhood effect*, Chicago, The University of Chicago Press.
Sassen, S. (1991), *The Global City,* Princeton, Princeton University Press.
Smets, P. and T. Salman (2008), "Countering urban segregation: Theoretical and policy innovations from around the Globe", *Urban Studies* vol. 45, No.7.
Solís, P. e I. Puga (2011), "Efectos del nivel socioeconómico de la zona de residencia sobre el proceso de estratificación social en Monterrey", *Estudios Demográficos y Urbanos*, No. 77, El Colegio de México.
Torres, H. (2008), "Social and environmental aspects of peri-urban growth in Latin American megacities" (UN/POP/EGM-URB/2008/10), paper presented at the United Nations Expert Group Meeting on Population Distribution, Urbanization, Internal Migration and Development, New York, 21-23 January [online] http://www.un.org/esa/population/meetings/EGM_PopDist/P10_Torres.pdf.
___ (2004), "Segregação residencial e políticas públicas. São Paulo na década de 1990", *Revista Brasileira de Ciências Sociais*, vol. 19, No. 54.
UN-Habitat (United Nations Human Settlements Programme) (2008), *State of the World's Cities, 2008/2009: Harmonious Cities*, Nairobi.
United Nations (2014), *World Urbanization Prospects: The 2014 Revision, Highlights* (ST/ESA/SER.A/352), New York, Population Division [online] http://esa.un.org/unpd/wup/Highlights/WUP2014-Highlights.pdf.
___ (2008), *United Nations Expert Group Meeting on Population Distribution, Urbanization, Migration and Development* (ESA/P/WP.206), New York, Department of Economic and Social Affairs [online] www.un.org/esa/population/meetings/EGM_PopDist/EGM_ PopDist_Report.pdf.
Welti, C. (ed.) (1997), *Demografía I*, Mexico City, Latin American Programme of Population Activities (PROLAP), National Autonomous University of Mexico (UNAM).
White, M., (1983), "The measurement of spatial segregation", *American Journal of Sociology*, vol. 88, No. 5.
Yanes Rizo, Pablo Enrique (2004), "Urbanización de los pueblos indígenas y etnización de las ciudades. Hacia una agenda de derechos y políticas públicas", *Ciudad, pueblos indígenas y etnicidad*, P. Yanes, V. Molina y O. González (coords.), Mexico City, Universidad de la Ciudad de México/Dirección General de Equidad y Desarrollo Social.
Zubrinsky, C. (2003), "The dynamics of residential segregation", *Annual Review of Sociology*, No. 29.

Annex 1

Technical note on the study of socioeconomic residential segregation

Measures of socioeconomic residential segregation: index of dissimilarity (Duncan index); exposure indices and global Moran's I index (see box V.2).

Variables of social segmentation: education level, considering only heads of household in the categories of low, medium and high education; an ad hoc socioeconomic index, and income.[31]

(i) *Index of socioeconomic status*. The index is based on the combined indices of consumer goods possession (IB), mostly electrical appliances, and overcrowding (IH), understood as the average number of people per bedroom. By measuring the number of people per bedroom, the intention is to represent the amount of physical space available to individuals within a home or housing unit.

For the consumer goods index (IB), a specific weighted index is created for each city, in four steps: (1) a goods penetration index is obtained for each city, corresponding to the percentage of households that own the good. Under normal conditions, this index should reflect the value of the good (the more it costs, the lower the penetration); (2) a scarcity index is calculated by subtracting the penetration index from 100; this index forms the basis of the weighting associated with the ownership of each good; (3) these penetration weightings are added together and then recalculated so that they are standardized and so that the households with all goods receive a score of 1,000; (4) the standardized weightings are added together and a quantitative index is obtained, whose theoretical range is from 0 (households without any of the goods considered by the index) to 1,000 (households that have all goods). The goods in question depend on the questions asked by each census. Distributions were analysed previously in order to ensure that they presented a normal pattern (with availability increasing in line with socioeconomic status), using other socioeconomic status variables, such as income and the education level of the head of household, for this purpose.

To calculate the overcrowding index (IH), the maximum value was determined for each city (only occupied private housing units, which account for more than 99% of the total in the countries studied, were considered). Dwellings with no bedrooms were assigned the maximum value, since it was considered that by definition they have a high level of crowding. To create an overcrowding index that can be combined with the goods index, an algorithm was designed that allows a theoretical range from 0 to 1,000, with 0 assigned to the households with the highest level of overcrowding in the country, and 1,000 to those with the least overcrowding. This algorithm is as follows: IH = 1,000 - (1,000 * Number of people per bedroom / Maximum value of people per bedroom in the city). Lastly, for each home or housing unit, the two indices are added together, thereby obtaining a total score of between 0 and 2,000. This socioeconomic index allowed for the construction of deciles, based on the distribution of the index in each city.

(ii) *Per capita income*. Census questionnaires on population and housing do not usually capture data on income. However, surveys do collect this data in Brazil, Mexico and Panama, which were part of the sample studied in this chapter. However, Mexico changed its method of gathering information between 2000 and 2010, which prevented comparisons between censuses.

(iii) *Education level*. Refers to the highest level of education attained by heads of household aged 25 and over, classified in three groups: basic (primary or pre-primary education); intermediate (secondary education, whether completed or not) and higher (university or technical education, completed or not).

Variable of sociocultural segmentation: ethnicity (indigenous, Afro-descendant and others); status of international migrant.

Estimate of the impact of migration on socioeconomic residential segregation: ad hoc procedure developed by CELADE-Population Division of ECLAC on the basis of factual and counterfactual values of the matrices of flow indicators (Rodríguez, 2011).

---

[31] The variables presented in this section are measured on the basis of available microdata from the 2000 and 2010 census rounds, supplied by CELADE-Population Division of ECLAC. Consequently, the results for income and other socioeconomic variables are not directly comparable with those used in other chapters of this edition of *Social Panorama of Latin America*, which are derived from household surveys.

Selected cities: cities with more than 1 million inhabitants (with the exception of Cuenca, Ecuador, which has fewer than 500,000 inhabitants), comprising several municipalities and with data available from the 2000 and 2010 census rounds.

Geographical scales: three geographical scales were considered: (1) "broad urban areas", including centre, periphery and others[32] (ii) minor administrative divisions (MIADs) and (iii) subMIADS, which vary between countries but which can be as small as city blocks at the most disaggregated level. The MIADs of the selected cities are listed in table V.A1.1:

Table V.A1.1

Latin America (selected cities): minor administrative divisions (MIADs) of the cities analysed

City	Minor administrative divisions
Buenos Aires (Argentina)	School districts I to XV Almirante Brown, Avellaneda, Berazategui, Cañuelas, Escobar, Esteban Echeverría, Ezeiza, Florencio Varela, General Rodríguez, General San Martín, Hurlingham, Ituzaingó, José C. Paz, La Matanza, Lanús, La Plata, Lomas de Zamora, Malvinas Argentinas, Marcos Paz, Merlo, Moreno, Morón, Pilar, Presidente Perón, Quilmes, San Fernando, San Isidro, San Miguel, San Vicente, Tigre, Tres de Febrero, and Vicente López.
Belo Horizonte (Brazil)	Centre: Belo Horizonte Subcentre or peripheral industrial area: Betim, Contagem and Sete Lagoas. Gentrified periphery (new periphery): Nova Lima and Lagoa Santa. Traditional near periphery: Pedro Leopoldo, Caeté, Sabará, Confins, Mateus Leme, Juatuba, Igarapé, Santa Luzia, Sarzedo, São José da Lapa, São Joaquim da Bica, Rio Acima, Raposos, Esmeraldas, Ibirité, Ribeirão das Neves, Mario Campos and Vespasiano. Traditional far periphery: Brumadinho, Itaúna, Florestal, Itabirito, Barão de Cocais, Santa Bárbara, Pará de Minas, Matozinhos, Jaboticatubas, Prudente de Moraes, Itaguará, Taquaruçu de Minas, Fortuna de Minas, Bonfim, Inhaúma, Rio Manso, Belo Vale, Baldim, Nova União, Capim Branco, Funilândia, Moeda, Itatiaiçu and São José da Varginha.
Brasilia	Centre: Brasilia Traditional near periphery: Águas Lindas de Goiás, Cabeceira Grande, Cidade Ocidental, Cristalina, Formosa, Luziânia, Novo Gama, Padre Bernardo, Planaltina, Santo Antônio do Descoberto and Valparaíso de Goiás. Traditional far periphery: Buritis, Unaí, Abadiânia, Água Fria de Goiás, Alexânia, Cabeceiras, Cocalzinho de Goiás, Corumbá de Goiás, Mimoso de Goiás and Pirenópolis.
Curitiba (Brazil)	Centre: Curitiba Industrial periphery: Araucária and São José dos Pinhais. Traditional near periphery: Almirante Tamandaré, Balsa Nova, Campina Grande do Sul, Campo Largo, Campo Magro, Colombo, Contenda, Fazenda Rio Grande, Itaperuçu, Mandirituba, Pinhais, Piraquara, Quatro Barras and Rio Branco do Sul. Traditional far periphery: Adrianópolis, Agudos do Sul, Bocaiúva do Sul, Cerro Azul, Lapa, Quitandinha, Tijucas do Sul, Tunas do Paraná and Doutor Ulysses.
Recife (Brazil)	Centre: Recife Subcentres: Jaboatão dos Guararapes and Olinda. Traditional near periphery: Abreu e Lima, Cabo de Santo Agostinho, Camaragibe, Moreno, Paulista and São Lourenço da Mata. Traditional far periphery: Araçoiaba, Igarassu, Ipojuca, Ilha de Itamaracá and Itapissuma.
Rio de Janeiro (Brazil)	Centre: Río de Janeiro Subcentre: Niterói Industrial periphery: Duque de Caxias, Nova Iguaçu and São Gonçalo. Gentrified periphery: Maricá Traditional near periphery: Belford Roxo, Itaguaí, Magé, Mesquita, Nilópolis, Queimados and São João de Meriti. Traditional far periphery: Guapimirim, Itaboraí, Japeri, Paracambi, Seropédica and Tanguá.
Salvador (Brazil)	Centre: Salvador Subcentre: Camaçari Gentrified periphery: Lauro de Freitas Traditional near periphery: Candeias, Dias d'Ávila, Itaparica, Madre de Deus, Mata de São João, São Francisco do Conde, Simões Filho and Vera Cruz. Traditional far periphery: São Sebastião do Passé, Mata de São João and Pojuca.
São Paulo (Brazil)	Centre: São Paulo Subcentre: Guarulhos, Osasco, Santo André, São Bernardo do Campo and São Caetano do Sul. Gentrified periphery: Barueri, Cotia, Mogi das Cruzes and Santana de Parnaíba. Traditional near periphery: Arujá, Caieiras, Carapicuíba, Diadema, Embu, Ferraz de Vasconcelos, Franco da Rocha, Itaquaquecetuba, Mairiporã, Mauá, Poá, Ribeirão Pires, Rio Grande da Serra, Santa Isabel, Suzano and Taboão da Serra. Traditional far periphery: Biritiba-Mirim, Cajamar, Embu-Guaçu, Francisco Morato, Guararema, Itapecerica da Serra, Itapevi, Jandira, Juquitiba, Pirapora do Bom Jesus, Salesópolis, São Lourenço da Serra and Vargem Grande Paulista.

32 Defined according to the criteria of proximity to the centre (centre-periphery contrast) and social composition (in order to distinguish, where possible, between the poorer traditional periphery and the new periphery containing pockets of wealth). Most cities have three or four "broad urban areas", since the central area is usually surrounded by an inner ring or "pericentral" area, as well as a periphery divided into a "traditional near periphery" and a "new far periphery". In some cities the centre consists of several minor administrative divisions (MIADs), while in others (Caracas, Guayaquil, Montevideo, Panama City and Quito, as well as Brazilian cities), it comprises a single central MIAD which accounts for a large proportion of the city's population. In a few cities, a fifth category, the "gentrified periphery", has been included in order to examine the phenomenon whereby peripheral spaces have been gradually occupied by affluent socioeconomic groups.
There are two reasons for using "broad urban areas". The first is to contribute to the debate on metropolitan changes and discussions on the validity of the sociodemographic contrast between centre and periphery, including the argument over the social diversification of the periphery. The second is to facilitate the comparative analysis of cities, since they all share a basic centre-periphery structure. Of course, the use of the broad category carries certain risks, such as masking processes that occur at a smaller, more disaggregated level —a risk that is controlled for by using other geographical scales in the analysis— and the possibility that the results will be dependent on the use of this territorial definition. Nevertheless, this territorial definition is based on official data and background information supplied by national experts.

Table V.A1.1 (concluded)

City	Minor administrative divisions
San José	City centre: San José, Goicochea, Tibás, Montes de Oca, Curridabat, Heredia (Cantón Central), Santo Domingo (Heredia), Belén (Heredia), Flores (Heredia) and San Pablo (Heredia). Near periphery: Escazú, Desamparados, Aserrí, Santa Ana, Alajuelita, Vásquez de Coronado, Moravia, Alajuela, Cartago and La Unión (Cartago). Far periphery: Mora, Atenas (Alajuela), Poás (Alajuela), Paraíso (Cartago), Alvarado (Cartago), Oreamuno (Cartago), El Guarco (Cartago), Barba (Heredia), Santa Bárbara (Heredia), San Rafael (Heredia) and San Isidro (Heredia).
Cuenca (Ecuador)	City centre: Cuenca First ring: Paccha, Ricaurte, Sinincay, Turi and Valle. Inner periphery: Baños, Llacao, Nulti, San Joaquín, Santa Ana, Sayausi, Sidcay and Tarqui. Outer periphery: Cumbe, Chaucha, Checa (Jidcay), Chiquintad, Molleturo, Octavio Cordero Palacios, Quingeo and Victoria del Portete.
Guayaquil (Ecuador)	City centre: Guayaquil First ring: Juan Gómez Rendón (Progreso), Morro and Eloy Alfaro (Durán). Inner periphery: Posorja Outer periphery: Puna and Tenguel.
Quito	City centre: Quito First ring: Conocoto and Cumbaya. Inner periphery: Alangasi, Amaguaña and Calderon (Carapungo). Outer periphery: Atahualpa (Habaspamba) and Calacali.
Mexico City	City centre: Coyoacán, Iztacalco, Benito Juárez, Cuauhtemoc, Miguel Hidalgo and Venustiano Carranza. First ring: Azcapotzalco, Cuajimalpa de Morelos, Gustavo A. Madero, Magdalena Contreras, Álvaro Obregón, Tlalpan, Xochimilco, Atizapán de Zaragoza, Coacalco de Berriozábal, Cuautitlán, Huixquilucan, Naucalpan de Juárez, Tlalnepantla de Baz and Cuautitlán Izcalli. Inner periphery: Iztapalapa, Tlahuac, Tizayuca, Acolman, Amecameca, Atenco, Cocotitlán, Coyotepec, Chiautla, Chicoloapan, Chiconcuac, Chimalhuacán, Ecatepec de Morelos, Huehuetoca, Ixtapaluca, Jaltenco, Melchor Ocampo, Nezahualcoyotl, Nextlalpan, Nicolás Romero, Papalotla, La Paz, Tecamac, Teoloyucan, Teotihuacan, Tepotzotlán, Texcoco, Tezoyuca, Tlalmanalco, Tultepec, Tultitlán, Zumpango and Tonanitla. Outer periphery: Milpa Alta, Apaxco, Atlautla, Axapusco, Ayapango, Chalco, Ecatzingo, Hueypoxtla, Isidro Fabela, Jilotzingo, Juchitepec, Nopaltepec, Otumba, Ozumba, San Martín de las Pirámides, Temamatla, Temascalapa, Tenango del Aire, Tepetlaoxtoc, Tepetlixpa, Tequixquiac, Villa del Carbón and Valle de Chalco Solidaridad.
Guadalajara (Mexico)	City centre: Guadalajara First ring: Zapopan Inner periphery: Tlajomulco de Zúñiga, Tlaquepaque and Tonala. Outer periphery: Ixtlahuacán de los Membrillos, Juanacatlán and El Salto.
Monterrey (Mexico)	City centre: San Pedro Garza García, Monterrey and San Nicolás de los Garza. First ring: Apodaca, Guadalupe, Santa Catarina and Santiago. Inner periphery: Cadereyta Jiménez, García, General Escobedo and Juárez. Outer periphery: Ciénaga de Flores, General Zuazua and Salinas Victoria.
Toluca (Mexico)	City centre: Toluca and Metepec. First ring: Lerma, Mexicaltzingo, Ocoyoacac and San Mateo Atenco. Inner periphery: Almoloya de Juárez, Calimaya, Chapultepec, Rayón, San Antonio la Isla and Xonacatlán. Outer periphery: Otzolotepec, Temoaya and Zinacantepec.
Panama City	Arraiján, La Chorrera, Panamá and San Miguelito.
Lima (Peru)	Ancón, Ate, Barranco, BellaVista, Breoa, Callao, Carabayllo, Carmen de la Legua Reynoso, Chaclacayo, Chilca, Chorrillos, Cieneguilla, Comas, El Agustino, Independencia, Jesús María, La Molina, La Perla, La Punta, La Victoria, Lima, Lince, Los Olivos, Lurigancho, Lurín, Magdalena del Mar, Magdalena Vieja, Miraflores, Pachacamac, Pucusana, Puente Piedra, Punta Hermosa, Punta Negra, Ricardo Palma, Rimac, San Bartolo, San Borja, San Isidro, San Juan de Lurigancho, San Juan de Miraflores, San Luis, San Martín de Porres, San Miguel, Santa Anita, Santa Eulalia, Santa María del Mar, Santa Rosa, Santiago de Surco, Surquillo, Ventanilla, Villa El Salvador and Villa María del Triunfo.
Santo Domingo (Dominican Republic)	City centre: Santo Domingo de Guzmán. Near periphery: Santo Domingo Este and Santo Domingo Oeste. Far periphery: Los Alcarrizos, Pedro Brand, Santo Domingo Norte, Bajos de Haina, Boca Chica and San Antonio de Guerra.
Montevideo (Uruguay)	Centre: Montevideo. High-income periphery: Colinas de Solymar, Paso de Carrasco, San José de Carrasco, Lomas/Médanos Solymar, Parque Carrasco, Shangrilá, El Pinar, Solymar, El Bosque, Lagomar, Altos de la Tahona, Barra de Carrasco, Colinas de Carrasco, Barrio Asunción, Lomas de Carrasco, Carmel and Quintas del Bosque. Low-income periphery: Seis Hermanos, Aeropuerto Internacional de Carrasco, Costa y Guillamón, Fraccionamiento sobre Ruta 74, Villa Paz S.A., Monte Grande, Safici (Parque Postel), Santiago Vázquez, Villa Porvenir, Villa Crespo y San Andrés, Villa Felicidad, Villa Aeroparque, Villa San Cono, Joaquín Suárez, Toledo, Las Piedras, Barrio Cópola, Fraccionamiento Camino del Andaluz, Villa San José, Villa San Felipe, Delta del Tigre y Villas, Juan Antonio Artigas, Progreso, Pajas Blancas, La Paz, Jardines de Pando, Santa Mónica, Abayubá, Viejo Molino - San Bernardo, Barrio La Lucha, Colonia Nicolich, Pando, Villa El Tato, Parada Cabrera, Fraccionamiento Progreso, Playa Pascual, Olmos, Estanque de Pando, Rural, Villa Hadita, Instituto Adventista and Cerámicas del Sur.
Caracas (Venezuela (Bolivarian Republic of))	City centre: Libertador (capital district) First ring: Baruta, Chacao, El Hatillo and Sucre. Inner periphery: Carrizal, Guaicaipuro, Los Salias, Plaza and Zamora. Outer periphery: Cristóbal Rojas, Independencia and Paz Castillo.

Source: Economic Commission or Latin America and the Caribbean (ECLAC).

Annex 2

Supplementary tables

Table V.A2.1

Latin America (8 selected countries): demographic and social indicators of selected cities, by broad urban area, 2000 and 2010 census rounds

(Percentages)

Country	Metropolitan area	Percentage of total population		Heads of household aged 25 and over with: low education level (primary or lower)		Heads of household aged 25 and over with: high education level (secondary or higher)		Percentage of households in top and bottom socioeconomic status deciles: Decile 1		Percentage of households in top and bottom socioeconomic status deciles: Decile 10		Average annual growth rates (per hundred, exponential): Total	Urban	Primary education or less	Secondary education or higher	Decile 1	Decile 10
		2000	2010	2000	2010	2000	2010	2000	2010	2000	2010	2000-2010	2000-2010	2000-2010	2000-2010	2000-2010	2000-2010
Brazil	Cities	100.0	100.0	63.1	47.4	14.0	21.0	[a]				1.3	1.4	-2.9	4.0	[a]	
	Centres	58.1	56.5	57.5	40.8	17.4	28.1	8.6	8.0	13.2	14.9	1.0	1.1	-3.4	5.3	-0.7	2.2
	Periphery	19.6	20.5	75.1	57.6	6.1	9.7	12.9	14.6	6.8	6.0	1.8	2.0	-2.6	7.5	1.5	2.0
Costa Rica	San José agglomeration	100.0	100.0	50.2	41.7	20.3	26.6	10.0	10.0	9.8	10.0	0.8	2.3	-1.7	2.5	-0.0	0.2
	Central	38.9	35.9	40.5	32.6	27.3	33.5	8.8	9.0	13.6	12.0	0.1	0.6	-2.0	1.9	0.2	-1.2
	Near periphery	45.5	47.1	54.4	44.9	16.4	23.3	10.7	10.3	7.9	9.4	1.2	3.1	-1.8	3.2	-0.3	1.6
	Far periphery	15.5	16.9	63.9	53.2	12.8	20.2	11.3	11.3	5.1	7.2	1.6	5.0	-1.7	4.1	0.0	3.1
Dominican Republic	Santo Domingo agglomeration	100.0	100.0	44.7	40.8	25.1	26.1	[a]				2.3	3.5	-0.9	0.4	[a]	
	Central	33.0	27.9	36.6	33.4	35.3	37.0	7.2	8.8	19.3	19.1	0.5	0.5	-0.9	0.5	2.0	-0.1
	Near periphery	38.6	37.9	42.9	38.2	24.5	26.8	8.6	8.9	7.5	8.5	2.1	5.3	-1.1	0.9	0.3	1.3
	Far periphery	28.3	34.3	57.3	50.5	13.1	15.2	13.0	12.5	2.5	3.3	4.2	5.1	-1.3	1.5	-0.5	2.7
Ecuador	Cities	100.0	100.0	41.5	39.5	21.3	26.3	[a]				2.0	[c]	-0.5	2.3	[a]	
	Centres	81.3	79.1	36.8	34.7	24.1	29.5	[b]	8.8	[b]	14.2	1.7		-0.6	2.2	[b]	
	Periphery	6.9	8.0	64.1	60.1	8.2	11.9		13.8		4.1	3.6		-1.0	4.7		
Mexico	Cities	100.0	100.0	44.8	32.8	19.4	23.7	[a]				1.7	1.6	-3.0	2.0	[a]	
	Centres	41.7	35.5	38.9	28.0	27.4	33.4	5.6	5.5	15.8	16.4	0.2	0.1	-3.2	2.0	-0.2	0.4
	Periphery	23.4	28.6	55.1	37.1	8.4	13.7	16.8	14.0	3.6	5.0	4.0	4.4	-3.8	5.5	-1.7	3.6
Panama	Panama City agglomeration	100.0	100.0	30.0	24.1	21.7	27.1	[a]				2.1	2.1	-2.2	2.2	a	
	Centres	78.5	75.6	28.1	22.4	23.6	29.2	9.5	9.0	11.8	12.3	1.8	1.7	-2.3	2.1	-0.6	0.4
	Periphery	21.5	24.4	37.1	29.6	14.4	20.4	11.4	13.0	2.5	2.6	3.4	3.7	-2.3	3.5	1.3	0.3
Uruguay	Montevideo agglomeration	100.0	100.0	49.9	30.4	16.8	26.7	[a]				0.3	0.4	-3.3	3.1	[a]	
	Central	80.6	77.1	47.3	27.5	18.7	30.6	8.3	9.2	11.3	9.3	-0.0	-0.0	-3.6	3.3	0.7	-1.3
	Affluent periphery	4.8	6.7	41.0	22.6	18.3	27.8	7.9	5.9	12.3	20.8	2.5	2.5	-4.0	2.8	-2.0	3.5
	Poor periphery	14.7	16.2	69.0	48.1	4.4	6.6	19.6	17.5	2.0	9.1	0.9	1.6	-2.4	2.6	-0.8	10.0
Venezuela (Bolivarian Republic of)	Caracas agglomeration	100.0	100.0	56.4	31.0	20.4	20.6	[a]				0.8	0.8	-6.0	0.1	[a]	
	City centre	49.4	48.1	57.9	30.7	17.0	17.7	9.2	9.1	5.8	5.4	0.6	0.6	-6.3	0.4	-0.1	-0.7
	First ring	24.9	23.8	46.7	27.5	32.7	30.6	8.6	8.8	20.8	18.8	0.4	0.4	-5.3	-0.7	0.2	-1.0
	Inner periphery	13.8	14.4	59.4	32.1	18.0	20.2	9.9	8.8	9.1	10.9	1.3	1.3	-6.1	1.1	-1.2	1.8
	Outer periphery	11.9	13.7	68.6	37.5	9.3	12.5	16.9	17.3	4.3	9.2	2.3	2.4	-6.1	3.0	0.3	7.5

Source: Economic Commission for Latin America and the Caribbean (ECLAC), on the basis of special processing of census microdata.

[a] The calculation is inadmissible, since the first and tenth deciles are prepared for each city and are therefore constant.

[b] The socioeconomic indicator could not be calculated because the 2001 census did not include questions on household goods.

[c] The calculation is inadmissible because urban and rural areas are defined at the level of administrative divisions, and are generally dichotomous (e.g. 100% or 0% urban).

Table V.A2.2a

Latin America (18 selected cities): total net migration by age and education groups, five-year periods prior to the 2000 and 2010 census rounds [a]

(Absolute numbers)

City	Net migration, 2010 census round									Net migration, 2000 census round								
	Total	Total heads of household	Age groups				Education groups (heads of household aged 25 and over)			Total	Total heads of household	Age groups				Education groups (heads of household aged 25 and over		
			0-14	15-29	30-59	60 and over	Low	Medium	High			0-14	15-29	30-59	60 and over	Low	Medium	High
Belo Horizonte	49 630	11 159	-1 273	51 084	-1 057	877	4 539	5 406	721	101 067	22 037	13 888	67 011	17 141	3 027	17 171	2 638	1 307
Brasilia	98 583	30 855	3 904	70 269	22 377	2 032	10 519	7 554	11 386	157 928	35 344	26 516	93 030	36 072	2 310	20 949	6 592	7 296
Curitiba	46 230	13 218	-283	37 218	8 960	334	3 493	3 824	5 544	111 213	31 458	18 408	57 427	32 023	3 355	18 028	7 887	5 000
Recife	-14 150	-7 565	-4 265	-240	-9 476	-169	-3 182	-2 414	-1 792	-1 401	-3 646	-2 370	4 091	-3 774	652	-1 849	-1 382	-621
Rio de Janeiro	-80 350	-37 206	-22 563	22 737	-59 456	-21 068	-9 053	-12 400	-15 331	-26 815	-29 216	-9 923	49 131	-48 928	-17 096	-1 722	-14 842	-12 337
Salvador	2 371	-4 191	-3 077	19 967	-13 832	-687	-2 451	-244	-1 243	21 040	98	-1 649	24 981	-3 671	1 379	152	-869	411
São Paulo	-182 803	-73 037	-76 789	101 741	-161 487	-46 268	-32 685	-26 369	-13 860	-227 394	-122 272	-77 713	127 162	-227 127	-49 716	-66 259	-31 598	-22 709
San José	-7 108	-3 817	-5 337	7 016	-7 843	-944	-3 719	-1 448	1 310	15 792	2 222	-190	13 438	1 900	644	1 448	362	435
Cuenca	8 997	1 865	555	7 446	642	354	882	645	264	15 009	3 772	2 140	10 059	2 281	529	1 954	1 127	496
Guayaquil	-7 487	-6 196	-3 328	7 152	-10 586	-725	280	-2 373	-3 966	44 694	7 790	6 078	27 502	6 712	4 402	6 397	1 616	-774
Quito	23 284	5 664	-1 179	29 875	-5 986	574	1 928	2 571	1 084	52 370	12 365	3 613	43 726	2 925	2 106	5 823	4 669	1 069
Guadalajara	2 107	2 641	-9 440	19 841	-9 162	868	-531	1 256	2 162	-7 234	-2 524	-7 713	10 106	-9 914	287	-2 697	-1 114	659
Mexico City	-149 018	-74 140	-45 799	25 156	-105 627	-22 748	-17 716	-25 888	-26 671	-59 159	-44 943	-39 800	62 883	-74 127	-8 115	-7 966	-16 027	-17 177
Monterrey	45 753	7 589	4 560	33 821	7 112	260	1 953	2 042	3 099	62 064	12 500	7 231	42 184	10 563	2 086	3 972	3 626	3 586
Toluca	40 599	13 670	8 261	8 690	21 768	1 880	2 178	2 298	8 524	1 441	2 254	554	-3 974	4 169	692	-77	50	2 004
Panama City	71 069	25 307	2 266	35 527	28 937	4 339	5 983	9 336	5 452	82 321	26411	6 083	41 270	30 298	4 670	7808	9347	4462
Montevideo	3 851	2 047	-2 681	15 799	-6 926	-2 341	-1 247	-2 072	-1 403	12 897	1 317	-818	18 032	-2 477	-1 840	74	-934	-1 363
Caracas	-72 083	-24 031	-15 427	-19 376	-32 979	-4 301	-5 612	-11 327	-4 675	28 246	-11 600	5 156	28 880	-8 699	2 909	-8 785	-4 633	373

Source: Economic Commission for Latin America and the Caribbean (ECLAC), on the basis of special processing of census microdata.

[a] The sum total of the age groups matches that of the total population (strictly speaking, those over four years old who may qualify as internal migrants, in other words, who responded to the relevant questions and resided in the country at the time of the census or during the five years prior to it). Conversely, the total sum of heads of household by education groups does not match the total number of heads of household, since the latter includes all heads of household, while the education categories only include heads of household aged 25 and over.

Table V.A2.2b

Latin America (18 selected cities): total net migration rates by age and education groups, five-year periods prior to the 2000 and 2010 census rounds

(Annual averages, per thousand inhabitants)

City	Net migration, 2010 census round									Net migration, 2000 census round								
	Total	Total heads of household	Age groups				Education groups (heads of household aged 25 and over)			Total	Total heads of household	Age groups				Education groups (heads of household aged 25 and over)		
			0-14	15-29	30-59	60 and over	Low	Medium	High			0-14	15-29	30-59	60 and over	Low	Medium	High
Belo Horizonte	2.0	0.3	-0.3	7.1	-0.1	0.3	0.4	1.0	-1.5	5.2	2.6	3.6	10.8	2.2	1.8	3.5	0.7	0.5
Brasilia	5.9	4.0	1.2	13.8	3.1	1.5	2.8	2.1	7.8	12.5	7.1	9.4	21.2	7.7	3.0	6.6	4.6	12.7
Curitiba	3.2	1.2	-0.1	9.0	1.4	0.2	0.9	0.6	2.5	9.3	6.8	7.5	15.3	6.7	3.4	7.1	6.6	5.5
Recife	-0.8	-1.4	-1.5	0.0	-1.3	-0.1	-1.0	-1.5	-3.1	-0.1	-0.8	-0.8	0.8	-0.7	0.5	-0.5	-1.4	-1.8
Rio de Janeiro	-1.4	-2.4	-2.6	1.6	-2.4	-2.7	-1.6	-2.7	-4.3	0.5	-2.4	-1.1	3.5	-2.4	-2.8	-0.9	-4.3	-5.4
Salvador	0.1	-1.6	-1.1	4.0	-1.9	-0.4	-1.3	-1.1	-3.4	-1.5	-0.6	-0.6	5.2	-0.7	1.4	-0.5	-1.4	0.2
São Paulo	-2.0	-3.5	-5.1	4.0	-4.0	-4.4	-3.4	-4.6	-3.0	2.8	-6.2	-4.9	5.1	-6.8	-6.8	-5.6	-7.4	-7.1
San José	-0.7	-1.2	-3.1	2.3	-1.8	-0.8	-2.8	-2.4	-0.4	1.8	0.9	-0.1	5.0	0.5	0.8	0.8	-0.1	-0.2
Cuenca	4.0	2.9	1.1	10.3	0.8	1.4	2.1	1.3	-2.8	8.2	7.7	4.8	17.1	3.8	2.7	5.2	6.2	0.8
Guayaquil	-0.6	-1.8	-1.3	2.1	-2.3	-0.7	-0.1	-2.1	-6.6	4.6	3.0	2.8	9.0	1.9	4.7	5.7	1.1	-2.6
Quito	2.7	2.1	-0.7	11.3	-1.8	0.7	0.7	-0.5	-1.5	7.4	5.9	2.3	19.3	1.1	3.2	5.2	3.2	-1.7
Guadalajara	0.1	0.5	-2.2	3.4	-1.2	0.5	-0.3	0.6	1.6	-0.5	-0.6	-2.0	1.9	-1.8	0.2	-1.5	-0.9	0.9
Mexico City	-1.6	-2.8	-2.7	1.0	-2.7	-2.3	-2.1	-2.4	-4.6	-0.7	-2.0	-2.2	2.4	-2.4	-1.3	-0.9	-2.0	-4.4
Monterrey	2.5	1.5	1.3	6.6	0.9	0.1	1.3	1.0	2.3	4.2	3.1	2.3	8.6	1.9	1.8	2.8	2.8	4.4
Toluca	4.8	6.2	4.3	3.4	6.5	2.9	2.7	2.9	18.4	0.2	1.4	0.3	-1.7	1.8	1.6	-0.1	0.1	8.6
Panama City	10.9	12.7	1.7	19.6	10.7	6.1	13.0	10.4	10.8	15.7	17.5	5.5	25.3	14.9	10.1	18.5	14.1	14.4
Montevideo	0.5	0.7	-2.5	9.0	-2.3	-1.6	-1.6	-2.0	-2.2	1.8	0.6	-0.7	10.0	-0.9	-1.3	0.1	-1.3	-3.6
Caracas	-4.3	-4.7	-5.9	-3.8	-4.5	-2.3	-4.2	-5.1	-4.8	1.7	-2.5	1.5	5.9	-1.3	1.8	-3.7	-4.8	0.4

Source: Economic Commission for Latin America and the Caribbean (ECLAC), on the basis of special processing of census microdata.

Table V.A2.3a

Latin America (22 selected cities): index of dissimilarity at the level of minor administrative divisions (MIADs) for three education groups, censuses conducted in the 2000s and 2010s, and absolute change between censuses

County	City	Low education level			Medium education level			High education level		
		2000	2010	Absolute change 2000-2010	2000	2010	Absolute change 2000-2010	2000	2010	Absolute change 2000-2010
Argentina	Buenos Aires	0.234	0.239	0.004	0.143	0.084	-0.058	0.422	0.414	-0.009
Brazil	Belo Horizonte	0.235	0.171	-0.064	0.140	0.061	-0.079	0.377	0.320	-0.057
	Brasilia	0.200	0.157	-0.043	0.138	0.057	-0.081	0.278	0.258	-0.020
	Curitiba	0.254	0.208	-0.046	0.144	0.061	-0.083	0.355	0.324	-0.031
	Recife	0.131	0.096	-0.035	0.075	0.062	-0.013	0.255	0.261	0.006
	Rio de Janeiro	0.207	0.162	-0.045	0.081	0.029	-0.052	0.324	0.298	-0.026
	Salvador	0.108	0.074	-0.034	0.088	0.037	-0.051	0.154	0.143	-0.011
	São Paulo	0.111	0.070	-0.041	0.050	0.046	-0.004	0.193	0.172	-0.021
Costa Rica	San José	0.177	0.176	0.000	0.091	0.088	-0.003	0.212	0.189	-0.023
Dominican Republic	Santo Domingo	0.103	0.106	0.003	0.050	0.044	-0.005	0.202	0.195	-0.007
Ecuador	Cuenca	0.326	0.317	-0.009	0.232	0.165	-0.067	0.322	0.306	-0.016
	Guayaquil	0.025	0.031	0.005	0.014	0.015	0.001	0.035	0.053	0.019
	Quito	0.041	0.039	-0.003	0.017	0.019	0.002	0.032	0.044	0.011
Mexico	Mexico City	0.120	0.145	0.024	0.065	0.087	0.023	0.258	0.259	0.001
	Guadalajara	0.082	0.092	0.009	0.037	0.061	0.025	0.180	0.203	0.023
	Monterrey	0.081	0.111	0.030	0.122	0.162	0.041	0.207	0.197	-0.010
	Toluca	0.194	0.194	0.000	0.081	0.041	-0.039	0.297	0.303	0.006
Panama	Panama City	0.086	0.074	-0.012	0.027	0.031	0.004	0.109	0.077	-0.031
Peru	Lima	0.156	0.166	0.010	0.073	0.117	0.044	0.306	0.285	-0.021
Uruguay	Montevideo	0.101	0.131	0.030	0.051	0.033	-0.019	0.129	0.150	0.021
Venezuela (Bolivarian Republic of)	Caracas	0.120	0.070	-0.051	0.057	0.073	0.015	0.220	0.169	-0.051
	Maracaibo	0.098	0.090	-0.007	0.047	0.050	0.003	0.177	0.154	-0.022
Simple average (including Brazil)		**0.145**	**0.133**	**-0.012**	**0.083**	**0.065**	**-0.018**	**0.229**	**0.217**	**-0.012**
Simple average (excluding Brazil)		**0.130**	**0.132**	**0.002**	**0.074**	**0.071**	**-0.002**	**0.207**	**0.200**	**-0.007**

Source: Economic Commission for Latin America and the Caribbean (ECLAC), on the basis of special processing of census microdata.

Table V.A2.3b

Latin America (18 selected cities): index of dissimilarity at the subMIAD level [a] for three education groups, censuses conducted in the 2000s and 2010s, and absolute change between censuses

County	City	Low education level			Medium education level			High education level		
		2000	2010	Absolute change 2000-2010	2000	2010	Absolute change 2000-2010	2000	2010	Absolute change 2000-2010
Brazil	Belo Horizonte	0.328	0.258	-0.069	0.213	0.124	-0.089	0.559	0.477	-0.082
	Brasilia	0.368	0.294	-0.074	0.238	0.179	-0.058	0.644	0.514	-0.130
	Curitiba	0.324	0.267	-0.057	0.185	0.139	-0.047	0.531	0.456	-0.075
	Recife	0.295	0.208	-0.088	0.182	0.125	-0.057	0.531	0.479	-0.052
	Rio de Janeiro	0.301	0.242	-0.059	0.158	0.131	-0.027	0.512	0.470	-0.042
	Salvador	0.289	0.207	-0.081	0.184	0.130	-0.053	0.597	0.487	-0.110
	São Paulo	0.277	0.212	-0.065	0.138	0.110	-0.028	0.488	0.453	-0.035
Costa Rica	San José	0.237	0.239	0.001	0.113	0.111	-0.002	0.309	0.280	-0.029
Dominican Republic	Santo Domingo	0.180	0.181	0.002	0.097	0.090	-0.008	0.372	0.351	-0.022
Ecuador	Cuenca	0.342	0.334	-0.009	0.239	0.181	-0.057	0.375	0.363	-0.012
	Guayaquil	0.285	0.286	0.001	0.111	0.121	0.010	0.451	0.457	0.006
	Quito	0.297	0.306	0.009	0.134	0.136	0.002	0.372	0.397	0.025
Mexico	Guadalajara	0.094	0.094	0.000	0.042	0.063	0.021	0.196	0.203	0.007
	Mexico City	0.136	0.150	0.014	0.070	0.087	0.017	0.269	0.260	-0.009
	Monterrey	0.086	0.111	0.025	0.126	0.162	0.037	0.209	0.197	-0.012
	Toluca	0.291	0.194	-0.097	0.138	0.041	-0.097	0.435	0.303	-0.132
Panama	Panama City	0.286	0.284	-0.002	0.123	0.145	0.022	0.408	0.393	-0.015
Uruguay	Montevideo	0.320	0.345	0.025	0.141	0.133	-0.008	0.448	0.472	0.024
Simple average (including Brazil)		**0.259**	**0.229**	**-0.030**	**0.141**	**0.121**	**-0.020**	**0.422**	**0.381**	**-0.041**
Simple average (excluding Brazil)		**0.231**	**0.223**	**-0.008**	**0.118**	**0.114**	**-0.004**	**0.352**	**0.329**	**-0.023**

Source: Economic Commission for Latin America and the Caribbean (ECLAC), on the basis of special processing of census microdata.
[a] A division smaller than a minor administrative division (MIAD).

Table V.A2.4a

Latin America (17 selected cities): index of dissimilarity at the level of minor administrative divisions (MIADs) for the top and bottom socioeconomic deciles, censuses conducted in the 2000s and 2010s, and absolute change between censuses

Country	City	Lowest socioeconomic decile			Highest socioeconomic decile		
		2000	2010	Absolute change 2000-2010	2000	2010	Absolute change 2000-2010
Brazil	Belo Horizonte	0.203	0.187	-0.016	0.341	0.233	-0.108
	Brasilia	0.177	0.158	-0.019	0.290	0.216	-0.074
	Curitiba	0.287	0.294	0.007	0.328	0.288	-0.040
	Recife	0.083	0.084	0.001	0.282	0.241	-0.040
	Rio de Janeiro	0.210	0.162	-0.049	0.320	0.240	-0.080
	Salvador	0.107	0.103	-0.004	0.159	0.129	-0.030
	São Paulo	0.159	0.131	-0.028	0.183	0.119	-0.064
Costa Rica	San José	0.121	0.133	0.011	0.239	0.177	-0.062
Dominican Republic	Santo Domingo	0.112	0.086	-0.026	0.343	0.298	-0.045
Mexico	Guadalajara	0.218	0.241	0.024	0.195	0.233	0.038
	Mexico City	0.264	0.241	-0.023	0.294	0.283	-0.011
	Monterrey	0.197	0.189	-0.008	0.263	0.260	-0.003
	Toluca	0.305	0.297	-0.008	0.321	0.299	-0.021
Panama	Panama City	0.038	0.080	0.041	0.197	0.192	-0.004
Uruguay	Montevideo	0.161	0.120	-0.041	0.133	0.086	-0.047
Venezuela (Bolivarian Republic of)	Caracas	0.120	0.132	0.013	0.352	0.340	-0.012
	Maracaibo	0.064	0.115	0.051	0.192	0.193	0.001
Simple average (including Brazil)		**0.166**	**0.162**	**-0.004**	**0.261**	**0.225**	**-0.035**
Simple average (excluding Brazil)		**0.160**	**0.163**	**0.003**	**0.253**	**0.236**	**-0.017**

Source: Economic Commission for Latin America and the Caribbean (ECLAC), on the basis of special processing of census microdata.

Table V.A2.4b

Latin America (16 selected cities): index of dissimilarity at the subMIAD level for the top and bottom socioeconomic deciles, censuses conducted in the 2000s and the 2010s, and absolute change between censuses

Country	City	Lowest socioeconomic decile			Highest socioeconomic decile		
		2000	2010	Absolute change 2000-2010	2000	2010	Absolute change 2000-2010
Brazil	Belo Horizonte	0.294	0.266	-0.028	0.486	0.324	-0.162
	Brasilia	0.334	0.302	-0.033	0.632	0.387	-0.245
	Curitiba	0.371	0.341	-0.030	0.493	0.390	-0.103
	Recife	0.220	0.192	-0.028	0.575	0.427	-0.147
	Rio de Janeiro	0.312	0.265	-0.048	0.512	0.389	-0.123
	Salvador	0.265	0.205	-0.060	0.605	0.467	-0.138
	São Paulo	0.348	0.300	-0.047	0.439	0.315	-0.124
Costa Rica	San José	0.251	0.249	-0.002	0.339	0.241	-0.098
Dominican Republic	Santo Domingo	0.264	0.245	-0.020	0.556	0.514	-0.042
Mexico	Guadalajara	0.243	0.250	0.007	0.213	0.233	0.020
	Mexico City	0.282	0.255	-0.027	0.303	0.290	-0.013
	Monterrey	0.202	0.189	-0.013	0.263	0.260	-0.003
	Toluca	0.453	0.307	-0.146	0.461	0.299	-0.161
Panama	Panama City	0.291	0.250	-0.042	0.581	0.589	0.008
Venezuela (Bolivarian Republic of)	Caracas	0.199	0.209	0.010	0.451	0.431	-0.021
	Maracaibo	0.350	0.379	0.029	0.434	0.416	-0.018
Simple average (including Brazil)		**0.292**	**0.263**	**-0.030**	**0.459**	**0.373**	**-0.086**
Simple average (excluding Brazil)		**0.282**	**0.259**	**-0.023**	**0.400**	**0.364**	**-0.036**

Source: Economic Commission for Latin America and the Caribbean (ECLAC), on the basis of special processing of census microdata.

Table V.A2.5a

Brazil and Panama (8 selected cities): index of dissimilarity at the level of minor administrative divisions (MIADs) for the poorest and wealthiest deciles of the income distribution, censuses conducted in the 2000s and 2010s, and absolute change between censuses

Country	City	Poorest decile			Wealthiest decile		
		2000	2010	Absolute change 2000-2010	2000	2010	Absolute change2000-2010
Brazil	Belo Horizonte	0.199	0.143	-0.056	0.407	0.389	-0.018
	Brasilia	0.221	0.184	-0.037	0.276	0.29	0.014
	Curitiba	0.273	0.199	-0.074	0.362	0.347	-0.015
	Recife	0.142	0.094	-0.048	0.314	0.334	0.019
	Rio de Janeiro	0.186	0.114	-0.072	0.381	0.366	-0.015
	Salvador	0.123	0.079	-0.044	0.16	0.155	-0.005
	São Paulo	0.126	0.049	-0.077	0.243	0.238	-0.006
Panama	Panama City	0.054	0.04	-0.014	0.21	0.179	-0.031
Simple average		**0.166**	**0.113**	**-0.053**	**0.294**	**0.287**	**-0.007**

Source: Economic Commission for Latin America and the Caribbean (ECLAC), on the basis of special processing of census microdata.

Table V.A2.5b

Brazil and Panama (8 selected cities): index of dissimilarity at the subMIAD level for the poorest and wealthiest deciles of the income distribution, censuses conducted in the 2000s and 2010s, and absolute change between censuses

Country	City	Poorest decile			Wealthiest decile		
		2000	2010	Absolute change 2000-2010	2000	2010	Absolute change 2000-2010
Brazil	Belo Horizonte	0.275	0.209	-0.067	0.587	0.572	-0.015
	Brasilia	0.341	0.256	-0.085	0.678	0.628	-0.05
	Curitiba	0.316	0.254	-0.062	0.574	0.528	-0.046
	Recife	0.22	0.164	-0.055	0.595	0.579	-0.016
	Rio de Janeiro	0.276	0.225	-0.051	0.62	0.612	-0.009
	Salvador	0.237	0.192	-0.044	0.62	0.591	-0.028
	São Paulo	0.292	0.211	-0.081	0.58	0.585	0.005
Panama	Panama City	0.238	0.217	-0.021	0.48	0.425	-0.055
Simple average		**0.238**	**0.19**	**-0.055**	**0.519**	**0.492**	**-0.031**

Source: Economic Commission for Latin America and the Caribbean (ECLAC), on the basis of special processing of census microdata.

Table V.A2.6

Latin America (14 selected cities): exposure indices for the top and bottom socioeconomic deciles, at the minor administrative division (MIAD) and subMIAD levels, 2010 census round

Country	City	Indicator	Scale	Scale
Brazil	Belo Horizonte	Exposure indices	MIAD	subMIAD
		Interaction	0.36	0.29
		Isolation	0.64	0.71
	Brasilia	Exposure indices	MIAD	subMIAD
		Interaction	0.37	0.26
		Isolation	0.63	0.74
	Curitiba	Exposure indices	MIAD	subMIAD
		Interaction	0.51	0.45
		Isolation	0.49	0.55
	Recife	Exposure indices	MIAD	subMIAD
		Interaction	0.42	0.31
		Isolation	0.58	0.69
	Rio de Janeiro	Exposure indices	MIAD	subMIAD
		Interaction	0.42	0.31
		Isolation	0.58	0.69
	Salvador	Exposure indices	MIAD	subMIAD
		Interaction	0.47	0.30
		Isolation	0.53	0.70
	São Paulo	Exposure indices	MIAD	subMIAD
		Interaction	0.37	0.27
		Isolation	0.63	0.73
Costa Rica	San José	Exposure indices	MIAD	subMIAD
		Interaction	0.45	0.38
		Isolation	0.55	0.62
Dominican Republic	Santo Domingo	Exposure indices	MIAD	subMIAD
		Interaction	0.43	0.26
		Isolation	0.57	0.74
Mexico	Guadalajara	Exposure indices	MIAD	subMIAD
		Interaction	0.43	
		Isolation	0.57	
	Mexico City	Exposure indices	MIAD	subMIAD
		Interaction	0.41	
		Isolation	0.59	
	Monterrey	Exposure indices	MIAD	subMIAD
		Interaction	0.44	
		Isolation	0.56	
	Toluca	Exposure indices	MIAD	subMIAD
		Interaction	0.38	
		Isolation	0.62	
Panama	Panama City	Exposure indices	MIAD	subMIAD
		Interaction	0.45	0.21
		Isolation	0.55	0.79

Source: Economic Commission for Latin America and the Caribbean (ECLAC), on the basis of special processing of census microdata.
Note: The isolation index was calculated for the tenth (the wealthiest) decile.

Chapter VI

Recent trends in social spending and social investment in young people

Introduction

This chapter examines traditional indicators[1] of social spending, which aim to measure the level of priority that has been accorded to it in the current economic cycle, as a global slowdown curtails growth in Latin America and the Caribbean following limited rallies after the international financial crisis of 2008-2009. It also gauges the procyclical impact of social expenditure and seeks to determine whether its more recent tendency to be countercyclical is holding. The chapter also provides an overview of the sectoral distribution of public social expenditure, developments and changes in it over the long and medium term and cyclical patterns in its component parts.

Because the focus of the 2014 edition of *Social Panorama of Latin America* is an in-depth gap analysis, the second part of the chapter is devoted to public social investment in young people, highlighting the imbalance between expenditure targeting this group and on the population at large. This section is an adapted summary of ECLAC contributions to the *Third Ibero-American Youth Report*, recently presented at the seventeenth Ibero-American Conference of Ministers of Education, held in Burgos, Spain, from 17 to 19 September 2014 (ECLAC/Ibero-American Youth Organization, Mexican Youth Institute (IMJUVE), 2014).

A. Social spending in Latin America

Social spending grew more slowly in 2012-2013 than in previous years. This came after three years of significant efforts to increase social public spending as well as expenditure to boost the economy and on general State administration to combat the global financial crisis and its after-effects. The increased social spending seen in the first few years of the decade was used to strengthen programmes to combat poverty, develop emergency job programmes and implement or extend unemployment insurance and productive development programmes aimed at creating new jobs. These measures succeeded in augmenting domestic demand in the countries under review. Social spending is currently growing at a slower pace as a number of countries face the need to cut fiscal deficits built up when addressing the crisis of 2008-2009, a sluggish world economy and consequent efforts to boost investment in non-social sectors.

1. Recent and long-term trends

In spite of ups and downs in the economic cycle over the past five years, including the global financial crisis of 2008-2009, the slight rally in the economy in the following years and the global slowdown since 2012, the trend in the region until 2013 was towards a real increase in the resources available for financing social services and cash transfers to households.

This rise was also reflected in the priority accorded to social spending at the macroeconomic level: in the early 1990s, social spending as a share of gross domestic product (GDP) stood at 13.8%, rising steadily, albeit slowly, in the biennia under review to reach 16.7% in 2006-2007. It then soared to 19.1% of the region's GDP

1 Measurements based on the official statistics of the countries, organized as per the functional (according to destination of funds) or administrative (according to origin of funds) classifications of public spending. For further information, see box VI.1.

in 2012-2013 (see figure VI.1). In the last year under consideration, social spending in the region (21 countries) amounted to nearly US$ 685 billion (at constant 2005 prices). In 2012 the overall growth trend in social spending in both absolute and relative terms began to weaken somewhat. This trend reversal has led to ever-slower growth in public social spending owing to the persistent fiscal deficits incurred by a number of governments to tackle the global financial crisis and to the expected falls in revenue owing to the slowdown in growth in most countries, with a few exceptions that include several countries in Central America and the Caribbean (see ECLAC, 2014a).

Figure VI.1
Latin America and the Caribbean (21 countries): [a] **public social spending as a share of total spending, 1990-1991 to 2012-2013** [b]
(Percentages of GDP and of total public spending)

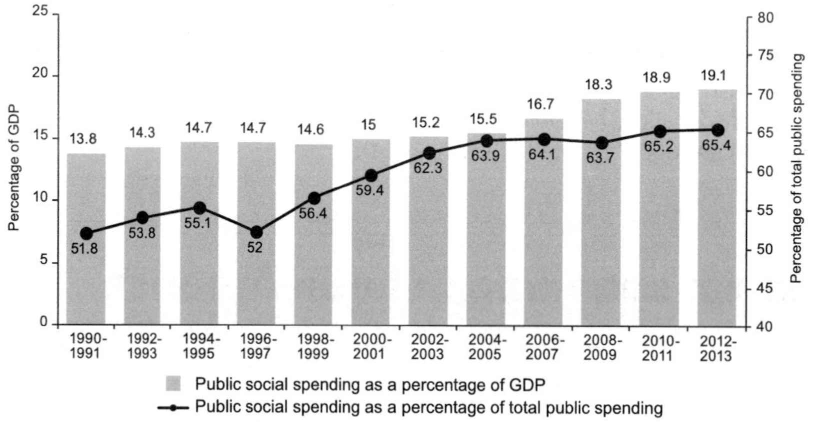

Source: Economic Commission for Latin America and the Caribbean (ECLAC), social expenditure database.
[a] Argentina, Bolivarian Republic of Venezuela, Brazil, Chile, Colombia, Costa Rica, Cuba, Dominican Republic, Ecuador, El Salvador, Guatemala, Honduras, Jamaica, Mexico, Nicaragua, Panama, Paraguay, Peru, Plurinational State of Bolivia, Trinidad and Tobago, and Uruguay.
[b] Weighted average of the countries.

Until the mid-2000s, social public spending had been markedly procyclical, as will be shown below. Even by 2005, however, several countries had embarked on systematic efforts to strengthen their social programmes, in particular those designed to combat poverty. The change in the pattern of social spending in the region is due to gradual measures to cope with external shocks: the escalation in food and fuel prices in 2008, the sustained rise in commodity exports which began in 2003; the worst of the world financial crisis towards the end of 2008 and in 2009; and, more recently, the climate of uncertainty across the world as the global economy slows.

These various developments had varying impacts on fiscal and social policy. In addition to the steps taken to shore up some of the major social programmes (to combat poverty and strengthen social protection, mainly through the solidarity-based or non-contributory pillar), spending (and taxes) were redirected, particularly in 2007 and 2008, to avoid the regressive effects of rising commodity prices. Subsequently, once the financial crisis had begun, governments adopted measures to stabilize domestic demand by increasing non-social public spending (especially through investment in infrastructure) and, above all, social spending, setting up programmes to create jobs, promote production (microenterprise lending) and launch housing projects. In some countries, setbacks in drafting and enacting legislation on investment projects and issues with implementation capacity led to delays in investment execution; more rapid responses were seen in the area of social spending. At the same time, greater fiscal priority was accorded to social spending as a share of total public expenditure, slowly going from 51.8% in 1990-1991 to 59.4% in 2002-2003 and then steadily climbing to 65.4% in 2012-2013. Some fluctuations and increases in the level of fiscal priority given to social spending were due, however, to contractions in non-social public spending and therefore to relative reductions in total public spending, mainly between 1999 and 2003 and once again from 2010 (see figure VI.2).

Figure VI.2

Latin America and the Caribbean (21 countries):[a] total public spending and biennial variation rates, 1990-1991 to 2012-2013[b]

(Percentages of GDP and percentage variation)

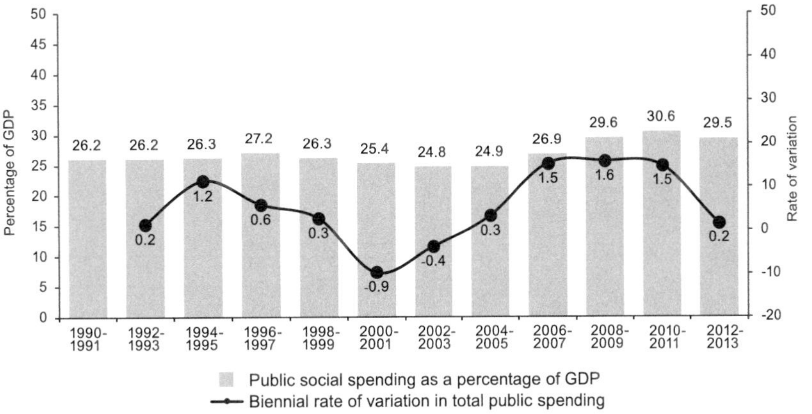

Source: Economic Commission for Latin America and the Caribbean (ECLAC), social expenditure database.

[a] Argentina, Bolivia (Plurinational State of), Brazil, Chile, Colombia, Costa Rica, Cuba, Dominican Republic, Ecuador, El Salvador, Guatemala, Honduras, Jamaica, Mexico, Nicaragua, Panama, Paraguay, Peru, Trinidad and Tobago, Uruguay and Venezuela (Bolivarian Republic of).

[b] Weighted average of the countries. The figures for total public spending are official figures using a functional classification of public spending and may not coincide with those obtained from an economic classification of spending. The regional figures are affected by the Brazilian official report's inclusion within total public spending of domestic and external debt refinancing, which was equivalent to 14.8% of total public spending on average over the last 4 years. For this reason, the data used for Brazil correspond to primary public spending.

Since 2010, several countries have embarked on fiscal reforms on both the revenue and the spending side in order to consolidate their public finances. This is because after some five years (from 2003 to 2008) of primary surpluses and falling public debt, the spike in public expenditure to finance measures to address the short- and medium-term effects of the global financial crisis led to a public accounts deficit as GDP stagnated or began to fall. Although the figures for 2010 show a continued countercyclical expansion in spending, this was accompanied by faster growth in social public spending and, in some cases, a decline in public spending in the economic and administrative spheres. At the regional level in 2010, social public spending grew by 7.9% compared with the financial crisis years of 2008-2009, and non-social spending by 7.2%. In 2011 expenditure in both categories was up, but public non-social spending rose at a faster rate.

Partial data for 2012 and 2013 point to a slowdown in social spending growth (3.5%) and a contraction in spending in non-social sectors, because, particularly in 2012, non-public social spending appears to have fallen (-5.2%). This trend held in 2013 although it was not quite as marked.

Among the countries for which data are available for 2012 or 2013, only in Mexico and the Bolivarian Republic of Venezuela did social spending fall in absolute terms in 2012. Colombia, Cuba and Peru saw social expenditure decrease in 2011 in respect of 2010 (see table VI.1).

Absolute changes in social spending do not, however, necessarily reflect the efforts made by countries to maintain it. Between 2011 and 2012, Brazil, Chile, Colombia, Costa Rica, Ecuador, El Salvador, Paraguay and Peru increased the level of macroeconomic priority given to social spending (while Chile, Colombia and Peru reversed the downward trend of 2010). What little data there are for 2013 suggest that this trend is likely to hold, but with rather more modest rises as a share of GDP (Colombia and Guatemala slightly increased social spending as a percentage of GDP, while levels in Chile remained unchanged).

Table VI.1

Latin America and the Caribbean (21 countries): total public spending, social public spending and non-social public spending 2008-2013 [a]

(Percentages of GDP and year-on-year percentage variation)

	Total public spending					Public social spending					Public non-social spending				
	2008-2009	2010	2011	2012	2013	2008-2009	2010	2011	2012	2013	2008-2009	2010	2011	2012	2013
								(percentages of GDP)							
Argentina	40.9	...	...	...	...	26.0	...	...	...	...	14.9	...	...	...	...
Bolivia (Plurinational State of)	36.5	36.8	35.0	34.4	...	12.2	12.3	11.7	11.5	...	24.3	24.5	23.3	22.9	...
Brazil	...	...	...	...	...	25.4	25.4	25.4	26.8	...	38.1	...	...	...	...
Chile	21.8	21.9	21.4	21.7	21.6	14.6	14.7	14.3	14.7	14.7	7.2	7.2	7.1	7.0	6.9
Colombia	19.3	19.7	17.7	18.8	19.7	13.4	13.7	12.3	13.1	13.7	5.9	6.0	5.4	5.7	6.0
Costa Rica	56.0	57.7	53.1	53.5	...	20.9	22.6	22.6	23.1	...	35.1	35.1	30.5	30.4	...
Cuba	76.8	70.0	66.7	...	...	40.7	42.2	36.5	...	...	36.1	27.8	30.2	...	...
Dominican Republic	20.4	19.5	18.8	...	...	8.1	7.3	7.1	...	...	12.3	12.0	11.7	...	...
Ecuador	29.3	30.8	32.0	32.7	...	7.1	8.1	8.1	8.3	...	22.2	22.7	23.9	24.4	...
El Salvador	22.8	24.0	25.8	24.4	...	13.2	13.4	14.7	14.8	...	9.6	...	...	...	...
Guatemala	14.6	14.9	15.2	14.5	14.3	7.5	7.9	7.6	7.5	7.6	7.1	7.0	7.6	7.0	6.7
Honduras	23.3	23.1	...	...	...	11.5	12.0	...	...	...	11.8	11.1	...	...	...
Jamaica	...	...	...	...	...	...	...	...	...	...	...	...	...	...	...
Mexico	19.5	20.2	20.1	18.5	...	10.6	11.3	11.4	10.7	...	8.9	8.9	8.7	7.8	...
Nicaragua	23.2	...	...	...	...	12.6	...	...	...	...	10.6	...	...	...	...
Panama	28.4	...	...	...	...	13.3	18.6	18.2	17.3	...	15.1	...	...	...	...
Paraguay	33.2	32.3	34.2	46.4	...	13.4	13.3	15.0	17.8	...	19.8	19.0	19.2	28.6	...
Peru	18.3	19.2	18.0	18.8	...	9.4	9.4	8.8	9.4	...	8.9	9.8	9.2	9.4	...
Trinidad and Tobago	35.2	...	...	...	...	12.1	...	...	...	...	23.1	...	...	...	...
Uruguay	31.8	32.1	32.5	...	...	23.5	24.2	24.1	...	...	8.3	7.9	8.4	...	...
Venezuela (Bolivarian Republic of)	30.4	23.9	32.2	29.9	...	18.8	17.3	22.8	21.2	...	11.6	6.6	9.4	8.7	...
Latin America and the Caribbean	**30.4**	**30.3**	**30.9**	**29.5**	...	**18.3**	**18.8**	**18.9**	**19.0**	**19.1**	**12.1**	**11.5**	**12.0**	**10.5**	...

Table VI.1 (concluded)

	Total public spending					Public social spending					Public non-social spending				
	2008-2009	2010	2011	2012	2013	2008-2009	2010	2011	2012	2013	2008-2009	2010	2011	2012	2013
	(rates of year-on-year variation)														
Argentina	...	...	...	...	...	...	...	...	...	...	...	...	...	...	...
Bolivia (Plurinational State of)	...	6.7	0.0	3.4	...	...	6.7	0.0	3.4	...	...	6.7	0.0	3.4	...
Brazil	...	3.7	2.0	4.3	...	...	7.4	2.7	6.6	...	...	1.3	1.5	2.7	...
Chile	...	5.6	3.3	7.0	3.8	...	5.9	3.0	8.3	4.1	...	5.0	3.9	4.5	3.1
Colombia	...	7.2	-4.3	10.8	9.0	...	7.2	-4.3	10.8	9.0	...	7.2	-4.3	10.8	9.0
Costa Rica	...	7.4	-3.8	6.0	...	...	12.9	4.5	7.5	...	...	4.2	-9.2	4.9	...
Cuba	...	-6.0	-2.1	...	...	...	6.9	-11.2	...	...	...	-20.6	11.7	...	...
Dominican Republic	...	3.4	2.2	...	...	...	-1.8	1.6	...	...	...	6.8	2.5	...	...
Ecuador	...	8.4	12.1	7.3	...	...	17.8	7.8	7.7	...	...	5.4	13.6	7.2	...
El Salvador	...	...	...	...	...	...	...	...	...	...	...	...	...	...	...
Guatemala	...	...	6.4	-1.7	2.3	...	...	0.2	1.6	5.1	...	...	13.5	-5.1	-0.7
Honduras	...	1.6	...	...	...	...	6.9	...	...	...	...	-3.7	...	...	...
Jamaica	...	...	...	...	...	...	...	...	...	...	...	...	...	...	...
Mexico	...	6.4	3.5	-4.4	...	...	9.4	5.0	-2.4	...	...	2.9	1.6	-7.1	...
Nicaragua	...	...	...	...	...	...	...	...	...	...	...	...	...	...	...
Panama	...	...	...	...	...	...	50.9	8.4	4.8	...	...	...	...	...	...
Paraguay	...	7.8	10.4	34.0	...	...	10.0	17.7	17.2	...	...	6.4	5.4	47.1	...
Peru	...	...	...	...	...	...	9.0	-0.3	13.2	...	...	...	...	...	...
Trinidad and Tobago	...	...	...	...	...	...	...	...	...	...	...	...	...	...	...
Uruguay	...	10.7	8.6	...	...	...	12.9	6.9	...	...	...	4.3	13.9	...	...
Venezuela (Bolivarian Repub ic of)	...	-24.0	40.4	-1.6	...	...	-10.8	37.3	-1.8	...	...	-45.3	48.6	-1.3	...
Latin America and the Car bbean	...	**7.7**	**5.6**	**1.1**	...	...	**7.9**	**4.9**	**3.5**	**3.1**	...	**7.2**	**7.4**	**-5.2**	...

Source: Economic Commission for Latin America and the Caribbean (ECLAC), social expenditure database.

[a] The figures for total public spending are official figures using a functional classification of public spending and may not coincide with those obtained from an economic classification of spending. The regional figures are affected by the Brazilian official report's inclusion within total public spending of domestic and external debt refinancing, which was equivalent to 14.8% of total public spending on average over the last 4 years.

(a) Long-term trends in social spending

The region's countries differ greatly both in the amount of resources they can effectively channel towards the social sectors and in the macroeconomic effort represented by their public social budgets. Of course, the capacity to assign greater macroeconomic priority to social spending depends on a host of economic, political and social variables. One of the determining factors is fiscal revenue, which sets a certain limit for the overall budget. Notwithstanding the rise in social expenditure as a percentage of GDP in the region (from 13.8% in 1990-1991 to 19.1% in 2012-2013), the initial and current levels of this indicator vary considerably between the countries. In 1990-1991 (or the most recent period for which data are available), countries such as Ecuador, Honduras, Mexico, Nicaragua and Trinidad and Tobago allocated less than 7% of GDP to social sectors, whereas Argentina, Brazil, the Bolivarian Republic of Venezuela, Costa Rica, Cuba and Uruguay earmarked 15% or more.

Except during certain periods, almost all the countries have made efforts to increase public social spending as a share of total spending (that is, the fiscal priority of social expenditure), often with the effect of pushing up social spending as a percentage of GDP. At the end of the period under review, the macroeconomic priority accorded to social spending had increased significantly in almost all countries. In 2012-2013 (or the most recent period for which data are available) every country in the region spent at least 7% of GDP on the social sectors. Only the Dominican Republic, Ecuador, Guatemala, Jamaica and Peru allocated less than 10% of GDP to these sectors, while Paraguay joined the group of countries that had been allocating more than 15% of GDP to social spending since the early 1990s (see figure VI.3).

Figure VI.3

Latin America and the Caribbean (21 countries): public social spending, 1990-1991 to 2012-2013

(Percentages of GDP)

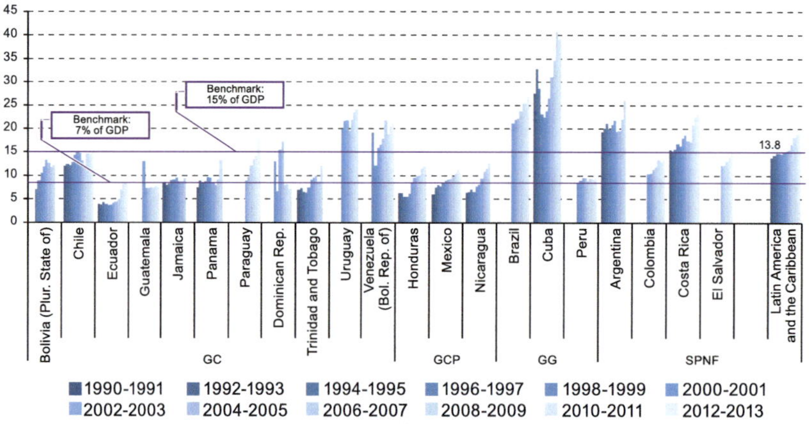

Source: Economic Commission for Latin America and the Caribbean (ECLAC), social expenditure database.

Note: CG: Central government; BCG: Budgetary central government; GG: General government; NFPS: Non-financial public sector (for Costa Rica: total public sector).

Despite persistent differences in the level of macroeconomic priority of social spending, some countries have made a proportionally larger effort to increase the percentage allocated to such spending. As a share of GDP, the macroeconomic priority of public social spending rose by 9.2% in Argentina between 1990 and 2009, by 8.7 percentage points in the Bolivarian Republic of Venezuela between 1997 and 2012, by 10 percentage points in Cuba between 1990 and 2011, by 10.4 percentage points in Panama until 2012 and by 8.9 percentage points in Paraguay between 2003 and 2012. In contrast, a comparison between the most recent data available (in most cases 2012-2013) and the initial series (1990-1991 or the most recent period for which data are available) shows no significant increase in the share of resources allocated to such spending by Chile, El Salvador, Guatemala, Jamaica or Peru.

But expressing social spending as a percentage of GDP masks even larger differences in amounts of resources actually allocated to the social sectors, which depend largely on each country's level of economic development (see figure VI.4). In 1990-1991 annual per capita social spending in the region averaged US$ 565 at constant 2005 prices; in 2012-2013, 22 years later, it had more than doubled to US$ 1,155. However, in countries such as Guatemala,

Honduras, Nicaragua and the Plurinational State of Bolivia, annual per capita spending remains below US$ 200, while in Argentina, Cuba, Trinidad and Tobago and Uruguay it exceeds US$ 1,600.

Figure VI.4
Latin America and the Caribbean (21 countries): per capita social public spending, 1990-1991 to 2012-2013
(Dollars at constant 2005 prices)

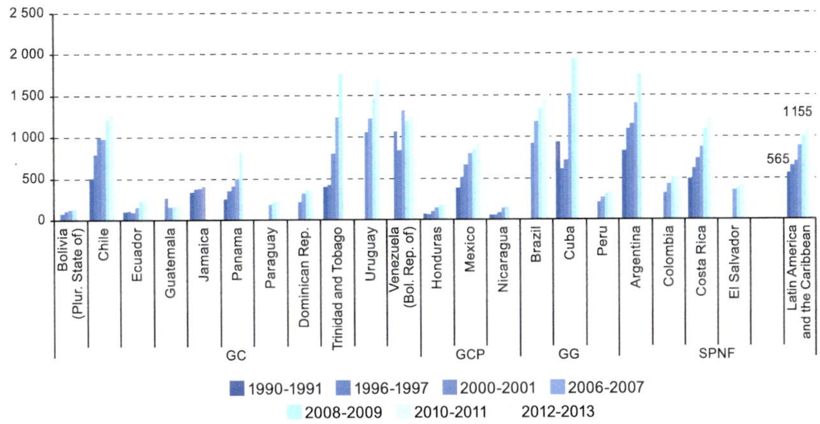

Source: Economic Commission for Latin America and the Caribbean (ECLAC), social expenditure database.
Note: CG: Central government; BCG: Budgetary central government; GG: General government; NFPS: Non-financial public sector (for Costa Rica: total public sector).

Heterogeneity in the macroeconomic priority of social spending and in levels of per capita spending does not make for a clear picture of whether these differences are due mainly to the size of the economies of the countries —which to a large extent shapes their ability to mobilize resources for the social sector— or if they stem from collective decisions and processes that have increased or reduced the role of the State in the provision of social services and enabled it to reasonably expand the overall government budget.

In order to ascertain whether there is a relationship between per capita GDP and per capita social spending, figure IV.5 correlates these two variables. The linear regression line may be used as a reference for identifying those countries that have made efforts consistent with their level of economic development and which, proportionately, have mobilized more resources, although this should not be taken as a normative pattern for the level of social spending in relation to GDP.

Figure VI.5
Latin America and the Caribbean (21 countries): ratio of per capita GDP to per capita social public spending, 2012-2013 [a]
(Dollars at constant 2005 prices)

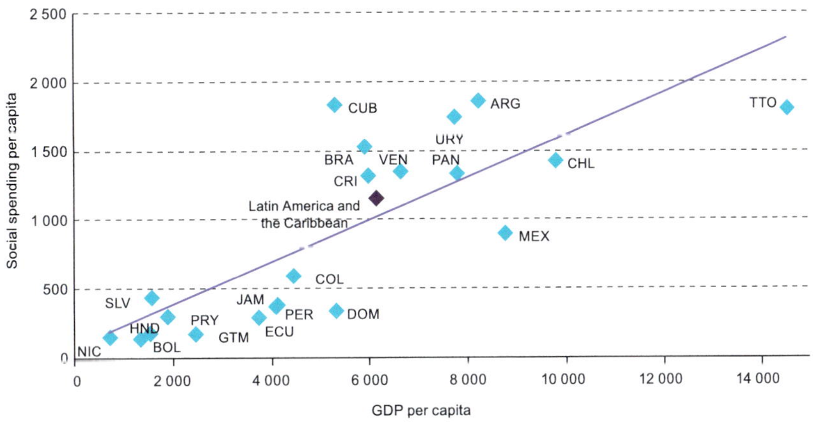

Source: Economic Commission for Latin America and the Caribbean (ECLAC), social expenditure database.
[a] 2012-2013 or the most recent biennium for which data are available (2010-2011 in most cases).

As indicated in the figure, certain countries in the region (Argentina, Bolivarian Republic of Venezuela, Brazil, Costa Rica, Cuba, El Salvador, Panama and Uruguay) mobilize an above-average share of resources, more than would be expected given their level of economic development. This does not mean that they mobilize an excessive amount of resources, since tax revenues in the region have tended to be low in recent decades and the pattern of social investment has been associated with the liberal economic models applied. However, even in the context of the region, some countries mobilize fewer resources than would be expected on the basis of their per capita GDP (see the countries below the regression line in figure VI.5). These countries would be well advised to forge new social and fiscal compacts in order to increase in a responsible manner their fiscal revenue as well as their provisions for economic and social expenditure (see ECLAC, 2014b) thus generating obvious synergies between social development, economic capacity-building for households and boosting domestic demand, levels of skills within the workforce and the competitiveness of countries. In the medium term, the virtuous circle created by the interplay between these factors would lay sustainable foundations for steady economic development and make countries less vulnerable to fluctuations in the world economy.

(b) How procyclical is social spending?

As a result of the measures adopted by the countries of the region to cope with the rising prices of food and other commodities, to attenuate the after-effects of the international financial crisis and to revive domestic economies, in recent years social spending has to some extent varied independently of the business cycle.

When social spending follows a procyclical pattern, this is chiefly because total public spending in the region rises, stagnates or falls in keeping with the business cycle. Thus, even when efforts are made to accord a higher fiscal priority to social spending, the tendency is for the latter to follow the pattern of total public spending. In the early 1990s, total public spending tended to be lower than at present, but social spending declined sharply (see figures VI.1 and VI.2). Thus, expansions in public spending, with a few exceptions, were fairly moderate and were in line with the business cycle, and falls in absolute terms were recorded at a time when GDP growth was slowing, although at no point did regional GDP fall during the period.

Thus, up to around 2004, total public spending was highly procyclical, sometimes with a certain lag in relation to the period of economic growth or contraction (see figure VI.6A). This "overreaction" in public spending in relation to the business cycle is associated with adjustments in non-social spending (mainly on economic sectors and general State administration). The fluctuations in this case were very sharp, in particular between 1991 and 2004, following ups and downs in the business cycle.

Since the early 1990s, governments have made significant efforts to increase or sustain social public spending, although fiscal responsibility led them to moderate their expansion whenever the pace of growth has slowed. This meant that social spending was also highly procyclical in line with higher GDP growth (elasticities of more than 1), but somewhat less procyclical in the face of slowdowns in the growth rate (elasticities below or equal to 1) (ECLAC, 2012). Since 2005, however, it has sometimes behaved countercyclically, in order to maintain or increase the resources allocated to the social sectors, for the reasons already discussed. This trend towards an expansion in social spending, particularly from 2005 to 2012, is clearly shown in figure VI.6B, even at a time of an outright contraction in GDP (in 2009), when growth in social spending also picked up significantly.

However, as noted above, the most recent data would suggest that trends towards maintaining or increasing social spending are weakening as a result of uncertainty concerning future global economic growth and the persistent balance-of-payment current account deficits in many countries, which could lead to a decline in fiscal revenue and a widening of fiscal deficits. This would suggest that social spending could well return to its procyclical pattern in 2013 and beyond unless action, underpinned by increased tax revenues as part of an effective improvement of tax collection systems, is taken to shore it up.

Figure VI.6
Latin America and the Caribbean (21 countries):[a] aggregate trends in total public spending, social public spending and GDP, 1991-2013[b]
(Annual percentage variation)

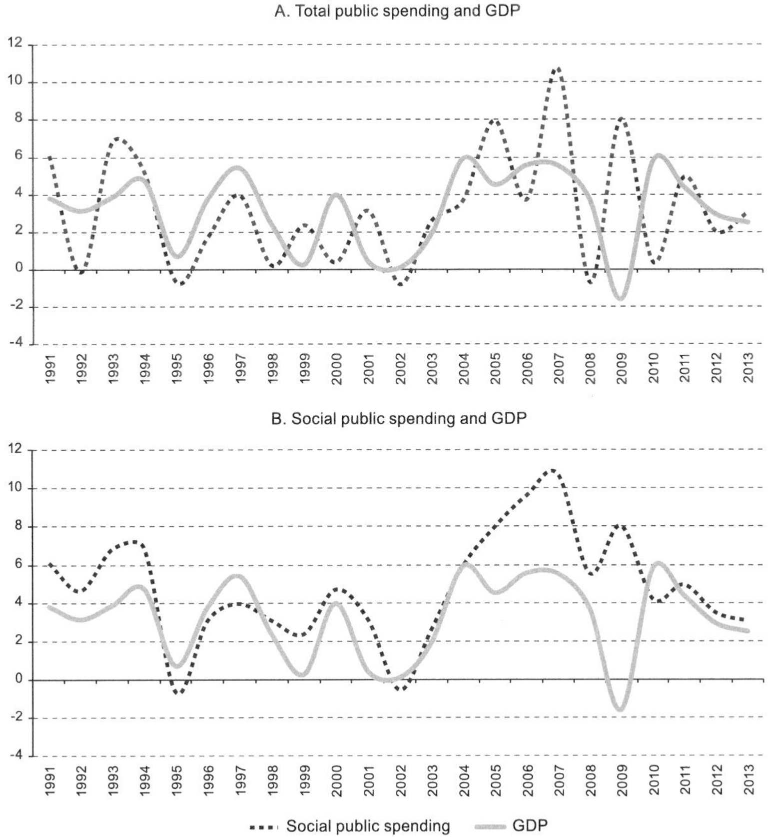

Source: Economic Commission for Latin America and the Caribbean (ECLAC), social expenditure database.
[a] Argentina, Bolivarian Republic of Venezuela, Brazil, Chile, Colombia, Costa Rica, Cuba, Dominican Republic, Ecuador, El Salvador, Guatemala, Honduras, Jamaica, Mexico, Nicaragua, Panama, Paraguay, Peru, Plurinational State of Bolivia, Trinidad and Tobago, and Uruguay.
[b] The figures for total public spending are official figures using a functional classification of public spending and may not coincide with those obtained from an economic classification of spending.

(c) Trends in expenditure by sector

As shown at the beginning of this section, social spending as a percentage of GDP has risen systematically at the regional level in all the periods under review. It is important, however, to look at the breakdown of expenditure by social sector (education, health, social security and social welfare, housing and others) (see figure VI.7).

Growth has not been uniform across all sectors. The ratio of social investment varies from sector to sector, and growth in any given sector also depends on how developed the institutional framework and social services coverage were at the start of the period under review, as well as on the pressures that various social groups can bring to bear on the State to obtain a more rapid increase in certain types of expenditure, on contractions in the economy requiring mobilization of welfare resources, and on the level of population ageing.

Generally speaking, the increase in social expenditure equal to 5.3 percentage points of GDP is largely attributable to greater spending on social security and welfare. The progressive ageing of the population in many countries in the region has meant that resources used to pay social security benefits have gradually increased. Although a significant proportion of these resources comes from revenues based on contributory social security schemes (in this case, public or mixed), more countries have gradually introduced solidarity mechanisms for financing social security payments in addition to the normal solidarity-based redistribution mechanisms that already existed within these systems.

Figure VI.7

Latin America and the Caribbean (21 countries):[a] social public spending by sector, 1990-1991 to 2012-2013[b]

(Percentages of GDP)

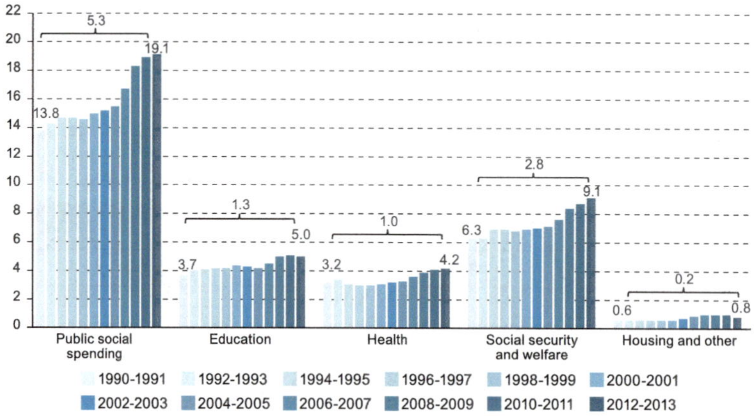

Source: Economic Commission for Latin America and the Caribbean (ECLAC), social expenditure database.

[a] Argentina, Bolivarian Republic of Venezuela, Brazil, Chile, Colombia, Costa Rica, Cuba, Dominican Republic, Ecuador, El Salvador, Guatemala, Jamaica, Mexico, Nicaragua, Panama, Paraguay, Peru, Plurinational State of Bolivia, Trinidad and Tobago, and Uruguay.

[b] Weighted average of the countries.

Although there is no disaggregated information that distinguishes between social security and non-contributory social protection systems, the data indicate that a number of welfare programmes were expanded (mostly during the 2000s) —especially anti-poverty programmes consisting of mechanisms for direct conditional or non-conditional transfers to households. In Argentina, from 2000 to 2007, spending on social assistance rose by almost 85% (even considering the fall of almost 20% in 2002); in Brazil (federal government), it tripled over the same period. In Chile, it went up by just 5.5% (with sharp falls in 2003, 2004 and 2006); in Colombia it almost doubled between 2004 and 2007, and in Costa Rica it has increased by more than 75% since 2002. Notwithstanding this expansion, it should be borne in mind that in 2007 public spending on social assistance in these and other countries for which this type of information is available represented as little as between 10% and 35% of the aggregate total for social security and assistance.

In the wake of the global financial crisis, various emergency programmes and other measures were implemented to avoid a contraction in the real economy (ECLAC, 2010). This accounts for much of the rise in social spending (equal to 1.8 percentage points of GDP) over the past five years. Most of this increase (three quarters of the total) was in social security and welfare. Since social security commitments usually show less elasticity to the business cycle, the increase was likely associated with strengthening or implementing social welfare programmes (including stepping up efforts to combat poverty through conditional and non-conditional transfers) targeting those persons and households most vulnerable to economic contraction, and with boosting the solidarity-based pillars of social security systems (or, more generally, of social protection systems).

The other sector in which there has been a noteworthy increase in spending (of 1.3 percentage points of GDP) over the past 22 years was education. This increase is related to the expansion in coverage of and access to primary education in the poorest countries, and secondary education in the remainder of them (in terms of infrastructure, and, above all, of current expenditure, associated mainly with the increase in teacher staffing) as well as, to a lesser extent, an expanded supply of public post-secondary education.

This has come at the expense of health sector expansion, which saw the level of macroeconomic priority afforded to it expand only very slightly (by 1 percentage point of GDP). Declining budgets for this sector usually mean that investments or reinvestments in infrastructure, renewal of equipment and replacement of medical supplies are sacrificed, which causes problems in the public health sector that have a negative impact on coverage and, above all, on the quality of services. It takes a long time to return to normal after such situations.

Lastly, the sector receiving the least attention is housing (which includes drinking water, sanitation, community infrastructure and, lately, the environment) despite the fact that practically all countries and major cities still have large pockets of substandard housing and segregation (see chapter V). There has even been a contraction over in the past biennium, owing in part to an expansion in the preceding period when housing was used as a tool to boost job creation and revitalize the region's domestic economies, particularly the construction industry.

Box VI.1
Updating social expenditure figures

To update social expenditure figures for this edition of *Social Panorama of Latin America*, data on the functional classification of public spending up to 2013 were obtained in accordance with the total and sectoral series published in previous editions. Information was obtained for up to 2012 or 2013 for 13 of the 21 countries reviewed; the decision to publish these figures was based on the realization that it is important to have recent data, even if they are only provisional, approximate or partial. The figures were updated during the third quarter of 2014, and the exercise was closed in early October.

In most cases, it was possible to collect data on central government budget execution; in a number of countries figures for actual spending were obtained from agencies with budgetary autonomy, local governments and non-financial public enterprises. Although differences in institutional coverage make comparisons between countries difficult, it was decided to publish the most comprehensive data available for each country except when they involved significant constraints for constructing a series for 1990-2013. This is because the Commission's primary interest is to report the amount of public social spending in each country as accurately as possible, in order to convey the effort being made by States in this area.

The following is a classification of the countries by institutional coverage of the social expenditure series used:

Institutional coverage	Country
Public sector (NFPS + FPE)	Costa Rica
Non-financial public sector (GG+NFPE)	Argentina, Colombia and El Salvador
General government (CG+LG)	Brasil, Cuba and Peru
Central government (BCG +AA)	Bolivia (Plurinational State of), Chile, Ecuador, Guatemala, Jamaica, Panama, Paraguay, Dominican Republic, Trinidad and Tobago, Uruguay and Venezuela)Bolivarian Republic of)
Budgetary central government (BCG)	Honduras, Mexico and Nicaragua

Where:

NFPS: non-financial public sector; FPE: financial public enterprises; GG: general government; NFPE: non-financial public enterprises; CG: central government; LG: local government; BCG: budgetary general government; AA: autonomous State agencies.

Considering that a number of countries only very recently adopted the classification system presented in the *Government Finance Statistics Manual* 2001 of the International Monetary Fund (IMF), which is harmonized with the 1993 System of National Accounts (SNA), the 1990-2013 series is not always compatible at the subfunction and/or subgroup level. Most of the countries publish the functional classification in aggregated form and use classifications of their own.

Data continuity problems brought about by the switch include a lack of information for the full series or for certain years and/or functions in particular cases. For example, there are no data for the Plurinational State of Bolivia between 1990 and 1994, for Colombia between 1990 and 1999 or for El Salvador between 1990 and 1992, and a change in the methodology used means that data for the series from 2004 to 2009 are not strictly comparable with those from previous years. No data have been included on Guatemala concerning the period between 1990 and 2009 since an important methodological change was made the following year; no data on social security in Nicaragua are available. It has not been possible to construct the complete series for certain other countries owing to a lack of information on Jamaica and Trinidad and Tobago between 1997 and 1999. The Dominican Republic publishes two social public spending series, one between 1990 and 2002 and the other between 2003 and 2010, with methodological differences meaning that the series can be compared overall but not at the sector-by-sector level. The Bolivarian Republic of Venezuela has series for central government social public spending from 1991 to 2012. The figures for Mexico relate to programmable spending of the budget public sector from the Federal Public Treasury Account until 2012.

Like previous editions, *Social Panorama of Latin America 2014* uses biennial averages to present social spending data. The indicators published are for total public social spending and its component functions and sectors (education, health, social security and welfare, and housing, sanitation and other functions not included in the above categories) as a percentage of GDP, in dollars per capita, and as a percentage of total public spending. In the case of this last indicator, official information from the countries is used, but these figures may differ from those based on other classification systems (such as economic or administrative classification of spending) because some include interest payments on the public debt and others do not, and because different methodologies are used to classify disbursements.

This 2014 edition, like those of 2012 and 2013, includes the change made by the countries in the base year for GDP in constant dollars, which means that levels of GDP have been re-estimated, and data used are therefore not necessarily comparable with those published in previous years. All calculations of public spending in constant dollars are expressed at constant 2005 prices.

The figures used to calculate the percentages are in current prices for each year and each country. These proportions are then applied to the GDP series in dollars at 2005 prices to obtain per capita social spending, expressed in dollars. This may result in certain variations in relation to the data in constant currency reported by the countries, which depend on the degree of appreciation or depreciation implicit in the official parity of each country's currency in relation to 2005, and also on the demographic data on which the per capita calculations are based.

Figures at current prices on total and social public spending and the sectoral breakdown of the latter are official data provided by the corresponding government bodies. Depending on the country, these may be directorates, departments, sections or units for planning or drawing up the budget or social policy within the ministries of the treasury, finance or the economy. In addition, information on budgetary execution was obtained from the countries' general accounting offices or treasury departments, and occasionally from central banks, national statistical institutes and national social and economic information systems.

The figures for GDP in dollars at constant 2005 prices are official ECLAC statistics; the population figures come from projections by the Latin American and Caribbean Demographic Centre (CELADE)-Population Division of ECLAC.

Source: Economic Commission for Latin America and the Caribbean (ECLAC).

This makes it difficult to develop and sustain programmes to provide housing (for the most part starting with sanitation programmes) or eradicate slums, thus affecting both the low-income population and, indirectly, the health sector, by making it harder to control vectors of infectious and contagious diseases that spread easily in the absence of access to drinking-water, sewerage and waste treatment systems.

Scanty investment in this area has also hampered or slowed environmental conservation initiatives involving the establishment of biodiversity conservation areas and implementation of measures needed for regulating human activity, in particular productive ventures, so as to prevent environmental degradation and pollution.

B. Social investment in youth: amount and distribution by sector[2]

It is estimated that in Latin America some 13.8% of public social investment is earmarked directly or indirectly for young people; this is equivalent to US$ 102 billion at 2005 prices and around 2.65% of regional GDP. Taking all of the countries together, if such spending were measured against a yardstick of an equal distribution across all age groups, there would be a shortfall of almost 47% in the share allocated to young people.

Estimations of social investment in youth conducted by the Latin American countries, unlike traditional classifications of public expenditure, have yet to be systematized at the regional level, thus complicating comparisons. Although previous studies have been carried out on the subject (ECLAC/UNFPA, 2011), it is clear that there is a dearth of information and that national budget execution does not account itemize youth population explicitly.

This chapter thus attempts to provide a consolidated overview of available data on social investment in youth, differentiating between spending in the education, health, social care and housing sectors. It also presents a conceptual framework outlining the key characteristics and classifications of social investment as well as the procedures used to estimate spending in each of the sectors (see ECLAC/OIJ/IMJUVE, 2014).

1. Social investment and classifications thereof

One of the most widely used definitions of social expenditure is that of the Organization for Economic Cooperation and Development (OECD), which considers it to be the provision by public and private institutions of benefits to, and financial contributions targeted at, households and individuals in order to provide support during circumstances which adversely affect their welfare (OECD, 2001). Public-sector social investment —unlike compensatory policies, which address the effects of an incident or a hazard that has already manifested itself (such as by defraying health expenses associated with treatment and rehabilitation rather than prevention)— aims to help prevent or prepare for adverse events, and to support and equip people for coping with them, rather than compensate those affected by, for example, market deregulation. These measures are particularly necessary in Latin America where neoliberal policies, in addition to failing to ensure sustained high growth rates, have had negative socioeconomic consequences for the population, leading to a widening of the gap between society's haves and have-nots (Urteaga, 2013).

From this perspective, public spending is not a cost for the economy but rather a series of investments that are necessary to ensure strong, lasting and shared growth, meet new social needs and safeguard economic, social and cultural rights (DESC). Social investment strategies set priorities with a view to supporting people throughout their

2 This section is an excerpt from chapter II of the Third Latin American Youth Report (ECLAC/OIJ/IMJUVE, 2014). This and other chapters was drawn up as part of a project implemented in 2014 by ECLAC and the Latin American Youth Organization (OIJ) on estimates of social investment in youth.

life cycle, focusing on groups that are subject to social exclusion (including women, young people and children) in fundamental areas of human development (such as education, health, employment and housing).

As noted above, social investment can encompass spending in both the public and the private sectors. However, public spending, particularly public social expenditure, makes up the bulk of it. Therefore, although these two categories are not strictly speaking the same, for the purposes of estimating the magnitude of social investment in youth, this chapter will consider public social expenditure on this population group. Public social expenditure can be defined as total resources allocated by the State for the provision of goods and services in various social sectors, especially education, health, housing and welfare (Espindola and Martínez, 2007).

In their annual public budgets, governments set out their priorities and objectives as expressed by their estimated income and expenditure. Budgets thus show the manner in which governments extract resources from society and redistribute them; in carrying out these two processes they reveal their true preferences and priorities (Guerrero and Valdes, 2001).

Young people can thus be the target population of public policies, and can benefit either directly from resources allocated exclusively to them or indirectly from policies targeting not them but their environment. Four types of social spending can be identified, which differ in the way in which young people benefit from it:

(i) Direct
This kind of social investment works through policies and programmes whose target population are young people, as direct beneficiaries. The basic eligibility criterion for these initiatives is simply to be young. This category includes training, youth employment and teen pregnancy prevention programmes. Depending on programme objectives, the target population may comprise some or all of the individuals within the age range for young people as defined by each country.[3]

(ii) Expanded
This kind of social investment is made through programmes that are not specifically aimed at young people but at a wider population of which they form part. Young people are therefore beneficiaries alongside other age groups. Spending (both current expenditure and investment) on education by the State on students at various levels (mostly in upper-secondary, post-secondary and tertiary education) represents the most substantial social investment made in young people. Other programmes, such as unemployment insurance, job training and formalization of own-account workers, can be categorized as this kind of investment. Not all Latin American countries have such programmes, and the resources allocated for them are far below State spending on regular cycles or levels of education.

(iii) Indirect
Another part of public spending that can be considered to be social investment benefits young people indirectly and only to the extent that they are part of households receiving resources allocated by the programmes. This category chiefly consists of initiatives targeting households, such as programmes to combat poverty, for housing and other subsidies and for sport and general community infrastructure. In most Latin American countries, "conditional cash transfer" or "co-responsibility" programmes are the most common of such initiatives, and they are the most significant in terms of resources allocated. They are non-contributory social protection schemes for families in situations of poverty or extreme poverty, and they are for the most part aimed at families with children. These programmes seek to combat poverty and its reproduction over time by improving levels of educational attainment and health.

(iv) General
Spending not specifically aimed at young people or their households but affecting the areas in which they live or spend time (such as investment in communities or neighbourhood unions) should also be considered investment in young people. Public investment in such areas as neighbourhood improvement, community infrastructure, water and sanitation, sports venues and green spaces falls into this category. Community initiatives to improve public safety carried out in conjunction with local authorities are of particular importance.

In addition to this classification based on beneficiary group, there are economic classifications that standardize information on government income and spending. The importance of these classifications lies in their usefulness for drawing up and interpreting budgets as they facilitate the analysis of budget policy and its impact at national level

[3] This chapter considers young people to be between the ages of 15 and 29; this is the operational definition used by ECLAC in its reports on youth and the age range most often used in legislation on young people in force in Latin America.

(Guerrero and Valdes, 2001). At the level of public finances, the three most widely used approaches are economic, administrative and functional classifications of public expenditure based on the questions "what are the funds being spent on?", "who is spending them?" and "why?" (Guerrero and Valdes, 2001). Answering these three questions provides detailed information on how a part of public resources is managed.

2. Procedure used to estimate the amount of social investment in youth

As noted previously, owing to the absence of comprehensive, sector-disaggregated studies on social investment in youth, there are variations in the methodology and sources employed to obtain the information used in this chapter to estimate the magnitude of social spending in the different areas considered, namely education, health, welfare and housing. Details of the procedures used for calculations in each sector are thus provided below.

While the OECD definition of social investment encompasses benefits provided and contributions made by the private sector, data on private social financing and spending is more difficult to gather. That is why the only relatively homogenous information available for the drafting of this chapter was on State spending targeting social sectors.

The data used on spending on education came from the functional distributions of public expenditure provided by countries which is compiled in the ECLAC social expenditure database.[4] Education spending includes annual public sector expenditure on various levels of education, which in most countries falls under central government spending.

To estimate total spending on education targeting young people, data was used on gross enrolment rates at selected levels of education and the share of pupils enrolled in public or private establishments. The information used, with the exception of the total amount of public spending on education, comes from the United Nations Educational, Scientific and Cultural Organization (UNESCO). These data enabled information provided by ECLAC on total public spending on education on young people aged 15 to 29 to be broken down, using data from the UNESCO Institute for Statistics, by the relative share of public spending in the three aforementioned levels of education. A separate estimate was made of spending on young people enrolled in upper-secondary and tertiary education (whether at universities or technical colleges). Estimates of per capita spending on both levels of education were made using the percentage of young people enrolled in public establishments.

The data from the UNESCO Institute for Statistics[5] do not cover every year; estimates could not be made for Honduras or Nicaragua, which were therefore excluded from the analysis of investment in education. The fact that disaggregated information on spending and enrolment in postsecondary education is only available for a limited number of years and for a handful of countries is an even greater constraint.

Estimates were made for around 2000, 2004, 2008 and 2012, the latest year for which data on most countries were available. The years selected allow examination of changes in the amount of social investment in young people in three subperiods characterized by different economic growth rates, changes in the order of priority afforded to the various components of social investment and the impact on the availability of public resources, particularly in the period following the crisis of 2008 and 2009.

The amount of social investment in young people's health was also estimated using a common accounting framework for public spending, but drawing on information from the database of the World Health Organization (WHO)[6] rather than the ECLAC public health expenditure database. As with education, the amount of public expenditure was compared based on the share of gross domestic product reported in both of these sources. It was found that in most Latin American countries the information on public health expenditure provided by the national offices of the Pan American Health Organization (PAHO) was more comprehensive than data on health spending provided by central governments. The decision was therefore taken to use the data reported by PAHO.

---

4 See [online] http://dds.cepal.org/gasto/indicadores/.

5 See [online] http://data.uis.unesco.org/.

6 World Health Organization (WHO)/Pan American Health Organization (PAHO), Global Health Observatory Data Repository [online] http://apps.who.int/gho/data/?theme=main.

Unlike investment in education, the data available on health are unsufficient for estimating the breakdown of spending between age groups each year. Studies carried out for OECD countries containing estimates of the distribution of public spending on health by age group were therefore used.

These studies show that health spending follows a characteristic pattern or profile in which the age and sex of the population are the main determinants of per capita expenditure. As figure IV.8 shows, health spending per individual is relatively high during the period running from pregnancy-related tests through birth and the first year of life (linked to the high costs associated with pregnancy and childbirth); it then falls to its lowest levels between the ages of 10 and 14. It subsequently rises, and at a faster rate for women, chiefly as a result of the costs related to motherhood. Public spending on health per individual begins rise again after the age of 50, particularly for men; the older the target population the faster the rate of increase.

Figure VI.8

Canada: profile of health expenditure by age and sex

(Index: average spending on the group aged 10 to 14=1)

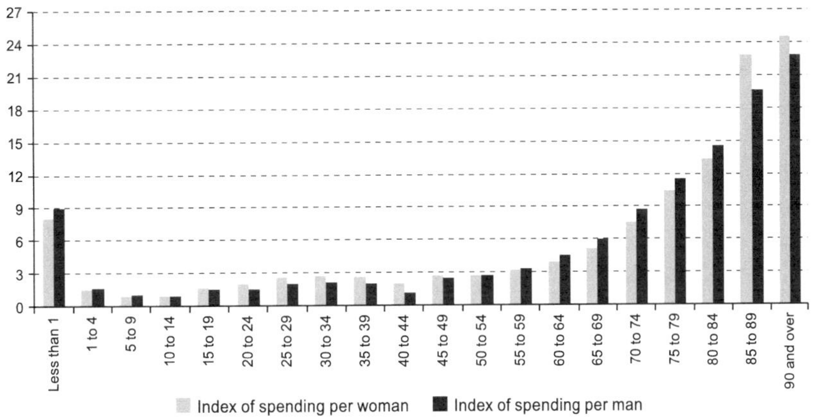

Source: Canadian Institute for Health Information (CIHI), National Health Expenditure Trends, 1975 to 2013 [online] https://secure.cihi.ca/free_products/NHEXTrendsReport_EN.pdf.

This health expenditure profile was used to estimate the amount of public resources allocated to health care for young people. As noted above, between the ages of 15 and 29 the higher costs for women than men are associated with motherhood. The figures were therefore corrected to account for the greater incidence of teenage and underage (girls younger than 15 years) pregnancy in Latin American countries, a pattern that has been noted by ECLAC (ECLAC/OIJ 2008) and the Latin American and Caribbean Demographic Centre (CELADE)-Population Division of ECLAC (Rodríguez, 2014) in other reports on young people.

This profile was used to estimate the total and per capita expenditure of Latin American countries on health. No other background information was available so it was assumed that the pattern of expenditure by age and sex has remained relatively constant since the beginning of the past decade. The trends in the share of spending on youth health in total public expenditure and changes in per capita expenditure presented below mirror very closely changes in the amount of public sector resources allocated to health and follow, to a lesser extent, changes in population structure in terms of age and sex.

Annual health spending per young person is low —less than US$ 500 per year in purchasing power parity (PPP) terms in almost every country– particularly when compared with expenditure per young person on education, which in most cases exceeds US$ 1,000 per year. This disparity reflects the fact that while per capita figures on education refer to young people who regularly make use of the resources invested (those enrolled in public educational institutions, that is, the effective beneficiaries of expenditure), in the case of health, the per capita amounts are based on the total of young people aged 15-29 (the potential beneficiaries of this expenditure). No data are available on numbers of actual beneficiaries of health systems, but these are a very small fraction of all potential beneficiaries, especially in the case of young people. As the expense profile shows, young people benefit from a small portion of total public resources allocated to health. Figures on spending per young person in hospital and primary health care settings (out of the total users of these public services) are likely much higher than those given above and on a level that is more comparable to public education expenditure per young person.

In order to compare per capita expenditure on health and education on the same basis, per capita education expenditure must therefore be considered in terms of the total number of young people, whether attending an educational institution or not. Furthermore, although in both cases estimates of expenditure on young people are made on the basis of total public spending (including capital expenditure) on the sector (and by level in the case of education) the incomplete data available on health indicate that expenditure is far higher on education: approximately 10% at most.

Social assistance spending on young people, by its very nature, varies greatly between countries and over time, and is chiefly made up of programmes (often to combat poverty) benefiting young people directly or indirectly. Unlike investment in education and health, there are no relatively homogeneous accounting frameworks covering most of the programmes through which the State allocates social assistance resources to different population groups. Spending on social assistance typically comes under the same budget heading as social security expenditure, which makes up a share of GDP that varies greatly from country to country depending on social security system coverage.

The amount of investment in social assistance for young people was therefore estimated by analysing conditional cash transfer programmes, the most common form of such assistance in the countries of Latin America, on which ECLAC has collected and systematized the information necessary to analyse, on a comparable basis, the resources the region's countries allocate to social assistance (Cecchini and Martínez, 2011).[7]

Although these programmes were first launched over 10 years ago, some countries either lacked this type of non-contributory social assistance or allocated very little resources to existing programmes. This chapter therefore only includes estimates of investment in social assistance for 2009, the most recent year for which systematized records are available.

The other component of social investment is public expenditure on housing, which, in addition to housing construction programmes, includes investment in basic water and sanitation services and other spending on improving community infrastructure (such as electricity, sports centres and community centres). There is an accounting framework for estimating aggregate spending on this component of functional expenditure in the various countries, but there are no records on its distribution by age group. There are, however, studies on certain countries showing how public spending on social housing programmes breaks down according to beneficiary-household income (IDB, 2011). The relatively high concentration of resources in housing and urban infrastructure programmes shows that the bulk of spending benefits households in the top three income quintiles; within this 60% of total households, about 70% of the resources benefits households in the first quintile. The remaining 30% is distributed among the two subsequent quintiles. In order to estimate the amount of social investment in housing and infrastructure allocated to young people it was assumed that this spending benefits young people in households in the three lowest-income population quintiles. Spending per young person in this component of social investment was calculated by dividing the total amount allocated in each country to housing and infrastructure programmes by the total number of young people aged between 15 and 24 benefiting from these resources (around 27% of all persons belonging to the poorest 60% of households).

3. Overview of social investment in young people in Latin America

Given that the way in which social investment in Latin America is measured differs from country to country, and that the figures presented below understate the actual amount of such investment made at all levels of the State, total social investment around 2012 can, for purposes of illustration, can be put at 19.1% of GDP, or around US$ 660 billion. Latin America and the Caribbean stands out in that the levels of macroeconomic priority given to public social spending vary greatly, ranging from just over 8% of GDP (in Guatemala and the Dominican Republic, for instance) to over 35% of GDP (in Cuba). But differences in the degree of budget execution decentralization and in the most common methods of reporting central government expenditure suggest that caution is advisable when comparing countries.

[7] See also [online] http://dds.cepal.org/proteccionsocial/.

According to estimates, out of total public expenditure on social investment, the region allocates around US$ 102 billion to social programmes which directly or indirectly benefit young people (US$ 183 billion at 2005 prices at PPP). The share of social public spending allocated to young people is 13.8%, which is equivalent to 2.65% of GDP for the Latin American countries under review (see table VI.2).

Table VI.2

Latin America (19 countries): social investment in young people, around 2012

(Percentages)

Country	Investment in young people as a percentage of social spending	Investment in young people as a percentage of GDP	Percentage of young people in the total population
Argentina	11.9	3.3	24.3
Bolivia (Plurinational State of)	24.2	2.8	28.2
Brazil	10.6	2.8	25.7
Chile	15.5	2.3	24.9
Colombia	12.5	1.6	26.3
Costa Rica	14.4	3.3	27.4
Cuba	26.0	9.7	20.4
Dominican Republic	17.8	1.4	26.8
Ecuador	31.4	2.6	26.7
El Salvador	12.1	1.6	30.2
Guatemala	19.1	1.8	28.4
Honduras	...	0.5	29.9
Mexico	18.0	2.1	26.4
Nicaragua	...	1.4	30.2
Panama	21.5	3.7	25.1
Paraguay	25.8	2.8	28.9
Peru	17.9	1.9	27.3
Uruguay	13.0	3.3	22.1
Venezuela (Bolivarian Republic of)	19.2	4.0	26.7
Latin America	**13.8**	**2.65**	**26.3**

Source: Economic Commission for Latin America and the Caribbean (ECLAC), social expenditure database and calculations on the basis of conditional cash transfer programmes and data provided by the UNESCO Institute of Statistics, World Health Organization and Inter-American Development Bank (IDB).

A breakdown of social investment in youth, according to the data available on the education, health, social assistance and housing sectors, is presented below. It is followed by a look at annual public expenditure per young person and the maximum amount of resources that a young person could receive if he or she were to benefit from all of the programmes simultaneously.

(a) Education

As noted above, social investment in youth is focused on education. Almost 60% of the resources allocated directly or indirectly to young people are used to fund education systems, particularly for coverage and operation at the upper-secondary level (which aims to provide students with some form of specialized knowledge and basic job-training tools) and post-secondary non-tertiary level (vocational and professional training programmes) and tertiary level (professional university education).

At least since the 2000s (when most countries made a definite effort to boost public social spending and sought to decouple it from the economic cycle as much as possible), spending on education has been rising steadily. This trend was enhanced by a steady increase in enrolment rates, especially at the secondary level. So, while total spending on education (as a simple average) in 2000 was 3.7% of GDP, by 2012 it had reached 5.2% of GDP against a backdrop of relatively sustained growth, with the exception of the period following the global financial crisis (see figure VI.9). The crisis led most countries to implement countercyclical policies that kept the resources allocated to education constant or even increased them, although they subsequently had to make adjustments as shown by the declining share of GDP allocated to education in 2011 compared with previous years.

Figure VI.9
Latin America (19 countries):[a] total public spending on education and expenditure on youth education as a share of GDP, and rates of change
(Base year: 2000=100)

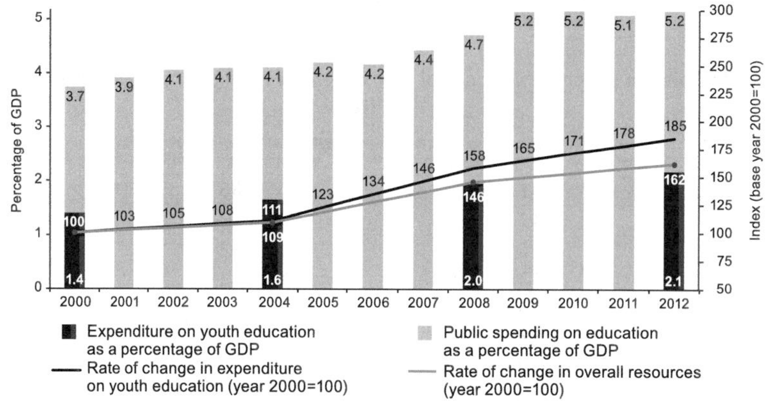

Source: Economic Commission for Latin America and the Caribbean (ECLAC), estimates on the basis of official figures from the countries provided by the UNESCO Institute of Statistics.
[a] Argentina, Bolivarian Republic of Venezuela, Brazil, Chile, Colombia, Costa Rica, Cuba, Dominican Republic, Ecuador, El Salvador, Guatemala, Mexico, Panama, Paraguay, Peru, Plurinational State of Bolivia and Uruguay.

Public spending on youth education, while of course lower than overall expenditure on education, has followed the same sustained upward trend, although there are insufficient historical data to ascertain whether there have been fluctuations associated with the business cycle. In 2012, public investment in education stood at nearly 2.1% of GDP (as a simple average), which is 0.7 percentage points more than in 2000. The lines in the figure show that the rise in youth education spending has at times outpaced growth in total expenditure on education, as upper-secondary and tertiary levels of education have been the main beneficiaries of this increased spending. This is because, with the exception of preschool levels, primary and lower secondary education had already expanded (in both enrolment and spending), principally in the 1990s (the last two levels are now mandatory in most countries of the region, which is not the case for upper-secondary education).

As shown in figure VI.10, in virtually all of the countries the level of macroeconomic priority given to youth-targeted spending on public education increased (that is, spending rose as a share of GDP). The exceptions were Colombia and Peru, in which it remained unchanged, and the Dominican Republic, where it contracted slightly. As mentioned above, as a simple average for the region, this priority increased by 0.7 percentage points of GDP. The sharpest rises in the macroeconomic priority given to this spending were seen in Cuba (by 4.7 percentage points; from 3.3% of GDP to 7.9% of GDP), followed by Ecuador (1.4 percentage points) and then by Paraguay (1.1 percentage points).

Figure VI.10
Latin America (17 countries):[a] public spending on youth education as a percentage of GDP, around 2000 and 2012
(Percentages)

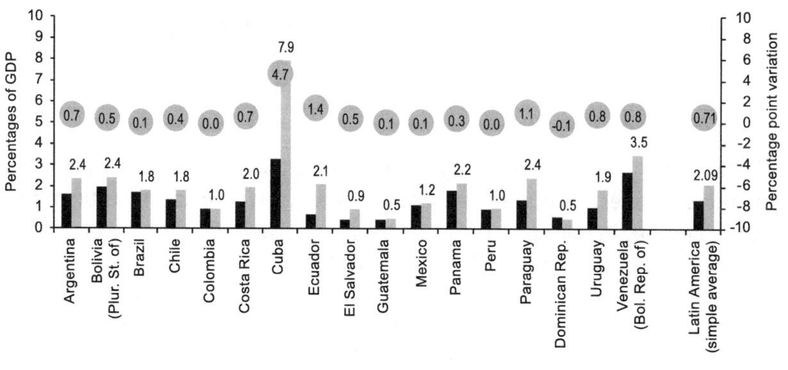

Source: Economic Commission for Latin America and the Caribbean (ECLAC), estimates on the basis of official figures from the countries provided by the UNESCO Institute of Statistics.
[a] Excludes Honduras and Nicaragua.

By and large, increases in the macroeconomic priority of youth education spending were in line with the greater macroeconomic priority of total public expenditure and the increasing priority of spending on education within overall public expenditure (usually at the expense of economic and administrative spending). But as stated above, youth education spending also increased somewhat in absolute terms, with its share of total education spending climbing in 2000 and 2012 as shown in table VI.3. The figures show that all of the countries saw an absolute increase in education spending at upper-secondary, post-secondary vocational and technical and tertiary levels.

Table VI.3

Latin America (17 countries):[a] public expenditure on youth education as a share of GDP and as a share of public spending on education, and per young person[b] around 2000 and 2012

Country	Public spending on youth education				Per young person			
	(as a percentage of GDP)		*(as a percentage of public spending on education)*		*(2005 dollars at constant prices)*		*(2005 PPP dollars)*	
	2000	2012	2000	2012	2000	2012	2000	2012
Argentina	1.6	2.4	32.6	35.3	1 137	2 263	2 601	5 176
Bolivia (Plurinational State of)	2.0	2.4	37.8	46.2	288	364	1 041	1 314
Brazil	1.7	1.8	35.5	31.3	1 627	2 060	2 919	3 696
Chile	1.4	1.8	35.4	42.9	2 095	5 749	3 514	9 644
Colombia	0.9	1.0	28.6	31.4	1 212	928	2 600	1 991
Costa Rica	1.3	2.0	26.5	26.3	1 884	2 511	3 676	4 900
Cuba	3.3	7.9	37.8	49.7	2 467	5 388	2 467	5 388
Dominican Republic	0.6	0.5	24.6	21.0	353	372	6 567	8 373
Ecuador	0.7	2.1	39.1	44.3	439	1 174	615	647
El Salvador	1.6	1.9	14.8	24.1	523	831	1 040	2 779
Guatemala	0.5	0.5	16.9	16.0	1 013	1 007	1 923	1 912
Mexico	1.1	1.2	33.2	32.4	2 417	2 112	3 696	3 229
Panama	1.8	2.2	37.8	51.4	1 304	3 318	2 504	6 369
Paraguay	0.9	1.0	28.6	52.1	722	1 068	2 222	3 288
Peru	2.1	2.4	32.2	34.1	560	981	1 242	2 175
Uruguay	1.0	1.9	39.4	41.9	862	1 997	1 589	3 682
Venezuela (Bolivarian Republic of)	2.7	3.5	27.8	32.4	5 269	3 156	9 551	5 721
Latin America (simple average)	**1.5**	**2.1**	**31.1**	**36.1**	**1 422**	**2 075**	**2 927**	**4 134**

Source: Economic Commission for Latin America and the Caribbean (ECLAC), social expenditure indicators in Latin America and the Caribbean and calculations on the basis of data provided by the UNESCO Institute of Statistics.
[a] Excludes Honduras and Nicaragua.
[b] Young people attending public educational establishments.

A look at public spending per young person enrolled at a public educational establishment helps to confirm the above. Even accounting for the fact that in most countries the number of young people enrolled increased significantly over these 12 years, per capita expenditure grew by 41% over the period (in PPP dollars), equivalent to an increase of US$ 1,207 per student per year PPP (in constant 2005 dollars the increase was just over US$ 650), as table VI.3 shows. Spending per young person fell only in the Bolivarian Republic of Venezuela, Colombia, Guatemala and Mexico, in part because increases in numbers of students enrolled at in public institutions outstripped absolute growth in resources. In countries such as Argentina, Chile, Cuba, Ecuador, Panama and Uruguay, meanwhile, public expenditure per student doubled (or more), albeit in a context of absolute increases in public education enrolment figures.

But the rate of growth in students enrolling at the upper-secondary level, and especially in the higher levels (non-university post-secondary and tertiary) does not necessarily lead to similar rates of expansion in enrolment in public education. In fact, in most countries where access to upper secondary and higher levels expanded there was a proportional decrease in the levels of enrolment in public education. This could help explain the sharp rise in expenditure per student in public education seen in table VI.4. Thus, in three of the four countries in which per-student spending declined (the Bolivarian Republic of Venezuela, Colombia and Mexico) enrolment in public education increased both percentage-wise and in absolute terms.

Table VI.4
Latin America (17 countries):[a] public spending on education per young person as a share of GDP per capita and percentage of young people enrolled in public educational establishments, around 2000 and 2012
(Percentages)

Country	Public spending on education per young person as a percentage of GDP per capita		Young people attending public establishments as a percentage of all young people enrolled	
	2000	2012	2000	2012
Argentina	25.3	33.0	75.5	71.5
Bolivia (Plurinational State of)	29.4	28.3	71.9	83.1
Brazil	36.9	35.9	66.1	59.0
Chile	32.0	60.9	51.7	25.3
Colombia	39.4	21.8	50.4	63.2
Costa Rica	45.3	43.8	62.3	63.7
Cuba	82.3	103.7	100.0	100.0
Dominican Republic	7.5	6.3	74.9	65.7
Ecuador	16.9	32.8	70.0	66.7
El Salvador	20.5	27.4	48.6	55.7
Guatemala	48.4	43.4	37.5	32.0
Mexico	31.2	24.2	75.0	76.5
Panama	31.8	44.4	85.6	77.5
Paraguay	48.6	62.0	58.8	51.9
Peru	22.5	23.0	66.1	55.4
Uruguay	17.3	26.6	89.3	83.3
Venezuela (Bolivarian Republic of)	100.3	49.2	60.6	70.6
Latin America (simple average)	**37.4**	**39.2**	**67.3**	**64.8**

Source: Economic Commission for Latin America and the Caribbean (ECLAC), estimates on the basis of official figures from the countries provided by the UNESCO Institute of Statistics.
[a] Excludes Honduras and Nicaragua.

Lastly, as table VI.4 shows, in a fair proportion of the countries spending per student grew more quickly than GDP per capita, a testament to government efforts to increase the resources allocated to public education, particularly at upper-secondary levels and in higher education.

(b) Health

As noted above, young people are, comparatively, the healthiest age group or population segment. This does not mean that they are spared the health issues that affect the rest of the population, but rather that they are generally in better physical condition to fight off infectious diseases, although they, too, can develop congenital, chronic or degenerative illnesses. They are also at a stage in life when particular sexual and reproductive health needs arise.

For young people, the major health events requiring specialized care are, for young women, pregnancy and motherhood, especially at early ages (adolescence). Young men face issues associated with alcohol and drug abuse, accidents, violence and the prevention and treatment of HIV.

Thus, when compared with spending on the rest of the population, the amount of resources allocated by States to youth health would appear rather low, but demand is markedly lower. Figure VI.11 shows public expenditure on health regon-wide (as a simple average) and spending on young people at various points of time for which the information required to make estimates was available. While total public spending on health around 2000 averaged 3.1% of GDP, spending on youth health was only 0.65% of GDP (less than 18% of total health expenditure). Trends in social spending are somewhat procyclical, as can be seen in 2003-2004 and 2010-2012 (with a peak in 2009 associated with the sharp contraction of GDP in some countries and, to some extent, countercyclical policies in investment spending on health, which were subsequently abandoned). Overall, spending on health increased by 1% of GDP between 2000 and 2012.

Figure VI.11

Latin America (19 countries):[a] total public spending on health and young people as a share of GDP, and rates of change in the absolute amount of total spending and spending on young people

(Simple averages of percentages and indices where 2000=100)

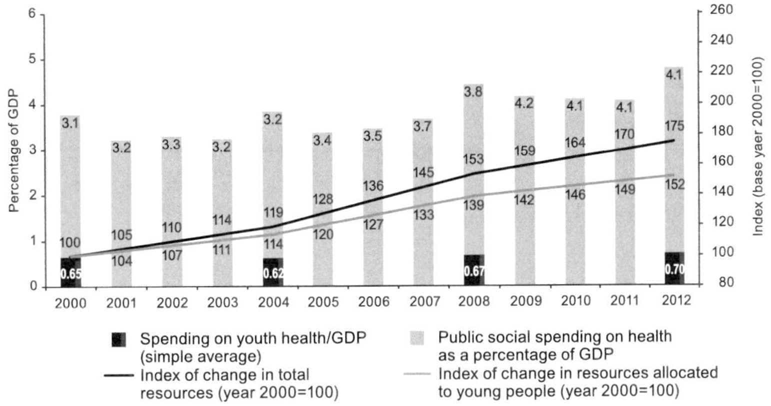

Source: Economic Commission for Latin America and the Caribbean (ECLAC), social expenditure database and information provided by the Pan American Health Organization (PAHO)/World Health Organization (WHO).

[a] Argentina, Bolivarian Republic of Venezuela, Brazil, Chile, Colombia, Costa Rica, Cuba, Dominican Republic, Ecuador, El Salvador, Guatemala, Honduras, Mexico, Nicaragua, Panama, Paraguay, Peru, Plurinational State of Bolivia, and Uruguay.

But while spending on health services for young people rose between 2000 and 2012 (by 12%, as a percentage of GDP), it grew more slowly than total spending on health. This meant that its relative share of overall health spending fell to 17.3% of total public expenditure on health in 2012 (as a simple average of the countries), as table VI.5 shows.

Table VI.5

Latin America (19 countries): health spending on young people, as a share of total public expenditure on health and a percentage of GDP, and total and per capita spending on health for young people,[a] around 2000 and 2012

Country	Health spending as a percentage of total public spending on health		Health spending as a percentage of GDP		Total public spending on youth health *(in millions of 2005 dollars)*		Per capita *(2005 dollars at constant prices)*		Per capita *(2005 PPP dollars)*	
	2000	2012	2000	2012	2000	2012	2000	2012	2000	2012
Argentina	14.9	13.6	0.7	0.8	1 227.8	2 243.9	132	225	301	515
Bolivia (Plurinational State of)	20.1	20.1	0.7	0.8	60.1	110.0	26	38	95	137
Brazil	19.4	16.4	0.6	0.7	4 317.1	8 059.9	88	158	157	284
Chile	15.7	14.5	0.5	0.5	531.9	836.6	142	194	238	326
Colombia	19.6	17.5	0.9	0.9	1 127.3	1 843.2	103	147	220	316
Costa Rica	18.4	17.6	1.0	1.3	167.3	366.1	159	278	310	543
Cuba	13.4	10.4	0.7	0.8	246.5	495.0	97	215	97	215
Dominican Republic	19.5	17.7	0.4	0.5	122.1	253.6	51	93	89	162
Ecuador	19.5	17.6	0.2	0.5	72.2	279.8	21	68	49	160
El Salvador	18.6	19.5	0.7	0.8	105.8	157.2	66	83	132	167
Guatemala	20.2	20.3	0.5	0.5	106.4	170.6	35	40	66	76
Honduras	20.9	21.4	0.8	0.9	57.8	115.5	33	49	77	114
Mexico	20.5	17.5	0.5	0.6	3 009.7	5 750.6	132	184	202	282
Nicaragua	22.2	21.5	0.6	1.0	34.7	77.6	23	43	60	112
Panama	19.0	16.0	1.0	0.8	125.8	236.6	149	248	285	476
Paraguay	19.7	19.9	0.6	0.9	50.7	99.3	34	51	106	158
Peru	20.4	18.2	0.6	0.5	363.5	693.2	49	85	109	188
Uruguay	12.4	10.9	0.8	0.6	131.4	165.0	169	219	312	404
Venezuela (Bolivarian Republic of)	19.7	17.9	0.5	0.3	596.9	538.9	89	67	161	122
Latin America (simple average)	**18.6**	**17.3**	**0.6**	**0.7**	**13 335**	**22 493**	**84**	**131**	**161**	**250**

Source: Economic Commission for Latin America and the Caribbean (ECLAC), social expenditure database and information provided by the Pan American Health Organization (PAHO)/World Health Organization (WHO).

[a] Young people aged 15-29.

The increase in spending in absolute terms has been substantial as the region has benefited from fairly sustained economic growth. The one major exception arose from the global financial crisis, with the impact of falling or slowing GDP felt chiefly in 2009. Between 2000 and 2012, spending on health for young people increased in absolute terms by 68.7%. But this growth was outstripped by the rise in total health expenditure, which, as a budget item, was up by some 75% as a simple average of the countries (see the lines in figure VI.11).

In keeping with the ongoing demographic transition and population aging, the countries allocating the smallest share of health spending to young people are Cuba and Uruguay (less than 11% of total health expenditure) although the share of GDP differs greatly, in part because of the disparities in their levels of GDP. By contrast, countries with less aged populations allocate a more significant proportion (more than 19%) of health expenditure to young people, as table VI.5 shows. This is the case in El Salvador, Guatemala, Honduras, Nicaragua, Paraguay and the Plurinational State of Bolivia.

Although these figures may appear relatively low when seen as a share of total public health expenditure and GDP, in absolute terms the amounts involved are significant. In 2012 some US$ 22.5 billion (at 2005 prices) was spent on health for young people (see table VI.5).

Naturally, absolute levels of spending differ greatly, due in part to the fact that numbers of young people vary from country to country. It is thus useful to carry out a comparative analysis of the potential target population, namely young people aged 15 to 29. In 2012, annual per capita expenditure on health per young person stood at US$ 250 PPP (at 2005 prices), which is 55% higher than at the turn of the millennium. In only one country did per capita spending on youth health contract: the Bolivarian Republic of Venezuela. Countries such as Brazil, Costa Rica, Cuba, the Dominican Republic, Ecuador and Nicaragua, meanwhile, saw significant per capita increases, of 75% or more over this 12-year period. Per capita spending on youth health in Ecuador nearly tripled. Despite these increases and with the exception of Costa Rica, these countries are not among those allocating the most resources to youth health (in terms of per capita spending). The countries spending US$ 400 or more on these services at PPP per young person in 2012 were Argentina, Costa Rica, Panama and Uruguay.

Lastly, most of the countries have made efforts to increase spending on young people by boosting the macroeconomic priority afforded to expenditure on youth health (as a share of GDP). This is principally owing to the overall rise in national health budgets in the countries of Latin America (see figure VI.12).

Figure VI.12

Latin America (19 countries): per capita public spending on health per young person as a share of GDP per inhabitant, 2000, 2004, 2008 and 2012

(Percentages)

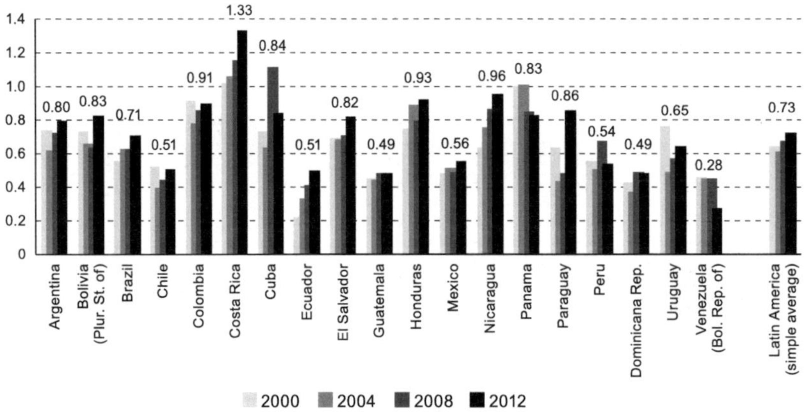

Source: Economic Commission for Latin America and the Caribbean (ECLAC), social expenditure database and information provided by the Pan American Health Organization (PAHO)/World Health Organization (WHO).

Box VI.2

Analysis of shared responsibilities in funding the response to HIV in Latin America

The human immunodeficiency virus (HIV) affects 1.6 million people in the region, with a rate of prevalence of 0.4% among the population at large. Some 60% of the HIV-positive people in the region are men, and around 75% live in Argentina, the Bolivarian Republic of Venezuela, Brazil, Colombia or Mexico. The prevalence of HIV is far higher among certain specific groups, particularly men who have sexual relations with men, and transsexual women, than in the general population. The young adult population is also one of the groups most at risk of contracting HIV: at least a third of new infections occur among young people aged 15 to 24.

In terms of treatment policies, 14 countries in the region now begin treating adults at a CD4 count of less than 500 cells/mm^3, thereby bringing the region gradually into line with new WHO standards. The coverage of antiretroviral treatment is uneven in Latin America, both between and within from countries. For example, in Argentina, the Bolivarian Republic of Venezuela, Brazil, Chile, Ecuador, El Salvador, Mexico, Nicaragua, Paraguay and Peru, over 60% of the population is covered by such treatment, while coverage in the Plurinational State of Bolivia reaches less than 20% of inhabitants. According to data from the Pan American Health Organization (PAHO), an estimated 792,000 people were covered in December 2013. However, in spite of the progress made on the public policy front, the epidemic continues to spread at a rate of more than 200 new HIV infections per day.

In respect of resources, in 2012 an estimated US$ 2.092 billion was allocated to financing the response to the epidemic in the countries of the region. The bulk of this, 70%, was earmarked for the treatment of people living with HIV[a], while approximately 20% was spent on activities to prevent transmission. One dollar out of every hundred spent went to prevention programmes for the most at-risk groups.

The Political Declaration on HIV and AIDS approved by the General Assembly of the United Nations in June of 2011 called for a redoubling of efforts to eliminate this twin scourge. An important point made in the declaration concerns the "shared responsibility" between governments and international cooperation (paragraphs 86 to 95). It urges the international community to continue to honour its commitment to co-finance the response to HIV and AIDS with a view to arresting the epidemic in countries lacking the necessary resources to do so, and calls on the governments of countries with the necessary means to take the lead in the fight against HIV.

The resources available to combat HIV have increased steadily in recent years, rising by 24% between 2008 and 2012. The region funds 93% of this amount from domestic resources, while 6% comes from international donors. Thus, in comparison with other regions with low-to-mid-income countries, Latin America leads the world in terms of funding the response to HIV with domestic funds, but this leadership does not encompass preventive programmes for the people most at risk.

It can therefore be said that, by and large, the region is not dependent on donors for funding this response. Nevertheless, the regional averages mask the financial fragility of a third of the countries in Latin America. Whereas Argentina, the Bolivarian Republic of Venezuela, Brazil, Chile, Colombia, Mexico and Uruguay provide 95% or more of the financing of the fight against HIV from domestic funds, Guatemala, Honduras, Nicaragua and the Plurinational State of Bolivia are dependent on donor funding to cover 40% to 55% of their response efforts.

A further important aspect to consider when analysing "shared responsibility" is dependence on donor resources in funding key programmes in the fight against HIV. For example, antiretroviral therapy and programmes to prevent the vertical transmission of HIV are financed principally from domestic funds in most countries of the region (13 countries provide 90% or more of such funding). However, there is a high level of dependence on donors for preventive programmes targeting the most at-risk populations, even in upper-middle-income countries such as the Bolivarian Republic of Venezuela, Mexico and Uruguay. This is the case, for instance, in 10 countries in the region for prevention programmes for men who have sex with men.

Figure

Latin America (17 countries): domestic financing of the response to HIV as a share of GDP, most recent year reported

(Constant dollars and percentages)

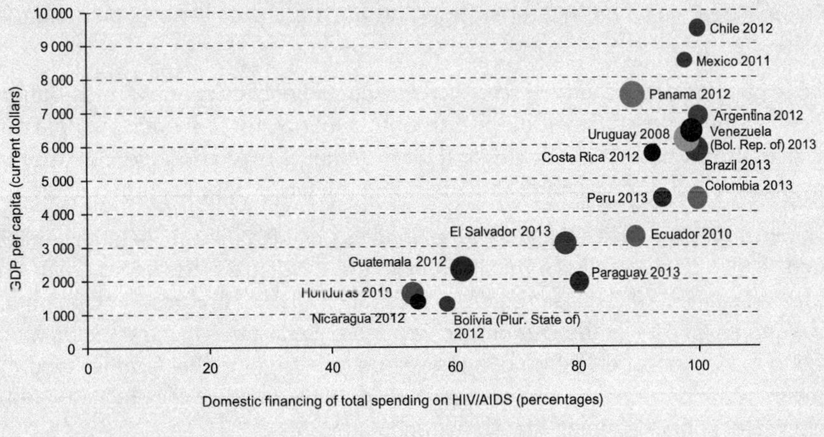

Source: Joint United Nations Programme on HIV/AIDS (UNAIDS), various years.
Note: The size of the circle denotes the prevalence of HIV.

Box VI.2 (concluded)

Although studies on the ways in which HIV is transmitted show that the majority of new HIV infections continue to occur in specific groups of the population, from a "shared responsibilities" viewpoint preventing HIV in key and vulnerable groups is a major weak point in the region's response to HIV. This is in a wider context in which (i) half the countries in the region are dependent on external resources to fund prevention programmes for these groups and (ii) of the aggregate US$ 20 million spent in 2013 in the 14 countries providing figures on the financing of and spending on HIV prevention programmes for key populations, 63% came from donor funds.

Even in countries in which most prevention activities are financed from domestic resources, prevention programmes for the most at-risk groups have a comparatively higher share of donor funding. It is unclear whether this dependence on donor support is a symptom of a lack of political commitment on the part of governments vis-à-vis the groups most at risk (sex workers and men who have sexual relations with men), or instead reflects the current mindset of donors, which prioritizes funding proposals targeting key populations, or a combination of both.

Careful thought needs to be given to this state of affairs, as the countries' ability to access international funds is likely to lessen as their economies continue to grow. In the light of the data provided by countries, it remains to be seen whether governments will assume responsibility for financing these crucial HIV prevention programmes when donor funding is less readily available.

Source: Joint United Nations Programme on HIV/AIDS (UNAIDS).

[a] Treatment of HIV is by means of antiretroviral drugs, and levels of coverage vary in Latin America and the Caribbean. Changes in WHO guidelines for initiating treatment have aggravated the gaps in treatment coverage.

(c) Social assistance and poverty reduction programmes

Social assistance programmes are long-established in Latin America. They have taken many different forms in various countries, but for the most part they have all sought a way to increase or at least safeguard the human capital of households.[8] In the past decade a new generation of such initiatives, known as conditional cash transfer programmes (ECLAC, 2006), was introduced and became the most widely used mechanism for combating the intergenerational transmission of poverty in the countries of the region (ECLAC, 2010).

The target population of such programmes varies from country to country, but generally the beneficiaries are families, especially those with children under 18 years old, living in poverty or extreme poverty. Young people indirectly benefit from these programmes as members of beneficiary households and in some cases may also receive benefits directly —sometimes up until the age of 29— as in the case with *Oportunidades* (opportunities) in Mexico, *Bolsa familia* (family grant) in Brazil and *Jóvenes en Acción* (young people in action) in Colombia.

From the first initiatives dating from the mid-1990s, these social assistance programmes have expanded steadily in Latin American countries, both in terms of population coverage and budgetary resources (ECLAC, 2010). Despite this, the regional picture remains mixed. The average budget allocated to conditional transfer programmes in the countries of Latin America amounts to around 0.3% of GDP. Ecuador's *Bono de desarrollo humano* (human development grant) programme had the highest budget relative to GDP (1.17%) at the end of the past decade, followed by Mexico's *Oportunidades* (0.51%) and Uruguay's *Asignaciones familiares* (Family allowance) initiative (0.45%). Other programmes are more modest in coverage and funding. Among them are El Salvador's *Comunidades Solidarias Rurales* (Solidarity in rural communities) and Paraguay's *Abrazos* programme, which although nationwide in scope, has a limited target population. These programmes have budgets in the order of 0.02% of GDP.

About 13% of the population of the countries reviewed belongs to beneficiary households, although the percentage varies depending on the scope of programmes and the proportion of poor or vulnerable people meeting the relevant eligibility criteria. Certain programmes are notable for their extremely broad coverage, but this makes it more likely that there will be errors of inclusion (households that are not in the target population).

Among the programmes with the largest budget are the *Bono Juancito Pinto* (Juancito Pinto grant) in the Plurinational State of Bolivia (Marco, 2012), *Bolsa Familia* in Brazil, *Familias en Acción* (Families in action) in Colombia, the *Bono de Desarrollo Humano* in Ecuador, *Mi Familia Progresa* (My family is making progress) in Guatemala, *Oportunidades* in Mexico and *Solidaridad* (Solidarity) in the Dominican Republic, the last of which benefited more than 20% of the population at the end of the last decade. It should, however, be kept in mind that families tend to be larger in poor and vulnerable segments of the population, so coverage in terms of the number of beneficiary households (the most commonly used unit of selection) is less than that shown in table VI.6.

[8] For further details of social assistance programmes, see ECLAC (2006).

Table VI.6
Latin America (16 countries): conditional transfer programmes, around 2009
(Percentages)

Country	Programme	Year	Population covered		Budget	Geographic area covered
			Percentage of population covered	Percentage of poor population covered [a]	Percentage of GDP	
Argentina	*Asignación universal por hijo*	2009	8.3	46.4	0.2	Nationwide
Argentina	*Programa de ciudadanía porteña*	2009	9.6	100.0	0.1	Local
Bolivia (Plurinational State of)	*Bono Juancito Pinto*	2009	17.5	32.4	0.3	Nationwide
Bolivia (Plurinational State of)	*Bono Madre Niño-Niña Juana Azurduy*	2009	3.5	6.4	0.2	Nationwide
Brazil	*Bolsa Família*	2009	26.4	84.6	0.5	Nationwide
Brazil	(PETI)	2008	0.5	1.6	0.0	Nationwide
Chile	*Chile Solidario*	2008	6.8	51.7	0.1	Nationwide
Colombia	*Familias en Acción*	2009	25.2	56.5	0.4	Nationwide
Colombia	*Subsidios condicionados a la asistencia escolar*	2006	0.6	1.4	0.0	Local
Costa Rica	*Avancemos*	2009	3.3	17.4	0.4	Nationwide
Dominican Republic	*Solidaridad*	2009	21.2	46.3	0.5	Nationwide
Ecuador	*Bono de desarrollo humano*	2009	44.3	100.0	1.2	Nationwide
El Salvador	*Comunidades Solidarias Rurales* (formerly red solidaria)	2009	8.2	17.1	0.0	Rural areas
Guatemala	*Mi Familia Progresa*	2009	22.6	39.7	0.3	Nationwide
Honduras	*Programa de asignación familiar (PRAF)*	2009	8.7	12.3	0.2	Nationwide
Mexico	*Oportunidades* (formerly *Progresa*)	2009	24.6	62.8	0.5	Nationwide
Panama	*Red de oportunidades*	2009	10.9	39.5	0.2	Nationwide
Paraguay	*Tekoporâ*	2009	8.6	13.9	0.4	Nationwide
Paraguay	*Abrazo*	2009	0.0	0.1	0.0	Nationwide
Peru	*Juntos*	2009	7.6	21.2	0.1	Nationwide
Uruguay	*Asignaciones familiares*	2009	11.6	84.6	0.5	Nationwide
Latin America (simple average)			**12.9**	**39.8**	**0.30**	

Source: Economic Commission for Latin America and the Caribbean (ECLAC), estimates made on the basis of data on non-contributory social protection programmes [online]: [http://dds.cepal.org/bpsnc/].
[a] Includes the indigent population.

The funding targeting young people in Latin America out of budgets for these programmes (directly or indirectly, and primarily through access to services) comes to little more than an estimated US$ 170 million region-wide. Brazil and Mexico allocate the largest amount of resources to conditional transfer programmes in the region: around US$ one billion each. Then, far behind, come Argentina, Colombia and Ecuador, which allocate around US$ 100 million each (see table VI.7). The remaining countries allocate amounts ranging from US$ 6 million to US$ 50 million, with the exception of El Salvador, whose rural development programme has a budget of US$ 1 million (at 2005 prices).

As can be seen in column 1 of table VI.7, the amounts allocated to young people as a share of total beneficiaries are fairly consistent across the board. There is also a certain correlation in that the higher the share of young people among a given programme's beneficiaries the smaller its coverage is (excluding programmes with very low coverage). This is because such programmes generally focus on the poorest households, which tend to be larger and have a higher proportion and children and young people (as dependent and inactive family members).

Taking the universe of analysis as the total number of young people aged 15 to 29, conditional transfer programmes cover 14% of all young people —a slightly higher proportion than for the total population (12.9%). As with general population coverage, some countries stand out for high coverage of young people: more than 18% in Brazil, Colombia, the Dominican Republic, Ecuador, Guatemala and Mexico.

Table VI.7
Latin America (16 countries): share of young beneficiaries and expenditure on social assistance programmes per young person, around 2009 [a]

Country	Population covered	Budget	Spending per young beneficiary	Spending per young beneficiary
	Young people benefiting from programmes as a percentage of the young population	Programme resources allocated to young people (millions of 2005 dollars)	(2005 dollars)	(2005 PPP dollars)
Argentina	11.8	174.8	150	342
Bolivia (Plurinational State of)	11.7	6.9	36	132
Brazil	21.7	1 050.9	96	172
Chile	6.3	35.3	134	225
Colombia	22.4	162.3	63	135
Costa Rica	2.3	17.8	612	1195
Dominican Republic	18.6	54.1	109	190
Ecuador	38.9	129.1	85	200
El Salvador	7.8	1.0	7	14
Guatemala	19.6	23.9	32	61
Honduras	7.7	6.8	41	96
Mexico	19.9	992.2	166	253
Panama	9.7	10.6	120	231
Paraguay	7.0	8.2	65	200
Peru	7.7	40.1	66	146
Uruguay	11.7	21.4	243	449
Latin America (simple average)	**14.0**	**171.0**	**127**	**253**

Source: Economic Commission for Latin America and the Caribbean (ECLAC), estimates made on the basis of data on non-contributory social protection programmes [online]: [http://dds.cepal.org/bpsnc/].
[a] Ongoing conditional transfer programmes in the countries.

In terms of expenditure per young beneficiary in 2005 PPP dollars, the regional picture is mixed. Average spending per young beneficiary is US$ 253 PPP, with Costa Rica spending the most (US$ 1,195 PPP), followed by Uruguay (US$ 449) and Argentina (US$ 342). After them comes a large group of countries spending between US$ 100 PPP and US$ 200 PPP per young person. El Salvador, with US$ 14 PPP, comes in last.

Programme components vary and thus do not lend themselves to comprehensive comparisons beyond overall coverage. How "well" the resources are used in terms of the type and comprehensiveness of assistance given to families and individuals cannot be reduced to figures.

(d) Housing

Public social spending on housing and basic services such as clean water, sanitation, slum improvement and community facilities is the item of social expenditure that receives the smallest proportion of resources. As noted above, budgets for these sectors depend on the business cycle and therefore fluctuate a great deal in line with each country's economic performance. However, some countries used investments in this area to address the recent global financial crisis by creating jobs in the public sector, thus boosting domestic consumption, which has sometimes made the sector's behaviour countercyclical.

In 2012, total expenditure on housing and basic services stood at 1.8% of GDP as a simple average for 19 countries in the region (see table VI.8). Although this figure is low, there are fairly large variations between countries, with some spending 0.5% of GDP or less (Chile, Ecuador, Honduras, Paraguay and the Plurinational State of Bolivia) whereas others allocate 3% of GDP or more (Cuba, Guatemala, Nicaragua, Panama and Uruguay). This inconsistent picture reflects not only the individual efforts countries make or the level of macroeconomic priorities that countries ascribe to public housing and basic services, but also depends on the degree of urbanization (whether they urbanized recently or decades ago) and, therefore, the amount of investment already made in this area.

Table VI.8

Latin America (19 countries): public spending on housing as a share of GDP and per young person between 15 and 29 years old, around 2012

Country	Public spending on housing as a percentage of GDP *(percentages)*	Public spending on housing per young person [a]		Public spending on housing per young person as a percentage of GDP per capita *(percentages)*
		(2005 dollars)	*(PPP dollars)*	
Argentina	2.0	955	2 185	21.2
Bolivia (Plurinational State of)	0.3	20	72	2.0
Brazil	2.1	776	1 392	17.6
Chile	0.5	299	501	4.6
Colombia	0.7	188	404	6.1
Costa Rica	2.4	820	1 600	19.7
Cuba	3.3	1 405	1 405	46.9
Dominican Republic	2.0	633	1 102	19.3
Ecuador	0.3	74	174	2.8
El Salvador	1.0	162	327	6.3
Guatemala	3.5	471	894	22.5
Honduras	0.2	17	40	1.4
Mexico	1.6	856	1 308	11.0
Nicaragua	3.6	272	707	25.6
Panama	3.8	1 867	3 583	45.5
Paraguay	0.2	23	70	1.5
Peru	2.4	622	1 378	25.0
Uruguay	3.6	2 005	3 697	40.2
Venezuela (Bolivarian Republic of)	1.4	549	995	10.4
Latin America (simple average) [a]	**1.8**	**632**	**1 149**	**17.4**

Source: Economic Commission for Latin America and the Caribbean (ECLAC), social expenditure database and Inter-American Development Bank (IDB), *Room for Development: Housing Markets in Latin America and the Caribbean*, Washington, D.C., 2012.
[a] Calculation based on the number of 15 to 29 year-olds in households belonging to the three poorest quintiles.

The disparity noted above is also evident in the amounts of spending indirectly benefiting young people. Most social housing programmes are aimed at poor and vulnerable families and are not youth housing programmes per se. The estimates provided here have therefore been made on the basis of the number and proportion of young people whose families benefit from social housing and urban development programmes (involving the installation of basic utilities at home). As shown in table IV.8, the simple average of spending on housing benefiting young people in the countries in the region is US$ 1,149 (2005 PPP dollars), their second highest item of expenditure after education.

Once again, spending per young beneficiary varies greatly from country to country, with Argentina, Panama and Uruguay allocating over US$ 2,000 PPP per young person and Honduras, Paraguay and the Plurinational State of Bolivia earmarking less than US$ 100 PPP per young person. However, higher values may reflect on the whole a greater degree of specialization of programmes, and lower values a broader scope.

The fourth column of table IV.8 also provides an indicator of relative efforts made by each country, by correlating spending per young person with GDP per capita. Region-wide, spending on housing per young person equals 17% of GDP per capita, although there still tend to be considerable differences between countries. One way to illustrate the relative efforts of countries and how different the absolute figures per young person are is to compare the absolute and relative effort made by the following countries: Brazil, which spends some US$ 1,400 PPP per young person (representing a relative effort of 18% of per capita GDP); Costa Rica, which spends US$ 1,600 (almost 20% of per capita GDP); Nicaragua, which allocates US$ 707 PPP (a higher relative effort at 25.6%); and Peru, whose relative effort is 25% of per capita GDP although this entails spending US$ 1,370 PPP per young beneficiary.

In most countries of the region, housing and access to basic services indeed remain a pressing concern, with precariousness and gaps affecting children, young people, adults and the elderly (see, for example, ECLAC/UNICEF 2010 and ECLAC 2013). Shortages or lack of housing affect young people directly, too, by making it harder to become independent and start a family of their own. It forces them to found their own mini-household within the dwelling, which affords them only a relative degree of autonomy and generally leads to overcrowding, or establish a second household, usually very small and often with difficulties in terms of access to basic utilities, on the same site as the main one.

Table VI.9 provides an estimation of the number of housing units required to meet total demand, especially from young people and young families. In the region, for the 17 countries considered, the total deficit is put at slightly more than 58 million dwellings. In line with current levels of public spending on housing and basic services, and assuming that all such resources are devoted specifically to the purchase or construction of social housing, it would take the region 100 years on average to meet current demand for this type of housing (by which time this shortfall would probably have grown worse because of family nuclearization, even in the context of a shrinking population in absolute terms). Excluding the countries with the highest levels of demand and lowest levels of spending (those that would need more than 100 years to remedy the current shortfall) brings the average down to 28 years, which appears more manageable because it does not encompass future demand.

Table VI.9

Latin America (17 countries): [a] **housing deficit and social spending required on the sector**

Country	Total deficit *(millions of dwellings)*	Deficit [b] as a percentage of total dwellings *(percentages)*	Market price of social housing [c] *(2005 dollars)*	Total deficit *(millions of 2005 dollars)*	Number of years needed to close housing deficit [d]
Argentina	3.8	32.0	30 310	116 661	23
Bolivia (Plurinational State of)	1.9	75.0	6 682	12 842	622
Brazil	19.2	33.0	19 923	381 660	17
Chile	1.3	23.0	28 793	36 635	49
Colombia	4.9	37.0	7 834	38 466	33
Costa Rica	0.2	18.0	11 753	2 611	4
Dominican Republic	1.1	41.0	19 333	21 180	22
Ecuador	1.9	50.0	14 100	26 864	154
El Salvador	0.9	58.0	12 845	12 191	68
Guatemala	2.5	67.0	13 992	34 455	32
Honduras	1.1	57.0	11 084	12 343	539
Mexico	9.8	34.0	17 861	174 260	12
Nicaragua	1.2	78.0	10 187	11 843	45
Panama	0.3	39.0	27 176	9 391	11
Peru	5.7	72.0	12 925	73 624	29
Uruguay	0.3	26.0	21 482	6 401	9
Venezuela (Bolivarian Republic of)	2.1	29.0	39 376	81 537	34
Latin America (simple average)	**3.4**	**45.2**	**17 980**	**61 939**	**100**

Source: Economic Commission for Latin America and the Caribbean (ECLAC), social expenditure database and Inter-American Development Bank (IDB), *Room for Development: Housing Markets in Latin America and the Caribbean,* Washington, D.C., 2012.

[a] Excludes Cuba and Paraguay.

[b] Includes the quantitative deficit (new dwelling shortfall) and the qualitative deficit (materials, overcrowding, infrastructure and lack of secure tenure).

[c] Market price of cheapest dwelling in main cities.

[d] Ratio between total deficit and annual public spending on housing.

States must therefore pay greater attention to this area of social policy that is so often neglected, since poverty and social exclusion and marginalization are caused not only by insufficient income but also by the development of subcultures of poverty created by residential segregation and a lack of stable housing or community infrastructure. There are too many examples to mention of the link between urban segregation and the development of ghettos, which puts large urban areas at risk of invasion by youth gangs. This leads to increasing violence and drug trafficking and further complicates matters for the already small number of State representatives on the ground, exposing young people to the world of drugs and urban violence and turning them into victims of social exclusion.

C. Final remarks

Recent trends point to slower growth in public social spending in 2012 and, particularly, 2013. This is attributable in part to the end of the surge in spending to address the effects of the international financial crisis and the current global economic slowdown. While these measures succeeded in increasing domestic demand in the countries, rates of growth in expenditure have tailed off at a time when the fiscal deficits created in some countries to mitigate the effects of the crisis of 2008 and 2009, a sluggish global economy and the subsequent efforts to prop up financial investment need to be reduced. Efforts therefore need to be redoubled in order to improve planning of expenditure and to develop and strengthen assessment mechanisms with a view to making more efficient and effective use of resources.

Part of this increased effectiveness and efficiency can be achieved by bringing spending more in line with the needs of various population groups, such as young men and women. By allocating resources to the general programmes and specific initiatives most likely to benefit the well-being of the population and to provide the necessary opportunities and capacities, a new development model can be built to reduce inequalities and help break the chains that transmit poverty from generation to generation.

Bibliography

Cecchini, S. and R. Martínez (2011), "Inclusive Social Protection in Latin America: a Comprehensive, Rights-based Approach", *Libros de la CEPAL*, No. 111 (LC/G.2488-P), Santiago, Chile. United Nations publication, Sales No. E.11.II.G.23.

ECLAC (Economic Commission for Latin America and the Caribbean) (2014a), *Economic Survey of Latin America and the Caribbean, 2014* (LC/G.2619-P), Santiago, Chile.

___ (2014b), *Compacts for Equality: Towards a sustainable future* (LC/G.2586(SES.35/3)),Santiago, Chile.

___ (2013), *Social Panorama of Latin America, 2013* (LC/G.2580-P), Santiago, Chile. United Nations publication, Sales No. E.14.II.G.6.

___ (2012), *Social Panorama of Latin America, 2012* (LC/G.2557-P). United Nations publication, Sales No. E.13.II.G.6.

___ (2010), *Social Panorama of Latin America, 2009* (LC/G.2423-P), Santiago, Chile. United Nations publication, Sales No. E.09.II.G.135.

___ (2006), *Shaping the Future of Social Protection: Access, financing and solidarity* (LC/G.2294(SES.31/3)), Santiago, Chile.

ECLAC/OIJ (Economic Commission for Latin America and the Caribbean/ Ibero-American Youth Organization) (2008), *Juventud y cohesión social en Iberoamérica. Un modelo para armar* (LC/G.2391), Santiago, Chile.

ECLAC/OIJ/IMJUVE (Economic Commission for Latin America and the Caribbean/ Ibero-American Youth Organization/ Mexican Institute for Youth) (2014), *Invertir para transformar. La juventud como protagonista del desarrollo*, Madrid, September.

ECLAC/UNFPA (Economic Commission for Latin America and the Caribbean/United Nations Population Fund) (2012), *Informe regional de población en América Latina y el Caribe 2011. Invertir en Juventud* [online] http://www.cepal.org/cgi-bin/getProd.asp?xml=/publicaciones/xml/8/47318/P47318.xml&xsl=/tpl/p9f.xsl.

ECLAC/UNICEF (Economic Commission for Latin America and the Caribbean/United Nations Children's Fund) (2010), "Pobreza infantil en América Latina y el Caribe" (LC/R.2168) [online] http://www.cepal.org/cgi-bin/getProd.asp?xml=/publicaciones/xml/6/42796/P42796.xml&xsl=/dds/tpl/p9f.xsl&base=/dds/tpl/top-bottom.xsl.

Espíndola, E. and R. Martínez (2007), "Gasto social en América Latina: una propuesta para su análisis. Reunión técnica. La medición del gasto social: avances y desafíos metodológicos. Borrador para discusión", Santiago, Chile, Economic Commission for Latin America and the Caribbean (ECLAC).

Guerrero, J. P. and Y. Valdés (2001), *Manual sobre la clasificación económica del gasto público. Programa de Presupuesto y Gasto Público,* Mexico City, Economic Research and Teaching Centre (CIDE).

IDB (Inter-American Development Bank) (2011), "Un espacio para el desarrollo. Los mercados de vivienda en América Latina y el Caribe", *IDEA*, vol. 26, September – December.

Marco, Flavia (2012), "El Bono Juancito Pinto del Estado Plurinacional de Bolivia. Programas de transferencias monetarias e infancia", *Project Document* (LC/W.492), Santiago, Chile, Economic Commission for Latin America and the Caribbean (ECLAC).

OECD (Organization for Economic Cooperation and Development) (2007), *The Social Expenditure database: An Interpretive Guide SOCX 1980-2003,* Paris.

Rodríguez Vignoli, Jorge (2014), "La reproducción en la adolescencia y sus desigualdades en América Latina. Introducción al análisis demográfico, con énfasis en el uso de microdatos censales de la ronda de 2010", *Project Document* (LC/W.605), Santiago, Chile, Economic Commission for Latin America and the Caribbean (ECLAC).

Urteaga, E. (2013), "Estado de bienestar e inversión social en Europa", *Comunitania. Revista Internacional de Trabajo Social y Ciencias Sociales*, No. 5, January [online] http://www.comunitania.com/numeros/numero-5/eguzki-urteaga-estado-de-bienestar-e-inversion-social-en-europa.pdf.

Publicaciones recientes de la CEPAL
ECLAC recent publications

www.cepal.org/publicaciones

Informes periódicos institucionales / *Annual reports*

También disponibles para años anteriores / *Issues for previous years also available*

- Estudio Económico de América Latina y el Caribe 2014, 222 p.
  Economic Survey of Latin America and the Caribbean 2014, 214 p.
- La Inversión Extranjera Directa en América Latina y el Caribe 2013, 160 p.
  Foreign Direct Investment in Latin America and the Caribbean 2013, 152 p.
- Anuario Estadístico de América Latina y el Caribe 2013 / *Statistical Yearbook for Latin America and the Caribbean 2013, 226 p.*
- Balance Preliminar de las Economías de América Latina y el Caribe 2013, 92 p.
  Preliminary Overview of the Economies of Latin America and the Caribbean 2013, 92 p.
- Panorama Social de América Latina 2013, 226 p.
  Social Panorama of Latin America 2013, 220 p.
- Panorama de la Inserción Internacional de América Latina y el Caribe 2013, 128 p.
  Latin America and the Caribbean in the World Economy 2013, 122 p.

Libros y documentos institucionales / *Institutional books and documents*

- Pactos para la igualdad: hacia un futuro sostenible, 2014, 340 p.
  Covenants for Equality: Towards a sustainable future, 2014, 330 p.
- Integración regional: hacia una estrategia de cadenas de valor inclusivas, 2014, 226 p.
  Regional Integration: Towards an inclusive value chain strategy, 2014, 218 p.
  Integração regional: por uma estratégia de cadeias de valor inclusivas, 2014, 226 p.
- Reflexiones sobre el desarrollo en América Latina y el Caribe. Conferencias magistrales 2013-2014, Enrique Peña Nieto, Marino Murillo, Luis Gonzaga Beluzzo, José Miguel Insulza, Winston Dookeran et al, 2014, 100 p.
- Prospectiva y desarrollo: el clima de la igualdad en América Latina y el Caribe a 2020, 2013, 72 p.
- Comercio internacional y desarrollo inclusivo: construyendo sinergias, 2013, 210 p.
  International trade and inclusive development: Building synergies, 2013, 200 p.
- Cambio estructural para la igualdad: una visión integrada del desarrollo, 2012, 330 p.
  Structural Change for Equality: an integrated approach to development, 2012, 308 p.
- La hora de la igualdad: brechas por cerrar, caminos por abrir, 2010, 290 p.
  Time for Equality: closing gaps, opening trails, 2010, 270 p.
  A Hora da Igualdade: Brechas por fechar, caminhos por abrir, 2010, 268 p.

Libros de la CEPAL / *ECLAC books*

129 Prospectiva y política pública para el cambio estructural en América Latina y el Caribe, Javier Medina Vásquez, Steven Becerra y Paola Castaño, 2014, 338 p.

128 Inestabilidad y desigualdad: la vulnerabilidad del crecimiento en América Latina y el Caribe, Juan Alberto Fuentes Knight (ed.), 2014, 304 p.

127 *Global value chains and world trade: Prospects and challenges for Latin America, René A. Hernández, Jorge Mario Martínez-Piva and Nanno Mulder (eds.), 2014, 282 p.*

126 Planificación, prospectiva y gestión pública: reflexiones para la agenda del desarrollo, Jorge Máttar, Daniel E. Perrotti (eds.), 2014, 250 p.

125 La crisis latinoamericana de la deuda desde la perspectiva histórica, José Antonio Ocampo, Barbara Stallings, Inés Bustillo, Helvia Velloso, Roberto Frenkel, 2014, 174 p.

124 La integración de las tecnologías digitales en las escuelas de América Latina y el Caribe: una mirada multidimensional, Guillermo Sunkel, Daniela Trucco, Andrés Espejo, 2014, 170 p.

123 Fortalecimiento de las cadenas de valor como instrumento de la política industrial: metodología y experiencia de la CEPAL en Centroamérica, Ramón Padilla Pérez (ed.), 2014, 390 p.
Strengthening value chains as an industrial policy instrument: Methodology and experience of ECLAC in Central America, Ramón Padilla Pérez (ed.), 2014, 360 p.

Copublicaciones / *Co-publications*

- *Decentralization and Reform in Latin America: Improving Intergovernmental Relations, Giorgio Brosio and Juan Pablo Jiménez (eds.), ECLAC / Edward Elgar Publishing, United Kingdom, 2012, 450 p.*
- Sentido de pertenencia en sociedades fragmentadas: América Latina desde una perspectiva global, Martín Hopenhayn y Ana Sojo (comps.), CEPAL / Siglo Veintiuno, Argentina, 2011, 350 p.
- Las clases medias en América Latina: retrospectiva y nuevas tendencias, Rolando Franco, Martín Hopenhayn y Arturo León (eds.), CEPAL / Siglo XXI, México, 2010, 412 p.
- *Innovation and Economic Development: The Impact of Information and Communication Technologies in Latin America, Mario Cimoli, André Hofman and Nanno Mulder, ECLAC / Edward Elgar Publishing, United Kingdom, 2010, 472 p.*

Coediciones / *Co-editions*

- *Regional Perspectives on Sustainable Development: Advancing Integration of its Three Dimensions through Regional Action, ECLAC-ECE-ESCAP-ESCWA, 2014, 114 p.*
- *Multi-dimensional Review of Uruguay, ECLAC-OECD, 2014, 190 p.*
- Perspectivas de la agricultura y del desarrollo rural en las Américas: una mirada hacia América Latina y el Caribe 2014, CEPAL / FAO / IICA, 2013, 220 p.
- Perspectivas económicas de América Latina 2014: logística y competitividad para el desarrollo, CEPAL/OCDE, 2013, 170 p.
  Latin American Economic Outlook 2014: Logistics and Competitiveness for Development, ECLAC/OECD, 2013, 164 p.

Cuadernos de la CEPAL

101 Redistribuir el cuidado: el desafío de las políticas, Coral Calderón Magaña (coord.), 2013, 460 p.
101 *Redistributing care: the policy challenge, Coral Calderón Magaña (coord.), 2013, 420 p.*

100 Construyendo autonomía: compromiso e indicadores de género, Karina Batthyáni Dighiero, 2012, 338 p.

99 Si no se cuenta, no cuenta, Diane Alméras y Coral Calderón Magaña (coordinadoras), 2012, 394 p.

98 *Macroeconomic cooperation for uncertain times: The REDIMA experience, Rodrigo Cárcamo-Díaz, 2012,164 p.*

Documentos de proyecto / *Project documents*

- La economía del cambio climático en la Argentina: primera aproximación, 2014, 240 p.
- La economía del cambio climático en el Ecuador 2012, 2012, 206 p.
- Economía digital para el cambio estructural y la igualdad, 2013, 130 p
  The digital economy for structural change and equality, 2014, 128 p.
- La cooperación entre América Latina y la Unión Europea: una asociación para el desarrollo, José E. Durán Lima, Ricardo Herrera, Pierre Lebret y Myriam Echeverría, 2013, 157 p.

Cuadernos estadísticos de la CEPAL

41 Los cuadros de oferta y utilización, las matrices de insumo-producto y las matrices de empleo. Solo disponible en CD, 2013.

40 América Latina y el Caribe: Índices de precios al consumidor. Serie enero de 1995 a junio de 2012. Solo disponible en CD, 2012.

Series de la CEPAL / *ECLAC Series*

Asuntos de Género / Comercio Internacional / Desarrollo Productivo / Desarrollo Territorial / Estudios Estadísticos / Estudios y Perspectivas (Bogotá, Brasilia, Buenos Aires, México, Montevideo) / *Studies and Perspectives* (The Caribbean, Washington) / Financiamiento del Desarrollo / Gestión Pública / Informes y Estudios Especiales / Macroeconomía del Desarrollo / Manuales / Medio Ambiente y Desarrollo / Población y Desarrollo / Política Fiscal / Políticas Sociales / Recursos Naturales e Infraestructura / Reformas Económicas / Seminarios y Conferencias.

Revista CEPAL / *CEPAL Review*

La Revista se inició en 1976, con el propósito de contribuir al examen de los problemas del desarrollo socioeconómico de la región. La *Revista CEPAL* se publica en español e inglés tres veces por año.

CEPAL Review first appeared in 1976, its aim being to make a contribution to the study of the economic and social development problems of the region. CEPAL Review is published in Spanish and English versions three times a year.

Observatorio demográfico / *Demographic Observatory*

Edición bilingüe (español e inglés) que proporciona información estadística actualizada, referente a estimaciones y proyecciones de población de los países de América Latina y el Caribe. Desde 2013 el Observatorio aparece una vez al año.

Bilingual publication (Spanish and English) proving up-to-date estimates and projections of the populations of the Latin American and Caribbean countries. Since 2013, the Observatory appears once a year.

Notas de población

Revista especializada que publica artículos e informes acerca de las investigaciones más recientes sobre la dinámica demográfica en la región. También incluye información sobre actividades científicas y profesionales en el campo de población.
La revista se publica desde 1973 y aparece dos veces al año, en junio y diciembre.

Specialized journal which publishes articles and reports on recent studies of demographic dynamics in the region. Also includes information on scientific and professional activities in the field of population.
Published since 1973, the journal appears twice a year in June and December.

Las publicaciones de la CEPAL están disponibles en:
ECLAC Publications are available in:

www.cepal.org/publicaciones

También se pueden adquirir a través de:
They can also be ordered through:

www.un.org/publications

United Nations Publications
PO Box 960
Herndon, VA 20172
USA

Tel. (1-888)254-4286
Fax (1-800)338-4550
Contacto / *Contact*: publications@un.org
Pedidos / *Orders*: order@un.org